Thraldom

Thraldom

A History of Slavery in the Viking Age

STEFAN BRINK

OXFORD
UNIVERSITY PRESS

OXFORD
UNIVERSITY PRESS

Oxford University Press is a department of the University of Oxford. It furthers the University's objective of excellence in research, scholarship, and education by publishing worldwide. Oxford is a registered trade mark of Oxford University Press in the UK and certain other countries.

Published in the United States of America by Oxford University Press
198 Madison Avenue, New York, NY 10016, United States of America.

CIP data is on file at Library of Congress
ISBN 978–0–19–753235–5

DOI: 10.1093/oso/9780197532355.001.0001

1 3 5 7 9 8 6 4 2

Printed by Sheridan Books, Inc., United States of America

Contents

Foreword and Acknowledgments

This book has a very long history. It began in the 1980s with trying to find place-name evidence in Scandinavia for slaveholding. The result was indeed meager; I was actually able to identify only a handful names. So I turned my attention to the kind of slavery—traditionally called *thraldom* in Scandinavia—that must have existed in prehistoric times, especially during the Viking Age. By prehistory in Scandinavia we mean before circa 1050–1100, when we have no written sources apart from the runic inscriptions. During a later phase of the Scandinavian slavery, which appears in our earliest written sources, some Latin documents, and in the provincial laws—that is, from roughly the thirteenth and fourteenth centuries—we are faced with a slavery that is in decline and finally abolished. To be able to try to understand pre-1100 slavery I therefore had to use every source available, to squeeze out any possible information. This research hence became very interdisciplinary, analyzing some continental or Arabic written sources mentioning Scandinavia, archaeology, runic inscriptions, Old Icelandic sagas, early law, place names, personal names, slave terminology, and comparative studies from other related cultures. The result of my research became a book published in Swedish in 2012. This present book is a revised translation and extensively extended version of that book.

I have had the fortune during these decades, during lectures, seminars, and private conversations, to discuss these problems with and consult some of our foremost experts in the field and I thank them all: Professors and Doctors Thomas Lindkvist, Gothenburg; Else Roesdahl, Aarhus; Frands Herschend, Uppsala; Sven Kalmring, Schleswig; Torun Zachrisson, Stockholm; Magnus Källström, Stockholm; Lisbeth Imer, Copenhagen; Dagfinn Skre, Oslo; Patrick J. Geary, IAS Princeton; Søren M. Sindbæk, Aarhus; Andreas Nordberg, Stockholm; Tore Iversen, Bergen; Andrew Reynolds, UCL London; Mats Widgren, Stockholm; Agnar Helgason, Reykjavík; Stephan Conermann, Bonn; Bjørn Poulsen, Aarhus; Matthias Toplak, Tübingen; Ben Raffield, Uppsala; Mads Dengsø Jessen, Copenhagen; Anna Kjellström, Stockholm; Volker Hilberg, Schleswig; Andres Siegfried Dobat, Aarhus; and the late Lennart Moberg, Uppsala, and D. H. Green, Cambridge.

Furthermore, I am grateful to Dr. Karen Bek-Pedersen, Aarhus, for her translation of the Swedish predecessor, which has not been an easy task, trying to find English counterparts for the Swedish terminology in disparate research fields, such as archaeology, history, runology, philology, and onomastics. The translation was made possible thanks to a generous grant from the Royal Swedish Academy of Letters, History and Antiquities in Stockholm. I am also very grateful to my colleague and friend Professor David N. Dumville, Cambridge/Aberdeen, for commenting on and improving large parts of the text. I am very much indebted to my wife, Helena, and our children, Hampus, Emma, and Anna, for allowing me to be absent, both mentally and physically, both while writing the Swedish book and while revising and rewriting this English volume. Finally, I am most grateful to two Institutes of Advanced Studies for inviting me as a Member/Fellow, in Princeton for the academic year 2017–2018, in Bonn at the Center for Dependency and Slavery Studies for the academic year 2019–2020, which afforded me the time and environment to finalize this book.

Bonn/Uppsala
April 2020

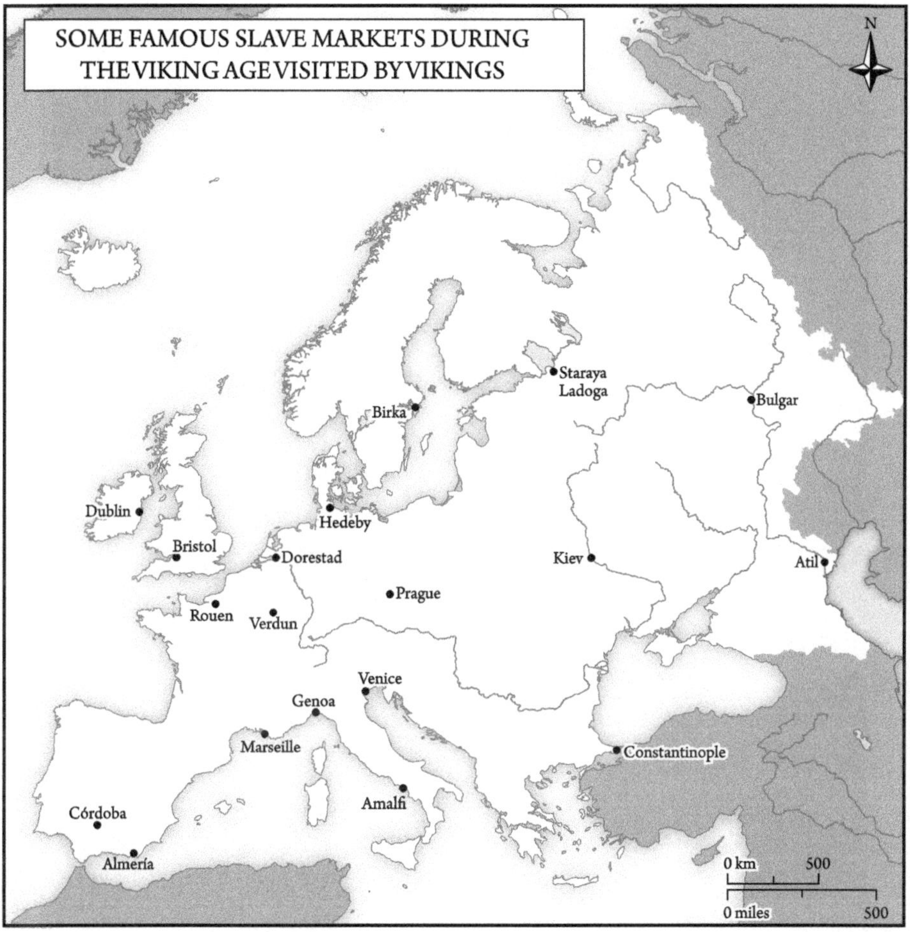

SOME FAMOUS SLAVE MARKETS DURING THE VIKING AGE VISITED BY VIKINGS
N
Staraya Ladoga
Birka
Bulgar
Dublin
Hedeby
Bristol
Dorestad
Kiev
Atil
Prague
Rouen
Verdun
Venice
Genoa
Marseille
Constantinople
Amalfi
Córdoba
Almería
0 km
500
0 miles
500

Prologue

One summer's day in 1627, more specifically on July 16, four ships approached the south coast of Iceland. On board the ships were North African corsairs—privateers or pirates—licensed by their homelands to plunder and raid across Europe. Three of the ships headed for Heimaey, the largest of the Vestmannaeyjar. The corsairs went ashore on the peaceful and utterly defenseless island. Brutally and ruthlessly the local population was raided. There was plundering and killing. Witnesses reported that a man had his head sliced off right under his eyes and that his body was then chopped up the way you would slaughter a sheep. The priest and psalmist Jón Þorsteinsson, who was famous in Iceland, knelt down to pray to God for help, but he, too, was soon slain. About thirty individuals of the small population were killed that morning. The majority of the islanders were taken prisoners and brought down to the harbor. Afterward, all houses were set on fire. An old woman and a two-year old child she was carrying walked too slowly for the liking of the North Africans and both she and the child were thrown into the fire.

The small farming and fishing community in Heimaey had nothing of value that the pirates could plunder. What they were after was people. Together with the fifteen individuals that a fourth ship had robbed from the mainland, a total of about 380 Icelanders were forced away from their homes in this year of terror 1627 in order to be brought to Africa and sold as slaves in Algeria.

One of the captives was the priest Ólafur Egilsson. He has described how the prisoners were divided up in Algiers. The captain took two Icelanders. Representatives of the Turkish sultan were given every eighth man, woman, and child, and then the rest were divided into two halves with the ship owners claiming one and the sailors the other. Ólafur's eleven-year-old son was given to the "king"; Ólafur himself was placed with some other Icelandic men in a house while his wife and two younger children were taken to another house. It seems that Ólafur, probably in his capacity of priest, functioned as some sort of leader or spokesman among the remaining Icelanders and because of this he was sent home to Denmark in order to obtain ransom with which his enslaved countrymen's freedom could be purchased. The sixty-year-old priest succeeded in reaching Denmark without any funds at all and also in collecting money for the purpose. This endeavor resulted in the rescue of some of the 380 Icelanders who were taken captive; the freedom of 34 was bought in 1635 (with public and collected means), 9 were bought free in 1644, 20 succeeded in purchasing their own freedom, 35 died of illness and hardship, and 282 stayed on, gone forever. Ólafur and his wife, Ásta, eventually returned to Heimaey, but they never saw their eldest son again. He was later sold as a slave in Tunis after which he disappeared without a trace.

A mere 390 years ago, Scandinavians thus became brutally acquainted with one of the worst aspects of humanity, slavery and captivity whereby people are robbed of all social and legal rights and turned into objects, tools whose lives are entirely in the hands of the slave owners. The slave raid of Iceland is only eight to ten generations past, no more than that. The memory of this awful event is still alive in Iceland.[1]

At one time Scandinavians also held slaves. This domestic slavery was prohibited during the Middle Ages. This black chapter of the history of the Scandinavian people is dealt with in this book.

[1] A contemporary document relates this strange enslavement of Icelanders in Heimaey: *En kort Beretning Om De Tyrkiske Søe-Røveres onde Medfart og Omgang da de kom til Island i Aaret 1627, og der borttoge over 300 Mennesker, ihjelsloge mange, og paa tyrannisk Maade ilde medhandlede dem. Sammenskreven af Præsten Oluf Eigilssen Fra West-Manøe, Som tillige blef ført derfra til Alger, og 1628 kom tilbage igien. Men nu af Islandsk oversat paa Dansk*, and the events have been treated by Þorsteinn Helgason 1997, Riise Kristensen 2003, and Munkhammar 2003 as well as noted by Davis 2001, p. 51. The travelogue of Ólafur Egilsson has now been translated into English, *The Travels of Reverend Ólafur Egilsson* (2016).

1
Introduction

Freedom, like love and beauty,
is one of those values better experienced than defined.
—Orlando Patterson, *Freedom* I, 1991, p. 1

A question of slavery is a question of freedom. What, then, is freedom actually and when did this social quality so fundamental to our times emerge? Did it always exist and has it always been defined in the same way? In connection with the bloodiest civil war we have ever seen—a war about personal freedom—Abraham Lincoln supposedly uttered, somewhat dejected, that he did not know any good definition of freedom. This statement remains valid today. A person from the secularized West has a different understanding of freedom than a Taliban in Afghanistan, a Hindu from India during the thirteenth century, or a Roman senator two thousand years ago in Rome.

One of the most prominent scholars of slavery, the American sociologist Orlando Patterson, believes that a notion of freedom may have emerged only when there was something to contrast it with, namely slavery. He defines slavery as a state in which a person is robbed of all human worth, wherein the life of the slave lies entirely in the hands of another person. A slave is a socially dead being.[1]

What we actually mean by "freedom" is a complex question. In European usage the term developed to mean the opposite of "slavery." As many great thinkers have found, among these the British anthropologist Edmund Leach, a social human being can never be completely free, which is an old key theme for many political ideologies—how great an encroachment on freedom, that is, restriction of personal freedom, are people prepared to accept in order to create a humane, mutually responsible, functioning society?

[1] Patterson 1982. See above all his detailed analysis of the concept of freedom in Patterson 1991.

Thraldom. Stefan Brink, Oxford University Press. © Oxford University Press 2021.
DOI: 10.1093/oso/9780197532355.003.0001

In an extensive analysis of what freedom is, Orlando Patterson reaches the conclusion that freedom, in the sense that we in the West attach to the concept, above all involves three dimensions: *personal*, *sovereign*, and *civic* freedom. Personal freedom ultimately implies that a person feels free to do what he wants to do, based on his personal preconditions. Patterson defines sovereign freedom as the freedom to do as one wishes without others influencing one's actions. Often, something one might do can have a negative impact on others; as is well known, one person's freedom can mean another person's lack of freedom. Moreover, many people have an urge to control not only their own life but also the lives of others. The extreme form of sovereign freedom is represented at one end of the social scale by the absolute ruler. For example, the Egyptian Pharaoh had unrestricted freedom to do what he wanted with his subjects. He had total power over all others, all of whom thereby had restricted freedom. At the other end of this social scale was the slave who lacked freedom in any sense, including the right to decide over his own life. Finally, Patterson defines civic freedom as the capacity of adult citizens to partake in the life and rule of society.[2]

As is explored later, it seems that in ancient societies sourcing new slaves consisted in taking captives during feuds, conflicts, battles, and wars. From classical authors we know that those defeated in war would be killed and, vice versa, if one had been defeated in war without dying in the fight one was considered dead even so. This was reality to the victor as well as the defeated. If anyone's life was spared in battle and he or she was taken captive instead, the victor could use the captive as a tool according to his own wishes until the captive died. Prominent Roman lawyers, such as Ulpian, Florentinus, and Justinian, referred to this fact, *res mancipium*, "the victor's power over his slave or possession," in order to morally justify slavery: a slave was a person who was the recipient of an advantage or a gift—his or her life had been spared when it rightfully should have been ended.[3] In *The Second Treatise of Government* (1690), the English philosopher John Locke expressed this eventually universal understanding and used it to defend slavery:[4]

[2] Dagfinn Skre (2014) has given an interesting reflection regarding the diachronic usage and misusage of the Scandinavian concepts of *fri* 'free' and *frihet* 'freedom', and what it meant to be "free" in early Scandinavian society.
[3] See Watson 1987 p. 8, Turley 2000 p. 3.
[4] Locke 1690 ch. 4:22.

> [A man] having, by his fault, forfeited his own Life, by some Act that deserves Death; he, to whom he has forfeited it, may (when he has him in his Power) delay to take it, and make use of him to his own Service, and he does him no injury by it.

This way of thinking is encountered in many cultures across our world. The American anthropologist Theda Perdue, who has studied slavery among the Cherokee of North America between the sixteenth and nineteenth centuries, has found that in all battles it was expected that the defeated enemies would be killed, and this was the normal practice.[5] In other words, North American Indians were just as cruel as European tribal warriors had been some thousand years earlier. In some individual cases, however, the Cherokee took certain people captive to use them as slaves. These were called *atsi nahsa'i*, people without tribal affiliation, and a person who did not belong to any tribe had no rights whatsoever, not even the right to his or her own life (something which, as we will see, had a counterpart in Viking society).

History shows that an individual feels freedom provided she experiences a sense of belonging to a social group or a society and is able to influence decisions made within that group or society. Historically, this group has often comprised only the male population (as in classical Athens) or even exclusively male aristocrats (as in classical Rome), leaving aside the remaining population.

In ancient Scandinavia, a person lacking family or the right to belong to a community was a social outcast and thus a "nonperson."[6] To be excommunicated from one's kin or community was the cruelest sort of punishment, legally comparable to execution.[7] These, then, are the three aspects that Orlando Patterson considers as constituting the foundations of our Western understanding of what freedom is.

There are many indications that the kind of clan society we perceive existed in Scandinavia during the Early Iron Age, about two thousand years ago, operated with the same type of social rules. We base this view primarily

[5] Perdue 1979. See also, with the same observation generally for Indian tribes in America, MacLeod 1928.

[6] See Wennerström 1933, Jacoby 1974, Breich 1994, Breen 1999, van Houts 2004, and Riisøy 2014.

[7] The social status of not belonging to a social group or some kin was such a predicament that one almost became dehumanized, something found in many "primitive" societies, as has been noted by several anthropologists, such as among the Yanomamo Indians in Venezuela: "To be outside of the kinship system is, in a very real sense, to be inhuman or nonhuman: real humans are some sort of kin" (Chagnon 2013 p. 142).

on the Roman historian Tacitus, who in circa AD 98 wrote *Germania*, a work on the Germanic tribes, who lived to the north of the Romans. It seems that already very early on in our history it was important to belong to a kin group, a community—otherwise one did not exist as a person. Therefore, the worst possible punishment that could be inflicted on someone, equivalent to being killed, was to be excluded from the community, from society.

In other words, it seems that a different conception of freedom existed among our early ancestors whereby freedom was not defined as a personal, individual freedom of an inviolable person, but rather as a right to belong to a community, to be part of a group; to be put outside of the group was the equivalent to not existing at all. It is against this background that we have to understand how our ancestors were able to accept and even justify the existence of slavery. If an individual ended up outside his or her community as a result of having been captured by neighbors in battle or having committed a serious crime and therefore been excommunicated, in normal cases this would result in that person being killed. If the person's life was spared, it was legitimate—according to the mode of thought of that time—to use this person as an implement without showing any human considerations at all. That individual was already de facto socially dead. The slave owner did nothing more than prolong that person's life for some time, unless he decided to kill his slave, which was of course also entirely legitimate according to contemporaneous views of the matter.[8] Hence, the study of slavery, being a subset of an integrated system of social interaction, forces us to analyze social relationships, economic preconditions, and cultural values in that society. Slavery must thus be considered in its relation to the entire economic system, social structure, and cultural preferences of a given society.[9]

[8] See, e.g., Benveniste 1973 p. 289.
[9] Siegel 1945 p. 363.

2

Difficulties of Defining Slavery and the Borders between Free and Unfree

The nature of slavery changes from one period of history to another, and, within a given period, it varies from one region to the next. Even in one particular spot at one moment in time, quite different kinds of slaves are found: the social division of labor and internal hierarchy of society have always been particularly marked among the servile masses, being intimately bound up with slavery itself.

—Pierre Dockès, *Medieval Slavery and Liberation*, 1982, p. 49

The person who wants to study slavery in bygone times must define what constitutes a "slave" or "thrall."[1] This may seem obvious, but that is, in fact, not the case. If nothing else, this description shows that views of slavery consist of much more than black and white poles because it operates with a rather complex scale of gray.[2] This is evident not least in the problems of defining what the different terms for "farmer" covered during the early continental Middle Ages (c. 400–1200), such as *servus*, *mancipium*, *ancilla*, *villicus*, *rusticus*, *villanus*, *colonus*, and so on; were they free farmers, semifree tenants, or unfree slaves?[3] To further obfuscate the issue, most of these Latin terms for "farmer" have undergone semantic changes over time so that, for example, *rusticus* 'free farmer' could refer later on in medieval times to a more or less semifree farmer who could be sold when the master sold his estate and who was tied to his farm and his land, while the old and indisputable term for a slave, *servus*, during the thirteenth century could refer to a type of tenant, such as in English law.[4] To confuse the terminology even more, in

[1] A selection of other scholars who are not mentioned in what follows, but who have defined "slave" and "slavery" are Phillips 1985 pp. 5 ff., Nordberg 1988 pp. 171 ff., and Zeuske 2018 pp. 7–40, 2019 pp. 194–205. General introductions to slavery are found in Rodriguez (ed.) 1997, Finkelman and Miller (eds.) 1998, and the Wikipedia article "Slavery."

[2] This is productively discussed in Kopytoff and Miers 1977.

[3] See, e.g., Bloch 1976 pp. 58 ff., Bonnassie 1991 pp. 294–295, Goetz 1993, Arnoux 2014, and Theuws ms.

[4] Hyams 1980 *passim* and Phillips 1996 pp. 80–81.

Thraldom. Stefan Brink, Oxford University Press. © Oxford University Press 2021.
DOI: 10.1093/oso/9780197532355.003.0002

France around the year 1000 the term *villani* indicated free farmers, while in England at the same time *villani* could refer to unfree persons.[5]

European society of the High Middle Ages may be described as tripartite, with *oratores, bellatores, et servi*—that is, those who pray (priests), those who fight (nobility), and those who work the fields (farmers).[6] It was not uncommon that a tenant—who was in principle a "free" farmer, although he did not own the land he worked, but had the use of it on paying an annual fee or rent for his tenancy according to the agreement made with the estate owner—was forced to stay on his farm and its lands and to be present on his farm every day of the year unless the estate owner had other wishes. It was even written into the contract that if any legal disputes arose, such matters were to be solved by the estate owner and not by any other independent legal body. The tenant was thus fettered to his farm and subjected to the estate owner's private jurisdiction.[7] From this it is clear that what we are dealing with is to all intents and purposes a "slave," even if the person in question was not formally classified as such during medieval times. The distinction between a slave and a semifree tenant was that the former lacked all legal rights and in a very concrete sense was owned by someone, while the latter was geographically confined, forced to work a certain farm, and from a legal point of view entirely in the hands of he who owned the land.[8]

This actual equation of slaves with many kinds of farm tenants during early medieval times was, of course, the condition for the dissolution of slavery. Those who were financially in charge of European society found a new method of production, which was more profitable and easier to administer than the old slavery system, namely the feudal system with contractually bound tenants. According to Marc Bloch, the great change took place when slaves passed into the class of "free" tenants during the tenth and eleventh centuries,[9] something that has been labeled the "feudal revolution" or the "feudal transformation."[10] Since Bloch, this has been most

[5] Fourquin 1988 p. 203, cf. Stenton 1971 pp. 477 ff.

[6] Duby 1973 pp. 187 ff., 1980, Bonnassie 1991 p. 325.

[7] Bonnassie 1991 pp. 229 ff.

[8] Lindkvist 1979 *passim*, esp. pp. 25–36, and Pelteret 2002 p. 85.

[9] Bloch 1975 [1933] pp. 33–91.

[10] Duby 1980 pp. 147 ff. and Poly and Bournazel 1980. I use—here and in what follows—"feudal" and "feudalism" in a rather "uncritical" way, knowing the difficulty of correctly defining the terms in the context of the Middle Ages, especially after the important deconstruction of the concepts by Susan Reynolds (1994). It is not my intention here to analyze what kind of "feudal" system that was introduced into Scandinavia and how it functioned; and Scandinavian historians have used the concepts in different ways, as a political explanatory tool, or as a socioeconomic description within a materialistic theoretical paradigm. My usage of "feudal" in this work takes aspects from both of these theoretical traditions. I refer readers interested in these aspects of Scandinavian history to, e.g., Lindkvist 1979, 2003; Gelting 1988, 2002; Skre 1998; Bagge, Gelting, and Lindkvist (eds.) 2011; Sindbæk and Poulsen (eds.) 2011.

fully described by Georges Duby,[11] who stresses that in no way did farmers become "free," but were subjected legally and socially to an estate owner, a system which Duby called *seigneurie banale*. By making slaves "free" and letting them become tenants, a more secure profit was obtained since the tenants paid an annual fee at a set time during the year, plus it was no longer necessary to monitor one's workers by the means of various penal systems since the farmers were tied to the land and to their farms in order to survive.[12]

The *Concise Oxford English Dictionary* (COD) defines a slave thus: "Person who is the legal property of another or others and is bound to absolute obedience."[13] A standard definition of slavery was given in The Slavery Convention of the League of Nations (1926): "the status or condition of a person over whom any or all of the powers attaching to the right of ownership are exercised."[14] Already in 1910, Herman J. Nieboer defined a slave as "a man who is the property of another, politically and socially at a lower level than the mass of the people, and performing compulsory labour," and argued, "the great function of slavery can be no other than a division of labour."[15] Orlando Patterson defines slavery as "the permanent, violent domination of natally alienated and generally dishonoured persons."[16] Another fairly basic definition by David Brion Davies says roughly that a slave lacks the right to make his or her own decisions and is someone else's possession and that the work or service of a slave is of a binding nature and warrants no financial compensation.[17] This is primarily an economic definition. A more socially orientated definition of a slave is, according to the anthropologist Edmund Leach, "a man or woman who has no recognized kin outside his owner's family (*familia*)."[18] In other words, a slave was the property of a slave owner; this compares to the Old Icelandic term for a thrall: *mansmaðr* 'a man's man'. Legally, a slave was without rights, but was nonetheless a legal subject in the

[11] E.g., Duby 1980.

[12] Lindkvist 1979. For an up-to-date discussion regarding this change from slavery to serfdom, see Rio 2017; see also Cavaciocchi (ed.) 2013.

[13] COD pp. 1132–1133.

[14] Turley 2000 p. 6; *League of Nations. Treaty Series*, vol 60 (1927), p. 263 (https://treaties.un.org/doc/Publication/UNTS/LON/Volume%2060/v60.pdf).

[15] Nieboer 1910 pp. 5, 7. Orlando Patterson (1977) has critically discussed Nieboer's definition.

[16] Patterson 1982 p. 13; for a critical remark on this definition, see Blackburn 1988 p. 278 n. 13, see also critical aspects *pace* Patterson in Schiel and Hanss 2014 pp. 14 and 17.

[17] Davies 1966 p. 31 ("his person is the property of another man, his will is subjected to his owner's authority, and his labor or services are obtained through coercion"), cf. Davies 1984 pp. 8 ff. Also Thomas E. J. Wiedemann (1987 p. 22) emphasizes the social aspect of slavery above the economic. For other definitions of slavery, see, e.g., Finley 1972 pp. 3 ff. and Dockès 1982 pp. 4 ff.; Iversen (1997 pp. 27–30) has also discussed definitions of "slave" and "slavery" (in Norwegian).

[18] Leach 1967 p. 14.

sense that slaves are often mentioned in laws where it is stipulated how the situation must be handled when a slave has done an injustice. The point, however, always is that the slave can never be his own spokesman in a court case and any legal compensation that a slave may be awarded belongs to his owner. Legally speaking, the slave lives through his or her owner, who in principle has unrestricted power over the slave's life and body; the master is allowed to beat, flog, and even kill the slave at his own will. Roman law makes the further distinction that a slave who lacked an owner (which must have been a highly unusual situation) was defined as *res nullius* (properly "land belonging to nobody," "nobody's property"), and as such a "nothing." This all means that a definition of slave and slavery actually needs to encompass an economic, a social, and a legal aspect,[19] which makes it difficult to construct a general definition; in fact, so difficult that the aforementioned Edmund Leach would have liked for one such to be eliminated from the scholarly discussion altogether![20]

Igor Kopytoff delved into the problem and has presented us with a comprehensive and thorough analysis of the different attempts to define "slave" and "slavery," and he did also try to find a general definition, but resigned and concluded:[21]

> "Slavery" may then be used not as an *analytical* concept but as an *evocative* one—much as we use "economics" and "politics," for all the endless debates about their true definition. "Slavery" evokes certain kinds of relationships and draws attention to them, but it is not a useful analytical component of general theoretical models intended for cross-cultural use.

In many cultures, terms for "slave" have no grammatical gender, but are neuter, which shows that a slave was not regarded as a human being, but as an object, a thing. This is the case with Latin *mancipium* n. 'slave'. Already Aristotle defined a slave as an "implement with a voice" (*instrumentum vocale*) that could, however—since the slave was a living being—be compared to a domestic animal.[22] This view of slaves is well illustrated by the

[19] A similar view has been proposed by Devroey 2006 p. 315.

[20] "The ambiguities of this word ["slave"] are indeed so confusing that sociologists might be well advised to eliminate it from their discussion altogether" (Leach 1967 p. 14). Kopytoff and Miers (1977) hold the same opinion.

[21] Kopytoff 1982, citation from p. 221.

[22] Aristotle, *Politics* 1:4 ("Thus, too, a possession is an instrument for maintaining life. And so, in the arrangement of the family, a slave is a living possession, and property a number of such instruments;

early Frankish-Salian laws *Pactus Legis Salicae* from the early sixth century and *Lex Salica*, of which the oldest version was issued during the reign of Pepin the Short (763–64) and was in force for Merovingian and Carolingian Francia respectively,[23] wherein one type of slave, *ancilla*,[24] was valued higher than a boar, but lower than a cow, while a *servus* was considered of equal value to a cow, but worth less than a horse or a bull.[25]

It is probably a significant point that, during the Scandinavian Viking Age, a slave lacked the social quality that can be translated as honor.[26] Nor did a slave have any human value, but only the value of an object. A free man had a value with which his kin must be compensated if he was killed. In Scandinavia this price was called *manhælghis bot*, *mansbot*, *mangæld*, *ættarbot*, or *baugr*; among the Anglo-Saxons it was called *wergild*; and among the Germans *wer(e)geld*.[27] If a slave was killed the requirement was to compensate to the value the slave had as a tool or the amount for which the slave had been bought as well as the financial loss incurred on the slave owner by the loss of the slave's life.[28] The code of honor, fundamental to the male ideal of the Scandinavian Late Iron Age, which is hard to define, but which involved an individual's reputation, could therefore not encompass slaves. A person lacking all honor was practically socially dead, which is also how Orlando Patterson characterizes a slave.

It may be that we are dealing with a social and moral shift in Scandinavia around the middle of the first millennium (which in Scandinavian archaeological terms is the shift between Early and Late Iron Age) in terms of how an individual's social status and exclusion were regarded. As seen earlier, it was fundamental to an individual during the (Scandinavian) Early Iron Age to belong to a community. If a person was excommunicated, this entailed social death. Belonging to a social group, a family, was clearly also of great importance during the Late Iron Age, but we must probably allow for a gradual shift

and the servant is himself an instrument which takes precedence of all other instruments.") Cf. Plato, *Laws* book 6 (776d ff.). About Aristotle's view on slaves, see also what follows.

23 See Rivers 1986 pp. 2 f. and Fischer Drew 1991 pp. 28 ff.

24 For the etymology of Latin *ancilla*, see Rix 1994 pp. 11–34.

25 See Table 1 in Bonnassie 1991 p. 18—*Pactus* II:8, 14, III:4, 7, 8, X:3, 4; *Lex Salica* II:3,4, XI:1,2. See also Fischer Drew 1991 pp. 74–75.

26 See Meulengracht Sørensen 1993.

27 See, e.g., von Schroeder 1893, Seip 1957, Angermann 1997, Erhardt 1997, Wormald 1997, 1998, Roth 1997, Esders 2011, 2015, Brink 2014c, and Skre 2017, and cf. the 2014 conference *Wergild, Compensation and Penance: The Monetary Logic of Early Medieval Conflict Resolution* (http://www.rm-calendario.it/wp-content/uploads/2332/Flyer-Wergild-Conference.pdf).

28 Cf. Karras 1993 p. 598.

with regard to this issue between these two (for Scandinavia) prehistorical periods.

This observation is also important on a general level since the opposite of slavery in most societies was the inclusion in society, clan, or family, hence not personal autonomy but citizenship (cf. Orlando Patterson definition earlier), civic rights, and belongingness and attachment to the social structure rather than detachment from it.[29]

During the Late Iron Age (AD c. 500–1100) it seems that the single individual became more prominent at the expense of the group. This accords with our current views of the Scandinavian society of the Late Iron Age. It appears that, during this period emerged a new kind of aristocracy, an upper social class not based on kinship or clan, and a new type of leader who was able—via alliances and connections and with his own group of warriors loyal to the leader rather than to the group—to act in a more independent way.[30] The concentration of power in society increased and the degree of social hierarchy probably also increased. Even within the landscape changes took place since these new aristocrats created their own new "residences," so-called halls, in Old Norse *salir* (sg. *salr*), which became the new social arena wherein power was exercised and alliances made.[31]

In order to highlight the complications of finding a simple yet satisfactory definition of a slave, we can consider the social situations of ancient Egypt and China. Here, all the Pharaoh's and the emperor's subjects were their respective "slaves" in the sense that they were his "possessions" with which he could in principle do as he wished; he could even kill them. Did these great societies then consist of nothing but slaves (with the Pharaoh and emperor as sole exceptions)? Moreover, certain slaves in ancient Babylonia, Egypt, the Roman Empire, and the Ottoman Empire even relatively late on were high-ranking officials with considerable and important societal functions to attend to regarding finances and the administration of society, just like high-ranking soldiers.[32] Did the high social rank of these officials then prevent them from being regarded as slaves?

[29] Kopytoff 1982 p. 221.

[30] For an attempt at an analysis of the aristocracy during the Late Iron Age, see Löwenborg 2010, V: pp. 1–14.

[31] Brink 1996b pp. 255–258. On the hall as a vertical social arena, see Brink 2005 p. 61. Today Scandinavian archaeologists often refer to the period *c.* 600–1000 as a "Hall Society."

[32] See, e.g., Erdem 1996 *passim*.

This problem is pushed to its limits if we consider slavery in Egypt, not during the time of the Pharaohs, but in medieval times—a mere 600–700 years ago—as in the Ottoman Empire, with its center in Turkey.[33]

It is not all that easy for a modern Westerner to comprehend that a slave could become the ruler of a whole country, but this was not as uncommon as one might imagine. The Egypt of the mid-thirteenth century and about three hundred years on features the peculiar phenomenon that a Muslim kingdom lasting for centuries, the so-called Egyptian–Syrian Mamluk Sultanate, had rulers who were all slaves, or to be correct, who had been slaves. To understand how this was possible, we have to go back some centuries to the time immediately after the death of the prophet Muhammad in Medina in 632.

After the death of Muhammad, extensive Arab conquests began, whereby many lands were put under Arabic-Muslim rule. The conquerors, however, appear not to have forced their religion onto the defeated peoples to any noteworthy degree. In the so-called Umayyad Caliphate (661–750),[34] which included Arabia, Persia, Syria, Egypt, and so on, Muslims made up only about 3–4 percent of the population even after some fifty years of Islamic rule. Arabs constituted a small, exclusive military aristocracy that did not wish to mix with the conquered and the infidels, so-called *dhimmis*. The only way for an infidel to achieve any position of power to speak of was to attach oneself as "client" to some member of an Arab tribe; Arabic society remained a decidedly tribal society for a long time. Scattered around the caliphate were Arab tribal groups placed as garrisons, and around these, clusters of infidel clients gradually sprung up, so-called *mawlā*. These *mawālī* did service as warriors, although not as cavalry, only as infantry. In time, these groups acquired a much stronger position and their discontent with their low societal position led to the so-called Abbasid Revolution in 747–750,[35] which was brought about first and foremost by Persian and Iraqi *mawālī* and which caused a radical and fundamental reshaping of Islamic society.

When the Arabs lost their role as rulers holding together the caliphate, cracks began to emerge partly between separate Muslim sects, such as *Sunnites*, *Shiites*, and *Kharijites*, partly due to ethnic conflicts, partly between different emirs attempting to obtain power.[36] The first Abbasid caliphs then

[33] What follows is a summary of Nordberg 1988 pp. 176–205, Segal 2003 pp. 103–117, Schultz 2006, Amitai 2006, Stiles 2006, de la Puente 2006, and Conermann forthcoming.

[34] See, e.g., Hawting 2000, Hämeen-Anttila 2014 with refs.

[35] See, e.g., Sha'bān 1970.

[36] See, e.g., Anthony 2012 and more generally Esposito (ed.) 1999 and Bloom and Blair 2002.

thought of reshaping the *mawālī* system into a base on which their state could be built. A *mawlā* thus became a loyal and faithful client to a caliph. Various *mawālī* came to function as auxiliary troops to the ruler, and their warriors began gradually to be obtained as slaves from southern Russia and central Asia. In this way, the army became ethnically separate from the population at large. This obviously caused tension in Baghdad, which is why Caliph Al-Mu'tasim chose to remove the Turkish slave troops to a separate administrative and military capital, Samarra, north of Baghdad. These slave troops and their officers, who were likewise slaves, came to influence and to a great extent rule the caliphate for a long time.

It is against this background that we are to assess the Mamluk Sultanate in Egypt from 1249 onward. That year, the last Ayyūbid sultan died. The Ayyūbids had, in the usual way, built up an army of slaves, the Mamluks (*mamlūk* 'a person who is owned', referring to white slaves), who were mostly taken from southern Russia (the Kipçak/Qipchaq Turks).[37] The trade in these slaves was mediated by Venetian merchants.

The Mamluk Sultanate was a form of military rule not unusual in the Islamic world, where a predominantly Arab population was dominated by an exclusively Turkic elite of freed military slaves. In order to become a Mamluk, a man had to be a Turk born to non-Muslim parents. This normally young boy (as young as 10–15 years old) could be enslaved by force or having been sold by his parents, and then traded to the Arabic world, often by Genoese and Venetian slave traders. He was bought by a ruling sultan and quartered in barracks where he would undergo a training program during the early years: receiving an introduction to Islam, which included recitation of the Qur'an; learning both written and spoken Arabic; and receiving instruction in the general doctrine of Muslim laws and obligations. In addition, there was military training: archery, use of the lance, polo and horse racing, and finally swordsmanship. After the completion of this curriculum the Mamluk received his manumission diploma, a horse, all the necessary equipment, and a share of his master's estate. He was then a free Muslim and a regular soldier.[38]

During the following centuries, the sultanate experienced a great many rulers, virtually all Turkish slaves, many of whom were probably not Arab speakers. When a general from one of the Mamluk groups was elected as the

[37] See, e.g., Schultz 2006, Mazor 2015 pp. 15–19, Conermann forthcoming.
[38] An excellent introduction to the Mamluks is Conermann forthcoming.

new sultan, he became completely dependent on the support of his group. Around 1400 there was a change when a Circassian slave succeeded in becoming commander-in-chief and proclaimed himself sultan (1382–1399). After this event, the trading of slaves from the Kipçak Turks ceased and instead it was predominantly Circassians from the Caucasus who were brought in as Mamluks.[39] In this way, a foreign rule endured in Egypt, with the small difference that the ethnic composition of the ruling classes and the warriors, the Mamluks, was changed. In the year 1516 the Ottoman Sultan Selim I defeated the Mamluk army in a great battle in Syria, and a Pasha was brought in to rule Egypt. The old ruling structures nonetheless still existed. Circassian slaves continued to be imported until the end of the eighteenth century, and the Mamluk military aristocracy came to dominate Egyptian society until the early nineteenth century, when the Albanian Muhammad Ali conquered and knocked out the old structure.

Even closer to us, geographically speaking, is the strange Ottoman Empire of which Constantinople became the headquarters after the city was conquered in 1453 as the last remains of the old Roman Empire, capital of the Byzantine Empire. During the reign of Murat II (1421–1451) (or perhaps already by Murat I) a particularly controversial institution was instigated, which was that all farming families in the Balkan area (and elsewhere) were forced to give up a young son who would become the sultan's slave and be brought up a soldier. This infamous so-called *dev(i)şirme* ("levy of boys") system, known in Balkan as the blood tax, was in operation right up until the early eighteenth century.[40] These selected boys, who would be taken to Constantinople, were called *kullar* (sing. *kul*). On the way to the capital they were circumcised and given a new, Muslim name. The majority were distributed among Turkish farming and soldier families where they spent some years working on the farms, learning the Turkish language and the Ottoman way of life. A small proportion—the bright ones—were picked out to be given an education in one of the sultan's palaces, an education lasting for fourteen years and including studies in Turkish, Arabic, and Persian in music, writing, poetry, theology, and law, obviously with the Qur'an as the hub of all learning. Other than this, they were educated to become soldiers so

[39] Mazor 2015 p. 20.

[40] Ménage 1991. Cf. Murphey 1999 p. 223; *pace* Hubbard and Kane 2013 p. 152. For a qualification of the *dev(i)şirme* as "pure slaves," see Yilmaz 2009, cf. Kunt 2014.

that at the age of about twenty they could be taken on as *Janissaries* (*Yeni čeri* or *Yeniçeri*),[41] the sultan's own soldiers (see what follows).

Until the fifteenth century the army actually did consist of these former slaves, but the higher-ranking administrators, such as viziers and governors of provinces, were Turks. With Mehmet II this, too, was changed so that all grand viziers, high-ranking officers, and administrators were *kullar* of Greek or southern Slavic ancestry. These distinguished *kullar* could marry, but in the eyes of the law their children were not slaves since they were born as Muslims. This was the key to the continuity inherent in the Ottoman societal structure; the status and wealth of high-ranking officials could not be passed on to the next generation since the children were Muslims and thereby prevented from entering service as *kullar*. The sultan was also able at any time to dismiss or have executed an official who was rightfully his slave. Moreover, the often-sizable fortune that a *kul* was able to amass was the property of the sultan, which meant that the wealth could not accumulate within certain families, as it did in western Europe—creating an upper class that took a ruling position in society. In this way, no alternatives to the Ottoman ruling dynasty were allowed to spring up and potentially threaten the existing order. Instead, a static order of society was preserved.[42]

An interesting register of slaves is preserved from the famous Topkapı in Istanbul, residence of the Ottoman rulers and the administrative center of the empire. The superintendent in charge of it, Cafer Aga, was called or had the title "The White Chief-Eunuch."[43] At his death in 1557 he had 156 slaves. Cafer Aga himself was, of course, slave to the sultan and, as his title points out, also a eunuch. Of his slaves, 52 were Bosnian, 24 Circassian, 22 Hungarian, 16 Albanian, 7 Croatian, 7 "Frenks" (Europeans from southern Europe: French, Italian, and Spanish), 4 Abazins, 3 German, 3 Greek, 2 Georgian, 2 Mingrelian, 1 Russian, and 1 Vhlach.[44] These slaves were hierarchically organized officials who looked after the financial and administrative affairs of the empire.

At the end of the sixteenth century, the Turkish writer (*şair*) Gelibolulu Mustafa Ali (1541–1600) wrote a handbook for the Ottoman elite, a kind of counterpart to the *Speculum Regale* or *Specula Principum* that were

[41] Ménage 1991 p. 212, Kunt 2014 pp. 326–327.
[42] For slavery in the Ottoman Empire, see, e.g., İnalcık 1979, Toledano 1982, 1998, Faroqhi 2017, and Wagner 2017 with a historiographical overview of research in the field.
[43] Kunt 2014 pp. 329–332.
[44] Fisher 1980 p. 34.

fashionable in Europe during the Middle Ages, of which the Swedish one is called *Konungastyrelsen* (OSw *Um styrilse konunga ok höfdinga*), in Norway *Kongespeilet* (ON *Konungs skuggsjá*).[45] When it comes to female slaves, he has this to say:

> *Cariyes* [slaves] who are degenerate can never gain the respect and affection of the great people. Female slaves whose talents are worthless can never find a place with people of good standing, or serve such masters in bed [...]. One must take very good care of the intelligent and efficient *cariyes*, especially those who serve in bed.[46]

He also expounds extensively on how well various ethnic groups function as slaves:[47]

> To hope that one can train and give good breeding to an Albanian, to hope for honesty from a foul Kurd, is like asking a chicken who is laying an egg to speak [. . .].
>
> Some things which cannot happen: a female slave who is Russian not to be immoral; male slaves from Russia to be courageous. Cossacks from this race are all heavy drinkers; they are more depraved than the black-eyed Araps [Blacks] and they are continuously drinking wine and *bozay* [a fermented berry drink]. They are the worst scoundrels in the world [. . .].
>
> Bosnians and Croats are for the most part honest and energetic. They have behaviour characterized by stout hearts, well built bodies, and are well brought up to have shy and bashful characters. In just the same way as Frenks, they are fine and smart, agile and handsome [. . .].

[In case of any doubts, Gelibolulu Ali was himself Croatian.]

> Most of the coarse Georgians are dirty. Even though they might wear satin, it is as though it were coarse linen on their bodies. Even the top of their heads is dirty (they are dirty from head to foot). From the perspective of their eyes and eyelashes, they are like Circassians; yet to think the two are the same is to be deceived [. . .].

45 See Moberg 1984, Holm-Olsen 1983, 1987; cf. Bagge 1987 and Schnall and Simek 2000.
46 Fisher 1980 p. 37.
47 Fisher 1980 pp. 40–41.

> But the Hungarians are clean, and in service are dextrous and quick. Although a few of them are bad, most are excellent slaves.
>
> Circassians and Abaza can be well trained. They are all brave. They have beautiful eyes, eyebrows and eyelashes. But here and there are a few who are obstinate and do not obey as they should.
>
> Wallachians, Moldavians and Transylvanians are all similar infidels in temperament. Some are beautiful, others bad and ugly. They are worse than Hungarians and Croats and are inclined to criminal behaviour. In the midst of them are the Bulgarian infidels, who are neither good nor beautiful, but are all a crowd of faithless individuals.
>
> The Amhars, Mariyes and Damuns, from Abyssinia are sweet slaves. They have a fine temperament; they feel great remorse even from a small reproach. The boys act like women in spreading out beds and mattresses and when speaking about and to their masters do it like girls.
>
> Nubians and Tekrudis, black-eyed Araps, have coarse temperaments and are of very common stock.

His final remark and summary is remarkable:

> It is written thus: most of these have no value. Their work is entirely unsuitable. The Circassians and Croats are of a good race, followed at some distance by the Hungarians and Frenks. Beware of all the rest.

Had this Gelibolulu Ali lived in the modern world, he would undoubtedly have received a phone call requesting him to be confronted with the Discrimination Ombudsman in order to explain himself and be given a proper reprimand, or perhaps more likely be charged with slander against an ethnic group—or, in his case, ethnic groups. What is interesting about this statement is the way in which Gelibolulu classifies human beings into different categories that refer to their function as slaves within the Ottoman Empire, whether they were honest, willing to work, cunning, beautiful, well built, and so on.[48]

[48] There are similar "handbooks" or slave-buying manuals, to the extent that they perhaps can be described as a genre of their own in the Muslim culture, just like the *Speculum Regale* in the Western world. One is written by a Cairene doctor, al-Amshati (d. 1496), who presents us with similar stereotypes as Gelibolulu Ali based on ethnic and/or geographic origin that were common in the Mamluk period: dark-skinned African slaves could be used for lowly domestic tasks; Greek males were obedient, serious, loyal, trustworthy, and intelligent and were valued for their good manners and excellent knowledge of the sciences; Armenians were considered strong, of good health and looks; light-skinned Franks were believed to be rough, courageous, miserly, stupid, and uneducated, but

Thus, the Ottoman Empire was decidedly a slave society during medieval and later times. Beside the aforementioned slaves who became soldiers and civil servants and who often came out of the Balkan region, there were also great numbers of slaves captured during war campaigns and female slaves bought at slave markets,[49] and also slaves owned by other slaves. Black male slaves from Africa were often castrated and became eunuchs and servants for families. Women from predominantly Southern Russia and Caucasus—especially Circassians and Georgians were sought after for their beauty—were bought in large numbers as sex slaves. In the home, slaves worked as servants and as sexual partners.[50] Wealth was sometimes measured by the number of sex slaves. Beautiful slave girls were sometimes given as gifts to people higher up in the system, to try to win the favor of one's superiors.

Officials in the service of the sultan were therefore predominantly slaves, which meant that an inheriting class of civil servants never came into existence. It happened that free Muslims attempted to bribe their own or their sons' way in as slaves in order to obtain high social standing as military officers or as officials. This system was in operation as late as far into the nineteenth century.

In the fourteenth century the Ottomans decided to create an additional army, the Janissary Corps (*Yeniçeri Ocağı*), consisting of young Christian boys who were recruited by force; the rule was to take only one per family. These boys, between ten and 18 years of age, should be physically healthy, handsome, unmarried, uncircumcised, and intelligent. The boys were rounded up in the center of the village, divided into groups and prepared for the march to Istanbul. There they were converted to Islam, circumcised, and given Islamic names. Those best qualified were deployed to the royal palaces. Their basic training took seven years, followed by another seven of specialized education. There were lessons in Turkish, Arabic, literature, Qur'an studies, and Islamic law and theology as well as administrative and military matters. A small cohort made it to the Topkapı Palace, where they received more training to prepare them for the highest offices. The rest were put in

very good and skilled at a variety of manual tasks, they were strongly religious but not trustworthy. Their women were good for nothing, being coarse, cruel, and merciless; light-skinned Circassians were ugly, vicious, evil, disloyal, and untruthful, and so on (Barker 2016, Conermann forthcoming).

[49] Fisher 1980 p. 26.
[50] McKee 2014 pp. 502–504.

mid-ranking administrative posts. Those who were not selected for school education were sent to a regiment to become a soldier in the military.

If we look at this Janissary system, it becomes clear that we cannot refer to it as "slavery" as such. The youths were not bought or regarded as chattel, and they were not marginalized or placed on the edge of society. On the contrary they might end up at the highest administrative or military posts. Still they were officially the sultan's *kullar*, "slaves." This last case illustrates the difficulty of defining a "slave," and the difficulty of semantically understanding and translating a term in a context of dependency.

The Ottoman Empire was a Muslim, Turkish state, which was in terms of the practical levels of politics and military ruled by slaves, who were Serbs, Bosnians, Croats, Greeks, Hungarians, Albanians, Circassians, Georgians, and Russians. Socially speaking, they had all come from poor farming backgrounds. Slavery in the Ottoman Empire was, in other words, of a military and political order, it had an important status function and a considerable sexual function, but—in marked difference to the situation in Roman society—it had neither financial nor production-orientated functions since slaves played no major working part in agrarian production. Roman slavery focused on production, Ottoman slavery on a sort of (service) consumption.[51] The Ottoman slave society was different from the slave societies we encounter during classical Roman times in southern Europe or in America in the eighteenth and nineteenth centuries. These examples highlight the difficulties in assessing and comparing slavery through time and space.[52]

Two basic distinctions must be included in the definition of a slave. First is the opportunity to influence one's own life and the right to one's own life, something that a slave did not have. He was purely a tool in the hands of his owner, and should the owner want to kill his slave—no matter how important a role the slave played, for example, administratively—he had every right to do so. The Norwegian Frostaþing Law (20), for example, states: "If a man kills his slave [*drepr þræl sin til dauðs*], he shall announce this on the same day, then he cannot be held responsible for the deed except in the eyes of God." The second essential distinction, which was of particular importance in ancient societies, is that the slave could never be part of a social network, a family, which implied, legally speaking, that the slave could never be a subject to the law. The owner of a slave had total financial, social, and legal power

[51] Segal 2003 p. 107.
[52] An interesting overview of the Byzantine slavery is given by Hadjinicolaou-Marava 1950.

over his slave. The slave lived through his or her master and was a social isolate with no option of choosing his or her own partner, with no kin-group, honor, or right to his or her own life. The slave's existence was alienation, degradation, and a constant risk of physical punishment, in the worst case resulting in death.

Physical punishment naturally led to the fact that the scars ensuing from beatings became a stigmatizing indication of caste, displaying who was a slave. Such corporeal chastisement and mutilation were, of course, also carefully regulated in old laws. The aforementioned Salian law, *Pactus*, which was in force in the Merovingian kingdom, specified that if a slave were to be punished this should be done in such a manner that the slave was to be tied to a ladder with his back bared and then receiving a certain amount (usually some inhumane number) of blows to the back with a stick that had to be the thickness of a little finger.[53] In Bavaria, in southern Germany, *Lex Baiuvariorum* (AD c. 740–745) allowed for slaves to be punished by cutting off a hand or putting out an eye.[54]

In order to study slavery and the lack of freedom during ancient periods, it is important not to let slavery of later times, particularly American slavery, become a filter through which slavery belonging to other periods is analyzed, something which William Linn Westermann has also pointed out: "we must first discard all the paraphernalia of modern slavery."[55] It is easy to be influenced by this, the best-known system of slavery, but—as was pointed out by Pierre Dockès in the epigraph to this chapter—it must be made clear that there are very big differences between one system of slavery and another. "New World slavery, and especially its Southern American variety," Igor Kopytoff warns us, "is a peculiar form [of slavery]."[56]

It is nonetheless important to a study of early Scandinavian slavery to seek analogies and be aware of the development of this human abomination in Europe on a general level, partly because Scandinavia has obviously always partaken in cultural exchanges with the rest of Europe, partly

[53] *Pactus* XL:6, see Fischer Drew 1991 p. 103 ("6. If the slave is guilty of such a crime that he who charged ought to require that he [the slave's lord] should hand over his slave to torture, he who charged should have rods prepared which are the size of the little finger and he should have a rack prepared where the slave can be stretched out.").

[54] *Lex Baiuvariorum* I:6, II:6, 11, 12. For the dating, see Eckhardt 1927 p. 68.

[55] Westermann 1968 p. 25. Also Igor Kopytoff (1982 p. 214) questions using the stereotype of the New World plantation slavery as the norm or model, a stereotype where "slavery is singularly monolithic, invariant, servile, chattel-like, focused on compulsory labor, maintained by violence, and suffused with brute sexuality."

[56] Kopytoff 1982 p. 225.

because comparative material is so much more significant for Scandinavia since it lacks the written sources from the time. The importance of comparative studies in research on slavery has earlier been emphasized by William D. Phillips Jr.: "Crosscultural comparisons proved to be essential, and connections had to be traced to different geographical areas and periods if the overall story of slavery were to be comprehensible."[57]

Ancient Philosophers' Views on and Historical Descriptions of Slavery

A kind of slavery has existed in most cultures of our world, because asymmetrical dependencies constitute a building block of all human social systems.[58] It is mentioned already in ancient Babylon. The *Law Code of Hammurabi* (c. 1754 BC) has parts dealing with slaves and slave owners, and we can see that a kind of time-limited slavery existed and there were also "State-slaves." The customs of marking a slave by mutilating him is obviously old, mentioned already in Hammurabi's law: "If the slave of a freed man strike the body of a freed man, his ear shall be cut off" (205), and to "remove" the mark or sign on a slave resulted in severe punishment, "If a barber, without the knowledge of his master, cut the sign off a slave on a slave not to be sold, the hands of this barber shall be cut off" (226), and "If any one deceive a barber, and have him mark a slave not for sale with the sign of a slave, he shall be put to death, and buried in his house" (227).[59]

According to the Old Testament, slaves were allowed among the Israelites. It says in *Exodus* (21:5) that a father could sell his daughter as a slave, however not to some foreigner, and in *Leviticus* (25:39) we learn that a poor man could voluntarily go into servitude ("If a countryman of yours becomes so poor with regard to you that he sells himself to you") and that you could buy slaves from "pagan nations" to be used as chattel slaves, whereas an indigenous slave should be treated leniently and not be sold abroad.

[57] Phillips 1985 p. ix.

[58] This latter was an observation made by Professor Rudolf Stichweh, Bonn, during the conference "Beyond Slavery and Freedom" at the *Bonn Center for Dependency and Slavery Studies*, November 7, 2019.

[59] Code of Hammurabi (online: http://www.wsu.edu/~dee/MESO/CODE.HTM), discussed by Professor Fernanda Pirie, Oxford, at the conference "Slaves, Serfs and Free Labor in Medieval Northern Europe" in Bonn, October 25–26, 2019.

As a research area, the topic has been overlooked for rather a long time, but during the twentieth century, for purely political reasons, it was given a lot of attention, which is why scholarly literature on slavery is confusingly copious.[60] It is easy to become disheartened and frustrated when dealing with such a tragic chapter of human history as slavery. But all historians who study topics pertaining to human cruelty must naturally always try to understand the past on its own terms and within the appropriate context to the extent that this is possible.

What thoughts, for example, did the Greek thinkers who laid the foundations for Western philosophy and morality harbor on slaves and slavery? Plato (427–347 BC) regarded slavery as a *mal nécessaire* and thought that slaves should be disciplined, punished, and directed "fairly" but firmly.[61] Plato thought it improper to enslave Greeks captured in warfare, but he had no scruples regarding the enslavement (or killing) of non-Greeks.[62] The conservative Aristotle (384–322 BC), Plato's apprentice in Athens, claimed it was impossible for slaves to live their own independent lives; they were the living property of their owners, natural and necessary implements in the possession of slave owners.[63] Like Plato, Aristotle notes that non-Greeks (Barbarians) were predestined by nature to be slaves and that states were founded on families which, in turn, consisted of free family members and slaves. Within the family there were two similar and essential types of affiliation: marriage and slavery. Both were necessary to the existence of the family and by extension to the survival of society (the state).[64]

The usual Greek term for "slave" was *andrapodon* 'man-footed creature', a term evidently constructed with the common term for "cattle" in mind, namely *tetrapodon* 'four-footed creature', which was to indicate that cattle and slaves belonged to the same category.[65]

[60] Zvi Yavetz says : "Thirty years ago practically every study of slavery was prefaced with a regret of the lack of attention the subject had received in modern research. Soon there will be cause to regret the fact that too much has been written, and not necessarily on its most important aspects. Much of the material published is trivial and dull, contributing little to the sum of acquired knowledge. Original ideas are few and far between"(1988 p. 141). The research and the literature on slavery during the classical period is immense; many important works are published in the German series *Forschungen zur Antiken Sklaverei*, founded by Joseph Vogt.

[61] Plato, *Laws* 777e, 778a.

[62] Plato, *Republic* 469b–c.

[63] Aristotle, *Politics* I:125a–b (Rackham ed. 1944). See Schlaifer 1936, Vlastos 1941 (both reprinted in Finley 1960), Garnsey 1996 pp. 107–127, Thalmann 1998; cf. Yavetz 1988 p. 156, Bradley 2000 p. 110.

[64] Aristotle, *Politics* I:253b (Rackham ed. 1944).

[65] Harvey 1988 p. 42 and Bradley 2000 p. 110.

Gradually, views on slaves were modified. For example, Euripides assumed that some were predestined to become slaves but that not all Barbarians—as opposed to Greeks—should be regarded as intended slaves, such as Aristotle had thought.[66]

Unfortunately, the Aristotelian definition of slaves in particular was used to defend slavery and the moral acceptance of slaveholding well into modern times.[67] To many conscientious thinkers, this Greek philosophical tradition has been a painful ideological burden to carry, not just because of the compound of ideas surrounding slavery as such, but also because Athens, prototype of the democratic society, was in practice constructed on and functioned due to an extensive slavery—during the fifth century BC there were some 60,000–80,000 slaves in a population of about 250,000.[68]

The thoughts of these Greek philosophers were taken on by Roman philosophers and lawyers.[69] In the Early Roman law compilation *Lex Aquilia*, from the third century BC, slaves were equated with livestock in the same way as was done in Greece.[70] During the first century BC, however, the Stoics instigated the notion that a slave was, in fact, a human being and not just an implement that could be compared to a head of cattle. This thought was adhered to by Seneca and by the lawyer Florentinus. The rules and regulations that treated slaves were included in laws that concerned the nation (*ius gentium*). The famous lawyer Ulpian wrote that mankind divides into three groups: free persons, slaves, and freed slaves.[71] In other words, the Romans accepted that all humans were exactly humans, albeit with the modification that the existing social order—consisting in free people, slaves, and freed slaves—held sway and that it was just. Cato the Elder wrote a handbook for landowners in which they were encouraged to get rid of everything that was unnecessary, such as worn out oxen, weak livestock, and old and ill slaves, in order to make their land use more efficient.[72] Cicero positioned himself close to the Aristotelian idea that certain people were by nature predestined to become slaves. Seneca further argued for an idea of a "decline of mankind,"[73]

66 See a discussion of this in Turley 2000 pp. 19 ff. and *passim*.

67 Cf., e.g., Jacoby 1994 p. 95.

68 Hopkins 1967 pp. 166, 168, cf. Bradley 2000.

69 An interesting review of how classical philosophers in Greece and Rome looked on slavery is presented by Douget 2016, see also Wiedemann 1981, Gardner 2011.

70 Bradley 2000 p. 111.

71 *Et cum uno naturali nomine homines appellaremur, iure gentium tria genera esse coeperunt: liberi et his contrarium servi et tertium genus liberti, id est hi qui desierant esse servi* (Ulpian *Digest* I:1.4).

72 Bradley 2000 p. 110.

73 See Moriarty 2011 p. 53.

which hinged on the notion that during some previous golden age there was no slavery, but when people introduced the evil of corruption the necessary consequences were administration, ownership, and slavery, which thus became legal. This idea of Seneca's was later taken up by Christian ideologies and was an argument in favor of slavery for as long as it continued to exist.[74]

The new philosophical forge of Europe during the Middle Ages comprised men of the Church, Christian thinkers. One of the most prominent, the Dominican monk Thomas Aquinas (c. 1226–1274), finds no theological problems in slavery, which is based on the idea that *ius*, the law, recognizes the existence of a master–slave relationship and that this is philosophically anchored and accepted by Aristotle, to whom he refers.[75] It is noteworthy, but actually also natural, that the new Christian Church took over the views on slavery that existed in the philosophy of Greco-Roman culture. The Christian view became a mixture of Roman philosophers' and lawyers' adaptations of the Stoics' thinking combined with the words of the Old and New Testaments. The Old Testament provided the idea that a situation in which a slave belongs to the same race and religion as the slave owner goes against Christian doctrine, although it took time for this notion to gain a foothold in reality. Not until Carolingian times was it stressed that within the Christian community nobody (no Christian, that is) could be reduced to a slave. Non-Christian foreigners of other ethnic origins, however, were potential slaves throughout medieval times and much later on in the colonies, even when these foreigners converted to Christianity. The Christian church fathers argued for the Christian community to be kept free from oppression and slavery, within the family, so to speak. Slaves existed as a necessary part of the social system. Although slaves were de facto human beings who were therefore potential targets to save in a religious sense, it was not the primary objective of Christianity to improve social conditions; it was the soul that needed to be saved, not the person, the physical body.[76]

As is well known, slavery existed long into the 1800s. As late as in 1962, slavery was abolished in Saudi Arabia, and in Mauritania in North Africa not until 1980.[77] However, in November 1981, a Mauritanian state review noted that slavery still existed and the same year a representative of the Anti-Slavery Society in London estimated that there were a total of 100,000 slaves in

[74] Verlinden 1988 p. 334.
[75] Brett 1994 pp. 3 ff., Garnsey 1996 pp. 15, 241.
[76] Verlinden 1988 p. 334, Garnsey 1996 pp. 157–235.
[77] Gordon 1987 p. 44, Bales 1999 pp. 80 ff., cf. Sawyer 1986 pp. 16 ff.

Mauritania. In 1993, the International Labour Organization (ILO), an agency of the United Nations (UN), reported that slavery exists in the country.[78] The Swedish newspaper *Dagens Nyheter* on August 10, 2007, published a short notice saying, "The West African desert country of Mauritania is praised for its decision to make slavery a criminal offence. Parliament decided late on Wednesday to make it punishable by up to ten years in prison to keep humans as slaves."[79] Would you believe it! As the newspaper stresses, slavery has been prohibited in the country since 1981, but has continued to be practiced, predominantly in the countryside.

In 1948, the UN adopted a general convention on human rights, which among other things states that slavery is prohibited. In 1953, the French ambassador in Saudi Arabia reported that in Jeddah a young male slave could be purchased for a sum corresponding to about £150 ($420) if bought privately while a girl less than 15 years of age could cost as much as £400 ($1,124) or more. The same year, the Sheikh of Qatar visited England in connection with the crowning of Queen Elizabeth II. In his retinue were slaves; the same happened when he returned in 1958.[80]

In 1956, John Laffin witnessed a slave auction in Djibouti, where more than two hundred slaves were sold. These were black Africans from Chad who had been brought there by Arabic slave traders. The buyers were mostly slave traders from Arabia who intended to transport the slaves to markets in Jeddah and Medina. Laffin recounts:[81]

> Men, women and children were brought from the warehouse and paraded on a raised platform so that all dealers could clearly see them. A trader would nudge a slave's jaw with a stick and a man would open his mouth to display his teeth. Another probe with the stick and he would flex his arm muscles. Young women were forced to expose their breasts and buttocks. A dispute developed over the virginity of a tall young ebony woman, and during the hour-long argument she was forced to squat while one of the most prominent buyers examined her with his fingers. She was terrified; her trembling was visible fifty yards away.

[78] See Segal 2003 pp. 204–205. On slavery in modern times, see also Greenidge 1958, Derrick 1975, Grace 1975, Sawyer 1986.

[79] *Det västafrikanska ökenlandet Mauretanien hyllas för sitt beslut att kriminalisera slaveriet. Parlamentet beslöt sent i onsdags att göra det straffbart med upp till tio års fängelse att hålla människor som slavar.* For a more recent discussion of slavery in Mauritania, see Ould Ciré 2014.

[80] Segal 2003 p. 199.

[81] Segal 2003 pp. 199–200.

> Occasionally children were sold in batches. They did not cry, mainly, I think, because they had no tears left, but they held tightly to one another and kept looking around as if for help. Boys of about ten or twelve had their anuses examined; homosexual buyers are fussy about disease.

That same year, 1956, the journalist James Morris wrote in *The Times* that among wealthy Saudi Arabian men, a young beautiful slave girl was considered a more than adequate present. More reports from the 1950s and 1960s further indicated that black Muslims who visited Mecca were the victims of assault and were sold into slavery.[82] Newspaper and television reports on people who disappear as slaves during conflicts and ethnic cleansings in parts of Africa continue to appear. Unfortunately, people are subjected to the atrocities of slavery even today.[83]

Research on Slavery

With the phase-out of the colonies and the abolishment of slavery, of which the American civil war formed the high point, a more in-depth scientific research into these evils was initiated.

During the communist era, slavery became a fashionable research topic, especially in what was then the Soviet Union.[84] This was expected, since slavery constitutes a principal stage in the historical materialist evolution theory, wherein slavery was a production method that preceded the feudal production method. With Marxist class theory as the starting point, the slave eras of various cultures were analyzed and particular attention was paid to slave revolts, which were regarded as examples of the revolutionary phase

[82] Segal 2003 p. 200.

[83] I am thinking, for example, of Asians working in households and in construction in the Middle East (see, e.g., http://www.hrw.org/en/reports/2004/07/13/bad-dreams; http://www.asiantribune.com/news/2012/11/27/slavery-saudi-arabia), forced labor even in Europe today (*The Guardian*, March 12, 2017), and also the "trade in sex slaves," human trafficking, that occurs today, especially with regard to young women who are lured on false premises to western Europe from the former Eastern Bloc and Soviet countries or from Southeast Asia and are kept here as veritable "slaves"; see, e.g., Sawyer 1986 p. 101, Bales 1999 pp. 34 ff., Williams (ed.) 1999, Cacho 2012, Davidson 2013, Jürgs 2014, Zeuske 2019 p. 161, and further in what follows.

[84] For short historiographies and references, see, e.g., Konstan 1975, Garlan 1988, Yavetz 1988, and Bonnassie 1991 pp. 8 ff. A Western historical-materialist synthesis treating slavery is found in Anderson 1996. An overview of how Marx and Engels analyzed slavery is given by Backhaus 1974 and Tomich 2004 pp. 9–27. For Scandinavia, see, e.g., Thomas Lindkvist's analyses of medieval farm tenants (1979).

from slave societies into feudal societies. During this period, a sharp distinction developed between the views of Western historians and Eastern Bloc historians in terms of how slavery operated in different cultures, especially the classical ones, and how this was to be analyzed scientifically.[85] The two most recent decades have provided a more balanced and fruitful climate for discussion, which has led to many good surveys of slavery across our world.[86] Lately, discussions have also been modified by the fact that an "Asian" mode or method of production with different sorts of social dependences has been given more attention.[87]

As far as Scandinavia is concerned, there are some early studies of slavery or "thraldom" (a native Scandinavian term that is used also in English, albeit nowadays with a rather archaic tone to it). The earliest is probably Matthias Calonius, *De prisco in patria servorum jure* (Concerning the law of slaves in the fatherland) (Åbo 1780), but an early, extensive, and exquisite study was presented in 1862 by Gustav Antonio Gjessing, "Trældom i Norge" (Thraldom in Norway), which is a comprehensive survey of Icelandic

[85] This dark chapter of scholarship history has been described in a well-balanced way by Zvi Yavetz (1988 pp. 113–175), and a critical historiographic overview is given by Konstan 1975, see also Schiel and Hanss 2014 pp. 11–12.

[86] An important—however, by some considered a controversial (see, e.g., Jew et al. [eds.] 2016)—contribution qualifying a Marxist analysis of slavery during the classical period was made by Moses Finley, who in a way lay a new foundation to build on in the study of early slavery (Finley 1980, [ed.] 1960).

A summary of today's state of research is found in, e.g., Orlando Patterson's significant work *Slavery and Social Death: A Comparative Study* (1982). An entertaining and brief research history is given by Thomas E. J. Wiedemann (1987 pp. 1–10); see also Patrick Manning's *Slavery and African Life* (1990), *Serfdom and Slavery: Studies in Legal Bondage*, ed. Bush (1996), *The Historical Encyclopedia of World Slavery*, ed. Rodriguez (1997), *A Historical Guide to World Slavery* (1998), *Macmillan Encyclopedia of World Slavery* (1998), Duncan Clarke's *Slaves and Slavery* (1999), *The Cambridge World History of Slavery*, vol. 1 (2011 ff.), Joseph C. Miller, *The Problem of Slavery as History: A Global Approach* (2012), David Brion Davies, *The Problem of Slavery in the Age of Emancipation* (2014), and Michael Zeuske, *Sklaverei: Eine Menschheitsgeschichte von der Steinzeit bis heute* (2018) and *Handbuch Geschichte der Sklaverei: Eine Globalgeschichte von den Anfängen bis zur Gegenwart* (2019), as well as the journal dedicated to the subject, *Slavery and Abolition* (1980 ff.). Igor Kopytoff, "Slavery" (1982) gives an interesting account of and research history on anthropological approaches to slavery.

Also the history of slavery in Europe has seen new important contributions, e.g. Charles Verlinden's *L'esclavage dans l'Europe médiévale* (1955–77), but above all from the legal perspective, William D. Phillips' *Slavery from Roman Times to the Early Transatlantic Trade* (1985), Charles Verlinden's excellent State of the Art-article in *DMA* 11 (1988) pp. 333–340, Pierre Bonnassie's *From Slavery to Feudalism in South-Western Europe* (1991), which is a broader and more in-depth study than what the title reveals, David A. E. Pelteret's *Slavery in early medieval England* (1995), a broad overview is given by Joseph C. Miller, "The Historical Contexts of Slavery in Europe" (2002), a short but excellent overview in Swedish of the European research tradition is given by Thomas Lindkvist "Från träl till landbo. Uppkomsten av det medeltida godssystemet i Europa och Norden" (2003).

[87] See, e.g., Vittinghoff 1960, Lichtheim 1963, Varga 1967, Hopkins 1978 p. 99, Watson (ed.) 1980, Bailey and Llobera 1981, Dunn 1982, Wiedemann 1987 pp. 6 ff., and McFarlane, Cooper, and Jaksic 2005, cf. Trakulhun 2014, for an interesting semantic discussion in Siam (present-day Thailand) for the introduction of the Western concepts of "slavery" and "freedom."

literature and Norwegian provincial laws. Also worthy of mention are Emil Sommarin's *Träldomen i Norden: Ett blad ur den svenska arbetsklassens äldsta historia* (Thraldom in Scandinavia: A page from the early history of the Swedish working class; 1917). Gjessing has later offshoots in Ruth Mazo Karras, *Slavery and Society in Medieval Scandinavia* (1988) and Tore Iversen, *Trelldommen: Norsk slaveri i middelalderen* (Thraldom: Norwegian slavery in the Middle Ages; 1997). The most recent works are *Trälar: Ofria i agrarsamhället från vikingatid till medeltid*, edited by Th. Lindkvist and J. Myrdahl (2003) and Stefan Brink, *Vikingarnas slavar* (Slaves of the vikings) (2012).

Furthermore, one could point to a scholar such as Marlis Wilde-Stockmeyer, whose book on thraldom in Iceland promotes the argument that particularly German scholars have systematically avoided treating thraldom and, when the topic has been dealt with, the picture has consistently been idealized by avoiding using the term "slavery" to designate this institution. Instead, says Wilde-Stockmeyer, the term "thraldom" and other euphemisms have been employed.[88] When the word *þræll* has been translated, it has been given interpretations such as 'Knecht', 'Hausgenosse', and 'Unfreier' and not, as she apparently thinks ought to have been done consistently, 'Sklave'. German scholars have discussed other social factions of society, such as women and warriors, but shied away from tackling slaves. She has a point here. Within Germanic scholarship, with its emphasis on Early Germanic society as a uniform community of free farmers, a group of socially unfree people probably presented a disturbing element. But in my opinion, she goes much too far in her criticism. A more decisive reason why slavery in Scandinavia has not been treated would be the scarcity of sources. Regarding the period prior to circa 1200, there is practically nothing that can be subjected to scholarly analysis. Wilde-Stockmeyer further criticizes earlier (German) research for being vague in its assessment of thraldom and for not wanting to give it its proper name, which should be slavery. Instead, various degrees of lack of freedom have been discussed. I think that Wilde-Stockmeyer goes over the top also with this issue. Earlier scholars were perchance more sensitive to the nuances that do, in fact, exist within Old Norse slavery. It is not a simple case of all thralls in Scandinavia having been purely working slaves, on par with livestock, which I hope this exposition will show.

[88] Wilde-Stockmeyer 1978.

Scandinavian literature is, proportionally speaking, nowhere near as plentiful as international literature with regard to the study of slavery. Within the Scandinavian discussion of thraldom, especially the issue of emancipation has been given attention. This is a logical consequence of the fact that, by the time written accounts began to emerge, slavery was on its way out of history. The sparse written sources we have for this field predominantly concern the abolition of slavery and how thralls were liberated (ON *frjáls*, No. and Da. *frels*, Sw. *fräls*) from slavery. The few medieval documents that relate to slavery concern exactly such emancipation. Also the provincial laws have many and detailed rules for how a thrall is legally brought into freedom. Exactly these research aspects, from the final phase of Scandinavian slavery, have been treated in great detail by scholars such as G. A. Gjessing, I. S. Landtmanson, Samuel Henning, Nils Ahnlund, Gösta Hasselberg, Clara Nevéus, Ruth Mazo Karras, and most recently Tore Iversen.[89]

During recent decades, slavery in Scandinavia has once more become the subject of scholarly attention. The catalyst for this discussion is no doubt the Norwegian historian Tore Iversen's aforementioned book and dissertation. One of those influenced by Iversen's ideas is the Norwegian archaeologist Dagfinn Skre, whose comprehensive thesis on the Iron Age and the Early Middle Ages in the province of Romerike attempts to set up a prehistoric model of society in which slaveholding constituted a significant element.[90] Moreover, Iversen, Skre, and other Norwegian scholars have recently taken part in a discussion about the origins of farm tenants (the *leilending* system of tenancy) in Norway wherein they have expressed the opinion that slaves were to a great extent transformed into tenants during roughly the twelfth and thirteenth centuries,[91] a model previously discussed by Thomas Lindkvist with regard to the Swedish case.[92] Lately, also the question of an existence of early (slave-driven) estates or main farms (Sw. *huvudgård*, Da. and No. *hovedgård*, Lat. *mansio*, *curia*) in Scandinavia during twelfth and thirteenth centuries has become a hot topic. Today, several scholars hold the opinion, albeit on a rather meager base of source material, that slave-powered main farms existed as forerunners for the estate system, with main farms and tenant farms, that we encounter in written sources from the thirteenth and

[89] Gjessing 1862, Landtmanson 1897, Henning 1930, Ahnlund 1935, Hasselberg 1944, Nevéus 1974, Karras 1988, and Iversen 1997.

[90] Skre 1998.

[91] See T. Iversen 1995, Dørum 1999, Sandnes 2000, and Skre 2002.

[92] See Lindkvist 1979.

fourteenth centuries and onward. Among the scholars who have discussed these aspects are, inter alia, the agrarian historian Janken Myrdal; the cultural geographers Mats Widgren, Clas Tollin, and Johan Berg; the medieval historians Thomas Lindkvist and Sigurd Rahmqvist; and the Danish historians Michael H. Gelting and Bjørn Poulsen, while Norway has contributed to the debate via the historians Tore Iversen and Hans Jacob Orning and the archaeologists Dagfinn Skre and Frode Iversen.[93]

My intention with this description of Scandinavian slavery is not to deliver yet another contribution to this already well-exposed question pertaining to the latter phase of thraldom. Instead, I want to attempt to throw some light on the earlier period for which there is no written documentation. The detailed rules and regulations about slaves contained in the provincial laws from the thirteenth to the fifteenth centuries will thus be treated sporadically here since my focus will be on older, "contemporaneous," sources, such as runic inscriptions, place names, archaeological remains, terminology, and in a more general way Old Icelandic literary sources. I think that such a study provides new, very important pieces of the obscure jigsaw puzzle that is prehistoric slavery in Scandinavia.[94] I will be using the terms "thrall" and "slave," and "thraldom" and "slavery," synonymously and rather arbitrarily, simply to underline that they are, in my view, practically identical.

Issues that I intend to discuss in the present work include: What did Scandinavian slavery look like qualitatively and quantitatively during the period AD circa 600–1200?[95] Is it possible to obtain an understanding of, for example, Viking Age thraldom, its constituent parts and extent, based on literary sources or on retrospective analysis—that is to say, might we dare to apply what we know about slavery during the fourteenth and fifteenth centuries to the Viking Age? Can other source material, such as runes, terminology,

[93] Lindkvist 1979, 2003, Gelting 1988, 2002, 2005, Rahmqvist 1996, Widgren 1998, 2003, Pedersen and Widgren 1998, Tollin 1999, Myrdal 1999, F. Iversen 1999, Skre 2002, Myrdal and Tollin 2003, Berg 2003, Poulsen 2012 and ms., and Poulsen and Orning 2019.

[94] See also the interesting analysis of Viking Age slavery in Scandinavia carried out by Mats Olsson (1999).

[95] My scope with this book is in a way similar to the scope of Alice Rio (2017) who analyzes slavery, unfreedom, and serfdom in Europe in the written records after the fall of Rome to around 1100 (but excluding Scandinavia because of the lack of written sources to be used for this region, p. 136 n. 3), a period with, as she writes, the "vexed question of the faith of slavery in the centuries following the fall of the Roman Empire. Historians of antiquity generally agree that the Roman model of slavery . . . died out some time during late antiquity. Estimates vary from as early as the second century AD to no later than the fifth. It is nevertheless absolutely clear that unfree people and unfree status continued being used throughout Europe for centuries after the demise of a recognizably 'Roman' style of exploitation. What precisely it *meant* to be unfree, however, is even harder to tell for this period than for the Roman world" (p. 1).

names, archaeology, and so on, strengthen such a retrospective method, or must we allow for a different substance of Viking Age thraldom? My hope is that a thorough analysis of all available source material can give us a new and more comprehensive picture of what slavery looked like in Scandinavia in the period before circa 1100 (which in Scandinavia is prehistory).

3

Slavery in Europe during Antiquity and the First Millennium

Some Case Studies

Many, probably most, historians of early medieval Europe view slavery as a Roman institution which had become marginal to or was fast declining in an early medieval society.

—Carl I. Hammer, 2002, p. 3

Generally, as we have seen, slavery seems to have existed at all times of human history, at least in all of the great civilizations known to us, such as the Chinese, Mesopotamian, Egyptian, and so on. In Europe there are indications that a very early form of slavery is linked to an ancient family constellation, which in Rome was known as *familia*, a primitive patriarchy headed by the *paterfamilias*. In such a family a slave could be regarded as occupying about the same social level as a wife, a concubine, a farmhand, or a child; none of these were allowed to own anything in their own name, they were not allowed to partake in political decisions, and they were not counted as part of the judicial community so that they were not able to act as witnesses. The difference seems to have been that everyone except the slave was included through kinship; the slave would hardly have been part of the kin group.[1]

David Herlihy writes: "*Familia* [. . .] originally meant a band of slaves."[2] This supposition that slavery grew out of a patriarchal family context was, among other issues, the thesis that Marx and Engels pursued in order to understand the origins of slavery. Attention was paid to and analyses carried

[1] Henrion 1941–1942, Herlihy 1985, 1991, Blackburn 1988 p. 264; cf. Brink 2008.
[2] Herlihy1991 p. 2.

Thraldom. Stefan Brink, Oxford University Press. © Oxford University Press 2021.
DOI: 10.1093/oso/9780197532355.003.0003

out on words such as Latin *famulus* 'household slave', originally: 'person belonging to a family', a word emanating from the Oscan *famel*,[3] and *familia* 'family', which according to Engels should perhaps be understood as 'slaves belonging to a particular owner (*pater*)'.[4] Also a word such as *puer* 'slave', which additionally had the meaning 'son', belonged to the same semantic sphere.

Slavery, then, has existed in Europe as far back as we can tell, that is to say, as far back as written records go. Slavery also played an important part in much earlier societies, such as the Babylonian and Egyptian civilizations. Orlando Patterson considers it plausible that no cultures have been entirely without slavery: "Probably there is no group of people whose ancestors were not at one time slaves or slaveholders."[5]

Particularly in the Roman Empire, slavery was fundamental to society and the many and prolonged wars provided Rome with a steady stream of new prisoners who became slaves. It is thought that, during the period 200–150 BC alone, as many as 250,000 individuals were enslaved by Rome.[6] In previous historiography slavery was thought to have decreased in Europe after the fall of Rome. In an important essay by the French historian Marc Bloch—which was published posthumously some years after he had been executed by the Nazis one summer night outside of Lyon—he showed that slavery did nonetheless carry on to at least the same extent as before. The reason was that the many wars during the fifth century provided the market with even more slaves, and the tough times that followed the exhausting wars and invasions led many poor people to either sell themselves as slaves or sell their children into serfdom. Bloch, however, assumes that some centuries later, around the eighth and ninth centuries during Carolingian times, slavery had decreased in both extent and importance. The reasons for this supposedly were, first, that the Church started reacting—not against slavery as such, but against keeping Christians as slaves—and, second, that the tenth century saw people who had previously been free *coloni*, freed slaves, and slaves who acquired land to inhabit, begin to merge into a new social group of peasants, tenant farmers, and serfs—in Latin *coloni*, *villani*, *bordari*, *cottari*, etc.[7] This brings

[3] Herlihy 1991 p. 2.

[4] Blackburn 1988 p. 266 and Rix 1994 pp. 35–53.

[5] Patterson 1982 p. vii.

[6] Hopkins 1967 p. 168.

[7] Fourquin 1988 p. 203. For a rather critical and different view on how slavery gradually dissolved in Europe, with an assumed agro-economic shift from agriculture based on slavery to one based on semifree tenants, see Dockès 1982 pp. 22–23 and *passim*. Dockès believes among other things that

us into the final phase of European slavery when slaveholding gradually ceased to be profitable.

A reorientation with regard to European slave trade has been initiated by the Harvard historian Michael McCormick, who has studied especially the trade routes between Europe and the Middle East during the latter part of the first millennium. McCormick notes the great import of silver, gold, and other trade goods that poured into Europe from the east and points out that the only significant trade commodity that in its extent can have constituted a profit corresponding to this is slaves. He thus reckons with a huge slave trade from Europe to the Middle East during the eighth and ninth centuries with Venice as an important trading hub.[8]

It would be natural to begin with the Greek and Roman civilizations of 2,000–3,000 years ago, from which we have a great literature and other written documents, but here I settle for a brief description of classical slavery in Rome.[9]

Slavery in the Roman Empire

It has been stated many times by many scholars that ancient Greece and Rome were both societies with economies based on slavery—on a large scale. Others have denied that especially Roman society should have been founded on slaveholding. Out of the assumed population of about 250,000 in Athens during the 500s BC it has been estimated that some 60,000–80,000 were slaves.[10] As far as Rome is concerned, it is contextually important to distinguish between early and late Rome, in other words Rome prior to year AD 1 and the Roman Empire of later times. Everyone who has dealt with slavery in Rome points out that during the earlier period slaveholding was of an

farmers and landowners were unable to financially calculate which was more profitable, slavery or rent-income from farm tenants. See also Wickham 2005 pp. 258–302.

[8] See McCormick 2001, 2002a, 2002b.

[9] A good general overview of slavery in Europe during ancient, classical times is given by Phillips 1985, see also Brockmeyer 1979, Dumont 1987, Bradley 1994, Garnsey 1996, Schumacher 2001a, Andreau and Descat 2006, Joshel 2010, Harper 2011, and Rio 2017. For analyses of Greek slavery, see, e.g., Beringer 1961, Cuffel 1966, Hopkins 1967, Finley 1978 pp. 54, 58–59, 1981, Wickert-Micknat 1983 p. 117, Garlan 1988, Rihll 1996, Garnsey 1996, and Vlassopoulos 2009. For a discussion of Muslim slavery especially in the Middle East, see Gordon 1987, Nordberg 1988 pp. 171–212, Lewis 1990, Segal 2003, Fisher 2001, Bradley and Cartledge 2011, Amiati and Cluse 2017, Gordon and Hain 2017.

[10] Hopkins 1967 p. 168.

entirely different nature compared with the later period. Slaves were fewer, were more integrated into the family, and were treated more humanely.

The Dutch legal historian Herman van den Brink highlights this in an interesting way. He notes that slavery was, in fact, a rather late phenomenon, which supposedly shows in the fact that the terms used to designate a slave during an older stage of the Latin language did not at all indicate "unfree" or "slave." This applies to the four most common terms for 'slave': *mancipium*, *famulus*, *puer*, and *servus*. The etymology of *mancipium* is hard to grasp and is polysemantic, since none of its meanings refer directly to the same category of meaning as 'unfree, slave'.[11] The etymology favored by classical authors, which is that a *mancipium* (pl. *mancipia*) was someone who was taken by "hand" (Latin *manus*), imprisoned, and taken away, is according to modern etymologists unlikely. The Dutch archaeologist Frands Theuws has shown that *mancipia* in the southern part of the Low Countries in the early eighth century apparently referred to certain dependent, nonfreeholding, but seemingly free farmers, not to slaves.[12] The oldest etymological layer of the word *famulus* (pl. *famuli*) 'slave' designates someone belonging to a family.[13] Both words, *famulus* and *familia*, probably had an origin in the Oscan language.[14] Originally, *famuli* thus referred to everyone who was part of the Roman *familia* over which a *paterfamilias* held power, in other words not just slaves, but also wife, children, servants, and other members of the household. The word *puer*, which was used unambiguously about a slave, among other things in order to name a slave by a specific slave-name, originally meant 'son, boy'.[15] Finally, we have the word *servus*, which is somewhat more problematic to etymologize, since it is probably a Latin loan from Etruscan. van den Brink puts the word into a historical context wherein, he holds, slavery only appears as a social phenomenon when we can detect urbanization, something that happens during Etruscan times on the Italian peninsula. The Romans, then, supposedly took over the phenomenon as well as the term for it from the Etruscans. van den Brink thus promotes the thesis that slaves were few in classical (early) Rome and that they were treated well. Slavery did not appear as a general social phenomenon until urbanization

[11] van den Brink 1974 p. 45, with references to fundamental exploration of this question by Reinach 1960 p. 20, Kaser 1971 p. 45; also cf. Nehlsen 1984.

[12] Theuws ms.

[13] See, e.g., Rix 1994 pp. 35–53, Buongiorno 2017.

[14] Buongiorno 2017.

[15] For a discussion on the use of *puer* meaning 'son' as well as 'slave' and the arbitrary use of these two meanings by the early theologians, see Garnsey 1996 pp. 220–235.

was underway, and this coincided with Etruscan supremacy, hence the loan of *servus*, according to van den Brink.

The aforementioned French historian Marc Bloch has written an excellent general introduction to the topic:

> In the Roman world of the first centuries A.D., the slave was everywhere: in the fields, in shops, in workshops, in offices. The rich kept hundreds or thousands, and one had to be quite poor not to own at least one. This is definitely not to say that servile labor had a monopoly on any activity, however humble. Many artisans were in a free condition, and innumerable fields were cultivated by peasants, small land-owners or tenant-farmers who had never been the property of a master. Vespasian reserved for the free workers of Rome those hard tasks that he refused to give to machines. Nonetheless, neither the material life of Greco-Roman societies, nor even their civilization at its most exquisite, could be conceived of without the existence of this forced labor. The Germans also had their slaves, either as servants or field hands. On the other hand, the Europe of modern times, with a few rare exceptions, has not known slavery on its own soil. For the most part, this transformation, one of the most profound that mankind has known, took place very slowly in the course of the high Middle Ages.[16]

Literature on slavery in the Roman Empire is tremendously extensive and reveals diverse opinions about central questions.[17] In the light of this, only a very superficial overview can be given in order to understand what slavery looked like in the Rome of classical times and in order for us later on to make

[16] "Dans le monde romain des premiers siècles, l'esclave était partout: aux champs, à la boutique, à l'atelier, à l'office. Les riches en entretenaient des centaines ou des milliers; il fallait être bien pauvre pour n'en posséder au moins un. Non certes que la main-d'œuvre servile eût le monopole d'aucune activité, si humble fût-elle; beaucoup d'artisans étaient de condition libre; d'innombrables champs étaient cultivés par des paysans, petits propriétaires ou fermiers, qui n'avaient jamais été la chose d'un maître; c'était au libre prolétariat de Rome que Vespasien réservait les rudes besognes qu'il refusait aux machines, Il n'en est pas moins vrai que ni la vie matérielle des sociétés gréco-romaines, ni leur civilisation même, dans ce qu'elle eut de plus exquis, ne sauraient se concevoir sans le secours de ce travail forcé. Les Germains eux aussi avaient leurs esclaves, serviteurs ou ouvriers de culture. L'Europe des temps modernes, par contre, à quelques rares exceptions près, a ignoré, sur son propre sol, l'esclavage. Pour sa plus grande part, cette transformation, une des plus profondes qu'ait connues l'humanité, s'est opérée très lentement, au cours du haut moyen âge" Bloch 1947 p. 30; English translation in Bloch 1975 p. 1.

[17] A few central works are Westermann 1955, Finley (ed.) 1960, 1972, 1980, 1981, Hopkins 1978, while modern works are Dockès 1982, Bonnassie 1991, Gonzales 1997, and Bradley and Cartledge (eds.) 2011.

use of this knowledge as a backdrop to our analysis of not only Scandinavian slavery but also the slavery we believe existed within the Germanic area.

Keeping slaves as part of the household, then, constituted an important foundation for the economy of the Roman Empire; Max Weber has even gone as far as defining the entire classical culture of antiquity as a slave culture,[18] while others have differing views, for example, Keith Hopkins.[19] Marc Bloch points out that slaves were found everywhere in society, they took care of household duties in the home,[20] they were craftsmen,[21] they worked as shepherds, they worked the fields in great numbers, and they were also used as miners.[22] Slaves could be bought, inherited, or given as gifts. As has been noted, it is traditionally held that the majority of slaves in the Roman Empire were acquired through conquest and military victories. The notion that the majority of Roman slaves were brought up at home or bought in peaceful circumstances has also been voiced,[23] although this seems doubtful to some.[24] A Roman could also become enslaved if he committed a grave crime. As is well known, however, a Roman could not become a slave in Rome. If a slave were caught thieving the punishment was death. If a free Roman were caught thieving it was stated already in the oldest known Roman law codex, the so-called Twelve Tables (c. 450 BC), that he was then to be killed or sold into slavery "on the other side of the Tiber."[25] Recently, Thomas E. J. Wiedemann has argued vigorously against a theory that focuses overly one-sidedly on warfare as the main factor in the acquisition of new slaves. He believes that the written sources are insufficient when it comes to bringing out two other important factors, namely kidnapping and children being either exposed immediately after birth or being sold by their parents.[26]

The English sociologist Keith Hopkins, who has studied the Roman slave society in detail, estimates that around the end of the first century AD there were around 2–3 million slaves in Italy and that they made up circa 40 percent of the total population. Kenneth Neill Cameron comes up with the

[18] Weber 1924 pp. 293 ff.; cf. Hopkins 1978 p. 99.
[19] Hopkins 1967 p. 172.
[20] See, e.g., Gonzales 1997 pp. 342 ff.
[21] See, e.g., Westermann 1942.
[22] See, e.g., Lauffer 1956–57.
[23] Schtaerman 1969 pp. 36 ff; cf. Watson 1987 p. 8.
[24] E.g., Hopkins 1978 p. 102.
[25] Watson 1987 p. 16.
[26] Wiedemann 1987 p. 22: "Our sources under-estimate two of the major and constant sources of new slaves in the ancient world, kidnapping and piracy in time of 'peace,' and the enslaving of new-born children exposed by their parents, or of not-so-new-born children sold by them to slave-traders."

following figure: during the reign of Claudius there were some 21 million slaves in the Roman Empire.[27] Even so, it must be said that slaveholding in Rome was by no means uniform across the centuries.

After the Etruscans had been ousted during the 500s BC and the clan-based society had disappeared during the 300s BC, the so-called Patricians came into power. They based their power on landownership and control of the senate. Already in the 400s BC they nonetheless had to share power with the upstarts in Rome, the nouveau riche Plebeians. It is thought that small and medium-sized landed estates dominated during these centuries, not just in Latium, but in many parts of Italy. Individual farmers could own their farms.

During the third and second centuries BC this would change radically due to the many wars. The aristocracy in Rome controlled the army and could, as a consequence of all the wars, amass great amounts of booty, in particular conquered areas of land, but also great numbers of slaves. This great landownership became extended because the farmers, who were also soldiers in the army, could no longer look after their farms and when they returned home after all the campaigns they were forced to either borrow great sums of money in order to begin farming their fields again or simply sell their possessions. In this way a great many farms ended up in the hands of senators. The economic and political polarization in society thus increased. In the course of only two centuries landownership in Rome changed radically.[28] Hence, it has been assumed that something fundamental happened around the fourth and third centuries BC, with a new agrarian economic system and a new "kind" of slavery, with large-scale employment of servile laborers working fields.[29]

This change of system in Roman society meant that free farmers were replaced with slaves and individual estates merged into bigger units, not always *latifundia*, which were large slave-run landed estates,[30] but also some smaller estates, which could be run by free farmers (of the sort that sold

[27] Cameron 1973 p. 190.

[28] Dockès 1982 pp. 51–52.

[29] Aspects discussed by Professor Pierangelo Buongiorno, Lecce/Münster, in a lecture at the Bonn Center for Dependency and Slavery Studies, Bonn University, January 27, 2020, see also later.

[30] *Latifundia* were a sort of large farms focusing on grain production or the production of fruit or olives on a large scale, predominantly in southern Italy, where the workforce was made up of great numbers of hard-driven work slaves, usually branded and chained. The overseer or warden was a *villicus*, who also had a slave background. See esp. Roux 1910, Tibiletti 1955, Russo 1999, and Launaro 2011. In recent studies the role of the *latifundia* in the Roman agrarian production has been very much toned down, as an exceptional phenomenon concentrated in a very few core regions, such as southern Italy (see Rio 2017 pp. 4–5 and n. 12), which should have consequences for historians' attempt to find "*latifundia*-like" units in, e.g., northern Europe in the Early Middle Ages.

their farms) or by slaves.[31] That the new owners of these great estates chose not to exploit the opportunity to turn these farmers into paid workers on their lands, but chose instead to import slaves on a huge scale is, according to Hopkins, attributable to the fact that this was much more profitable since slaves could be forced to work twice as much as paid workers (tenant farmers).[32] A slave was actually expensive to acquire, but to many wealthy Romans this did not pose a great problem. The smaller estates were merged into large units, which provided the owners with great yields generated by working slaves inhumanly.[33]

This hypothesis of Hopkins' goes completely against the grain of the traditional historical explanation that if a landowner were given the choice of having slaves or farmers work his land then he would choose the latter, as was the case, for example, when feudalism emerged. The reason why the former option prevailed in Rome may be that the significant economic profit that could be obtained enabled wealthy people to buy great numbers of slaves. In a different work, Hopkins has pointed out that it was above all in central Rome that the exploitation of slaves on landed estates was extensive and that this was supposedly not the case in more peripheral areas of the Roman Empire.[34]

The fundamental pillar of society was, as mentioned, "the family," *familia*, in which the father, *paterfamilias*, had unrestricted power over the lives of the family members. At the bottom of this family hierarchy were, of course, the slaves, whose prospects included beatings, floggings, being sold, or being killed. A slave did not have his own name, but was known by his owner's name: *Marcus*' slave was called *Maricipor* (a formation based on *puer* 'boy'). The slave was an object, a thing.

Important information about classical slavery can be found in epigraphic inscriptions from the Roman Empire and also from *Germania superior* and *inferior*.[35] Interestingly, inscriptions commemorating slaves are found fairly often. From their *cognomen*[36] we can ascertain where these slaves originally

[31] Hopkins 1978 p. 9.
[32] Hopkins 1978 pp. 110–111.
[33] See also Dockès 1982 p. 52.
[34] Hopkins 1967 p. 172.
[35] On names of slaves in epigraphic inscriptions, see, e.g., Solin 1971, 1990. *Germania superior* consisted of present-day southern Germany and northeast France, *Germania inferior* was situated to the north of that, in present-day northwest Germany, Belgium, and the Netherlands.
[36] In practice, all Roman men of high social standing had at least three names: a first name (*praenomen*), a family name (*gentilicum*), and a sort of byname (*cognomen*), which was commonly used as the addressing form in nonofficial situations; e.g., *Nero Claudius Drusus*, *Marcus Aurelius Scaurus*.

came from. An example is *Felix Germanus*, which is Felix from "Germania."[37] Unfortunately, there are many sources of error to take into account since, according to Varro (*La Lingua Latina* 8.21), one could give a new slave a name that indicated not where he originated, but where he was bought.

In his world history, the historical materialist Kenneth Neill Cameron has greatly emphasized what also Max Weber and Marc Bloch have stressed, which is that the Roman Empire was a slave society, one founded on slave work:[38]

> The basic labor everywhere was slave labor. The Roman legions were supplied with their armaments by slave labor (in the "Gallic" and other mines). The famed "Roman roads" over which these legions marched were built by slaves. The architectural wonders of Rome, the Colosseum, the Forum, the Baths of Caracalla, on whose ruins tourists gaze today, were constructed by slave gangs owned by building contractors. The great aqueducts were built and maintained by slaves; the sewers of Rome were built by slaves and maintained by slaves. Slave labor predominated in manufacturing. In the potteries of Arretium, 123 out of 132 workers were slaves. The 9 workers who were not slaves were craftsmen, some of whom signed their wares. And this, in general, was the relationship of slave labor to paid labor: the paid worker was a skilled worker, the slave the laborer.

Keith Hopkins argues similarly,[39] stressing that there are, in fact, only two examples of slave societies in Europe: ancient Greece and the Apennine peninsula during Roman times. His definition of a *slave society* is that, in one such, slaves supposedly make up a sizable demographic component (more than 20 percent) and play a vital part in production. Peter Garnsey has written: "There have been slaves in many societies, but very few slave societies,"[40] whereas Allen J. Frantzen is of the opinion that "Early Germanic, Scandinavian, Irish, and Anglo-Saxon societies were slave-holding but were not 'slave societies' to the extent that either ancient societies, such as Rome, or New World societies (the American South) were."[41] After collecting the different opinions and arguments of the matter, Alice Rio has also arrived

[37] Lazzaro 1993.
[38] Cameron 1973 p. 187.
[39] Hopkins 1978 p. 99.
[40] Garnsey 1996 p. 2.
[41] Frantzen 1994 p. 6.

at the conclusion that "The Roman Empire is one of the very few societies in history that are generally agreed to deserve the 'slave society' label."[42] In this connection, the distinction made by David Turley must be noted, since he distinguishes between *societies with slaves* and *slave societies*. In the latter, there was exploitation of slaves on a large scale, usually in farming and mining, while in the former slaves were found to a lesser extent, mostly as servants in the home, as "objects of prestige," for sexual services and so on. This is a relevant distinction, but one that much previous research has not considered directly and the designation "slave society" has therefore often been applied to societies that had any form of slavery at all.[43]

Peter Garnsey's definition of a slave society is as follows:[44]

> In a genuine slave society (as distinct from a society with slaves, or a slave-owning society), slaves are numerous, but the crucial issue is not slave numbers, but whether slaves play a vital role in production. In a pre-industrial society with, inevitably, an agrarian base, this means that they should form the core of the agricultural labour force, more particularly on the estates of the wealthy.

This is very much an economic definition of a "slave society," whereas other scholars give the social a more prominent place in a definition.[45]

There must have been a great influx of slaves to the center of the Roman Empire as a consequence of the continuous campaigns so favorably carried out, especially during the time of the Republic. During the second and third Punic Wars in the first century BC, about 2,000 slaves were taken at the capture of Lilybaeum, and furthermore 5,000 Hirpinians, 30,000 Tarentines (Tarentum in southern Italy), 3,000 Mandurians, 5,700 Macedonians, 20,000 Sardinians, 5,632 Histrians, 700 Ligurians, 2,500 Boeotians, 150,000 Epirotes, 10,000 Spaniards, and 50,000 when Carthage was conquered and destroyed, according to Livy, Aurelius Victor, and Orosius.[46] The huge amount of new slaves coming to Rome mostly passed through the famous slave market on the island of Delos, where, according to Strabo, as many as 10,000 slaves could be sold in just one day, a number that should probably be taken with

[42] Rio 2017 p. 4.
[43] Turley 2000 pp. 4–5, 62 ff.
[44] Garnsey 1996 p. 2.
[45] See, e.g., Bradley 1994 p. 30 and the important discussion on the problem by Vlassopoulos 2016 pp. 95–99, Zeuske 2019, and the contributions in Lenski and Cameron (eds.) 2018.
[46] Yavetz 1988 p. 2.

a good pinch of salt. Delos reached its peak as a slave market around 130 BC; then, following a final devastation in 48 BC, it ceased to exist altogether. Instead, the markets moved to other places, predominantly Rome.

A consequence of these incessant campaigns and the steady stream of new hordes of slaves was that agriculture in the Roman Empire, particularly in the central regions, changed in nature. The many small farms disappeared one by one and were replaced, as mentioned, by *latifundia*, or other kinds of large farms, where many slaves were placed as workers. The former smallholders were either employed as soldiers or became part of the massively expanding Roman population within which they figured as a sizable city proletariat (*plebs urbana*).

Modern reckonings of the number of slaves in Italy indicate that just before the beginning of the Common Era there were as many as 2–3 million slaves, making up about 30–40 percent of the population.[47] A different estimate says that around the time of the Principate (27 BC–AD 284) there were circa 6 million slaves in the Roman Empire out of a total population of an estimated 60 million people.[48]

Another effect of the existence of a large and toughly managed slave population was the so-called slave revolts,[49] a phenomenon that—as mentioned—has caught the attention particularly of Marxist and historical-materialist scholars who have studied slavery in ancient societies.[50] Several slave revolts took place during a fairly short period of time (c. 140–70 BC) of which one of the best known, besides the Spartacus revolt, is a revolt that began in Sicily in 135 BC and was led by a Syrian slave, Eunus from Apamea. Within a short time, the revolt had spread across Sicily and the slave army counted an unfathomable (if we can rely on the sources) 200,000 men, which, if nothing else, gives us an understanding of how many slaves were captured during campaigns and existed within the Roman Empire. Only after Rome sent military troops to Sicily was the rebellion put down. Following this episode, it was prohibited for slaves to carry arms.

The perhaps best-known slave revolt began in 73 BC when a certain Spartacus (109–71 BC), a slave from Thrace, succeeded in inducing his colleagues at the gladiator school in Capua to rebel and take up arms.[51]

[47] Brunt 1971 pp. 121–130, Hopkins 1978 p. 9, Fitzgerald 2000 p. 3.

[48] Scheidel 1997.

[49] On the slave revolts or the slave wars, see, e.g., Vogt 1957, 1965, 1975, 1983, Volkman 1961, Dockès 1982 p. 56, Bradley 1989, Shaw (ed.) 2001, Harrison 2006 pp. 142–166, Urbainczyk 2008, Schiavone 2013. For a minimalist view on slave revolts, see Wiedemann 1987 pp. 47 ff.

[50] For an excellent exposition, see Verlinden 1988 p. 335.

[51] Shaw (ed.) 2001, Schiavone 2013; cf. Harrison 2006 pp. 155–163.

During the subsequent three years, Spartacus managed to gather an army of 120,000 slaves under his command and embarked on a regular war against Rome. Not until the Roman senate handed over the empire to Crassus, one of the greatest landowners, who mustered an army of 50,000 men of whom he paid 30,000 out of his own pocket, could the slave army be defeated in 71 BC.

An obvious reason why slave revolts could take place in southern Italy, especially in Sicily, during this time and on this scale, is that those who were kept as slaves in this area were predominantly herders who took care of livestock on the great estates that specialized in animal husbandry. These slaves naturally led active lives; they were not fettered to farm and land. The possibilities for similar slave revolts were minimized during the later Republic when the system of *villae*, a kind of estate, emerged.[52] The great *latifundia* of earlier times, with large cattle herds taken to pastures, were superseded. The new system involved the emergence of *villae*, great and small self-supporting estates, but also specialized *latifundia* continued to exist, with large slave populations who were, however, attached to a *villa*, lived in huts, and were superintended by a warden (*villicus*).[53] A *villa* has been described as "a cluster of houses, usually surrounding one or two yards, a manor as well as work sheds and outhouses"; belonging to this were farms, individually situated or gathered into villages, while a *latifundium* could consist of sizable agricultural grounds with great slave shelters or including several *villae*.[54]

Spartacus' slave revolt had a decisive influence on the political development of Rome. After the senate handed over power to Crassus, who became a consul, there was a period during which the old system of the senate changed into a dictatorship, the Principate. The first ruler of this, Caesar, came to shape this new system, which was held together by a standing, salaried army and an advanced fiscal-administrative apparatus that could ensure the foundations for a solid economy. Emperor Augustus refined this power base, among other things by introducing a tax on landownership (*tributum*), a tax on "movable property" (*tributum capitis*), inheritance tax and sales tax alongside revenues from selling slaves or buying their freedom, and, finally, customs duties. The main part of the army was

[52] See, e.g., Smith 1997, Frazer (ed.) 1998, and Becker and Terrenato (eds.) 2011.
[53] Dockès 1982 pp. 62–63; cf. Bodel 2011.
[54] Dockès 1982 p. 65.

stationed along the *Limes*, the borders of the Roman Empire against the "Barbarians" to the north.

At an ordinary Roman *villa* there were different kinds of slaves. Uppermost in the hierarchy was the warden or the bailiff (*villicus*) and his wife, below him were various kinds of foremen and further down craftsmen followed by other household slaves (*mediastini*). At the bottom of the slave hierarchy were work slaves, who were often chained.[55] Since the estate owner was only rarely present at his estate, the warden was an important figure with considerable power, which is why it was essential to find as competent and faithful a person as possible to fulfill this role. In Scandinavia, the counterpart to this *villicus* was, as we shall see, the *bryti*, a superintendent or estate manager. It was the task of the *villicus* to supervise the farming, ensure no slaves fled, ensure that the work slaves were properly chained, and oversee the cooking (which his wife was in charge of) and distribution of the food.

Roman slavery was, from a financial point of view, only one of the ways in which the urban upper classes seized on a large enough surplus to maintain their lifestyle. During the second century AD slavery began to lose its significance in Rome. Slaveholding no longer provided a sufficient profit. During the fourth and fifth centuries slavery decreased even more, partly because the number of slaves declined since no new slaves were brought into the system, but first and foremost because the distinction between semifree tenants and unfree slaves had become practically nonexistent.[56]

It thus seems clear that the nature of slavery changed during the time of the Roman Empire. In pre-Republican times slaves appear to have led relatively tolerable lives, closely affiliated to the people on the farm to which they belonged. In Republican times conditions changed due to the large crowds of war prisoners captured during the continuous campaigns. These prisoners were brought into the Roman economy as slaves via, inter alia, the creation of great *latifundia*. During the Principate slaveholding became differentiated; lack of legal freedom was general, but a social hierarchy within the slave population became ever more noticeable. It is generally thought that slaveholding decreased dramatically during the fourth and fifth centuries and was superseded by farming by smallholders.

[55] Dockès 1982 p. 70.
[56] Hopkins 1967 p. 176.

Slavery in Europe after the Fall of Rome

In the early fifth century, the proud Roman Empire collapsed.[57] The former empire was divided into the Byzantine Empire, which continued to exist as a cohesive unit for another thousand years, and western Europe, which was torn apart by wars and extensive migrations. When the Germanic Visigoths, led by Alaric, conquered Rome in 410, many Romans (and their slaves) ended up as slaves to the Goths. Other invasions, for example, by the Huns in 452, the Vandals in 455, and the Heruli in 476, had similar outcomes—many new slaves were taken. During the Ostrogothic rule of Theodoric (493–526) we acquire laws in the shape of the so-called Theodoric's Edict (*Edictum Theodorici*), which describes conditions in Italy. During this time, slavery became predominantly rural.[58] The situation of slaves worsened significantly compared to what had been common during the last phase of the Roman Empire. The slave owner's power over his slaves was greatly intensified. He could kill his slave if the latter fell afoul of the law, the slave could be burned alive if he had had sex with a widow (even if she had given her consent), the slave could not marry and a female slave was her owner's concubine, the slave could be arbitrarily transferred from one estate to another to work there or to a semifree tenant to work on his farm, in which case it would seem unlikely that the tenant would treat the slave any kinder than the slave owner did. The semifree tenant, *colonus*, was, however, not much better situated than the slave in terms of legal and financial matters during this time.

When the Langobards obtained power over Italy in 568, new rules controlling the lives of slaves were brought in. In the law compilation or edict of King Rothari (*Leges Rotharis* or *Edictum Rotari* from 643), *aldii*—who were a kind of semifree, according to Katherine Fischer Drew, legally "halfway between the slave on the one hand and the freeman on the other"[59]—were sided with *servi ministeriales*, who were a specific category of slaves, often of Roman origins, with particular craft skills and who lived in the household of the slave owner. These two categories of slaves, skilled craftsman slaves

[57] I do not treat all slave societies of Europe here, but give brief overviews of the slavery we encounter in some parts of Europe, mainly in the old Germanic-speaking area in northern Europe. On southern Europe, see, e.g., Verlinden 1955, 1977, Yavetz 1988, Bonnassie 1991, Garnsey 1996, Harper 2011, Rio 2017. Also, Muslim slavery in the Middle East and in North Africa is of great interest to comparative studies, see, e.g., Gordon 1987, Willis (ed.) 1985, Lewis 1990, Segal 2001, and Harrison 2006.

[58] For the account that follows, see Verlinden 1988 p. 335. See also Rio 2017.

[59] Fischer Drew 1956 p. 18.

of Roman origins and slaves of non-Roman origins, were legally and financially distinct from *rusticani*, agricultural work slaves, in such a way that a *rusticanus*, who had occupied the lowest level on the Roman social scale, was only worth half as much as a *servus ministeriales* and an *aldius*, who were at the bottom of the Langobard social scale.[60]

Interestingly, *rusticani* were transformed as a social category since they were agricultural workers and as such very distanced from their owners, so that *rusticani* took on the character of semifree tenants, while *servi ministerialis* remained slaves strictly controlled by their owners.

With King Liutprand's capitularies[61] (712–744), the presence of the Church becomes more tangible in the legal perception of slaves. With Liutprand's Langobard Law, *manumissio in ecclesia* is introduced, which is the possibility to grant freedom to a slave in a church, and also the possibility for a slave to, with his owner's permission, become a priest. This change in the use of slaves was of importance to the subsequent few centuries, when an extensive number of churches were established in the form of privately owned churches built by feudal magnates and noblemen on their main estates. These churches became financial entities, which was the property of the owner, *patronus*, who could sell it and who also presided over churchly matters. It was not uncommon that the *patronus* had one of his slaves as the church priest in order to fully control church, priest, and congregation and to preclude the bishops' involvement.[62]

To return to the "heartland" of the Roman Empire, the Apennine Peninsula, that is modern Italy, it can be ascertained that as long as the empire existed a probably large proportion of the population was made up of slaves. For various reasons that have been eagerly discussed by scholars for a long time and that were indicated earlier, slavery as it existed during the heyday of the Roman Empire collapsed. One reason was the absence of wars resulting in recently conquered peoples and areas, which put a stop to the influx of slaves; another reason was the new financial trend with estates, main farms and "semifree" tenants on the farms belonging to the estate that proved more economical and administratively efficient.[63] Slave trade, however, continued during early medieval times with new slaves coming in from, for example,

[60] See also Fischer Drew 1956 pp. 18–19.

[61] Capitularies were royal decrees and regulations that came to complement and alter the Frankish laws. (See *Monumenta Germaniae Historica*: http://bsbdmgh.bsb.lrz-muenchen. de/dmgh_new/.)

[62] Cf. Brink 1991 p. 115.

[63] Cf. Wickham 2005 pp. 286–293, Harper 2011 p. 502.

the Balkans. "Less intensive" slaveholding appears to have existed until about 1000, but—as was pointed out previously—if one is to believe Michael McCormick, this slave trade was not modest, but rather extensive, especially during the eighth and ninth centuries, with Venice as the trade hub.[64]

In later medieval times, slavery strangely enough had a boom in Italy, particularly toward the end of the Middle Ages and during the sixteenth century. In spite of slavery ending in other parts of western Europe, it had a renaissance in Italy. It was especially in ports, such as Genoa and Venice, that slaves were common, and the reason for this must be that there was an import of slaves to these ports. It is estimated that 4–5 percent of the population of Genoa during the fifteenth century consisted of slaves while inland towns, such as, for example, Florence, could only boast a few hundred. It was characteristic of this "slave renaissance" in Italy that the slaves were, in fact, exclusively young women from the areas north and west of the Black Sea, Russians, Tartars, and others, who were used within the household as some sort of exclusive possessions.[65]

Germany and the "Germanic" Area

Very little is known of any potential slavery among the Germanic speaking peoples of northern Europe during the first half of the first millennium. The main source remains Tacitus' *Germania*, which is unfortunately problematic and in many respects hard to interpret;[66] from our viewpoint this concerns especially what Tacitus means when he writes *servus*—does this designate a slave or a tenant?[67] Tacitus' description of slaveholding among the Germanic

[64] McCormick 2002a.

[65] On this "slave renaissance" in Italy, see Epstein 2001 *passim*, esp. pp. xi–xiii.

[66] The evaluation of Tacitus' *Germania* as a historical source has oscillated considerably over the years. Scholars in the nineteenth century, such as Karl Müllenhoff (1870–1908) took the text more or less at face value, which also can be said of Rudolf Much's, however important, contribution (1937), but with the critical readings by especially Eduard Norden (1923) it was understood that *Germania* was very much part of a learned literary tradition, full of reused ideas and motifs (*Wandermotive*). A recent critical approach has been taken by Allan A. Lund (e.g., 1991 pp. 1951–1954, and Lund 1995), who considers *Germania* essentially useless as a historical source; and Krebs 2011 and Jansson 2013 are written more or less in the same vein. A general introduction to Tacitus' *Germania*, with discussions of critical source problems relating to the work, is given by Anthony R. Birley (1999), Günter Neumann and Henning Seemann (eds.) 1992, Jan-Wilhelm Beck 1998, and for a recent sound historiographic analysis and a discussion of *pro et contra* arguments, see J. B. Rives 1999 pp. 56–66.

[67] See, e.g., Thompson (1957), who represents a minimalist view on slavery in Germany after the fall of Rome: "Indeed, there is no evidence that domestic slaves existed on any appreciable scale among the Germans, and Tacitus denies that it existed at all." (p. 17) Thompson bases this statement on his interpretation of the passages in Tacitus' *Germania* where slaves are mentioned. In, e.g., chapter 25:1 the word *servus* occurs, which he interprets rather as a sort of farm tenant. And the existence of slaves

peoples in chapters 24 and 25 is famous and often cited. In chapter 24, Tacitus describes the Germanic peoples' partiality for games and gambling, their obstinacy, but also their honesty, which can lead to their undoing and self-inflicted slavery:

> Surprisingly, gambling for them is a serious matter, in which they engage when sober; so recklessly do they win and lose that when all is gone they stake their bodily freedom on the last and final throw. The loser willingly becomes a slave; although perhaps the younger and stronger, he suffers himself to be bound and sold. Such is their persistence in a thoroughly bad business: they themselves call it honour. Slaves of this sort they exchange in trade, to free themselves from the shame of victory.[68]

In chapter 25, we then find the famous description of how slaves functioned within Germanic society:

> The other slaves they do not use as we do, with designated duties throughout the household; each one controls his own holding and home. The master requires from him, as from a tenant, some amount of grain or livestock or clothing, and only so far must the slave submit; the wife and children perform the other domestic chores. Seldom do they beat a slave or punish him with shackles and hard labour, yet they are apt to kill him: not through harsh discipline, but in a fit of rage as they would a foe, except that the deed is unpunished. Freedmen rank little higher than slaves. They rarely have any influence in the home, and never in the state, excepting only those tribes ruled by kings. For there they surpass both the free-born and the well-born; among the others, unequal freedmen are an indication of freedom.[69]

in chapter 20:2, he says, "proves nothing: the fact that slave and free children grew up together is inconclusive for the existence of domestic slaves." (p. 17 n. 2) He does not, however, deny that slaves existed—as great numbers of war captives—but his point is that Germany during this period was not a "slave society." (p. 229) See also the discussion in Wiedemann 1987 p. 5.

[68] *Aleam, quod mirere, sobrii inter seria exercent, tanta lucrandi perdendive temeritate, ut, cum omnia defecerunt, extremo ac novissimo iactu de libertate ac de corpore contendant. Victus voluntariam servitutem adit: quamvis iuvenior, quamvis robustior adligari se ac venire patitur. Ea est in re prava pervicacia; ipsi fidem vocant. Servos condicionis huius per commercia tradunt, ut se quoque pudore victoriae exsolvant.* (The Latin text, here and later, is from http://www.thelatinlibrary.com/tacitus/tac.ger.shtml). Here and later I cite the English translations from James Rives' translation of Tacitus' *Germania* (1999), p. 87. For an analysis and commentary of what Tacitus says about slaves, see also Much 1937 pp. 230–236 and *passim*.

[69] *Ceteris servis non in nostrum morem, descriptis per familiam ministeriis, utuntur: suam quisque sedem, suos penates regit. Frumenti modum dominus aut pecoris aut vestis ut colono iniungit, et servus*

What Tacitus describes here is first the fact that a free person could hand himself over into slavery, something we know was practised much later in Scandinavia among other places. What baffled Tacitus was, however, not the possibility of voluntarily entering slavery as a consequence of debt, criminal offense, or inability to provide for oneself, but as the outcome of obstinacy and honesty in gambling, which was, according to Tacitus, common practice and was taken seriously by the Germans. Whether this describes actual practices or whether it is a reflection of Roman culture or has been passed through a Roman filter is uncertain. When Tacitus goes on to describe slave-holding, we encounter something that we today could hardly term regular thraldom or slavery, but rather a sort of tenant system with (semifree?) farmers placed on small dependent farms who had to pay a rent in kind to their master. This, of course, looks much like the system that replaced slavery in Europe during medieval times, with semifree tenants inhabiting leased farms and paying rents, farmers who were socially comparable to slaves and legally occupying the middle ground between the free and the unfree, since their master's private jurisdiction was frequently what was practised; in other words, they were outside common law. In this instance, we should probably believe Tacitus. If slavery among the Germanic peoples was conceived in the same way and played the same role as it did in the Roman Empire, Tacitus would presumably have remarked on this, but since he describes a digression in relation to Roman slavery, the impression is that his account carries a certain evidential weight. But the decisive question is, of course, what it is Tacitus is describing and whether his terminology leads us astray. He employs the term *servus*, which in his day referred to a proper slave, be it in the household or at a *latifundium*. Germanic society supposedly deviated quite radically from Roman in this respect so that the term that Tacitus employs for a "dependent" or "unfree" person may not be entirely adequate. What he actually describes instead is a sort of tenant system wherein farmers occupied their own (albeit dependent) farms. It is noteworthy how he stresses that a master could kill his farmer without any legal repercussions, which demonstrates that the legal position of such individuals was low and that they were subjects to their master's authority. What we might plausibly deduce from Tacitus'

hactenus paret: cetera domus officia uxor ac liberi exsequuntur. Verberare servum ac vinculis et opere coercere rarum: occidere solent, non disciplina et severitate, sed impetu et ira, ut inimicum, nisi quod impune est. Liberti non multum supra servos sunt, raro aliquod momentum in domo, numquam in civitate, exceptis dumtaxat iis gentibus quae regnantur. Ibi enim et super ingenuos et super nobiles ascendunt: apud ceteros impares libertini libertatis argumentum sunt.

description is that "slavery" among the Germanic peoples was dissimilar to its Roman counterpart.

Tacitus treats slaves a further three times in his *Germania*. In the well-known and much discussed chapter 40, in which Germanic people's worship of the goddess *Nerthus* is described, it is said that in an island in the "ocean" there is an unpolluted grove with a sacred, covered carriage, which only the "priest," the one in charge of the cult, was allowed to touch. This carriage is occasionally driven around among the people and at such times peace and feasting rule. Once this is done, the carriage is taken to a secret and secluded lake where it and the idol or symbol of the goddess that is kept covered up inside it are washed in the lake. This washing is carried out by thralls (*servi*), and when this task is finished "the lake at once engulfs them" (*Servi ministrant, quos statim idem lacus haurit*). The reason for drowning the thralls in the lake is said to be that "there is as a result a mysterious fear and a sacred ignorance about something seen only by those doomed to die" (*Arcanus hinc terror sanctaque ignorantia, quid sit illud, quod tantum perituri vident*).[70]

Naturally, this unique description has fired the imagination of many a scholar, and there have been heated discussions about how this should be interpreted and whether the description has any truth to it. There is no doubt that the name of the goddess is likely to be genuine. It is, indeed, formally the same as the name of the goddess Sw. **Njärd* (OSw **Niærþer*), whom we encounter in cultic place-names in Sweden, and of the god ON *Njǫrðr*, who is known from Old Norse mythology.[71] That the slaves are sacrificed in the way described has, moreover, been linked to several so-called bog bodies, which are sacrificed humans who have been found in north German and Danish bogs and some of whom were evidently killed.[72]

In his description of the Swedes, whom Tacitus calls *Suiones*, who are said to live out in the ocean and to have their forte in fleets besides in men and weapons, occurs a noteworthy statement.[73] Weapons, Tacitus says, are not carried permanently and by all, but are locked up and guarded, a duty carried out by a slave (*servo*). The incentive behind this is said to be that the location

[70] Rives 1999 p. 93.

[71] Why the goddess name *Nerthus*, which corresponds to a regular PGmc **Nerþuz*, results in a West Norse *Njord* (ON *Njǫrðr*) as the name of a male deity and an East Norse **Njärd* (OSw *Niærþer*), which in all likelihood is to be understood as the name of a goddess, is a classic problem that has not yet been solved in all its aspects. See Rives 1999 pp. 292–294 and Vikstrand 2001 pp. 101–102 for this intractable problem.

[72] See, e.g., Glob 1965 and Bergen (ed.) 2005, see also the discussion of "sacrificial slaves," Germ. *Opfersklaven*, later.

[73] Cf. Svennung 1962.

out in the ocean prevents sudden enemy attacks, but also the fact that armed men with little to do easily end up in fights that may have fatal outcomes. It is also in the king's interest, according to Tacitus, not to have a nobleman or a freeborn guarding the weapons, nor a freed slave. Instead, he has a thrall guarding the weapons. This in many ways recalls the king's unfree steward, administrator, or farm manager, or the Roman emperor's *servi principis*, *puer regis*, and so on, who were part of the *familia Caesaris* and whom we encounter in Rome,[74] but also in later history, since the *bryti* in Scandinavia may have had a similar background, as we shall see.

Finally, Tacitus tells in chapter 45 of the *Sitones*: "The tribes of the Sitones begin where the Suiones end" (*Suionibus Sitonum gentes continuantur*).[75] They are said to be like other Germanic people except for the fact that their ruler is a woman (*quod femina dominatur*). This is not to Tacitus' liking and he gives the following judgment: "so much do they sink not merely below freedom but even below slavery" (*in tantum non modo a libertate sed etiam a servitute degenerant*). This statement may be taken as a hint regarding the status of women in Rome at that time.

Scholarship on slavery during the period after the fall of Rome is extensive. An early as well as excellent work is Agnes M. Wergeland's *Slavery in Germanic Societies during the Middle Ages* (1900–1902). Based on Germanic laws, she proposes the following definitions of what characterized a slave in the Germanic area during medieval times:

1. The slave is an article of property,
2. The slave has no personal rights,
3. His existence is vested in that of his master,
4. Aside from his relation to his master, the slave has no place in society.[76]

Since the Merovingian kingdom and later on the Carolingian kingdom were structural continuations of the Roman agro-economic system, we must assume that the *villa*-system with its slaveholding was adopted and continued. Relatively large slave populations existed on estates, often placed in outhouses and sheds on the main farm, directly under the control of the estate owner and his steward. These slaves who worked at the estate were called *servi manuales* and were thus differentiated from those who acquired farms

[74] Weaver 1972, Blackburn 1996 p. 162, and Schumacher 2001b; cf. Bosl 1978.
[75] Rives 1999 p. 96.
[76] Wergeland 1900 p. 110.

to work for themselves, *servi casati*, who were socially much closer to the "free" tenants (*coloni*).[77]

The Merovingian and Frankish kingdoms seem to have had a good supply of slaves. A legal system had been created that more or less mechanically sentenced free individuals to slave status, the selling of children into slavery occurred, something that increased in financially poor times, and many slaves were captured during the numerous wars that were fought; warfare in these times has been called "manhunt" and kings, such as Clovis' sons in the German part of the Frankish kingdom and Dagobert in Gascony,[78] organized regular slave-hunting expeditions.[79]

An interesting instance regarding slavery in northern Europe during the first millennium comes from the Merovingian, originally Salian, compilation of laws *Pactus Legis Salicae*. In a legal clause probably dating to 507–511 there are regulations on how to retrieve slaves who have been taken prisoner and brought presumably to Anglo-Saxon England or possibly to Scandinavia.[80] This clause states the recommended procedures for buying or granting the freedom of a slave, namely to bring up the case with the foreign *thing*-assemblies.

The famous English historian E. A. Thompson in an early but excellent little article (*Slavery in Early Germany* 1957), attempted to come to grips with the troublesome issue of slavery in Germany, and his study can be used generally with regard to the Germanic area. Thompson discusses predominantly the first four centuries AD and he raises several questions for which he then seeks answers in the few, mainly classical, sources that are available. He establishes that a society wherein slaves constitute a financially important part requires a well-functioning slave trade and one such quite clearly existed, especially around *Limes*, the border between the Roman Empire and the Germanic-speaking people to the north, where the trading of slaves took place in both directions. He dismisses as less probable the notion that a great many Germanic slaves were found within the Germanic area. The reason for this—to which he often returns—is the difficulty of getting such a slave, who had perhaps been captured from a neighboring people and who in all likelihood spoke the slave owner's language, to stay put. The possibilities

[77] Dockès 1982 p. 92. For the elusive and complex social category, the *coloni*, they have been reevaluated in modern research, resulting in a most complex picture, see Rio 2017 p. 5 and n. 11.

[78] During ancient times, this was a province in southwestern France; it later became part of Aquitaine.

[79] See Bonnassie 1991 *passim* and Dockès 1982 p. 92.

[80] Wood 1983 p. 5.

for escape must have been immediate and overwhelming. The great Roman slave populations could be controlled by detaining them in large *latifundia* or in guarded mines, but as far as is known this practice had no counterpart in Germanic areas. The numerous wars fought by the Germanic peoples were mostly feuds with neighbors, so the prisoners that could potentially be taken were also neighbors; therefore, the inclination to escape must have been constant.[81] During this early period, the only option must, according to Thompson, have been to place slaves as "smallholders" on their own farms, which would provide an incentive for them to stay put. Early Germanic slavery would thus, if Thompson's plausible hypothesis can be shown to have validity, have consisted of unfree people who ran smaller dependent farms, probably above all in areas of new colonization. This form of slavery cannot have been particularly extensive, but it nonetheless constituted a significant element of society at the time. Nowhere was wealth measured in slaves, as is evidenced, for example, during a later period of history in Ireland; for this predominantly cattle-oriented society the current value unit was instead heads of cattle, ON *fé*, Latin *pecus*.

Slave trading ought, Thompson ascertains, to have gravitated toward the Rhine area due to the good turnover of this type of goods and the high price that slaves fetched here. In the slave trade that obviously existed, slaves were captured or bought mainly in order for them to be sold on. In an analysis of certain classical sources, he further claims to establish that slavery also tended to be more extensive in the regions closest to the Roman Empire. For example, the *Marcomanni*, *Quadi*, and *Alemanni* appear during the Roman Iron Age to have had sizable populations of slaves. This is supposedly backed up by an agreement between Marcus Aurelius and the *Marcomanni* in which the former demanded the release of 13,000 prisoners, and in another case the *Quadi* handed over no fewer than 50,000 prisoners of whom we know that many were taken as slaves. With such high numbers of captives there existed, according to Thompson, the basis for an extensive slave trade.[82]

Thompson concludes his analysis by stating that the number of slaves within the Germanic area during Roman times must have been low and that where slaves existed these were predominantly of non-Germanic origins, probably placed on their own small, dependent farms. Thompson makes the important point, which we can transfer to our analysis of Scandinavian

[81] Cf. Dockès 1982 p. 93.

[82] On large numbers of enslaved war captives, as when entire towns or regions were conquered during Hellenic–Roman times; cf. earlier discussion.

slavery, that extensive slaveholding requires an extensive and well-functioning slave trade with recurring slave markets.

Carl I. Hammer has recently presented a view of slavery in Germany, more precisely in Bavaria, that digresses markedly from Thompson's. He states already in the preface: "I intend to show why Bavaria deserves to be classified as a 'large-scale slave society,' perhaps one of the clearest examples that ever existed."[83] These two scholars thus reach diametrically opposed results. This comes down to their respective starting points. Hammer follows Orlando Patterson's sociological definition of what a slave is, while Thompson takes his departure from Tacitus' description and instead analyzes slavery in terms of legal and financial aspects. The advantage of Hammer's research is that he has been able to analyze a great deal of contemporary documents, laws, capitularies, church and monastery archives, etc., which gives him a marvelous base of material from which to proceed. But, as I reiterate many times in the present book, the analysis of the terminology and semantic-legal definitions remains a decisive problem to the discussion. One problem with Hammer's research is that he accepts unconditionally the terms he finds in his sources and reads them *verbatim*. He seems to think that if it says *servus* then it indicates a slave, while other scholars might moderate and refer to a serf, bondsman, or a free or unfree tenant in order to approximate the social or legal capacity that this *servus* actually had.[84] I think that in this respect Hammer to some extent reverts to a simplification of reality, which recalls the black-and-white definition of a human being given in Roman laws: a human being could be either free or unfree. He emphasizes that his research "concentrates on persons who can be fitted into unambiguously servile categories,"[85] which is a difficult and delicate task when it comes to the analysis of early medieval documents.[86] Even so, Hammer's research is important and of great interest and he produces good arguments for Bavaria having had an extensive slavery during this period albeit, and in this he is not so unambiguous, of a different character—from slaves doing agricultural work on large farms (*villae*); large groups of female slaves who worked in textile production at mills; *servi casati* or *coloni*, who were slaves occupying and running their own farms but paying rents to their masters, and thus a sort of unfree tenant

[83] Hammer 2002 p. x.
[84] Cf. Davies 1996.
[85] Hammer 2002 p. 13.
[86] Cf. Cathy Pearson's review of Hammer's book in *Speculum* (Pearson 2005) and also Hans-Werner Goetz's critical review in *American Historical Review* (Goetz 2003).

who were legally speaking slaves but socially speaking hard to distinguish from free tenants; to *adalschalks* (*servi principis*, *puer regis*, or *ministerialis*),[87] which corresponded to the *servi* that were part of the *familia Caesaris*—the Roman emperor's "household" slaves who carried out advanced administrative tasks;[88] or for that matter the slaves who looked after the administrative and financial affairs of the Ottoman sultan in Topkapı in Istanbul or the high-ranking slaves who were part of the Russian administration in medieval times.[89]

In today's research, there is no consensus with regard to what happened to the huge community of slaves from the heyday of the Roman Empire.[90] Of the aforementioned scholars, it is evident that Verlinden, Duby, and Bonnassie all reckon that slaves continued to form a large demographic group within society after the dissolution of the Roman Empire. Others, such as Bloch, Dollinger, Ganshof, and others, hold the opinion that the Church contributed to the emergence of a view of slaves that counted them as human beings rather than as implements, which must have given them a different and better position within society—an opinion that few seem to share today. As usual, the problem comes down to ambiguity in the terminology. What is meant by the term *servus* (pl. *servi*) in Carolingian Europe? Was it an unfree or (semi)free farmer? This unsolvable conundrum has been discussed by Hans-Werner Goetz.[91] His answer is that nothing can be said for sure, since we cannot know how the word was used.

The Hamburg-Bremen Archbishop Rimbert's hagiography of his predecessor, *Life of Ansgar*, includes a chapter on slaves among the Nordalbingians (VA 38),[92] referring to the people living in Nordalbingia, north of the river Elbe (Latin *Alba*), roughly corresponding to modern-day Holstein in northern Germany. In the middle of the ninth century some slaves who had been captured in "Christian lands" had escaped from their suppressors and had come to the Christian Nordalbingians, "who, as is well known, live next to the pagans" (*qui proximi noscuntur esse paganis*) in the hope of finding a refuge there. But when the slaves arrived there they were taken captive once

[87] See Bosl 1978, Nehlsen 2001. Cf. Wergeland 1901 pp. 401–402.

[88] Blackburn 1996 p. 162 and Schumacher 2001b.

[89] On the latter, see, e.g., Hellie 1982 pp. 461 ff.

[90] Two Swedish works from the great number of contributions discussing this are Gustafsson 1986 and Olsson 1999 pp. 13–16.

[91] Goetz 1993. For a semantic discussion of the word, see, e.g., Dumont 1987, Pârvulescu 2010, Buchwitz 2012, Arnoux 2014.

[92] The Latin text is from *Vita Anskarii auctore Rimberto*, ed. by G. Waitz, the English trans. by C. H. Robinson (see *VA* in bibliography).

more and were fettered, which means that they were enslaved: "Some of them they sold to pagans, whilst others they enslaved, or sold to other Christians" (*Quorum alios iterum ad paganos vendebant, alios suo mancipabant servitio aut aliis christianis venundabant*). This outrageous breach of conduct among Christians had become known to Ansgar. Following a divine revelation, Ansgar traveled to the area north of the Elbe and succeeded in bringing people to release their slaves.[93] What Ansgar resented was hardly the fact that Christians kept slaves, which was common during these times when also the Church had many slaves, but that exactly Christians, people from "Christian lands," were enslaved. At this time, the Church had successfully achieved, in the Frankish kingdom among other places, the right for Christians not to be sold as slaves.

With the feudal agrarian revolution, slavery is assumed to have decreased in importance. The landowning upper classes found it financially more profitable to release their slaves and instead employ them as peasants on small farms belonging to their estates. This appears in certain areas to have taken place on a large scale and may form the origins of a much discussed group of semifree farmers in France known as *colliberti*.[94] These could have been the *servi manuales*, purely work slaves, who existed in great numbers at the *latifundia* and large *villae* and who were in the ninth and tenth centuries collectively transferred from slave status to that of semifree tenants who continued to have strong ties to their masters.[95] In Anglo-Saxon England, we encounter corresponding social groups known in Wessex and Western Mercia as *coliberti*, but in the remaining parts of England as *gebur*.[96] This group, *coliberti*, were distinct from another large faction of freed slaves, *servi*, of whom a sizable group seem to have been *servi casati* who, like the *cotsetla*,[97] occupied their own farms and could therefore fairly readily be transformed into tenants. This process is, of course, also the background for the semantic

[93] This episode, when Ansgar is redeeming Christian slaves in Hamburg, is also highlighted by Adam of Bremen in his *Gesta* (1:29), referring to Rimbert's *Vita*.

[94] For the continental *colliberti*, see Bloch 1975 [1928] pp. 93–149; On *col(l)iberti* in Anglo-Saxon England, see Finberg 1976 pp. 66, 215–217 and Stenton 1971 p. 477. The term *colibertus* obviously contains the Latin *collum* 'neck' and *libertus* 'a freed man' and as such it corresponds to the Scandinavian *fräls* < *fri-hals*, ON *frjáls*, lit. 'free-neck' (see Hellquist 1948 p. 242), Gothic *frei-hals* m. 'free man, freedom' (on the phonetic development of the word, see Brate 1887 pp. 30–31).

[95] For a discussion regarding the development of the *servus*/*serf* and *serfdom* in Europe, see, e.g., Bush 1996 pp. 199–246.

[96] Stenton 1971 pp. 475–76, Finberg 1976 pp. 65–66, 216–219, 221–222, 226.

[97] Finberg 1976 pp. 217–222.

shift of the word *servus*, which referred in classical antiquity to a 'slave', but which came to refer in medieval times to a semifree "tenant," a serf.

During the second half of the first millennium there existed in the present-day German area of the Frankish kingdom a type of slavery, which was no more distinct from slavery in the Frankish areas generally than regional variation warrants. In the new eastern parts, slaveholding was rather unusual in contrast to the western parts. In the same way as happened in continental Europe, various lower social classes merged into one working class toward the end of the first millennium, a class that in the German areas was called *hörig* and that was successor to the *servi casati*. The lowest-ranking slaves, the purely working slaves of the great estates (*mancipia*), became the social group known as *leibeigen*, serfs.[98]

As concerns the Frankish kingdom, it should also be stressed that the quite stereotypical picture of society that has been assumed in previous scholarship, with vassals and estate owners who held authority over hordes of semifree tenants, has recently been modified in such a way that the free tenants and their role have been brought to the fore with regard to the eighth, ninth, and tenth centuries. It is emphasized that these free tenants were linked together by communal ties and common work in the fields and that they exercised "collective power" at their *thing*-sites and assemblies. Tenants in the Frankish kingdom were free since they were frequently also warriors, a fact that is underlined by capitularies issued by Charlemagne in 807–808 in which he attempts to preserve the system of enrolling (especially poor) tenants in the army.[99] In other words, Scandinavian research still needs to consider these free tenants and their role in societal development during medieval times, a picture that does not digress all that dramatically from the late medieval Scandinavian societies, with a strong element of free tenants.[100]

Pierre Dockès has—rather boldly—summarized how he regards the development from the fall of the Roman Empire in the fifth century until the High Middle Ages. He assumes that there existed during the fifth, sixth, and seventh centuries a large element of not all that heavily exploited free farmers and tenants of which a sizable proportion was made up prior to this of slaves who were then emancipated at the fall of the Roman Empire. The

[98] Perrin 1955 and Fourquin 1988 p. 204. One may note, as was pointed out earlier, Frands Theuws believes that, at the beginning of the 700s, *mancipia* were probably not slaves in the southern Netherlands.

[99] Dockès 1982 pp. 99–100.

[100] I discuss the extent and the role of the free farmer in Scandinavia later.

eighth and ninth centuries saw, according to Dockès, a return to large-scale farming with the emergence of great estates with *latifundia*-like specialization with extensive slave work and exploitation as well as impoverishment of smallholders.[101] During the latter part of the tenth and in the eleventh century a new kind of political feudalism arises, which George Duby has called *seigneurie banale*,[102] within the area formerly constituting the Frankish kingdom and based on strong feudal princes, possession of strong fortifications, and a new kind of warrior: heavily armored cavalry. Yet again the semifree tenants become the basis of agrarian economy in the High Middle Ages; what is problematic about them is, as was mentioned earlier, the difficulty of separating out all classes of especially tenants and the extent of their freedom or lack of freedom.

Ironically, the eastern parts of Germany were hit by a new wave of peasant bondage in the latter half of the fourteenth century. Following agrarian crises and the Black Death, large tracts of farming land were abandoned. These were taken over by the German aristocracy and included in their already great domains. The German princes allowed these aristocrats to usurp formerly royal jurisdiction, which gradually led to an "old fashioned" legal and financial power over the subordinate farmers.[103]

Slavery in Anglo-Saxon England

Slavery in Anglo-Saxon England—that is from the time of the Roman loss of Britain and the colonization of southern parts of the island by Germanic speaking peoples of northwestern Europe until the viking-descended William the Conqueror from Normandy defeated King Harold II Godwinsson in the Battle of Hastings 1066—is relatively well known, particularly in the latter part, since we have written sources from that period. These sources are predominantly law codes issued by various kings, chronicles, and other sorts of official documents. Particular importance with regard to the discussion of the extent of slavery has been placed on the "Domesday Book" (1086), which is the extensive tax-register of England produced by the

[101] Dockès 1982 p. 101.
[102] Duby is believed to have minted the concept of *seigneurie banale* in his book on the tenth-century society in the Mâconnais (Duby 1953); cf. the discussion by F. L. Cheyette 2002 p. 301 and *passim*.
[103] Fourquin 1988 p. 207; cf. Rothenhöfer 1967 pp. 26 ff.

Norman government. A great deal of discussion has focused on the extent of the validity of its evidence in this context. Opinions are divided. "Domesday Book" shows that an average of 10 percent of the English population were at this time slaves.[104]

Relatively thorough research has been carried out on Anglo-Saxon slavery, and we now have two recent books treating the topic: David A. E. Pelteret's *Slavery in Early Mediaeval England* (1995) and David Wyatt's *Slaves and Warriors in Medieval Britain and Ireland, 800–1200* (2009). Apart from these, there are important shorter contributions by Frederic Seebohm, Frederic W. Maitland, Paul Vinogradoff, Frank M. Stenton, Dorothy Whitelock, H. P. R. Finberg, Eric John, and John Blair.[105]

Slavery of one sort or another existed in England during Roman times and throughout the Anglo-Saxon period. In contrast to the Roman Empire, England was obviously never a "slave society": that is, it never relied on slave work for agriculture and mining. The British ecclesiastic Gildas in the sixth century wrote in his *De excidio Britanniae* ("The Ruin of Britain") that the recently arrived English (*Saxones*) enslaved many of the native Britons.[106] It was, however, far from all indigenous Britons who became enslaved; a British aristocracy lived on into early Anglo-Saxon England, albeit with a lower *wergild* than the English aristocracy.[107]

But even warfare and warlike conflicts between Anglo-Saxon population-groups led to the capture and enslavement of people of Anglo-Saxon origins.[108] Some of these were presumably sent to the great slave markets of this period, such as Bristol or Marseille in southern France, to be sold there. It seems to have been with this in mind that Pope Gregory the Great (c. 540–604) sent Abbot Augustine to Kent in 597 to "convert" the Anglo-Saxons. The story is told by Bede (c. 673–735) in his *Historia ecclesiastica gentis Anglorum* (from 731) in such a way that the pope had noticed that some English slave boys (*Angli*) had been seen at a slave market in Rome and supposedly had said that they have the faces of angels [*angeli*] and such people ought to be together with the angels of Heaven, thus linking the name of the population to angels.[109]

104 Pelteret 1985 p. 122; cf. Wyatt 2009. See, moreover, Maitland 1897 pp. 26–66.
105 See, e.g., Seebohm 1890, Maitland 1897, Vinogradoff 1911, Whitelock 1952 pp. 108–114, 1979, Finberg 1964, John 1966, Kirby 1967, Stenton 1971, and Blair 1991.
106 The exposition that follows is based mainly on Pelteret 1985, 1995, and 2014.
107 Pelteret 1985 p. 120.
108 Whitelock 1952 p. 111.
109 *Bede* Book II, chap. 1; Pelteret 1985 p. 120.

Bede told another story (Book IV, chap. 22), which is interesting in this context. During a conflict between the Northumbrian and Mercian overkingdoms in 679, Imma, a young *thegn* (a grade of Anglo-Saxon aristocrat) was injured, lying on the battlefield as if dead all that day and the next night among the bodies of the slain. He managed to bind his wounds, got up and walked away, but was discovered and taken prison and led before one of King Ethelred's nobles. When asked who he was, he answered that he was a peasant, a poor man. The noble decided his life should be saved. After being a prisoner for some time, people notice that he did not behave like a peasant, and he had to confess who he was, a thegn of the king. The nobleman thus decided he ought to be killed, but he could not break his promise, so he sold him to a Frisian man in London who allowed Imma to buy his own freedom. The story illuminates a detail, which Bede comments on, namely the condition that an imprisoned warrior should be killed while an imprisoned peasant should be enslaved.[110]

Of great significance to the understanding of slavery in Anglo-Saxon England are clauses about slaves in the early Anglo-Saxon law codes. The earliest source in this respect is King Æthelberht's Law of Kent from around 600, of which the oldest manuscript (*Textus Roffensis*) is from the 1120s. King Æthelberht was the first English king who converted to Christianity and one of the first to become a sort of "overking" of several Anglo-Saxon overkingdoms.[111] Judging by this law, the kingdom of Kent, just like the rest of Europe, was a strictly hierarchical society with slaves at the bottom. One group of these slaves was made up of *birele*, which literally means "the one who carries the drinking cup" (King Æthelberht's Law §14, 16).[112] These slave women are mentioned in the law in order to regulate cases in which a *birele* has been raped. Compensation for this should be based on the social position of the owner of the *birele*: a man of the uppermost layer of society should be compensated with 12 shillings, a free farmer with 6 shillings, and an owner of lower standing should receive a compensation of 50 or 30 pence. Slave women's "honor" was closely regulated in this law. If a slave woman belonging to the king was raped, compensation amounted to 50 shillings (§10), while slave women of the "second" class, so-called grinding-slaves

[110] Pelteret 1985 p. 120 and Strickland 1992 pp. 46–47, also mentioned by Whitelock 1952 p. 111.

[111] Regarding Anglo-Saxon overkingship and the problematic term *bretwalda/brytenwalda/bretenanwealda*, see York 1981, Wormald 1983, Fanning 1991, Keynes 1992, 1999, Dumville 1997, and Charles-Edwards 2000.

[112] See Pelteret 1995 p. 44.

(*grindende þeowa*, §11) who were slaves grinding meal with hand-querns, or those belonging to the "third" class were recompensed to the owner with, respectively, 25 and 12 shillings. A male slave could be a *theow* (*þeo*[*w*], §90), of whom it is stated that, if he stole, he must repay double the amount of value. He could also be an *esne* (§85–88), who could apparently marry, since the law clause mentions that an *esne* could have a wife (§85), which probably indicates that an *esne* could have his own household and perhaps his own farm, making him an early Anglo-Saxon counterpart to the *servi casati* whom we encounter on the Continent. A strange middle ground is apparently occupied by the *laet* mentioned in Æthelberht's Law (§26), but in no other Anglo-Saxon sources, and is in all likelihood an Anglo-Saxon counterpart to the *laetus* that appears in various linguistic forms used in continental laws.[113] Here it says that if you kill a "laet" of the uppermost class you must pay 80 shillings, if you kill one of the second class you must recompense with 60 shillings, and of the third class with 40 shillings.[114] Presumably, this grading depends, as with the *birele*, on the master's social status.

Since Anglo-Saxon England was primarily an agricultural society, there were certain kinds of farming slaves, plowmen, according to "Domesday Book," which meant that they also had to look after the oxen that pulled the plow. They could also be shepherds and swineherds. Female slaves seem mainly to have carried out household chores, which is indicated at least by terms for such, for instance *dæge* 'baker', and *birele* 'the one who carries the drinking cup'. An interesting will from the end of the tenth century, of the noblewoman Æthelgifu, moreover mentions that slaves could fulfill other, even more advanced, services and offices in Anglo-Saxon society, since her household comprised also a priest, special female singers who were to sing in the church, and a goldsmith, all of whom were slaves.[115]

Slaves were presumably acquired primarily via warfare and slave raids among the Welsh and the Scots, but also, as has been mentioned, through internal feuding that took place between the kingdoms of England, especially until the eighth century. In these cases, the men were usually killed while the women and children were enslaved. Many slaves were bought or

[113] On this Kentish *laet*, see Finberg 1976 p. 57. The etymology of the word is obscure, but the word has counterparts (see later). Seebohm (1911 pp. 483–487) compares the Kentish *laet* with the Old Norse *leysing*, and finds that the wergild for the three classes, of both *laet* and *leysings*, were identical, and therefore he sees a parallel, so the *laet* was some kind of freed slave on his way to become totally free from bondage.

[114] *Gif* [*man*] *læt ofslæhþ ðone selestan .lxxx. scill. forgelde gif ðane oðerne ofslæhþ .lx. scillingum forgelde ðane þriddan .xl. scillingum forgelden.*

[115] For a philological analysis of terms for slaves in Anglo-Saxon England, see Girsch 1994.

sold also at the famous slave market in Bristol even into the eleventh century, while Scandinavian vikings might take slaves in England and ship them to the slave market in Rouen in Normandy, France. Dorothy Whitelock nonetheless asserted that the majority of slaves in Anglo-Saxon England consisted of formerly free people who had been enslaved because of crimes, such as incest, theft, or working on a Sunday, or due to inability to pay their debts and fines.[116] It is probable that people unable to provide for themselves could have voluntarily made slaves of themselves.[117]

King Alfred, the much admired king of the West Saxons (871–899), introduced laws that made it illegal to kill one's slaves according to one's own whims, as had previously been practised. Some human worth was, in other words, ascribed to slaves in the late ninth century. Instead, slaves were to be disciplined and controlled by means of beatings and floggings.

A slave had no *wergild*; that is, there was no price (no value as a human, only as an implement) by which to compensate his family if he were killed.[118] Instead, a slave had a value or price as a slave, namely 60 shillings to be paid to the owner if the slave were killed.[119] For crimes committed by a slave, for example, theft or fleeing, the punishment was normally death. For lesser crimes, the slave could expect floggings.[120] There is an interesting agreement from the tenth century between Anglo-Saxons and a Welsh people, *Dûnsæte*, wherein the value of a slave is given alongside the values of various types of livestock:[121]

horse	30 shillings (i.e., 1 ½ pound)
mare	20 shillings (i.e., 1 pound)
man (slave)	1 pound
untamed donkey	12 shillings
ox	30 pence
cow	24 pence
pig	8 pence
sheep	1 shilling
goat	2 pence

[116] Whitelock 1952 p. 112, 1979 p. 59; cf. also Pelteret 1985 p. 122, incl. n. 22.
[117] Cf. Whitelock 1952 p. 112, Pelteret 1985 p. 122, incl. n. 23, 126.
[118] Hough 1999 p. 469.
[119] According to Whitelock 1952 p. 108, the price of a slave was 1 pound, which was the equivalent of eight oxen.
[120] Whitelock 1979 p. 57.
[121] Pelteret 1985 p. 86.

The value of a slave is given here as 1 pound (that is, one third of the value of the aforementioned 60 shillings). In other words, a slave was valued at four oxen and at two-thirds of a stallion.

In Latin documents from Anglo-Saxon England, the words *servi* and *ancillae* appear unequivocally to have designated 'slaves'.[122] In "Domesday Book" they usually occur together with the register of tools and utensils created for a lord's estate. The term *villanus* (pl. *villani*) is more problematic, since it can refer to free as well as unfree farmers.[123] The same probably goes for other terms, such as *bordarii* and *cottarii*.[124] The usual native words for slaves are *esne* and *theow*, of which an *esne* seems in early Anglo-Saxon laws to have been able to have his own farm and is thus a counterpart to the Continental *servus casatus*.[125] In a contextually interesting will from the eleventh century it is evident that the person writing the will wanted that all his men were to be granted freedom and each one of them should be given a place (presumably a single house) and a cow and seed for food.[126] In other words, it appears that many slaves in Anglo-Saxon England had their own little place to inhabit, including a cow and a field.

Earlier in the Anglo-Saxon period there were five general terms for 'slave (regardless of gender)' and 'male slave', which were *þeow(a)*, *þræl*, *þegn*, *esne*, and *wealh*. Gradually, *esne* disappeared and later on also *wealh*. During the whole period, the words *þegn*, *esne*, and *wealh* also had other parallel meanings: *þegn*—replacing OE *gesith*—additionally indicated 'companion, member of a nobleman's guard, warrior, a king's retainer, aristocrat',[127] *esne* additionally 'hired worker, worker, man',[128] and *wealh* additionally 'foreigner, Briton, Welshman'. Also the word *Briton* could denote a 'slave'.[129] In other words, it was only *þeow(a)* and *þræl* that exclusively denoted 'slave'.[130]

David Wyatt has argued that slavery in Anglo-Saxon England was much more widespread than has previously been imagined.[131] He may be right in

122 On *servus*, see Loyn 1991 pp. 362–363.
123 Maitland 1897 pp. 36–66, Stenton 1971 pp. 477–478.
124 Stenton 1971 p. 477.
125 Finberg 1976 p. 57.
126 Whitelock 1930 pp. 68–69.
127 See Loyn 1955.
128 It is of interest that OE *esne* etymologically is a cognate to ON *ǫnn* and *ǫnnungr* (see *ánauðigr*, *ǫnn*, and *ǫnnungr*, later).
129 Whitelock 1952 p. 111.
130 A comparison of terms for unfree and free people in early and late Anglo-Saxon England, respectively, was given by Finberg 1976 pp. 65 and 218.
131 Wyatt 2009 *passim*.

this, but, when he has attempted to argue his case by referring to extensive slavery in Scandinavia during the same period, he commits an unfortunate fallacy, since we have no sources in Scandinavia that can either confirm or refute such an assertion.[132] His argument is more solid when he points out that the slaves mentioned in "Domesday Book" are male slaves. Apart from these, there must have been female slaves and their children. Therefore, we cannot rely solely on "Domesday Book" when estimating the number of slaves in Anglo-Saxon society.

Anglo-Saxon slavery seems to have decreased dramatically after the Norman conquest in 1066 (that England traded and transported slaves far into the nineteenth century is a different matter).[133] The reason was the same as on the continent—it became unprofitable and unfashionable to keep slaves, it was cheaper and simpler to employ more or less free tenants who paid a rent for the farms they worked or who worked as forced labor. A century after the Norman conquest of England, slavery ceased to exist in society. This constituted a change so thorough that the most common word for a slave, *þeow*, also fell out of use in the English language.[134] New classes of farmers emerged during this time. One such is *famulus*, who was a landless man, not an unfree slave, most often employed as a plowman.[135]

Slaves in Ireland

In the Ireland that was not yet influenced by vikings, that is prior to about 800, unfree people (*dóer*) existed.[136] These suffered various degrees of lack of freedom or, rather, they were to various extents tied to and dependent on their masters who were in turn able to a greater or lesser extent to control the lives of these people, something that was strictly regulated in Old Irish law-compilations. The first type, which is for legal reasons usually reckoned among the unfree, is *fuidir* (pl. *fuidri*), literally 'semifree', also referred to as 'tenants at will'.[137] It has been supposed that a *fuidir* had his direct

[132] See my review of Wyatt's book in *Early Medieval Europe* (Brink 2011).
[133] Pelteret 1985 p. 132.
[134] Pelteret 1985 p. 132.
[135] Postan 1954, Pelteret 2002 p. 93.
[136] The exposition that follows, on slavery in Ireland prior to the Viking Age, is based predominantly on Kelly 1988 *passim*.
[137] Kelly 1988 p. 33.

counterpart in the "semifree" *laet* that existed in Anglo-Saxon Kent.[138] A *fuidir* did not merit any honor-price (presumably identical to *wergild*) and he never owned any land. Even so, some *fuidri* had the right to leave their lord, who had to compensate him in some way. Moreover, the *fuidir* could enter into legal contracts with his master. A *fuidir* was entirely in the hands of his master in such a way that the latter was fully able to control the everyday life of a *fuidir* by assigning him particular work-tasks. The master was responsible for feeding and clothing a *fuidir* and for paying any fines for offenses that he might commit. On the other hand, the master received any legal compensation for wrongs committed against a *fuidir*: these did not go to the wronged *fuidir* himself. A person could become a *fuidir*, for example, by leaving or being forced away from his family. At the lowest end of this scale were criminals who were unable to compensate for their offenses but instead became *fuidri* to some lord. It has been supposed that a *fuidir* represented a transitional status for a person who had lost his property or had been penalized.[139]

A *senchléithe* 'inherited serf' was a step further down on the scale of lacking freedom. The name in fact means 'old dwelling place' and refers to the fact that a *fuidir*, whose ancestors had inhabited the same land for three generations, could strangely enough be "degraded" to *senchléithe* according to Old Irish law. He was tied to the land and could not leave his lord. If the master sold his estate, the *senchléithe* was part of the purchase, irrevocably bound to the land.

At the bottom of the societal pyramid were the work-slaves, *mug* 'male slave' and *cumal* 'female slave',[140] who lacked all rights and were equated with livestock. Their background was that they had been captured during warfare, perhaps from a neighboring petty-kingdom, were "foreigners" bought as slaves in slave markets or were Gaels who had been unable to pay their way out of some offense they had committed. In some Gaelic law compilations it is also evident that parents sometimes sold their children into slavery. A slave was not subject to the law, he did not count as a witness, and all legal contracts were handled by his master. A runaway slave had no rightful refuge. Since Christianity was introduced early on, before the 430s, in Ireland, there were already in the sixth century some mitigating rules pertaining to slaveholding.

[138] Charles-Edwards 1972 p. 9.
[139] Brady 1994 pp. 128–129.
[140] Brady 1994 p. 129–130. On Old Gaelic *maug*, *mug* 'slave', see Mees 1998 p. 380.

Laws against unrestrained sexual abuse of female slaves came in the form of rules to the effect that, if a man had sexual intercourse with a slave woman he was obliged to sell her as well as compensate for the damages, but if he made her pregnant he must make her free. This applied in spite of the great importance of slaveholding even until the arrival of vikings in Ireland, which shows among other things in the fact that *cumal* or *cumalach* 'female slave' came to be considered a specific unit of value in Gaelic society,[141] in the same way as *fé, fæ* 'head of cattle' was in ancient Scandinavia.

Slaveholding apparently changed its nature in Ireland following the arrival of vikings around 800.[142] The great quantities of Viking-Age silver found in Ireland are in many cases linked to vikings' activities in the country and to their slave trade. Prior to the arrival of vikings, slaves appear to have been predominantly "property," but, following the ingress of vikings, slaves became first and foremost "goods," which could be sold for silver. Irish chronicles contain many accounts of how vikings wrecked churches and monasteries, plundered them for silver and treasures, and took many prisoners. It seems as if the Scandinavian raids during the first half of the ninth century primarily took the form of quick raids on ecclesiastical settlements, in which mainly valuables were taken and perhaps also one or more priests or abbots as hostages, with the aim of squeezing out even more money. In the second half of the ninth century regular slave raids appear to have been part of the vikings' strategy, since great numbers of people were captured. Dublin, which was dominated by Scandinavians during the Viking Age, became a central point in this extensive slave trade. On an island off Dublin, Dalkey Island, many slaves seem to have been gathered and traded at a slave market.

Gradually, the Irish adapted to the ways of the vikings; there is even proof of Scandinavians and Irishmen cooperating in warfare and taking great numbers of prisoners. In the eleventh century, the slave trade became very important all across the Irish Sea, with Dublin and probably also the Isle of Man as important central places.[143] In the fights between vikings and Irishmen, and internally among Irish petty kings, cattle and people were the sought-after items. Year after year during the eleventh century Irish chronicles tell of one Irish king attacking another, taking, as it says, 600 cows and 50 people, 200 cows and 20 people, and so forth. In 1022, it is said the *Ulaid*, the inhabitants

[141] Cf. Herlihy 1985 p. 38.

[142] Viking Age slave-trading in Ireland has been treated by Holm 1986, whose important contribution I refer to later.

[143] See also Bromberg 1942 on Wales.

of what is now Ulster in Northern Ireland, took many vikings prisoner; but nine years later, in 1031, the chronicles report that the *Ulaid* were raided by vikings who took 3,000 cows and 1,200 people.[144] This type of "warfare" was to a great extent the result of internal strife between Irish overkingdoms. Entire fleets of warships could be hired as part of these fights, most often fleets belonging to Scandinavians stationed in Dublin and elsewhere and paid in kind with cattle and slaves. These widespread slave raids culminated around 1115, following which warfare in Ireland changed. Many slaves were therefore of native Irish or Scandinavian descent. But also foreign slaves were brought, probably in fairly big numbers, to Ireland. The slave trade was facilitated through Bristol,[145] which was an important port for slave transports to and from Dublin right up until William the Conqueror prohibited such trade and Westminster Council issued a general prohibition against all trading of slaves in England in 1102.

Spain

Obviously, slavery existed in Spain already in Roman times, in the same way as everywhere else in the Roman Empire, particularly in connection with the extensive mining that took place on the Iberian Peninsula. Later on, when the Visigoths conquered Spain, we acquire more information about slaveholding, among other things from the laws of the Visigoths. Slaves were very common. It was not unusual for a landowner or an ecclesiastical unit to own several hundreds of slaves, sometimes even thousands. It was symptomatic of the stance adopted by the early Church toward the question of slavery that the Sixteenth Council of Toledo decided that a provincial church could not have a full-time priest unless it owned at least ten slaves. If a church and a priest were in possession of a mere ten slaves, however, it was considered poor.[146]

The great majority of slaves in Visigoth Spain had been brought up inside the system. It required only one of the parents to be a slave for a child to automatically be a slave. Partly, new slaves were brought in through wars and slave markets, for instance slaves from Sardinia and the British Isles. That the

[144] Holm 1986 p. 335.

[145] Thus according to St. Wulfstan of Worcester (*Vita Wulfstani* II:2); see Bromberg 1942 p. 265 n. 6 and Pelteret 1995 p. 77.

[146] The account that follows is based mainly on Eisenberg 2003.

whole society was a "slave society" shows in the fact that legislation was such that poverty often led to the loss of freedom. It was common for poor people during bad times to "voluntarily" give themselves up to slavery. Also the selling of children into slavery occurred. Anyone sentenced for committing crimes, even if the offense was of a minor kind, was often punished with the loss of freedom. The entire legal system seems to have had as its objective the transfer of poor people into the unfree state.

When a person passed into the unfree state, he or she became "socially dead." This shows in among other things the fact that the former spouse had the right to remarry after only one year, as if his or her former spouse had died. Also in legal terms, a slave was socially "dead." The common legal term for a slave, *mancipium*, was grammatically of neuter gender as if the person in question were a thing, an object,[147] and in the eyes of the law the slave owner had complete power over the life of the slave. Punishment in the form of beatings and floggings was part of everyday life, although people did not stop at this, but also engaged in mutilating faces and in castration or quite simply in killing the slave. In 650, a law was issued that prohibited such acts, but it is clear that they continued in spite of this. Several decades on there are reports of slave owners chopping off hands, noses, lips, ears, and feet, even putting out eyes or in other ways mutilating the slave's body.[148] This was, of course, not an expression of any inherent harassment within society, but was to serve as warnings to other slaves, keeping them in their proper place.

As in many other societies, there were distinctions also in Spain between different kinds of slaves. The king and high-ranking officials could keep slaves as part of the administrative apparatus and in other ways. These highly qualified slaves (*idoeni*) were socially distinct from the great masses of work slaves (*vili*).[149]

As is well known, there was much upheaval in Spain at the beginning of the eighth century. In 711 the victorious Muslim army crossed the straits of Gibraltar and embarked on a conquest of the Iberian Peninsula. By 720 it had defeated the kingdom of the Visigoths, except for Galicia in the northwest. The Muslims carried on into France, but were stopped by the Franks led by Charles Martell at the famous Battle of Poitiers in 732. Following this, the

[147] Cf. Duby 1973 p. 42.
[148] Bonnassie 1991 p. 73.
[149] See Bonnassie 1991.

Muslims withdrew and consolidated their power in Spain, which came to be called *al-Andalus*.

In this Muslim al-Andalus, slavery, of course, operated as in other medieval Muslim countries.[150] Primarily female slaves were sought after for sexual purposes. Daniel Eisenberg stresses that many slave women in al-Andalus lived better and freer lives than their free sisters; concubinage allowed them to move about freely in the cities, have better access to education, and have a fuller emotional life, and it enabled them to manipulate their masters in many ways. Granting freedom was common, and a child born to a free man and a slave woman was free from birth, which, according to Eisenberg, is a significant factor in the emergence of the strong bonds between mother and son that are still found today in Hispanic culture. Estimates reckon that circa 10–20 percent of the population of al-Andalus were slaves, with the majority consisting of people coming in from the outside. To begin with, many slaves seem to have come from eastern Europe and the Balkans, often via France.[151] When this slave trade, traditionally understood as being primarily carried out by Jewish slave traders, was discontinued it was replaced with the trading of black slaves from Africa. During the entire period, however, Christian slaves were also taken from the Christian areas of northern Spain and from France, in practice only women and children, since the men were killed. These proportionately very few slaves were particularly sought after. They were seen as desirable sexual partners and became mothers of many aristocrats and rulers. News of these women and children kept in sexual slavery reached Christian Europe, and appeals and requests to free them fueled the wish to go to war against the "infidels" and to create anti-Islamic propaganda.[152]

Summary

It can be established that during the second half of the first millennium in Europe, from which we have detailed written sources, there is a sliding social and legal scale within society, comprising unfree work slaves, semifree tenants, and free farmers. The unfree and the semifree could, however, from a legal point of view be better off than free farmers, since the former could

[150] Lewis 1990.
[151] Lewis 1990 p. 11.
[152] Eisenberg 2003 p. 759.

count on their master's protection. Finally, there were unfree officials with leading positions in society as well as free civil servants of lower social status.

At the bottom of this societal hierarchy were slaves without any sort of freedom, they were pure chattel slaves (*servi manuales*, slaves who worked with their hands); there were those who lacked a farm to run and to inhabit (*mancipia infra casam* or *mancipia non casata*) and who were often referred to in contemporary sources as "people belonging to the estate" (*servi salici* or *hommes propres*).[153] Within agricultural life there were unfree people, Latin *servi*, and in Bavaria there was a special category of *servi quotidiani* 'daily slaves', which seemingly implied that these had to work every day on main farms, while others were called *servi casati* "housed" slaves or slaves who lived on farms.[154] In Anglo-Saxon England there existed corresponding categories in *kotsetla*, who occupied a *kot* (single house),[155] or in *esne*, a category of slaves apparently running a farm and able to marry.[156] A particular category consisted of household slaves (*familia*) who were referred to as *pueri*, *mancipia*, *ancillae*, and *servi*.

On this sliding scale, between free farmers and pure slaves, there was a kind of semifree tenant (*homines cum casa et substantia*) who might be called *coloni*, *rustici*, *masarii*, and *manentes*. In Early English (Kentish) laws there is a corresponding category of farmers, *laet*, which probably springs from the same origins as the continental *litus*, *latus*, and *lazzus*.[157] These semifree tenants became the usual category of farmers within feudal European agriculture during later medieval times.[158] Carl I. Hammer, however, has rightfully emphasized that although the categories encompassing the working classes were fluid in terms of everyday life, where it must have been hard to distinguish between slaves working as millers, blacksmiths, or stewards and free men working at slave chores, such as plowing, herding animals, or spreading manure in the fields, then the legal distinction was rather sharp.[159]

[153] Cf. Duby 1968 pp. 38, 192.
[154] Fourquin 1988 p. 204 and Hammer 2002 pp. 11 ff.
[155] Lindkvist 1979 pp. 32 ff. and *passim*.
[156] Stenton 1971 pp. 473 ff. and Finberg 1976 p. 57.
[157] Bloch 1975 [1928] pp. 148–149, Finberg 1976 p. 57; cf. Fischer Drew 1988 p. 2.
[158] Verlinden 1988 p. 336.
[159] See Hammer 2002 *passim*.

4
Scandinavian Slavery

> *He began also to buy Danish and Slav boys and to redeem some from captivity so that he might train them for God's service. Of these he kept some with him, whilst others he sent to be trained at the monastery of Turholt.*
>
> —Rimbert, *Vita Anskarii* 15

Since slaves and slaveholding are regulated in great detail in most of our medieval provincial laws, it has usually been deduced from this that thralls existed in great numbers and constituted a necessary precondition for society at the time.[1] For a discussion on Scandinavian slavery during late medieval times, Niels Skyum-Nielsen's (1979) short, but comprehensive, survey is useful; for an understanding of the widespread occurrence of thralls in our provincial laws I recommend three excellent in-depth studies by Clara Nevéus (1974), Ruth Mazo Karras (1988), and Tore Iversen (1997).

Excellent overviews of how medieval thraldom has been regarded are presented by Peter Foote, Niels Skyum-Nielsen, and Clara Nevéus in *Kulturhistorisk lexikon för nordisk medeltid* (*KL* volume 19). The sources referred to by these authors are, of course, the Icelandic sagas for the West Norse tradition and the oldest provincial laws for the East Norse tradition.

An indirect, but contemporary, testimony of slaveholding in Scandinavia is found in Rimbert's *Life of Ansgar*, a hagiography set in the ninth century, which is Early Viking Age. Rimbert describes how Ansgar and his helper Autbert visit Denmark in the early ninth century and:

> made diligent search for boys whom they might endeavour to educate for the service of God. Harald also gave some of his own household to be

[1] See, e.g., Wessén 1945 p. 172, on the mention of slaves in the Guta Law.

Thraldom. Stefan Brink, Oxford University Press. © Oxford University Press 2021.
DOI: 10.1093/oso/9780197532355.003.0004

> educated by them; and so it came about that in a short time they established a school for twelve or more boys. (VA 8)

This must refer to slave boys who could be bought and educated to become preachers of God. It is not unlikely to imagine that these slave boys were the sons of captured Christians who had been brought to Denmark. It can be assumed that such boys had a Christian background and also knew the local language so that it was exceptionally clever to buy their freedom and then school them to become priests or preachers. This topic also occurs in a different part of the *Life of Ansgar*:

> He began also to buy Danish and Slav boys and to redeem some from captivity so that he might train them for God's service. Of these he kept some with him, whilst others he sent to be trained at the monastery of Turholt. (VA 15)

Presumably the "Christians who were held captive," according to Rimbert's first account from Birka (VA 11), were held in Birka as slaves.

Adam of Bremen, the author of the History of the Hamburg diocese and its bishops (*Gesta Hammaburgensis Ecclesiae Pontificum*) from circa 1073–1076, relates an episode when Ansgar's successor as archbishop, his biographer Rimbert, in the late ninth century visited "*Sliaswig*" (probably to be understood as Hedeby[2]) observed a group of Christians dragged away in chains as prisoners. According to Adam, Rimbert was able to break the shackles by praying and also to buy them free with his own horse.

If we focus on Sweden, we find thralls in wills made in medieval times wherein some free person grants his or her thralls their freedom. In 1259 Bengt Sigtryggsson bequeaths his estates to the Franciscans of Skara and sets free four persons who were born in slavery (*Quator personis in servitute natis plenam libertatem condonaui*), and whom the vicar of Rådene and his *stabularius* Omerus know by name (*DS* 457).[3] The will of Johan Eriksson from 1268 states:

[2] Adam of Bremen, *Gesta*, ch. 1:41. Cf. Sawyer 2002 p. 72; Adam writes in ch. 1:57: *apud Sliaswich, quae nunc Heidiba dicitur* (at Schleswig, which now is called Hedeby), in ch. 2:35: *apud Heidibam, quae Sliaswig dicitur* (at Hedeby, which is called Schleswig), and in ch. 4:1: *apud Sliaswig, quae et Heidiba dicitur* (at Schleswig, which also is called Hedeby).

[3] Cf. Nevéus 1974 p. 184.

> *Hærmodo quem pater meus dedit libertati do fundum curie cum domibus in faldunge. cum pascuis pecorum que dicuntur wlgariter fang oc fiargang. sibi & heredibus suis in perpetuum possidendum*
>
> to Härmod, to whom my father granted freedom, I leave a farming plot with buildings in Fållinge as well as cattle pastures, commonly known as *fang oc fiargang* (acquisition [of hay fodder] and pasture), to be owned from now on by him and his heirs. (*DS* 532)[4]

Bengt Magnusson writes in his will from 1269 (*DS* 541) that he grants freedom to Asker in Brunnby and Nicolaus in Sörby (*Item do libertatem ascero in brunnaby & Nicolao in sørby*).[5] This important testament indicates that these two former slaves lived in Brunnby and Sörby, respectively, which would seem to indicate that they were either thralls at one (of the) farm(s) that would then have been run by a *bryti*, or that they had their own (tenant) farms.

In 1272, Peter Erengisleson writes his will wherein he bequeaths monetary gifts to all Swedish monasteries and hospitals, distributes his farms and possessions, and "gives back" the woman Helena her freedom as well as that of her existing four and any future children, and that he leaves "P.," *bryti* (*uillico*) of Forsheda, 20 mark sterling (*Item mulierem quandam actenus iugo seruitutis pressam libertati restituo cujus nomen est helena. eum filio & tribus filiabus uel ab ea in posterum nascituris. Jtem pro redemtione uoti mei quo uoui me ierusalimam profecturum committo. P. uillico de forsith. XX. Marcas sterlingorum*) (*DS* 559).[6]

In Viglog Nilsson's will from 1279 (*DS* 615) he sets free at his death all unfree persons belonging to him, regardless of gender, in all of his estates (*Ceterum omnes utriusque sexus mihi seruili condicione prorsus astrictos in omnibus mansionibus meis tam legatis pro anima mea quam aliis a iugo seruitutis eximens post mortem meam asscribo plenarie libertati*).[7] Johan Karlsson's will from 1279 (*DS* 695) is of similar wording as he grants to all of his unfree people of both genders their full freedom forevermore (*Preterea omnes vtriusque sexus mihi seruili condicione attinentes plena & perpetua libertate manumitto*).[8]

[4] Cf. the Swedish translation in Nevéus 1974 p. 184.
[5] Cf. Nevéus 1974 p. 184.
[6] Cf. Nevéus 1974 p. 184.
[7] Cf. Nevéus 1974 p. 184.
[8] Cf. Nevéus 1974 p. 184.

A will of remarkable contents is made by the lawman of Värend in Småland, Folke Karlsson, in 1282: "To Brynulf carpenter I grant freedom as well as 2 oxen, 4 cows and *duas horas annone*, to be received from Hov or 'hwæm.' Also to Sigge and his brother I grant freedom and the possessions they have with them" (*Brynulpho carpentario do libertatem duos boues. quatuor vaccas. & duas horas annone, & recipiat ista de huf aut hwæm. Siggoni eciam & fratri eius do libertatem cum rebus quas habent*) (*DS* 742).[9]

A woman named Ingeborg in Glänås writes in her will in 1282: "Furthermore, I grant freedom to all of my unfree people" (*Jtem omnibus mancipiis meis confero libertatem*) (*DS* 755).[10] In the same way, Sigge Guttormsson in 1283 grants "All of my unfree people . . . full personal freedom" (*Mancipiis meis omnibus securam & propriam confero libertatem*) (*DS* 762).[11] In 1284, Ragnvald Ingesson announces from his deathbed that he bequeaths to the friars of Alvastra his estate in Östraby and grants freedom to six domestic thralls (*Item sex uernaculis confero libertatem*) (*DS* 786).[12]

An unusually extensive will is made by Christina Fastesdotter of Landsjö in 1258 (*DS* 855):

> May thus future descendants and those now living know that to the monks of Alvastra, with whom I choose my gravesite, I have bequeathed an estate belonging to me in *swecia* [Sweden, probably meaning the Old Swedish *Svitjod*, the region around Lake Mälaren] which is called Ramshammar with all thereto belonging, except for all unfree people (*mancipia*) to whom I grant freedom. [. . .]
>
> Moreover, it is my will that my estate in Närke which is called Fällersta shall be sold including mill and all moveable items belonging to it, except for the unfree people to whom I grant freedom, and that 5 *marcas denariorum* of the sum shall be paid to each monastery. [. . .]
>
> But what may remain leftover of the purchasing sum of that same estate [= Västby] shall together with the purchasing sum of the buildings and other goods—except for the unfree people to whom I have granted freedom—be put together with the purchasing sum of the estate of Fällersta and paid as specified above. Moreover, I grant the following people freedom: Margareta and Ragnhild from Tift, Manne, Sven, Erngund, Erik, Hermund

[9] Cf. Nevéus 1974 p. 185.
[10] Cf. Nevéus 1974 p. 185.
[11] Cf. Nevéus 1974 p. 185.
[12] Cf. Nevéus 1974 p. 185.

> from Landsjö, furthermore Sigge Lång's sons Johannes and Ragnvald. Additionally, I announce to all that Havard, Sven and Cecilia are free.[13]

Somewhat later Johan Sixtensson announces in his will from 1275 that: "To all of my unfree people (*Mancipiis*) I have granted freedom" (*DS* 866), while Björn, dean of Bälinge, in his will "grants freedom to my thrall woman (*ancille*) and her baby child" (*DS* 871),[14] which shows that even priests long into medieval times owned slaves. Filip Jonsson in his will from 1285 grants "full freedom to all my unfree people, men and women, at my estates and elsewhere" (*omnibus seruis meis & ancillis*) (*DS* 890).[15]

In the 1270s, Knut Jarl's daughter Cecilia writes in her will: "To five unfree people (*mancipiis*)—those whom my son Birger would care to choose—I grant freedom" (DS 900), which should probably be taken to mean that Cecilia does not grant all of her thralls freedom, but only five of them, whom the son Birger is given the honor of selecting. Filip Karlsson at the same time grants "freedom to all unfree people whom I own, men and women" (*seruis & ancillis*) (*DS* 901), while Brynolf Haroksson of Fiskeby in the 1280s grants "Johannes, son of my slave woman (*ancille*), complete freedom" (*DS* 902), and Håfrid Sigtryggsdotter in 1286 grants "Tova and her two little children" freedom (*DS* 925).[16] In the will of Nils Ubbesson from 1286 he grants freedom "to all unfree people (*mancipia*) belonging to me, wherever they may be [. . .]. Nysäter [. . .] I leave to Ragnvald with all thereto belonging goods, except for the unfree people; to Björn [. . .] 11 *oras terre* [OSw *ørisland*] in Skämma [. . .] except for the unfree people" (*DS* 911) and so on.[17] All of these wills are made within a few decades in the latter half of the 1200s.

Three wills are of particular interest. In 1310 Asmund Lang grants "to Karelus [. . .] freedom as well as a horse and saddle" (*DS* 1656), which would seem an unusual gesture toward a former slave. The will of the nobleman Magnus Johansson (Ängel) from 1292 (*DS* 1737) bequeaths estates and lands around Lake Mälaren (i.e., central Sweden) to various monasteries and rounds off by saying that he finally grants freedom to all his thralls and female thralls: "And to my unfree men—bought as well as domestic—and unfree women I grant full freedom" (*Seruis etiam meis tam empticijs quam*

[13] This long letter (SDHK nr 762) in Latin can be read here: http://sok.riksarkivet.se/sdhk; Translation in Nevéus 1974 p. 187.

[14] Cf. Nevéus 1974 p. 186.

[15] Cf. Nevéus 1974 p. 186.

[16] Cf. Nevéus 1974 p. 187.

[17] Cf. Nevéus 1974 p. 187.

vernaculis et ancillis, plenam confero libertatem).[18] From this it is evident that he had bought some of his male slaves while others had been born and raised on his estates. Finally, we have a unique will by Margareta Ragnvaldsdotter from sometime before 1277 in which she announces:

> Whether I become well or not, I bequeath to the *bryti* (*Villico*) Sten in Frövi 2 *ørisland* of land and grant him, his wife and child freedom. In the same manner, I also grant freedom to the sole *bryti* (*Villicum solum*) in Tängstad. Furthermore, I grant, should I not become well, complete freedom to all unfree people, men and women, belonging to me.[19]

In this will, we are given several noteworthy pieces of information. First, it is clear that a *bryti*, who was normally a manager or steward of someone's estate, could in the 1270s be unfree. With this in mind, it is not so easy to understand what sort of slave a "sole *bryti*" was since it appears that a *bryti*, as far as we can tell, managed an estate, presumably with a number of slave workers. Perhaps this "sole *bryti*" had a farm in Tångstad and ran it himself. Finally, we can ascertain that Margareta's goodwill when it comes to granting her slaves freedom was only to be realized in case of her death. In case of her living on for some time yet, she intended, indeed, to keep her unfree people, men and women.

If nothing else, this shows us partly that thralls still existed at the end of the 1200s, most likely on the *bryti*-estates belonging to free people, and partly that it had become "fashionable" or was considered a deed pleasing to God among privileged classes in society to bequeath estates and lands to monasteries and convents and to grant freedom to slaves. It is not clear from these medieval wills and letters whether ordinary farmers had thralls to whom they could grant freedom. All of these letters concern Götaland in southern Sweden, most prominently the province of Småland, and in a few cases east central Sweden, around the Lake Mälaren.

An interesting passage from the Borgarþing Law, which was in force in the Oslo region of Norway, informs us that during Christian times thralls were given some sort of funeral on par with men who were found washed ashore on the beach and who had a haircut according to Old Norse tradition and

[18] Cf. Nevéus 1974 p. 189.
[19] See Nevéus 1974 p. 189.

custom, hence probably meaning these men presumably were of Nordic origin.[20] In chapter 9 it says:

> *nest kirkiu garðe skall grava man manna. oc menn þæir er rekner ero a siouarstronðu oc hava har skurði norøna.*[21]
>
> Slaves' graves should be dug closest to the church yard and the graves of men who are "thrown up" [that is: washed ashore] on the beach and have their haircut to Norse style.

The law paragraph is actually rather difficult to interpret; was only a "slave" with a Nordic hairstyle to be buried, and how did they know the dead person was a "slave"? Furthermore, as stated several times, we cannot be sure if ON *man(s)manna* (sg. *mansmaðr*) is to be understood as "slave" or not in all the cases the word occurs in the laws, however, it seems odd if the dead person in this case, being buried outside of the consecrated graveyard (but "closest to the churchyard," hence the wall demarcating the graveyard) was not to be understood as a "slave." Otherwise one would expect the person to be buried inside. And what was indeed a "Nordic hairstyle"?

[20] Cf. Skyum-Nielsen 1979 p. 131.
[21] *NGL* 1 p. 345.

5

Where Did the Slaves Come From?

Dvalði daprt of skilða
(drifu, þeirs eptir lifðu)
ferð, en fengin urðu
fǫgr sprund (Danir undan).
Láss helt líki drósar;
leið fyr yðr til skeiða
(bitu fíkula fjǫtrar)
fljóð mart (hǫrund bjartir).

The pitifully scattered crowd was delayed;
the Danes who were still alive fled away,
but fair women were captured.
A lock secured the girl's body;
many a maiden went before you to the warships;
bright fetters bit greedily into the flesh.

—from a poem by Valgarðr á Velli[1]

The transition from free human being to unfree slave could happen in different ways. Most common—numerically speaking—was probably captivity resulting from warfare and other forms of conflict, but a person could also pass into slavery more or less voluntarily and such thraldom could be for a limited time. Many slaves were, of course, born to slave parents and thus to slavery. During times of trouble, such as certain periods of the first millennium AD, the risk of ending up in slavery must have been imminent for people.

Thralls, then, could be obtained in war (as prisoners of war) or as booty resulting from campaigns and raids. A well-known episode that relates of

[1] The Old Norse text and the translation is from the Skaldic Project (https://skaldic.abdn.ac.uk/m.php?p=verse&i=4693); Kari Ellen Gade (ed.) 2009, "Valgarðr á Velli, *Poem about Haraldr harðráði* 9," in Kari Ellen Gade (ed.), *Poetry from the Kings' Sagas 2: From c. 1035 to c. 1300* (Skaldic Poetry of the Scandinavian Middle Ages 2), Turnhout: Brepols, pp. 307–8. Valgarðr's poem is preserved in Snorri's *Heimskringla* III:94 and appears in normalized form in Finnur Jónsson's *Skj* BI: 360 ff. The episode has been discussed by Foote and Wilson 1970 p. 67 and Meulengracht Sørensen 1993 p. 162.

Thraldom. Stefan Brink, Oxford University Press. © Oxford University Press 2021.
DOI: 10.1093/oso/9780197532355.003.0005

manhunts appears in a poem from right before the middle of the eleventh century by the Icelandic skald Valgarðr á Velli, which he composed in honor of the Norwegian King Haraldr harðráði (see epigraph). Haraldr had raided in Sweden and Denmark. He visited the area around Roskilde in Denmark, where he killed men or drove them to flee. The beautiful women, however, he captured (*en fengin urðu fǫgr sprund*). They were imprisoned, supposedly by hand- or foot-chains, and brought to the ships (*láss helt líki drósar, leið fyr yðr til skeiða bitu fíkula fjǫtrar*). This has been taken as an example of how women were captured and taken away as thralls. To assume that the male Scandinavian vikings would not have captured beautiful young women as part of their raids and plunder expeditions in order to use them for sexual purposes is likely to represent a viewpoint reflecting a modern person's ethical, humane sensibilities, polished by almost a millennium of cultural influences from Christian sexual taboos, more than Viking Age reality. Among one of our few contemporary accounts describing Viking Age Scandinavians is Ibn Fadlan's (see later), a proof of sexual exploitation of female slaves, which was probably the rule rather than the exception.[2]

Large numbers of captives are mentioned also in many chronicles. The question is how many of these eventually ended up in Scandinavia and in Iceland. This question is of direct importance to the assessment of how common slaves were in Scandinavia. As is discussed later, by all appearances, relatively few people were captured in the Frankish kingdom through viking raids and brought home. This has been assumed to be because the vikings were after precious metals and easily convertible goods. Continental churches and monasteries were well equipped with such treasures, while the Irish ones were more sparsely decked out. On the Continent, humans were therefore captured as hostages to be exchanged for luxurious articles, while in Ireland humans were captured and sold at slave markets, especially in the Muslim areas. It seems, in other words, as if the primary purpose was not to take slaves, but to exploit such unfortunate captives as valuable commodities of exchange, convertible into money, precious metals, and luxury articles.[3]

[2] See, on this topic, Ruth Mazo Karras (1990 p. 141).

[3] Holm 1986 pp. 318, 328, 330, P. Sawyer 1997a p. 10, 1997b p. 252, Nelson 1997 p. 29, and Ó Corráin 1997 p. 96. However, in the present toxic and highly polarized public discourse in Sweden and elsewhere, reflected in op-eds and cultural pages in major newspapers (and esp. in "social media"), it is possible today to write: *Vikingarna förde med sig östeuropeiska trälar och en och annan hustru—de flesta svenskar härstammar sannolikt snarare från trälarna än från den avsevärt mindre vikingaöverklassen* ("The Vikings brought with them East European slaves and the occasional wife—most Swedes probably derive from the slaves rather than from the significantly smaller Viking

The Frankish Annals make it clear that humans were captured and probably enslaved on the Continent, in all likelihood sold at slave markets. In the Annals of St. Bertin, which deal with the Frankish kingdom in the ninth century, the entry for 834 narrates that a Danish fleet arrived that year in *Frisia* and devastated a great tract of land. The Danes went to the trading center of Dorestad, which they sacked, and many people were killed and some taken prisoner. In 841, Danish pirates sailed through the English Channel and attacked Rouen, which was plundered. People were killed or captured. In January 863, a viking fleet sailed up the Rhine toward Cologne. After the sacking of Dorestad the vikings sacked a major estate, which many Frisians had escaped to with their goods. The estate was captured, the property seized, and a great many Frisians were taken captive.[4]

Adam of Bremen relates in his *Gesta* (ch. 2:43) how Hamburg in the beginning of the eleventh century (c. 1010–20) was ransacked, obviously by Slavic Vends, and many priests and many Christian townspeople were abducted in captivity, probably—or most certainly—to be sold off as slaves at some slave market.

Thralls could also be bought in slave markets. In a famous episode from *Laxdæla saga* (12, 13) it is told how during the tenth century the Brännö Islands (*Brenneyjar*) off Gothenburg served as a meeting place for kings every third year, when negotiations, trading, drinking, entertainment, games, and all manner of fun took place (*skemmtan mikil, drykkjur ok leikar ok alls kyns gleði*). Here, slaves could also be sold and purchased. The Icelander Höskuldr Dalakollsson came here to meet the Norwegian king, who traveled there with his "meeting levy" (*stefnuleiðangr*).[5] During his visit, Höskuldr bought from the merchant *Gilli inn gerski* and for a very high price an extremely beautiful albeit apparently mute slave woman. That same night he slept with her and the next morning he gave her, presumably still in a state of euphoria

aristocracy") (by Marcus Priftis in *Svenska Dagbladet*, SvD Kultur, April 1, 2014), without presenting any evidence or citing any research (for example, that of authors cited in this chapter—prominent professors of the field from Ireland, England, and Scandinavia, working in these areas for decades) and without intervention by the editors of the newspaper, asking the author to substantiate the claim, in a normal, editorial way. Of course, it would be most interesting if this was the case, and we would have to partly rewrite our viking history, but the stance of research today does not support such a view. The present Swedes, those who might have an ancestry very far back in what is Sweden today, cannot derive from a viking aristocracy; some might, but overwhelmingly the Swedes derive from the farming community, which made up 90–95 percent of the population in Sweden even up to the middle of the nineteenth century (SCK, HSS p. 45). But this kind of obvious statement is, in the present tone of public discourse, of course too "dull" and "unsexy."

[4] *The Annals of St-Bertin* I pp. 30, 50, 104.

[5] I am grateful to Professor Lars Lönnroth, Gothenburg, who drew my attention to this episode.

continuing on from the nightly exercises, a beautiful garment (which he had probably bought for and intended to give his wife). Back in Iceland it turned out that the slave woman was not so silent after all. Her name was *Melkorka* and she was the daughter of the Irish King *Myrkjartan*. The thrall woman Melkorka later gave birth to Höskuldr's son, *Óláfr Pái* (Olaf the Peacock), who became one of the greatest of chieftains in Iceland and father of Kjartan, the hero of *Laxdæla saga*.

Rather than buying slaves, it seems to have been more common for Scandinavians to sell captives, especially at slave markets in the Muslim areas, in al-Andalus, i.e., Spain (such as Pechina, Almería, Córdoba) and North Africa; in eastern Europe and in what are now Russia, Belarus, and Ukraine; at Atil/Itil, Bolghar/Bulgar, and Kiev; in central Europe, at Rome, Prague, and Rouen; and certainly also in Scandinavia, at Hedeby and Birka.[6] This may be taken to indicate that thralls in themselves were not coveted as such; precious metals and luxury goods constituted the attraction.[7]

To many people in ancient times, the apparently unlikely act of selling one's child as a slave or giving up one's freedom and placing one's life in someone else's hands was the only way to quite simply survive. Whether this is what lies behind the inscription on a strange Sumerian clay tablet with cuneiform characters from circa 2100–2000 BC is uncertain. This early inscription describes in all details a court case wherein a father sold his daughter as a slave for 2 ½ shekels (c. 21 g) worth of silver.[8]

Hunger and poverty were the reality of medieval Europe.[9] Chronicles and annals constantly return to macabre communications about people dying of hunger, sometimes in huge numbers. At times, hunger even drove people to take up cannibalism, which was reported several times in the tenth and eleventh centuries, for instance in France.[10]

Also in Scandinavia a person could enter thraldom as a consequence of financial difficulties, whereby the debtor submitted himself to the one to whom the debt was owed and was "voluntarily" enslaved. This so-called *debt-slavery* was obviously a reality in medieval times.[11] This is the situation in

[6] P. Sawyer 1997b p. 252, Nazmi 1998 pp. 138–151 and 191–197, Třeštík 2001, Jankowiak 2013, pp. 139–144.

[7] Cf. Krag 1982 p. 214.

[8] The Sumerian clay tablet can be seen in the British Museum in London.

[9] Curschmann 1900, Lucas 1930, Brink 2008 pp. 12, 22.

[10] Bonnassie 1989.

[11] Miller 1990 pp. 148–149 and Meulengracht Sørensen 1993 pp. 161–162. For debt-slavery among the Lombards in Italy, where a debt of more than 20 solidi, which the individual was unable to pay, led to permanent slavery, whereas a debt between 6 and 20 solidi led to temporary slavery, see Fischer Drew 1956 pp. 14–15.

which a person could end up, according to the oldest Icelandic law compilation, *Grágás* (Ib:3–4, II:103–105), if he were unable to provide for himself and his family; alternatively he could surrender his children to debt-slavery (*Grágás* Ib:53, II:185). Debt-slavery ended when the debt was regarded as paid. There is only one instance of debt-slavery in the Icelandic sagas, namely in *Ljósvetninga saga*, wherein a person ends up in thraldom because of a debt he cannot pay.[12]

Adam of Bremen has in his *Gesta* given a vivid description of Scandinavian vikings. They are, he claims, totally disloyal to each other, and as soon as one of them has taken another captive, he will without pity sell him off as a slave to a friend or a stranger. And if a man has committed against his king or has been caught for some other crime, they prefer to be beheaded before being flogged. Adam continues to say that other forms of punishment [apart from execution and flogging] are not found among these people, except "the axe or slavery."[13]

Crimes could be atoned for by the offender entering into slavery, presumably for a limited period of time. In the Law of Scania (*Skåne*) (130) the following can be read:

> If a man steals and is handed over to the king's official, he shall become a slave in the king's manor until he is redeemed from this or until he is given freedom. But he cannot lawfully be taken from thence into another man's power. If he becomes free again and subsequently is killed, a full man's compensation shall be paid for him; but if he is killed at the king's manor and in servitude, then it is paid for him as the king wishes and his kinsmen cannot take action for his killing, because he stole himself into the power of another man.[14]

In Andreas Sunesen's *Paraphrase* (76) of the Law of Scania this is explained in the following way:

> Also a free man, who is caught for felony and brought to the thing, may be sentenced to either hanging or to mutilation or other injury on the body, but he can also be sentenced to disgraceful thraldom, however accordingly, so that he shall carry the burden of thraldom on the King's estate and never

[12] See Miller 1990 p. 343 n. 17.
[13] Adam of Bremen, *Gesta*, chap. 4:6.
[14] Tamm and Vogt (eds.) 2016 p. 78.

> can he be passed on to someone else's ownership; he may either end his miserable life there or turn back to his former free condition. If he is slain, while he is a thrall, he shall not be compensated to paternal or maternal ancestry, but to the King or his agent as for a thrall.[15]

This shows us that the one who committed a serious crime could, according to the Law of Scania, either be sentenced to death, to maiming, or to slavery, and the latter could apparently be for a limited time. It is a point of interest that when the free person entered thraldom, he found himself legally on the thrall's level; that is, he was owned by his master and it was the latter who would receive any compensation if the thrall were harmed or died. The thrall's former kinsmen had no right to compensation. In Denmark, as on Gotland according to the Guta Law, a person could end up in or enter into slavery for a limited time.

Also *gæf*-thraldom should be regarded as a special form of voluntary thraldom. The term OSw *gæfþræll* occurs in the Law of Uppland (*Upplandslagen*), the Law of the Södermän (*Södermannalagen*), and in the Law of the Östgötar (*Östgötalagen*), but it is only in the last-mentioned that we get some slight knowledge of what a *gæf*-thrall was.[16] In the Book of Inheritance (§ 11) of this law it says that one is not allowed to give away lands or other possessions of the rightful heirs, as had previously been decreed by law, and not give away oneself as a *gæf*-thrall because this was forbidden by Birger Jarl.[17] In other words, a *gæf*-thrall was someone who had given away his possessions and his farm to someone other than his heir, thus making himself a *gæf*-thrall of that other person and being provided for by him for the rest of his life.[18] The concept of *gæf*-thrall seems to resemble the institution later known as *sytning*, and further to the south in Scandinavia as *flatföring*, which was to give over one's farm and possessions to someone in return for being provided for for the rest of one's life, hence to "retire as a pensioner," but with one important difference, namely by giving up one's judicially free status.[19] As Ragnar Hemmer writes in his analysis of the position of the

[15] My free translation from *DGL* 1 p. 151.

[16] See Hemmer 1932, C. Nevéus in *KL* 19 col. 23, Nevéus 1974 pp. 89–90.

[17] *Nu ma egh man iorþ ælla annat gozs giua undan rættum aruum sua sum før uar i laghum ok egh sik til gæftræls guia: þy at þæt gaf birghir iarl af* (Now no man may give away from the legal heirs land or other property, which is stated before in the law, and not give oneself as a *gæftræll*; because this was given [decided] by Birger Jarl). Cf. also the Book of Inheritance § 12 and the Book of Manslaughter § 17:2 in the same law.

[18] Hemmer 1932 p. 233.

[19] See Charpentier 1896 and Hasselberg, Iuul, and Pirinen 1959.

gæf-thrall, it must be assumed that a *gæf*-thrall was not in as "unfree" a position as a regular work thrall, even if the *gæf*-thrall was legally speaking probably equated with an ordinary thrall.[20] The former did not enter thraldom because he had committed a crime or due to insolvency, but because he had become unable to provide for himself due to illness or old age. The word is probably a compound including an adjective indicating possibility, OSw *gæf*, based on the verb *giva* 'give' and thus indicating someone "giving" himself into thraldom.[21]

The *gæf*-thrall institution when we have it documented, that is, in thirteenth-century Sweden, implies, in my opinion, that at least during this period the type of thraldom known here can hardly be compared to the deeply depraved slave system known in classical Rome or to American slavery. If that were the case, nobody—however great their need for nursing—would have voluntarily given themselves up to slavery. Rather, this probably indicates that thraldom was some sort of "social contract," a patron–client relationship, which, admittedly, almost certainly included unpleasantries, such as penal elements, sexual abuse, and other inhumane treatments. We are, it should be stressed, talking about a thraldom in medieval Sweden, when slavery was on the retreat. Thraldom during earlier times, such as the Viking Age, may have been very different in Scandinavia.

It should probably be considered a special case when a free person was put into thraldom against his or her will. Evidence for such a unique case comes from an early letter (*DS* 75) issued by the Danish King Valdemar I in circa 1177 wherein he requests of Bare and Atte in Okome, Faurås in Halland, that they release a formerly free woman from thraldom:

> Furthermore, we command Bare and Atte from Okome to give back freedom to the woman whom they have put into slavery [*servitutem*], thus turning a free woman into a thrall woman [*ancillam*]. If they do not obey this Our order, they shall be killed by Our majesty's avenging sword. But if the aforementioned woman's brothers owe them anything then they must without further ado restore to them what is rightfully theirs.[22]

[20] Hemmer 1932 pp. 235–237.
[21] Cf. Hellquist 1948 p. 321 and Nielsen 1976 p. 142.
[22] The letter is translated into Swedish in Nevéus 1974 p. 182; my English translation is based on that.

It appears from this letter that the woman in question was apparently taken as some sort of pawn for a debt owed to Bare and Atte by her brothers so that she was kidnapped and enslaved.

Something similar is discussed in another Danish letter from 1201 (*DD* I:4 nr 32), a testament of Archbishop Absalon:

> Eskil bath-attendant(?) [*bathsuen*] he granted freedom. The women whom Niels *stabularius* had made unfree and put into thraldom must, wherever they be, be granted freedom along with their children. The woman who was taken from the hundred of Bjäre in Skåne he granted freedom along with her children.—Kristian cook, who was unlawfully taken as thrall, he granted freedom.[23]

Practically all of these different ways of ending up in thraldom are described in the Old Icelandic law codex, *Grágás*.[24] These different causes of servility form the basis of the categorization of thralls that can be detected in Old Norse society and that is reflected, as we shall see, in the native thrall terminology (see what follows). Lastly, it may be noted that the Gulathing Law as well as the Frostathing Law in Norway distinguish between "native" and "foreign thrall."[25]

We can sum up this chapter by reproducing Peter Foote's table of how a person could end up in thraldom:[26]

1. By birth (being born into thraldom)
2. As prisoner of war and captive (abroad)
3. By purchase (buying slaves and captives of war)
4. By debt or owing money (entering thraldom in order to pay off a debt)
5. By punishment (being sentenced to thraldom for having committed a crime)
6. By voluntary submission (giving oneself over to thraldom, for example on becoming unable to provide for oneself)

[23] Translated here from the Danish translation in Nevéus 1974 p. 182.

[24] Cf. Foote 1977 pp. 52 ff. and Jón Hnefill Aðalsteinsson 1986 p. 41.

[25] GuL 262; FrL 10:40; cf. Krag 1982 p. 218.

[26] P. Foote in *KL* 19 (1975) cols. 14–15; cf. also Niels Skyum-Nielsen's (1979) and Jón Hnefill Aðalsteinsson's (1986 p. 41) comparisons.

6

Thralls in Old Norse Poetry and Sagas

Óðinn á jarla, þá er í val falla, en Þórr á þrælakyn
Óðinn owns the chieftains who fall in combat,
but Þórr owns the thrall kin

—*Hárbarðsljóð* 24; my trans.

The natural starting point for all discussion of thralls in Scandinavia has always been the eddic poem *Rígsþula*[1] (Fig. 6.1). It gives an allegorical picture of society wherein named persons represent social classes, among these also thralls. The poem describes how each person (= social class) behaves, looks, and acts, and what names he or she is known by. It has therefore been natural to let the descriptions of the thrall's work ("make stone fences, manure the fields, feed swine, herd goats, and cut peat") throw some light on the kinds of tasks thralls were given in ancient times.

Unfortunately, *Rígsþula* must be approached with the utmost caution, especially if the intention is to use it as a source for prehistoric Scandinavia.[2] It is a very special poem—Erik Noreen has called it "peculiar and quite unique both formally and in reality"[3]—a mythical allegory wherein the main character *Rígr*, which is what the god *Heimdallr* calls himself in this poem, carries what is supposedly an Irish name (= Ir *rí*, Old Gaelic *ríg* 'king'). Claus Krag probably represents an extreme position; he dismisses it as a source for knowledge of thraldom altogether: "The poem has no source value whatsoever for the time in which slaveholding was a social reality."[4] We do not know either

[1] *Rígsþula* is not included in *Codex Regius*, only in *Codex Wormianus*, but is traditionally reckoned as an *Edda*-poem.
[2] Cf., e.g., Young 1933, Scher 1963 p. 397, Hill 1986, Dronke 1992 pp. 671 ff., 1997 p. 201, and most recently and extensively Dillmann 2003.
[3] *egendomlig och rätt enastående både formellt och reellt*, Noreen 1926, p. 94.
[4] *Kvadet har overhodet ingen kildeverdi for den tiden da trelleholdet var en social realitet*, Krag 1982 p. 212.

Thraldom. Stefan Brink, Oxford University Press. © Oxford University Press 2021.
DOI: 10.1093/oso/9780197532355.003.0006

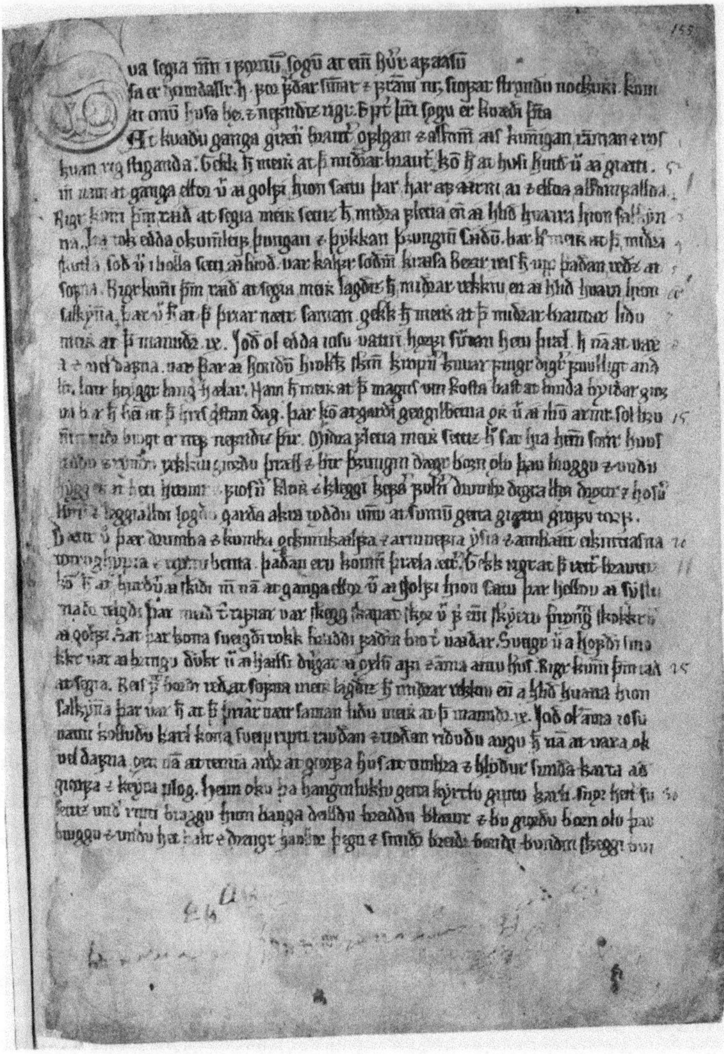

Fig. 6.1 The beginning of the poem *Rígsthula* in the manuscript *Codex Wormianus* (AM 242 fol.), dated to circa 1350. (Arnemagnean collection in the University library of Copenhagen; free e-book: https://codexquadruplum.wordpress.com/2016/05/04/codex-wormianus-am-242-fol/ or https://handrit.is/en/manuscript/imaging/en/AM02-0242#page/77v++(155+of+162)/mode/2up.)

where or by whom it was written down. Several scholars reckon with an Irish influence on the poem. Three of the scholars who have pointed to possible Irish loans are Einar Ólafur Sveinsson, J. I. Young, and Gísli Sigurðsson.[5] Also the dating of the poem is problematic. It has been suggested that it was written anytime between 900 and 1300.[6] A minority of scholars have regarded *Rígsþula* as early, tenth or eleventh century,[7] while a majority have dated the poem to the twelfth century[8] or, like Jan de Vries, Klaus von See, and Andreas Heusler, even later, to the thirteenth century.[9] However, there are modern scholars who, at least tentatively, place *Rígsþula* as early as the Viking Age.[10] Einar Ólafur Sveinsson established in his analysis that nothing in the poem indicates that it is later than the tenth century.[11] If it is deliberately archaic and written at a much later time then we are dealing with a very skillful and historically aware piece of work. In other words, it will not do to use the controversial poem *Rígsþula* uncritically or without reservations as a source for the cultural history of ancient times, particularly the social history.[12]

[5] Einar Ól. Sveinsson 1962 pp. 251–253, 287–291, Young 1933 pp. 100–105, and Gísli Sigurðsson 1988 pp. 82–85.

[6] Cf. A. Holtsmark in *KL* 14 col. 235, Dronke 1997 pp. 178–179 and Dillmann 2003. A good historiographic overview of the problem is given by Frederic Amory (2001), who, after analyzing earlier scholarship on the composing and date of *Rígsþula*, concludes his own opinion in the following—in my opinion—rather convincing way (p. 17):

> To conclude: with Rîgsþula, in all probability, we have to do with a poem that grew out of a folktale of the origin of the Norse estates, which is to say the three Indo-Germanic social groups of nobles, freemen, and slaves. A god such as Heimdallr was made responsible for the creation of these estates by having him sleep with their ancestral progenitrices from three generations, of which the oldest gave birth to the thralls, the next older to the freeborn, and the youngest to the nobility. This sexual scenario was in brief the nonhistorical core concept of Rîgsþula in its incipient, folkloric phase of development. When the folktale entered history in the tenth century as an oral-formulaic poem, to be recited to viking audiences at royal courts or popular festivals, it must have acquired its Irish linguistic and literary coloring and assimilated to its scenario the model kingship of Harald Fair-Hair, which is refounded mythically by Rîgr konungr at the fragmentary end of the poem.

[7] E.g., A. Bugge 1905 p. 212, Finnur Jónsson 1920 p. 193, Einar Ól. Sveinsson 1962 pp. 268, 287–288, 291, Meißner 1933 p. 128, and Nerman 1969 ("about the year 1000"). Nerman's arguments are given a positive assessment by Fidjestøl 1999 pp. 145–150.

[8] von See 1961, 1981 pp. 95–96, Holm-Olsen 1974, I: p. 282, Simek 1993 pp. 264–265, Karras 1988 pp. 60 ff., and Skovgaard-Petersen 1994 pp. 42–43.

[9] de Vries 1967 p. 127, von See 1981 pp. 95–96, Heusler [1906] 1969 pp. 184–188.

[10] Meulengracht Sørensen 1993 p. 164.

[11] Einar Ól. Sveinsson 1962 pp. 287 ff.

[12] For a critical opinion of the poem as a source of cultural history, see most recently Dillmann 2003 pp. 622–623.

The relevant section on thralls in *Rígsþula* reads as follows:[13]

Ióð ól Edda	Edda gave birth to a child
ióso vatni.	which was poured with water
Hǫrvi [vafði	he was wrapped in linen
hǫrund] svartan.	the black [dark-skinned] boy
[Hǫfug vóru augu] –	Heavy were his eyes –
hétu Þræl.	they called him Thrall.
Hann nam at vaxa	He started to grow
ok vel dafna.	and thrive.
Var þar á hǫndum	On his hands
hrokkit skinn,	the skin was wrinkled
kropner knúar,	gnarled knuckles
[kartnegl,]	[shriveled nails = onychauxis]
fingr digrir,	fingers thick
fúllikt andlit,	ugly face
lotr hryggr,	stooped back
langer hælar.	long heels.
Nam hann meirr at þat	Then he started
magns um kosta	to prove his strength
bast at binda	bind bast fiber
byrðar gørva.	make burdens.
Bar hann heim at þat	Carried to the house
hrís gerstan dag.	sticks every day.
Þar kom at garði	There came to the farm
gengilbeina.	a girl from far away [or bow-legged].
Aurr var á ilium,	Gravel in the foot sole
armr sólbrunninn,	sunburned arms
niðrbiúgt nef –	crooked nose –
nefndiz Þír.	she was called *Þír* [female slave].

[13] Old Icelandic text: Dronke 1997 pp. 163–165; my translation.

Miðra fletia	In the middle of the bench
meirr settiz hon –	she sat down –
sat hiá henni	beside her sat
sonr hús[s].	the son in the house.
Rœddo ok rýndo,	They talked and whispered secrets
rekkiu gørðu	prepared the bed,
Þræll ok Þír,	*Þræll* and *Þír*,
þrungin dœgr.	arduous were the days.
Bǫrn ólu þau,	Children they begot
biuggu ok unðu.	built and thrived.
Hygg ek, at héti	I think they were called
Hreimr ok Fiósner,	Whiner and Barn farmhand,
Klúrr ok Kleggi,	Bungler and Cleg [or Clod],
Kefser, Fúlner,	"He who shares the bed with a thrall-woman"
	and Stinker [or The Ugly],
Drumbr, Digraldi,	Log and Fatso,
Drǫttr ok Hǫsvir,	Slacker and Gloomy [or The Gray],
Lútr ok Leggialdi.	Stoop back and Longlegs.
Lǫgðu garða,	Made stone fences,
akra tǫddu,	manured the fields,
unnu at svínum,	fed up swine,
geita gættu,	herded goats,
grófu torf.	cut peat.
Dœtr vóru þær	There were daughters
Drumba ok Kumba,	Clod and Log,
Økkvinkálfa	Calf shit-heap [or Fatlegs]
ok Arinnefia,	and Soot-Nose,
Ysia ok Ambátt,	Loudmouth and Thrall-woman,
Eikintiasna,	Braggart [or The consumedly randy],
Tǫtrughypia	Ragamuffin [or Shabby],
ok Trǫnubeina.	and Cranelegs.
Þaðan ero komnar	From them comes
þræla ættir.	the thrall lineages.

The poem, thus, is an allegory of how society came together socially. Particularly interesting to us is, of course, the names of the thrall children born to *Þræll* and *Þír*, which is discussed later.[14]

Thralls also appear in other eddic poems. *Vǫlundarkviða* (st. 39) mentions the thrall *Þakkráðr*, who is called "the best of my thralls" (*Þakkráðr, þræll minn inn besti*). In *Þrymskviða* an *ambótt* is mentioned several times. The poem tells of how the *jǫtunn* Þrymr has stolen Þórr's hammer *Mjǫllnir* and in return for it he demands Freyja in marriage. The *æsir* gods do not agree to this exchange and therefore hold an assembly to discuss the matter, at which Heimdallr suggests that Þórr dress up as Freyja, something Þórr is wary of:[15]

20. *Þá kvað þat Loki,*	Then Loki said,
Laufeyiar sonr:	the son of Lauvey,
"Mun ek ok með þér	"I can serve you
ambótt vera:	and be your *ambótt* [here obviously
vit skolom aka tvau	with the meaning 'bridesmaid']
í iǫtunheima!"	we two shall travel
	to the worlds of the giants!"

On their arrival among the *jǫtnar* Þrymr prepares a great wedding feast. Þórr alone eats a whole ox and eight salmon and drinks three casks of beer. Þrymr is amazed at this, speaks up, and says that the bride is displaying an unusual appetite, to which Loki responds:

26. *Sat i alsnotra*	Before them sat
ambótt fyrir	the cunning *ambótt* [bridesmaid]
er orð um fann	and found an answer
við iǫtuna máli:	to the giant's question:
"Át vætr Freyia	"Freyja has not eaten
átta nóttom,	for eight days,
svá var hón óðfús	so much she loved to come
í iǫtunheima!"	to the worlds of the giants!"

[14] In chapter "Thralls' Names in Scandinavia."
[15] *Edda* ed. Neckel pp. 109–110; my rather free translation.

This seems to indicate that the word *ambótt* could also be used in an extended sense, not just for a 'slave woman'. The meaning 'concubine, a woman with whom a man cohabits without being married' is known,[16] but apparently it could also, according to *Þrymskviða*, have the meaning 'hand maid, bridesmaid'.

Helgakviða hundingsbana II 2–4 contains an enlightening episode. King Hundingr sends men to Hagall's farm in order to search for the hero Helgi. Hagall had been Helgi's foster-father. As Helgi was unable to escape he dressed in a thrall woman's clothes (*klæði ambottar*)—which was doubly degrading, not just dressing as a woman but also pretending to be a thrall—and went to grind corn. The men could not find Helgi, but Blindr the malevolent (*Blindr inn bǫlvísi*) said that piercing are the eyes of Hagall's slave woman (*þý*); eddic heroes often have piercing, penetrating eyes.

The story of the thrall woman Herkja, who was the mistress of the hero Atli in *Guðrúnarkviða III* (Third Lay of Gudrun) is well known and interesting—albeit problematic. Herkja blabs to Atli that she has seen Þjóðrekr and Guðrún together, which makes Atli enraged. Guðrún therefore undergoes an ordeal in order to prove that she is innocent of this accusation by picking up some gemstones from the bottom of a boiling cauldron. She manages to do so without damaging her hands and this is proof of her innocence. When, however, Herkja is forced to do the same thing, she burns her hand badly. Once the thrall woman has thus proved herself guilty of lying, she is punished by being buried, presumably alive, in a "foul" bog (*í mýri fúla*), as the poem has it, likely to be understood as a swampy, stinking wetland.[17] The narrative contains two strange details; one is the ordeal, which is a sort of ordeal by fire,[18] only in this case with heated gemstones, the other is the burial (presumably while alive) of the one who has been found guilty of lying. The harsh punishment probably links to the fact that the woman was a slave. This passage of the poem may, of course, be seen in relation to the so-called bog bodies known from southern Scandinavia, which some scholars assume are the bodies of slaves.[19]

[16] See Fritzner, article *ambátt*, and Karras 1990 pp. 154–155. On the *frilla*-institution in Iceland during the Viking Age and Early Middle Ages, see Karras 1990 and Auður Magnúsdóttir 2001, 2008.

[17] The Old Icelandic adj. *fúll* means 'rotten, stinky, unclean, detestable' etc. (see, e.g., Fritzner, article *fúll*).

[18] On ordeal by fire, see Bartlett 1986, Pilarczyk 1996, and, for Scandinavia, Miller 1988, Nilsson 2001.

[19] On the Danish bog bodies, see, e.g., Glob 1965.

In *Atlamál in grænlenzko* (Greenlandic Poem of Atli), which indulges in fights, bloodshed, and death like any Hollywood movie, there is the interesting story of the opponents in strife, Atli and Hǫgni. Atli had defeated Hǫgni and his companions, following which Beiti, who is Atli's *bryti*—that is, a thrall of rather high social standing—points out that Hǫgni's life might be spared because of his courage, and instead the cowardly thrall Hjalli could be killed since the latter could already be seen as half dead:[20]

61. *Beiti þet mælti* — *– bryti var hann Atla –*
Tǫko vér Hialla, — *en Hǫgna forðom!*
Hǫggom vér hálft yrkiom: — *hann er skapdauði;*
lifira svá lengi, — *lǫskr mun hann æ heitinn.*

62. *Hræddr var hver gætir,* — *helta in lengr rúmi,*
kunni kløkkr verða, — *kleif í rá hveria;*
vesall léts vígs þeira, — *er skyldi váss gialda,*
ok sinn dag dapran, — *at deyia frá svínom,*
allri orkosto, — *er hann áðr hafði.*

63. *Tóko þeir brás Buðla* — *ok brugðo til knífi:*
æppi illþræli, — *áðr odds kendi;*
tóm léts at eiga, — *teðia vel garða,*
vinna it vergasta, — *ef hann við rétti,*
fenginn léts þó Hialli, — *at hann fiǫr þægi.*

64. *Gættiz þess Hǫgni* — *– gørva svá færi! –*
at árna ánauðgom, — *at undan gengi:*
Fyrir kveð ek mér minna, — *at fremia leik þenna;*
hví mynim hér vilia — *heyra á þá skrækton?*

61. Then Beiti was saying — – he was Atli's *bryti* –
Let's catch Hjalli — and let Hǫgni be!
Since he already is half-dead — he is ready for slaughter
however long he will live — he will always be called a sluggard.

[20] Old Icelandic text from *Edda* ed. Neckel pp. 250–251, followed by my rather free translation. (Many words and expressions invite several alternative translations.). For the thrall name *Hjalli*, see Høverstad 1909.

62. Afraid was the "stew keeper,"
must have felt cowardly,
miserable over their fight,
and the gloomy day,
disappeared from the site,
hid in all corners,
which he had to pay for,
when he had to die away from his swines,
and all reward,
which he otherwise had.

63. So they took Buðli's cook-thrall,
and the miserable thrall screamed,
and took to the knife,
already before he felt the point of the knife,
he said he had plenty of time,
to carry out the most dirty work,
happy would Hjalli be then,
to manure the fields well,
if only he could live,
if he only could live.

64. Hǫgni acted then
as an envoy for the thrall,
For me it is a simple thing,
why should we here want to hear
– which few would do –
that he should get off:
to encourage this game,
this screaming?

It is interesting that different terms for "thrall" occur in these stanzas: *bryti*, *hvergætir* m. 'cook' (originally: 'the one who tends to the cauldron'), *bráss* m. 'cook' (linked to the verb *brasa* 'light the fire, roast', cf. Da. *brasa* 'fry in fat in a pan' (*stege i fedtstof på en pande*),[21] and the modern Swedish slang expression *brassa käk* 'cook'),[22] *illþræli* n. 'the bad thrall' (from ON adj. *illr* 'bad'),[23] and also the adjective *ánauðugr* 'living under duress'.[24]

Further on in the same poem, Atli mentions how he paid a dowry for Guðrún, thirty thralls and seven good thrall women (*þræla þría tigo, þýjar siau góðar*) and moreover an amount in silver; it was obviously a beautiful and highborn woman he was marrying:[25]

[21] https://ordnet.dk/ddo/ordbog?select=brase,2&query=brase.

[22] This word *bráss/brass* is attested only here; it is thus a so-called *hapax legomenon* (de Vries 1962 p. 54). On the verb *bras(s)a* 'cook, roast, fry', see *SAOB* col. B4166, article *brasa*.

[23] On the interesting word formation, the second element *þræll* occurs with an *ia*-suffix extension *þræli* (< *þrahil-ia-*); cf. e.g. *illgresi* 'weed' to *gras* n. 'grass', a type of formation encountered especially in Old West Norse—see, for example, Olson 1916 p. 180.

[24] These words are discussed in detail later.

[25] Old Icelandic text from *Edda* ed. Neckel p. 255, followed by my rather free translation.

95. *Mund galt ek mœrri*
þræla þriá tigo,
– sœmð var at slíko –,
meiðma fiǫlð þiggia,
þýiar siau góðar
silfr var þó maira.

95. A dowry I gave
and thirty thralls,
– such was honorable –
with expensive jewelry,
and seven good thrall-women,
but silver even more.

One entire eddic poem, *Grottasǫngr* (Song of Grotti), concerns thralls. The plot is that the Danish King Fróði bought two slave women (*ambátt*) from King Fiǫlnir in Sweden, Fenja and Menja.[26] He set them to work the great quern Grotti, whose nature was such that it ground out whatever was spoken out loud as a wish. Fróði wanted the slave women to grind out gold, peace, and happiness for him. Instead, the slave women ground out an army led by the sea-king Mýsingr, who killed Fróði. Mýsingr then took both the quern Grotti and the two slave women with him on his ship and told them to grind out salt, which they did to such an extent that the ship finally sunk into the sea, and because of all the salt that had been ground out the seawater became salty and remains so even today.

A narrative concerned with morality about thralls in early Iceland is found in *Geirmundar þáttr heljaskins*, which forms the introduction to the great *Sturlungasaga*.[27] The story tells of two settlers, the twin brothers Geirmundr and Hámundr, sons of the Norwegian King Hjǫrr from Hordaland, who settled in Iceland toward the end of the ninth century. The tale explains Geirmundr's strange byname, *heljarskinn* 'with skin as black as Hell (*Hel*)'. During the king's absence from Norway the queen gave birth to twins. Both were unusually large and incredibly ugly. But the worst aspect of their ugliness was, according to the tale, that they were so dark; nobody had seen such dark-skinned children. Simultaneously, a slave woman gave birth to an extraordinarily beautiful—fair-skinned—child. When the queen became

[26] Axel Koch (1898 p. 262) has interpreted both names of the female slave thus: *Fenja* (*Fenia*) is compared to a word that occurs in dialects found in the province of Hälsingland, *fanor* f. pl. 'uncleanliness, chaff and husks in grain', deriving from **făna* 'husks' on which the verb **fenia* 'remove chaff from grain (through grinding)' is based. This verb, employed as a *nomen actionis* ("the removal of chaff") has, he supposes, passed into a *nomen agentis* ("one who removes chaff"), while *Menja* (*Menia*) is supposedly based on the word *man* n. 'thrall'. Whether a verb **menia* 'being a thrall, to thrall' was constructed in the same way he does not discuss.

[27] Krömmelbein 1994, Seelow 1994 pp. 698 ff., McTurk 1997, Jochens 1999 pp. 80–81, and Clunies Ross 2006 pp. 39–40. This narrative appears also in different versions of *Landnámabók* as well as *Hálfs saga ok Hálfsrekka*, see Clunies Ross 2006.

aware of this, she quite simply exchanged her twin boys for the child of the slave woman. The years passed, but after three years a court skald realized that something must be wrong since the children acted the way they did. The queen admitted what she had done and showed the king the twin boys. When he had seen them, he could tell that they must be his sons, although he declared that he had never seen boys as dark-skinned (*heljarskinn*) as these.

There are three versions of this tale. The version contained in *Landnámabók* narrates that King Hjǫrr had gone on a campaign in Bjarmaland, which would be somewhere close to modern-day Finland. There, he had taken as hostage the daughter of the King of Bjarmaland and then brought her back to Norway. Later on, she gave birth to a pair of twins who were very dark of complexion.

We find here that the saga narrators are concerned with pointing out and explaining ugliness. Such ugliness is usually identified in the sagas as darkness.[28] One variant of *Geirmundar þáttr* explains the ugliness of the twins by stating that they were born to a non-Scandinavian.

It is very clear that the author follows a particular "thrall-motif" characterized by set patterns that recur whenever thralls are described and mentioned in Old West Norse literature—thralls apparently fulfilled certain functions within the narrative strategy.[29] The thrall was always dark, short, stupid, gloomy, and ugly,[30] in sharp contrast to the hero, who was tall, fair, happy, well-spoken, and extremely handsome. The picture of the thrall was, in other words, to contrast the free human being.[31] It is thus clear that we are dealing with literature and that one must, also in this respect, approach the poem with the utmost caution if we want to deduce historical facts from it.

This literary motif recurs over and over again in Norse texts. Thralls were not just ugly, they were also cowardly, like Þorðr in huglausi 'the cowardly', who appears in *Gísla saga Súrssonar* (Saga of Gísli Súrsson).[32] Þorðr was so cowardly and stupid that he let himself be deceived into putting on someone else's clothes after which he was killed instead of the owner of the clothes.

The free farmer (*hauldr*) was the norm and the point of departure for a life worth living; this was contrasted by the thrall who lived an unworthy,

[28] Jochens 1999 pp. 80 ff.
[29] See, e.g., Wilde-Stockmeyer 1978 pp. 93–148.
[30] See, e.g., *Egil's saga* (ch. 85); cf. Gjessing 1862 p. 141.
[31] Meulengracht Sørensen 1993 pp. 161 ff.; cf. Foote 1977 p. 50.
[32] Cf. also *Eyrbyggja saga* (ch. 37) with similar thrall-topoi.

honorless life. The famous speech that Sǫlvi klofi made to "King" Arnviðr in Sunnmøre, included in *Egils saga*, constitutes a good example of this.

> *Þótt þetta vandræði hafi nú borit oss at hendi, þá mun eigi langt til, at sama vandræði mun til yðuar koma, þuíat Haralldr ætla ek at skjótt man hér koma, þá er hann hefer alla menn þrælkat ok áþjáð, sem hann vill, á Norð-Mæri ok í Ravmsdal. [. . .] En at ǫðrum kosti munu þér vilja taka vpp þat ráð, sem Naumdælar gerðu, at ganga með sjálfuilja í ánauð ok geraz þrælar Harallz.*

> Although this misfortune has happened to us now, it won't be long, before the same misfortune will happen to you, because it is my belief that *Haralldr* soon will come to you, once he has enslaved and oppressed all of those he wants, on Nordmøre and in Romsdal. [. . .] Otherwise you will have to do as the Naumdælingar, voluntarily give up your freedom and become *Haralldr*'s slaves.[33]

The same saga often employs the stylistic trait of describing handsome people as tall and fair while ugly ones are short and dark haired. This contrast is used to describe the two children of Skallagrímr, the brothers Þórólfr and Egill, of whom the former is said to be tall and handsome to look at, he was strong, stronger than his peers, and was the best at sports and physical exercise, he was cheerful of mind and liked by all, his father and mother loved him dearly; Egill, on the other hand, is described as *mjǫk ljótr ok líkr feðr sínum, suarta á hár* "very ugly and like his father, with black hair."[34]

Egils saga also contains the famous dispute between Egill's son Þorsteinn and Steinar, son of Egill's old friend Ǫnundr.[35] The quarrel began when Steinar let his cattle graze in a lush pasture, Stakksmýr, which belonged to Egill and Þorsteinn. When this was repeated the following year, Þorsteinn tried to talk Steinar into stopping this bad practice, but the latter refused to give up the pasture and had his thrall Grani guard the cattle. Þorsteinn then got angry and went up to the pasture, killed Grani, and drove the animals away. The following winter when Steinar was in Snæfellsströnd he met a

[33] *Egil's saga* ed. Jónsson pp. 7–8, my translation; cf. Egil's saga in *The Complete Sagas of the Icelanders* 1 p. 35 (trans. B. Scudder).
[34] *Egil's saga* ch. 31.
[35] What follows is based on *Egil's saga* chs. 83–86.

thrall, Þrándr, who was bigger and stronger than others. The thrall was expensive, for sure, "one and a half the price of an average thrall," but Steinar bought Þrándr. Safely home again, Steinar revealed what he wanted Þrándr to do the following summer, namely guard the cattle armed with an axe and if Þorsteinn or any of his farmhands prevented grazing in the disputed pasture, Þrándr was to kill them with the axe. So it happened, as one might expect, that Þrándr drove the cattle into Stakksmýr, Þorsteinn was told of the mischief and went up to the pasture again. A conversation of classical Icelandic saga format took place between Þrándr and Þorsteinn, upon which "Þorsteinn lifted his axe and gave Þrándr a hard blow on his neck so that the head fell down onto the chest."

The whole affair escalated until it was to be taken to the spring assembly and Steinar struck a deal with the legal expert Tungu-Oddr, who promised to help him with the case. In the spring the two of them set off and had many people with them. Steinar summoned Þorsteinn for the killings of the thralls to "half outlawry" for either killing. "For such was the law when thralls were killed, if no compensation had been paid by the third sunrise; but two cases of half outlawry should be reckoned as equal to one case of outlawry." In other words, Steinar intended to have Þorsteinn sentenced as *skógarmaðr*, an outlaw. Then the spring assembly began. People arrived with many followers and put up their tents near the thing-site. Þorsteinn, who was a *goði*, had much authority at the assembly, but Steinar went on the offensive in the negotiations. When the judges retired for counsel in the evening, a crowd of men were seen riding alongside Gljúfurá with their shields glistening in the evening sun. They rode up to the assembly site. Foremost rode a man in a blue cloak, gilded helmet, and gold-inlaid shield, with a sword in his belt and carrying a spear with gold-decorated shaft in his hand. This was Egill Skallagrímsson with eighty selected and well-equipped men. Egill dismounted and asked whether his old friend Ǫnundr, Steinar's father, was at the assembly. Ǫnundr spoke out and said that was the case and gave him a friendly greeting. The case now took a turn so that Þorsteinn and Steinar handed over the settlement of the case to their fathers, at which point Ǫnundr asked Egill to find a solution to the dispute. The next day Egill went to the thing-site along with Þorsteinn "and their entire entourage," a great crowd of men, and began pronouncing judgment in the case. First, Egill described how his father, Skallagrímr, took ownership of this land and how he distributed land among his friends and followers, including Áni at Ánabrekka, where Ǫnundr and Steinar now lived. Then he reproached Steinar for entering Þorsteinn's land and emphasized that the killing of the two thralls must remain uncompensated and that had they been free men whom Þorsteinn had killed they could still not have been compensated for. Þorsteinn had the legal right to these killings. Steinar was sentenced to give up his lands at Ánabrekka, without any compensation.

The tale of this dispute has an authentic element in the description of how a society without any repressive power, that is to say without any kind of "police," may have functioned. One acquired right by being stronger than one's opponents, by being legally cleverer and above all by being able to refer to the past, calling on ancestors, customs, and traditions. We get a description of how disputes were solved in an oral culture that lacked any superior royal power or a "police." The thrall's function in this context was that he could be bought and used as an implement of revenge or to carry out unlawful deeds; in this case Þrándr was requested to carry out a killing on behalf of his master.

A very interesting case of something that is developed further later, namely various degrees of unfreedom or the fluid lines between thrall and subordinate—servant—subject, is mentioned in one of the most "literary" of the sagas: *Njáls saga*. The introduction tells of the beautiful and obstinate Hallgerðr Hǫskuldsdóttir. She had a *fóstri* (foster-father) named Þjóstólfr. This Þjóstólfr is said to come from the Southern Isles (he was *suðreyskr*), which means from the Hebrides, and is described as a strapping fellow and a rowdy fighter who had killed many, but never paid compensation for anyone. Among others he killed Hallgerðr's first husband, Þorvaldr, because he abused his wife. After hitting one of Hǫskuldr's farm workers, Þjóstólfr sought refuge with Hallgerðr and her new husband, Glúmr. But yet again Þjóstólfr succeeded in making a nuisance of himself. A final showdown came in the autumn, when he was asked together with the farmhands to bring the sheep down from the mountains. "Looking for sheep is not my line," said Þjóstólfr.[36] "Besides, I'm not going following in the footsteps of your slaves' [*þrælum þínum*]. But if you go yourself, then I'll come with you." As said, then done. Glúmr went along, and when Glúmr and Þjóstólfr found themselves alone in Þverfell tempers burst for both of them. Glúmr said: "There's no bad company unless it comes from home. Now I have to put up with insults from you, a bonded slave! [*þú ert þræll fastr á fótum*]."[37] Þjóstólfr responded:

[36] *Njals saga*, ed. Cook (1997), ch. 16, p. 22.

[37] The expression *fastr á fótum* seems to be idiomatic about a thrall, lit. "fixed feet, tied at the feet"; it occurs in among other places *Grágás* 229 (see more sources in Fritzner, article *fastr* 2). Cleasby-Vigfússon translates it as "feet are bound fast to the soil," which appears a very literal but

"You'll find out whether I'm a slave or not, for I'm not about to yield to you."[38] The quarrel between them ended with Þjóstólfr killing Hallgerðr's second husband, Glúmr, with an axe-blow to the shoulder, splitting the shoulder blade and the collarbone.

There are several interesting details in this tale. First, one might note that Þjóstólfr is said to be Hallgerðr's *fóstri*. This word cannot be entirely synonymous with OSw *fostre*, which apparently designated a thrall brought up in the home (see later). In Iceland a *fóstri* could be a 'foster-father', 'foster-brother', or 'foster-son'.[39] In the eddic poem *Helreið Brynhildar* 11:2 (Brynhild's ride to Hel) there is a reference to a foster-father:[40]

Reið góðr Grana,	On Grani rode the good
guldmiðlandi,	giver of gold,
þars fóstri minn	where my foster-father
fletiom stýrði;	ruled the house;

In the same way, Fránmarr jarl was the foster-father (*fóstri*) of the beautiful Sigrlinn, daughter of King Sváfnir, who is mentioned in the prose prologue to the poem about Helgi Hjǫrvarðsson (*Helgakviða Hjǫrvarðzsonar*).

Foster-fatherhood was, of course, not a slave task in early Iceland, which the example of Fránmarr jarl, if nothing else, shows us. The descriptions in *Njáls saga*, however, give cause for hesitation with regard to Þjóstólfr's social position. One wonders why Glúmr scorns Þjóstólfr for being a thrall. Was he perhaps a *leysingi*, a freed thrall? We never obtain a certain answer to this. Even so, it is noteworthy that a *fóstrman* n. in Iceland was unambiguously a thrall, namely a thrall who had been fostered and grown up together with

rather incomprehensible translation; it is my conviction that the expression had other, considerably more pejorative, meanings, which is indicated by Lars Lönnroth (2006 p. 57) in his translation with "wretched thrall (*usel träl*)." Perhaps the expression alludes to thralls being fettered by a foot shackle after being purchased at a slave market, or after the day's work, during the night, to prevent the slave from running away? There is a metonymical expression in some early laws, such as *fæst a føtær* (ÖgL "The book concerning land," Sw *Jordabalken*, 10), roughly meaning "to witness against a dead man" (where his feet are used as a kind of pars pro toto for the man, hence metonymically) (cf. Pettersson 1959 p. 97), however this use of *foot/feet* for a "man" seems far-fetched.

[38] *Njals saga*, ed. Cook (1997), ch. 17, p. 22.
[39] See, e.g., Fritzner, article *fóstri*.
[40] *Edda* ed. Neckel p. 216; my trans.

the free children of the household,[41] and a foster-sister was a female thrall who had from childhood been fostered as a playmate and companion to her young mistress, as is evident from *Sigurðarkviða in skamma* (70):[42]

þvíat hánom fylgia	For him will follow
fimm ambóttir,	five *ambótt,*
átta þiónar,	eight *þjónn,*
øðlom góðir,	of noble birth,
fóstrman mitt	my foster-sister
ok faðerni,	and patrimony,
þat er Buðli gaf	that which Budle gave
barni síno	to his child.

Here, we might note that *fóstrman* n. is mentioned in connection with the thrall designations *ambátt*/*ambótt* and *þjónn*. This is cause to consider whether ON *fóstri* might not also contain a semantic layer that would explain why Glúmr so unduly accuses and scorns Þjóstólfr for being a thrall (*þú ert þræll fastr á fótum*).

In Iceland, a *fóstri* could also mean a foster-son, as is evident from the prose introduction to *Grímnismál*:[43]

> *Óðinn ok Frigg sáto í Hliðskiálf ok sá um heima alla. Óðinn mælti: "sér þú Agnar, fóstra þinn, hvar hann elr bǫrn við gýgi í hellinom? En Geirrøðr, fóstri minn, er konungr ok sitr nú at landi."*
>
> Óðinn and Frigg sat in Hliðskiálf and looked around all worlds. Óðinn said: "Can you see Agnar, your *fóstri*, where he begets children with a giantess in the cave? But *Geirrøðr*, my *fóstri*, is King and rules over a land."

In the previously mentioned *Egils saga* there is another interesting passage describing the bonds of affection and love that must have existed between many a child of the house and his or her wet nurse, who was a thrall woman breast-feeding and caring for the small child. In the saga it happens one day

[41] Note the neuter gender of the word, thus here *man* n. 'thrall, man or woman or as a collective'. Fritzner (article *fóstrman*) translates the word as "Thralls that have grown up in the household" (*Trælle som ere opvoxne i Huset*).

[42] *Edda* ed. Neckel p. 213; my trans.

[43] *Edda* ed. Neckel p. 54; my trans.

that Egill's father, Skallagrímr, was playing a ball game and had as opponents his son Egill and a young man named Þorðr. Toward evening the game became heated and Skallagrímr began to get bad-tempered. In his anger he accidentally grabbed Þorðr, whom he threw to the ground so hard that he died. Then he took hold of Egill. But Þorgerðr brák, who was Egill's wet nurse (*ambátt*), saw this. She started shouting abuse at Skallagrimr out of concern for the son whom she had nursed. This was not to the father's liking, and he chased the thrall woman out onto the edge of Digranes, from where Þorgerðr jumped off the cliff and into the water. Skallagrímr picked up a boulder, which he threw at her, and it hit her between her shoulders. The thrall woman died from this and was never seen again. Later that same evening, when it was time to eat supper, Egill was nowhere to be found. He was out of his mind with rage against his father who had lost his temper and killed his wet nurse. Before he came to eat he went into the cook shed and up to the man who looked after Skallagrímr's workshop and valuables and who was his favorite slave. Egill directed a fatal blow toward him and killed him, upon which he went and sat at the table. Nothing was said of the matter during supper, and what had happened was never spoken of between them again.

In *Eyrbyggja saga* there is an episode involving the thrall Egill. This episode is introduced in the following manner: "Thorbrand of Alftafjord had a slave called Egil the strong. He was the biggest and strongest of men, and was unhappy with his lot as a slave, and often asked Thorbrand and his sons to give him his freedom, offering to do whatever he could to earn it."[44] The opportunity came when the *Breiðvíkingar* were holding their annual ball games. Egill was asked to kill one of the *Breiðvíkingar*, Bjǫrn, Þorðr, or Arnbjǫrn, whereby he would obtain his much desired freedom. As said, then done. Egill set off on the day when he was to carry out this deed. His intention was to enter the smoke-filled room where the *Breiðvíkingar* were spending time and, unnoticed, kill one or more of them. He managed to approach the building without being discovered, but when he came through the door he stepped on his shoe strap so that he fell headlong and noisily to the ground. He was discovered, his feet were bound, and he was asked to reveal the reason for his visit. Egill truthfully told them that it had been his intention to kill one or more of them. The next day they brought Egill up to a mountain gorge and killed him. Then follows an interesting development of the situation: "It was law in those days that if a man killed another man's slave, he had to take the

[44] *Eyrbyggja saga*, ed. Quinn (1997) ch. 43, p. 184.

compensation payment of twelve ounces of silver to his home, beginning his journey there no later than the third sunrise after the killing of the slave. If the payment for the slave was legally made, there was no case to be answered for the killing of the slave."[45]

An interesting episode is narrated in *Ágrip* and concerns a time when Hákon Jarl was in Sørtrøndelag, Norway.[46] *Ágrip* is a somewhat unusual source in comparison with the other sagas treated here.[47] Toward the end of his reign, Hákon had clearly developed a taste for women and, according to the Christian author of *Ágrip*, a quite ungodly lust for all sorts of skirts, wives as well as daughters. One clearly gets the drift that these excesses of the flesh will be the downfall of Hákon, and this is indeed what happens. In this case, Hákon was in Melhus (< *Meðalhús*) and had taken a shine to a woman named Guðrún Lundasól, a byname meaning approximately 'she who is like a sun in Lunda', and she accordingly lived at Lunda in Gauldal. With this simple stylistic detail the author of *Ágrip* has communicated to us that Guðrún was both incredibly beautiful and popular back home in Lunda. Hákon sent his thralls to fetch her and bring Guðrún to Melhus in order for the two of them to, as the author hints at, commit fornication (*til ósæmðar*). But when the thralls sat down to eat they were overpowered by a large group of men that Guðrún had managed to get together, and so the kidnapping failed. Guðrún then let Hákon Jarl know that she had no intentions of sharing his bed unless he sent his mistress, Þóra from Remol, packing. So this was the sore spot for "the sun from Lunda." Hákon Jarl, of course, was of no such intent; as an earl he was able to both have his cake and eat it. Instead, he himself set off for Lunda with all his men in order to fetch Guðrún. However, a man named Halldór from Skerðingssteðja became aware of this move and gathered together a great number of armed men from all over Gauldal. When the earl saw this impressive and armed crowd he realized, as it says in *Ágrip*, that he had been deceived, upon which he sent away all his men. Afterward, he and his thrall Karkr—whom Snorri calls both Karkr and Þormóðr karkr, while in *Jómsvíkinga saga* he is called Skopti karkr—rode off until they came to a hole in the ice (presumably on the river Gaula). There they drowned his horse and placed his cloak and his sword on the ice, presumably so that

[45] *Eyrbyggja saga*, ed. Quinn (1997) ch. 43, p. 186.
[46] The same episode is found in a slightly different version in chs. 48–50 in *Ólafs saga Tryggvasonar*, ed. Finlay and Faulkes (2016), pp. 182–185.
[47] See M. J. Driscoll's "Introduction" to *Ágrip*, ed. Driscoll (2008) pp. ix–xviii.

anyone following them would think that Hákon had fallen into the river and drowned. Then they went to a cave in Gauldal, which is still known as *Jarlshellir*, according to the author of *Ágrip*.

During the night, the thrall had visions in this cave (as is proper for a saga) to the effect that Hákon was nearing the end of his life. As a last resort, they therefore went to his mistress Þóra in Remol and she hid the two men in her pigsty.

Shortly after, a group of men arrived at Þóra's farm to search for Hákon, but they did not find him. Then they threatened to burn down the entire farm. When Hákon Jarl heard this and with the prospects of being tortured by the men if he revealed himself he asked the thrall Karkr to slit his throat (*lét þrælinn skera sik á barka*). In this way a man who had lived a filthy life died in a filthy place, a pigsty; thus the indignant eulogy of the Christian author of *Ágrip*.

There are, of course, several interesting angles to this tale. The Christian bias with its moralizing is obvious. Of interest to us, however, is the relationship between the Norwegian ruler and his trusted thralls, particularly his helper Karkr, who attracts special attention. *Ágrip* deals with the political history of Norway from the late ninth century till the early twelfth century, and the text is preserved in only one manuscript (AM 325: II 4to), which can be dated to the first half of the thirteenth century.[48] This ought to mean that when *Ágrip* was written as the work of one author or as the recording of a narrative that had been passed on orally, thraldom was probably still in use, even if it was petering out. It is with this in mind that *Ágrip* should be approached in order to discover how the author describes the relationship between a thrall and a regent. It appears unproblematic, indeed almost natural, that a king or a *jarl* could have as his closest companion a thrall. This, of course, compares to what is indicated on the Hovgården runestone (see later), where we are told of a *bryti* who looked after the king's farm. Perchance Karkr should be seen as analogous to this, as Hákon Jarl's *bryti* or some other trusted thrall who was close to the regent?

Perhaps also the ending of this tale about Hákon Jarl's erotic expedition to Sørtrøndelag, which led to his ruin, is of importance. It says that the thrall Karkr was the one who displayed Hákon's severed head, an action that Karkr apparently expected would contribute to the sparing of his life. That, however, was not the outcome, since Karkr was hanged anyway—according to

[48] See *Ágrip*, ed. Driscoll (2008) p. ix, with references.

Snorri in *Heimskringla* his head was cut off.[49] It is possible that one can deduce from this that Karkr was, indeed, close to the regent and to some extent he was therefore somewhat prominent in society, but as a thrall he lacked any legal status and therefore he was mercilessly executed.

To sum up, it can be established that qualitative characteristics concerning thralls and their circumstances in prehistoric times can hardly be deduced from the Icelandic sagas. The picture that is drawn up in these sources—that the thrall was dark-skinned, ugly, and stupid, a conception the Scandinavians shared with the people of the continental Middle Ages[50]—is far too much of a stereotype and a cliché for it to be considered reliable.[51] To employ Old Icelandic literature as the starting point for a description of slavery in Scandinavia can thus be described as rather a rash and venturous undertaking. However, the saga literature provides us with thirteenth-century *ideas* about the variable roles of slaves within working farmsteads in tenth- to eleventh-century Iceland.

[49] In ch. 49 in *Ólafs saga Tryggvasonar*, ed. Finlay and Faulkes (2016), p. 185.
[50] Jochens 1999 p. 88.
[51] For a discussion of thralls in the Icelandic sagas, see Gjessing 1862, Foote 1977, Karras 1988, and Meulengracht Sørensen 1993 pp. 161–164.

7
Thralls in Runic Inscriptions

Toki blacksmith raised this stone after Thorgisl,
. . . who gave him gold and freedom.

—*DR* 58

One might expect—if one is of the opinion that thralls made up a large part of Scandinavian society in the Viking Age—that thralls would be mentioned frequently in runic inscriptions, which are together with place-names our most important contemporaneous linguistic source material from the Viking Age. But this is not the case. In fact, probably only six (perhaps nine) thralls are mentioned in the around three thousand runic inscriptions from Scandinavia, and those mentioned—a *bryti* (possibly four *brytar*), a blacksmith, and four *fostrar*—are unlikely to have been ordinary work slaves, but presumably persons with a fair degree of social esteem. This is remarkable. If thralls constituted a large proportion of the population, as is sometimes assumed, it would be expected that at least some people of outright thrall status would be mentioned in some inscription or other. That individuals from the bottom layer of society, that is to say pure work thralls, would appear often in runic inscriptions can, of course, not be expected. But the fact that not a single thrall is mentioned is worth noting.

Terms for thralls occur in a few inscriptions, but apparently as bynames rather than appellatives. Moreover, persons who seem to be freed thralls occur in runic inscriptions, hence not thralls but free human beings with a past as slaves. For these, the terms OSw *løysi* m., *løysa* f. are used. In Old West Norse areas these are paralleled by ON *leysingi* m., *leysingja* f., terms that have, indeed, never been found in runic inscriptions.

The examples that we have of thralls occurring or of words that fall within the semantic range of 'slave' are the following:[1]

[1] The transliterated runic inscriptions and the translations that follow are taken from *Samnordisk runtextdatabas* (http://www.runforum.nordiska.uu.se/samnord/), in some case slightly modified by me after my readings.

Thraldom. Stefan Brink, Oxford University Press. © Oxford University Press 2021.
DOI: 10.1093/oso/9780197532355.003.0007

Fig. 7.1 On this runestone from Hørning, Jutland, Denmark, the smith Toki is said to have been freed (*frials*) from slavery. (Photo: Erik Moltke, National Museum, Copenhagen, CC-BY-SA.)

The Hørning stone (*DR* 58; Fig. 7.1) from Hørning parish, Hjelmslev hd, in northern Jutland, Denmark, carries this inscription:[2]

tuki smiþr riþ stin ift þurkisl kuþmutaR sun is hanum kaf kul ok frialsi

[2] Here and in what follows are indicated—as is commonly done within runology—in semibold (and *sans serif* font) the transliterated runic inscription, i.e., the runes as they occur on the stone in transliterated form; in italics a normalized text (here in Old Danish or Old Swedish); and in inverted commas a translation.

Toki Smithr resthi sten æft Thorgisl GuthmundaR sun, æs hanum gaf gul(?) ok frælsi.
"Tóki Smith raised the stone in memory of Thorgísl Gudhmundr's son, who gave him gold(?) and freedom (or: . . . made him a member of the family and gave him freedom)"[3]

In the inscription on the Hørning stone there is, for sure, no term that may be translated as 'thrall'; instead, it emerges that a person, Toki smith, was "freed," that is, he was given freedom by his master, Thorgisl. This inscription is historically very significant. A blacksmith was often a well-esteemed craftsman. In King Æthelberht's Law (560–616), an early Anglo-Saxon law for the kingdom of Kent, there is a reference to the king's official blacksmith.[4] Among Swedish place-names from, in all likelihood, the Late Iron Age, the place-name *Smedby* (< *SmiþarbyR*) is not uncommon. Even so, such names always occur as part of a complex of names that are best interpreted as prehistoric central places.[5] What we get here, then, is proof that a smith could be a thrall. That a pure work thrall, at the bottom of society, should raise a rune stone, even if he had been freed, does not seem plausible. Instead, this Toki smith must be reckoned as having a fairly stable social status. This notion is strengthened by the fact that the same Toki smith appears to have raised yet another rune stone, the Grensten stone (*DR* 91) at Middelsom in Jutland, the inscription of which reads:

: tuki : smiþr : risþ : l : stin : þisi : aiftiR : l : Rifla : sun : askis : bianaR l : sunaR : kuþ : hiab : þaRa : salu :
Tóki smithr résth[i] stén thæssi æftiR Rifla/Ræfla, sun Æsgis BiarnaR sonar. Guth hialpi théRa sélu
"Tóki Smith raised this stone in memory of Hrifli, son of Ásgeirr Björn's son. May God help their souls."

The important deduction that can be made following this discussion is that in Viking Age Scandinavia blacksmiths could be unfree and, as such, thralls.

[3] Cf. Moltke 1981 p. 316.
[4] *Gif cynings ambihtsmið oþþe laadrincmannan ofslehð, meduman leodgelde forgelde,* "If [he] slays a smith in the king's service, or a messenger [?] belonging to the king, he shall pay an ordinary wergild" (King Æthelberht's Law 7, here cited from *The Laws of the Earliest English Kings*, 1922 pp. 4–5).
[5] See Hellberg 1979 pp. 145 ff. and Brink 1996b p. 242 and *passim*.

Fig. 7.2 The runestone U 11 at Hovgården on the island of Adelsö, Lake Mälaren, Sweden, from probably the second half of the eleventh century, where a *bryti*, Tolir, a king's estate manager, is mentioned. (Photo: H. Faith-Ell, Swedish National Heritage Board.)

A slave of this kind must be assumed to have had a certain social standing that was based on his skills as a craftsman.

bryti

The word *bryti* has a very exciting albeit problematic background, which is discussed in the next chapter. The word probably appears on four Scandinavian rune stones.

On the Hovgården rune stone (U 11; see Fig. 7.2) on Adelsö (OSw *Alsnø*) in Lake Mälaren, Sweden, which according to Ann-Sofie Gräslund's classification is to be dated to the second half of the eleventh century (Pr 4),[6] the following can be read:

[6] Gräslund 1991–1992, 1998, 2006.

raþu runaʀ ret lit rista toliʀ bry[t]i i roþ kunuki toliʀ auk gyla litu ris . . . þaun hion eftiʀ . . . k merki srni . . . hakun baþ rista
Raþ þu runaʀ. Rett let rista Toliʀ bryti i Roþ kunungi. Toliʀ og Gylla letu ris[ta . . .], þaun hion æftiʀ [si]k(?) mærki . . . Hakon baþ rista
"Interpret the runes! Tólir the *bryti* of *Roþr* had them rightly carved for the King. Tólir and Gylla had [the runes] carved . . . this married couple as a landmark in memory of themselves(?) . . . Hákon ordered (it) be carved"

The inscription tells of Tolir, the king's (or a king's *jarl*'s) *bryti* in *Roþ* (or by *roþ*). The question discussed later is whether such a *bryti* was a thrall, an unfree slave, which would be the traditional interpretation of the term. The appearance of a *bryti* in so prominent a rune stone, raised on a royal estate and clearly very closely linked to the king is, of course, remarkable and requires an explanation.[7]

On a much-damaged rune stone from Gillberga (Sö 42; Fig. 7.3), Västerljung parish, Hölebo hd, in Södermanland, Sweden, the following can be read:

sigualti r[aisti . . . -kil br]utia sin
Sigvaldi ræisti . . . kel, brytia sinn
"Sigvald raised . . . -kel, his *bryti*"

[7] Mats G. Larsson and Staffan Fridell (2013) in an interesting article have re-analyzed this runic inscription and think they are able to reconstruct some missing runes and amend the inscription. In their opinion, the inscription should be read:

raþu : runaʀ : ret : lit : rista : toliʀ : bry[t]i : i roþ : kunuki : : toliʀ : auk : gyla : litu : ris. . . ʀ : : þaun : hioa : eftiʀ. . .[au]k : merki hakun • baþ : rista srni[-]. . .
Rað þu! Runaʀ rett let rista Toliʀ, bryti i Roð, kunungi. Toliʀ ok Gylla letu ris[ta runaʀ þessa]ʀ, þaun hion æftiʀ [ku]nung mærki. Hakon bað rista . . .
"You interpret! The runes Tole, *bryti* in Roden, had rightly carved for the King. Tole and Gylla had these runes carved, this married couple, [as a] memorial after the King. Håkon ordered [it] be carved . . . " [My trans.]

The main difference with this interpretation compared with the traditional one is that one should expect two different Håkons mentioned in the inscription, one Håkon, the King, and another Håkon, being what is proposed to be a *jarl* (a royal ombudsman or administrator; cf. Eng. *earl*)—which then would have a counterpart in the expression, *iarls bryti i Rodhs bo*, found in the Östgöta Law—who then is the one who ordered the inscription to be made. This new interpretation does not fundamentally change the function and status of the *bryti* in the inscription; he is still to be seen in a royal context. As I discuss later, Magnus Källström (2015) has recently dismissed Larsson and Fridell's suggestion of two different "Håkon."

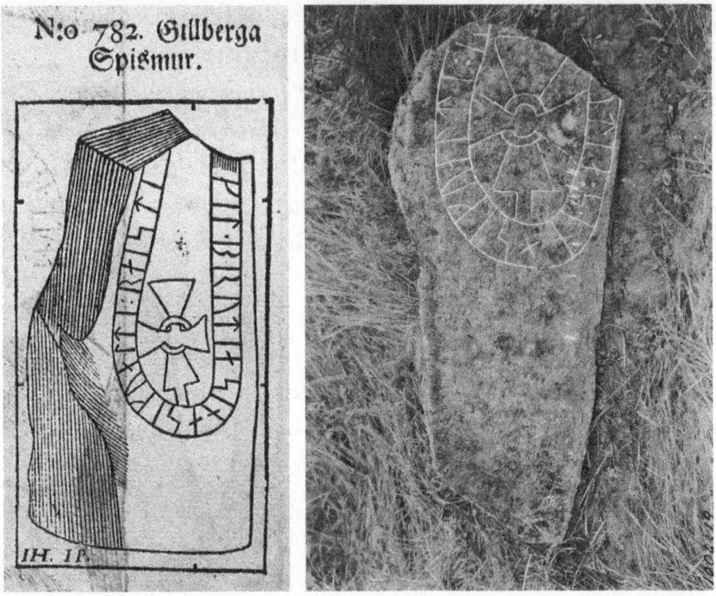

Fig. 7.3 On this damaged runestone (Sö 42) from Gillberga, Västerljung parish, in Södermanland, Sweden, a *bryti* (*. . . utia*) is probably mentioned. (Photo: H. Faith-Ell, Swedish National Heritage Board.)

The damaged word -utia has commonly been taken to stand for brutia. If this is the case, then we are dealing with the word *bryti*. However, there is no way of ascertaining any context that could provide further information on who this *bryti* was. The inscription is much too damaged for this.

On the Randbøl stone (*DR* 40; Fig. 7.4) in Jutland, Denmark, this can be read:

> **tufi bruti risþi stin þansi aft lika brutia þiR stafaR munu þur kuni miuk liki lifa**
>
> *Tofi bryti resþi sten þænsi æft lika brytia. ÞeR stafaR munnu Þorgunni miok længi lifa*
>
> "Tófi *bryti* raised this stone in memory of the *bryti*'s wife (or helpmate). Very long will these staves live for Þorgunnr"

According to this runic inscription, Tófi *bryti* raised the stone in memory of his wife (*lika*), which is made clear by terming her the *bryti*'s wife (*lika brutia*). The word *bryti* apparently occurs as a byname, but it is also clear that

Fig. 7.4 On the Danish runestone from Randbøl (DR 40) another *bryti* is mentioned, who has erected the stone after his wife. (Photo: Erik Moltke, The National Museum of Denmark, CC-BY-SA.)

this Tófi actually was a *bryti*, since the wife's epithet mentions this. The by-name can therefore be interpreted quite literally.

In Sønder Vinge, Middelsom hd, near Viborg in Jutland, Denmark, there is a peculiar rune stone (*DR* 83; Fig. 7.5), the inscription on which is hard to interpret and offers many alternative readings:

> **-u(þ)(i) : b(i) – (l)i [or] bruti : risþi : stin : þensi : uftiʀ : uruku auk : kaþu : bruþr : sino : tuo : . . . sarþi : auk siþ : r(a) (t)i [or] siþ:riti : saʀ : monr : ias : auþi : mini : þui**
>
> *[G]uþi [or] Øþi <bi--li> [or] Bryti resþi sten þænsi æftiʀ Urøkiu ok Kaþu, brøþr sina twa . . . særþi ok seþ. Ræti(?) [or] seþretti(?) saʀ mannr æs øþi minni þwi*

Fig. 7.5 Another *bryti* is mentioned on this runestone from Sønder Vinge, Denmark (*DR* 83), from circa AD 1000. (The National Museum of Denmark, CC BY-SA.)

> "Guþi [or] Øþi <bi--li> [*or*] bryti raised this stone after Órøkia and Kaþa, his two brothers . . . wounded and bewitched(?). May the one who disturbs this monument become perverse and an evil spirit [*or*] a sorcerer(?)"

We cannot know for sure whether the second word in this inscription should be read as <bi--li> or bruti. If the latter reading is accepted then we have a case of the word *bryti* occurring as the byname of someone named *Guþi* or *Øþi*. But since the potential appearance of the word *bryti* here is so uncertain, this inscription will not be included in the further discussion.

All three (certain) runic inscriptions containing the word *bryti* are historically tremendously important[8] and are analyzed and discussed in greater detail in the next chapter.

fostri/fostra

The words *fostri*, *fostra* appear four times in Swedish runic inscriptions from the Viking Age (the words are discussed in the next chapter).

On the Nolgården stone (Vg 13; Fig. 7.6) in Karleby, Leksberg parish, in Västergötland, Sweden, this can be read:

> **x þorir x skuba x risti stin : þikno : iftir ÷ kitil x sun : sin :x auk x (u)ftir : olaf x stro : sino**
> *ÞoriR Skorpa ræisti stæin þenna æftiR Kætil, sun sinn, ok æftiR Olaf, fostru sina*
> "Þorir skorpa raised this stone in memory of Kætil, his son, and of Olaf, his *fostra*"

Here, the farmer Þorir sko(r)pa has raised a stone and carved memorial words in honor of his son Kætil, but at the same time also of—what has been interpreted as—his female *fostra*, who, interestingly, was named *Olof*/*Olaf* (which is a woman's name, < *Ōlǭf*). However, the runes are actually **olaf x stro**, which could be understood as a personal name (*Olaf*) and her biname (*stra*), which, according to the context, all the same could have been his female "fostra." Thus, if the traditional reading of this inscription is correct, we can see that Þorir apparently had great affection not only for his son but also for his *fostra* Olaf, who, it can be assumed, grew up and was fostered on the farm together with the free children of the household. A few kilometers to the north, near Leksberg Church, there is another rune stone (Vg 11) whose inscription reads:

> **þorir x skurba x raisti x stin : þino : ift(i)(r) [:] (k)(i)til x sun : sin**
> "Þorir skorpa raised this stone after his son Kætil"

[8] See greater detail in Brink 2008 *passim*.

Fig. 7.6 On this runestone (Vg 13) from Karleby Nolgården, Leksberg parish, in Västergötland, Sweden, *Þorir skorpa* has raised a stone after his son and after Olaf **stro**, or, if we can accept a misspelling, his *fostra* (**-stro**). (Photo: H. Faith-Ell, Swedish National Heritage Board.)

On a rune stone (Sö 20 Fig. 7.7) from Smedsta in Hölö parish, Daga hd, in Södermanland, Sweden, there is a much-damaged inscription that has been taken to potentially contain the word *fostri*, but the emendation must be considered uncertain:

uþmunr ti : riti: stin : þensa * abtiʀ : þurfas : fu . . .
[G]uþmundr <ti> retti stæin þennsa æftiʀ Þorfast, fa[þur] / fo[stra] [sinn]
"Gudhmundr . . . raised this stone in memory of *Thorfast*, his *fo* . . . "

Fig. 7.7 A *fostre* is probably mentioned on the runestone (Sö 20) from Smedsta, Södermanland, Sweden, where only the first two runes have survived. (Photo: Magnus Källström, Swedish National Heritage Board.)

On another rune stone in Södermanland, near Jäder Church (Sö 97; Fig. 7.8) in Österrekarne, the evidence for *fostri* is unambiguous:

asgautr : raisti : stin : þena : . . . . . . (r)(l) : faþur : sin x fostra : arna
Asgautr ræisti stæin þenna . . . faþur sinn, fostra Arna
"Asgautr raised this stone after (. . .) his father, Arni's *fostri*"

It is not entirely easy to interpret this damaged inscription. It seems as if the deceased had a *fostri* named Arni. Perhaps it was his "foster-son." Did he then have the status of a thrall, or was he a free man?

On a runic inscription on a rock face near Såsta (U 163; Fig. 7.9) in Täby parish in Uppland, Sweden, the rune carver has used several binding-runes (marked with = in the transliteration) so that there is a stave with two subordinate twigs on either side:

k=lamal as=auk=a n=sa=u=kain=fa auk + farulfr + litu + rista x ili tfs=l'fR +
þuri + R=ufa=kþ=au=mr=a s=lin x auk x kamal x iftiR x fusra sin f-str x iaRk

Fig. 7.8 Another *fostre* is mentioned on a runestone (Sö 97) from Jäder, Södermanland, Sweden (where the "*fostra Arna*" is carved on the side of the stone). (Photo: H. Faith-Ell, Swedish National Heritage Board.)

> *Gamall ok Svæinn ok Farulfr letu rista hælli æftiʀ Þori, faþuʀ sinn, ok Gamall æftiʀ fostra sinn . . . f[a]str hiogg*
> "Gamall and Sveinn and Farulfr let carve this stone slab in memory of Thórir, their father; and Gamall in memory of his *fostri* . . . -fastr cut"

In this instance, three brothers carved runes on a rock surface in memory of their father. But, interestingly, one of the sons, Gamall, wanted also to honor his *fostri*. Not a *fostra*, who could then be assumed to have been his wet nurse when he was little and who, if the earlier mentioned episode from *Egil's saga* can be believed, could be taken to have been very close to him. Instead, it is clearly a male *fostri*. Might we have here a parallel to Hallgerðr's *fostri* from the

Fig. 7.9 This rock face has a beautiful eleventh-century runic inscription in Såsta in Uppland, Sweden, where a man, *Gamall*, is commemorating his *fostre*. (Photo: H. Faith-Ell, Swedish National Heritage Board.)

episode in *Njáls saga* mentioned previously? In Iceland, as discussed earlier, a *fostri* could be a foster-father (alternatively foster-brother or foster-son). Gamall's *fostri* possibly compares to Hallgerðr's *fostri*, who was presumably a thrall, but it is more likely that he was Gamall's foster-father.

Løysi

If the words *fostri*/*fostra* are not unambiguous examples of terms for thralls, the next example, OSw *løysi* 'one who is loose (free, freed)', is not a term for a thrall either, but rather for a freed thrall. The word seems to appear in only

Fig. 7.10 On this badly damaged runestone (U 696) from Veckholm, Uppland, Sweden, a *løysi* 'freed slave' is probably mentioned. (Photo: N. Lagergren, Swedish National Heritage Board.)

two Viking Age rune stones, both of which are in Swedish Uppland. On a severely damaged rune stone near Veckholm Church (U 696; Fig. 7.10) in Trögd this can be read:

. . . -- * (r)(a) -- a * st-. . . -t * a-ui * (l)ausa * s-- * --. . . -- * ilbi * sial hans

and since the inscription is so badly preserved it is not so easy to normalize and interpret it, but one possibility is this:

. . . ræ[is]a st[æin] [a]t A[l]ve(?) / Ø[l]ve, løysa(?) s[inn] . . . hialpi sial hans,

which can mean:

> ". . . raised this stone in memory of Alve(?), his freed . . . [may God] help his soul"

If the interpretation is correct, then this inscription would concern a freed thrall, Alve(?), in memory of whom a rune stone was raised, which must have been highly unusual, even if the thrall had been freed.

On the Björkeby stone (U 168; Fig. 7.11) from Östra Ryd parish in Danderyd, Sweden, which is no longer preserved (apart from a fragment discovered in 2017), the following was inscribed:

> **[hu=lmstin'ranfastr' aystin * litu auka' stain * at * fasta' lusa * sin * -- þoru ybiR * iak]**
> *Holmstæinn, Ragnfastr, Øystæinn letu haggva stæin at Fasta, løysa(?) sinn [ok] Þoru. ØpiR hiogg*
> "Holmstæinn, Ragnfastr and Øystæinn let carve this stone after Fasti, their and Thora's freed. Øpir cut"

Presumably, this Fasti was a trusted former thrall to the three brothers and their mother. It is remarkable—and highly interesting—to commemorate a former thrall in this way, raising a costly memorial to him and have the best renowned and most fashionable among Uppland's rune masters, Øpir, who cannot have been cheap, carry out the work.

We have, then, two examples of freed slaves occupying social positions of such esteem that the families concerned have chosen to raise (doubtlessly) costly rune stones in memory of them. Had they been regular work slaves, and as such legally tools, *instrumentum vocale* 'implements with voices', this would—of course—never have happened.

thræll

The old church in Bø, in Telemark, Norway, presents what is called runic "church graffiti" (N A104) that stems from medieval times. The inscription, which is long for a piece of "graffiti," reads:

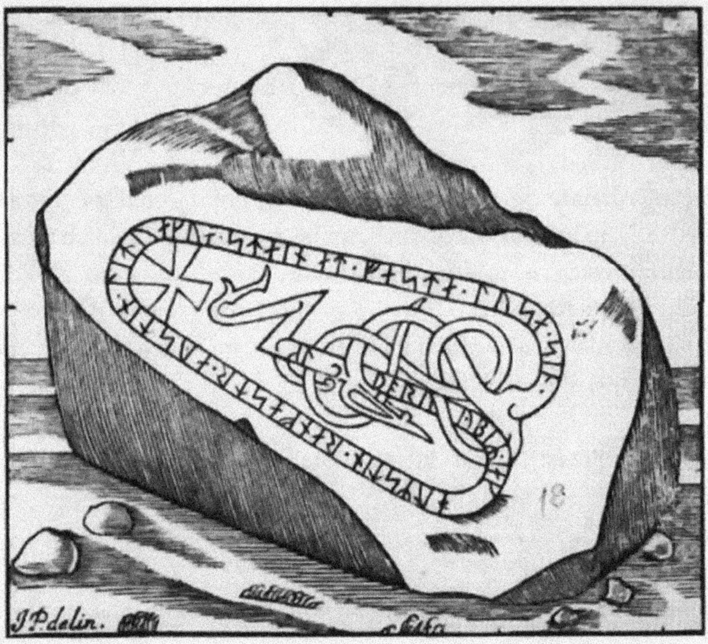

Fig. 7.11 This runestone U 168 was destroyed in the nineteenth century, but luckily we have a drawing from 1750, where we can read how a *løysi* 'freed' has been given his freedom. A fragment of this stone was rediscovered in 2017. (Ill. from Peringskiöld, *Monumenta*, 1750.)

> **suæfn banar mer : sot er bna fion sfinkata : fials ibui hect ærfaþe : øuk huhis hui --(t)i ÷ þris unsela ÷ þt sklu raþa**
> *Svefn bannar mér, sótt er barna, fjón svinkanda, fjalls íbúi, hests erfaði, ok heys víti, þræls vansæla. That skulu ráða*

Which may perhaps be translated thus:

> 'I get no sleep, children are sick; hatred of the worker, mountain-dweller; hard work for the horse, and damage to the hay; misfortune of the thrall. This you must interpret.'

The impression is that someone sitting in the church must have stopped listening to the sermon of the priest and instead scribbled fairly random messages on the wall. He is tired, the children are ill, and things are generally very bad; life is full of toil and evil, for the worker, the horse, and the thrall. Now you interpret these runes if you can! Perhaps the jumbled inscription is to be understood in this manner? However, this is the only inscription we have in Scandinavia in which the word *þræll* appears and it is from medieval times (hence post-1100). As it stands, the inscription provides no substantial information about thralls in the Middle Ages other than that the writer thinks it is a great misfortune to be a thrall.

This is what our Scandinavian runic inscriptions from the Viking Age and the Middle Ages have to say about Scandinavian thraldom during the Viking Age. It is not a great deal.

Among the Proto-Nordic runic inscriptions, belonging to the period circa AD 150–800, there are, however, some exciting inscriptions, normally consisting of simply a personal name or a title, that contain the Proto-Nordic **þewaʀ*, a word that is analyzed in the following chapter.

8

Terms for Thralls and Their Meanings

Every attempt to grasp the meaning of words which were in use in a distant epoch can deepen our understanding of the community which used them and of its customs.

—A. Ya. Gurevich, 1992, p. 209

A good starting point for a discussion of the terminology for thralls is found in a paragraph of the Norwegian Gulathing Law (GuL 198): *Tvær ero hans hinar bezto ambatter. Seta. oc deigia. oc tveir þrælar: þionn oc bryti*, "two are his [the farmer's] best female slaves [*ambáttir*]: *seta* (she who sits inside, and weaves?) and *deigja* (she who bakes, the housekeeper); and two male slaves [*þrælar*]: *þjónn* and *bryti* (the farm overseer)." It emerges from this that in the West Norse area *ambátt*, *ambótt* seems to have been an umbrella term for female slaves,[1] while *þræll* was the male counterpart. This pair we also find in another paragraph in the Gulathing Law (GuL 61), *þræll eða ambott*, moreover in some Icelandic sagas: in *Hálfs saga ok Hálfsrekka* where it is told how King Hjǫrleifr gave Handir and Hrindir land to occupy and also thralls (*þræll ok ambátt*),[2] and in *Gísla saga Súrssonar* (25) it is said that Ingjaldr had *þræll ok ambátt; þrællinn hét Svartr, en ambáttin hét Bóthildr*, likewise the ambiguous *Vǫlsa þáttr* (*þræll ok ambátt*). On the other hand, *Rígsþula* presents, as was seen previously, the pair *þræll* and *þír*, while *Atlamál in grœnlenzko* and *Hervarar saga ok Heiðreks* both have *þræll* and *þý* as the general terms for, respectively, male and female slaves. The other terms occurring in the cited paragraph of the Gulathing Law, *seta* and *deigja*, were female slaves with specific functions, similar to the male terms *þjónn* and *bryti*.[3]

[1] Cf. Karg-Gasterstädt 1942 p. 320.

[2] *kongr gaf þeim Hanndi ok Hrindi land at bua aa ok þar med þræl ok ambatt*, *Hálfs saga ok Hálfsrekka*, ed. Seelow, p. 175.

[3] For the following discussion regarding the development of languages and word's etymology, see Appendix 2.

Thraldom. Stefan Brink, Oxford University Press. © Oxford University Press 2021.
DOI: 10.1093/oso/9780197532355.003.0008

The same pair of words, *þræll* and *ambótt*, which are general designations of, respectively, male and female slaves, was supposedly commonly used across the Scandinavian area, at least in Norway and western Sweden (albeit not in the Svea regions, i.e., eastern, central Sweden of today). In the Older Västgöta Law, the section on thieving (17 and 19) contains the general pair: *þræl ok ambut*. Moreover, the famous Skara-Charter from 1335,[4] which is regarded as the final and official document that abolishes thraldom in Sweden, states that: *alt Mankyn ælder qvinkön, sum i Wæsgözko ældir Wærinsko* [probably an error of *Wærmsko*] *Laghsaghu födhes af krisnum Manne ældir Kono, maa aldrigh þræl ælder ambut wæra ælder þetta namn bæra*,[5] "all of man- or woman-kind, who is born to Christian man or [should presumably be *and*] wife within the jurisdiction of Västergötland or Värmland must never be *þræl* or *ambut*, or be so called." It can therefore be assumed that *þræll* and *ambótt* were the general designations for, respectively, male and female slave during early medieval times across Scandinavia.[6] Whether this were also the case in prehistoric times is uncertain, but in all likelihood, it was not.

The most commonly occurring term for a male slave during medieval times (and, as it happens, the Viking Age) was ON *þræll*, OSw, ODa *þræl*, which has, at least in Old Swedish and modern Swedish, also yielded a verb, *träla* 'to work like a thrall, to toil.' The word can probably be derived from a Proto-Nordic **þrahilaʀ* or **þrāhilaʀ*,[7] which some scholars link etymologically to Goth. *þragjan* and OE *þrægan* 'to run.' The word *þræll* may thus have had an earlier meaning of 'the one who runs (errands) for someone.' A link to a verb meaning 'to run' seems to provide a good point of departure for the etymology of the word, although this is disputed by some etymologists.[8] They claim that the meaning 'runner, someone who runs (errands)' does not match the word *þræll* when the heavy work of a slave is considered. I find, based on the thesis I promote in this study of the development of the institution of slavery, that the meaning of 'errand boy', 'servant' fits excellently and it is also an earlier meaning of, for instance, *ambátt* (< *ambactus*), as well as many other slave terms.[9] The word *thrall*, however, is very problematic. It

[4] See Hasselberg 1944.

[5] *DS* 3106. On *Wærinsko* for *Wærmsko*, see Henning 1930 pp. 86–87 and Hasselberg 1944 pp. 78–79.

[6] See, e.g., Henning 1930 p. 86 and Nevéus 1974 p. 26. It is noteworthy that both these sources are from Västgötaland, which means that the statements are somewhat uncertain with regard to the part of the region influenced by the *Svear* (Swedes).

[7] See, e.g., Björkman 1900 p. 19, de Vries 1962 p. 625, and Nielsen 1976 pp. 426–427.

[8] Thus de Vries 1962 p. 625, who considers the etymology of the word uncertain.

[9] On the word *ambactus*, see Green 1998 p. 15 and Scardigli 2002 pp. 567–568.

has been taken to be an exclusively Nordic word so that its occurrence in other languages is due to borrowings.[10] The word is therefore discussed in detail later.

ambátt, ambótt

The word ON *ambátt, ambótt* f., OSw *ambut, ambot, ambat,* which designates a female slave, is generally thought to be a loan from the Gallo-Latin *ambactus* 'servant' (cf. Eng. *embassy*, Sw. *ämbete*, Da. and Germ. *Amt*, etc.).[11] It was borrowed into Proto-Germanic as well as into Medieval Latin. There are many indications that the word was brought in via the Visigoths.[12] The origins of the word is an Old Gaelic **amb*(*i*)*aktos* 'servant, companion' (which is in turn the root of the Gallo-Latin *ambactus* 'official').[13] This Old Gaelic word is presumed to have the original meaning 'one who walks or runs about' or perhaps 'one who herds (and guards) livestock', constructed from *amb*- 'around' and a stem belonging to PIE **ag*- 'drive, lead', thus presenting a meaning close to the one discussed here for the word *þræll*. *Ambátt* seems to have been one of many words, relating to legal issues pertaining to the private and the public spheres, that were borrowed into Proto-Germanic already from Old Gaelic (e.g., ON *arfr* 'inheritance', *eiðr* 'oath', *friðr* 'peace', *gísl* 'hostage', and *ríki* 'realm, kingdom'; cf. Old Gaelic *-*rîgs*, Gall. -*rix*, OIr *rî*, Goth. *reiks*, OE *rica* 'ruler, king', Latin *rex*),[14] thus in very distant times (probably more than two thousand years ago). The Old Norse word (*ambótt*) has since then possibly been borrowed into Late Old English as the Middle English *ammbohht*;[15] OE *ambiht, embiht, ymbiht* m. 'servant', which existed already in Early Old English,[16] obviously shared its roots with the Nordic word, and was an early borrowing into Proto-Germanic from Gallo-Latin. The word occurs in Gothic as *andbaht* 'official, servant' as in *andbahti* 'office, service'

[10] See, e.g., Pelteret 1995 p. 264 and P. Foote in *KL* 19 (1975) col. 15.
[11] Kuhn 1973 p. 258 and Kluge *EW*, article *Amt*.
[12] See von Olberg 1991 p. 208, with further references.
[13] Mees 1998 p. 375, Orel 2003 p. 18.
[14] Feist 1939 pp. 48–49, de Vries 1962 p. 8, Nielsen 1976 p. 8 and *passim*, von Olberg 1991 p. 207.
[15] Brate 1884 p. 32 and Björkman 1900 p. 226. The reason supposedly being that ME *ammboht* has an *o* in the stem form, while the OE counterpart, *ambiht, ambeht*, has an *i*(*e*).
[16] Pelteret 1995 p. 264; Björkman (1900 pp. 226–227) states: "This would then be a case of a Celtic word being introduced into English through Scandinavian," but ends up with a tentative: "I prefer to leave the question of the nearest origin of the word unsettled." See also Pons-Sanz 2013 p. 420 with references.

where the prefix *and-* has been understood as resulting from influence from the preposition *and*.[17]

It may be noted that the word discussed here appears in Germanic languages partly in a weak masculine as well as a strong masculine variant, OHG *ambaht*, OSax *ambahteo*, Goth. *andbahts*, OE *ambeht*, etc. (< **ambahta-*) 'official, civil servant', and partly in a neuter variant, Goth. *andbahti*, OSax *ambaht*, OE *ambiht*, *embeht*, OHG *ambahti* (> *Amt*), ON *embætti* (< **ambahtja-*) 'office, service'.[18] In Germanic languages, then, we have to reckon with one loanword for the official and one for the office. It is remarkable that in all Germanic languages, with the exception of Old Norse, this is a masculine word designating an 'official'. In Scandinavia, a term corresponding to PGmc **ambaht-* never occurs with masculine gender. Instead, the word has come to refer to a female servant, a slave woman. This situation has not previously been discussed, as far as I am aware. The only explanation I can find for this anomaly is that there was already a word for a male slave in Scandinavia, namely *þræll*, wherefore **ambaht* came to have its gender changed so that it referred to a female slave.[19]

deja

Another designation for a female thrall is a term encountered in the aforementioned Gulathing Law, namely ON *deigja* (< **daiȝiōn*), which is a derivation of the word *deig*, meaning 'dough', and thus means 'one who bakes'. During later stages of the Scandinavian vernacular languages this word, MNo. *deigja*, MSw. *deja*, has secondarily acquired meanings such as 'milk maid', etc.[20] A direct counterpart is found in Old English *dæge* 'bakeress, milk maid', which forms part of the term *hlæfdige* (< *hlāf-dæge*),[21] which is

[17] An alternative etymology of Gothic *andbahts* has been suggested by Hjalmar Falk (1886 pp. 341 ff.).

[18] Kluge *EW*, article *Amt*, Much 1937 pp. 157–158, Lehmann 1986 p. 36, Carlton 2019 *passim*. Vladimir Orel (2003 p. 18) reconstructs the word as a strong masculine *a*-stem PGmc **anđbaxtaz*, presumably based on Gothic *andbahts*, while Guus Kroonen (2013 p. 24) reconstructs a weak masculine *an*-stem, **ambahta-* (cf. Carlton 2019 p. 54).

[19] It is likewise noteworthy, as was pointed out earlier, that the word *ambótt* could acquire an extended semantic meaning since the word was (secondarily) used about a 'frilla', but in *Þrymskviða* also about a 'servant girl, bridesmaid'.

[20] Olson 1916 p. 66, de Vries 1962 p. 75 and Hellquist 1948 p. 137.

[21] Holthausen 1934 p. 161. On the development *hlāf-dæghe* > *hlæfdige*, see later. The *bryti* and *deigja* are mentioned as being socially equal in, e.g., the Gulathing Law (198), Erik's Law of Sjælland (3:19) and in the Västgöta Laws (ÄVgL, Book of Inheritance 16, YVgL, Book of Inheritance 21).

'bread-bakeress', later developing into *lady* and in medieval times coming to mean 'a mistress in relation to servants or slaves; the female head of a household'.[22] The masculine counterpart to the English *lady* is *lord* (see later), while the masculine counterpart of *deigja* in Scandinavia can be assumed to have been *bryti* (see later).[23]

man n., *mansmaðr* m. (*mansman* n.?)

Particularly in Old Icelandic we find the term *man* n. 'thrall, female thrall or thralls collectively'. It is, then, a neutral word, which moreover includes meanings such as 'househould, including children, thralls and other servants'.[24] According to Gjessing, the word occurs only in Scandinavian, not in other Germanic languages.[25] That is to say, it shows great similarities to the semantically related *hjón* n. The word *man* n. is probably an older Proto-Nordic *gamannʀ*,[26] i.e., constructed with a (probable) collective *ga*-prefix to *man*, cf. Goth. *gaman*. The *ga*-prefix as well as the neuter gender of the word could indicate an earlier meaning of 'servants, thralls' or similar. As Emil Olson has pointed out, this little group of individual, neutral designations for a person all show strongly derogatory meanings (Sw. *man*, *våp*, *troll* and OSw *fol* 'fool').[27] In for example the Frostathing Law the compound *mansmannr* occurs (as *mansmanna* and *mansmönnum*), wherein the belonging of the person to someone else is explicit. The word means 'a person who belongs to a man' and is explained as an *ánauðigr maðr* (see later).[28]

líni

In a name-*þula*, a list of names, preserved in *Codex Wormianus* we encounter the word ON *líni* m., which is usually translated as 'thrall, servant', but which must originally have meant 'one who works with flax or linen'.[29] The word

22 *OED*[2] 8 p. 582.
23 See Gjessing 1862 p. 158.
24 Fritzner, article *man* n., and Olson 1916 p. 77.
25 Gjessing 1862 p. 313.
26 So, e.g., de Vries 1962 p. 378.
27 Olson 1916 p. 78.
28 See Fritzner, article *mansmaðr*.
29 de Vries 1962 p. 357.

appears to be unique, a *hapax legomenon*, and has been discussed by Dag Strömbäck, who regards it as an *an*-stem derivation to ON *lín* n. 'flax' and regards the following as related formations: ON *fjósi* to *fjós* 'stable, byre', and *mjólki* to *mjólk* 'milk'.[30]

ánauðigr maðr

In the Older Västgöta Law (the Book on Manslaughter, 2) occurs another word designating a thrall or, rather, a person who was previously a thrall. A freed thrall is described here using the adjective *ánauðigr* 'enslaved' (*ætlæddan man . . . þæn annøþoghær havir farit* 'a free man, who has been enslaved'),[31] a word that has disappeared from use, but that occurs in our old languages such as OSw *an(n)øþugher*, ODa *an(n)øthughær*, ON *ánauðigr* 'enslaved, unfree'.[32] This word occurs also in the Östgöta Law and in the archaic Pentateuch Paraphrase.[33] The word, which Vendell translates as 'enslaved',[34] must be constructed on ON *ánauð* f. 'suppression, need, force, thraldom' in the compound *ánauðarmaðr* 'thrall',[35] which in turn is assumed to have been derived from a verb, corresponding to the Gothic *ananauþjan* 'force, subject someone to force'.[36]

The Icelandic ethnologist Jón Hnefill Aðalsteinsson discusses the contextually interesting ON word *ǫnnungr*, which at first glance could be taken to be related to *ánauðigr* and which occurs only a few times in Old Icelandic literature: in the law codex *Grágás* and in Snorri's *Edda*.[37] The word is commonly supposed to mean 'thrall'.[38]

Etymologically, *ǫnnungr* is to be separated from *ánauðigr* since the word appears to be derived from a ON *ǫnn* f. 'work, toil',[39] OSw *an(d)* f. 'work

[30] Strömbäck 1935b p. 114.
[31] See Holmbäck and Wessén 1946 pp. 24, 43.
[32] This adjective was encountered earlier in *Atlamál in grœnlenzko* 64.
[33] See ÖgL, Collin and Schlyter (eds.) 1830 p. 238.
[34] Vendell 1894 p. 3.
[35] *NO* p. 28 and Holmbäck and Wessén 1946 p. 43 n. 40. The OSw and ODa medieval forms often display double consonants (*ann-*), which is thought to be due to a shift in the accent and a shortening of the initial vowel, see Brøndum-Nielsen 1952 pp. 44–49.
[36] Holmbäck and Wessén 1946 p. 43 n. 40, Orel 2003 pp. 282–283.
[37] Jón Hnefill Aðalsteinsson 1984, cf. Fritzner art. *ánauð* and *ánauðigr*.
[38] Thus, e.g,. *Lexicon Poeticum* p. 663, Björn Þorsteinsson 1966 p. 127, and Jón Jóhannesson 1969 p. 300. In modern Icelandic, *önnungur* is translated as 'þræll' (*ÍO* p. 848).
[39] The etymology of this word is not entirely clear, even though the basic meaning of 'work' appears reasonable; see de Vries 1962 pp. 687–688, with references, as well as Hellquist 1948 pp. 19–20 and Bjorvand and Lindeman 2007 pp. 831–832.

the soil in spring and autumn, especially about harvesting',[40] a word that has shifted from meaning 'work' to 'the time for a certain type of work'. In Swedish dialects, the word occurs as *ann*, *and* 'busy time of work' and in compounds such as *anntid* 'harvest time', *höand* 'time for making hay', etc.[41] The ON *ǫnnungr*, Icelandic *önnungur*, is a derivation, with an individualizing -*ung*-suffix, to *ǫnn*, which most likely shows that the original meaning of the word must quite simply have been 'worker'. The word ON *ǫnn* derives from PGmc **azn*- (probably **az(a)niz* f.),[42] as in OHG *arn* f., *aren* m. 'harvest' (< **az(a)ní*-), and has cognates in OE *esne* m., OHG *asni* m. 'worker, slave', Goth. *asans* f. 'harvest', *asneis* m. 'day laborer', etc. The two parallel forms in *as-/es* and *ar-/er* are the result of a grammatical shift, *s* > *z* (> ʀ > *r*) according to Verner's Law.[43]

In a chapter on *Mannaheiti* ("terms for people") in *Skáldskaparmál*, Snorri says: *Heitir ok þræll kefsir, þjónn, ǫnnungr, þírr*,[44] "a thrall may also be called *kefsir*, *þjónn*, *ǫnnungr* and *þírr*." In a so-called *þula*, a listing of names or words, in this case a listing of words for thralls and servants, it says: *þjónar, þrælar, þírr, ǫnnungar, verkmenn, kefsar ok vílmegir*.[45] In the first case, *ǫnnungr* appears in a context relating exclusively to thralls, in the second case together with words meaning 'thrall' as well as 'servant, worker'. In the Icelandic law codex *Grágás* appears a section that discusses *ǫnnungsverk*: "The work that someone does by order of the householder is called *önnungsverk*."[46] Jón Hnefill's interesting conclusion is that this term was used for a person occupying a position between an unfree thrall and a free worker in early Iceland. It is possible that he is right. On the other hand, one could argue that this is an example of the fluid transition that I think existed in prehistoric times between different types of servants, so that an *ǫnnungr* was a man who could be used or hired to carry out farm work, a free or unfree worker.

[40] *SAOB* 1 col. 1280 and Hellquist 1948 pp. 19–20.

[41] Rietz 1867 p. 8. From my own dialect, *Färilamålet* in the province of Hälsingland, Sweden, I am acquainted with a word *ann* f. 'harvest time'.

[42] Orel 2003 p. 31.

[43] See Feist 1939 pp. 58–60, Hellquist 1948 pp. 19–20, Torp *NEO* p. 476, Bjorvand and Lindeman 2007 pp. 831–832. For Verner's Law, see later.

[44] *Snorra Edda, Skáldskaparmál*, vol. 1, ed. Faulkes, p. 106.

[45] From an anonymous *þula*: *Manna heiti* (see, e.g., *Skj* A:1, 661; B:1, 662–663).

[46] *Grágás* 1 (*Kristinna laga þáttr* 17) p. 35: *Þat erv avnongs verk. ef maðr viþr hvern dag þar er bvande vil.*

Terms Based on the Stem *þeu̯-

Rígsþula's designation for the female slave, *þír* f., is a word closely related to another known term for a female slave, namely *þý* f. (< **þeu̯jō*),[47] which presumably occurs in the dative singular, *þýio*, in the eddic poem *Helgakviða Hundingsbana* II (st. 2). The word appears also in Old Swedish, but only in the compound *þybarn* 'illegitimate child' (actually 'female slave's child') and in the Old Gotlandic *þysun* 'illegitimate son.'[48] These words belong to a large group of words within the Germanic languages, which by a so-called Siever's shift resulted in two closely related stems **þeu̯-* and **þeg-*,[49] showing meanings such as 'slave, servant,' two bases on which many words were constructed with gender-specific suffixes.[50]

Direct counterparts to ON *þý* f. are OE *þéowe, þéowu* f.,[51] OSax *thiu, thiwi* f., OHG *thiu, diu, diuwa* f. and Goth. *þiwi* f.[52] The forms *þý* and *þír* must have sprung from separate case forms, depending on the development of the diphthong *eu*. If a *j* followed immediately after the diphthong, a *j*-mutation would occur (pl. *þýjar*, cf. Goth. *þiujōs*, but sg. *þír* from **þiwīʀ*).[53] The ON form *þír* f. (< **þeu̯īʀ*)[54] has probably also emerged when ON *þý* f. (< **þeu̯jō*) in some cases adopted an *iō*-stem declension, in the same way as the word has come to develop *i*-stem declension in Old High German.[55] It is interesting to observe how etymologists have struggled with this word *þír* f. and with other feminine *iō*-stems that have an ultimate *-r* in the nominative (which is otherwise case indicator for masculine). Bengt Hesselman has provided a

[47] Sophus Bugge in *ANF* 4 (1888) p. 125, de Vries 1962 p. 629.

[48] Olson 1916 p. 75.

[49] See Karg-Gasterstädt 1942 pp. 322, 326.

[50] We possibly ought to reckon with two parallel stems, **þēu̯a-* and **þĕu̯a-*, respectively, but it appears reasonable to reckon with analogous formations and connections, which seems obvious in some cases.

[51] Pelteret 1995 p. 305; OE *þir* f. 'slave woman' is in all likelihood a loan from ON *þír*, cf. somewhat incorrectly Pelteret 1995 p. 316. Cf. Sara M. Pons-Sanz (2013 p. 69) discussion of the OE *ðīr*.

[52] See Feist 1939 p. 499, cf. p. 352 (Goth. *mawi*); Wright 1910 pp. 37, 71, 91. The latter regards Goth. *þiwi* f. to have been constructed from Goth. *þius* m., which seems an unnecessary detour. Gottfried Schramm (1957 p. 167) reconstructs a form **-þiwī*, inflected as an *ī-/ijō*-stem, and interestingly enough (see discussion later) emanating from a PGmc **þegwī*. In his opinion, similar to the opinion expressed by Wright, **-þiwī* f. is to be understood as a development from **-þewaz* m. as a result of "movierung" (gender-change). Also Vladimir Orel (2003 p. 419) is of the opinion that *þiwi* is "[d]erived from **þeʒwaz*."

[53] Noreen 1892 p. 212, 1923 p. 142, and Otto von Friesen in *ANF* 19 (1903) p. 252.

[54] de Vries 1962 p. 611.

[55] See Karg-Gasterstädt 1942 pp. 308–309, who shows that OHG *thiu* displays gen. sg. forms such as *thiuua* alongside *thiuui*, whereby the word in the former case is declined as a *jō*-stem, in the latter as an *i*-stem.—The ON form *þír* f. has apparently caused problems (see, e.g., Noreen 1923 pp. 77, 142, 264, de Vries 1962 p. 611, Wessén 1966 § 27, Iversen 1973 § 13.2).

plausible explanation for this, although he stresses that the history of the *iō*-stems constitutes one of the murkiest issues of the Proto-Nordic grammar.[56] He writes that the majority of these words are what he calls "person and animal-feminines"; that is to say, they don't refer to objects, but to people, so-called individual concrete words. Earlier attempts to explain this nominative indicator *-r* in these feminine words have been to assume the existence of an earlier *-īʀ* (< *-īz*) in this position, which supposedly has been replaced analogically—for instance from feminine adjective *i-* and *u*-stems—by *-ĭʀ*, i.e., with a short vowel. Hesselman, however, considers this a cumbersome and less plausible detour—and rightfully so. His elegant explanation is aware of the fact that in relation to words for persons and animals the nominative marker *-r* can more easily be explained in such a way that an earlier *-īʀ* has been influenced by ending in the vocative, that is the addressing form, and changed into *-iʀ*; for example the vocatives of **wulȝīʀ* (> ON *ylgr* 'she-wolf') and **hildīʀ* (> ON *hildr* 'battle') had in Proto-Germanic *-i* or *-ī* endings (this latter *-ī* was subsequently shortened to *-i*). In this way, according to Hesselman, a "feminine gendered word category" emerged where "person and animal-words" that originally were feminine *iō*-stems took on a nominative *-iʀ*, borrowed from the *i*-stems, and to this group our example of *þíʀ* supposedly belonged.[57] Elias Wessén qualifies this theory by emphasizing that *þíʀ* belonged to a small group of so-called gender-changed (Germ. *Movierung*, Sw. *movering*) feminines that in sg. nom. had PGmc **-ī* which took over the nominative ending ʀ from the feminine *i*-stems and root stems (such as *kýr* 'cow', *sýr* 'sow').[58] Later Dietrich Hofmann has explained the *-r* in *þír* as initially representing the nominative singular ending, which eventually was understood as a declensional ending, and therefore incorporated into the stem.[59]

Also, words for 'male slave, servant' were constructed on the same stem, **þeu̯-*, such as Goth. *þius* m.,[60] OHG *theo, deo* m.,[61] OSax *dio-* m., OE *þéow*,

[56] Hesselman 1913 p. 21.
[57] Hesselman 1913 p. 28.
[58] Wessén 1966 § 95.
[59] Hofmann 1955 §§ 236 and 399.
[60] Evidenced only as nom. pl. *þiwōs* and gen. pl. *þiwē*; Wright 1910 pp. 37, 89, Feist 1939 pp. 497–498, and Braune (and Ebbinghaus) 1973 p. 65.
[61] Evidenced only once in OHG, namely in the early continental Frankish law compilation *Pactus legis Salicae* (Tit. 26 § 2, p. 97); see von Olberg 1991 p. 203. The word is, however, evidenced in compound personal and place names. In certain manuscripts of *Lex Salica* occurs the word *theoleodi* 'wergild for a servant' ("Knechtsmanngeld"), containing OHG *theo* and the word *leodi* 'wergild', which is based on Salian-Frankish *leod*, OHG *liut*, cf. ON *lýðr* 'people' (< PGmc **leuðiz* m.) (von Olberg 1987 pp. 416–417).

þéowa m.,[62] and ON *þírr* m. In Scandinavia, the stem occurs in early runic inscriptions as Proto-Nordic *-þewaʀ*.[63]

On a hartshorn amulet from the sixth century recently discovered at Sorte Muld, Ibsker parish, in Bornholm, Denmark, is the inscription: **balika ar- . . . . (f)ulaz þewaz.**[64] The inscription is very hard to comprehend. However, the word *þewaʀ* is clear. The word is not evidenced in the old languages wherein a parallel to Goth. *þius* m. (< **þeu̯az*) would have resulted in either ON **þjór* or **þér/*þær*, in the same way as we have the variants ON *sjór* and *sær* from Proto-Nordic **sewaʀ* (< **siaw-*) 'sea, lake'.[65] We encounter this word especially as the second element in some Proto-Nordic compounded men's names (in the same way as in Proto-Germanic personal names[66]), probably in three different forms: As *-þér*, in names such as *Sigþér*, *Eggþér*,[67] wherein *-þér* is gradually reduced to *-þir*; as *-þjófr*, which is probably correctly assumed to have developed from **þjór* (< **þeu̯aʀ*), which is a form in all likelihood based on an accusative **þeu̯* > **þjó*,[68] presumably influenced by or linked to the word *þjófr* 'thief' (< PGmc **þeuƀaz*);[69] and perhaps also as **-þýr*,[70] which in unstressed positions as second elements developed into *-tyr*,[71] in names such as *Angantyr* (< *Hanganþýr*).[72]

[62] For the OE words, see comparisons in Liebermann *Die Gesetze der Angelsachsen* 2:1 pp. 220–221. On the weak variant *þéowa* m., see Hempl 1901 p. 427.

[63] These names ending in *-þewaʀ* are discussed later. Gottfrid Schramm (1957 pp. 70 ff.) gathers these names under the umbrella term "Götterknecht" (servant of gods).

[64] *DR* AUD2002:131U.

[65] Wessén 1927 p. 117 (110–118), 1966 § 39, Seip 1929, and de Vries 1962 pp. 575–576.

[66] In Germanic names such as Gothic *Alatheus* for an Ostrogothic young king of the Greuthungi around AD 370s–380s (Woolf 1939 p. 207, Schramm 1957 pp. 15, 72); OE *Angeltheow*, son of Offa, mythic king of Mercia (Woolf 1939 p. 40); OE *Ecgtheow*, the father of Beowulf; OE *Ongentheow*, a Swedish king in Beowulf, also mentioned as *Ingenþeow* or *Ongendþeow* in Widsið (Schramm 1957 p. 35); *Wealtheow*, queen in Beowulf; *Flaccitheus* († *c.* 475) and his son *Feletheus*, kings of the Rugii (Feletheus from 475 to 487) (*PLRE* 2: 473, Woolf 1939 p. 241, 261, Schramm 1957 p. 72); *Ulitheus*, a Gothic king mentioned by Procopios (*The wars of Justinian* p. 249); Goth. *Godosteus* (Schramm 1957 p. 74); OHG *Herideo* (Schramm 1957 p. 72); a.o. Many of these, and other personal names in **-þewar*, are discussed later.

[67] Noreen 1923 pp. 253, 258 and de Vries 1962 p. 609.

[68] From PGmc **þeu̯a-* derives the following variants that occur in Old Scandinavian languages: **þér-/*þǽr-* and (if the combination *-eu̯-* occurs as the final sound or before a consonant, and also with a shift of the accent) **þjó*, which must derive from the accusative **þeu̯* > **þió* with inverted accent. See Wessén 1966 § 39.

[69] Wessén 1927 p. 117, Orel 2003 p. 422; cf. de Vries 1962 p. 613, von See 1964 p. 10.

[70] Fulk 1988 p. 115.

[71] Thus according to Brøndum-Nielsen 1950 p. 102. The fact that the name occurs in other Germanic languages speaks in favur of this, OHG *Angandeo*, OE *Ongenþeow*, and similar, which points toward a Common Proto-Germanic form **Anganþew-*.

[72] It is possible that *-tyr* in *Angantyr* derives from the form **Anganþér*, wherein the second element came to be associated with the name of the deity *Týr* (de Vries 1962 p. 10); Gordon (1935 p. 170 n. 1) suggests that *-týr* may be a substitution for *-þér* due to "etymological misunderstanding," while Brate (1887 p. 34 n.) assumes a change according to a sound law *þ* > *t* following *n*.

The ON *þírr* m.—found in two enumerations of words for slaves and servants by Snorri in *Skáldskaparmál* and in a *þula* (see earlier), which seems to be a masculine counterpart to the feminine *þír* f. dicussed previously—is rather difficult to etymologize. As Sophus Bugge has noted, the word cannot be understood as identical with Goth. *þius* m., OSax *dio-* m., OE *þéow*, etc. Bugge's suggestion is that it is derived with another suffix to the stem *þeu̯-*.[73]

Adjectives have also been constructed from the same stem, **þeu̯-*, e.g., OE *þéow* 'unfree,'[74] as well as verbs, e.g., ON *þjóna* (< **þeu̯anōn*) 'serve,'[75] OHG *dionôn*, *dionen* and ON *þjá* (< **þeu̯an*) 'treat as a slave, suppress, torment,' Goth. **þiwan* (in *gaþiwan* and *anaþiwan*), OE *þéowian*, OHG *dewên*. Later (?) formations include words such as ON *þjónn* m. (< **þeu̯anaʀ*) 'servant, slave,' OE *þéowen* 'thrall, servant' (cf. *þéowian* 'make somebody a slave'), ON *þján* f. (< **þeu̯anō*) 'suppression,'[76] and ON *þerna* (< **þeu̯ernō*) 'servant girl,' Sw. *tärna*.[77]

Elisabeth Karg-Gasterstädt has discussed in an etymological analysis this latter word, OHG *thiorna*, which appears in the sources with the same meaning as OHG *thiu* f. where, however, the former is considered a later formation, often used as a designation for the Virgin Mary in early religious texts. The word *thiorna* is assumed to be a specifically German formation later borrowed into the other Germanic languages.[78] The Scandinavian word *tärna*, *tærne*, *terna*, ON *þerna*, which in medieval times designated a 'young servant girl to a mistress,' has obviously, as mentioned already, been borrowed from German. The male counterpart, 'young male servant,' was OHG *thegen*, which is, of course, paralleled by ON *þegn*, modern Scandinavian *tegn*.

This exposition results in the conclusion that the Germanic languages contain a multitude of words for 'slave, female slave, servants' that are assumed

[73] Bugge 1873 p. 317. Maybe *þírr* m. is a secondary development to the feminine *þír* f. (**þeu̯īʀ* f. nom. and **þeu̯īʀaʀ* m. nom.?) where the ultimate *-r* in the feminine word has been perceived as a radical *-r*. On the other hand, since the word seems only to be found twice, and both times in a kind of *þulur*, lists of words, and not within any context in a law, saga, or poem, maybe the word is to be understood as an occasional formation, as a masculine counterpart to the feminine *þír*, and never in actual use in the language?

[74] von Olberg 1991 p. 203.

[75] According to de Vries (1962 p. 614) the Proto-Nordic form **þeu̯anōn* did develop into **þiau̯anōn* due to analogic influence from *þjónn*.

[76] See Karg-Gasterstädt 1942 p. 323, Holmbäck and Wessén 1946 p. 43 n. 40 and de Vries 1962 p. 612.

[77] Peter Foote in *KL* 19 (1975) col. 15 includes this word in his register of terms for thralls.

[78] Already Emil Olson (1916 p. 76) suggested that OSw *thærna* is "probably" a loan from OSax *thêrna* (< *thiorna*) or MLG *dêrne*, with the sound shift *d* > *þ*.

to have been constructed from one and the same stem **þeu̯-* (< **þaiu̯-*) (: PIE **tek^{w}-* 'sprint, run, move', **tek^{w}o-* 'runner').[79] Vladimir Orel postulates two gender-specific etymons: PGmc **þeʒwaz* m. (for, e.g., Goth. *þius*, ON *-þer* and *þý*, OE *þeów*, etc., cf. Sanskrit *takvá-* 'quick' < **tek$^{u̯}$u̯ós*, derived from PIE **tek$^{u̯}$-* 'to run') and **þeʒwjō* f. (for, e.g., Goth. *tiwi*, OE *ðéowe*, OHG *diu*, etc. to be derived from the afore **þeʒwaz*, or PIE **teku̯ī*, after Hirt). Why the *-ʒ-* in this postulated stem is not evidenced in any of these Germanic words for 'slave, servant' is puzzling, and is discussed later.

This PIE root **tek$^{u̯}$-* 'to run' is found in words such as OInd *tákti* 'hurry', *takvá-h* m. 'runner', Lith. *tekù* 'sprint', Latv. *teksnis* m. 'runner/servant', OIr *techid* 'flee, escape'. Based on this root—or via paradigmatic linkage—Germanic languages then constructed feminine words with an *-ī-*, *-iō-*, or *-jō-*suffix, such as, e.g., ON *þý* f., *þír* f., Goth. *þiwi*, OHG *thiu*, *diu*, OSax *thiu*, *thiwi*, OE *þéow(u)*,[80] and with an *-a-*suffix masculine words, such as ON *þírr*, *-þér*, *-þjófr* (< **þjór*), and **-þýr* (> *-tyr*), Goth. *þius*, OE *þéow(a)*, OHG *theo*, *deo*.[81] In the same way as with the word *þræll*, if the suggested etymology is correct, it can be assumed that an earlier basic meaning for this group of words from **þeu̯-* was 'one who runs, does errands'.

This common and hitherto generally accepted etymology has recently been questioned by Subhadra Kumar Sen, who points out several reasons why a new etymology must be sought.[82] The etymology hitherto accepted assumes that the stem **þeu̯-* goes back to a PIE **tek^{w}-* 'sprint, run, move', whereby problems arise with regard to the masculine derivation **þeu̯az*, which we find in Goth. *þius*, since this word in its Proto-Indo-European form had **tek^{w}-wó*, alternatively **tek-wó*. A word of this form must undergo the First Germanic Sound Shift, also called Grimm's Law,[83] so that a PGmc **þeχu̯a-* (> **þehu̯a-*) arises. But, as was shown by the Danish scholar Karl Verner in the 1870s,[84] if the Proto-Indo-European main stress was on the ultimate syllable of the word, as in this case, then this shift would go even further, so that PIE *k* > PGmc *h* (*χ*) > PGmc *g* (*ʒ*). This law of Verner's implies,

[79] See the usual etymological dictionaries, e.g., Walde-Pokorny 1 p. 716, Feist 1939 pp. 497–498, Pokorny 1959 p. 1059, de Vries 1962 pp. 609, 629, Lehmann 1986 p. 362, and Mallory and Adams 1997 p. 491.

[80] The somewhat complicated circumstances of word formation for the feminine words have been commented on by Olson 1916 pp. 74–75.

[81] One of the earliest to enumerate these related words (< *þewa-*) was Sophus Bugge (1873 p. 317).

[82] Sen 2004.

[83] See, e.g., Wessén 1979 pp. 9–10.

[84] On Verner's Law, see, e.g., Wessén 1966 pp. 34–35.

says Sen, that a PIE *tek^w-wó* would not result in a PGmc **þeu̯a-*, but rather in **þegu̯a-*, whereby this *g* ought to appear in certain forms in the old languages. We are therefore, Sen argues, in need of a new etymology and he attempts to instead link to the PIE root **teu-* 'swell, grow', which accordingly should result in PGmc **þeu-*. He must then reckon with a semantic development of this PIE **teu-* from 'swell, grow' to 'strength' and to 'strong (man)' in order for the equation to be solved. This should then explain the occurrence of Goth. *þiu-magus* 'servant' (literally 'servant-boy') and we should find the same root in, for instance, Goth. *þiunda*, ON *þjóð* 'people', which would then be formations based on a collective suffix PIE *-tā*; thus PIE **teu-tā* 'many strong (men)'. Similarly, the Gothic *þiu-magus* should then, says Sen, have originally meant 'a boy strong enough to do physical work'.

Kenneth Shields Jr. has recently discussed Sen's analysis.[85] He agrees with Sen regarding the fact that we have a problem in explaining the expected form **þegu̯a-*. Shields establishes that the previously applied PIE root *tek^w-* is not probable and suggests a root **tek-*, however not with a meaning 'run, sprint, flow', but instead 'bear (bring forth), get, carry'. This PIE root is encountered in many words for 'child', such as Greek *tékos*, *téknon* 'child', OInd *tákman-* 'child', as in ON *þegn*, OE *þegn*, and OHG *degan*. However, Shield's suggestion still leaves the problem that, if we reckon with a PIE **tek-*, then certain word forms (such as PIE **tek-wó-*) should result in **þegu̯-*, not in **þeu̯-*. His solution to this problem is to reckon with an analogical change and the analogy should have taken place in connection with the Proto-Germanic word **þeu̯-ða* 'people', ON *þjóð*, and so on.

The end result is that we still do not have any widely accepted etymology of these words for 'slave' based on the stem **þeu̯-*. We will have to settle with the fact that one option is 'someone who runs (errands)', another 'child'. Noteworthy, however, is that both these meanings frequently occur in words for exactly 'slave'.

Even so, I think it is possible to save the earlier etymology, which so elegantly explains words within this semantic sphere, appearing as both **þeu̯-* and **þeg-*, thus grammatical variants of the supposed PIE root *tek^w-*. A possibility not yet brought into the discussion is that forms with an expected **þeg-*, for example in Goth. *þius*, could be explained by assuming analogy with the supposedly much larger group of names in **þeu̯-* within this group

[85] Shields 2006.

of words that did not have the main stress on the latter part, the *ultima*, of the word.

In northern Europe, we then get the pairs Goth. *þius* m. (: *þiwi* f.), OE *þéow(a)* m. : *þéow(u)* f., OHG *theo* m. : *thiu* f., ON *-þér/*-þjór* m. : *þý* f., thus PGmc **þeu̯az* m. : **þeu̯jō* f., which designated respectively a male and female slave or servant.[86] It is possible that these "original" conceptual pairs for 'slave, servant' from the Germanic areas paralleled the Latin pair *servus–ancilla* (and *puer–puella*).[87]

It is uncertain whether the word Scand. *tegn*, ON *þegn* 'warrior, servant', OSw *þæghn*, OE *þegen* 'servant' also belongs here.[88] Reasons for including it have been given by Elisabeth Karg-Gasterstädt, who, following an in-depth etymological analysis, assumes that *tegn* (in her opinion < **þeg-n-az*) is to be regarded as a variant of (wherein *g* : *w* shift according to Siever's Law), and therefore linguistically very close to, the word ON *þerna* (< **þeu̯-ern-ō[n]*); a parallel could then be the words Goth. *magus* 'boy' and *mawi* 'girl', showing the same shift *g* : *w*.[89] In this way, also *tegn* could potentially be assumed to derive from the PIE root **tek*^{w}- 'run'. Normally, *tegn* is thought to derive from a different root, namely PIE **tek-* 'bear', in Greek *téknon* (*τέκνον*) 'child',[90] but there are according to my opinion semantic reasons that speak in favor of Karg-Gasterstädt's etymology, which says that the stem of *tegn* (< **þeg-naz*) is a variant of the stem of ON *þerna* (< **þeu̯-ern-ō[n]*). Jan de Vries hints at this other possibility and notes as an alternative etymology of ON *þegn* an earlier Proto-Germanic form **þeganaʀ*, which would be a variant of **þegunaʀ* (> *þjónn*).[91] Sara Pons-Sanz notes that OE *þegn* could have the meaning 'slave', or rather 'young slave', in tenth-century Northumbria.[92] In this context, one could also point out the interesting OE *þinen* f. 'servant' (< **þeghninjō*).[93] Finally, also the Scandinavian word *tjuv/tyv* 'thief' (< **þeuƀaz*), ON *þjófr* m., Goth. *þiufs*, *þiuhs*, OHG *dioh*, OE *þêof*, could be mentioned, all of which are,

[86] Cf. Karg-Gasterstädt 1942 p. 323.

[87] Cf. von Olberg 1991 pp. 203–204, Arnoux 2014 p. 62.

[88] See Krogmann 1938 p. 191 and Feist 1939 p. 498. Perhaps to be compared to ON *þjónn* m. previously, see de Vries 1962 p. 614. For an in-depth semantical analysis of the West-Germanic OE *þegn*, OS *thegan*, see Carlton 2019 *passim*.

[89] Karg-Gasterstädt 1942 p. 326, cf. Orel 2003 p. 418, see also Carlton 2019 p. 109 f. and *passim*.

[90] See, e.g. Olson 1916 p. 55, Green 1965 pp. 99, 101, and Orel 2003 p. 418. Guus Kroonen (2013 p. 536) has given an alternative, interesting etymology, well worth considering, namely that the word denoted not a 'child' or a 'young man', but instead a 'retainer'.

[91] de Vries 1962 p. 607; on the etymology of the word *þjónn* see p. 614.

[92] Pons-Sanz 2007 p. 14.

[93] On this last-mentioned word, see Odenstedt 1995 pp. 140, 142.

however, regarded as derived from the PIE root **teup*- 'squat (in order to hide)',[94] although the etymology of this word is uncertain.[95]

thrall

Since *ambátt*, *ambótt* is quite clearly a loanword for a female slave, although it may be an old loan, we might consider testing whether also *thrall* (< *þræll*) has come into the Scandinavian languages as a loan. It can be established that counterparts of *þræll* do not occur in other Germanic languages, only the Scandinavian ones; OE *þrǣll* (ME *þrăll*) was apparently borrowed into Anglo-Saxon from Old Norse.[96] This shows that the word cannot be a Proto-Germanic native word, which means that it could be a loanword from a non-Germanic language. One possibility could be to link it to Celtic, specifically an Old Irish word that appears in Middle Irish as *tráill* and that has been connected to the word *þræll*.[97] Such a possibility would moreover fit well factually since many thralls in Scandinavia had been brought from Ireland and since many Scandinavians in the Viking Age traded slaves in and from Ireland.

Evidently, the possibility of a borrowing from Old Irish can, however, be dismissed since this Irish *tráill* is as far as can be ascertained likewise a borrowing from Old Norse. Carl Marstrander has produced very good arguments that this *tráill* was only brought into Old Irish in the tenth century as a borrowing from Old Norse *þræll*.[98] He also shows that a basic form **þranhila*-, regarded by some etymologists as linked to ON *þryngva* with a basic meaning of 'one who is under compulsion', can be dismissed, since an Old Irish form **trámaill*, derived from a nasalized Scandinavian *ǽ*, would in that case be expected. Marstrander moreover assumes that the basic form commonly applied, **þrahila*- or **þrāhila*-, cannot be correct either; instead, he wants to relate our Scandinavian word to OHG *drigil* 'servant' (< **þrehila*-,

[94] Nielsen 1976 p. 453.

[95] de Vries 1962 p. 613, Lehmann 1986 p. 362, and Orel 2003 p. 422.

[96] See Björkman (1900 p. 19), who explains that OE and ME *ll* like ME *ă* can only be explained as loans from Scandinavian languages, wherein *ll* < *lʀ*, while the *þrǣl* (pl. *þrǣlas*) occurring in OE arose from some Scandinavian grammatical case, resulting in ME *þrēl* (pl. *þrēlas*). Sara M. Pons-Sanz (2913 p. 69–70) discusses this word and makes an attempt to understand the OE *ðrǣl(l)* as an internal Anglian derivation of a PGmc **þrahilaz*, but finds this less probable, on the ground that Björkman explains.

[97] de Vries 1962 p. 625.

[98] Marstrander 1925.

þreȝila-).[99] A link to OHG is, however, not necessary as I see it. Rather, Old Scandinavian *þræll* must be considered an exclusively North Germanic word that is not encountered in other Germanic languages. There is probably no reason for regarding it as a word borrowed into Scandinavian from elsewhere, since related word formations—if not the same words—are found in West as well as East Germanic languages in OHG *drigil* (< **þrehila-*/ **þreȝila-*) and OE *þrægan* 'sprint' and Goth. *þragjan* 'sprint'. To thus apply an earlier base form **þrahila*, as for example Elof Hellquist does, appears possible.[100]

A. Gjessing believes that the word *þræll* cannot be derived from the stem **þra-* 'run', since the word occurs only in Scandinavian languages wherein the meaning 'run' is not (any longer) evidenced for this stem, "just as also the thralls cannot ever have been particularly well-known for their speed except when their lives were at stake."[101] Instead, he reckons it to have derived from the stem **þrau*, which is supposedly also found in OHG *drûen*, Eng. *threat*, ON *þrá* 'force' and similar meanings, so that the earlier meaning of the word *þræll* should have been 'one who suffers', 'one who is forced'.[102]

In an interesting explanation T. Michaelsen and Sv. Stech Jr. discuss the Slavic word *otrok* and its potential relationship to our Scandinavian *þræll*.[103] The word *otrok* is found in all Slavic languages with meanings such as 'servant' or 'child, especially young boy'. The previous etymology of the word was based on an earlier meaning of 'someone with no right to speak'. They show that this etymology is in all likelihood false and instead they identify Slavic **trok-* with Proto-Germanic **þrah-*, which they consider must be a direct counterpart.[104] It is pointed out that in Indo-European languages a

[99] Wilde-Stockmeyer 1978 p. 41 understands OHG *drigil* as identical to ON *þræll*, albeit "historisch offenbar selbständig entwickelt" (historically obviously developed independently). Fick, Falk, and Torp (1909 p. 190) suggests that this may be the etymological background of *thrall* ("Wenn an. *þræll* hierher gehört"), but in this case not from PIE **trĕgh*, **tragh*, but from the PIE root **trēkh*, **trahk*, which would then result in PGmc **þregila*. See, moreover, Lehmann 1986 p. 3.

[100] Wilde-Stockmeyer 1978 p. 41 follows an earlier suggestion by Fick, Falk, and Torp (1909 p. 190), that *þræll* was derived from an earlier **þranhila-*, on the OSw stem *þrængia* 'force', and thus with the meaning 'one who is forced', which semantically speaking fits well. There are, however, arguments that speak against such a proposal, see Marstrander (previously) and Olson 1916 p. 25. It must be added that Fick, Falk, and Torp (1909 p. 190) include as possible background to *þræll* the very same **þrahila* as does Hellquist.

[101] Gjessing 1862 p. 315: *ligesom ogsaa Trællene vel aldrig have været synderlig kjente for Hurtighed uden hvor det gjaldt Livet.*

[102] Gjessing 1862 pp. 315–316.

[103] Michaelsen and Stech 1963.

[104] One can note that apparently already Fick, Falk, and Torp (1909 p. 190) were aware of this possibility, since they include in their discussion of the word *thrall* OSlav *trŭkŭ* and Slovenian (actually, I have understood, rather Croatian) *trčati* 'to run', and point to Old Gallic *ver-tragos* 'Windhund (greyhound)': "vgl. asl. trŭkŭ Lauf. nslov. trčati laufen. Daneben tragh in gall ver-tragos Windhund."

multitude of words for 'slave, servant' have had a basic meaning of 'one who runs (errands)', such as *þius*, *þewar*, *þý*, and so forth.[105]

Michaelsen and Stech Jr. see a possibility of etymologically linking *þræll* to the large group of words deriving from **þeu̯-*, such as *þius*, *þewar*, *þý*, and so on, if one supposes that the Indo-European root **tek-* / **tok-* 'to run' had a parallel root **trek-* / **trok-* with the same, perhaps enhanced, meaning: 'to run – fast', and they provide parallels for such a development. This etymology, linking the entire group of words that all have the semantic contents of 'slave, servant' deriving from the earlier meaning 'to run (errands for someone)', seems attractive. Greek provides the examples of *trého* (τρέχω) 'sprint, run', *tróhos* (τρόχος), *tróhis* (τρόχις) 'runner, messenger, servant',[106] *trohílos* (τρόχίλος) '(the bird) sandpiper', as well as the name *Trohílos*, one of Demeter's priests, where the last-mentioned word and the name appearing to possibly be linguistically related to an Old Norse **þrahilaʀ*.

I think, in other words, that there are grounds for supposing that the word *þræll* (< **þrahilaʀ*) can be assumed to be a formation native to North Germanic, apparently an *-ila*-derivation of the previously discussed stem **þrah-* with the probable meaning 'to run (errands for someone)'.[107] The original meaning of *þræll* (< **þrahilaʀ*) could then be 'one who runs (errands), does services, often (constantly?) and quickly'. Whether this hypothesis will hold remains to be shown by future scholarship.

hapter and *est*

It is common development within the entire Indo-European linguistic area that terms for foreigners have taken on the semantic contents of 'slave', which obviously relates to the fact that captives or kidnapped foreigners were often enslaved. That taking captives during warfare was the most common way of acquiring slaves in classical times is evidenced by a word found in many Indo-European languages and encountered all over the continent, in Romance languages as Latin *captus*, *captivus*, in Celtic languages as Welsh

[105] On this, see also Marstrander 1925 p. 175, with more PIE examples.
[106] See Feist 1939 p. 500 and Lehmann 1986 p. 362.
[107] On the use of *-ila*-suffix in order to construct so-called *nomina agentis*, see Kluge 1899 p. 10, Olson 1916 pp. 23–26. The in terms of word formation related appellatives *karl* and *jarl* are assumed to be formed without a middle vowel, thus **karlaz* and **erlaz* (Olson 1916 *loc. cit.*).

caeth, OIr *cacht*, and in Germanic languages as ON *haptr*, OSw *hapter*,[108] where the meaning of the words varies between 'captive' and 'slave'.[109] In the case of Sweden it may be noted that the nationality designation *est* (pl. *ester*) 'Estonian' occurs during medieval times with the apparent meaning of 'thrall, unfree',[110] which probably shows that Estonians could be brought to Sweden and become enslaved.

kæfsir

Another word that has been taken to mean 'thrall' and that appears in the old languages is ON *kæfsir* (*kæfsi*), *kæpsir* m. (< Proto-Nordic **kaƀisia*).[111] This word is very obscure and lacks any obvious derivation.[112] It is probably a word borrowed into Old Norse, or even Proto-Nordic. It has been suggested that it could have been borrowed from Latin *captivus*, but that explanation leads to linguistic muddles.[113]

A paragraph in the Book of Marriage (*Giptar bolker* 4:3) in the Older Västgöta Law (VgL) deals with the case of how a slave (*þræll*) could marry a wife:

> *Vill þræll fa huskono giui tva öræ til þem ær hana a. ækki kiæpsir i barnum*

> If a thrall wants a wife [he shall] give two *ørar* to the one who owns her. The *kiæpsir* has no [part or] legal right to the children. (My trans.)

And similarly, in the Book of Marriage (*Giptar balker* 29) in the Östgöta Law (ÖgL), it is again regulated that a *kæfsir* has no right to his children:

> *nu gangær fostre manzs æfte fostru: þa a egh kæfsir i barnum:*[114]

[108] The word has been assumed to be constructed from the verb **hafjan* 'capture' (de Vries 1962 p. 209), from the PIE root **kap-* 'take, catch' (Olson 1916 p. 5).

[109] Mees 1998 p. 363 n. 8.

[110] Söderwall (article *ester*), Lindroth 1916 p. 198, *SAOB* (article *est*), see moreover the chapter on Älmeboda.

[111] de Vries 1962 p. 304.

[112] See de Vries 1962 p. 304.

[113] See de Vries 1962 p. 304. The Latin word *captivus* could, however, possibly be a loan via some other mediating language, which would explain the form. One possibility for understanding the Scandinavian word is suggested by Kluge *EW* p. 481 (article *Kebse* f. 'concubine').

[114] ÖgL, Collin and Schlyter (eds.), 1830, p. 111.

Now a man's *fostre* goes after [i.e., marries] a *fostra*, then a *kæfsir* has no [part or] legal right to the children. (My trans.)

First to be noted is that in the Västgöta Law we are dealing with a *þræll*, whereas in the Östgöta Law the slave is a *fostre* (and his "wife" a *fostra*). There is a social and legal difference between a *þræll* and a *fostre*, in that the latter had a higher social standing in society and was given a higher value in legal cases; the penalty was three to four times higher for a *fostre/fostra* than for a *þræll*. However, the outcome of a case where an unfree man had offspring with an unfree woman is identical in both laws; the children which the slaves had begotten belonged not to them, but to the owner of the slave. This is what should be expected in early medieval laws, the owner of a slave owned both the slave and also the offspring.[115]

The word occurs three more times in Old Scandinavian, twice in *Snorra Edda*, in *Nafnaþulur* as a name for men, obviously thralls (*kefsar*), and in *Skáldskaparmál* (81. *Mannaheiti*): *Heitir ok þræll kefsir, þjónn, önnungr, þirr*, "(A) thrall is also called *kefsir, þjónn, önnungr, þirr*." The third occurrence (*kefsir*) is in the poem *Rígsþula* (9) in the enumeration of names for male thralls. In these examples, in the Old Norse poetry, the word seems exclusively to be placed in a slave context.

The problem is the Old Swedish legal clauses: how is the word *k(i)æfsir* to be understood? The word is etymologically obscure,[116] and the context in the short sentences does not help us regarding the semantics; the person alluded to must be the thrall who is denied his children. But is the word a term for a slave? Jan de Vries assumes that the word denoted a slave ("sklave"), with the remark: "eig. der unfreie mann in seinem verhältnis zu der sklavin, mit der er zusammenlebt,"[117] which is pretty much what we are able to squeeze out from the two, short legal clauses.

Everyone who has discussed the word can, of course, see the link to a word found in West Germanic: Germ. *kefse* 'concubine' (*Nebenfrau*), OHG *kebis* (ninth century), *kebisa* (eleventh century), OE *cefes* 'concubine', etc., a word the etymologists derive from **kaƀisō* f.[118] or * *kabisjō*. An early attempt was

[115] The word and the link to marriage, cohabitation, concubinage, and illegitimate children has been discussed in an interesting, not yet published article by Dr. Cecilia Ljung (ms.).

[116] Cf. Kluge in *EW*^{6} p. 199b "Das wort (*kabisjō*) ist etymologisch leider ganz dunkel"; de Vries 1962 p. 304 "Das wort is dunkel"; H. Schröder 1906 p. 523 "Ist das wort germanisch(?)," etc.

[117] de Vries 1962 p. 304 ("actually, the unfree man in his relationship with the female slave, with whom he cohabit", my transl.).

[118] Rooth 1963.

hence to link the word to Lat. *cap(i)tio* 'prisoner of war' and *captivus* 'prisoner',[119] which seems like a rather obvious and natural possibility, but thus leads to decisive linguistic difficulties. Elmar Seebold has recently derived Germ. *Kebse* f. 'concubine' from a PGmc **kabisjō* to the stem in Germ. *Kaue* and *Koje* 'hut, room with no window', which in its turn is a loan from Lat. *cavea* 'cage, den, cavity', giving *Kebse* the original meaning 'Bettgenossin' (bedfellow; I assume a euphemism for concubine).[120] However, the leap from 'cave' to 'bedfellow', seems daring, to say the least, and the proposal does not convince. Recently Gabriele von Olberg has presented us with a research history of the word *Kebse* and the different attempts to explain its background.[121]

Also, the etymon for the Scandinavian masculine word is difficult to understand; Evald Lidén postulates **kaƀisjō-* to be derived from an *s*-stem **kaƀis-*,[122] and Emil Olson thinks he is able to give that word the meaning 'woman, concubine' (*kvinna, frilla*), to which *kæfsir* according to him is to be a derivation with an *-ia*-suffix.[123] It seems perhaps like an unnecessary detour to first reconstruct a feminine word (*kaƀisjō*) to which a masculine *kæfsir* then was derived from, but I assume Olson wanted to link his etymology to the well-known West-Germanic words *kefse* f. This Scandinavian masculine word is not known in the West Germanic languages. It seems to be an exclusively Old Scandinavian (or even a Proto-Nordic) word.

A new and interesting etymology has been possible to consider after the Slavic philologist Karl H. Menges' discussion of a Polish word *kobieta* 'female person, woman, wife', also found in several other Slavic languages: Ukrainian *kob'ita*, Belarussian *kab'ěta*, Slovak *kobieta*, Czech *koběta*, etc., for which he is of the opinion that it is probably a loanword for 'girl' from Uralic.[124] I think it is possible to see the background to *kefsir* in the light of Menges' discussion, and this is probably the possibility with the greatest potential to explain the Old Scandinavian word *kefsir*, *k(i)æfsir* (probably also the West-Germanic word *Kebse* etc.), namely that it is to be derived from a word of Old Slavic origin for a woman or girl, which was borrowed into Old Scandinavian in the Viking Age as **kabis*, with, as Emil Olson probably correctly assumed, a meaning 'woman, concubine'.

119 See de Vries 1962 p. 304 and Kluge EW[24] p. 481 for refs.
120 Kluge *EW*[24] p. 481.
121 von Olberg 2000.
122 Lidén 1894 p. 64.
123 Olson 1916 p. 7.
124 Menges 1983.

This loan hypothesis seems so much more plausible, since we know that Scandinavians, probably especially "Swedes," took many slave girls and women as slaves and concubines during their slave raids and trades in the Slavic world in the east during the Viking Age. We know of several Arabic historians, such as Ibn Fadlan, Ibn Rustah, Ibn al-Athīr, and others, who mention how Scandinavians (*Rūs*) took especially slave girls and woman, and used them as concubines. The story of the burial of a Rūs chieftain, accompanied by his slave concubine on the pyre, witnessed by Ibn Fadlan, is famous,[125] but the same Arabic author also describes how Rūs regularly were accompanied by beautiful slave girls for trading and that each one of the Rūs had a slave woman who was said to serve him, wash his head, cook food, and make drink, as well as another woman who slept with him.[126] These Arabic authors, thus, talk frequently of the Rūs keeping slave women as concubines, and even burying them with their dead master.

If this hypothesis is correct, the word **kabis* is to be seen in the same category as many other words for 'slave', as *haptr*, *slav*, *est*, *wealh*, *doûlos*, etc., of people becoming slaves who were caught, captured, or bought, where the word was brought with the "object," so to say, a common route for new loanwords into any language. The word, *kefsir*, *k*(*i*)*æfsir*, which is the one which has survived in our sources in only five cases, must either be a masculine derivation with an *-ia*-suffix to this word **kabis*, as already Emil Olson hence postulated,[127] or an OSlav. loanword that was associated with words of, and aligned to, this grammatical category, such as *hirðir*, *læiknir*, *hlytir*, *spillir*, *deilir*, (*bog*)*sveigir*, etc., and the original meaning must be 'a man (not necessarily a slave then!) who has and sleeps with a slave woman (a concubine)'.

This philological and etymological analysis can probably be placed in a wider (pre)historic context, namely in the Viking Age slave trade in the East, and the usage of bought or captured slave girls of Slavic origin as concubines by Rūs (Scandinavian/"Swedish") "vikings." These Scandinavians must have heard a word used by the Slavs for a 'girl', which the Scandinavians perceived as or then transformed into **kabis*, a word they brought back to Scandinavia, probably with several concubines of Slavic origin. To this word, a new word was formed in early Viking Age Scandinavia, *kefsir*, *kæfsir*, for a male who had a concubine (from the beginning probably of Slavic origin).[128]

[125] See, e.g., Montgomery 2000.
[126] See Brink 2012 p. 47.
[127] Olson 1916 p. 7.
[128] For this subchapter on *kæfsir*, see Brink 2019a.

muslegoman

There is a strange word in the Östgöta Law (Book of Settlement, 34), *muslaghumaþer* m., which according to Schlyter and Vendell translates as 'a wanted runaway slave'.[129] The word occurs also in the Guta Law as *muslegu maþr*. The relevant section of Östgöta Law (ms A) says: *takær mulslaghu* [mss B, C, F: *muslaghu*] *man ælla hæst a gangu. ællar uxa ok lysir laghlika þa a han firi örtugh*, "If someone takes hold of a runaway thrall or a stray horse or ox and announces it according to the law, he shall be given an *örtugh* for this."[130] More clarity is provided by the Guta Law: *Ier þrel a laupstigi, ok ier lyst eptir at kirkiu ella þingi, þa ier þann muslegu-mader (muslaghu maþær), ok bytir engin þrigildi fyri þann, sum stiel mat at sir, utan sett skal hwar ater hafa, en til ier; þa en ietit ier, þa fullar þet engin fyri muslegu-mann,*[131] "If the slave is on the run, and has been proclaimed at the church, or at the assembly, then he is a fugitive [*muslaghu maþær*]. And no one is to pay a triple fine for anyone who steals food for themselves, but each shall have their own back, if it remains. If it has been eaten, then no one is to make amends for the fugitive [*muslaghu maþær*]."[132] Carl Johan Schlyter's opinion was that already Vedell translated the word correctly when he regarded the word as a compound of *mus* 'mouse' and *ligga* 'to lie (down)', thus a comparison of the runaway thrall who hid himself in wretched hiding places to a mouse hiding away in a hole.[133] The same translation is given by Elias Wessén: "originally a man who lies like a mouse, i.e., hides in whatever holes and hideaways he can find."[134] The only alternative interpretation is offered by Johan Ihre, who reckons the first element to be linked to a verb *musla* 'hide, abscond, run away'.[135] At any rate, we can establish that the word does not refer directly to a thrall, although the person referred to with this epithet appears in the context of thralls in the relevant section of the Guta Law, but obviously to someone who runs away and hides, which must be assumed usually to have been a slave. The use of the

[129] "*en förrymd och efterlyst träl*," Schlyter *Gloss.*; Vendell 1894 p. 23. The Östgöta Law's manuscripts have *mulslaghu man* (ms A), and *muslaghu man* (mss B, C, F) (ÖgL, Collin and Schlyter [eds.] 1830 p. 222).

[130] ÖgL, Collin and Schlyter (eds.) 1830 p. 222. Cf. Freudenthal 1895 (*Bygda balkær* 34); Holmbäck and Wessén 1933 pp. 220–221.

[131] Cited from Säve 1859 p. 38.

[132] *Guta Lag* (*GL*), ed. Peel, p. 86. Cf. Swedish trans. by Holmbäck and Wessén 1943 p. 234.

[133] Schlyter *Gloss.*, article *muslaghu maþer.*

[134] Holmbäck and Wessén 1943 p. 285 n. 16: *egentl. en man som ligger som en mus, d.v.s. gömmer sig var han kan i hål och gömslen.* Cf. *Guta Law* (*GL*), ed. Peel, pp. 199–200.

[135] Schlyter *Gloss.*, article *muslaghu* maþer; *Guta Lag* (*GL*), ed. Peel. pp. 199–200.

word *muslaghu maþær* is an obvious pejorative metaphor for a man who is hiding in a hole like a mouse.[136]

slave

Although the term *slave* does not exist in the slave-terminology lexicon of early Scandinavia, it is, for the sake of comparison, interesting to discuss its background and use.

In an exciting philological exposition, Emile Benveniste has investigated words that display the double meaning of 'slave' and 'foreigner' (= 'enemy').[137] Greek, during Homeric times, had the word *doûlos* (*δοῦλος*) 'slave'.[138] The word lacks an etymological basis in Greek, but related words are found in non-Indo-European languages in Asia Minor. The word is therefore assumed to be a very early loanword from one of these Asian languages. In Latin, the most common word for 'slave' was *servus*. Already the famous Roman lawyer Justinian gave a plausible and, considering the views of slaves during his time, justified etymology of the word. In *Institutes* (I.3.3) Justinian says:

> *Servi autem ex eo appellati sunt, quod imperatores captivos vendere iubent ac per hoc servare nec occidere solent: qui etiam mancipia dicti sunt, quod ab hostibus manu capiuntur.*[139]
>
> The name 'slave' is derived from the practice of generals to order the preservation and sale of captives, instead of killing them; hence they are also called *mancipia*, because they are taken from the enemy by the strong hand.[140]

In spite of Justinian's early etymological attempt, the case of *servus* seems to resemble that of Greek *doûlos* (*δοῦλος*) in that it has been supposed impossible to find an etymological basis for the word in Latin (although there have been attempts[141]); closest at hand is the verb *servāre*, as Justinian intended, but which, according to Benveniste, is probably better translated as 'guard'.[142]

136 Pettersson 1959 pp. 184–185.
137 Benveniste 1973 pp. 289–294.
138 Cf. Gschnitzer 1964, 1976.
139 https://droitromain.univ-grenoble-alpes.fr.
140 http://amesfoundation.law.harvard.edu/digital/CJCiv/JInst.pdf; cf. Watson (1987 p. 8).
141 See, e.g., Tovar 1971, cf. Persson 1912 p. 563.
142 Benveniste 1973 p. 292; see also the discussion by Pârvulescu 2010 pp. 115–116.

Benveniste emphasizes, however, that from a legal as well as a social point of view it is difficult to imagine that a slave could have had such tasks. An attempt to save the "guard"-hypothesis by Adrian Pârvulesco, by giving the word another "semantic link," and by comparing *servāre* and *servus* with, according to Pârvulesco, the semantically close word-pair retain and retainer,[143] is for me difficult to follow. Instead, the word may be a loan from the (poorly known) Etruscan language, which seems to have contained the stem *servi-*, *serve-*.[144] Latin *servus* would then, if we follow Benveniste, have an Etruscan origin. In other words, in both Latin and Greek the two words for 'slave' may have been borrowed from other neighboring languages, from neighbors with whom these peoples fought and from whom they took slaves.

In ancient as in later civilizations, slaves were outside of socially organized society. Slaves were taken as captives during wars and battles fought predominantly with neighbors. In other words, "stranger" became synonymous with "enemy" and thus also with "slave." The word *slave*, Scandinavian *slav*, French *esclave*, German *Sklave*, and so on, are most likely to be understood in the same way as Greek *doûlos* and Latin *servus*. The word probably originates as an ethnic designation, *sloveninu*, for a Slavic person, coined from a south Slavic linguistic form,[145] probably Serbian or a related dialect (cf. Slovenia).[146] From this word the Byzantine Greek *Σκλαβηνοί*, *sklavênoí*

[143] Pârvulesco (2010 p. 192) semantically links *servāre* and *servus* to *retain* 'to keep attached to one's person or engaged in one's service, to engage, hire', and *retainer* 'a dependent or follower of some person of rank or position; one attached to a house, or owing it service'. The *servus* should hence originally be more like the "half-free" *serf*, we know from later times in Europe. I am of the opinion that the slave/*servus* status probably has to be seen in a much more cruel, alienating, and dehumanized context, already from the beginning. However, Pârvulesco gives in his article an exellent and comprehensive research history (with references) to the etymological discussion of the word *servus*.

[144] This etymology by Benveniste (1973 pp. 292–294) of the word *servus* 'slave' is accepted by, e.g., *LEW* (2 p. 527), but, hence, according to the new etymology proposed by Pârvulescu 2010 it *is* possible to derive *servus*—whereby he follows Benveniste in that the word cannot be of an Indo-European origin, but is rather a Latin formation (a proposal he does not explain or expand on)—from the verb *servare* 'to keep, retain' as a *nomen postverbale* with an original meaning 'retained (for service), hired'. Helmut Rix (1994 pp. 54–87) is also critical of Benveniste's etymology and background in Etruscan, but he proposes instead an Indo-European background to the word, where the PIE root had a meaning 'watch, observe', and he is of the opinion that Latin *servus* from the beginning had the meaning 'shepard (Germ. *Hirte*)' and sees this in the light of the famous Transhumance of sheep on the Appeninian peninsula (which thus must be considered to be very early). For other attempts to etymologize *servus*, see Vendryes 1935, Guenther 1960, Tovar 1971, Lambertini 1984.

[145] This identification and etymology was already presented by Friedrich Ludwig Karl Weigand in *Deutsches Wörterbuch* (1909 col. 877): "hervorgegangen aus der byzantinischen Benennung der südslaw. Völker *Σκλαυηνοί*, *Σκλαβηνοί* (im 6. Jh. n. Chr.) [. . .] daher in Italien im 8./9. Jh., mlat *Sclavi* als Bezeichnung der als Leibeigene verkauften slawischen Kriegsgefangenen" ("comes from the Byzantine designation for South Slavic people *Σκλαυηνοί*, *Σκλαβηνοί* (in sixth century AD) . . . [and] therefore in Italy in the eighth/ninth century the Middle Latin *Sclavi* was used as a description for sold servile Slavic war-captives"), cf. Korth 1970 p. 145.

[146] Cf. Aebisher 1936, Verlinden 1943, 1988 p. 338, Benveniste 1973 p. 293, Łukaszewicz 1998, and Arnoux 2014 pp. 60–63. However, there are attempts to explain the word in other ways, derived from

has later been formed, resulting in an ethnic designation *sklavoi* being the source of the variant forms of the word "slave" found across the Western world.[147] The Arabic word *saqāliba* (which is discussed later) has alo been seen as a development from the same word, Byzantine Greek *Σκλαβηνοί*, *sklavênoí*, shortened to *Σκλάβοι*, *sklávoi*.[148]

Scandinavia has probably borrowed the word form Middle Low German.[149] In all likelihood, the word *slave* for 'slave' is not ancient, but rather recent. The reason for its spread and success has to do partly with the fact that slaves of Slavic origins were taken in great numbers—according to many scholars Slavic lands were the main supply region for slaves—,[150] especially via France to Spain (al-Andalus), and partly that the old and within the Latin world most common word for 'slave', namely *servus*, underwent a semantic shift toward the end of the first millennium and came to refer to a 'tenant', that is a free or semifree farmer who farmed someone else's land against paying the owner a fee.[151] This shift results in the word *servus* being used in medieval times, and later as English *serf*, about just such a 'tenant', which means that a new word was needed to cover the semantic field formerly occupied by *servus*, and this seems to have been *slave*.[152]

val

The same goes for *val* (< **walha-*) 'Celt, foreigner (southerner)', which appears in the adjective Sw. *välsk* 'southern' and the compound noun *walnut* (Sw. *valnöt* 'nut from the Roman countries') and in *Wales* and *Wallonia*.[153]

a nonethnic word, cf. Korth 1970. According to Renée and Henry Kahane (1962 p. 360) the meaning of "slave" occurred first in the ninth century AD, when the ethnonym *Sklav-* 'Slav' semantically shifted to a common noun, *sklav-* 'slave' (cf. Weigand above); according to Alberto Manco (2008 p. 271 n. 1) this happened in the tenth century.

147 For the shift *slave* ~ *sklave*, see Frings 1942.

148 Nazmi 1998 p. 74, Epstein 2001 p. 18, Pohl 2013, Zeuske 2018 pp. 51–52. Fr. Weigand wrote already 1909 (col. 877): "bei den spanischen Arabern im 10. u. 11. Jh. *sikláb*, Pl. *sakálibah*" ("[used] by Spanish Arabs [hence in al-Andalus] in the 10th and 11th C. *sikláb*, Pl. *sakálibah*"), which is to be understood, I assume, that Weigand was of the opinion that the Arabic word *saqāliba* (sg. *siklāb*) evolved in al-Andalus in Muslim Iberia as late as in the tenth and eleventh centuries, a stance difficult to uphold.

149 Hellquist 1948 p. 986.

150 See, e.g., Henning 2003 p. 271.

151 Cf. Phillips 1985 p. 57.

152 Phillips 1996 pp. 80–81.

153 Hellquist 1948 p. 1305.

Fig. 8.1 The famous Tjurkö bracteate from Blekinge, Sweden, with its intricate runic inscription written in the Old Futhark. (Photo: Ulf Bruxe, The Historical Museum/SHM, Stockholm, CC BY.)

The word occurs already on the famous Tjurkö-bracteate from Blekinge (Fig. 8.1), whose inscription from the middle of the first millennium reads: **wurterunoRanwalhakurne heldaRkunimudiu**, which is usually normalized as: *wurtē rūnōR an walhakurnē HeldaR Kunimundiu*,[154] and translates approximately as: "HeldaR made the runes on the southern corn (= gold) for KunimunduR." The "southern corn" is apparently a *kenning* (a sort of a metaphor) for the gold from which the bracteate is made, gold that must then be supposed to have come form the south.

The Old English counterpart, *wealh*, pl. *wealas*, with the earlier meaning 'foreigner, Briton (of Gaelic origin), Welshman' had in Anglo-Saxon times acquired the secondary meaning 'slave', due, supposedly, to the many fights during which Britons and Welsh were taken captives.[155] In her analysis of the word, Margaret Lindsay Faull finds that the shift in OE *wealh* from 'Celt' to

[154] See, e.g., Düwel 2006 pp. 14–16.
[155] A. Bugge 1905 p. 43, Hellquist 1948 p. 986, Benveniste 1973 p. 293, Faull 1975, Girsch 1994 p. 51 n. 3.

'foreigner, slave' must have taken place already by the end of the seventh century.[156] The feminine counterpart was OE *wîelen* (< **walhinjō*).[157]

vassal

Like the term *slave*, the word *vassal* is not found in the indigenous early Scandinavian slave terminology, but it is of interest to analyze from a semantic, comparative point of view. A *vassal* refers to a liege answering to a king, emperor, bishop, prince, or some other overlord during medieval times and it is formed on the Latin *vassus*, which in turn proves to be a loan from Celtic, represented by OIr *foss* 'slave, servant' and deriving from **gwas*- 'human being, young man, servant, slave'.[158] In other words, it has been rather common for neighboring peoples to borrow their word for 'slave' from the neighbor; at times even ethnic designations for those neighbors have come to be used as words for 'slave' (as with *wealh*).

In order to link back to what was said by way of introduction to this type of word for 'slave', we find a sharp distinction in ancient times between a 'free man' and a 'slave' wherein the free was a person born into the social community, into society (*ingenuus*) and who as such had all the rights attributed to a man. The opposite was thus a person who did not belong to the community, but was a stranger. A stranger was a potential enemy and if a stranger (= enemy) was taken captive in war then he consequentially became a slave.[159]

bryti and *lavard*—*lord* and *lady*

As is already apparent, thralls did not at all constitute a homogeneous group. Many were pure work slaves on farms, presumably equated with livestock, but there were also slaves who performed specific tasks, such as *deigja* (see earlier), and in a few special instances highly qualified tasks. With this we draw close to the borderline to trusted servants and officials. One such—as

156 Faull 1975 p. 35.
157 Odenstedt 1995 p. 142.
158 von Olberg 1991 pp. 231 ff. For a very energetic discussion, or rather deconstruction, of the terms and concepts of *vassal* and Lat. *vassus*, see Reynolds 1994.
159 Benveniste 1973 p. 294.

has commonly been assumed—originally unfree servant who appears relatively early as a comparatively well-esteemed person is the ON *bryti*.[160] If the word is to be regarded as native it should derive from Proto-Nordic **brŭtjan* and is then a *nomen agentis* constructed on the stem of the weak verb OSw *brytia*, ON *brytja* 'break into pieces, break asunder'. This term has long been assumed to originally designate 'one who breaks (bread and distributes food)'.[161] The word appears in Old Scandinavian with meanings such as 'manager (of someone else's property), farm bailiff, particularly one who in return for a share in the yields runs and farms someone else's farm'.[162] The word *bryti* has also been borrowed into Finnish as *ruttio*, *ruttia* 'steward, slave'.[163] It has been assumed that a *bryti* was originally the foremost among thralls, a particularly trusted thrall, whose job it was to watch over the other thralls and to distribute food (bread) among them.

A *bryti* must originally have been some sort of farm manager, a bailiff watching over the other thralls. On studying written medieval sources, *bryti* appears to have undergone a shift in meaning, from (unfree?) 'farm steward' to 'ombudsman, especially within the royal management' to then decrease in social status and come to refer to a 'farmer, especially tenant'.[164]

It is interesting that this word *bryti* occurs at least twice, probably three times, on runestones. On the famous rune stone by Hovgården on Adelsö in Lake Mälaren, central Sweden, the following can be read: **raþu runaʀ ret lit rista toliʀ bry[t]i i roþ kunuki toliʀ auk gyla litu ris . . . þaun hion eftiʀ . . . k merki srni . . . hakun baþ rista** (U 11), which has been normalized as: *Rað þu runaʀ. Rett let rista Toliʀ bryti i Roð kunungi. Toliʀ og Gylla letu ris[ta . . .], þaun hion æftiʀ [si]k(?) mærki . . . Hakon bað rista*, "Interpret the runes! Tólir the *bryti* of *Roþr* had them rightly carved for the King. Tólir and Gylla had [the runes] carved . . . this married couple as a landmark in memory of

160 Cf. Lindquist 1944 p. 225, Wührer 1981, Gissel 1981, Authén-Blom 1981, and Brink 2014b.

161 Thus, e.g., Hans Hildebrand *SM* 1 p. 81 and Olson 1916 pp. 13 and 22–23.

162 See Fritzner art. *bryti* and Söderwall, art. *bryti*.

163 de Vries 1962 p. 62.

164 That the position of the *bryti* changed during medieval times is entirely apparent, most clearly in Denmark. Here, the originally unfree and later on free farm manager—assuming this can be taken as the early social status of a *bryti*, as seems to be generally accepted (see literature that follows)—developed into becoming a sort of steward (*villicus*), especially in the king's service, in terms of the administration of taxes and of justice. During the later part of the Middle Ages (after the thirteenth century), *bryti* (*villicus*) becomes a designation for a farmer, practically synonymous with a tenant, and the term *bryti* is often used as contrast to a tax-paying farmer. See Velschow 1840, Erslev 1898 pp. 90, 101, 226, 252, Hjärne 1947 p. 36, Skrubbeltrang 1957, Riis 1970, Gissel 1981, Myrdal and Tollin 2003, Brink 2014b, and Poulsen and Orning 2019 *passim*.

themselves(?) . . . Håkon ordered (it) be carved." This historically very important inscription is not all that easy to interpret.[165] Elias Wessén reckons the stone to have been raised at the king's request and that this king is the Håkon who ends the inscription.[166] It is at his request that the *bryti* Tolir had the runestone raised. Wessén states: "The inscription on the Hovgården stone testifies to the fact that a *bryti* and his spouse could to a great extent benefit from his master's esteem and goodwill."[167] Many scholars have compared the runic evidence to a passage in the Östgöta Law that mentions *iarls bryti i roþzs bo*, although the rune stone refers to a king's *bryti*, which in von Friesen's reading describes a "manager of an estate,"[168] but in Wessén's interpretation the "king's ombudsman in Roden."[169] In an in-depth study, Erland Hjärne has argued against Wessén's suggestion and presents good arguments why Tolir was not a *bryti* in a district named Roden, but instead at the royal estate of "Hovgården" on Adelsö, and thus a farm manager.[170] As mentioned earlier, Mats G. Larsson and Staffan Fridell have in an interesting article re-analyzed this runic inscription and think they are able to reconstruct some missing runes and amend the inscription. In their opinion, the inscription should be read: **raþu : runaR : ret : lit : rista : toliR : bry[t]i : i roþ : kunuki : : toliR : auk : gyla : litu : ris. . . R : : þaun : hioa : eftiR. . .[au]k : merki hakun • baþ : rista srni[-]. . .** *Rað þu! RunaR rett let rista ToliR, bryti i Roð, kunungi. ToliR ok Gylla letu ris[ta runaR þessa]R, þaun hion æftiR [ku]nung mærki. Hakon bað rista . . .*, "You interpret! The runes Tole, *bryti* in Roden, had rightly carved for the King. Tole and Gylla had these runes carved, this married couple, [as a] memorial after the King. Håkon ordered [it] be carved . . . " [My trans.] In their opinion there are two individuals, Håkon, a king and a *jarl* (a royal administrator), and they link this *jarl* to the above mentioned *iarls bryti i roþzs bo* in the Östgöta Law. Magnus Källström has discussed this interpretation and can, after a thorough analysis of the runestone, dismiss the idea of two different "Håkon," and also the word *Roden* (< *Roþ*), which he is inclined to interpret as OSw *roþ* 'waterway, sea route'. Although not being explicit on the actual function of the

[165] See especially Elias Wessén in *Upplands runinskrifter* 1 (1940) pp. 11 ff., Hjärne 1947 pp. 21 ff., Larsson and Fridell 2013, Källström 2015.

[166] Wessén in *Upplands runinskrifter* 1 (1940) p. 12. Hjärne 1947 p. 66 interprets it in the same way.

[167] *Inskriften på Hovgården-stenen vittnar om att en bryte och hans maka kunde i hög grad åtnjuta sin herres aktning och välvilja, loc. cit.*

[168] von Friesen 1913 p. 58: *förvaltare på ett gods.*

[169] Wessén in *Upplands runinskrifter* 1 (1940) p. 12: *konungens ombudsman i Roden.*

[170] Hjärne 1947 p. 81, cf. p. 37.

bryti, it seems Källström leans toward Hjärne's interpretation as *Tolir bryti* being the manager/steward on the royal estate here.

On a rune stone in Gillberga, Västerljung parish, Hölebo hd, in Södermanland, there is a badly damaged inscription: **sigualti r[aisti . . .—kil br]utia sin** (Sö 42),[171] which can presumably be translated as "Sigvaldi raised . . . (after) . . . (Thor)kel, his *bryti*" where **brutia** may be an oblique form of *bryti*. At Randbøl in Jutland there is a Viking Age rune stone (dated c. 965) with the following inscription: **tufi bruti risþi stin þansi aft lika brutia þiʀ stafaʀ munu þur kuni miuk liki lifa** (DR 40), in normalized form: *Tofi bryti resþi sten þænsi æft lika brytia. Þer stafar munnu Þorgunni miok længi lifa*, "Tófi *bryti* raised this stone in memory of the *bryti*'s wife (or helpmate). Very long will these staves live for Þorgunnr." The Randbøl stone, the only Danish rune stone that appears to be standing in its original location, has been called Denmark's ugliest rune stone, but it carries an unusually beautiful and gripping message.[172] With it, the *bryti* Tófi has raised a memorial to his wife (*liki*) Þorgunnr. In Denmark, rune stones have long been regarded as indicators of power and authority in the landscape and commonly linked to the "aristocracy" and an upper social stratum, and presumably rightly so,[173] although this generally accepted thesis has recently been—not questioned, but—qualified by Gunhild Øeby Nielsen.[174] Even so, the traditional interpretation, spearheaded by among others Erik Moltke, which is that the term *bryti* in this inscription "should be understood to refer to the king's bailiff," is probably correct.

In the cases of the Hovgården stone and the Randbøl stone, a *bryti* has raised and had carved a rune stone, while the Gillberga stone says that a stone was raised to commemorate a *bryti* (if the reading of its inscription is correct). All this runic evidence states unequivocally that a *bryti* was a highly esteemed man, a servant of course, as the Hovgården stone mentions, but not at all some "slave" belonging to the bottom of society. Instead, he was a trusted official, probably an estate manager, whose work brought him into close contact with kings and other important men.

[171] Erik Brate and Elias Wessén translate the inscription in *Södermanlands runinskrifter* (1924–1936) p. 32 as: *Sigvalde reste (denna sten efter) Torkel (?) sin rättare* (Sigvalde raised [this stone after] Torkel [?] his bailiff). Why they prefer the translation *rättare* (bailiff) for **brutia** is not explained.

[172] Moltke 1981 p. 296.

[173] E.g., Sawyer 2002 p. 33.

[174] Øeby Nielsen 2004 p. 162, 2005; see also *Runesten, magt og mindesmærker*, ed. G. Øeby Nielsen (Hikuin 32), Højbjerg 2005.

The consensus presented in handbooks regarding the *bryti's* supposed original unfree status actually surprises when the sources are examined. The *bryti* can be assumed to have a sort of slave-status in, for instance, the Frostathing Law (XI: 21):

Umm haullz rétt á bryta sínum
Haulldr scal taca .iij. aura talda á bryta sínum oc þióni oc deigiu oc setu. en á öllum öðrum mansmönnum .ij. aura. En þræll scal taca .ij. lutum minna rétt en dróttinn hans. En ef þræll lýstr annann þræl þá scal svá hit sömu. en dróttinn á ecki á því.[175]

About a *hauld's* right for his *bryti*
A *hauld* shall take three *aura* in fine for his *bryti* and *thión* and *deigia* and *seta*, but for all other *mansmannum* two *aura*. And a thrall shall take two-thirds less in fine than his owner. But if a thrall kills another thrall, then the fines should be the same, but the owner has nothing to do with this.[176]

And in the Östgöta Law (Book on Trading, 12):

Nu sitær bryti i bo manzs ok han ær þræll hans: til þæs bos skal tilseu man vara: han skal köp gæra ok egh þrall hans.[177]

Now a *bryti* sits on a man's farm and he is his thrall : the farm he [the thrall, obviously] shall look after. He [the owner] shall trade and not his thrall.[178]

And in the Östgöta Law (Book on Manslaughter, 14):[179]

Vm brytia gildi, æn þer dræpnir uarþa : ok iui hærra þukka æn þerra mæn dræpas.
Nu uarþær dræpin kunungxs bryti i upsala bo. han ær gildær at fiuratighi markum: þöm a kunnungær taka sua gaf birghir iarl i lagh. för uaru þæt tolf markær. §. 1. Nu uarþær dræpin iarls bryti i roþzs bo. han ær gildær at niu markum. þöm a iarl taka. §. 2. Nu uarþær biskups bryti dræpin i stafs bo ok

175 *NGL* I p. 234.
176 My free translation from Hagland and Sandnes' (1994 pp. 177–178) Norwegian translation.
177 ÖgL, Collin and Schlyter (eds.) 1830 p. 162.
178 Cf. Holmbäck and Wessén 1933 p. 168 Swedish translation, which I have slightly modified.
179 ÖgL, Collin and Schlyter (eds.) 1830 pp. 46, 59–60; Holmbäck and Wessén 1933 p. 62. Clara Nevéus (1974 pp. 88–89) argues convincingly that *bryti* in this legal paragraph must be an unfree person.

stols han ær gildær at niu markum þöm skal biskupær taka. §. 3. Nu uarþær laghmanzs bryti dræpin. han ær gildær at siax markum. þa skal han haua stallara ok stekara ok fiuratighi sæssa a sialfs sins kust. §. 4. Nu uarþær þæn dræpin sum nam gær i garþe bondans sum fæt a. ligge ogildær. uarþær han dræpin utan garþ þæs ær fæt a uari gildær sum skilt ær. §. 5. Nu uarþær dræpin bonda bryti han ær gildær at þrim markum. þöm a bondin taka. nu kallar annar brytia ok annar bolaxs man: þa a han uitzsorþ uita mæþ eþe fiughurtan manna at han uar bolaxs man ok egh bryti: uari sua gildær bolax man sum bonde.

Of fines for *brytar*, if they get killed; and of noble men's honor fine, if their men are killed.

Now a king's *bryti* is killed in *Uppsala bo*; he is to be compensated with forty *marker*, them shall the king take. This Birger Jarl gave as law; it used to be twelve *marker*. §1. Now a *jarl*'s *bryti* in *Roþs bo* is killed; he is to be compensated with nine *marker*, them shall the *jarl* take. §2. Now a bishop's *bryti* in staff's and seat's *bo* is killed; he is to be compensated with nine *marker*, them shall the bishop take. §3. Now a lawman's *bryti* is killed; he is to be compensated with six *marker*. Then he shall have *stallare* [cf. Lat. *stabularius*] and cook and forty oarsmen at his own expense. §4. Now a man is killed who steals in a farmer's farm, who owns the stolen goods; he lies uncompensated. If he is killed outside of the farm, he is still to be uncompensated. §5. Now a farmer's *bryti* is killed; he is to be compensated with three *marker*, them shall the farmer have. Now one says that he was a *bryti*, and the other that he was a copartner; then he has the right to prove with fourteen men's oaths that he was a copartner and not a *bryti*. A copartner is to be compensated as a farmer.[180]

From the last citation in the Östgöta Law, it seems clear that the compensation of a killed *bryti* does not represent a "wergild," the honor price of a man, instead it looks like a compensation for the loss of a *bryti*'s labor, therefore the falling scale from the king down to a farmer. The *bryti* is understood as a "tool," working for a king, jarl, bishop, lawman, or a farmer. This has—rightly or wrongly—been taken to represent an earlier state of affairs.

From the Västgöta Laws and also the Danish Laws it is not certain whether a *bryti* was of free or unfree legal status,[181] while in the Svea Laws it is clear that the *bryti* was a free farm-manager; however, the Danish legal

[180] My trans. Cf. the trans. to Swedish by Holmbäck and Wessén 1933 p. 62.
[181] Nevéus 1974 pp. 69–70.

historian Poul Johannes Jørgensen is of the opinion that "it is not evident from the word itself that the bryti is a slave, but originally he probably was that as a rule."[182] The three runic inscriptions treated here, in which a *bryti* appears, speak a rather different language from, for example, the clause in the Frostathing Law. There is nothing here to prove that we are dealing with an unfree person; instead, we encounter a sort of servant/steward/manager (free or unfree). These runic inscriptions—contemporary evidence—are 100–200 years older than the provincial laws. One possibility is therefore that the lack of freedom came in during the Late Viking Age/Early Middle Ages, but such a view will be hard to prove.

Perhaps the sections that deal with the *bryti* in the Law of Jutland can throw some light on this problematic issue. In this law, the *bryti* practically never appears as ombudsman/steward, nor in the Law of Sjælland or the Law of Scania, but instead almost exclusively as a person mentioned in connection with the property belonging to his master, his patron. It is clear that he was not able to act as his own master at the thing assembly, but had to rely on his master speaking on his behalf with the exception that if a *bryti* or his family were subjected to violence then he could bring an action against somebody without the intervention of his lord or in cases where the *bryti* himself had his own *bryti*.[183]

> A bailiff [*bryti*] and a slave [*threl*] and one who is house-led [*fletførth*[184]] can be no man's guardian, as they are not their own guardian. (I:31)

> There should be eight men of truth [*sannend men*] in each district [*heræth*], two in each quarter [*fiarthing*], but from the partnership [*fælegh*] more than one. All of them shall have property in that quarter where he is a man of truth, and be at least a bailiff [*bryti*] in a partnership and not a tenant-farmer (II:1)

> A tenant-farmer is his own householder and against him one can commit gang crime, but not against a bailiff [*bryti*], because with respect to what is done against a house held by a bailiff [*bryti*], it is for the householder to take

[182] Nevéus 1974 p. 114, Jørgensen 1974 p. 195: "at det ligger ikke i selve ordet, at bryden er træl, men oprindelig har han vistnok regelmæssigt været det," cf. Poulsen and Orning 2019 p. 218.

[183] Tamm and Vogt (eds.) 2016 pp. 251, 264, 266, 267. The Jutish Law (*Codex Holmiensis*) in facsimile, see http://www.kb.dk/permalink/2006/manus/41/dan/. The Law of Jutland in modern Danish translation: http://ribewiki.dk/da/Jyske_Lov; Cf. Riis 1970 pp. 6 f.

[184] See the discussion of *flatföring*, *sytning*, and *gæf*-thrall earlier. An ODa *flatføring* was hence someone who had handed over his farm to someone else, in return for protection and food during his old age, hence a kind of retired person. In these cases that person got some kind of "slave-status," as we can see from this law paragraph.

> action. But if something is done against the bailiff's [*brytis*] members or his wife, then the bailiff [*bryti*] can himself raise the complaint without his householder. (II:32)
>
> The nominated men shall be eight in each district [*heræth*], two in each quarter [*fiarthing*], and they should be men with three marks, real householders [*aðelbonde*] and not bailiffs [*bryti*] and not tenant-farmers [*lanbo*]. (II:50)
>
> If a nominated man dies or goes on a pilgrimage or leaves the region [*sysl*] or the district [*hæret*] or becomes a bailiff [*bryti*], then the men of his quarter shall mention another and the official have him swear as is said before. (II:56)

This situation, which the law clauses in the Law of Jutland describe, appears to speak of a "patron–client" relationship and actually need not have its origins in a "free–unfree" dichotomy, but rather in some sort of relationship of dependency or service. What we find here is actually rather confusing: In the first case the *bryti* seems to be on par with a slave [*threl*], and in the second it is stated that a *bryti* should have property and could be a *sannend men* ("men of truth"[185]), hence used in legal cases, which seems to be contradicted by the fourth and the fifth cases, where it says that nominated men for a jury had to be householders and not *brytar* nor tenant-farmers, and in the fifth case, where a man nominated to a legal jury could not be a *bryti*, and then again in the third case we learn that the *bryti* had to rely on his householder (owner?/ owner of the farm?). The majority of these cases, however, places a *bryti* in some "patron–client" relationship, where they normally could not be used as subjects in court cases.

In Old Norse languages another word occurs within the same semantic sphere, namely ON *lávarði*, *lávarðr* m. 'lord', OSw *lavardher* m. 'lord, master', which is a loan from OE *hlaford*, *hlæford*, a compound of *loaf*, OE *hlāf* 'bread' and *ward*, OE *weard* 'manager, guard'.[186] This word provides the basis for the English designation of nobility *lord*. It is, of course, tempting to compare OSw *bryti* to the OE *hlæfbrytta* m. 'steward (servant)', a compound of *hlāf* 'bread' and *brytta* m. 'servant, lord', etc., yielding 'the one who breaks the bread', a

[185] For the concept of *sandemæn* in the Law for Jutland, see Skautrup 1934 and Per Andersen 2014 *passim*.

[186] de Vries 1962 p. 349.

word that occurs only once and on that one occasion in a letter of emancipation from 1330–1350.[187] This Old English word is, of course, semantically very close to *lord*, OE *hlāford* (< *hlæfweard*) 'one who guards the bread', OE *hlāfæta* 'one who eats the bread (servant, slave)', a word occurring only in the earliest of the Anglo-Saxon laws, Æthelberht's Law (25): *ceorles hlāfæta*, a *ceorl*'s servant/slave,[188] and *lady*, OE *hlæfdige* 'bread-bakeress',[189] the second element in *lady* (*-dige* < *-dæge*) is to be linked to Gothic *deigan* 'to knead', which result in the meaning '(female) bread-kneader', hence the one who bakes the bread.[190] These Old English appellatives lack direct counterparts in other Germanic languages, although I think that the word *bryti* belongs to the same semantic sphere. The words relate of a time when a sort of "food-community" constituted a unifying institution with a bread-baker (female servant), a bread-guard (male official of a higher rank than the following), bread-distributor (male servant of a higher rank than ordinary servants, slaves), bread-eaters (slaves, workers, servants) and we actually have preserved the word for the gathering of the "food-community," the common meal; it was known in Old English as *hlāfgang* 'the going to eat bread'.[191]

The Old English phenomenon of the "food-community" gathering around the bread (i.e. food) is highly interesting,[192] and it was probably widespread since German provides a semantic counterpart to *lord* (< *hlāfweard*) in the word *brotherr* m.: "herus, der seinen leuten brot gibt, welchen

[187] Bosworth and Toller *ASD* p. 132, Bosworth and Toller *ASD* Suppl. p. 548, and Pelteret 1995 p. 292.

[188] Bosworth and Toller *ASD* p. 540.

[189] *OED*[2] 8 p. 582, cf. Pelteret 1995 pp. 292–293. As Alfred Bammesberger (2002) recently has discussed, the word *lord* is to be derived from a PGmc **hlaiba-warda-*, whereas *lady* from PGmc **hlaiba-daigijôn-*. The development of the OE forms is rather complicated, as Bammesberger shows, where the vowel in the first syllable in *hlæfdige* (> *lady*)—for an expected **hlæfdæge*—probably is to be understood as an *i*-umlaut and the vowel in the second syllable is to be explained by weakening, *æ* > *i* (*-dæge* > *-dige*). The *ā* in OE *hlāford* is probably to be understood as analogically introduced from the simplex *hlāf* 'bread'. See also the discussion of *lord* and *lady* by Hoops 1908, and Sievers 1909, 1927.

[190] See Kluge and Lutz 1898 p. 117 and Skeat 1882 p. 282.

[191] Bosworth and Toller *ASD*Suppl. p. 548.

[192] For an interesting discussion of the partially semantically parallel words *lev*, OHG *leip*, OE *hlāf*, ON *hleifr*, Goth. *hlaifs* (< **hlaiba-*) and *bröd*, Germ. *broth*, Eng. *bread* (< **brauða-*), see Schrader 1896 pp. 5–11. It seems a similar institution, a collective or retinue around the "bread," was also found in Slavic areas. Christoph Witzenrath (2016 pp. 18–19) has discussed, or rather intimated this, when analyzing a term for a kind of slave in early Russia, the *kholop*, a word related to Western Slavic *khlap* "indicating a slave," but also denoting a 'boy' (which hence has a counterpart in, e.g., Latin *puer*, and other terms discussed in this book), see also the discussion by Clarence-Smith 2014 pp. 121–125 (the standard Russian word for "slave" is *rob* or *rab* [*раб*] and *rabynya* [*рабыня*]). Witzenrath places these words in a lexical field "centred around the family, on the *pater familias* or the lord of the family, or the leader of the sworn Varangians, who was to assign bread rations"(2016 p. 19). And he continues with suggesting that the Russian word for 'bread', *khleb* (*хлеб*), is "likely" a borrowing from ON *hleifr*.

altpatriarchalischen sinn auch das ags. *hlâford*, vieleicht *hlâfveard*, verkürzt in engl. *lord*, enthält" ("the master of the house [Lat. *herus*], who gives bread to his people, in the old patriarchal sense, (see) also the ags. *hlâford*, perhaps *hlâfveard*, shortened in Eng. *lord*"),[193] hence 'bread-lord', the one who distributes bread to his subjects. It would be a small step to link this to some ancient institution within the Germanic-speaking area, perhaps some sort of cultic, sacrificial meal, and so on. However, I do not think that is the case, but rather believe the Anglo-Saxon "bread/food-community" to have another, more recent background within the frame of running large farms/estates in a feudal agrarian system. From the Continent, there is evidence of the existence of large farms/estates during Carolingian times, a kind of estates run with the aid of slaves. An estate was owned by some important man, a bishop or a king, and often by a vassal to a bishop or king. On the continent as well as well as in England, where the countryside was deforested and claimed for agrarian cultivation early on, crop growing was the single most important form of agriculture,[194] and therefore porridge and bread were by far the most common food intake for the majority of people. The slaves on a main farm did not have free access to their food, of course; in ancient times food was always a scarce resource. It must be assumed that someone had the task of guarding the food (*hlāfweard*) and that the food, that is the bread, was distributed among the slaves (*hlāfæta*) by especially trusted slaves (*hlāfbrytta*), a kind of farm steward, when it was mealtime (*hlāfgang*).

I have not been able to demonstrate any direct parallel institution in Scandinavia. Instead, our area offers recollections of a different kind of "food-community," which appears considerably more archaic, namely the group of people who gathered for special sacrificial meals in heathen times. The best-known sacrificial meals that have been described are the so-called sacrificial feasts in Lade in Trøndelag, which Snorri Sturluson describes in the saga of Hákon the Good in *Heimskringla*. During these, cooked horsemeat was eaten, toasts were dedicated to the gods, for peace and for prosperity, and also so-called memorial toasts (ON *minni* n.) were drunk; that is, people drank to the deceased. This episode has been considered by certain scholars to be a late falsification, while others deem Snorri's narrative reliable and consider it historically authentic to a great extent.[195] Of greatest interest to us, however, is a short passage in the peculiar and ancient *Guta saga*. This

193 J. Grimm and W. Grimm, *Deutsches Wörterbuch* 2 (1869) p. 405.
194 See, e.g., Miller and Hatcher 1978 p. 14.
195 See, e.g., Sundquist 2002 pp. 184 ff. for a discussion and references to literature.

archaic narrative exists in an appendix in the manuscript from circa 1350 that contains the Guta Law, the provincial law for Gotland during medieval times. *Guta saga* contains the famous passage that describes the heathen sacrifices of the Gotlanders:

> *Firir þan tima ok lengi eptir siþan troþu menn a hult ok a hauga, vi ok stafgarþa ok a haiþin guþ. Blotaþu þair synum ok dytrum sinum ok fileþi miþ mati og mungati. Þet gierþu þair eptir vantro sinni. Land alt hafþi sir hoystu blotan miþ fulki. Ellar hafþi huer þriþiungr sir. En smeri þing hafþu mindri blotan miþ fileþi, mati ok mungati, sum haita suþnautar, þy et þair suþu allir saman.*[196]

> Prior to that time, and for a long time afterward, people believed in groves and grave howes, cult sites and *stafgarþa*, and in heathen idols. They sacrificed their sons and daughters, and cattle, together with food and ale. They did that in accordance with their ignorance of the true faith. The whole island [i.e., Gotland] held the highest sacrifice on its own account, with human victims, otherwise each third held its own. But smaller assemblies held a lesser sacrifice with cattle, food, and drink. Those involved were called "boiling-companions" [*suþnautar*], because they all cooked their sacrificial meals together.[197]

We have here a description of a sacrificial "food-community" and we are even given the term for such a ritual sacrificial "food-community," namely *suðnautar*. This word is a so-called *hapax legomenon*, that is a word that occurs only in this one instance. Beyond that it is entirely unknown in Old Norse languages. The word has the stamp of authenticity and the appearance of great age. It is a compound of the words *suða* 'to cook', which is obviously closely related to the modern Swedish verb *sjuda* (< **siuðan*) and Old Gotlandic *nautar*, OSw *nøtar* (sg. OSw *nøtr*, ON *nautr* and OSw *nøti*, ON

[196] *Guta Saga*, ed. Christine Peel (1999), p. 4.

[197] Christine Peel's English translation, with some minor changes by me, in her excellent edition of *Guta saga* (*GL* p. 278) There are several difficult words here, such as *stafgarþa*, the word occurs still today in place names on the island, but has still not been explained etymologically and historically (a brave and thorough attempt was made by Ingemar Olsson 1976; cf. Axel Kock in *ANF* 28 (1912) pp. 199–205, and *GL* pp. 290–291); *fileþi*, which seems to have included livestock, probably especially sheep, but presumably also horses (see *GL* pp. 291–292); *suþa* 'to cook', a word related to ON *seyðir* 'cooking pit' and ON *sauðr* 'sheep' and to Old Gotlandic *sauþr* 'well, spring' and Goth. *sauðs* f. 'sacrifice' (see, e.g., Hellquist 1948 p. 916), with other words displaying a semantic content relating to cooking, often mutton, in connection with sacrifice, *suþnautar* obviously contains this word *suþ-* and an unusual OSw *nautar, nøtar* 'companions' (see Olson 1916 p. 2; cf. Germ. *Genossen*).

nauti) 'team, gathering, group of people', where the final element is related to the Sw. verb *njuta* (at the Ablaut stage *naut-*), which has various earlier meanings such as 'capture, use, eat, and enjoy'. The latter element has a direct counterpart in German *genossen* (sg. *genosse*) 'comrades'.[198] The earlier meaning of Old Gothlandic *suþnautar*, OSw **suþnøtar* would then be 'those who share food at a sacrificial meal'.[199]

We are faced, then, with two different kinds of "food-communities." The Scandinavian *suðnautar* was a group of people who gathered for a sacrificial meal at a *blót* and what was cooked (ON *sjóða*) on a fire or in a cooking pit (ON *seyðir*) was meat, horsemeat, pork, beef, or mutton (cf. ON *sauðr* 'sheep'). The Anglo-Saxon *hlāfgang* was a group of people who were given food by a *hlāfbrytta* who broke and distributed bread. No cultic associations can be demonstrated for the latter "food-community," which appears rather to have been a purely profane mealtime, or rather feeding time, for servants and slaves on a large farm/estate.

Against this background I think it is reasonable to hypothesize that the term and the phenomenon of *bryti* came into Scandinavia at the same time as we adopted farming of a feudal agrarian sort, or perhaps rather the kind of "tributary society" Chris Wickham discusses, where the relations were as those between patrons and clients, unlike feudal relations between landlords and serfs,[200] and where estates had a main farm/manor that was run with the aid of slaveholding. Within such a unit there must have been a trusted slave who acted as foreman for the slaves, a *bryti*. This function, foreman on a large farm, has apparently developed over time to take on more trusted tasks, as farm manager, and later on in the twelfth century a *bryti* (Lat. *villicus*)—at least in Denmark—became a royal steward,[201] hence high up the social ladder, until it decreased in social value during medieval times when it came to refer to a farm tenant. It is possible that *bryti*—as perhaps also *deigja*—came in at

198 ON *nautr* m. and *nauti* m. are, as their relation to German *genosse* shows, a formation with a prefix *ga-* with a collective meaning, comparable to formations such as *granne*, ON *granni* (< **ga-raznan*) to ON *rann* n. (< **razna*) 'house', cf. *gränd* (< * *ga-razniþō*) 'small settlement district', ON *sessi* m. (< **ga-sessan*) 'bench mate (on a ship)' to ON *sess* m. (< **sessa*) 'rowing bench', like the closely related, albeit obviously based on a collective *-ia*-suffix, OSw *farunøti* (< *fara-ga-nautia-*) 'those who travel together' from the verb *fara* 'travel', OSw *skipnøti* (< **skip-ga-nautia-*) 'naval district' from *skip* 'ship', etc. (Brink ms; cf. Hj. Falk in *ANF* 3 [1886]: 187–188, S. Bugge 1896, 1905, Kock 1905, Kauffmann 1910). Axel Kock's suggestion that these forms are older juxtapositions, where a word in dat. pl. merged with *-nautr* followed by an assimilation *mn* > *nn* (*kaupum nautr* > **kaupunnautr* > *kaupunautr*), seems less convincing, especially due to the occurrence of Germ. *genosse* etc.

199 On such ritual food teams, see Hauck 1950.

200 Wickham 2005 passim, cf. Poulsen and Sindbæk 2011 pp. 13–14.

201 Poulsen and Orning 2019 pp. 216–217, 228.

the same time as the term and phenomenon of OSw *lavarder*, ON *lávarðr*, *lávarði*, were borrowed from Anglo-Saxon (< *hláfweard*) since the terms belong together semantically and perhaps also chronologically. A *bryti* was at the earliest stage the "bread-distributor," that is the steward or manager who distributed bread (food) to those who worked, servants and slaves. He was thus a *primus inter pares* for the slaves, probably a counterpart to the *villicus* that existed in *latifundia* in the Roman Empire. These terms possibly belong to an even earlier Proto-Germanic collective institution, the **hiwa*.[202]

If these terms are not Proto-Germanic, there are reasons to regard the *bryti*, and perhaps the *deigja* as well as quite clearly the *lávarðr*, as being among the numerous Scandinavian cultural borrowings that have come in from Anglo-Saxon England, probably during the Viking Age. The origin and function of the *bryti* deserves a critical and detailed historical-semantic examination.[203]

fostri/fostra

In the Old Swedish lexicon we find the words *fostri* m. and *fostra* f. as terms for a kind of slave. The words mean approximately 'slave/female slave born and brought up at home',[204] which indicates that these thralls were not captured in war, but were born and brought up on the farm.[205] In Sweden a *fostri/fostra* was probably, as in Iceland during the same period of time, a slave/female slave who grew up with the "freeborn" children of the farm household. This distinction between indigenous slaves and acquired slaves also shows in a document from Uppland in 1292 (*DS* 1737).[206] The Book of Inheritance of the Older Västgöta Law (4:2) states that if a widow wanted to enter into a new marriage she could not part from house and children unless the children owned a slave or female slave, specified as a *fostri* or *fostra*, who could run the household. This clause reveals that the *fostri* was apparently more trusted and had a different social and legal position than other thralls, a position recalling the one allotted to a *bryti*. That the *fostri* was, however, unfree is evident from the fact that a *fostri* could be sold (ÖgL: The Book Concerning

[202] On this, see Brink 2008.
[203] For an analysis of the *bryti* and the Proto-Germanic collective **hiwa*, see Brink 2008.
[204] Olson 1916 pp. 15, 61.
[205] Gösta Hasselberg 1944 pp. 85 ff. has written an excellent little "excursus" on the *fostri* in medieval Sweden, which is referred to later. Cf. also Strid 2006 pp. 104–105.
[206] Cf. Hasselberg 1944 p. 86.

Land 23) and that children born to a *fostri* outside of marriage belonged to the *fostri*'s master (ÖgL: The Book Concerning Matrimony 29). The trusted position of the *fostri* is further verified by a clause in the Younger Västgöta Law (The Book Concerning Matrimony 11), which says that an "unfree *fostra*" was entrusted with the master's keys.[207] The fine for adultery with a *fostra* was four times higher than for an ordinary slave woman and half that of a free woman. If we consult the Östgöta Law, we find that the term *fostri* is used to refer to a thrall who occupies a special legal position. It says (ÖgL: The Book Concerning Accidents and Wounds 16, 31:1) that in questions of received wounds and strikes a *fostri* and other thralls were on equal par, but the penalty for killing a *fostri* was a full 8 *marker* where a thrall was valued at 3 *marker*. It is also evident that a *fostri* could own property and moreover in the book on matrimony (29) that a free person could marry a *fostri*/*fostra* with the effect that any children born in such a marriage would be free. Finally, it is noteworthy that a *fostri* had, in certain circumstances according to the Västmanna Law (The Book Concerning Personal Security 25:9), so independent a position that he could fulfill military duty, which seems very strange, since this was the prerogative of free men.

The picture becomes even more complicated when we take into account the previously discussed runic material. The word *fostri* occurs in two Swedish runic inscriptions. Both cases concern a man. In Sö 97 appears an "Arne's fostri" who must be assumed to be a foster-brother of the deceased who is commemorated rather than a regular thrall. In U 163 a son honors the memory of his father, but also his *fostri*, who remains unnamed. Perchance this *fostri* was Gamall's foster-father. These two pieces of evidence in no way indicate that a *fostri* was a slave, but instead that one such was regarded as a member of the family, which was also the case for *fostri* and *fostra* as mentioned in the laws. Was the border between a foster-brother or foster-father and a thrall brought up within the family (*fostri*/*fostra*) fluid during the Viking Age? This is a question that can presumably not be answered by the preserved source material that we have at our disposal.

[207] Cf. Carlsson 1942.

"servant"—patron–client

We actually know very little about the thrall's circumstances during prehistoric times in Scandinavia. In all likelihood, it is way off the mark to compare the situation of a Scandinavian thrall with that of a slave in classical Roman times or with an African slave in North America during the eighteenth and nineteenth centuries. But the problem is also considerably more limited geographically and chronologically. In his study of the abolishment of slavery in Sweden, Gösta Hasselberg establishes that thraldom, as it can be observed in our provincial laws, is very different in the Svea Laws (for central and eastern Sweden) compared to the Göta Laws (for western Sweden).[208] He therefore wants to discuss two separate kinds of thraldom during the period in which thraldom was being abolished in Sweden. Niels Skyum-Nielsen has since emphasized that this means we must reckon with more kinds and types of thraldom in earlier periods during which chronological differentiation and regional variation probably occurred.[209] It is therefore noteworthy that thralls are mentioned in practically all the old provincial laws, except for the Hälsinge Law (valid for northern Sweden).[210] Does this imply that there were no thralls in northern Sweden in the Early Middle Ages?[211] Judging by the etymological evidence for terms for thralls, such as the status of the *bryti* indicated in the Law of Jutland, the status of an *ǫnnungr* according to Snorri and to *Grágás* in Iceland, and the status of a *fostri* according to the Swedish provincial laws, the different designations for "thralls" can indicate different degrees of lack of freedom and different kinds of dependencies in relation to a superior. A basic meaning is, nonetheless, obviously 'servant'. This, naturally, does not necessarily mean that a relationship of extreme suppression should always be assumed to exist between the servant and the one who uses

[208] Hasselberg 1944 p. 53.

[209] Skyum-Nielsen 1979 pp. 127–128.

[210] Cf. Henning 1930 p. 93 and Hasselberg 1944 pp. 62–63.

[211] Henning (1930 p. 93) believes that since thralls are never mentioned in the Hälsinge Law this is because the thrall institution had been abolished by the time this provincial law was recorded in writing, which seems a plausible assumption. This makes it possible to use this when it comes to dating the redaction of the Hälsinge Law. If the Skara Charter from 1335 can be regarded as an official proclamation of the abolition of slavery in Sweden, which is likely, this ought to mean that the Hälsinge Law was compiled sometime after 1335 (and before 1347; see Henning 1930 pp. 94–95). However, we know that often obsolete law rules are to be found in medieval laws, which means that in this case we cannot be sure that the omission of slaves in the Hälsinge Law is a consequence of an official proclamation of abolition, but instead mirrors a situation where slavery actually did not exist in this northerly part of Scandinavia in the Middle Ages (and presumably also in earlier periods).

the service; instead, such relationships were more akin to "patron–client" setups.

In this connection, it becomes impossible not to include in the discussion some words for "warrior" that existed in the Scandinavian languages of prehistoric and medieval times, namely ON *rekkr*, OSw *rinker*, ON *karl* and ON *sveinn*, OSw *sven*. *Rekkr/rinker*, and *karl* occur also with the meaning of 'warrior' in Anglo-Saxon, as *rinc* and *ceorl*. Beginning with the word *sven*, Runic Swedish *svæinn*, ON *sveinn*, this shows earlier meanings such as 'lad, young man', but also 'herder, servant' and 'unfree, thrall'.[212] OHG *swein* and OE *swain* have meanings such as 'swineherd', but also 'warrior'.[213] Noteworthy in this connection is the fact that Bishop Absalon of Lund in his will of 1201 granted freedom to among other slaves Eskil his "bath-attendant(!)" ("Eschillum *bathsuen* libertati donauit"; *DD* I:4, 62. 4). Moreover, it may be noted that in the Gulathing Law, for western Norway, *sveinar* are owned by farmers.[214] The word *sveinn/sven* (< **swaina-*) is a very old formation corresponding to PIE **suoi-no-*, whose stem is a locative form of the reflexive pronoun **sve*, **svo* 'own' (cf. Latin *suus* 'own'),[215] with the meaning 'one who is owned'. An earlier meaning of *sveinn/sven* would then have been 'one belonging to the house',[216] which goes well with both a young lad and a thrall. We thus find here a complete spectrum of meaning ranging from 'thrall, servant' via 'lad, young man' to 'warrior'.

The word *rink*, OSw *rinker* m., ON *rekkr* m. 'man, warrior, hero', OE *rinc* 'man, warrior', OHG *rinch*, occurs in Latinized form in the Salian Laws as *rencus*, where it has a semantic component of 'unfree' as well as 'young', according to Gabriele von Olberg,[217] and from these laws' use of the word she deduces this meaning: *noch nicht erwachsener (schwacher), im Wachstum befindlicher Mann, also im rechtlichen Sinne: "der Unmündige"* ("not yet grown-up [weak], a man in growth, also in a legal sense: 'the underage', the dependent"). In other words, *rink* occurs in Early Germanic times with the meaning of a 'young, perhaps unfree, warrior'. It is noteworthy that a Salian *rencus* could apparently be of both free and unfree status according to these early laws.[218]

212 See, e.g., Fritzner, article *sveinn*, and Söderwall, article *sven*.
213 *SAOB* (article *sven*) and Wilde-Stockmeyer 1978 pp. 47–48.
214 Cf. Olsson 1999 p. 17.
215 Falk and Torp 1903–1906 pp. 694, 868 and Olson 1916 p. 55.
216 Olson 1916 p. 55.
217 von Olberg 1991 pp. 236–238.
218 von Olberg 1987 p. 421.

A *karl* (< **karlaz*) was a 'farmer, man' generally speaking. But its appearance in certain place-names, *Karlaby*, as well as in compounds, *húskarl* '(royal) guardsman' and in OE *ceorl* 'farmer, freeman, warrior' reveals a more complex context. It cannot be excluded that the word *karl* in Old Scandinavian may also have been a designation for a thrall, an unfree man (which is obviously not the case in Old English). That this is the case for the derived form ON *karli* is fairly clear.[219] The etymology of the word discloses that a meaning-component indicating 'old' must be reckoned with (the word is derived from PIE **ger-* 'to age').[220] The words *sveinn/sven* and *karl* thus seem to make a pair, "young man"–"old man" and "young warrior"–"adult warrior," respectively.

This is a theme that we encounter with some frequency in the Old Germanic world, a division of a retinue or a contingency of warriors into two age categories.[221] A very illustrative example is found in Anglo-Saxon England, probably during the earlier part of this period, where the king's *fyrd*, that is his retinue or army, was divided into OE *duguð* and *geoguð*. We come across this division in, for instance, *Beowulf*, but also in other sources.[222] The word OE *geoguð*, *geogoð*, *iuguð* f. 'youth, young man', OSax *iuguð*, OHG *iugund*, Goth. *jund-s* (cf. Latin *juventus*), are, of course, the same as English *youth*, derived from West Germanic **juȝunþ-* or **juwunþ-*, corresponding to OE *geong* > *young*.[223] In the plural the word thus means 'young men, youths', while the word OE *duguð*, *dugoð* is related to the verb Sw. *duga* 'good enough' and the adjective Sw. *duktig* 'capable, clever, good' and shows a range of meanings in West Germanic languages, such as 'skill, strength; splendor, honor; help, gift; luck', but also 'group of warriors, retinue',[224] and from earlier sources we know that we must reckon with a more narrowly defined meaning: 'able retinue (of mature warriors)'. Richard Abels has explained this division in the following manner:[225]

> The distinction between "tried men" (*duguth*) and "youths" is crucial to a proper understanding of early Anglo-Saxon lordship. In Bede's day, the following of a king or of a great noble was divided into his *geoguth* and his

219 See the discussion of *karli* later.
220 Olson 1916 p. 24 and de Vries 1962 p. 301.
221 See for example Schlesinger 1953 *passim*.
222 Abels 1988 p. 218 n. 113 and Enright 1996 p. 203.
223 Holthausen 1934 p. 141 and *CDOEE* p. 550.
224 Holthausen 1934 p. 79.
225 Abels 1988 p. 32.

> *duguth*. The former were young, unmarried warriors who, having as yet no land of their own, resided with their lord, accompanying him as he progressed through his estates. When a retainer of this sort had proved himself to his lord's satisfaction, he received from him a suitable endowment, perhaps even the land that his father had held from the lord. This made him into a *duguth*, or, as Bede put it, a "companion [*comes*] or tried warrior [*emeritus miles*]." He ceased to dwell in his lord's household, although he still attended his councils; rather, he lived upon the donative, married, raised a family, and maintained a household of his own.

By the gift that a *duguð* had received he was, of course, tied more closely to his lord. And when a young king gathered his warriors, these *duguð*s must turn up with their own following, in the same way as when they attended council during times of peace. A king's retinue (*fyrd*), then, consisted of his household retainers (*geoguð*) and his "tried" warriors (*duguð*), who had their own properties, and their own smaller retinues.

Was then a *sveinn/sven* or a *karl* a thrall or was he a free warrior? Are *sveinn/sven* and *karl* to be interpreted in the same way as Anglo-Saxon *geoguð* and *duguð*? This is a question that requires a solution and is developed in a concluding chapter.

***þeu̯- in personal names**

As mentioned before, the element **þeu̯-* occurs in several Old Norse personal names.[226] On the ferrule of a sword scabbard found in Thorsberg in Angeln, Schleswig (Fig. 8.2), occurs the runic inscription **owlþuþewaʀ**,[227] which has generally been transcribed as a personal name *Wulþuþewaʀ* (possibly *Wulþuþewaz* if the ferrule originates in the West Germanic area, as has been suggested).[228] The occurrence of this name in an early runic inscription (third century AD) creates a range of problems.[229] The final element *-þewaʀ* (*-þewaz*) nonetheless appears to be certain.

In the discussions of this name it is clear how scholars have struggled with a compound wherein the first element potentially consists of the name of

[226] See also Haubrichs 2004.
[227] *DR* col. 21, Antonsen 1975 pp. 29–30, Moltke 1981 pp. 98–99, and Andersson 1993 p. 46.
[228] Odenstedt 1990 p. 116, cf. Andersson 1993 p. 46.
[229] On this, see Andersson 1993 pp. 46 ff. and Peterson 2004.

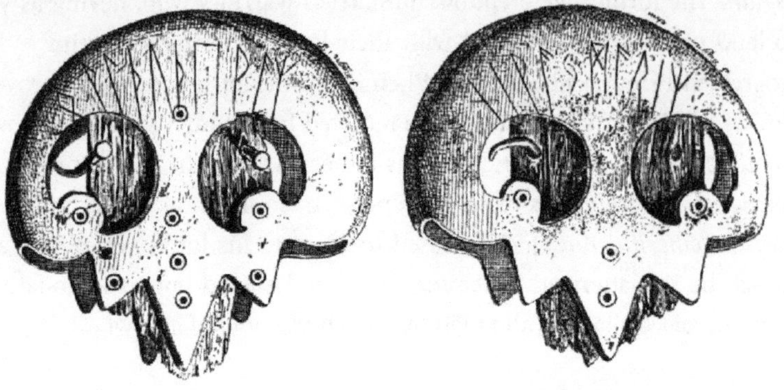

Fig. 8.2 During excavations in the Thorsberg Moor peat bog in Angeln, Germany, in the middle of the nineteenth century, a bronze chape belonging to a scabbard from circa AD 200 was found with a runic inscription **owlþuþewaz / niwajēmariz**. (Wiki Commons, https://upload.wikimedia.org/wikipedia/commons/4/47/Thorsberg_Ortband.png; and for credentials: https://commons.wikimedia.org/wiki/File:Thorsberg_Ortband.png.)

a deity (*Ullr*) or a word for "luster and splendor" (cf. Goth. *wulþus*) and a final element that, if encyclopedias and dictionaries are consulted, means 'slave (unfree)'. Some scholars, for example Thorsten Andersson,[230] assume that we are dealing with a so-called variation name, wherein the first and last elements can be combined quite arbitrarily without any demands for semantic concord between the elements, while Fred Wulf is even more categorical in his interpretation.[231] Other strained and strange explanations and arguments have been made. Ivar Lindquist believes the name to contain the word **wulþuʀ* 'honor, splendor' and that the name carried the meaning of 'one who has splendid servants'.[232] Elmer H. Antonsen translates the inscription **owlþuþewaʀ niwajemariz** as "Wolþuþewaz [servant of Ullr] of immaculate repute,"[233] a rendition that does not chime very well with a designation/name containing *-þewaz*, given the meanings attached to this word in literary times. Carl Marstrander has assumed that the issue is not of a personal name, but the name of the actual sword,[234] an interpretation that has received

[230] Andersson 1993 p. 51.
[231] Wulf 1994 p. 39.
[232] Lindquist 1940 p. 52.
[233] Antonsen 1975 p. 30.
[234] Carl Marstrander in *Viking* 16 (1953) p. 12.

little acceptance. The question that has caused the most trouble is whether this form *Wulþuþewaʀ* constitutes an appellative or a personal name (be it meaningful or not).

An argument that speaks against seeing the name of the deity *Ullr* in this name is that the first element would then be expected to appear in the genitive and that we would not find a stem-composition, which, in fact, we do. The criticism is justified; one would undoubtedly expect a genitive linkage in a compound meaning 'Ullr's servant'. However, one can probably not be entirely categorical. There are examples to prove that stem-compounds are possible in cases such as this. One such is, by way of example, the personal name *Þōriʀ*, which could potentially be a compound made up of the name of the deity *Þórr* and ON *vér* (< **wīhaʀ*),[235] usually translated as 'cult-leader' (i.e., a formation related to adj. *vi/væ/vé* 'sacred' and *vi/væ/vé* n. 'pagen cult place'), and thus be a Proto-Nordic **Þunra-wīhaʀ* 'Þórr's priest, cult-leader of Þórr'.[236] Absolute certainty that *Wulþuþewaʀ* does not contain the name of the deity Ullr, therefore, cannot be established. I think this possibility must remain open.[237]

Better semantic concord between the first and second element is exemplified in another compound, OE *Wealhtheow*, a woman's name that occurs in *Beowulf* and that has a male counterpart in ON *Valþjófr*.[238] Here, the known meaning of the second element *-theow* (< **þewa*) has been regarded as chiming with that of the first element *Wealh-* (< **walha-* 'Celt; stranger'); a Celt or foreigner who has been captured in war and enslaved has been considered as having historical and semantic relevance.[239] In the words of Leonard Neidorf: "Interpreting her name as a dithematic form consisting of *wealh-*, 'foreigner,' and *-þēow*, 'slave,' they have understood these elements to form a meaningful compound (i.e.,'foreign slave') designed to call attention to the Danish queen's personal history."[240] The opinion of, for example, Elias Wessén is that the name originates, instead, from a nickname for a slave, a

[235] Cf. Vikstrand 2009 p. 10.
[236] See Kousgård Sørensen 1989 p. 6–7 and Peterson 2007 p. 232.
[237] See Kousgård Sørensen 1989, Andersson 1993 pp. 41–43 and the summarizing discussion by Per Vikstrand 2009 p. 16.
[238] The element *-þjófr* has, as mentioned earlier, developed from *-þewaʀ*. It may be noted that a son of jarl Sigvarðr (Earl Siward) of Northumbria (c. 1030s and 1040s) was called *Valþjófr*, in OE *Walþeow*. The memorial poem *Valþjófsflokkr* was composed in honor of him (see http://abdn.ac.uk/skaldic/m.php?p=text&i=1422).
[239] The first element in this woman's name has also been considered an adj. **wala* 'beloved, chosen' (Gordon 1935 pp. 169 ff.), *valr* 'the dead' (in, e.g., *valkyria*) (Damico 1984 pp. 59 ff.) etc.
[240] Neidorf 2018 p. 75.

Sw. *välsk* or "southern" slave.[241] But the problem is that *Wealhtheow*, as she appears in *Beowulf*, is a highborn and gold-bejeweled woman, King Hroðgar's queen, and by no means a slave or unfree female servant. E. V. Gordon therefore hesitates in the face of this question: "It would be strange, however, if a lady of such dignity and gentle breeding, whom the poet calls *þeodnes bearn* [. . .] were also regarded by the poet as a type of 'foreign servant' or captive bond-woman."[242]

This inherent opposition within the name has, naturally, led to an extensive discussion among scholars in order to find explanations.[243] Helen Damico, for instance, presents a discussion of the topic in order to bring together a highborn queen named *Wealhtheow*, among other things by linking the name by way of association to the *val-* that occurs in the word *valkyrja*, and believes that the queen's name was chosen so that she would be associated with the function of a valkyrie.[244] Leonard Neidorf has recently given the name *Wealhtheow* an interesting analysis and discussion. He is of the opinion, building on an idea by E. V. Gordon,[245] that the first element is not *wealh-* 'foreign (slave)', but from **wala-* 'chosen, beloved', and therefore *Wealhtheow* should be understood as 'chosen or beloved servant'.[246] He also highlights the idea presented by Stefan Jurasinski that the names in *Beowulf*, such as *Wealhtheow*, are semantically empty, hence that these names were not designed to reflect meaningfully on their bearers (a problem discussed elsewere in this chapter).[247] On the other hand, as has been stressed by Maria Boehler among others, the name *Wealhtheow* (in the same way as two other women's names in *Beowulf*, *Freaware* and *Hygd*) "nicht historisch bezeugt sind," hence seems to be made up by the poet, to create some association, link, pun, or whatever, which—if Boehler is right—means that a name such as *Wealhtheow* was created for some purpose (see suggestion later), and for *Hygd* to explain the link to *Hygelāc*, etc.[248] If the poet or scribe(s) of the

241 Wessén 1927 p. 118.

242 Gordon 1935 p. 169. Cf. also Björkman 1919, Robinson 1964, and Hill 1990 p. 106.

243 See the opinions by different scholars, such as Frederick Klaeber, Thomas D. Hill, Andy Orchard, cited by Neidorf 2018 pp. 75–76.

244 Damico 1984 pp. 58 ff. Damico's argument is described as *spekulativ och utan övertygande kraft* ("speculative and lacking the power of conviction") (Andersson 1993 p. 48); "Damico (*Wealhtheow*) goes too far in the other direction, however, by seeking to make Wealhtheow more important in the poem than she actually is" (Enright 1996 p. 6 n. 10); and "The etymological relationship Damico argues seems implausible" (Hill 1990 p. 107). Joseph Harris (1986) also finds many improbabilities in Damico's hypothesis.

245 Gordon 1935.

246 Neidorf 2018.

247 Jurasinski 2007.

248 Boehler 1930 pp. 243–247.

Beowulf poem intended to have the names represent certain semantic information of that character in the poem or not, will probably continued to be dicussed, depending on how to understand the background to the poem.[249]

Michael Enright has argued that *Wealhtheow* played a central role in the hall and within the retinue of warriors (*comitatus*) as "she who carries the cup and gives out drink" and that the name is to be understood as a sort of built-in critique by the *Beowulf* poet.[250] The most important episode takes place in King Hroðgar's famous hall, Heorot, where our hero Beowulf arrives and is given an honorable seat among the king's sons, after which Queen Wealhtheow enters and the following scene is played out:

Ðær wæs hæleþa hleahtor, hlyn swynsode,
word wæron wynsume. Eode Wealhþeow forð,
cwen Hroðgares, cynna gemyndig,
grette goldhroden guman on healle,
ond þa freolic wif ful gesealde
ærest East-Dena eþelwearde,
bæd hine bliðne æt þære beorþege,
leodum leofne; he on lust geþeah
symbel ond seleful, sigerof kyning.
Ymbeode þa ides Helminga
duguþe ond geogoþe dæl æghwylcne,
sincfato sealde, oþ þæt sæl alamp
þæt hio Beowulfe, beaghroden cwen
mode geþungen medoful ætbær;
grette Geata leod, Gode þancode
wisfæst wordum þæs ðe hire se willa gelamp,
þæt heo on ænigne eorl gelyfde
fyrena frofre. He þæt ful geþeah,
wælreow wiga, æt Wealhþeon,
ond þa gyddode guþe gefysed,
Beowulf maþelode, bearn Ecgþeowes:
"Ic þæt hogode, þa ic on holm gestah,
sæbat gesæt mid minra secga gedriht,

[249] For a new and totally different take on the background to the poem, which has implications for interpretations of aspects such as the names in the poem, see Bo Gräslund's book *Beowulfkvädet: den nordiska bakgrunden* ("The Beowulf Poem: The Scandinavian Background") (2018).

[250] See Enright 1996 pp. 189 ff.

þæt ic anunga eowra leoda
willan geworhte, oþðe on wæl crunge
feondgrapum fæst. Ic gefremman sceal
eorlic ellen, oþðe endedæg
on þisse meoduhealle minne gebidan!"
Ðam wife þa word wel licodon,
gilpcwide Geates; eode goldhroden,
freolicu folccwen to hire frean sittan.
Þa wæs eft swa ær inne on healle
þryðword sprecen, ðeod on sælum,
sigefolca sweg, oþ þæt semninga
sunu Healfdenes secean wolde
æfenræste. [251]

So the laughter started, the din got louder
and the crowd was happy. Wealhtheow came in,
Hrothgar's queen, observing the courtesies.
Adorned in her gold, she graciously saluted
the men in the hall, then handed the cup
first to Hrothgar, their homeland's guardian,
urging him to drink deep and enjoy it,
because he was dear to them. And he drank it down
like the warlord he was, with festive cheer.
So the Helming woman went on her rounds,
queenly and dignified, decked out in rings,
offering the goblet to all ranks,
treating the household and the assembled troop
until it was Beowulf's turn to take it from her hand.
With measured words she welcomed the Geat
and thanked God for granting her wish
that a deliverer she could believe in would arrive
to ease their afflictions. He accepted the cup,
a daunting man, dangerous in action
and eager for it always. He addressed Wealhtheow;
Beowulf, son of Ecgtheow, said:

[251] *Beowulf*, ed. Klaeber (https://sourcebooks.fordham.edu/basis/beowulf-oe.asp), or http://ebeowulf.uky.edu/ebeo4.0/CD/main.html.

"I had a fixed purpose when I put out to sea.
As I sat in the boat with my band of men,
I meant to perform to the uttermost
what your people wanted or perish in the attempt,
in the fiend's clutches. And I shall fulfill that purpose,
prove myself with a proud deed
or meet my death here in the mead-hall."
This formal boast by Beowulf the Geat
pleased the lady well and she went to sit
by Hrothgar, regal and arrayed with gold.
Then it was like old times in the echoing hall,
proud talk and the people happy,
loud and excited; until soon enough
Halfdane's heir had to be away
to his night's rest.[252]

Enright's analysis of this text passage is that here we encounter an archaic ritual in the hall, a solemn drinking ritual in which the queen had a central and ceremonial role to fulfill, which is evidenced by the hierarchical organization inside the hall.

Thomas D. Hill discusses a contextually interesting aspect when he points out that, among others, Merovingian kings on the continent married lowborn women or slave women, a topic treated by the English historian Janet Nelson. She shows that this odd "communion" was intended to give the king and his descendents a degree of exclusivity since it allowed him to distance himself from the highborn families by not marrying any of their daughters.[253] The best-known marriage of this sort is probably that between Clovis II and the Anglo-Saxon slave woman Balthilda, who was, however, not just any slave woman, but a noble English princess.[254] In other words, Hill imagines that Wealhtheow should be understood in this same way, as a foreign slave woman whom King Hroðgar has married. Hill might have been able to further his argument by noting, for example, Gro Steinsland's analysis of kingship according to Old Icelandic poetry, above all in *Skírnismál*, where she believes that a king could make himself exclusive by marrying the daughter

[252] *Beowulf*, trans. Seamus Heaney (2000 pp. 41–42).
[253] Nelson 1986 pp. 4–5.
[254] Cf. Nelson 1986 and Stafford 1983 p. 3.

of a *jǫtunn* 'a giant';[255] not a slave, right enough, but a social outsider, a foreigner. The problem with Hill's interesting hypothesis is that it can hardly be said to explain the name *Wealhtheow*, which Hill also realizes, and he therefore proposes his hypothesis with great caution.[256] In the continued discussion of this name I nonetheless think that Hill's suggestion should be taken seriously and should be developed, but that another aspect also needs to be brought into the discussion in order to understand the name *Wealhtheow* as well as her high social standing.

A problem rarely discussed in connection with *Wealhtheow* is the observation made by Elias Wessén, which is that this name must have an Old Norse origin (in Old English guise). He establishes that all the Old English names ending in *-þeow* are Old Norse and in this he relies on those English philologists who regard Old English personal names ending in *-þeow* as unknown. The names ending in *-þeow* that occur in *Beowulf* all seem to be applied to Scandinavians. Wessén's conclusion is that the two closely related names *Wealhtheow* and *Valþjófr* are both Scandinavian names, containing the element **-þiwi* 'female servant' and **-þewaʀ* 'male servant', respectively. These were originally appellatives meaning 'a captive servant from a Celtic (Roman) land, war captive, slave', which came to be used as a personal name. *Wealhtheow* was thus, according to Wessén, "probably a highborn woman captured by the Danes in a foreign land (Britain, Gallia), whom Hrodgar granted freedom and took as his wife."[257]

In *Beowulf*, there are at least two other persons whose names end in **-þeu̯aʀ*, OE *-þéow*, which are *Ecgþéow* (= ON *Eggþér*), Beowulf's father and a great hero, and *Ongenþeow* (= ON *Angantýr*), a Swedish king who was killed by Eofor. Ivar Lindquist, among others, has assumed that the man's name *Eggþér*/*Ecgþéow* (< **Agiþewaz*) contains the word PGmc **agjō* 'point, edge' and has the semantic meaning of 'servant carrying a sharp weapon',[258] which must then be assumed to be an appellative or "title" for a type of warrior carrying a sword.[259] The name also occurs in a stanza of *Vǫluspá* (42):[260]

[255] Steinsland 1991 pp. 119 ff. and *passim*, 2004 pp. 81–84.

[256] Hill 1990 p. 110.

[257] Wessén 1927 p. 111: *troligen [ha] varit en av danerna i främmande land (Britannien, Gallien) rövad kvinna av ädel börd, som Hrodgar frigivit och tagit till sin gemål.*

[258] Lindquist writes (1940 p. 52): *den som har med egg beväpnade tjänare, d. ä. hirdmän* ("he who has servants armed with edged weapons, i.e., retainers").

[259] Lindquist 1940 p. 52; cf. Gjessing 1862 p. 49. On the name, see Lena Peterson, *LUP* p. 37.

[260] Lena Peterson (*LUP* p. 37) notes that ON *Eggþér* is notional, which is incorrect, as the name obviously appears in *Vǫluspá*.

Sat þar á haugi	"Sat there on the mound
ok sló hǫrpu	and played the harp
gýgjar hirðir	giants' guard
glaðr Egðir;	the merry Egðir;
gól um hánum	and by him crowed
í gaglviði	in gallows forest
fagrrauðr hani,	a bright-red rooster
sá er Fjalarr heitir.[261]	who's name is Fjalarr."[262]

It emerges that the word *þewaʀ* is evidenced in three other early runic inscriptions. In the ancient sacrificial bog of Illerup in Jutland a shield handle (Fig. 8.3) has been found carrying the inscription: **laguþewa.**[263] This inscription must be from circa 200 AD. The lack of a final rune -**z** (-**ʀ**) is confusing;[264] it has been assumed that the rune carver may have forgotten it,[265] that we are faced with a weak by-form,[266] or that we are dealing with a West Germanic name form (*-þewaz*) in which -z has fallen away.[267] Lena

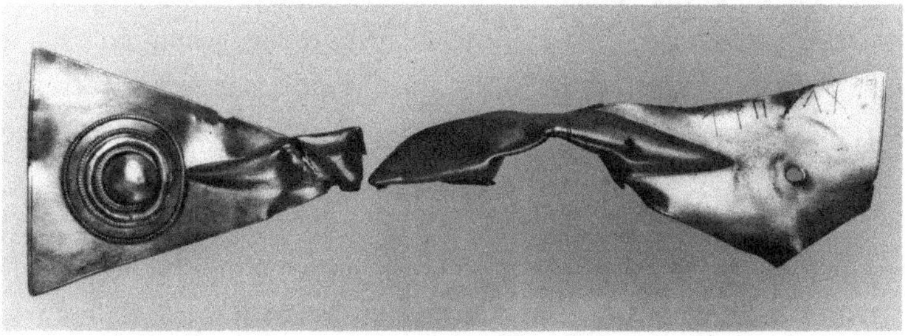

Fig. 8.3 During the large excavation of weapon deposits at Illerup, Jutland, Denmark, a shield handle from circa AD 200 was found with a runic inscription **laguþewa**. (The National Museum of Denmark, CC BY-SA; https://www.runesdb.eu/advanced-queries/d/im/q/r/r/1~2/f/175/p/2085/c/8d9099410b2b5915b5f159246f452698/.)

[261] Normalized text from Sophus Bugge in *Norrœn fornkvæði* (Christiania 1867).
[262] My translation.
[263] Stoklund 1987.
[264] Cf. Nielsen 1993 p. 86, 2000 *passim*, Peterson 2004 and the interesting discussion of this problem by García Losquiño 2015 pp. 54–62.
[265] Moltke 1981 p. 101.
[266] Stoklund 1987 p. 293.
[267] Antonsen 1987 p. 24. Stoklund (1987 and 1995 p. 345) has since argued against Antonsen's "West Germanic" theory.

Peterson considers it likely that the rune carver missed out the final rune so that we have a misspelling of *Laguþewa*ʀ (*-þewaz*).[268] Practically everyone who has discussed the inscription reckons *Laguþewa* to be a man's name, perhaps the owner of the shield, possibly its maker, and some have suggested that this is an appellative. Also the first element has caused much puzzlement. If this set of runes had semantic transparency to people at the time, that is to say if **laguþewa** is to be understood as a compound appellative or a variation name with a meaning recognizable to people at the time, then the first element has been seen predominantly as ON *lǫgr* m. 'water', although some have seen it as *lǫg* n. pl. 'law(s)'.[269] Marie Stoklund believes that the first element should be understood as **lagu** 'water' since the name then falls within a group of names that she labels "nature-words." Among these **staina**- 'stone' in the personal name **Stainawarija**ʀ on the Rö rune stone is taken as proof that such a group of words existed.[270] This argument surprises, and this specific example probably cannot be used in that way. As Lars Hellberg has convincingly shown, the first element in this personal name—or this title!—contains the word *stone* (< **staina**-) in the known sense of 'hill- or ringfort', which semantically speaking goes very well with the final element of the name. *Stainawarija*ʀ would then mean 'guardian of the fortress', 'defender of the fortification, hillfort' and would go back to an earlier appellative with an actual function;[271] thus it is hardly to be regarded as a variation name that occurred by chance. It is more plausible to point to variation names containing **Wid*- 'forest'.

Lena Peterson is, as usual, categorical in the stance she adopts. In spite of the fact that we are dealing with a period from which the written evidence consists in a handful of words and names,[272] Peterson is in no doubt when she asserts that:[273] "an interpretation of the first element as corresponding to the plural OWScand *lǫg* 'law' is impossible." Marie Stoklund is more

[268] Peterson 2004 p. 672.

[269] See the unbiased discussion in Michael Barnes 1984 p. 65. In her discussion of the runic form, Lena Peterson (2004) rejects the scholars who have voiced the possibility of seeing the word *lǫg* 'law' in the first element since no parallels wherein the first element of compound names have plural forms can be demonstrated. From what we know about how variation names are formed, namely that they are stem compounds, the first elements cannot contain the word *lǫg* 'law' (since this would in that case not appear in the declined form *lagu*-).

[270] Stoklund 1987 p. 292.

[271] See, e.g., Hellberg 1975 p. 99.

[272] We have only about 350 runic inscriptions from the period before AD 700 (Nielsen 2004 p. 639), and several of these contain only single words. About seventy of these come from the continent.

[273] Peterson 2004 p. 661.

cautious in noting that: "it can hardly have anything to do with n. pl. **lagu*, ON *lǫg* 'law,'" [274] an opinion that seems more justified given how little we actually know. Even so, everything indicates—based on today's knowledge of linguistics—that the first element is ON *lǫgr* m. (< **laguz*) 'water, sea,' but I do not think that we can completely dismiss the possibility that **laguþewa** should be regarded as originating from an appellative constituting a designation or a "title," perhaps of a law-speaker, someone whose task it was to know and recite the laws. And what if, against all expectations, a new runic find were to turn up containing a variation name in which the first element shows case composition, which would deviate from what we know about variation names today, all of which are stem compounds. I think that with regard to certain variation names it may be imagined that they are based on appellatives not necessarily stem compounded. Such appellatives have, of course, made up the pattern for the emergence of compound names, which were developed into a principle known as variation names that in time made it possible rather freely to mix and match first and second elements (see further in what follows).

The Swedish King *Ongenþéow* (= ON *Angantýr*, Proto-Nordic **Anganaþewar*), which appears in *Beowulf*, contains, according to Ivar Lindquist, a word ON *angan* 'pleasant sensation' and is interpreted as 'one who has happy servants'![275] The name also occurs in Old Norse literature.[276] Various suggestions for interpretations of the name have been made.[277]

On a newly discovered—actually as late as 2009—rune stone from Hogganvik, Mandal, Vest-Agder, in southern Norway, dated to circa AD 350–400, the start of the inscription begins with what obviously is a man's name, read as **kelbaþewas**, genitive of a man's name *Kelba-þewaʀ* (Fig. 8.4) The first element in that compound has been linked to Scand. *kalv*, Eng. *calf* (< PGmc **kalƀaz*), but the stem vowel indicates a related stem **kelƀ-*, which has been assumed to maybe denote a heifer.[278]

[274] *det [kan] næppe have noget at gøre med n. pl. *lagu, vn. lǫg, 'lov'*, Stoklund 1985 p. 10.

[275] Although this postulated meaning 'one who has happy servants' for *Ongenþéow* seems undeniably rather far-fetched, it has some semantic affinity to the meaning Leonard Niedorf postulates for the name *Wealhtheow* 'chosen or beloved servant' (above earlier).

[276] See, e.g., Lind 1905–1915 col. 29.

[277] See, e.g., Schramm 1957 p. 149.

[278] See the description of the archaeological excavation, the readings of the runes, and the discussion of the inscription by several runologists in Tsigaridas Glørstad, Johansson, and Stylegar 2011, Knirk 2011, Schulte 2011, 2013, García Losquiño 2015 p. 58.

Fig. 8.4 On a newly (2009) discovered runestone from Hogganvik, Mandal, Norway, dated to circa AD 350–400, a man's name **[s]kelbaþewas** is inscribed in the Old Futhark. (Wikimedia Commons CC-BY-SA 3.0; https://en.wikipedia.org/wiki/Hogganvik_runestone#/media/File:Hogganviksteinen_03.JPG.)

A runic inscription from a rock surface in Valsfjord in Norway (AD c. 400) reads: **ek hagustaldaz þewaz godagas**, which can be interpreted as "I HagustaldaR [am] *þewaR* ('guardsman, servant' or similar) to *GodagaR." In this instance one ought to be able to assume a priori that this HagustaldaR was GodagaR's thrall, but the name *HagustaldaR* appears to contradict that possibility.[279] Instead, everyone who has discussed the inscription has chosen to regard HagustaldaR as a 'Gefolgsmann', a guardsman, a retainer, warrior, and the like.[280] This fact forces us to reconsider the etymology of **þeu̯aR*, alongside all words for 'thrall, unfree', in my opinion.

It is clear—as all historical linguists know—that a word-meaning current during historical times cannot be assumed without further ado to have been

[279] Some have even understood this as a term, *haugstaldaR* '(young) warrior', but commonly it has been interpreted as a man's (by-)name (Antonsen 1975 p. 46, Reichert 1987 p. 417, Andersson 1993 p. 46).

[280] Krause 1966 pp. 124–125, Wulf 1994 p. 39, Antonsen 2002 p. 227, and Spurkland 2005 p. 48. A deviant etymology of the name *Hagustaldaz* is given by Lena Peterson (*LUP* p. 9; cf. Beck 1999) who considers the name to derive from an appellative **hagustaldaz* 'owner or manager of a plot of land', which supposedly should occur in secondary meanings in the OE (pl.) *hægstealdas* 'young warriors', OHG *hagustalt* 'bachelor', OSax *hagastald* 'young man; servant', an appellative apparently containing the word **hagu-* 'plot of land' and a derivation of the verb **staldan*, corresponding to Goth. *gastaldan* 'obtain, acquire'.

current for the same word also during prehistoric times.[281] There is nothing strange about this, it is only what is to be expected. Language is by definition in constant flux and so the meanings of words change over time. Some 3,000–4,000 years ago, the word Sw. *åker* 'arable field' (cf. Eng *acre*) did not mean "field that is worked and sown," but probably "place to which livestock is taken (for grazing)."[282] Agrotechnical development, in the form of a transition from a mobile pastoral culture to a stationary sedentary agriculture as the primary industry in the West, easily accepts such natural shifts in meaning. Changes in society have come about in the same way; terms for official positions and sociolegal status have changed semantically over time. Richard Diebold has in a similar way discussed the possibility for accessing an earlier meaning for the word *konung*, Eng. *king*, PGmc **kunungaz*, **kuningaz*. He establishes that during the thousand-year-long period that separates OE *kyning* from Eng. *king*, status, role, symbolic value, and sociopolitical function of the office of king has changed radically so that the present meaning has very little to do with the earlier (earliest?) meaning of the word.[283] In other words, the question needs to be asked whether the meaning 'thrall, slave' that we can deduce from certain words in written medieval sources, also had currency during prehistoric times. The answer is likely to be: hardly.

This question must also be seen in the light of a clear reorientation within scholarship in recent years whereby set assumptions have been questioned. A fundamental reorientation has been presented by the English historian Susan Reynolds in her important book *Fiefs and Vassals* (1994) in which she discusses in detail terms and concepts that have to do with relationships of dependency and official positions within the upper social strata of the feudal society of Europe during the Middle Ages. Her main result may be summed up in the statement that it is not possible to understand and assess earlier conditions correctly based on the terminology and conceptual orientation current during later periods of time, an argument that already Marc Bloch put forward much earlier.[284] Although terms and concepts may have lived on into later periods, the societal context has changed. This means that this realm of conceptions cannot be transferred onto an earlier period, which has often been done without further ado within history

281 Cf., e.g., Girsch 1994.

282 Sw. *åker*, PGmc **akra*, apparently derives from PIE **agros*, formed on the root **ag-* 'drive' (cf. Latin *agere* 'drive, lead' etc.), and is thought to have the basic meaning 'field to which livestock is brought' (see standard etymological dictionaries).

283 Diebold 1987, esp. pp. 35–36.

284 Bloch 1921, 1933, 1947.

research as well as philology. In Scandinavia, Tore Iversen has in a fruitful way discussed the concept of "thrall" along similar lines, whereby he rejects the simplified identification of 'slave' and instead emphasizes that we are dealing with a social spectrum in early society that operated with "patrons" and "clients" with varying degrees of dependency and of free/unfree circumstances.[285]

It is clear from what has been said thus far that we cannot assume that the meanings 'slave, thrall, unfree' given in dictionaries and encyclopedias are also adequate for and representative of prehistoric times. Already the etymological comparisons presented show that one of the frequently occurring basic meanings is 'servant'. There is nothing to prevent a word that in earlier times meant '(free) servant' from changing unto '(unfree) servant, thrall' in later times. In other words, there is nothing to stop for example the word *þræll* from having the semantic meaning of 'servant', thus indicating some sort of dependency between authority and subjects, perhaps warriors, such as in a "patron–client" relationship.

Here we have the likely explanation of a vital part of the problem with, for example, *WulþuþewaR* that has been discussed here. Several Old Germanic personal names are illustrative in the context, many of which contain the name of a deity as the first element or a word for God, such as OHG *Ansedeus* (eighth century) wherein the first element is related to ON *áss* 'god',[286] the Vandal *Gotthæus* (the sixth century),[287] in Gothic form **Guþþius*, likewise OHG *Gotadeo* 'servant of God' and the name of an abbess OSax *Godesdiu*, thus '*servus Dei*',[288] OE *Incganþeow*, which appears in *Widsið*, translated as 'servant of the god Ing', OHG *Irmintheo* 'servant of the god Ermin/Irmin' (cf. the world pillar *Irminsul*);[289] moreover, names of this type are known as names of kings and leaders, such as the Gothic *Arintheus* from the fourth century,[290] corresponding to ON *Arnþjófr*, the *Angelþéow* 'servant of the Anglians' who is known from the royal genealogy for the kingdom of Mercia in England, and so on.[291] Henry Sweet discusses the word OE *láttþéow*, which he believes to be an earlier *ládþéow*, containing the words *lád* 'path' and *þéow* 'servant', and translates as

[285] Iversen 1997 *passim*.
[286] Förstemann 1900 p. 130.
[287] Wrede 1886 p. 85, Schönfeld 1965 pp. 112–113.
[288] Schlaug 1962 p. 96.
[289] Förstemann 1900 p. 483.
[290] Schönfeld 1965 p. 26.
[291] Förstemann 1900, and Gordon 1935, cf. also Williams 2001. In the light of these names it is reasonable to consider the first element of ON *Angantyr* to contain a theophoric name **Angan* or a

"*minister itineris*," approximately 'pathfinder'. It is, however, apparent, Sweet says, that the word is employed in a "nobler signification."[292]

These names have semantic parallels in names such as the Ostrogothic *Gudiscalcus*, Visigothic *Godescalc*, Old Saxon *Godescalc*, and Burgundian *Ingescalcus*, OHG *Engilscalc*,[293] which are names where the first elements are the word *God* or in the last example, a god or a *heros eponymos*, but have the word PGmc **skalkaz* 'servant, slave' as their second element (cf. the word *marshall*, Sw. *marskalk*, and also as a man's name, OSax *Marscalc*,[294] a compound of PGmc **marha* 'horse' and a word ON *skalkr* 'servant, slave', Goth. *skalks*, OE *scealc*, OHG *scalc*, thus originally a 'stableman, stable-thrall', but in modern times indicating a royal master of the horse, an equerry, and in France the highest military rank in the army!).[295]

We probably have to place the Italian use of *Ciao!* as an everyday greeting within the same cultural semantic field, since the expression derives from an earlier (*vostro*) *schiavo* '(your) slave'.[296] This greeting appears to have originated among sophisticated upper-class people, without any hints of irony or thoughts of solidarity, but as a refined and elaborate way of showing politeness by verbally indicating humility and subservience.[297] Furthermore, terms such as *servus dei*, *famulus* (*famula*) *dei* and *ancilla dei* soon came to be used within the Catholic Church, and the wording *Servus servorum Dei* 'slave of the slaves of God', *famulus* (*famula*) *Domini Ihesu Christi* 'slave(s) of the Lord Jesus Christ' came to be a stock phrase used in all papal letters and charters.[298]

We have a similar custom, again what is understood emerging among the upper strata in society, when greeting someone with *servus* '(your) slave', which is nowadays common in central Europe, i.e., in southern Germany, Austria, Poland, Slovenia, Croatia, Slovakia, Hungary, and Südtirol.[299] A

designation for a deity. Against this, however, speak the many names (of which several are so-called *Óðinsheiti*, i.e., by-names for Óðinn) such as *Siftýr*, *Hertýr*, *Gautatýr*, etc., that are obviously based on ON **týr* 'god', pl. *tívar* 'gods' (Simek 1993 pp. 129, 284).

292 Sweet 1880 p. 152.

293 Schramm 1957 pp. 72–73, Schlaug 1962 p. 96, Schönfeld 1965 p. 115, and Wilde-Stockmeyer 1978 p. 46.

294 Schlaug 1962 p. 130.

295 *SAOB*, article *marskalk*, von Olberg 1991 pp. 221 ff., and de Vries 1962 p. 482.

296 Originally an old Venetian salutation, *s-ciào vostro* or *s-ciào su* "I am your slave" (*Treccani. Enciclopedia Italiana di Scienze, Lettere ed Arti*, art. *ciao*; online: http://www.treccani.it/vocabolario/ciao/).

297 Epstein 2001 p. xi.

298 Duggan 2003, Pons-Sanz 2007 p. 13, Wyatt 2009 p. 256, and Buongiorno 2017; cf. Girsch 1994 pp. 39–42.

299 *Duden. Wörterbuch der deutschen Sprache*, art. *servus* (online: https://www.duden.de/rechtschreibung/servus).

Swedish equivalent is the greeting *tjänare* or *tjenare*, which today is only part of the colloquial language. It is an interjectional usage of the noun *tjänare* 'servant', originally in courtesy language, such as *eder* (*ödmjuke*) *tjänare* (your humble servant), where the attributes eventually have been lost.[300]

This cultural code is found already in the early Church, used by the early theologians, such as Paul, Lactantius, Augustine, and so on, where they label themselves as "slaves of the Lord."[301] This custom is furthermore probably to be linked to the early Roman *familia* institution, where the members of the household, the *famuli*, were to be equated to "slaves" under the *pater-familias*, and where a young male, a *puer*, was equated with a "slave," which later develops into the situation where the word *puer* could be used to designate a "boy" as well as a "male slave."[302] I think this may be the background to the usage of names for kings and noblemen as the "slave (or servant) of X," such as *Gudiscalcus*, *Ansedeus*, *Guþþius*, *Incganþeow*, *Angelþéow*, where the X could be a god (*Guþ*, *Áss*, *Irmin*, *Ing*) or a people (*Angels*).

What we have here, then, is an example of an early *cultural code*, just like compound theophoric names wherein the first element indicates a named deity or an appellative for god(s) and a second element that, in literary times, indicates meanings such as 'servant' and 'slave', names that were—which is remarkable and important in this context—given to kings and leaders within society. An Irish parallel to this is *Gilla Patrick*, which translates literally as "Saint Patrick's servant." The expression contains the Old Gaelic word *gilla* 'servant, young boy', which is often used as preceding saints' names and as a part of names.

The name *Wulþuþewaʀ* on the ferrule from Torsbjerg has semantically and chronologically probably to been seen within the same cultural code and category of names. All in all, this speaks in favor of the possibility that the word **þeu̯aʀ* during early times (the first millennium) had the meaning 'servant', apparently (at least among other meanings) with a high social rank,[303] but that it underwent a shift in meaning later on, presumably toward the end of the first millennium, into 'unfree servant'.

As was mentioned earlier, Fred Wulf discusses some of these names ending in **-þeu̯aʀ* and rejects the possibility that this word had the meaning 'servant' (e.g., of a deity), as well as the possibility of translating these names and giving

300 *SAOB*, art. *tjänare* (online: http://www.saob.se).
301 Garney 1996 pp. 220–235; note his observation, citing Jerome: "It is a mark of great dignity and merit to be slave of the Lord and not a slave of sin" (p. 234).
302 Cf. Brink 2008 pp. 10–11, with references.
303 Cf. Spurkland 2005 p. 48.

them semantic contents;[304] as is well known, proper names lack etymological meanings. One of his arguments is that, for example, **owlþuþewaz** cannot contain the name of the deity *Ullr* "because names of individual gods are not evidenced/ do not exist in this early period" (*denn Namen von Einzelgöttern kommen in so früher Zeit nicht vor*). As far as we know, names of deities are assumed to be lacking from Proto-Nordic personal names in the sources available to us. But since these are very few indeed it is in my opinion overly rash to be categorical in this respect. The interesting question that must be put is whether these very early names belong to a period during which proper names may have been linguistically equal to appellatives, and as such etymologically transparent, so that a self-evident semantic understanding of names such as *StainawarijaR*, *WulþuþewaR*, *HlewagastiR*, and so on was apparent to the users themselves. I don't, for example, think that the perfectly, for a Germanic variation-name, compounded OSax *Godesdiu* for an abbess was given to, or took this name, by accident or out of whim, a name which means *servus Dei*, and is a common name or self-designated phrase for a priest, nun etc.[305] It seems likely that names such as *WulþuþewaR*, *HlewagastiR*, *Laguþewa*(R) could have had etymological transparency during the Roman Iron Age; at least the previously discussed names ending in **-þe̯uaR* appear to indicate this, since they fall into such a clear pattern wherein a **þe̯uaR* did service to a deity, a people, a (noble)man, or perhaps a legal assembly (*lagu-*), even if this latter interpretation is not the most obvious based on the knowledge we currently have.

Due to etymological considerations, then, we must question and discuss the slave-terminology in great detail in future research, particularly the earlier meanings of the terms.

Further arguments can be obtained through anthropological comparisons. In an interesting comparative study between the early Scandinavian society and a kinship-based agrarian society in Africa, the anthropologist Finn Fuglestad makes the following reflections.[306] The dichotomy "free–unfree," which he assumes in his work to be a Greek "invention," does not exist in this African society. Instead, various *degrees of dependence* in relation to the clan

304 Wulf 1994 p. 39.

305 This abbess, sometimes called *Äbtissin Godesti von Sachsen*, was the daughter of Bernhad I, duke of Saxony, and was hence named as abbess both at the monastery in Meteln (in 992) and in Herford (in 1002), Mecklenburg; however Gerd Althoff intimates that we perhaps are dealing with two different abbesses with the same pious name, *Godesdiu* (see Althoff 1984 p. 353).

306 Fuglestad 1979 pp. 72–73.

chieftain exist. The unfree person was an integrated part of the social group and thereby in possession of certain rights. Fuglestad addresses the overly one-sided view of thraldom by focusing on freehold and landownership and comes up with the presumably justified criticism that it is not possible to extrapolate backward in time on the basis of circumstances described in written sources no earlier than the twelfth century, as has been done uncritically. The changes that took place during the Viking Age and early medieval times, with a demographic expansion, a new religion, the introduction of Roman law and so on, would have constituted a veritable "revolution," he emphasizes (and rightly so), leading to extensive social and linguistic changes.

If we summarize the results of this semantic-etymological analysis, we find that terms for slaves appear to cluster around (at least) four semantic fields:[307]

1. One who is a member of a family or a household such as "household servant," that is, a person who waits on people and partakes in tending the farm and fields. To this belongs terms such as Latin *famulus*, OSw *fostre* and *fostra* (to Sw. *föda* [*upp*] 'to bring "feed" [up]' at home), *gæfþræl* ('one who has sold himself as a thrall to get support'), ON *deigja*, *seta*, *bryti*, and perhaps *sveinn* ('one belonging to the household'?).
2. One who sprints, runs errands, and does services for someone, such as OE *birele* f. 'one who carries around the drinking cup', ON *ambótt*, all the terms deriving from *þeu̯az* (< **tek*- 'sprint, run'), *þegn* (?) and perhaps *þræll*.
3. Ethnic terms for "war captives, enemies," indicating captivity, such as designations for neighboring peoples or other ethnic groups, or words borrowed from neighboring peoples, for example ON *haptr*, Sw. *slav*, OSw *est*, Latin *captus*, OE *wealh*, Welsh *caeth*, Greek *doûlos*, Latin *servus*, *vasall* 'servant' (from Gallo-Latin *vassus* 'slave, servant') and Goth. *frahunþans*. Among the northeast American Indians slaves were generically knowns as *Pawnees*, although they could have other tribal origin.[308]

[307] See also the interesting, albeit somewhat dated, etymological comparison of words for "slave" and "servant" in Buck 1949 pp. 1332–1337.
[308] MacLeod 1928 p. 644.

4. Designations for a "child, boy, young man," such as in Latin *puer* ('boy, slave'), *vassus* 'slave, servant' (from a Gaelic word for 'child', compare Welsh *gwas* 'child, servant'), *rinker/rekkr* (Latinized in the Salian Laws as *rencus* 'unfree, minor'), *þræll* (?).

What we can also conclude from this linguistic analysis is that dependency and the lack of freedom did not constitute absolute categories, but should be considered on the basis of a sliding semantic scale, which allows for discussion of various degrees of dependency between a master and a subject, as Finn Fuglestad has it. On the one hand, we have pure work slaves, chattel slaves, without any legal rights and living in social misery. On the other hand, we have people who have voluntarily become someone's slave and probably have some social standing, perhaps a special social bond to his or her master,[309] or who are trusted officials and managers. This is presumably what we detect in the shift in meaning with respect to *Wulþuþewaʀ*, discussed earlier. In the final chapter I pick up this thread and develop the issue further.

The question, finally, is how the name of the highborn Queen *Wealhtheow* of *Beowulf* is to be understood. I think this name must be considered in the light of the above discussion of how **þeu̯aʀ* could designate highborn "servants" in early times, individuals of the uppermost societal elite with a function to fulfill for the people or with a special association to something or someone. I think Elias Wessén had a significant point in thinking that *Wealhtheow/Valþjófr* constituted a sort of nickname for a Sw. *välsk*, hence a "southern," slave, even if he was not right.

Instead, I want to see the name in the light of Thomas D. Hill's suggestion, alongside Janet Nelson's research on how the Franks married queens and what Gro Steinsland believes the ideal wife to have been for a Norse king during prehistoric times, namely that there was an ideological reason for marrying a social "outsider," a female slave, or the daughter of a *jǫtunn.*

Queen *Wealhtheow* may have been a female war captive taken by the Danes, presumably highborn, Welsh, British, Anglo-Saxon, Frankish, or "southern"—one who could be given the epithet "female servant from *wealh*, i.e., the neighboring people, the enemy, the 'South' "—and who due to her "outsider-ness" was suitable as the spouse for the King of the Danes, *Hrōðgār* (the son of King *Healfdene* 'the half Dane').

309 Cf. Leach 1967 p. 13.

9

How Were Thralls Used?

lögðo garða,
akra tǫddo, unno at svínom,
geita gætto, grófo torf.

—*Rígsþula* 12

Almost everyone who has written about thraldom in Scandinavia, and the thrall's tasks in Old Norse Society, has, as mentioned previously, taken as a starting point the Old Icelandic poem *Rígsþula*. The relevant stanza of *Rígsþula* states that the thrall was to "bind bast and do burdens" (whatever the poet meant by that) "and bring home brushwood the whole day"; a little later it states that the thrall's children should "make stone walls, manure the fields, herd and feed the swine, herd goats and dig peat" (see epigraph).

As I emphasized in an earlier chapter, *Rígsþula* must be approached with great caution. The poem should definitively not be used as a source for history or for prehistory. For this it is far too complicated and problematic. In spite of these caveats, much speaks in favor of the fact that the tasks mentioned as thrall's work could have been carried out by exactly thralls.

Another "unhistoric" and considerably later, but nonetheless fully plausible, description of a thrall's life and work has been written down by the Swedish author Artur Lundkvist, with *Rígsþula* as a kind of latent mental reference, which forms a reflective backdrop in his novel "Slaves for Särkland" *Slavar för Särkland*:[1]

[1] Lundkvist 1978 p. 102: *Trälarna är nödda att arbeta så mycket som deras ägare kräver av dem och så långt de förmår, därefter kommer den frihet som är deras: att fylla buken likt kreatur för att orka fortsätta slitet, att sova i halmen på golvet i trälhuset och göra sina kvinnor med barn, i den mån inte deras ägare förekommer dem.*

Men i arbetet är bonde och träl på många sätt jämställda, bonden kan för sin heders skull inte gärna arbeta mindre eller sämre än sin träl.

Tillsammans hugger de ner träden på svedjan, för undan det bästa timret och bränner återstoden till aska, trälen hackar upp marken som ännu ryker av branden och bonden följer efter och sår, trälen gräver diken kring åkern och bonden plöjer åkern med stutarna, som en trälkvinna eller ett trälbarn driver på med käpp i hand.

Bonden fodrar kreatur och svin, trälen mokar ut gödseln, trälkvinnan mjölkar i trästävan, bondhustrun kärnar smör och ystar, trälkvinnor och trälbarn driver boskap, getter, får och svin ut på markerna, vaktar dem och ansvarar för dem med sina liv, bonden slaktar och gällar, frossar på blodkorv och stekta testiklar, trälfolket tar hand om avfallet.

Thraldom. Stefan Brink, Oxford University Press. © Oxford University Press 2021.
DOI: 10.1093/oso/9780197532355.003.0009

> The thralls are forced to work as much as their masters demand of them and as much as they are able to do, after which the freedom comes which is theirs: to fill the belly like an animal to be able to continue with the drudgery, to sleep on the straw on the floor in the slave house and make their women pregnant, insofar as their masters did not anticipate them.
>
> But in the labour a farmer and a thrall are in many ways equal, the farmer can for the sake of his honour not work any less or worse than his thrall.
>
> Together they chop down the trees on the swidden land, carry away the best timber and burn the rest to ashes, the thrall hoes up the land which is still smoking from the fire and the farmer follows behind and sows, the thrall digs trenches around the arable land and the farmer plows the field with the bullocks, which a slave woman or a slave child drives with a stick in hand.
>
> The farmer feeds cattle and pigs, the thrall mucks out the dung, the slave woman milks in the wooden pail, the farmer's wife churns butter and curdles [cheese], slave women and slave children drive cattle, goats, sheep and pigs out to the pastures, herd them and are responsible for them with their lives, the farmer slaughters and gelds, gorges on blood sausage and fried ballocks, the slave people take care of the waste.
>
> The slave's work is not always heavier but always deemed less and he toils not by free will or seemingly voluntarily as the farmer, all the same there is a kind of balance between farmer and slave, and what unites them is no less important than what divides them.

Rígsþula as well as *Slavar för Särkland* are pieces of literature and were not written as scientific historical works, although the author of *Rígsþula* is chronologically speaking considerably closer to the events treated by both authors, namely the thraldom in Scandinavia; indeed, the Icelandic(?) poet or scribe may well have lived in a society wherein thralls still existed or had existed until quite recently, which is why it is common today to maintain that a fairly high degree of accuracy ought to be attached to the author's presentation in order to throw some light on a possible historical reality.[2]

Trälens göra är inte alltid tyngre men ständigt mindre ansett och han sliter inte frivilligt eller till synes frivilligt som bonden, ändå råder ett slags balans mellan bonde och träl, och vad som förenar dem är inte mindre viktigt än det som åtskiljer dem.

[2] On such considerations, particularly of the historical value of Old Icelandic literature, see the discussion in Preben Meulengracht Sørensen 1991 and 1993, Theodore M. Andersson 1964, 1967, 2003, and Andersson and Miller 1989.

Also Artur Lundkvist's presentation appears historically reasonable and would slot into a peasant society of the type hinted at by a legal clause in the Frostathing Law, which states that an ordinary farm in Trøndelag, Norway, had twelve cows, two horses, and three thralls (or servants/farmhands).

A male thrall's work tasks probably varied a great deal depending on what function he fulfilled in society.[3] Pure work thralls probably existed, at least on royal farms and chieftains' farms, most likely also to a great extent on large farms, and perhaps also to some extent on ordinary farms.[4] A special task for a thrall, as mentioned, was to function as executioner,[5] which, of course, goes well with the fact that a thrall is often used when someone is to be murdered in the Icelandic sagas. As will be discussed in connection with archaeological evidence, there are grounds for assuming that these pure work slaves lived in byres and stables or rooms adjoining to such outhouses where animals were kept. These thralls were probably given the most monotonous, heaviest, and dirtiest jobs, such as digging, plowing with an ard, spreading manure, and cleaning away dung; compare the Frostathing Law's statement regarding work tasks for someone who had been a thrall: *oc tók hann hvárki til repis ne til reko* ("and he picked up neither rope nor spade").[6] And young thrall-boys were probably given the work of herding cattle, sheep, and goats. An animal that thralls were probably not allowed to handle was the horse, this was the farmer's privilege; perhaps the thrall might be allowed to tend to and feed the horse.

It must have been true that in Scandinavia certain thralls had other, more skilled and highly valued tasks. In the case of *brytar*—discussed in-depth previously—this seems certain. A *bryti* was, at least during the Viking Age, a sort of farm steward who ran a (presumably large) farm owned by the king or by a nobleman; an example is the *bryti* Tolir who is mentioned on the Hovgården runestone. A skilled and presumably highly regarded trade was the blacksmith's. This shows, as mentioned earlier, if nothing else in the occurrence of the word in place-names (*Smedby*) and in legal clauses in the Early Anglo-Saxon laws. As the inscription on the Hørning rune stone shows, thralls during the Viking Age could be blacksmiths, presumably for some nobleman. One such (perhaps two) is the Tóki smith who appears in the Hørning rune stone inscription in Hjelmslev in Denmark (*DR* 58): "Tóki

[3] Cf. Gjessing 1862 pp. 149 ff.
[4] See Myrdal 2011.
[5] Gjessing 1862 pp. 160–161.
[6] FrL 10:47; cf. Skyum-Nielsen 1979 p. 144 and Krag 1982 p. 217.

Smith raised the stone in memory of Thorgísl Gudhmundr's son, who gave him gold(?) and freedom (or: . . . made him a member of the family and gave him freedom)." It seems to have been so that this Thorgísl Gudhmundr's son was Tóki's master and that he granted him freedom and showed his appreciation by leaving some of his fortune to the freed slave, perhaps as seed money for his new life in freedom. It is maybe the same Tóki smith who appears on the Grensten stone in Middelsom (*DR* 91): "Tóki smith raised this stone in memory of Hrifli, son of Ásgeirr Björn's son." If this is the case, it must indicate that Tóki was a socially rather highly regarded man who had the resources to raise two rune stones.

This fact, that slaves could be blacksmiths and that smiths were often highly regarded craftsmen, is evidenced also by the legal clause in King Æthelberht's Law (560–616), mentioned earlier, which treats the king's unfree official smith. In early medieval Bavaria the situation was similar. It is stated in *Lex Baiuvariorum* that a blacksmith was particularly important and that even if he were unfree he was highly valued.[7] Around the middle of the eighth century the Bavarian Duke Odilo donated to the monastery of Mondsee several beekeepers, three blacksmiths, a cook, and a wine maker. In 908 a suffragan bishop acquired through trade with the monastery of Freising a smith, a potter, a baker, and a fisherman. But smiths could also be free. The freeborn blacksmith (*ingenuus faber*) Afbaldus settled in a "slave homestead" in Lauterback in 820/821 and married a female slave, Kisa, with whom he had two unfree children. According to Bavarian law, if a free man had a child with an unfree woman then the child would be unfree. Unlike Roman law, according to which the child's legal status was determined by the mother's, there was only one way of securing the freedom of children in Bavaria, namely if both parents were free; all other combinations that included one unfree party resulted in the child being born as a slave, a situation known as *deterior conditio* in Latin. This system, which also existed, for example, in China, resulted in the significant increase of the slave population within such societies.

A female slave's work tasks are discernible partly from the discussion of terms for female slaves discussed previously.[8] These must to a great extent have been occupied in running the household (cf. the *deigja* 'bread-bakeress'). That many female slaves with newborn children were also given

[7] Hammer 2002 p. 21.
[8] See Myrdal 2003, 2011; cf. Gjessing 1862 pp. 155 ff.

the task of being wet nurses seems reasonable to assume and may find some support in the previously summarized anecdote from *Egil's saga* about the affection between Egill and his *ambátt*. A supplement to this is found in the Older Västgöta Law, which rules that if a female slave has children and the father is a free man then the father of the children must compensate the slave's owner for the loss of labor days in connection with childbirth until the female slave "is able to turn quern and milk cow" (Book of Marriage, 6:3). Grinding seed on a hand mill,[9] milking cows,[10] sheep, and goats as well as doing laundry were presumably tasks performed by female slaves. In the Gulathing Law (57:6) it says that carrying water from the well was also the duty of the female slave.[11]

Grinding seed, presumably by hand mill, occurs several times as the work of female slaves in various eddic poems, so frequently that it seems safe to assume that this task was strongly linked to female slaves on a farm, otherwise this theme would hardly have been used so often in the poems. In *Helgakviða Hundingsbana II*, the hero Helgi dresses up in a slave woman's garments and goes to grind seed, which should be understood in such a way that this work was typical for a female slave, so that Helgi would not be found out. Also in the poem *Helgakviða Hundingsbana I* (st. 35; see later) it is made clear that grinding seed must have been a task that was identified as a female slave's work on a farm. Here, a derogatory remark is made about a man who spent time near the querns and kissed the slave women (*á kvernom, kystir þýiar*). *Grottasǫngr* tells of how the Danish King Fróði buys two strong female slaves from the Swedish King Fjǫlnir so that they can turn the magical mill *Grotti*. Female slaves were used specifically for grinding not only in Scandinavia but also in Anglo-Saxon England. In early laws from Kent (King Æthelberht's Law from c. 600), female slaves are ranked with regard to the penalties that must be paid if they were raped. If a man had sexual intercourse with the king's slave woman (*Gif man wið cyninges mægdenman geligeþ*), he must pay a compensation of 50 shillings. If the slave woman was a *grindende þeowa*, that is to say a slave who ground (seed), the fine was 25 shillings, but if she was "third class," the fine was only 12 shillings. If a man forced himself onto a

[9] Thus, e.g., *King Valdemar's Law for Sjælland*, 13 (*DGL* 8 p. 228).

[10] Grinding and milking are mentioned in the *Older Västgöta Law*, Book of Marriage, 11 (*SGL* 1, Collin and Schlyter [eds.] p. 147).

[11] Tore Iversen (1997 pp. 123–124) emphasizes how little the written sources tell us of tasks and work of slave women.

slave woman belonging to a nobleman (*eorles*), a *birele* "one who carries the drinking cup, one who serves," he must pay a fine of 12 shillings. If a man had sexual intercourse with a *birele*-slave woman belonging to a tax-paying man, that is an ordinary farmer, he must pay 6 shillings as compensation and if she was "second class" the fine was 50 *sceattas*, but if she was "third class" the payment was only 30 *sceattas*.

It should probably not be underestimated that buying and taking captive women as slaves for sexual purposes was part of slaveholding in the Viking Age.[12] In this context it is natural to point out the existence of so-called *bortmagad*, that is a sort of "well-being slaves," literally, however, "female table servants," that the Frisian Law distinguishes from *ancilla pecuariae*, ordinary work slaves.[13] *Bortmagad* refers to female slaves in a home who apparently, according to the Frisian Law, *Lex Frisionum*, could be used as sexual partners.

That female slaves were the objects of love in Scandinavia may be indicated by the aforementioned passage of *Helgakviða Hundingsbana I*, stanza 35:

Þar mun Hǫðbroddr	There *Hǫðbroddr* shall
Helga finna,	find *Helgi*,
flugtrauðan gram,	a chieftain who doesn't flee,
í flota miðiom,	in the middle of the fleet.
sá er opt hefir	He has often
ǫrno sadda,	fed the eagles,
meðan þú á kvernom	while you by the querns
kystir þýiar![14]	were kissing slave women![15]

[12] Iversen 1997 pp. 154–157, Karras 1994, and Brink 2019a; cf. Hellie 1982 pp. 115 ff.

[13] *Lex Frisionum* XIII:I: *Qui cum ancilla alterius, quae nec mulgere nec molere solet, quam bortmagad vocant, moechatus fuerit, solidorum XII mulctam domino eius cogatur exsolvere*, "He who fornicates with another man's slave (*ancilla*), who neither milks nor grinds [with hand quern], and who is called *bortmagad* [Eng. *table maiden*, Germ. *Tischmagd*], must pay a fine of 12 solidi to her master" (see, e.g., http://www.keesn.nl/lex/lex_en_text.htm#Stupro). Cf. von Olberg (1987 p. 421), who emphasizes that a *bortmagad* was a young, minor female; see also von Olberg 1991 pp. 227 ff.

[14] *Edda* ed. Neckel p. 131.

[15] My trans. (Cf. Erik Brate, *Eddan* 1978 [1913], p. 155.) The stanza is difficult to translate. Björn Collinder in his "free" translation into Swedish of the *Edda* has realized that Helgi "kissed the slave woman," but Collinder writes that this happened by the "mill," which is anachronistic and not grammatically congruent with *á kvernom* (*Den poetiske Edda*, trans. B. Collinder, 3rd ed. Stockholm 1972, p. 172).

The passage should probably be understood so that Helgi is described as the hero he was, who never fled from his ship and who fed eagles, that is to say he killed many men, but "you," coward and struck by love-sickness, stood by the grinding querns (hand mills of stone) and engaged in lovemaking with slave women (*kystir þýiar*), who were presumably grinding seed.

Another eddic poem, *Guðrúnarkviða III*, begins by narrating how the hero Atli had a slave woman named Herkja, who had previously been Atli's *frilla* or mistress (*Herkja hét ambótt Atla; hon hafði verit frilla hans*). It is clear that slave owners kept certain slave women as mistresses for a longer or shorter time; presumably until he bought a younger and more attractive slave woman.

It seems that we must reckon with polygyny in Scandinavia in the Viking Age, or at least that a (wealthy) man could have a wife and one or several concubines, even living in the same household.[16] This is evidenced in the old Norse sagas, hinted at on runestones and commented on by Adam of Bremen in his *Gesta* (4:21), who claims that the "lecherous" Swedish males, each have, after their capability, one, two, three or more wives at the same time, and rich men and princes have so many they can not be counted! It would not be an adventurous guess to assume that many of these concubines and "extra wives" may have been slave women brought from foreign countries.

The perhaps most important evidence for Scandinavians keeping slave women as concubines is found in Ibn Fadlan's description from the early tenth century. Ibn Fadlan, or *Aḥmad ibn Faḍlān ibn al-ʿAbbās ibn Rāšid ibn Ḥammād*, as was his impressive full name, was evidently sent by the caliph of Baghdad for diplomatic negotiations with and religious mission among the Turkish peoples to the north. From his travel descriptions, selected parts are included in works from the twelfth century and later.[17]

During his visit to the king of the *Saqāliba* people,[18] it happened that Ibn Fadlan encountered a people who were called *Rūs* and who are generally

[16] See Auður Magnúsdóttir 2001, 2008, Raffield, Price, and Collard 2017b, esp. p. 169.

[17] The following discussion is based on Montgomery 2000 (cf. Stig Wikander's translation from 1978 pp. 64–69).

[18] The Arabic word *Saqāliba* (or *Sakaliba*) is a Byzantine loanword, a corruption of Greek *Σκλαβηνοί sklavênoí*, shortened to *Σκλάβοι sklávoi* "Slavs" (see Kahane and Kahane 1962, Nazmi 1998 p. 74, Epstein 2001 p. 18, Pohl 2013, Zeuske 2018 pp. 51–52). The semantics are very complex: it can in the Arabic sources denote slaves, especially white slaves, but also Slavs, or Volga Bulghars, mercenaries, and even white men and western Europeans, as discussed during a Near Eastern and Islamic Studies seminar by Professor Eduard Mühle, Münster ("The Perception of Slavs/Saqaliba in Arabic Sources of the 9th–12th Centuries") at the Institute of Advanced Studies, Princeton, November 22, 2017. Standard lexica have: "the designation in mediaeval Islamic sources for the Slavs and other fair-haired, ruddy-complexioned peoples of Northern Europe" (EOI 8 p. 872), and "the

taken by scholars to be Swedes (cf. *Ruotsi* and *Roslagen*) who traded by the Volga. The description given of the Rūs is detailed and appears to concur with what is known from archaeological finds from Gotland and Sweden at the same time, that is, the early tenth century. Ibn Fadlan's description of how the Rūs sacrifice to their gods and idols for good luck in trade is famous, as is his description of preparations for the funeral and cremation of a Rūs chieftain.

Ibn Fadlan's description of the preparations and rituals surrounding the chieftain's funeral is extensive, and many aspects are apparently reliable, but for our purposes it is of interest that one of the chieftain's slave women had a significant role to play in the ritual. Following his death, the slave women were asked who among them wished to die with her master. Once the choice of woman had been made, she was given over to two other slave women, who washed her feet and followed her everywhere. During the period in which preparations were carried out, taking up several days, the slave woman is said to have been drinking and singing every day, "happy and high-spirited." When the day came for the funeral pyre to be lit, with the chieftain and his slave woman, a ship was brought up onto dry land and rigged out. Later, an older woman entered the proceedings; she was known as the "angel of death" and was to kill the slave women later on. On this day, the slave woman went from tent to tent among the Rūs and had sexual intercourse with the men who afterward apparently said to her: "Greet your lord and tell him that I did this out of love for him." Toward evening they led the slave woman to a sort of "gate" where a ritual was carried out in which the "gate" apparently constituted a metaphor for the Otherworld, the realm of the dead. The slave woman was then given great amounts of beer to drink, probably in order to intoxicate her and numb her mind. When she was groggy she was led into a tent and six men entered to have sexual intercourse with her. Then they placed the slave woman next to her master, two held her hands and two held her feet, upon which the "angel of death" put a rope around her neck and gave the ends to two men who pulled at them. She herself stuck a broad knife in between the slave woman's ribs several times, while the two men strangled

Slavs and other fair-haired, ruddy-complexioned peoples of northern Europe; ethnic groups of central or eastern Europe; white slaves of European origin; Germanic tribes" (EOI Gloss. and Index p. 308). For an authoritative discussion of *Sakāliba*, especially the difficulties of placing these people at a geographical location, see P. B. Golden in EOI 8 pp. 872–878. See also Nazmi 1998 pp. 74–97, Mishin 1998, and Watson 2001.

her. The slave woman and her master were then placed on the ship, which was set alight.[19]

It is clear from this that a chieftain among the Rūs had more slave women. In another place, Ibn Fadlan describes how the king of the Rūs had four hundred men (presumably his retinue) in his "castle," who interestingly are said to fall with him and let themselves be killed for him. Each one of these men had a slave woman who is said to serve him, washing his head, cooking food, and making drink, as well as another one who sleeps with him. Often the king or possibly individual warriors, Ibn Fadlan is not clear on this point, have sexual intercourse with these slave women in the presence of his comrades-in-arms.[20] Exactly this fact that such erotic flagrancies took place quite openly among the Rūs, without any shame, is something that clearly shocked Ibn Fadlan and he returns to this on several occasions. When, for example, he describes the Rūs as filthily unclean and akin to stray donkeys he says that they live on the shores (of the Volga) in houses with ten to twenty people in each. They are said to have with them beautiful slave women, intended for the slave traders. Indignant, Ibn Fadlan writes:

> One man will have intercourse with his slave-girl while his companion looks on. Sometimes a group of them comes together to do this, each in front of the other. Sometimes indeed the merchant will come in to buy a slave-girl from one of them and he will chance upon him having intercourse with her, but <the Rūs> will not leave her alone until he has satisfied his urge.[21]

From this eyewitness account, it appears reasonable to conclude that the Swedes of the Viking Age (if they are to be identified with the Rūs) must have had a fairly shameless attitude to sexuality. Copulation was clearly not something that was reserved for privacy behind closed doors.

In connection with this there is reason to pay attention to sexual slavery in other well-known Christian and non-Christian slave societies. Sex slaves were kept in classical Rome,[22] but the best known is probably the sex slavery that existed in the Arab world and in the Ottoman

[19] For this famous episode, see the translation in Montgomery 2000. For an analysis of Ibn Fadhlan's text, see also Montgomery 2008 and Jonsson Hraundal 2013, and for ritual aspects of the text, Warmind 1995 and Schjødt 2010.

[20] Wikander 1978 p. 69.

[21] Montgomery 2000 p. 9.

[22] See, e.g., Pomeroy 1975 and Kolendo 1981.

Empire.[23] It has been claimed that here the most common reason for acquiring slaves was to exploit them sexually.[24] At any rate, the primary role of slaves in Muslim countries was not to carry out physical work; here, slavery was not an economical method of production.[25] During the slave raids that were carried out, the men and older women were often killed while the young women were captured. Ibn Battuta (*ʾAbū ʿAbd al-Lāh Muḥammad ibn ʿAbd al-Lāh l-Lawātī ṭ-Ṭanǧī ibn Baṭūṭah*), a Moroccan scholar and traveler in the Sudan in the fourteenth century,[26] tells of how he journeyed with a caravan consisting of 600 slave women,[27] and even around the middle of the nineteenth century the Lithuanian George Schweinfurt encountered a slave caravan consisting of 150 women in North Africa.[28] A eunuch, a castrated man, was placed as the guardian of a harem or the slave women of a household. There has been a long-standing idea that slave traders in what is now France castrated young slave boys in order to increase their price before selling them on southward into Muslim Spain;[29] and it was believed that especially Jewish slave traders specialized in such procedures,[30] however newer research strongly opposes such claims.[31] Large numbers of castrated young men, meant to be sold as eunuchs to the Muslim world, were "produced" at well-known slave-trading places, such as Venice, Verdun, and the Andalusian region of Spain.[32] In Muslim slave markets, eunuchs fetched the highest prices, followed by young beautiful white women who could be used as concubines, a more polite word for sex slaves.[33] As is well-known, this system survived for a long time. In 1908, the Turkish ruler Abdul-Hamid still had a harem of 370 women and 127 eunuchs.[34]

[23] See, e.g., Toledano 1982, 1998, Willis (ed.) 1985, Gordon 1987, Nordberg 1988 pp. 199–205, Erdem 1996, and Marmon (ed.) 1999.
[24] Gordon 1987 p. 79.
[25] Nordberg 1988 p. 172.
[26] See the impressive article about Ibn Battuta and his journeys in Wikipedia (https://en.wikipedia.org/wiki/Ibn_Battuta).
[27] Bovill 1968 p. 96.
[28] Schweinfurt 1874 pp. 346–347.
[29] McCormick 2001 p. 754, *pace* Toch 2014.
[30] Verlinden 1988 p. 337; cf. Eisenberg 2003 p. 759.
[31] See Toch (2014), who has some devastating criticism of especially Verlinden on this matter.
[32] Constable 1996 pp. 96–97.
[33] Mowafi 1981 p. 12, Gordon 1987 p. 80, Zilfi 2010, and McKee 2014. Slaves were nonetheless found everywhere in society: within the family, as workers, and in the household, to a great extent as soldiers, etc. Most interesting is perhaps the existence of slaves and eunuchs in very high-ranking positions within administration and management; see, e.g., Mire 1985 pp. 104–105 and Nordberg 1988 pp. 176 ff.
[34] Gordon 1987 p. 90.

In a thesis treating the slavery of Egypt and the Sudan during the nineteenth century, Reda Mowafi establishes that the most important driving force within this system was to consider the great need for young women. Regular work slaves actually appeared very rarely. Instead, it was concubines that were wanted, preferably young, white women. In Egypt, a man could only have four wives, but as many concubines as he wanted, as many as he could afford. These slave women, in harems and private households, were used for household chores as well as the sexual services they were required to perform in accordance with their owner's wishes.[35]

In the Ottoman Empire, which dominated the Middle East and southeastern Europe after the conquest of Eastern Rome in 1453, that is Byzantium, harems and the keeping of slave women for sexual purposes were also widespread over an extended period of time.[36]

As emphasized earlier, presumably a great many young women were also taken captive and sold into thraldom in Scandinavia in order to serve mainly as sexual concubines. It has even been claimed that the capture of female slaves was more common than the capture of men in Anglo-Saxon England,[37] something that is impossible to prove due to the difficulties involved in confirming that hypothesis from the sources. It might be possible to argue for this by claiming that the men were usually killed in the fighting and that those who survived were executed on the spot, while women and children were taken as slaves, but this would be mere guesswork. Concerning the conditions in Scandinavia, Tore Iversen believes that the slave owner's sexual exploitation of his slave women must be regarded as a common occurrence and "a matter of routine" (No. *rutinemessig*).[38]

A late offshoot of this trade in sex slaves is witnessed in Europe today. It is called "trafficking": predominantly young girls from former eastern bloc countries, such as the Baltic countries, Poland, Moldavia, Chechnya, Belarus, and others, are enticed to come to western Europe, where they are deprived of their passports, are raped and frightened into obedience, and placed in brothels as regular sex slaves. In 1998, the newspapers of Genoa reported that a gang, kidnapping or luring Nigerian girls to Europe in order to use them as sex slaves in brothels, had been splintered. The girls were auctioned in Genoa

[35] Mowafi 1981 pp. 10 ff. On the Muslim capture of slaves in Europe and Africa far into the 1800s, see also Davis 2001.

[36] See, e.g., Zilfi 2010.

[37] Thus Karras 1994 p. 17. Cf. Pelteret 1981 pp. 102 ff.

[38] Iversen 1997 p. 154.

and the price of these Nigerian girls varied from ten thousand to thirty thousand dollars, depending on looks and age.[39]

The question of women's apparently obvious control of their own sexuality and the legal protection that they enjoy in this respect at different times is a (political) mine field of research.[40] What was the difference—from the point of view of the individual—between being captured by a viking and exploited as concubine and probably household slave on his Scandinavian farm, and a twelve-year-old noble girl who—without her consent—was married off to a completely unknown sixty-year-old nobleman, possibly in another country with another language, in order to serve as his sexual partner and bearer of his children? Hopefully, the time between the duties was more pleasant and less demanding for the latter. Both, however, were sexually abused according to our Western moral standards. Legally speaking, both ends of the latter transaction were in full accordance to the law, while in the former only the action that took place in the captive's homeland was illegal. In the perpetrator's homeland, it was law that the owner had the right to have sexual intercourse with his slave. Historical examples of this abomination are many; one is Charlemagne's third wife, Hildegard, who is said to have been constantly pregnant from the age of fourteen until her death at the age of twenty-four.[41] Hildegard, for sure, lived in the eighth century, but, if we are entirely honest in our indignation, then we must acknowledge that Swedish law in the twenty-first century apparently allows a teenage girl to be married off to an unknown man without her consent and without intervention of the Swedish legal system.[42] This is indicative of political cowardice and is both morally offensive and legally indecent. Thus, a woman's right to her own body and her freedom to make her own choices in life are difficult and sensitive topics even today.

The question of sexual exploitation is linked to the question of "honor" in these cultures. As in many cultures around the world—ancient, old, and (unfortunately also, reintroduced in western Europe) current—the honor of a family or kin is related to the chastity of the young, unmarried women. This led to the absurd consequence in the laws and customs that the master killing a slave did not particularly give rise to any legal or social condemnations, but

[39] See Epstein 2001 pp. 2–3.

[40] A frightening report is found in Barry 1984.

[41] Bullough 1991 p. 17.

[42] The weakness of our politicians and the intellectual "nomenclatura" of Sweden is conspicuous in this respect; for a nonsentimental description of the concept of honor in cultures around the Mediterranean and in Muslim countries, see, e.g., Barry 1984 pp. 179 ff.

if an "outsider" had sexual intercourse with that same master's slave women (or any female dependent of that family), there was a vigorous response; the authority held by the master and the family was breached and this led to severe legal punishments, if not revenge killings and feuds. Sex with another person's slave woman was one of the topics most frequently treated in the Barbarian (Germanic) law codes.[43]

On the whole, it is frighteningly complicated to discuss slavery and sexuality during the (Early) Viking Age, that is, prior to the moral code of the Christian Church permeating society, since we—apart from Ibn Fadlan's indignant description—know very little about what pre-Christian sexuality was like in Scandinavia.[44] That it was not fenced in by moral reservations, but presumably quite explicit can also be discerned from noting Adam of Bremen's great indignation at the unseemly behavior and shameful songs with sexual overtones that the *Svear* (Swedes) apparently performed as part of the heathen cult activities at Old Uppsala in the late eleventh century.[45] But was sexuality entirely free? Perhaps not, since hardly any culture at any time displays that kind of polycoity.[46] Sexuality appears to have been controlled by social conventions—for instance, a highborn person does not engage in sexual behavior with a lowborn person (unless it takes place in secret), regardless of whether the person in question is a captive or not. A legal clause from the Visigothic Law of Spain can serve as an example; it treats the (improbable) scenario of a free woman engaging in sexual behavior with an unfree man, something that was considered as going against nature. In this case the law said she must die—she and the male slave should be whipped in front of the judge and then burned. But if a free woman would marry a slave who belonged to someone else, or fornicate with him, then the judge should separate them and sentence them to punishment, which was one hundred lashes each. In the patriarchal, phallocratic Visigothic society it was nonetheless—of course—entirely legitimate for a male slave owner to exploit his female slaves as he wished. There were no obstructive restrictions or legal clauses to prevent that.[47]

The extent to which sexual exploitation of slaves was completely free of social restrictions is, however, a question over which opinions are divided. Ruth

[43] See Rio 2017 pp. 231–232 and the sources in n. 93.

[44] For a discussion of this sensitive topic, see Jochens 1991, Karras 1992, Auður Magnúsdóttir 2001, 2008, Price 2005, and Raffield et al. 2017b.

[45] Adam of Bremen, *Gesta*, ch. 4:27.

[46] Cf., however, Goody 1976 p. 42 and Karras 1990 p. 143, 1994 p. 19.

[47] Bonnassie 1991 pp. 72–73.

Mazo Karras represents the restrictive opinion,[48] while, for example, the expert Orlando Patterson in his studies of the topic has found only one society in which it was socially stigmatizing for a man to have sexual intercourse with his female slave, namely among the Gilyaks of southeastern Siberia.[49]

The question of "sexual lust" is also a flammable topic—is it socially or biologically conditioned and how has it been expressed during different periods of our history? The questions are mounting and the research field is mined, but I think that, in summary, it is safe to assume that Nordic vikings on raiding expeditions brought slave women home to Scandinavia not only to have them bake, clean, and cook.

[48] Karras 1994.
[49] Patterson 1982 pp. 50, 229–230.

10

Evidence for Thralls in Scandinavian Place Names

It has for a long time been assumed that thralls can be traced in Scandinavian place-name material.[1] As we have seen, different kinds of slaves could be referred to with special terms. It would therefore be expected that those terms would appear in place names. Close analysis shows that it is very hard to interpret and isolate these elements in place names with much certainty. The only reasonably certain place-name element that actually helps us is ON *þræll*, Sw. *träl*, Da. *træl*, No. *trell*.

This result chimes with what is found in, for example, England. Here, too, we have a good many terms for slaves. But an analysis of the Anglo-Saxon place-name material reveals very few, if indeed any, certain examples of place names containing slave designations. One of the most common terms for "slave" OE *þéow(a)* thus seems not to occur at all in place names.[2] The word *wealh*, which appears with the meaning 'slave', does occur here and there in English place names,[3] but since the word also has the meaning 'Briton (of Celtic descent), Welshman' as well as 'foreigner', then it cannot be said for certain that all *wealh*-names have denoted settlements with slaves.[4]

Tore Iversen has identified some terms that he reckons appear in Norwegian place names.[5] He classifies them according to various degrees of probability. Of those listed here, some designations must be said to constitute very uncertain indicators; one such is *folk*, which may find various other and more probable explanations (the man's name *Folke*, gen. pl. of *folk* 'people', etc.). The element *man* is interesting, but also in this case several

[1] See, e.g., Olsen 1926 pp. 97 ff. In the analysis that follows, I come to the same result as Bent Jørgensen (1995 p. 8), namely that there are very few cases where slaves are found in place names (in his case, discussing the word *træl*).

[2] Faull 1975 p. 33, cf. Pelteret 1995 p. 320.

[3] Zachrisson 1927, Ekwall 1953, Smith 1956:2 pp. 242–243, Finberg 1964 p. 34, Cameron 1980, Watts and Prince 1982, and Wakeford 1984.

[4] Faull 1975 and Pelteret 1995 p. 320.

[5] Iversen 1997, 2003.

Thraldom. Stefan Brink, Oxford University Press. © Oxford University Press 2021.
DOI: 10.1093/oso/9780197532355.003.0010

options can be considered. To assume from the beginning that place names with *Man-* would contain the word *maðr* in the meaning 'thrall' is rather hazardous, even if the possibility that the word sometimes occurs in a narrower semantic sense should not be neglected. It is more plausible that, in the cases where *Man-* occurs in place names with the possible meaning 'thrall', this is rather to be understood as the word *man* n. 'thrall, female slave or slaves collectively'.[6] Nor is there anything to directly support that the word *kot* 'little house' should have indicated living quarters for thralls specifically. Instead, some place names, *Kallakot* and the like, are interesting in this connection. They are found in several places around the North Sea. This name has usually been interpreted as an earlier **kaldakot* 'the cold little house'. However, it may also be that the name is instead an appellative **karlakot*, a compound of *kot* 'single house, cottage' and *karli*, which appears as a man's name in *Landnámabók*, especially for thralls![7] **Karlakot* could then mean 'thrall's or thralls' *kot*'.[8]

Generally, I think that many of Iversen's examples of place names potentially relating to thralls must be weeded out. The only fairly certain examples are names containing *Træl-*, while some of the listed names might contain *ambátt*, *þý*, and perhaps *man*.

In Denmark there are also traces of thralls in place names. The most certain example is probably *Trellerup* near Roskilde (Threlthorp 1203, Threllethorp c. 1376) and other names in *Træl-*. Uncertain but possible additions to this list are *Manderup*, which is found among other places near Roskilde (Manthorp 1268), *Manstrup* in Vendsyssel (Manstrvp 1462), and *Mandø* near Tønder (Mannæø 1200s), which may contain gen. pl. and sg. of ODa *maþr* or perhaps rather *man* n. In some Danish place names *brytar* can be traced, for instance in *Brydeballe* in Lolland (Brydeball 1422), *Brydegård* near Assens in Fyn (Brydegaard 1484), *Brøderup* in the district of Bårse, Præstø (Brydæorp 1401), *Brøttrup*, Slet hd, Jutland (Brutitorp 1200s), and *Bryrup* near Skanderborg in Jutland (Brythorp 1416).[9] The village of *Nørre-Sæby*

[6] Fritzner, article *man* n., and Olson 1916 p. 77.

[7] See the discussion on the name *Karli* and the word *karli* later.

[8] The word **karli* (probably unrecorded in the sources; see what follows) and the place name *Karlakot*, *Kaldakot*, *Caldecott*, etc., deserve detailed scrutiny. The word *kot* n. is evidenced late in Scandinavian languages (see de Vries 1962 p. 327) and might be a loan from OE *cot*, considering the distribution of the names. I have previously discussed place-names such as *Kallakot* in western Sweden (Brink 1997b p. 80), presenting an interpretation that I am now inclined to partly revise along the lines staked out here; due to young sources it is difficult to determine whether *Kallekot*, etc., has a background in *Kaldakot* (< *kaldr* 'cold') or *Karlakot* (< **karli*/*Karli*); cf. Iversen 1997 p. 249.

[9] Hald 1957 cols. 273–274 and Gissel 1981 p. 26.

in Nørre hd, Lolland, appears in King Valdemar's thirteenth-century Land-Register as *Brytisæby* and is said there to be the king's property. The same goes for *Brøns* (*Brytyenes*) parish near Tønder.[10] Much speaks in favor of the two latter examples revealing a *bryti* (*villicus*) in royal service, of the kind discussed previously.

Turning to the Swedish place names for an impression of how common slaveholding was during prehistoric and early medieval times, the answer would be that thralls were particularly uncommon in Sweden. Thralls would—judging by the names—have made up only something like one per mille (‰)of the population of the country. This is to be seen against estimates of thralls making up 20–30 percent of the Norwegian population during that period,[11] and 30–40 percent of the Icelandic population.[12] The few names that can be listed are the following: *Trälarp* in Nye parish, Östra hd, Småland (Trelutorp 1541, Treletorp 1551, Treletorp 1558); *Trälarp*, noted in 1927 as an abandoned village belonging to Bosgården in the hamlet and parish of Vistorp, Vartofta hd, Västergötland; †*Trälaryd* in Väderstad parish, Göstring hd, Östergötland (trælarydh 1447); *Trälsilt* in Knäred parish, Hök hd, Halland (Trælsryt 1407, Threlsrodht 1470, trelsrydh 1475)—in this name we probably have gen. sg. of the word *träl* in the first element, and where the second element *-ryd* was replaced with *-hult*;[13] *Trälebo* in Älmeboda parish, Konga hd, Småland (Trellebo 1667); *Trälebo*, a hamlet in Ettak, Velinge parish, Vartofta hd, Västergötland; *Trälebo* in Gryts parish, Hammarkind hd, Östergötland (Trählbo 1725); *Trälbo*, a village in Gällaryd parish, Östbo hd, Småland, and possibly †*Trälbo* in Torsö parish (now Otterstad parish), Kålland hd, Västergötland (Trälboo 1536); *Trälsätter* in Vånga parish, Finspångalän hd, Östergötland (Trælsæter 1420); *Trälket* (Trelicke 1540) in Halna parish and the neighboring †*Trälket* (now *Åkersberg*) (trälickie 1552) in Fägre parish, both in Vadsbo hd, Västergötland, which are thought to have constituted one settlement unit and derived from an OSw *Thrælalykkia*;[14] and finally *Trulletorp* (< *Trältorp*) in Grödinge parish, Svartlösa hd, Södermanland. Several of these names lack medieval written forms and it is therefore uncertain whether all represent early medieval names containing *träl* 'slave'.

[10] Hald 1957 cols. 273–274.
[11] Benedictow 1996 pp. 174 ff.
[12] Gísli Sigurðsson 1988 p. 31.
[13] See Ståhl 1948 p. 32.
[14] According to Ivar Lundahl in *SOSk* 11:2 pp. 60, 72.

Apart from OSw *þræl*, the word *bryti* occurs here and there in southern and middle Swedish place names. In the cases where the word occurs in names ending in, for example, *-by* and *-stad* we are likely faced with the pre-Christian word meaning 'unfree(?) farm manager'. It can probably be assumed that the background for an OSw *Brytiastadhir* or *Brytiaby(r)* was either that a *bryti*, a "king's *bryti*" (as in the inscription on the Hovgården rune stone in Adelsö) or a *bryti* of an estate occupied the farm as manager of a royal or of some nobleman's property, or that a *bryti* (perhaps a freed one such) acquired or established a farm here. In some interesting cases, place names containing *bryti* occur within what we call central-place milieus, which are places thought to have had a central administrative function during the period roughly AD 600–1000. One such example is undoubtedly *Brottby* in Össebygarn parish, Vallentuna hd, in Uppland (j brytioby 1473, brytteby 1514, Brytby 1550). The settlement is centrally located in Attundaland, right by Långhundraleden, the old waterway from Trälhavet, a name of part of the Baltic Sea, up to Uppsala and central Uppland. Settlements neighboring *Brottby* include *Karlby*, *Gillberga*, *Husa*, and *Vada*, with the famous great burial mounds, which indicate an "aristocratic" central-place milieu. In this case, we would be dealing with a "managerial farm" occupied by a *bryti*. Moreover, it can be noted that the name *Brollsta* appears in a peripheral location to the northeast, a name Lars Hellberg has assumed to be derived from an earlier *Brytia-løstir* 'the *bryti*'s outfield'.[15] Centrally located within its own settlement district is also *Brottsta* in Fors, town of Eskilstuna, Södermanland (ij brythiastu*m* 1409, i Brythiastom 1414, i brythiastom 1450, i Brythiasthu*m*/-stom 1453, i brytijestom 1461, i bryttistha 1486). Once more, Lars Hellberg has noted this name and points out that the farm was situated some 3 kilometers west of *Tuna*, a name indicative of a central place, along with *Karlaby*, *Hov*, and *Fröslunda*.[16]

Brötsta (Jn brytiestum 1331) in Grödinge parish, Svartlösa hd, Södermanland, is known today as *Snäckstavik*, which was presumably the naval port for Svartlösa *hundari* (cf. *snækkia* 'war ship'), which is why the *bryti* who appears in the name has been assumed by Carl Ivar Ståhle to be a royal *bryti*.[17] In the vicinity of Brötsta, Lars Hellberg notes, appears *Svartalöt*, the old thing-site of the *hundari*, as well as *husaby*, now *Husby* in Grödinge.[18]

[15] Hellberg 1975 p. 102.
[16] Hellberg 1975 pp. 102–103.
[17] Ståhle 1946 p. 178.
[18] Hellberg 1975 p. 102.

Bröttjestad in Bredaryd parish, Västbo hd, Småland (ii brytiastadhom 1369, i bröttiestad 1594), likewise appears in the interesting context of a central place. The settlement borders on *Draftinge*, which is probably a derailed **Drav-Tuna* 'Tuna by Lake Draven', and *Karaby* (< *Karlaby*).[19] *Bröttjestad* in Slaka parish, Hanekind hd, Östergötland (j brytistatha 1381, i Brytyngxstadum 1408, i Britingxstadum 1420, j brytingsxstadhom 1454, j brytestada 1457, j brytigxstadhe 1465, brytiastada 1502?), between Vikingstad and Linköping, is interesting since the name shows up in two parallel forms during medieval times, *Brytiastadhom* and *Brytingsstadhom*, of which the latter variant apparently contains a designation for an inhabitant, *bryting*, which is perhaps to be understood as 'someone who lives in Bröttjestad'. This farm is not located in any obvious central-place milieu, and the *bryti* mentioned in this name is then perhaps best regarded as farm manager of a prehistoric estate. *Bryttby(n)* in Film parish, Oland hd, Uppland (Brötieby 1505, brytaby 1525?, j Brijteby 1545), perhaps has a special—late medieval—background and may be linked to the mining industry that has been carried out here near Dannemora since olden days. Lars Hellberg has interpreted the name in that way.[20]

The word *bryti* has moreover been assumed to appear in †*Bryttiaholm*, an islet near (Forn-)Sigtuna in Håtuna parish, Håbo hd, Uppland (prediolum dictum Bryttiaholm attinens ville veteri Sictunie 1348),[21] here perhaps referring to a royal *bryti*, as well as *Bryggholmen* in Valby parish, Trögden, Uppland (Bryttieholmen 1551), an island in Lake Mälaren, although it is uncertain what historical background this latter name has.

The name *Brytegården*, which occurs with some frequency, can be assumed to describe the farm occupied by the *bryti* of an estate. There are, as becomes evident later, examples from medieval records that support such a conclusion. †*Brytegården* in Ununge parish, Närdinghundra hd, Uppland (brythia gardhin 1460, brytio gardhen 1460, i brytiagarden 1491), is probably comparable to the *bryti*-farm that exists on an estate, with mill, cottages, and village, in Skebo during late medieval times (Skedboo qwærn jærnhyttona brytigardehe*n* oc torpp th*er* vnder liggia 1444, Skeedboo qwærn oc jærnhyttona oc brtiagardhen me*dh* thøm torpo*m* ther vnder liggia 1444). According to Karin Calissendorff, this *bryti* refers to the manager of the iron works of Sankta Klara monastery by Skebokvarn, which is the oldest

19 On *Bröttjestad*, see Hellberg 1975 p. 103, 1984–1985 p. 24, and Fridell 1996 p. 25.
20 Hellberg 1975 p. 102.
21 Thus Hellberg 1984–1985 p. 22.

iron works in Uppland, from 1440.[22] Other *bryti*-farms are encountered in late medieval times in the hamlet of Bärby in Giresta parish, Lagunda hd, Uppland (brytia gorde*n* 1453 or.); in Landeryd parish, Hansekind hd, Östergötland (j brytiagardenom 1408 or.); and in Trökörna parish in Viste hd, Västergötland (brytiagordhen); in †*Bryttegården*, a farm in the now vanished hamlet of Sätuna, in the city of Uppsala (een gård i Sätuna . . . hettandes Bryttegården 1594), †*Bryttgården* in the hamlet of Viksta, Viksta parish, Norunda hd, Uppland (Brytiagarden i vixstade 1473), †*Brytjegården*, a vanished farm in Magra parish, Bjärke hd, Västergötland (Bryttyagarden och halft rennene 1467, en øde thompt oc hether bryttye gardhen 1468). In the former **Husa*(*r*), which today appears as *Hossmo*, a parish in Möre in Småland, there was, judging by a medieval letter, a *bryti*'s farm (J husamo en brytia gard 1393).[23]

There is a *Brytiathorp* in Stjärnorps parish, Gullberg hd, Östergötland, known today as *Bryttjorp* (j brytiathorpe 1399, j brytiathorpe 1431), another is *Bryttorp* in Gryts parish, Hammarkind hd, also in Östergötland (brytiætorp 1453). *Bryttsät*(*t*)*er* in V. Husby parish, Hammarkind hd, Östergötland (Bryttsetter 1650) is surrounded by several -*torp* and -*säter* farms, which may have been managed by the *bryti* of Bryttsäter. Lars Hellberg proposes the interesting hypothesis that this farm was originally given to a *bryti* who had been the manager of *husabyn* in nearby Västra Husby, which is by no means unlikely.[24] In Småland there are some examples of *Brytiarydh*: *Bröttjaryd* in S. Hestra parish, Västbo hd (brythiaryt 1346, in brytiarydh 1350),[25] and *Bröttjaryd* in Söraby parish, Norrvidinge hd (Brötteryd, Brötieryd 1546).[26] *Brytängen* and *Brytåkern* also occur here and there, which can in some cases be assumed to contain our word *bryti*; the first elements are, however, open to interpretation.

This meager result can probably be explained in different ways. One is that thralls in active "service," so to speak, were not candidates for lending their names to settlements and fields. Only if exclusively one or more thralls lived at a farm would there be grounds for referring to this farm with a characterizing qualifier. In this context, it is interesting to note whether the first

[22] Calissendorff 1982–1983 p. 25.
[23] See Hellberg 1979 pp. 133, 161 n. 111.
[24] Hellberg 1975 p. 103.
[25] This name, *Brötjaryd*, in Södra Hestra parish, Västbo, is discussed by Roland Otterbjörk (1965 p. 129) in an article analyzing the oldest legal document (from 1330) written in Old Swedish, where the name form *bryrite* is identified with this *Brötjaryd* (Brytiarydh 1350).
[26] See Fridell 1992 p. 37.

elements appear in the singular or plural. From the aforementioned names, it is evident that *Trälarp*, †*Trälaryd*, *Trällebo*, †*Trälbo*, *Trälket*, and *Trältorp* apparently contain gen. pl. *Thræla-*, indicating a group of thralls, while *Trälsryd* and perhaps *Trälsäter* seem to contain gen. sg. *Thræls-*, indicating an individual thrall. We know very little about the running of farms in prehistoric times and thus about whether the thralls who might have existed there lived on the farm—in their own house or in the byre—or whether they were made to tend and work singular farms, as a kind of precursor to tenant farms. The previously mentioned clause in the Frostathing Law is contextually very interesting. It mentions a presumably "ordinary farm" in Trøndelag, Norway, during the twelfth and thirteenth centuries—a farm with twelve cows, two horses, and three thralls (or servants).[27] If the thralls lived on the farm, for example in the byre, as is hinted at from Eketorp ringfort on Öland,[28] there was no reason to point out the thralls in a place name. If, however, singular farms were run by thralls then, of course, their personal names might appear as qualifiers in compound place names. One possibility of tracing them would be if thralls could be shown to have names so distinctive that these can be identified in a corpus of names. Name-giving traditions for Scandinavian thralls must therefore be investigated.

The situation surrounding the occurrence of *bryti* in Swedish place names is a different case. There are more of these, but there is also the inherent uncertainty of whether we are dealing with unfree *brytar* in all instances, rather than free managers of estates during the late Middle Ages, when slavery had been abolished. The majority of the many *Brytegården* we encounter probably have such a background.

[27] FrL 4:44; Krag 1982 p. 210, Hagland and Sandnes 1994 p. 221, and Iversen 1997 p. 115.

[28] Personal communication from Professor Frands Herschend, Uppsala; cf. Nordström and Herschend 2003 pp. 58 ff.

11

How Were Thralls Identified?

vm han rijstir man at bathum nosum
thz ær threls merke oc ey frels mans

"If he slits a man at both nostrils
that is the mark of a slave and not of a free man"
—King Valdemar's Law for Sjælland

That many thralls *looked* different is apparent, partly from all the names of thralls that refer to dark complexions, partly from the fact that many thralls were war captives or bought in distant places. But since the thrall was an important financial resource it was common also to mark thralls so that, if they fled, they could be caught and returned.

From slavery especially in antiquity—but also later—we know that slaves could be marked and differentiated by cutting off all or parts of the ears, by branding with glowing iron or by tattooing the owner's name onto the slave's body.[1] In the Muslim world, slaves could be marked by having their nostrils slit.[2] Precisely scarring of the face, primarily by cutting off part of one or both ears or other soft parts, seems to have been common, a method also used for marking reindeer and sheep. This detestable practice, however, did not disappear with the fall of the Roman Empire. Mutilation and other ways of scarring the slave's body, especially the face, carried on into post-Roman times. It seems to have been particularly common to chop off the nose, sometimes the ears, a foot, a hand, the tongue, or the lips. There is even evidence that slaves were scalped; that is, they did not just have their heads shaved, but the roots of their hair were torn out.[3]

If any slave succeeded in fleeing, most slaving societies of ancient Europe had a strict set of regulations that effectively sentenced to death anyone who helped a runaway slave. An example of this is a law from Genoa in Italy

[1] Brink 1997a p. 454, Casares 2014 p. 106.
[2] Segal 2003 p. 77.
[3] Bonnassie 191 p. 20.

Thraldom. Stefan Brink, Oxford University Press. © Oxford University Press 2021.
DOI: 10.1093/oso/9780197532355.003.0011

around 1300. If a free person there helped, offered protection to, or stole a slave, the penalty was a fine of 50 lira or more (for instance, corresponding to several years' salary for a craftsman) plus the value of the slave to be paid to the slave owner on top of the loss of one hand. Exactly the amputation of a hand was, of course, devastating to someone who made their living from using their hands. A peculiar aspect of this law from Genoa was that the punishment for allowing a slave to be transported (into freedom) by boat was 100 lira or, if the perpetrator was unable to pay, the loss of a foot. With the physical repression there existed also a spatial repression that fettered slaves to a particular place. In Genoa, if a slave—without valid "passport"—was caught more than 10,000 paces outside of the town, the "finder" could demand a reward of 2 lira from the owner of the slave.[4]

Sometimes, slaves that were particularly prone to escape could be given special markings, as for instance in France around 1400, when a slave who had run away had his jaw marked in a characteristic way.[5] E. A. Thompson emphasizes that physical markings and mutilations could also have a preventive effect. He believes that facial or bodily marking or mutilation could discourage the slave from fleeing since he was so easily identified as a slave and could therefore readily be caught and returned to his master.[6]

Another physical characteristic of slaves was that they often had visible scars and marks caused by abuse, something that was noted in the introduction. It was, after all, the job of the slave owner to foster, dominate, and suppress a slave, which happened mainly by means of flogging and beating the slave,[7] not so seriously that the slave was damaged and lost the ability to work, but superficially, in order to cause pain and induce fear. This continuous chastisement meant that slaves in antiquity had extensive scars and wounds on their bodies, which was obviously stigmatizing and contributed further to the fact that they were differentiated from and despised by society. As has been pointed out by Thomas E. J. Wiedemann, physical punishment was considered right and just in ancient times. The classical world tolerated violence to an extent that frightens a modern person. Physical discipline was part of the consolidation of the social order: husband toward wife, parents toward children, and free toward unfree, and the unfree could always beat the animals. Thus, the philosopher Ammonius, when he thought his

[4] Epstein 2001 pp. 118–119.
[5] Epstein 2001 p. 119.
[6] Thompson 1957 p. 23.
[7] Cf. Wergeland 1900 p. 109, Finberg 1976 p. 61, and Skyum-Nielsen 1979 pp. 134–135.

students had eaten too much food, could let a slave be flogged before the afternoon class, just to exemplify the need for self-control. Sometimes, certain slave owners got carried away by their temper, resulting in purely sadistic punishments of slaves. Vedius Pollio ordered a slave boy, who had broken a precious crystal vase, to be punished by having him thrown into a fish pond wherein a shoal of lampreys slowly killed the boy, or when Emperor Hadrian became irritated with his secretary and had one of his eyes put out.[8]

Very little is known about how female slaves were treated in order to show that they were slaves. From Anglo-Saxon England it is known that one way of differentiating slave women from free women was to cut the hair off the slaves.[9]

If similar practices are sought in the Scandinavian sources, that is, ways of physically marking thralls, nothing is actually found. This is hardly down to Scandinavian slave owners being more empathetic or philanthropic in their outlook, thus refraining from marking and physically mutilating their slaves, but as a consequence of the poor source situation. All the more unique is, therefore, a passage from King Valdemar's Law for Sjælland (28), from medieval Denmark,[10] which says:

> *En vm swa kan comma at annar takir nokir frelsan man oc rijstir han a andre noos. tha bode han fare fierthung manbota. En vm han rijstir man at bathum nosum. tha bode han fore halwa manbødir. for thy at thz ær threls merke oc ey frels mans.*

Which in English translation reads:

> But if it so happens that someone takes a free man and slices one nostril, then a quarter of a man's compensation shall be paid for it. But if he slices both nostrils of the man, then he shall pay half a man's compensation, because that is the mark of a slave and not of a free man.[11]

[8] Wiedemann 1987 pp. 24–25.
[9] Finberg 1976 p. 57.
[10] *DGLL* 7 p. 94, cf. p. 211. This passage is from a section of King Valdemar's Law for Sjælland called the "Book of Inheritance and *orbodemål*" (Da. *orbodemål*, Sw. *urbotamål* relates to heinous crimes [*orbode*, *urbota* 'not possible to compensate for'], which led to excommunication or execution), however, appears only in late medieval and late manuscripts (here cited from the so-called Rantzau Manuscript from c. 1430, KB Copenhagen), but which is thought to reflect earlier (early medieval?) legal practice (*DGLL* 7 p. 1).
[11] Tamm and Vogt (eds.) 2016 p. 129.

In the preceding paragraphs of the same medieval Danish law there are rules for how to treat legal situations in which someone has had an eye put out (ch. 26), an ear cut off (ch. 27), both ears cut off (ch. 27), or the nose cut off (ch. 28).

The Danish legal clause can be compared to a passage in the Old Norwegian Gulathing Law (259) about how to punish a female slave who steals:[12]

> *En ef stelr leysingia mannz eða ambott her alen, þa scal skera af henne annat eyra. En ef hon stelr annat sinn, þa scal skera af henne annat eyra. En ef hon stelr hit þriðia sinn, þa scal skera af henne nef, þa heiter hon stuva oc nuva, oc stele æ sem hon vill.*[13]

> But if a man's freed woman steals or a native slave woman, then one shall cut off one of her ears. But if she steals a second time, then the other ear shall be cut off. But if she steals a third time, her nose shall be cut off; then she is called "*stuva* and *nuva*" [stumpy and stubby], and then she can steal as she likes.[14]

This must mean that also in Scandinavia the bestial custom, common in other cultures, of physically mutilating the face of a slave was practiced. With regard to early Denmark the issue was not just any sort of facial marking, such as cutting off an ear, cutting out the tongue, or the like, but slitting both nostrils.

Maybe this horrible way of marking or branding a slave has a reflection in what is probably a *trope* in two Old Norse sagas, in Latin in Saxo Grammaticus *Gesta Danorum*,[15] and in the fantastic *Hrólfs saga kraka*, taking place around the middle of the first millennium, a saga with strong

[12] Cf. Krag 1982 p. 216.

[13] GuL § 259.

[14] My translation. This paragraph shows that a *leysingi*, a freed woman, was not to be considered totally free, she was still under some kind of influence and power of a master (this gradual process of becoming free is discussed by Tore Iversen 1997, 2003). The expression *stuva oc nuva* comes out as some kind of a saying, for someone who has been mutilated in the face by having ears and nose cut off. The words are ON *stúfa* f. to *stúfr* m. 'stump, snippet, bit; penis' and *(h)núfa* f. 'hump', a word related to dialect words with meanings such as 'pig with short ears', 'a cow without horns', 'tack', 'something trimmed', etc., and the Norwegian verb *nuva* 'truncate, curtail' (see, e.g., de Vries 1962 pp. 245, 555, Hellquist 1948 p. 526).

[15] In Book 2 of *Gesta Danorum*, Saxo relates the episode thus: "As it chanced, during the silence of that night Hialti, a warrior who surpassed all the other nobles of the court in his proven worth, had gone off to the country to the embraces of a wanton. When the crashes that arose from the distant fighting fell on his amazed ears, he preferred to set bravery before lust and to seek the deadly test of war rather than wallow in the smooth enticements of love. Can we guess what affection for his monarch burned in this soldier, who reckoned it better to risk his safety in obvious danger rather than save himself for pleasure? Yet he could have pretended ignorance and put forward the excuse of his

links to the Anglo-Saxon poem *Beowulf*. Saxo retells an episode where the hero warrior Hjalti punishes his mistress by cutting of her nose, thereby disfiguring her, according to Saxo, so she would lose her "good looks" and become ugly. Perhaps Hjalti also knew that by cutting of her nose, she not only lost her "good looks," but also was degraded as a potential slave woman. In *Hrólfs saga* we are told of a battle, the Last Stand and the Fall of King Hrólfr and his men. Before the battle one of the warriors, Hjalti "the Magnanimous," asks his mistress whether she would prefer two men of twenty-two or one of eighty. She says the former, with the consequence that he bites off her nose;[16] he then goes to join the doomed battle:

> *Þessu næst er þat at segja, at Hjalti inn hugprúði gengr til húss þess, sem frilla hans er inni. Hann sér þá glöggliga, at eigi mun vera friðsamligt undir tjöldum þeira Hjörvarðar ok Skuldar. Lætr hann þó kyrrt vera ok lætr sér ekki í brún bregða, leggst nú með frillunni. Hún var kvenna fríðust. Ok sem hann hefir verit þar um hríð, sprettr hann upp ok mælti til frillunnar: "Hvárt þykkir þér betri tveir tvíelleftir eða einn áttræðr?" Hún svarar: "Tveir tvíelleftir þykki mér betri en áttræðir karlar." "Þessara orða skaltu gjalda," sagði Hjalti, "þín hóra," ok gekk at henni ok beit af henni nefit. "Kenndu mér um, ef nokkurir fljúgast á um þik, ok vænti ek, at flestum þykki lítil gersemi at þér upp frá þessu." "Illa gerðir þú til mín ok ómakliga," sagði hún. "Ekki verðr við öllu sét," sagði Hjalti.* (*Hrólfs saga kraka* ch. 49)
>
> Next there is to tell, Hjalti the Magnanimous went to the house of his mistress. It was then that he saw clearly that peace was not being prepared in the tents of Hjorvard and Skuld. But Hjalti raised no alarm, and his expression showed no concern. He lay now with his mistress; she was the fairest of women. After he had been there for a while, he sprang to his feet and said, "Which do you think better, two twenty-two-year-olds or one eighty-year-old man?"
>
> She answered, "I think two twenty-two-year-olds better than men of eighty."

absence. At his departure his mistress started to ask how old a man she should marry, if she were to lose him. Hialti told her to come close as if he wished to whisper something, but, resenting that she needed a successor to his love, made her ugly by cutting off her nose; a disfiguring wound was left as punishment for her lustful question, for he reckoned that the loss of her good looks should restrain her lecherous inclinations" (*Saxo Grammaticus*, vol. 1, trans. Fisher, p. 56).

16 See Jesse Byock's discussion on this odd episode, *The Saga of King Hrolf Kraki*, ed. Byock (1998) p. 85 n. 76. Cf. Johannesson 1978 pp. 109–110 and Shippey 2010 p. 20.

> "You will pay for these words, you whore," said Hjalti, and he went up to her and bit off her nose. "You can blame me if anyone fights over you, but I expect that from now on, most will think you scarcely a treasure."
>
> "You treat me miserably," she said, "and it is undeserved."
>
> "Everyone," said Hjalti, "can be fooled by scheming."[17]

Why does Hjalti in his anger call his mistress a whore and bite off her nose? Probably to humiliate her as much as possible and for all future, to "brand" her as a slave woman, by mutilating her.

We understand from this that in the Middle Ages it was considered acceptable to punish a thrall by very brutish means. The hardest punishment of all is found in, for example, the previously mentioned paragraph of the Gulathing Law (259):

> *En ef stelr þræll her alen, þa skal drepa hofuð af hanom . . .*

> But if a native slave steals, then one shall decapitate him . . .

Marking or branding a thrall seem to have very ancient roots. Already in the Code of Hammurabi from Mesopotamia, the oldest law codex known to us (from 1790 BC), it says that if a slave hits a free man, both his ears should be cut off as punishment.[18]

Another way of marking or branding a slave, discussed during recent years by archaeologists and osteologists, are the filed or modified teeth, where one or several lines have been filed down on the front teeth. Examples of this custom are found on decapitated individuals, assumed to be slaves, found in double burials. Hence filed teeth could have been a physical characteristic of a slave, in the same way as slit nostrils or cut-off ears or nose. The problem is, however, that we seem to find this kind of modified, filed teeth also on buried "ordinary" persons. This is discussed later.

Yet another way of "marking" a slave was, of course, to give him or her a special slave name, a derogatory name, which whenever it was said out loud abused the slave and placed him or her at the bottom of society. Here, it may be possible for us to get a better insight into the conditions since the source situation regarding personal names is not exactly good, but somewhat better.

[17] *The Saga of King Rolf Kraki*, trans. J. Byock pp. 71–72.

[18] *Codex Hammurabi* 205 (http://www.wsu.edu:8080/~dee/MESO/CODE.HTM, cf. http://www.thenagain.info/webchron/middleeast/hammurabicode.html).

12
Thralls' Names in Scandinavia

> *Ketill son þeirra . . . hafði verið í vestrvíking og haft (úr) vestrvíking þræla írska; hét einn Þormóðr, annar Floki, þriðji Kóri, fjórði Svartr og Skorrar tveir.*
>
> Ketill their son . . . had been in West-Viking
> and from this journey he got Irish slaves;
> one was called *Þormóðr*, another *Flóki*,
> a third *Kóri*, a fourth *Svartr* and two named *Skorri*'
>
> —*Landnámabók* 45 (my trans.)

Our knowledge of thralls' names in Scandinavia is limited due to the poor source situation. We can, however, turn to other cultures with written sources that can tell us how unfree people were named. Such an example comes from medieval Italy.[1] From this it emerges very clearly that slave owners often gave their slaves new names after capturing or buying them. Slaves often changed their names when they were baptized or on being freed.

In classical Rome, it was normal to give a slave a name that was derived from the slave owner's name, adding the suffix *-por* (< *puer* 'boy, slave') so that *Marcus*'s slave was called *Marcipor*.[2] Also the word *servus* could be used as part of a slave's name, for example *Eros Aurelii s*(*ervus*) 'Eros Aurelius' slave'.[3] During later Roman times, slaves' names were given more freely. Varro has an interesting explanation of how slaves could be named:[4]

> There are two ways in which names can be derived; one is arbitrary and the other natural. It is arbitrary to impose whatever name anyone wishes—for instance, when three men buy one slave at Ephesus, often one of them will

1 Epstein 2001 pp. 24–33.
2 See Brink 1997a.
3 Löffler 1995 p. 1297.
4 Varro, *De Lingua Latina*, 8, 9, 21.

Thraldom. Stefan Brink, Oxford University Press. © Oxford University Press 2021.
DOI: 10.1093/oso/9780197532355.003.0012

> derive the name from that of the trader, e.g., Artemidorus, and call him Artemas, while another will call him Ion after Ionia, the district where he bought him, and third Ephesius because he was bought at Ephesus; so everyone calls his slave something different after different things, just as he likes.[5]

The Finnish scholar Heikki Solin has in a number of books and articles highlighted the onomasticon for slaves in Classic Greek and Latin inscriptions. Beyond the tripartite names just described, slaves were also given simplex names. Many of them seem to be names of gods and goddesses in the Greek and Roman mythological pantheon. The most common Greek slave name was *Dionysius, -ia*, followed by *Demetrius, -ia* and *Apollonius, -ia*, whereas in Rome the most common slave names where *Hermes, Eros, Onesimus, -e*, and *Alexander*.[6]

In order to increase the control of slaves, the city of Florence decided in 1366 to keep records of slave sales. These statistics contain complete physical descriptions of slaves and give their names. Often, a slave's old name was known. Thus, two female Tartar slaves were originally named *Cetehe* and *Cafisa*, but they were given the names *Margerita* and *Caterina* by their slave owner. Another female Tartar slave was called *Ersamabi* prior to being captured, but was then given the name *Lucia*, which was later altered to *Caterina*.[7]

In records (1392–1399) kept by a Venetian notary, Bernardo de Rodulfis, is a register of what names slaves obtained on being baptized:[8]

A Bulgarian *Stanna*	after baptism: *Baxilia*
A Tartar *Maria*	after baptism: *Bartolomea*
A Bosnian *Radoslava*	after baptism:—
A Tartar (unnamed)	after baptism: *Caterina*
A Russian *Malgarita*	after baptism: *Cita*

A few names seem to have become particularly popular with regard to female slaves in medieval Italy. From Genoa in the fifteenth century, over one thousand female slaves are recorded by names and a full 80 percent of these had one of the following names: *Lucia, Maddalena, Margherita, Maria, Marta*, and, the most common of them all, *Caterina*. What is interesting is that

[5] Here translated from Wiedemann 1981 p. 34.
[6] Solin 2001 p. 312. See also, for Greek slave names, Masson 1972.
[7] Epstein 2001 p. 25.
[8] Epstein 2001 p. 25.

several of these indicated ethnic origins: *Marta* was given mostly to Tartars, *Margherita* to women from Abkhazia, *Caterina* to Maurs and Turks, and so forth. As far as male slaves are concerned, the source situation is not as good from medieval Italy. An apparent reason for this is that the Italian slavery of the fourteenth and fifteenth centuries consisted mainly of female slaves within the household; of the male slave names that are known, *Giorgiora* seems to have been the most popular.

From medieval East Scandinavia, contemporary or early evidence of slaves and their names is very sparse.[9] Often, those who occur named are recently freed slaves, in OSw *løysi*, corresponding to ON *leysingi*, twice on rune stones and a few times in medieval documents granting freedom to a thrall. Two *løysar* are named on two rune stones from Uppland, **Faste** (U 168) and **Alvi** (U 696). Particularly from Småland, letters have been preserved that declare that someone has been freed from thraldom, for instance a *Härmod* in 1268 (*DS* 532), and in 1282 the lawman Folke Karlsson in his will grants freedom to the thrall *Brynolf* carpenter (*Brynulpho carpentario*) and allots him cows and seed grain (*DS* 742). In 1272 Peter Erengisleson grants freedom to the female thrall *Helena* as well as her son and three daughters (*DS* 559). As is clear from these names, they cannot be considered specifically thralls' names. They are typical Old Swedish personal names (*Faste*, *Alvi*, *Härmod*, *Brynolf*, and *Helena*). This is the case for all the thralls that are freed during the second half of the thirteenth century and are mentioned in wills, they all have what we would consider "normal" names: *Asker*, *Nicolaus*, *Margareta*, *Ragnhild*, *Manne*, *Sven*, *Erngund*, *Erik*, *Hermund*, *Sigge Lång*, *Johannes*, *Ragnvald*, *Havard*, *Cecilia*, *Tova*, *Sten*, and *Olle*.[10] Judging by these names, then, thralls had the same sort of names as the rest of society,[11] with perhaps only *Sigge Lång* and *Tova* standing out a little. We must, however, be reminded that we do not know whether these freed slaves were given new "ordinary" names at the same time as they were given freedom. There are, in fact, indications that thralls in Sweden had derogatory names if it is safe to assume that they were similar to some known medieval names for servants, such as *Mus* 'Mouse', *Tore havresäck* 'Tore oatsack', *Rävunge* 'Fox cub', *Rask* 'Swift', and the like.[12]

9 For a general overview of names of thralls with references to literature, see Löffler 1995 pp. 1296 ff. and Brink 1997a pp. 454 ff.

10 These freed male and female slaves appear in the wills treated earlier.

11 Cf. Ekbo 1947 p. 270.

12 Hildebrand *SM* 2 p. 262.

In the West Norse areas, the situation is somewhat better, obviously because of the Old Icelandic literature.[13] In numerous poems and sagas, thralls appear with their names and also in several places in *Landnámabók* (Ldn).[14] We find practically the same naming traditions in the west as in the east; thralls often had names of the same sort as free people, that is to say "normal" Norwegian personal names.[15] There are, however, two deviating categories that emerge from the material. The first one is made up of personal names that testify to foreign descent. The largest group of foreign names of thralls consists of Irish-Celtic names, such as *Kormákr* (Ir *Cormac*), *Dufan*, *Dufþakr* (Ir *Dubhthach*), *Kjaran*, *Melkolfr*, and in all likelihood originally also *Njáll* (Ir *Niall*); among women's names we have *Melkorka* (Ir *Mael-Curcaich*).[16] *Landnámabók* (45) tells of a certain Ketill who raided in the west and took Irish slaves captive: *Ketill son þeirra . . . hafði verið í vestrvíking og haft* (*úr*) *vestrvíking þræla írska; hét einn Þormóðr, annar Floki, þriðji Kóri, fjórði Svartr og Skorrar tveir* ("Ketill their son . . . had been in West-Viking and from this journey got Irish slaves; one was called *Þormóðr*, another *Flóki*, a third *Kóri*, a fourth *Svartr* and two named *Skorri*"). A famous episode from *Landnámabók* tells of two settlers from Telemark, *Ingólfr* and *Leifr*. The latter went on viking raids in Ireland and killed many men. Therefore he was called *Hjǫrleifr*. He also took ten prisoners and made them thralls and, according to *Landnámabók*, they had names such as *Dufþakr*, *Geirrøðr*, *Skjaldbjǫrn*, *Halldór*, and *Drafdrit*. Some of these thralls' names are Old Norse, others are Irish. A man who had previously been a thrall—a *leysingi*—apparently captured in Scotland, is *Hundi skotskr* (*Hundi hét leysingi Uðar, skotskr*, Ldn 84).

Another famous episode from *Landnámabók* tells of how the female settler *Auðr djúpauðga*, when she took land in Iceland, had twenty freed slaves with her, probably from Ireland. One of the thralls was *Erpr*, whom Auðr later gave Sauðafellslǫnd to live in, and about this thrall *Landnámabók* says that he was the son of Earl Meldún of Scotland and his wife Myrgjol, daughter of Gljómall, King of Ireland.[17] Another one of them, called *Vífill*, later became an important man in Iceland.[18] In *Landnámabók* we are also told that the founder of Reykjavík, Ingólfr, had a thrall with this name: *Vífill ok Karli*

[13] On names of thralls in Old Icelandic literature, see Jochens 1999.

[14] Cf. Wilde-Stockmeyer 1978 pp. 55–68.

[15] Lind 1905–1915 *passim*.

[16] Olsen 1926 p. 97, Heller 1988, Gísli Sigurðsson 1988 pp. 30 ff., Sayers 1996, O'Donoghue 1997, Brink 1997a, Jochens 1999.

[17] Jón Hnefill Aðalsteinsson 1986 pp. 37–38.

[18] Strömbäck 1935a p. 56, Jón Hnefill Aðalsteinsson 1986 p. 36.

hétu þrælar Ingólfs (Ldn 6). *Vífill* has earlier been interpreted as either a word **vífill* 'dung beetle' or as originating from a designation for a cult leader, **vífill* from the adjective *vi* (< **wīha-* 'sacred'). In all likelihood, however, William Sayers is right in suggesting that *Vífill* as a personal name in Iceland has Irish origins.[19]

Also the name *Karli* is of interest in this context. Whenever this name appears in *Landnámabók*, it seems always to be applied to thralls or to freed thralls, an example being the *leysingi Karli Konálsson* (Ldn 22), another the just-mentioned *Vífill ok Karli hétu þrælar Ingólfs* (Ldn 6). The name *Karl* is of course the same as the appellative *karl* 'freeborn man', while the derivation *Karli* seems to have referred to thralls.[20] Whether this is typical for Iceland is unknown; the name occurs a couple of times on Viking Age rune stones in Sweden,[21] obviously not in a slave context. More "normal" names are *Grani* and *Þrándr*, who are mentioned as thralls in *Egils saga* (83).

Pejoratives constitute the other category of thralls' names: *Gríss* 'pig' is what one of Skalla-Grímr's *leysingar* is called (Ldn 24); other names include *Flóki þræll* 'he with the tangled hair' (Ldn 19, 45), *Kolr þræll* 'the black', *Loðinn* 'hairy one', *Nagli* 'nail' (*Nagli skozkr at kyni*, "Nagli, Scottish by descent"); *Þórir dúfunef* 'Tore dove-nose' is the name of one of Yxna-Þórir's *leysingar* (Ldn 62); and the name *Svartr* 'the black, dark skinned' seems to have been especially common. The last-mentioned, *Svartr* and as a byname *Svarti*, came to be used pretty exclusively for thralls and then, of course, in a pejorative sense.[22] In *Gísla saga Súrssonar* several named thralls appear: *Kolr* 'charcoal' (1), *Þórðr hinn huglausi* (13) '*Þórðr* the shiftless', *Með Ingjaldr var þræll og ambátt; þrællinn hét Svarti en ambáttin hét Bóthildr* (25) (*Ingjaldr* had a *þræll* and an *ambátt*; the *þræll* was named *Svarti* 'the black one, dark

[19] Sayers 1996.

[20] *Karli* is (from what I can see in the sources) only found as a man's name, never as an appellative. That said, we probably have to assume a lost **karli* (something John Kousgård Sørensen, 1984 p. 116, is inclined to do for Old Danish), which is the background to the name *Karli* and which probably is to be found in the compound *Kaldakot* etc. (see earlier). The word **karli* could be looked on as a derivation of *karl* (< *karlaz*) with a possessive suffix *-an* (PGmc **karlan-*; with the meaning of 'a man who is own by another man', or, less likely, with a possessive or diminutive suffix *-ia*) (cf., e.g., Hellquist 1922 p. xvii). It is notable that the Old-Scandinavian man's name/byname *Karli, Karle* is a seldom-occurring name (see Kousgård Sørensen 1984 pp. 115–116), and is only found 2–4 times in Viking Age runic inscriptions (Peterson 2007 pp. 146–147). In one case, on Ög 44 (*Karli ræisti stæin þannsi æftiʀ Karl, faþur sinn* "Karli raised this stone in memory of Karl, his father"), the son seems to have been given a hypocorism of his father's name. The man's name *Karli* is also found in Old English as *Carle* etc. (see Björkman 1910 pp. 76–78, Tengvik 1938 p. 152). It is interesting, when discussing this name *Karli* in a thrall context, that a word *kalle* (< *karli*) is found in old Swedish dialects with a meaning 'begger (*tiggare*)' (Rietz p. 309).

[21] Peterson 2007 pp. 146–147.

[22] Olsen 1926 p. 97 and Jochens 1999 p. 87.

skinned' and the *ambátt Bóthildr*). We see that these thrall's names are entirely in line with the thrall topos that exists in Old Icelandic literature: the thrall was dark-skinned, short, stupid, ugly, and wrinkled.

Th. Høverstad has discussed a thrall name, *Hjalli*, found in the *Vǫlsunga saga* (ch. 37) and the poem *Atlakviða*. This Hjalli had an unfortunate fate in the narrative, in that king Atli (i.e. Attila the Hun) had his heart cut out (instead of the heart of the hero Hǫgni). The name is probably to be understood as a derivate of ON *hjallr* 'elevated place', for example in a byre, a loft or haymow in a cattle house; an explanation which seems fitting for a thrall (living in the byre).[23]

As far as names of female slaves are concerned, we know of the *Þorgerðr* from *Egil's saga* (40) who had fostered Egill from when he was a baby: *Þorgerðr brák hét ambátt Skalla-Gríms*. *Þorgerðr* is a common name for a woman, but her byname, or nickname, *brák*, is interesting. The first possibility could be to identify it with ON *brák* f. 'a tool for leather working', which, however, seems rather odd for a name. A second possibility, which fits better in a slave context, is the word ON *brak* n. 'noice, fracas, rag, brawl' related to ON *braka* vb 'fight, brawl, etc.',[24] which would be fitting for an unruly or hotheaded person. As we saw in the episode when Grímr and Egill were playing, this *Þorgerðr brák* angrily scolded Grímr, which probably is a hint to her hot temper. Furthermore, we know the name *Bóthildr* from *Gísla saga Súrssonar* (see earlier), and in *Landnámabók* (99) occurs a *Haki* and a female slave *Bót* (*Haki þræll hans ok Bót ambátt hans*).

Most of the evidence for similarly derogatory names (actually designations) for thralls occurs in the listing (*þula*) of thrall's names, actually "synonyms" for thrall (*præla heiti*) that is found in the previously mentioned eddic poem *Rígsþula*. Here, it is said that *Thrall* (*Þræll*) and *Slavegirl* (*Þír*) had the boys *Hreimr* ('Screamer') and *Fjósnir* ('the one who lives in the byre'),[25] *Klúrr* ('Clumsy') and *Kleggi* ('Stumpy; hay-sack or botfly'), *Kefsir* ('he who sleeps with a slavegirl') and *Fúlnir* ('Stinky'), *Drumbr* ('Clumpy, Stupid') and *Digraldi* ('Fatso'), *Drǫttr* ('Lout') and *Hǫsvir* ('The gray [old?] one'), *Lútr* ('crooked, slouch; dishonest, liar') and *Leggialdi* ('long-legged; bony') as well

[23] Høverstad 1909 pp. 101–102.

[24] de Vries 1962 p. 53, who, however, has a short stem vowel for *brak* and *braka*, whereas *Þorgerðr*'s nickname *brák* has a long *ā* in the saga manuscript. Fredrik Tamm (1890–1905 pp. 65–66) hints, in his etymological dictionary, that this female nickname is to be linked to Sw. *bråk* n. 'noise, trouble' and *bråka* vb 'make noise, brawl' (both with originally long *ā*), see also Torp *NEO* p. 38; both the latter etymologists assume a long *ā* for ON *brak* and *braka*.

[25] See Strömbäck 1935b pp. 107–108.

as the girls *Drumba* ('clumsy; dim') and *Kumba* ('gawky, [wooden] block, fatso'), *Økkvinkálfa* ('she with fat, stocky legs; thick-calves; shit-heap from a calf') and *Arinnefja* ('stove-nose; black-nose, one who has a sooty nose'),[26] *Ysja* ('hot-tempered') and *Ambótt* (term for a female thrall), *Eikintjasna* ('very horny; great prattler'), *Tǫtrughypja* ('slut, shabby one, ragtag') and *Trǫnubeina* ('crane-legs; one with long skinny legs'). These would not be ordinary names, but rather metaphorical names and above all strongly pejorative designations that were considered suitable for thralls, such as "crane-legs," "black-nose," "crooked-back," "byre-dweller," "fatso," "clumpy," and so on.

In the eddic poem *Vǫlundarkviða* (39) appears the thrall name *Þakkráðr*:

Upp rístu, Þakkráðr,	Raise up *Þakkráðr*
Þræll minn inn bezti	my best slave

Þakkráðr is a byname of uncertain origins. John McKinnell has cautiously suggested that the name seems to have Germanic origins,[27] but it is uncertain how it is to be interpreted. In the third poem about Guðrún[28] we find the female thrall's name *Herkja*, which is probably constructed from a verb *herkja* 'dragging oneself forward slowly and cumbersomely', from the verb *harka* 'drag, drudge',[29] in other words a derogatory name.

In summary, it seems that, on the one hand, thralls were not to any great extent given special thrall's names, but ordinary Scandinavian names seem to have been used. We must nonetheless keep in mind that, in the cases where contemporary early documents mention *leysingar*, *løysar*, that is freed thralls, these can, of course, have taken or been given new "normal" personal names on being granted freedom and may thus have had characteristic thralls' names earlier on. On the other hand, special thralls' names do seem to have been in use; the names listed in *Rígsþula* are, however, problematic in this context, since they look rather like literary constructions. In the cases where thralls' names deviate from "ordinary" names, the talk is partly of foreign names, frequently Irish-Celtic, partly of highly pejorative names. This last

[26] This translation of *Arinnefja* seems more probable than 'eagle-nose', which has been suggested by among others Fry 1977 p. 65 and Dronke 1997 p. 165. The translation 'stove-, soot-nose' has also been suggested by Professor Gottskálk Þ. Jensson, Reykjavík (personal communication) as already Gjessing 1862 p. 46.

[27] McKinnell 2001 p. 123.

[28] *Guðrúnarkviða III* i the *Edda*.

[29] See Fritzner, article *harka*, *herkja*.

category must be taken into consideration, since such names are definitively evidenced (*Gríss*, *Mus*, *Svartr*, *Loðinn*), but also keeping in mind the fact that this type of name fully concurs with the ways in which thralls are characterized in Old Icelandic literature, namely as swarthy, filthy, stumpy, short, ugly, and so on. Perchance it is thus possible to trace thralls, possibly freed thralls who kept their old thralls' names or whose thralls' names were used in naming, in certain place names and especially in places where names of smaller farms occur together, so that a system or pattern within the naming tradition becomes visible. The parish of Älmeboda in southern Småland, southern Sweden, constitutes just such an exciting case.

13

The Special Case of Älmeboda Parish in Southern Småland

In the southernmost part of the province of Småland, Sweden, in Konga hd, lies the parish of Älmeboda. This parish shows, according to Nils Ödeen,[1] the highest density of *måla*-names in Småland (see Fig. 13.1). This is a name type that probably belongs to the High Middle Ages, with a sizable majority presumably coined in connection with a wave of new settlements in the twelfth and thirteenth centuries. The word *måla* was reckoned already by the Lund professor Andreas Stobæus, in his *De Scania antiqua* (1706),[2] to be related to the verb *måla* 'to measure (time or space)', and as a place-name element it may then have signified divided and measured out units of agricultural land, that is farms in the outback. Emil Olson translates the word as 'outfield in the outback/forest' (*intaga å utmark*) and points to the compound OSw *utmale*, which he translates as 'a measured land in the outback for an outfield'.[3] Eric Elgqvist presents a contextually important letter from 1354 from which it emerges that the knight Magnus Niclisson buys half an *attung* in Snyttringe and also seventeen small plots that are called *maler* or *humper* (*terram meam ibidem in decem et septem mensuris terre dictis malum siue humppum DS* 5039).[4] This, then, provides as synonym for *måla* the word *hump*, a word that in dialects in the province of Östergötland means 'separate plot of land; land placed in the outback or within another settlements' land'. Other synonyms for these outfields were *fjäll* (OSw *fiælder*) or *urfjäll* (OSw *urfiælder*). Support for this etymology is also provided by the place names *Repemåla* and *Stångamåla*, wherein the first elements apparently refer to the

[1] Ödeen 1927; these names are discussed also in Brink 2002a. For a modern analysis of the *-måla* settlements, see Strid 2006.
[2] See Sahlgren in *NoB* 1919 p. 84.
[3] *å utmark till intaga avmätt jord*, Olson 1916 p. 215.
[4] Elgqvist 1963 pp. 16–17; Ericsson 2012 p. 151.

Thraldom. Stefan Brink, Oxford University Press. © Oxford University Press 2021.
DOI: 10.1093/oso/9780197532355.003.0013

Fig. 13.1 Map of Älmeboda parish, southern Sweden.

measuring (with a rope or a measuring stick) of land [5] as does the land unit *mål* used in the northern province of Hälsingland.[6]

[5] Cf. Ljunggren 1951 p. 192. For alternative interpretations of these names, see Strid 2006 pp. 80–81.

[6] See what follows.

A different etymology of *måla* is presented by Robert Norrby in his dissertation *Ydre härads gårdnamn* (1905). He believes that the word belongs together with the word *mål*, which we encounter in compounds such as *giftermål* 'marriage', *folkmål* 'dialect', and *klagomål* 'complaint', a word that secondarily shows meanings such as 'agreement, court case', whereby the place-name element then concurs with the term OSw *male* 'agreement, settlement (of a case)'. Place names ending in *-måla* may, Norrby imagines, refer to an agreed tax payment, a rent, how much the tenant is to pay to the landowner. This would correspond to an Old Norwegian *máli*, which in the oldest Norwegian laws referred to a 'lease contract for several years'.

K. G. Ljunggren has subsequently analyzed the word OSw *male* and believes the interpretation of the word meaning 'agreement', 'set agreement', and in this case referring to 'rent, lease payment', is unlikely, but instead means 'something measured off or measured out', albeit with reference to time, thus indicating the amount of time agreed between landowner and tenant regarding the latter's use of the land.[7] In an earlier article I listed the frequent *-måla*-names of Älmeboda parish in southern Småland and discussed their first elements as well as the origins of these settlements. Without discussing the place-name elements, I presented Ödeen's theory about the history of *måla*.[8]

Recently, Jan Paul Strid has treated the *måla*-settlements of Småland in an in-depth study and has discussed the linguistic problem of *måla*. He presents and discusses previous scholars' attempts at understanding the word and the name element. His discussion leads to the conclusion that Norrby's rather than Ödeen's suggestion is correct. Strid treats a very large group of Scandinavian words, including *male*, *máli* as simplexes and in compounds. Following Strid's extensive and convincing exposition there can be no doubt that the words and compounds he deals with show meanings relating to 'rent agreement' and the like.[9] Strid's claim—that the argument for Old Norse *male*, *máli* meaning 'something measured out', or a related *mal*, cannot be proved, and that each and every instance analyzed by him supposedly shows the meaning 'agreement'[10]—can nonetheless, in my opinion, be qualified and

[7] Ljunggren 1951.

[8] Brink 2002a pp. 119 ff.

[9] Jan Paul Strid (2006 pp. 125 ff.) also discusses other problematic place-name elements, such as *-benning*, *-bygget*, *-bygd*, seeing in these the same semantic contents as in *-måla*, namely 'rent agreement', 'leased land'. I think this analysis has great merits, where he presents the hitherto most plausible explanation of these groups of names.

[10] Strid 2006 p. 20.

discussed. There is a word *mål*, which Strid has overlooked or perhaps does not know—namely, the aforementioned term *mål* that occurs in northern Sweden and in Trøndelag, Norway, among other places in cadastrals from Hälsingland during the sixteenth century, and that refers to an area measured out for cultivated land.[11] As Sölve Göransson has shown, this *mål* belongs to the large group of land units that refer to the capacity of the field with regard to seed. This *mål* is, of course, linked to the *mål* and *mæling* that occur in the old Norwegian territories, Jämtland and Trøndelag, referring to the area a man could harvest in one day, hence again a measured area.[12] Gunnar Bodvall and later on Ingvar Jonsson have thoroughly analyzed and calculated the size of a *mål* in Hälsingland, which has varied over time. In other words, the existence of the word *mål* as referring to a measured-out plot of land has been unambiguously evidenced.[13] The question is whether this is the meaning encountered in the *måla*-names of Småland. Without taking any decisive stand in this issue I think the possibility ought to be considered.

The spread of the *måla*-names is also very interesting since they occur gathered together in the eastern part of Småland as well as in the provinces of Blekinge and the southern part of Östergötland.[14] The name type shows a concentration around the border between Blekinge and Småland, with the highest density occurring in Älmeboda parish in Konga hd.

Within this parish there are over forty *-måla*-names. This—together with the less common names ending in *-boda* and *-hult*—reveals that Älmeboda parish actually first appeared as a settlement district (Sw. *bygd*) in this period, (perhaps twelfth–) thirteenth–fourteenth centuries. There are no names containing name elements from the Viking Age and older, such as *-löv*, *-stad*, and others, nor any *-torp* names, within the parish. The names indicate an apparently extensive and late colonization of new land in these border regions.

When studying the qualifiers, the first elements, of the *-måla*-names of the parish, the following results emerge (including tentative suggestions for meanings of the first elements, with comments following):[15]

[11] On this *mål*, see Dovring 1951 p. 129, Göransson 1961, Jonsson 1971 pp. 80 ff., and Brink 1994 pp. 151–152.

[12] On this, see Jonsson 1971 p. 81 with references.

[13] It can be excluded that this Norwegian–Norrlandic *mål* has to do with 'rent agreement' or similar, since in the province of Hälsingland we actually never have had privileged classes (Sw. *frälse*) with estates and tenants of the sort common in southern and middle Sweden (see, e.g., Brink 1994 pp. 126 ff., 2013a and 2014a).

[14] See distribution map in Strid 2006 p. 13.

[15] If nothing else is stated, the earlier name forms are taken from OAUs.

Arpemåla (arpamal 1418) < mbyn. **Arpe* 'filth-pig'(?).
Askaremåla (askaramal 1327) < mbyn. *askare* 'box-maker'.[16]
Boamåla (Bowemole 1445) < mn. *Bove* 'a wide boy'(?).
Botamåla (Botamola 1539) < mn. *Bote* 'ragamuffin'(?).
Broddamåla (Bruddamaala 1338) < mn. *Brodde*.[17]
Brunnsmåla (Brundzmåla 1545) < *brunn* 'well'(?).
Bubbamåla (Bobbemållа 1580) < mbyn. *Bobbe* 'oaf' or 'fatso'(?).
Bönemåla (bønamaala 1453) < mn. *Bøne*(?) 'noisy clumsy one'(?).[18]
Estamåla (estremole 1445, estamåla 1557) < *esta*- 'Estonian'.

Eric Elgqvist notes that this word, *esti*, existed in 1352 as a man's by-name, 'man from Estonia', in Denmark, and furthermore remarks on the strange circumstance that Söderwall's dictionary of the medieval Swedish language states that *ester* was a common designation for thralls toward the end of the Middle Ages.[19] Hjalmar Lindroth presented this interpretation even earlier.[20]

Fösingsmåla (Forsyngmol 1515 Larsson 1980 p. 269, Fösingzmåla 1545) < mbyn. *Fösing* 'rash one, cheeky one'(?).
Gammalsmåla (gamalsmåla 1540) < mn. *Gamal* 'the Old One'.
Germundamåla (germundemåla 1545) < mn. *Germund*.
Gubbemåla (gubbemåla 1545) < mbyn. *Gubbe* 'Old Man'.
Gunnamåla (gwnnemaala 1482) < mn. *Gunne*.
Häggesmåla (Hæggesmla 1462) < mn. *Hægge*(?).
Iremåla in Tingsås parish (Iramålla 1580) < *ira*- 'Irishman'.[21]
†*Kantemåla* (kantemala 1467) < mbyn. *Kante*(?) 'pauper'(?).
Karpemåla (karpamåla 1545) < mbyn. *Karpe* 'great gabbler'(?).
Kavsjömåla (Kaffsømole 1445 Larsson 1980 p. 272, Kafzmålla 1631) < ?.
Korpemåla (korpamaala 1453) < mbyn. *Korp* 'thief'(?) or 'dwindler'(?).[22]
Krusamåla (Kyrwsemaale 1498) < mbyn. *Kruse* 'curly-haired one'(?).
Kråksmåla (kroxmåla 1545) < mbyn. *Krok* 'wretched one'(?).
Krämmemåla (krämemala 1545 Larsson 1980 p. 272, kremaremåla 1557) < mbyn. *krämare* 'trader' or 'horse-swindler'(?).

[16] See also Elgqvist 1963 p. 2 and Strid 2006 p. 90.
[17] Cf. Strid 2006 p. 86.
[18] This form is to be found in OAUs; L.-O. Larsson 1980 p. 269 has the form *Bønømale*.
[19] Elgqvist 1963 p. 3, *SAOB* (*est*).
[20] Lindroth 1916 p. 198 and Strid 2006 p. 88.
[21] Cf. Strid 2006 p. 88.
[22] Larsson 1980 p. 272 presents the form *Korpemale* 1453.

Kuppramåla (Kupamåla 1545 Larsson 1980 p. 274, kupparamåla 1560) < probably *koppare* 'copper-smith'; according to Elgqvist comparable to MLG *kuper* 'cooper'.[23]

Kuramåla (Kuramåla 1545) < *kure* 'Latvian; Kurlander', possibly in gen. pl.[24]

Lekaremåla (Lekaremala 1545 Larsson 1980 p. 274, Lekaramålla 1580) < *lekare* 'player, actor'.[25]

Lummamåla (lumemåla 1545) < probably mbyn. *Lume* 'dimwit'(?).[26]

Läppamåla (Læppemaale 1498) < mbyn. *Læppe* '(he with the hanging?/ big?) lip'.

Lönemåla (Linemåle 1545 Larsson 1980 p. 275, Lönnemåla 1580) < mbyn. *Löne*(?)

Makrismåla (Makelsmåla 1545 Larsson 1980 p. 275, makersmåla 1560), according to Elgqvist containing an Old Swedish counterpart to MLG *maker* 'maker'.[27]

Munkamåla (mwnchamalæ 1483 or.), may have belonged to a monastery?[28]

Persmåla (pedersmåla 1545) < mn. *Peder.*

Puppramåla (puperamåla 1545) < *puppare* 'shitter' from dialect *puppa* 'shit'.

Rävemåla (Räffwemåla 1440, Reffuamala 1545) < probably gen. pl. of *räv* 'fox' (pejorative).[29]

Sjuamåla (siømale 1483) < *sjö* 'lake'.[30]

Skarmansmåla (skartingzmala 1467, skarmandzmåla 1545, skarpmandsmåla 1570) < mbyn. **Skarpman* from *skarp* 'shrunken, lean, sharp, dry', or according to Elgqvist rather a borrowing from MLG *scharman* approximately 'forester'.[31]

Skräddaremåla (Skrædaramala 1344) < *skräddare* 'tailor'.[32]

23 Elgqvist 1963 p. 2 and Strid 2006 p. 90.
24 Cf. Strid 2006 p. 88.
25 Cf. Strid 2006 p. 90. A hamlet named *Lekaremåla* (Lekaremåla 1545) is also found in Vissefjärda parish, Konga hd.
26 Larsson 1980 p. 274 has the form *Lomamåla* 1545.
27 Elgqvist 1963 p. 2
28 Larsson 1980 p. 275 has the form *Monekamalæ* 1483. Cf. Strid 2006 p. 133.
29 Larsson 1980 p. 276 has the form *Roffwemala* 1545.
30 Larsson 1980 p. 276 has the form *Siomale* 1483.
31 Elgqvist 1963 p. 2.
32 Cf. Strid 2006 p. 91.

Skuntamåla (Skuntemåla 1538, skuntamåla 1545) < mbyn. *Skunte* from *skunt* 'dirt, shit, uncleanliness'.

Spritsmåla (sprismale 1418) < mbyn. *Sprit.*

Stänkelsmåla (Stenckelsmåle 1545 Larsson 1980 p. 278) < mbyn. **Stänkel*(?) 'long one, post-like'(?).

Summemåla (soma maala 1451,[33] somamale 1470s, Sumamål 1545) < from **sum(m)i* 'Finn'(?).[34]

Suttaremåla (sutaremåla 1545) < *sutare* 'shoemaker'.[35]

†*Tantemåla* (Tantemale 1487 Larsson 1980 p. 278) < mbyn. *Tante* or mbyn. *Tanta* 'village fool'(?).

Toramåla (tordamaala 1451) < mn. *Tord.*[36]

Torlandsmåla (Torlaxamåla 1545 Larsson 1980 p. 279) < mn. *Thorlak*?

Vinnamåla (Winjamale 1453 Larsson 1980 p. 279, windemåla 1545) < possibly a river- or lake-name **Vindal/Vinde.*

To a large extent, the qualifiers, the first elements, in these names consist of personal names or personal bynames. Moreover, the frequent use of Middle Low German words and artisan designations is noteworthy, as is the use of craftsman's designations, such as *askare* 'box-maker', *krämare* 'trader', *koppare* 'coppersmith', *lekare* 'player', *skräddare* 'tailor', and *sutare* 'shoemaker'.[37] In a few cases, a river or lake name seems to appear as the first element or a "normal" medieval man's name, such as *Tord* and *Germund.*

Quite unique interpretations have been made in the case of three of the *-måla*-names in this parish, namely *Estamåla, Kuramåla,* and *Summemåla.* These three names, together with *Iremåla* (Yiramola 1538, Iremåla 1571, Iramålla 1580) in the bordering parish of Tingsås to the west, have been seen to contain ethnic designations: *est(er)* from Estonia, *kur(er)* from Kurland, *Summ(ar)* from Finland (Suomi), and *ir(er)* from Ireland.[38] The interpretations are enticing. That *est-* may appear in *Estamåla* is entirely possible,

[33] Larsson 1980 p. 278 has the form *Somemoole* 1451.

[34] Cf. Strid 2006 pp. 90–91.

[35] The name *Sutaremåla* (Swderemaale 1490s, Larsson 1980 p. 294, Sutaremåla 1545) is found also in Vissefjärda parish, Konga hd. Cf. Strid 2006 p. 91.

[36] Larsson 1980 p. 279 has the form *Tordamoola.*

[37] To this category belongs in all likelihood also *Sneremåla* in Vissefjärda parish, Konga hd, recorded 1545 as *Sniderемåla* and probably containing the occupation description *snidare* 'strapwright, saddler' (see Söderwall art. *snidere* and *rem*). Strid 2006 pp. 90–91 has gathered a great number of *-måla* names containing medieval designations for artisans.

[38] Lindroth 1916, Ödeen 1927, Strid 2006 p. 88, and others; it may be noted that a man's byname *Ire* 'man from Ireland' is included by Assar Janzén in *Personnamn* (Nordisk kultur 7), Stockholm 1947 p. 245.

just like *kura-* in *Kuramåla* and *ira-* in *Iremåla*; whether a word for a "Finn" (*summe* or the like) appears in *Summemåla* must be regarded as less certain. Against these interpretations, the relevant place names have commonly been understood to recall how captive thralls from Estonia, Kurland, Finland, and Ireland acquired or were placed on farms in southern Småland.[39] Of course such an interpretation is uncertain, but it is nonetheless enticing and still well worth considering. If it is correct, then we would here have examples of how foreigners were placed as thralls on *-måla* farms in Småland. Naturally it may also be imagined that people from the countries in question voluntarily moved here and occupied the farms, but the concentrated geographical links between the farms whose names testify to the presence of Irishmen, Estonians, and Latvians rather speaks in favor of the former option, especially in the light of what emerges in the following.

The most striking aspect is how often pejorative bynames seem to appear as first elements in the *-måla*-names of Älmeboda parish, names coined on in many cases incredibly derogatory words:[40] **Arpe* from Småland dialect *arp* n. 'filth, dirt, dandruff, scabies on the head', *arp* 'dried snot, nose-slime' (Småland), *arp* 'a rather thick layer of dried out dirt, sometimes on the feet and legs of people' (Halland), *arpe* 'ingrained dirt on the body' (Halland), *arpe* 'dirt-crust on clothing, under the feet' (Södermanland), adj. *arpen* 'dried in heaps, stiffened, bunched up; frayed, uneven, rough, sulky', *arpor* 'shit-stains' (Småland), cf. Norwegian *arpe* m. 'dirt, unclean hair'; *Bote*, which may be formed on Småland dialect *bote*, occurring with meanings such as 'mended, patched clothes', 'worn trousers that cannot be mended', which may indicate a pejorative name *Bote* 'ragtag' or similar; *Bove* may be linked to Norwegian dialect *bov* 'large, broad person'; *Bubbe* from *bobb* 'short, stocky person; abscess, pimple', *bobbe* 'buffoon', *bobb* 'short, stocky person; pimple (in the face)'; a probable man's byname **Bøne* is possibly to be linked to Norwegian dialect *buna* 'work hard and clumsily' and 'rumble and brawl'; *Fösing*/*Fusing* may be understood as a man's byname, constructed with an *-ing*-suffix to the dialectal *fus* 'eager' we find also in *framfusig* 'cheeky, impetuous', whereby *framfusing* 'cheeky person' is evidenced; *Gammal* 'Old'; *Gubbe* 'Old Man'; **Kante* would function as a pejorative man's byname constructed from a dialectal *kant* appearing in expressions such as *kant och klar* 'totally poor, without the slightest means'; *Karpe* from Swedish dialect *karpa* 'prattle,

[39] For a discussion of the actual background for these names, see Strid 2006 p. 108.

[40] If nothing else is stated, the words that follow are taken from Ödeen 1927 *passim*, OSDs and/or Rietz and the Norwegian dialect words from Torp *NEO*.

blether', 'cackle'; *Korp*, which in dialects has the secondary meaning of 'thief, burglar', but should maybe be seen as linked to the Norwegian dialectal *korp* n. 'wrinkled bark on deciduous trees', cf. *korpna* 'draw together into wrinkles and knots, shrink', or why not in the sense of (*korp*)*svart* '(pitch)black' (from the bird name *korp* 'raven'); *Krämare* is obviously based on the word *kram* 'goods', but in dialects *krämare* occurs also with the meaning of 'horse-dealer, horse-trader, rascal'; *Krok* perhaps from *krok* 'wretched person', related to *krake* 'crock', cf. *kamp-kroka* 'lean horse' and *kroke-bagge* 'obstinate and pig-headed person'; the man's byname *Kruse* can, of course, be associated with curly hair, but may also be linked to the Norwegian dialectal *krusa* f. about a 'tardy person'; a *lekare*, that is a traveling player, actor, or performer, was in medieval times often of very low social standing and placed outside of society, which shows in the famous *Lekarerätten*, "Player's Law," in the Older Västgöta Law;[41] there might be a man's byname in *Lume*, based on *loma* 'walk heavily and slowly', Norwegian dialect *luma* 'saunter, walk idly'; *Læppe* presumably from *läpp* 'lip', perhaps referring to 'he who has hanging, big or distinctive lips'; *Puppare* from southern Swedish dialect *puppa* 'to shit' and as a noun *puppa* 'bad woman' (Småland), cf. *fylle-puppa* 'drunken female'; *Räv* from the animal designation *räv* 'fox', a name that was highly pejorative in medieval times; *Skarpman* from *skarp* 'shrunken, lean, sharp, dried out', cf. *skarping* 'lean and unpleasant person'; *Skunte* from *skunt* 'filth, shit, uncleanliness'; perhaps a man's byname **Stänkel* existed, formed on the word *stång* 'pole', a word *stengel* 'beam, support, measuring stick' exists in Norwegian dialects, understood by Torp as a diminutive form of the word *stång*; a supposed man's byname *Tante* or a woman's byname *Tanta* can be linked to the Swedish dialectal verb *tana* 'be foolish', cf. *tanta* f. 'dimwit, silly female', *tantig* idiotic, foolish', and *tanting* 'daft person'. In nearby Linneryd parish, Konga hd, there existed a †*Horkarlsmåla* (Horkarlsmåla 1545), containing the unflattering name or designation *horkarl* 'lecher, whoremonger'.[42]

This theme is repeated in several other *-måla*-names in other nearby parishes in which the first element contains men's bynames such as *Bus*(*s*)*e* from Swedish dialect *buse* 'troll, ghost, devil', 'evil person', 'wolf, viper', 'scarecrow'; *Fugge* from Norwegian dialect *fugg*(*e*) m. 'thick and clumpy person dressed in many badly fitting garments'; *Kagge* from Swedish dialect *kagg*(*e*)

[41] Holmbäck and Wessén 1946 pp. 197–200, see also what follows.

[42] The same name, *Horkarlsmåla* (Horkarlsmale 1515), is found also in Högsby parish, Handbörds hd, Småland.

'castrated bull, evil person', Norwegian dialect *kagge* 'big belly, short and stocky body'; *Labbe* from Swedish dialect *labb* 'large, bulky, rough hand or foot', adj. *labbug* 'clumsy, rough', *labba* 'dirty, unclean'; *Puke* from *puke* m. 'devil, ghost', 'scarecrow', also 'skinner'; *Påke* from *påke* 'daft person', adj. *påken* 'fat and flabby'; *Sigge* from Swedish dialect *sigg(e)* 'castrated male, gelded boar, boar with only one testicle, gelded billy-goat', *sigge* 'boar unsuitable for reproduction service', 'bloke with just one testicle' (derogatory term); *Skräp* from *skräp* 'rubbish'; *Slatte* to Norwegian *slatta* 'sordid person', 'shabby woman', Danish *slatte* 'dirty, untidy woman', adj. *slatten* 'limp, unclean', cf. Swedish dialect *slattra* 'scruffy person'; *Snagge* from *snagg* 'short' and *Spinke* from *spink(e)* 'skinny, lean person'.[43]

This extensive occurrence of strongly derogatory personal names and personal designations as the first elements of place names can hardly be coincidental.[44] The question is how this can be explained. In Nils Ödeen's opinion the explanation is this: "In the beginning of the thirteenth century the first *måla*-farms sprung up in Konga hd, to begin with partly established by the class of people that had previously been enslaved, but later on by the free farming class of the old agricultural villages."[45] These *måla*-farms were, then, occupied by *løysar*, freed thralls, according to Ödeen. This theory of Ödeen's has later been supported by Strid with extensive and new reference material.[46]

There are probably various possibilities for understanding the medieval colonization of this tract of land:[47] (1) the farms were run by thralls who were dependent on the farmer on a main farm; (2) outfields in the outback were allotted to *løysar*, freed thralls, where these could cultivate new ground and establish farms (it is uncertain whether a *løysi* had free rights to the land or whether he ended up as a tenant of the one who freed him); (3) we are dealing

[43] Further derogatory man's (by)names in -*måla*-names are discussed in Strid 2006 *passim*.

[44] It must be stressed that in this connection I have chosen, in my selection among various meanings of the appellatives contained in these man's (by)names, to present negative, pejorative connotations. Many of the personal (by)names mentioned here can also be given other, nonpejorative explanations, which must be emphasized, such as *Sigge*, a hypocorism of *Sigurd*, etc., but the interpretations given here should be seen in the light of the total amount of pejoratives, which I think may be decisive in this case. Also, Magnus Olsen (1926 p. 101) notes that many probable thrall or *leysing* farms in Norway have strongly derogatory names.

[45] Ödeen 1927 p. 471: *Vid 1200-talets början växa de första måla-gårdarna upp i Konga hd, till en början delvis uppbrutna av den folkklass, som under äldre tider varit trälbunden, men senare även av den fria bondeklassen i den gamla åkerbruksbygden.*

[46] Strid 2006 pp. 96 ff.

[47] For a discussion of various early medieval colonization models in Småland, see especially Tollin 1999 and Strid 2006 *passim*, with references.

with an entirely controlled colonization so that tenant farms were measured out and distributed, but remained dependent on a main farm—these tenant farms could be run by free tenants, by thralls, or by freed thralls; (4) there was an entirely free colonization of the outback, by freed thralls or free farmers, whereby free tax-paying farms emerged.

From these possibilities, the third is probably to be preferred; this describes a situation wherein units of forested land were distributed with rent-paying agreements (*måle*) or were measured out (*målats*)—based on the notion presented that *måla* referred to a "measured out plot of land for a farm with fields for cultivation"—and were distributed as tenant farms, in both cases run by free people, freed people, or thralls. This explanation seems to best account for the naming custom detectable in the first elements of the *måla*-names.

A name such as *Munkamåla* (mwnchamalæ 1483) hints that, if monks did not occupy the farm, it was at least in the possession of a monastery, perhaps Nydala monastery. Also the taxation of these farms during the 1500s indicates that hardly all newly established farms were free farms (that paid tax, not rent [Sw. *avrad*] to some landowner), but rather that many were established as tenant farms under secular or ecclesiastical nobility or monasteries. Jan Paul Strid has productively discussed the early medieval colonization in Småland and the decisive role of the nobility and the Church in this context.[48]

The qualifiers of the *-måla*-names are indisputably of great interest in this context. Since so surprisingly many names contain decidedly pejorative epithets, such as 'the shitty one with dandruffed hair', 'the fat and stocky buffoon', 'the great babbler', 'shitter', 'stinker', 'the shrunken lean one', 'filthy one', 'the black(-skinned) one(?)', 'fox', as do many examples from outside Älmeboda parish, 'the short and fat one who looks like a knot or a pimple', 'troll, devil', 'the daft one with badly fitting clothes', 'the gelded one', 'bungler', 'the fat-bellied one', 'the idiot', 'fatso', 'the castrated pig', 'sordid one', 'lecher, whoremonger', and so on, there seems to be cause for assuming that the category of individuals that are pointed out by all these pejorative names cannot have belonged to any of the well-regarded social classes. We seem to be dealing with people from the lowest rung on the social ladder.

This observation is supported by the usage in our provincial laws of strongly derogatory, nickname-like terms referring to representatives of

[48] See Strid 2006 pp. 96 ff.

the lowest social layer within the farming society, those who had a particularly low legal status during medieval times in Scandinavia. These might be called *horstakka* 'mutilated adulterer', *rishofþi* 'illegitimate child (born in the forest)' (cf. ON *hrísungr*), *hæraþspiækker* or *lurker landafæghir* 'vagabond', and *muslaghu maþer* 'runaway slave (who hides in the forest)'.[49]

The question that cannot be answered is whether all the *måla*-names have to do with thralls or with *løysar* or other persons from the lowest social orders. The possibility, expressed earlier, that a freed thrall presumably took or was given a new name if his or her former name had been as derogatory as those just listed might be taken to point in the direction that here we are dealing with actual thrall's names. This, however, must remain a hypothesis to which no proof can be found, unfortunately.

A reasonable hypothesis would, however, be that these *-måla*-farms were supposedly distributed in the twelfth and/or thirteenth century along with rent-paying agreements or were measured out (cf. *mål*) in the outback and were allotted to free tenants, freed thralls, *løysar*—who were "transformed" into tenants—or pure thralls. These farms have since—in ordinary fashion—been named by the surrounding neighbors who employed the thralls' names, or the previous thralls' old names, when speaking of their farms, and *not* the current (and presumable fairly unknown) new personal names, which these thralls had taken or been given on receiving their freedom.

Eric Elgqvist has cautiously, but with interesting observations, argued in favor of an ecclesiastical interest in southern Småland, with many Church estates in the area.[50] One possibility, which could therefore be considered, is that the Church (presumably the Bishop of Växjö) sectioned off land for cultivation (in former commons?) for thralls or for thralls who had been freed (by the Church?).

If this hypothesis—that many of the *-måla*-names of Älmeboda bear witness to the presence of thralls—has any relevance, this may speak in favor of the fact that some farms that were established in the twelfth and thirteenth centuries were run by thralls. Since this happens at the period in history when the thrall system was dissolved, many of these people would immediately have become *løysar*.

[49] C. I. Ståhle 1965 cols. 175–176.
[50] Elgqvist 1963 pp. 5 ff.

Perchance what we see in Älmeboda is therefore one part of the great transformation that takes place in northern Europe from the ninth century and onward, with extensive new settlements being established. Perhaps we are seeing an example of how Church and nobility abolish slavery, by freeing the slaves and letting them (Eng. *serfs*, Latin *servi casati*) cultivate their own fields and run their own farms as tenants.

14

Thralls in the Archaeological Material

Can We Excavate Slavery?

The nuanced opinions of historians on the relationship between the legal status of being free or unfree . . . makes it almost impossible [for archaeologists] to contribute to this debate on the basis of material culture. What we can do is contribute to the debate on the economic status of peasants.

—Frands Theuws

It is especially difficult to identify slaves archaeologically.[1] Detlef Gronenborn has recently explored in an interesting way the possibilities for tracing slaves and slavery in prehistoric times, his anthropological analogies being especially valuable. His analysis of what archaeological excavations can yield in this connection leads to negative results, which shows how hard it is to trace slaves in archaeological material.[2] In a unique study of various types of prehistoric chains and shackles, Hugh Thompson outlines the occurrence of this material in Europe, of which the majority— unsurprisingly—stems from the period between 100 BC and AD 400, that is Roman times. As Thompson show, chains and fetters of this type are apparently very rare in Northern Europe in post-Roman times: two examples come from Ireland in the early seventh century,[3] while others come from the Czech Republic, Slovakia, and Bulgaria in the period 900–1200.[4] A couple of Viking Age (slave?) shackles

[1] See Roesdahl 1980 pp. 27–28, Seiler 2001 p. 25, Gronenborn 2001 *passim*, Zachrisson 2003, and Theuws ms.
[2] Gronenborn 2001.
[3] Scott 1978 and Thompson 1993. Note that the former (p. 229) is not certain that we are dealing with "slave-collars" in this case, but poses the (vaild) question: "Is it not possible that instead of being used to secure slaves or hostages, the decorated Lagore collars might have been used for favourite animals as a way of showing the esteem of the master for his pet (while at the same time keeping the 'pet' safely restrained?").
[4] See Henning 1992, cf. Fontaine 2017.

Thraldom. Stefan Brink, Oxford University Press. © Oxford University Press 2021.
DOI: 10.1093/oso/9780197532355.003.0014

are discussed later. A source-critical problem with these chains and fetters is that we cannot know whether they were intended for slaves, for animals, or for criminals who were imprisoned. Thompson suggests they should probably be seen in the context of slavery, and he has good arguments for this. The chains and shackles that have been found are of four types: (1) foot-fetters, (2) hand-shackles, (3) neck-shackles, and (4) long chains with multiple neck-shackles (sometimes hand-shackles).[5] Especially the fourth type, of course, recalls slave transportation, where slaves were bought and sold at slave markets and were tied together with neck-chains in one long line.

In an interesting article, Erhard Cosack and Peter Kehne (1999) discuss various chains that have been found during archaeological excavations of a "germanische Siedlung," a settlement from Germanic times, in Niedersachsen, dated to the first centuries AD. Their interpretation is that these finds testify to a rather extensive Germanic-Roman slave trade during the period in question.

The Danish archaeologist Klavs Randsborg has considered in particular the problem of tracing slavery in archaeological material,[6] and in a contextually important article states, "for prehistoric periods, slavery can only be studied in a rather unsatisfactory way. It is always difficult to discuss social anthropological concepts by means of mute material data."[7] He concludes that the life of the "deprived," i.e. the "slaves," of Scandinavia can, only be studied through the literary sources, as there are no certain archaeological indications of living quarters for slaves, of their work.[8] The same conclusion has recently been reached by the Dutch archaeologist Frands Theuws: "The nuanced opinions of historians on the relationship between the legal status of being free or unfree and the relation between peasants and land owners in terms of dependency/independency makes it almost impossible to contribute to this debate on the basis of material culture. What we can do is contribute to the debate on the economic status of peasants."[9] However, it is not uncommon for archaeologists to speculate about the existence of slaves when excavations are interpreted.

As an early example, we could take the archaeological excavations carried out in Attica in Greece, where there existed many and important silver mines

[5] For shackles identified for slaves and the slave trade in Europe, see also Henning 1992.
[6] For general archaeological reflections pertaining to prehistoric class society, see Hodges 1989.
[7] Randsborg 1986 p. 155.
[8] Randsborg 1986 p. 158.
[9] Theuws ms.

in Lavreotiki already in the 900s BC. By all appearances it looks as if large numbers of slaves were used as workers in these mines. From the names listed in preserved records of slaves from circa 400 BC it is possible to detect where these people originated from. Reviews of archaeological excavations carried out there, however, reveal hardly any positive evidence for the existence of slaves on the site, which among other things is explained by a rapid adaptation by the slaves to the existing Greek culture, which must, of course, be regarded purely as an argument *e silentio*.[10]

Executions and ritual killings of people seem to have occurred within the frame of pre-Christian religion and culture of Scandinavia, which is indicated by archaeological as well as written sources.[11] Presumably, it was predominantly criminals and thralls who were used as human sacrifices, but occasionally it was assumed that the gods demanded a nobler sacrifice. Such slaves—obviously very often war captives—have been called Germ. *Opfersklaven* or *sacrificial slaves* and are known from several early cultures, for example the Aztec Empire in Mexico.[12]

Some of the so-called bog-bodies that have been found especially in Denmark and that can normally be dated to the period from the Late Bronze Age until the beginning of Roman Iron Age,[13] are hardly criminals that have been put to death. For example, some of these murdered individuals have had their clothes tidily folded up and placed close to their bodies, something that would not be expected for a criminal. P. V. Glob cautiously imagines that, for instance, the famous Grauballe-man was one of the "cult slaves" that Tacitus mentions.[14] Of particular interest is the find of a bog-body from southern Jutland that showed a special hairstyle considered typical for a Suebian free man, based on a description given by Tacitus (*Germania* chapter 38) and on Roman stone carvings. By all appearances he was a slave, a war captive from the area around the river Elbe.[15] Still, it must be considered rather bold to regard these bog-bodies from pre-Roman times as sacrificed slaves, since we have no knowledge of whether the institution of slavery existed in Scandinavia during this early stage. A more reasonable interpretation would be to regard these bog-bodies as belonging to people who were ritually

[10] See Morris 1998.
[11] Cf. Hemmendorff 1984 pp. 7–8, Nordenstorm 1994, and recently and comprehensively Wikström af Edholm 2020.
[12] Evans 2008 p. 451, Zeuske 2018 pp. 23–47, 2019 pp. 206–221.
[13] Glob 1965, Fischer 1979.
[14] Glob 1965 p. 136.
[15] Randsborg 1986 p. 158.

(killed and?) deposited in water or mires and of which some were probably war prisoners or captives.

I use the word "sacrifice," well aware of the fact that to historians of religion such a use of the term is considered incorrect. According to today's standard definition a sacrifice must be directed toward the gods.[16] In the examples that follow, the case is instead that thralls were killed and placed to accompany the deceased free person, presumably to serve them in Valhǫll or in the chthonic realm of Hel. In other words, according to the terminology of history of religion the case is rather of ritual killing. The stipulated definition given within history of religion causes a separation between the scientific and nonscientific use of "sacrifice" within many languages, which is unfortunate. One can, as is well-known, "sacrifice" oneself when a corner is given during a football, ice-hockey, or *bandy* match—the latter to use as an example of a Nordic sport and one of the most fun games to play (in my opinion)—an often heroic deed, which, however, is not done in order to assuage any deities, but to help the team. Keeping in mind this problem, in this chapter I use "sacrifice" with an extended meaning (against the definition given by historians of religion), thus including ritual killing of people. Moreover, it must be kept in mind that the possibility of thralls having been killed without any ritual actions and simply thrown into the grave to benefit the deceased free person in their next life may be worth considering.

In Scandinavia, a number of so-called *double graves* have been found, that is, burials in which two persons have been placed in the same grave. It is not uncommon that the deceased was accompanied in the grave by a dog or a horse. And considering what the previously mentioned muslim Ibn Fadlan wrote about the burial of the Rūs chieftain, a thrall may in the same way have been put to death to follow his or her master on the last journey.[17]

Furthermore, the woman—in all likelihood a slave, according to the traditional interpretation—who followed "her queen" in the ship burial from Oseberg in Norway is famous. It turns out that this burial was particularly elaborate, with magnificent grave goods and constructions. As a whole, this burial seems to bear witness to an extended ritual, possibly lasting several years![18]

[16] See, e.g., Widengren 1971 p. 159 and Henninger 1987 pp. 544 f.

[17] I am grateful to Dr Andreas Nordberg, Stockholm, for references to literature on possible thrall burials and to Professor Frands Herschend, Uppsala, for inspiring conversation about, in this case, the possibility of tracing slaves in archaeological material. See also Nordberg 2002 p. 22.

[18] Gansum 2002 pp. 271 ff., Price 2010, 2014, see also Herschend 2000, and see also what follows. It is interesting that recent scientific analyses on the younger woman in the burial may hint at the

This can be complemented by what the Persian explorer and geographer Ibn Rustah (*Aḥmad ibn Rusta Iṣfahānī*), who had traveled with some Rūs to Novgorod, wrote about the burial of an apparently Scandinavian chieftain in the Volga area around 900: When a chieftain among them dies, his followers make a grave for him in the shape of a spacious house and place him therein. Beside him they lay his clothes, gold bracelet, amounts of food, vessels, drinks, and minted coins. With him they also place the woman he loved, and this while she is still alive; the door to the grave is closed, and she dies.[19]

There is an unusual, albeit contextually interesting, poetic fragment, dated by Finnur Jónsson to the tenth century,[20] preserved in *Landnámabók* (*Sturlubók* 27). The narrative surrounding the poem tells of how Ásmundr died and was buried in a grave-mound, *Ásmundarleiði*, where he was placed in a ship together with a thrall (*Ásmundr var beygðr í Ásmundarleiði ok lagðr í skip ok þræll hans hjá honum*). Later on, a voice was heard coming from the mound, declaiming the following poem (in my free translation):[21]

Einn byggi ek stǫð steina	I was placed in the stone cairn
stafnrúm Atals hrafni,	in Atal's raven (= ship)
erat of þegn á þiljum	alone in the stem-space
þrǫng, bý ek á mar ranga.	where I am my own master on the boards.
Rúm er bǫðvitrum betra,	Room is for the battle-wise better
brimdýri knák stýra,	—the sea-monster (= ship) I can steer—
lifa man þat með lofðum	than to live among men
lengr, en illt of gengi.	if you feel bad about the company.

possibility that she comes from Iran or thereabout (Holck 2006), a possibility which however has not been substantiated in later DNA analyses. To further complicate the picture, Fedir Androshchuk (2005) has argued that there instead is a man buried in the grave, actually with quite interesting arguments.

[19] Ohlmarks 1983 p. 173; cf. Nordenstorm 1994 pp. 267–268. There has been a discussion whether some very interesting Viking Age double burials in Russia and Ukraine can be seen in a Rūs cultural context, and hence have something to do with Scandinavian mortuary practice, see, e.g., Androshchuk and Zotsenko 2012 pp. 169–173, also discussed by Raffield et al. 2017b pp. 169–172. This has been described for some burials at Pìdgìrcì (Podhorce in Polish, Podgorcy in Russian), close to Lviv in present-day western Ukraine, in the former Kievan Rūs' realm, where a male with weaponry of probably Scandinavian origin or link, hence probably a Rūs warrior, was buried with a woman (the wife or a concubine?), see Liwoch and Müller-Wille 2012.

[20] *Skj* B2:I p. 173, cf. https://skaldic.abdn.ac.uk/m.php?p=verse&i=1298&v=&x=0.

[21] The stanzas have been translated by Judith Jesch (2005) thus: "Alone I inhabit the place of stones (= mound), the stem-space of Atall's raven (= ship). I dwell on the steed of the frames (= ship); it is not crowded for the man on the deck-planks. Space is better for the battle-wise one than bad companionship; I am able to steer the surf-animal (ship); that will live for long among men." See also http://skaldic.abdn.ac.uk/m.php?p=verse&i=22247.

The poem is not all that easy to translate, but the gist of it appears to be approximately this:[22] "I alone inhabit the ship (or stem) room within the stone cairn/burial mound, there is no throng on the boards/deck where I live. The spacious quarter is, however, better for the warrior than (being part of/ being surrounded by) a whole entourage that irritates you." It is best to rest alone in one's grave is what the voice seems to say. After this incident, the thrall was therefore removed from the ship inside the mound (*Eptir þat var leitat til haugsins ok var þrællinn tekinn ór skipinu*). It is very possible that this poetic fragment goes back to the tenth century and that the author(s) of *Landnámabók* understood the narrative that surrounds the poem correctly. This would imply that, in the tenth century, it happened that thralls were killed and were put into the same graves as their owners, but the buried man in this case, the free man, did not want any (bad) company, but wanted to journey by himself.[23]

In *Sigurðarkviða in skamma* (65–70), composed in the old metrical foot of *fornyrðislag*, the dying Brynhildr explains in her parting speech how she wants to be cremated alongside her already deceased husband and her servants or thralls and two hawks:[24]

Biðia mvn ec þik	I beg you still
bœnar einnar,	a prayer,
—sú mun í heimi	—in this world
hinzt bœn vera!—	which is my last prayer—
Láttu svá breiða	Erect on the plain
borg á velli,	a mound so big
at und oss ǫllom	that all will
iafnrúmt síe,	fit inside
þeim er sulto	of those who died
með Sigurði.	with *Sigurð*.
Tialdi þar um þá borg	Then furnish this grave
tiǫldom oc skiǫldom,	with hangings and shields
valaript vel fáð	expensive textiles from the south
ok Vala mengi;	and many deceased,
brenni mér inn húnska	burn me with the Hun [= *Sigurð*]

[22] Cf. *Skj* B1:I p. 173.
[23] Cf. Nordenstorm 1994 p. 268.
[24] Old Norse text: *Edda*, ed. Neckel (1936) p. 212. My rather free translation. Several passages are particularly hard to translate and suggestions for translation and interpretation are very diverse.

á hlið aðra.	on the other side.
Brenni inom húnska	Burn on the other side
á hlið aðra	of the Hun [= *Sigurð*]
mína þióna	my servants [= thralls?]
meinom gǫfga:	with exquisite jewelry,
tveir at hǫfðom,	two by the head,
ok tveir haukar;	and two hawks;
þá er ǫllo skipt	then everything will be divided
til iafnaðar.	and properly arranged.
Liggi okkar enn í milli	Also lay between us
málmr hringvariðr,	the ring-sword
egghvast éarn,	the sharp iron,
svá endr lagit,	placed in such a way
þá er vit bæði	that it is with us both
beð einn stigom	as when we lay in the bed
ok hétom þá	and called ourselves
hióna nafni.	man and wife.
Hrynia honom þá	You will not find him
á hæl þeygi	on his heals
hlunn blik hallar	the door to the hall
hringi litkoð,	has a splendid ring,
ef hánom fylgir	I will follow him
ferð mín heðan	on my parting
—þeygi mun vár fǫr	—my departure shall not
aumlig vera!—	be dishonorable!
Þvíat hánom fylgia	With him shall follow
fimm ambóttir,	five slave women
átta þiónar,	eight servants [= thralls?]
øðlom góðir,	of noble descent
fóstrman mitt	my foster-father
ok faðerni,	and my paternal inheritance,
þat er Buðli gaf	that which *Buðli* gave
barni síno.	to his children.

These poetic stanzas describe what would likely be an upper-class burial from the Vendel Period/Early Viking Age (c. 600–900). The nobleman in his well-equipped grave—apparently what is referred to is a chamber grave hung with tapestries—besides his weapons and finery was given five female thralls and eight servants, presumably thralls, and also her *fóstrman*, a thrall raised in the household, as well as one or more hawks—possibly trained goshawks, a rare and precious gift.

This chimes with the aforementioned Oseberg burial, wherein grave goods worthy of a queen were deposited. Terje Gansum has carried out a new and interesting analysis of this burial.[25] When the grave was constructed in the 830s, it was apparently surrounded by many rituals that may have gone on for an extended period of time—months, perhaps years. After construction of the grave was begun, a ship was dragged up to the grave and the building of a grave chamber aft of the mast begun. The chamber was decked out and equipped, among other things, with a wagon, sleds, beds with carved posts and down covers, cloth, tapestries and other textiles, containers of food and berries, and as many as eight wooden chests with locks. Two women were buried in the chamber, one of whom is, then, supposed to have been sacrificed in order to accompany the other woman into death. Moreover, the decapitated head of an ox was deposited along with ten decapitated horses and three dogs. The grave chamber was subsequently covered with turf and half a mound was constructed. The peculiar thing is that half the ship appears to have jutted out of the grave; it was not entirely covered to begin with. After what is regarded as many and extended rituals had taken place, the exposed part of the ship was then covered with soil and great amounts of stones and a complete mound was built over the entire ship burial. The traditional interpretation is that a highborn "queen" was buried in the Oseberg ship together with her female slave.

Klavs Randsborg defines a "slave burial" as a grave with a person with no grave goods placed on top of or, as can be assumed on the basis of a grave from, for example, Stengade, beside another person. It may also be assumed, he states, that slaves were in certain cases put into separate graves, as was sometimes done with horses.[26] The question is, then, how that person can be identified as a slave. It must also be kept in mind that not all decapitated people found in graves should be interpreted as slaves, but perhaps rather as murderers and criminals.[27]

Randsborg treats this problem in a subsequent article wherein he introduces a stipulative definition specific to archaeology of what constitutes a slave burial: "we must actually rephrase the concept of slavery in order to

[25] Gansum 2002, se also Price 2010, 2014.
[26] Randsborg 1980 pp. 133 ff.
[27] A. Reynolds 2009, and for Scandinavia, see also Gardeła 2011, 2013.

make it operational for archaeological studies."[28] What archaeologists are able to identify are, according to him, certain material aspects relating to social groups and individuals of low social standing within the society at the time, particularly those whose lives were in the hands of others. These could include criminals (that is, individuals who broke the contemporary social code), outsiders, war captives, foreigners, and others who had no natural bonds to the local society. The various possibilities that Randsborg operates with in order to detect "slaves" within the archaeological material leads to a whole range of uncertain factors and includes many potential types of individuals and social groups, such as criminals, cripples and lame people, perhaps homosexuals, and other deviants alongside slaves. The probably "safest" indication of slaves within archaeological source material is made up of those cases consisting of so-called double graves, particularly those wherein one of the buried individuals has been tied up, decapitated, mutilated, or placed within the grave in a humiliating position.

In other words, double burials are archaeologically interesting in the present context.[29] In her review of Viking Age grave material from the towns of Ärvinge and Kymlinge in Spånga parish in Stockholm, Anita Biuw has found twelve certain and eight uncertain double burials.[30] A special case is a cremation containing three men. The burials are usually dated to the ninth or tenth century. All burials contain a wealth of finds, with many sacrificed animals and items of great value. The grave types are usually mounds or large cairns. Also in Birka around twenty double graves have been found. In Spånga as well as Birka these are in many cases to be considered high-status graves; the Birka graves, for example, include the wealthy chamber graves of 644, 735, 750, and 834. Biuw's tentative conclusion is that these double graves are possibly those in which a thrall has been placed, alternatively that we are dealing with *suttee*,[31] which are cases in which the wife (or, as in Ibn Fadlan's example, slave woman) of a deceased nobleman chose or was forced to follow her husband or master into death and was buried with him. Biuw's caution with regard to interpreting these double burials as slave burials is, in my opinion, well founded and should be emulated.

[28] Randsborg 1986 p. 155.

[29] For a discussion of many of the double burials excavated in Scandinavia, which are presented in what follows, see also Gardeła 2013.

[30] Biuw 1992 p. 293.

[31] See for example Stein 1978 on the *suttee* tradition in India.

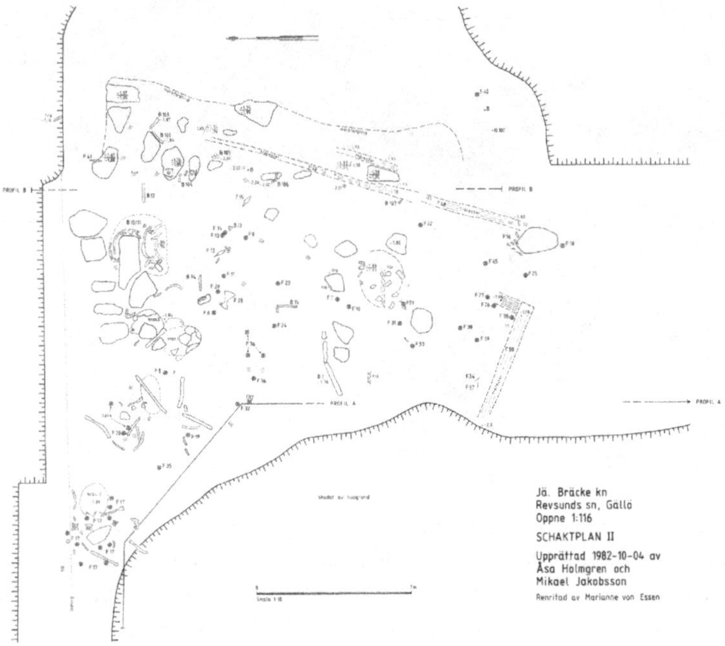

Fig. 14.1 A Late Viking Age primitive kind of chamber grave from Gällö, Jämtland, northern Sweden, which contained four individuals, a horse, a dog, and probably a blackcock (Sw. *orre*), an iron axe, five arrowheads, two knives, and thirteen pearls. The objects and remains of skeletons are difficult to identify in the plan, but two of the sides of the chamber grave are identifiable. (Jamtli Museum, Östersund; Thanks to Dr. Kristina Jonsson for providing me with the plan.)

A grave from Gällö in Revsund (Raä 91:1), Jämtland, Sweden, proves how hard it is for an archaeologist to correctly interpret what is excavated. The grave, which was excavated in 1982 and is situated in modern-day Gällö, near the shores of Lake Revsundssjön, had no markings above ground (in other words, a grave on flat ground). We are dealing with a chamber grave (3.5 x 3.5 m), constructed with pine timber and as such it is a fairly unusual grave type. In the grave was found—mixed around—the remains of four people, a horse, a dog, and probably a black grouse (Sw. *orre*) as well as an iron axe, five arrow points, two knives, and thirteen beads (Fig. 14.1). The grave is dated to the Late Viking Age (AD 900–1050). Why have four people been buried together, and with such exclusive grave goods? Is this a nobleman whose horse, dog, and slaves have followed him into the grave?

Fig. 14.2 The double burial from Bollstanäs, Uppland, Sweden, dated to circa AD 700–800, where a 20- to 40-year-old man had been cremated together with domestic animals, such as dog, horse and fowl, and equipment. On top of the pyre were two decapitated men, who have been assumed to be the young man's slaves. (Photo and permission to publish by Ove Hemmendorff.)

One of the first to pay attention to double burials was Ove Hemmendorff during the excavation of a grave field near Bollstanäs in the province of Uppland, Sweden.[32] Here, he excavated a grave field that was in use from the seventh century until the eleventh century. In a mound (8 x 1 m) that stood out from the rest he encountered two decapitated men (Fig. 14.2). They lay embedded in a funeral pyre wherein a 20- to 40-year-old man was burned together with domestic animals, such as dog, horse, and fowl, and equipment. The two decapitated men were about 17–22 and 20–40 years old, respectively. Both had been executed with a cut through the third cervical vertebra, separating the head from the body. All indications point to dating the grave to the Late Vendel Period (c. AD 700–800). Hemmendorff interprets this grave in such a way that the two decapitated were probably thralls of the deceased, cremated man and that they were executed and buried as "travel companions."

Judging by this, in comparison to the remaining graves in the Bollstanäs grave field, the exceptional burial mound containing such a strange burial, and in the light of the deposited grave goods, such as dog, horse, bird, and

[32] Hemmendorff 1984, see also Seiler 2003.

perhaps lynx (fur) and others, it seems reasonable to assume that the deceased and cremated man was a chieftain of the village, a sort of "village aristocrat." It was, at least, hardly any ordinary farmer who was given two decapitated men to accompany him on his way to the realm of the dead.

Lena Holmquist Olausson has described another grave, which she excavated at the Black Earth (*Svarta jorden*) in Birka, Sweden. Along the edge of a stone-packed terrace, a stone cairn was found under a Viking Age cultural layer. Underneath the stone packing two human skeletons were found, one of which was lying partially on top of the other. The upper skeleton was placed in an unnatural, distorted position, resting on the right side with the right arm behind the back. The left arm and the legs were bent. The right leg was stretched right up toward the upper part of the body. This individual, who turned out to be a 177 cm tall and sturdily built man of 20–30 years, had been decapitated and the head was placed near the chest. The right foot was missing. No grave goods could be related to this man. The other, lower burial was an ordinary Birka grave. It was a man of 40–50 years of age whose weapons had been deposited in the grave along with beads and other possessions. Close to the older man lay also an elk horn, which is why the grave has become known as "the elk-man from Birka." This Birka grave can be dated to the transition from the Vendel period into the Viking Age, that is to say circa AD 800. Holmquist Olausson's interpretation of the grave is that a middle-aged man—a semi- or fully professional warrior—was buried with his weapons and equipment. On top of this man was placed a younger man, who had first been decapitated and brought to the gravesite on a wooden stretcher. She assumes that the younger man was a slave. It is interesting to note that this young man also had his teeth modified/filed (see later).[33]

Holmquist Olausson also mentions a double grave in Fjällinge in the province of Skåne, Sweden.[34] Here, two skeletons lay on top of each other in a pit. The upper had the legs pulled up and was decapitated with the head being placed near the pelvis. Moreover, the lower legs appeared to have been cut off; the victim's foot-bones were missing.

Torun Zachrisson has pointed out a grave find from the Vendel Period from Grimsta in Fresta, the province of Uppland, Sweden.[35] Here, a man (aged 20–40) has been executed and burned in a fire together with horse, dog, bird of prey, and personal items. The remains of the fire were later gathered together

[33] Personal communication by Lena Holmquist Olausson.
[34] Holmquist Olausson 1990 p. 178.
[35] Zachrisson 2003 pp. 90 ff.

and taken to Grimsta burial ground, where they were covered over with a packing of stones. In the middle of the stone packing there is a rectangular area on which two young men were apparently placed, one in his late teens, the other aged 20–40. They appear to have had their feet tied together. The men had been decapitated and placed face down in the grave. Both heads were placed on top of the victims' backs. One of the skulls shows an open wound that may have been fatal and that perhaps reveals that the killing did not take place in an entirely peaceful manner. Subsequently, a mound was built on top of the grave. Zachrisson interprets, in all likelihood correctly, these two men as thralls.

Anton Seiler has pointed out some upper-class burials from Uppland, Sweden: in *Ottarshögen* in Husby, Vedel parish, a veritable "royal mound" (Fig. 14.3a and b), the cremated remains of a man as well as a woman have been found, although only masculine accoutrements occur, such as belt fittings and game pieces. In an equally impressive Viking Age mound in Husby-Långhundra, the so-called *Gullhögen*, also in Uppland, the same scenario was found; two urns, one containing the bones of a middle-aged man, the other the bones of a young woman. Near the urns was found a sword driven down between some stones. In both cases, Seiler believes, and probably rightly so, that we are dealing with a man who was buried together with his younger female slave.

In the cremation layer of a Viking Age stone setting from Arninge, Täby parish, in Uppland, numerous gold, silver, and bronze items were found along with gaming pieces and six combs. The strangest aspect, however, is the large amount of burned bones that was found, a total of 90 liters (corresponding to roughly 60 kilos). Following an osteological analysis, it could be determined that the bones stemmed from eleven dogs, seven horses, and one bird of prey as well as fish; there were also remains of five human beings, three middle-aged men, one young woman, and one older person whose gender could not be determined. How this burial is to be interpreted is uncertain, but there is nothing to disprove that thralls were buried here.[36]

At Flakstad in northern Norway some burials in a grave field excavated in the 1980s have ben reanalyzed using stable isotopes ($\delta^{13}C$, $\delta^{15}N$) and ancient mitochondrial DNA (mtDNA). In this grave field ten individuals were analyzed, where at least two graves contained double burials, and one (heavily disturbed and fragmented) potentially a triple grave[37]

[36] Seiler 2003 pp. 79–80.
[37] Naumann et al. 2013.

(a)

Fig. 14.3a The large mound, called *Ottarshögen*, named after a fictitious(?) king *Ottar*, at Vendel, Uppland, Sweden. (Photo: T. Öhrström, Upplandsmuseet CC BY-NC-ND; https://digitaltmuseum.se/011013957308/ottarshogen-i-vendels-socken-uppland-1979.)

(b)

Fig. 14.3b Drawing of *Ottarshögen* by Johan Peringskiöld (1654–1720). (https://sv.wikipedia.org/wiki/Fil:Ottarsh%C3%B6gen_i_Vendel_(Peringski%C3%B6ld_1725_s013).jpg.)

The isotope analyses indicated a strong differentiation between individuals, identifying different sources of protein intake. Of the ten individuals analyzed, seven had, according to the isotope analysis, marine food as their mainstay, whereas for three individuals, all of them found in double burials, the isotopes indicated a diet with predominantly terrestrial protein sources. The ancient mtDNA analysis was undertaken in order to investigate probable maternal kinship between the individuals, as well as to establish genetic origins of people. As for the former, although the sample from Flakstad represents only a small localized population, one would expect to find some shared kinship, however, even if approximated, the results suggested the examined individuals do not represent a particularly maternally inbred population. The isotope analyses indicated that there must have been a social differentiation in this sample of individuals, where some in the double burials (slaves?) had the same marine diet as the individuals in single graves (free farmers?), but a few individuals in the double burials had a different diet, coming from terrestrial protein sources, probably indication persons of a higher social status. As for the possibility of establishing genetic origin of the individuals, Naumann et al. do not give any hints in the paper.

A very interesting, however, difficult to interpret, early tenth-century burial was excavated at Kaupang, Vestfold, Norway.[38] Four individuals were buried in a furnished boat, a man and a women were placed head to head, the woman had a baby placed at her hip, and a second woman was placed sitting up (Fig. 14.4). Is this a married couple with a baby child and a slave woman? Why have they been buried at the same time? Killed through illness? If the second woman is to be interpreted as a slave woman, why is she sitting up in the stern, as if she was steering the boat with the steering oar? This complex burial epitomizes the difficulties of analyzing archaeological remains and to put them in a context.

In Denmark, some truly extraordinary examples have been found. One peculiar gravesite—which, admittedly, does not belong in this context, but requires a different interpretation—was made near Kumle Høje in Langeland. Two young men were found in a grave, one of whom was placed face down, facing and on top of the other one. The grave is probably dated to the Early Viking Age (ninth century). The excavators thought they were

[38] Ka. 294–297. See Blindheim and Heyerdahl-Larsen 1995, Stylegar 2007 pp. 95–100, 122–123, Price 2010; also discussed by Raffield et al. 2017b. pp. 170–171.

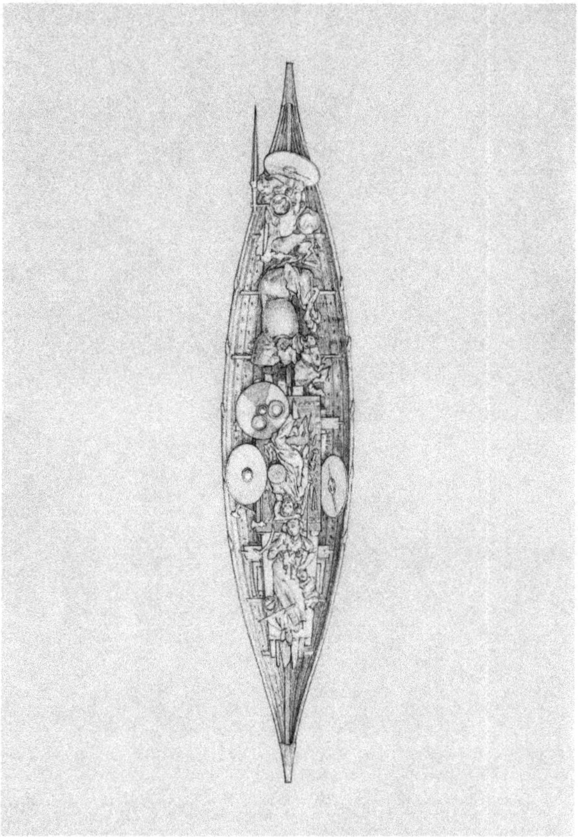

Fig. 14.4 An early tenth-century boat burial with four buried people inside, from Kaupang, Vestfold, Norway. (Reconstruction by Þórhallur Þráinsson. Permission to publish by Neil Price.)

able to establish that the men's feet were tied together.[39] It is possible that this grave should be interpreted as the grave of two homosexuals who were executed and given a degrading burial. There are strong indications that people had a very negative attitude toward homosexuality and transvestism during the Viking Age,[40] when an insult alluding to the recipient being a homosexual or dressing in women's clothes could constitute reason enough for killing the person who made the insult.[41]

[39] Kristensen and Bennike 2001 pp. 12–15.
[40] See, e.g., Meulengracht Sørensen 1980 and Gunnora Hallakarva ms.
[41] About verbal insult and composition of insulting poetry (*níð*), see Ström 1973, Almqvist 1974, and Meulengracht Sørensen 1980.

Fig. 14.5 The double burial from Lejre, Själland, Denmark. The beheaded man (to the right) was placed on top of the buried man (to the left). (Reconstruction by Mirosław Kuźma in Gardeła 2017 p. 107. Permission to publish by Leszek Gardeła.)

In the 1940s, interesting excavations were begun at Lejre in Sjælland, Denmark. One of the examined mounds turned out to contain a double burial. Underneath lay a rather small man on his back in the usual stretched out manner. He was equipped with a knife, a whetstone, and a buckle. On top of him lay another man in an unnatural position. He was placed on his stomach, bent down over the first man and with his hands and feet gathered together, which reveals that they had been tied together. The body was

Fig. 14.6 A Viking Age burial from Gerdrup, Sjælland, Denmark, with one man and one woman, where the woman was equipped with weapons, while the male had his hands and feet tied together and his head was broken apart or even pulled off. Large boulders have been placed on top of the woman. (Reconstruction by Mirosław Kuźma in Gardeła 2017 p. 183. Permission to publish by Leszek Gardeła.)

decapitated and the head placed face down near the left shoulder.[42] We are in all likelihood dealing with a man who was buried and whose slave was executed and thrown into the grave to accompany him on the journey to Valhǫll (Fig. 14.5).

In Gerdrup near Roskilde in Sjælland, a Viking Age grave has been examined, containing a female and a male skeleton. The woman was equipped

[42] Andersen 1960 p. 26 and Bennike 1985 pp. 108–109.

with weapons and on top of her large stones had been placed, while the man seems to have been buried with his feet tied together and probably also his hands (Fig. 14.6). His neck had been broken or rather it had been pulled apart when he was hung, which leads the excavators to believe that the man was a thrall who was killed and buried together with the woman.[43] This is, however, an interpretation that can be discussed. The gravesite in Gerdrup is especially interesting, albeit difficult to interpret.

Similarly, a grave was found at Stengade in Langeland, Denmark. In a sizable chamber grave (200 x 140 cm) was found a very tall (about 190 cm) buried man about 25 years of age, equipped with a silver-inlaid spear (Fig. 14.7). Next to this man lay another, shorter man (c. 175 cm) of 30–35 years of age. His feet were gathered together on top of each other, which suggests they were tied together. His left arm was bent across his body so that his hand was placed in his crotch. His right arm was bent across his body so that his hand was placed near his buttocks. This strange position of the hands can be explained in such a way that his hands were tied together in the crotch. The shorter, older man was, moreover, decapitated.[44] The head was placed by the right shoulder with the top of the head turned toward the neck.

This peculiar grave at Stengade has been interpreted by the excavator Jørgen Skaarup as the grave of a slave and his master. The interpretation is in all likelihood correct. The gravesite at Stensgade has been taken to represent the grave field of an ordinary settlement in the tenth century, but this particular grave deviates in the sense that it is a rather large chamber grave containing a very tall young man equipped with weaponry. There is reason to believe that he was a prominent person, given the grandeur of the weapons and the grave. The deceased had also been given a slave whose hands and feet were tied together and who was decapitated prior to the burial. The intention may have been that the youngster should be accompanied by his slave on the journey to Valhǫll.[45]

I think that this Stengade burial shows—also in the light of the Bollstanäs burial and of the double burials at Flakstad, Norway—that it is reasonable to hypothesize that slaves or thralls certainly did exist in Scandinavia during the

[43] Christensen 1981, Birkebaek 1982–83, Christensen and Bennike 1983, Bennike 1985 p. 117, Gardeła 2011 pp. 351–55.
[44] Skaarup 1972, 1976 pp. 57–58.
[45] Skaarup 1976 p. 183.

Fig. 14.7 A reconstruction of the double burial from Stengade, Sjælland, Denmark. (Reconstruction by Mirosław Kuźma in Gardeła 2017 p. 149. Permission to publish by Leszek Gardeła.)

Viking Age, but that it was perhaps *predominantly* the privilege of the upper classes to keep such. This hypothesis finds support in the conclusions drawn by Ove Hemmendorff, in the reasoning of Lena Holmquist Olausson in connection with the "elk-man" from Birka, in the interpretation by Naumann et al., where only potential high-status individuals were found in double burials (together with slaves?), in the analyses of "aristocratic" double burials in Uppland by Anton Seiler,[46] and in the analysis carried out by Kerstin Engdahl on burials characterized as human sacrifices.[47] The purpose of slaves to this

[46] Seiler 2003 pp. 77–87 (esp. p. 80).
[47] Engdahl 1990 pp. 3, 17, 41.

social group seemingly was to keep them as workers and servants, but apart from that it was considered prestigious for the owners to be able to keep one or more slaves. Perhaps slaves were found predominantly in the better-off households of society, albeit slaves no doubt must have been found also on ordinary farms. This would imply that we should hardly imagine great crowds of work thralls during the Viking Age in Scandinavia, working side by side with common farmers (who would be their owners). Instead, I think that slaves found on the lowest rung of the social ladder to a large extent functioned as workers who carried out the heaviest and dirtiest agricultural tasks and as servants in the households of noblemen and wealthy farmers, and furthermore at more ordinary farms there were to be found one or two slaves in the household or working the fields.[48]

It must nonetheless be stressed that the above hypothesis is an argument *e silentio* in the sense that the preserved probable slave burials, the double burials, are burials in which slaves were executed to follow their masters into the grave.[49] Whether the slaves that these burials contain constitute a representative segment of the slaves that existed in society at the time is very uncertain, perhaps unlikely. The hypothesis finds no support in, for instance, the section of the Frostathing Law describing a "normal" Trøndelag farm as housing three thralls (or servants), even if the passage is not entirely clear regarding this point.[50] Perchance Dagfinn Skre is right in assuming that slaves were not given burials, but were simply disposed of or dug down as fertilizer in the dung heap as was done with animals dead from accidents or diseases and other cadavers.

An example that highlights the complexity of the problem is found in the exceptional archaeological excavations at Kalmergaarden, Tissø, in Sjælland.[51] By the entrance to the Tissø settlement compound, at the old crossing of the Halleby stream, two dead and decapitated men were found. Their grave seems to be marked by a large stone, and the deceased have been placed or rather shoved into a small grave close by the stone (Fig. 14.8). The skeletons were earlier dated to around the twelfth and thirteenth centuries,

[48] An interpretation along this line is indicated also by Klavs Randsborg (1980 p. 135).

[49] There are also double, even triple graves, which are difficult to interpret whether they contain a slave or not, such as the Viking Age grave field at Kopparsvik on Gotland, discussed by Matthias Toplak (2018 pp. 87–88).

[50] See Krag 1982 p. 210, Iversen 1997 pp. 115–118; it is not a requirement to translate the word used in the laws as 'thralls'. Also 'servants' is possible (see for example Fritzner art. *mansmaðr*).

[51] See Bennike and Christoffersen 1981, Bennike 1985 pp. 106 ff., and Jørgensen and Pedersen 1996 p. 35.

Fig. 14.8 Two executed men found beside a large boulder at Kalmergården close to Tissø, Sjælland, Denmark. Both have been beheaded and more or less thrown into a pit, probably during the Late Viking Age. (The National Museum of Denmark; thanks to Dr. Mads Dengsø Jessen for providing me with the photo.)

but new analyses point to Late Viking Age, probably around the middle of the eleventh century.[52] The two decapitated men seem to have been executed and buried, or perhaps better, thrown into one or two pits. One was a 35- to 50-year-old man; the other, who was 20–35, may have been executed at a later date. One man had a prominent lower jaw and seems, in the wording of the excavators, "hardly to have been particularly handsome."[53] The other man had a stiff hip, the femoral head was joined to the hip socket, and he

[52] Personal communication from Dr. Mads Dengsø Jessen, The National Museum, Copenhagen, Denmark; see also Jessen and Olsen, forthcoming.

[53] Bennike and Christoffersen 1981.

must have had great difficulty walking. The leg would have pointed outward in an almost 90-degree angle. Both men had been decapitated and their heads had been placed between their legs, toward the crotch. The men have been thought to be criminals, which is, however, perhaps contradicted by the fact that one was severely crippled. In the light of, for example, the Stengade grave, it might also be supposed that the two decapitated men were slaves. However, what speaks in favor of the notion of these two men being executed as criminals could be, first, the circumstance that the place of execution and of burial is close to border of a hundred district, between Ars hd and Løve hd. Execution places often had such liminal situations.[54] Second, the heads of the executed have been placed between their legs, faces turned toward the pelvis, which was considered a disgraceful position suitable for criminals and malefactors. There is reason to believe that the placement of the head may be indicative of the person's social position. A decapitated criminal and scoundrel who had both lost his social status and legitimacy and was also despised by society could have his head placed between his legs, which must have been considered a deeply offensive placement. A thrall, on the other hand, was not necessarily despised, but may in presumably many cases have been loved and respected by his or her owner and family. If a thrall was put to death in order to follow his or her master into the grave, the head might be placed not in a degrading position, but in a way that was neutral or respectful toward the executed individual.

The archaeologist Mats Roslund has in a rather ingenious way analyzed pottery and is probably able via this source material to indicate the existence of slaves taken in eastern Europe.[55] Roslund manages to show a radical change in pottery style around AD 1000 in eastern Denmark and southern Sweden, where within a generation (c. 980–1050) a new kind of Slavic style ceramics emerged. He interprets this as a technological as well as a stylistic and social change within society. His theory is that this kind of Baltic ceramics was brought to Scandinavia with female slaves captured (or bought?) from the northern shore of the Baltics, from Rügen and Mecklenburg-Vorpommern in today's Germany, in what was then inhabited by the Slavic Obodrits and Wends (and perhaps even Sorbs). These slave women were placed at farms (ordinary or perhaps rather estate-like farms) where they produced this new ceramic, which was then sold at major trading markets. It is very difficult

[54] See A. Reynolds 2009.
[55] Roslund 2005, 2007, 2021, in press, and ms.

to ascertain how many of these slaves we are talking about, and it is also, as Roslund himself states, probable that there was a large regional difference in terms of where such slaves were found. I would assume they have been found in southern Scandinavia (particularly in Skåne and Sjælland) and perhaps also at marketplaces such as Lund and Birka.

Returning to the question of finds of shackles and fetters, which may indicate the existence of a slave trade and the use of slaves, which was more generally discussed earlier, there are some (albeit very few) finds from Scandinavia and northern Europe, places that were in contact with viking Scandinavians.

In the proto-town of Birka in Sweden, at least one iron shackle has been found, which probably can be interpreted as a shackle for a slave (Fig. 14.9).[56] This is not a particularly daring hypothesis, since Birka probably (or rather certainly) saw a lot of slaves sold and bought at a local slave market, which we assume must have been present in Birka, and also slaves used as chattel and especially craftsmen in the town. It has recently been noticed that the small houses found within the town wall of Birka must have created terrible living conditions, not particularly suitable for people, but where slaves could have been kept.[57] It is, however, in my opinion important *not* to equate Birka with the rest of Sweden at that time. I think the living conditions and the mix of people found here from many places abroad, many free tradesmen, but also probably many slaves, made the multi-ethnic, multicultural Birka very different from its surrounding areas.[58]

Finds of Viking Age shackles and fetters, which might be linked to a slavery or a slave trade, are actually very rare, apart from the just-mentioned shackle from Birka. One shackle from the tenth century is found in Dublin, Ireland (Fig. 14.10), which probably is to be seen in the context of viking Scandinavians dominating that town in this period.

Another interesting artifact is the newly discovered picture stone obviously depicting a raiding party with one individual who seems to be fettered with a neck shackle, being led to a ship (Fig. 14.11). The stone, broken in two pieces, was found during an excavation of the medieval churchyard at Inchmarnock, Scotland, in 2001–2002. It has been dated to the Viking

[56] See Ny Björn Gustafsson's interesting discussion (2009 pp. 89–96).

[57] See the interviews by Benny Eriksson for Swedish Television (SVT), citing Dr. Gunnar Andersson, Stockholm; Professor Neil Price, Uppsala; and others (Eriksson 2017).

[58] Another iron fetter from the Viking Age is found in Skedala, Halland, Sweden (SHM 11773), but this is of another kind and different from the shackle found in Birka (see photo at https://historiska.se/upptack-historien/object/877507-fjatter-av-jarn/), and it is not obvious that the Skedala fetter could have been used for a slave (SHM Coll.).

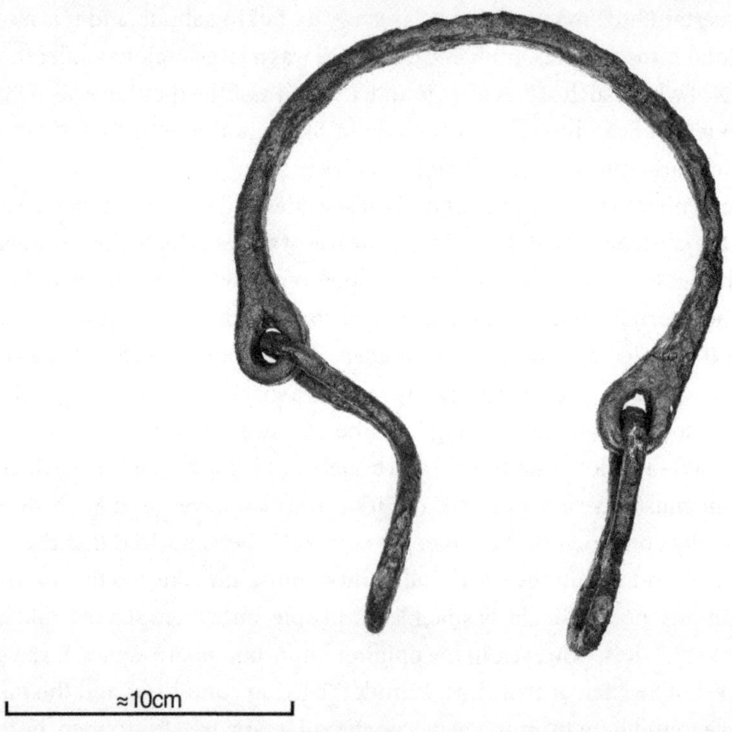

Fig. 14.9 Iron shackle (probably for a slave) found in the "Black Earth" at Birka, Björkö, Sweden, during archaeological excavation in 1872 (SHM 5208). (Photo: Christer Åhlin, Historical Museum/SHM, Stockholm; CC BY 2.5 SE.)

Fig. 14.10 A tenth-century iron slave shackle found at the archaeological excavation at St John's Lane, Dublin.

(a)

(b)

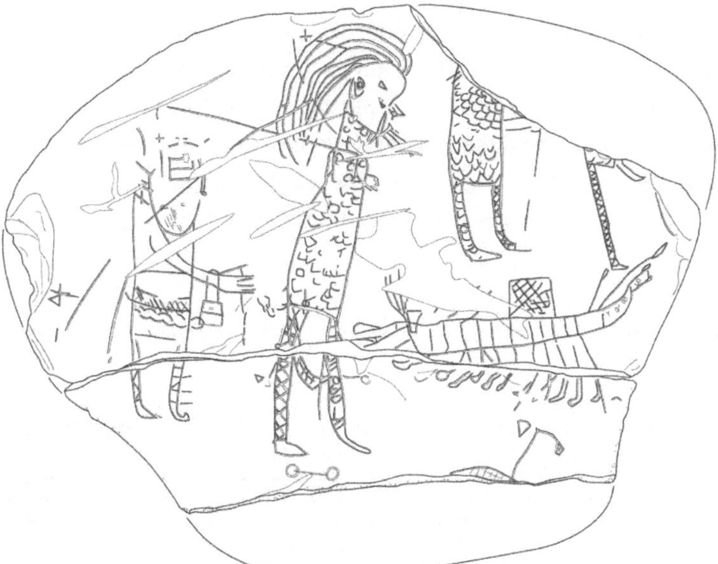

Fig. 14.11a and b This Viking Age picture stone from Inchmarnock, Scotland, is probably depicting a person being captured and fettered with a neck shackle. (Permission to publish by Headland Archaeology, UK, Ltd.)

Period,[59] and it is tempting to place the object in connection with the many viking raids in the area.

At another proto-town and slave-market, Haithabu (Hedeby), on the border between Germany and Denmark, six shackles have been found, five in the harbor (Fig. 14.12), which probably (or certainly) are to be linked to the slave trade.[60] When Petra Westphalen commented on these finds in her comprehensive description and analyses of iron finds from Haithabu, she did not definitively label them as shackles for slaves, but was more cautious, also mentioning the possibility of a usage for legal punishment ("Strafvollzug") or fetters for animals ("Viehfessel"), although one gets the impression that she prefers to see them in a slave context.[61] Sven Kalmring is, however, in his ample and most interesting description and discussion of the excavation and finds from the Haithabu harbor, inclined to see them in context with war captives and slaves.[62] As mentioned previously, we know from written, contemporary sources that Haithabu was an important slave market in the Viking Age, strategically positioned as it was between Denmark and Slavic tribes, and the Baltics and the North Sea.

Very similar to one of the cylinder-shaped shackles found at Haithabu, another find that may be understood as a slave shackle, was found at the Danish ring-fortress Trelleborg on Sjælland (Fig. 14.13).[63] The caveat for this interpretation is that the excavator, Poul Nørlund, identified the shackle as a horse-fetter, and he gives an interesting explanation that supports his interpretation.[64] The shackle was found in a burned pit (*brøndagtige*

[59] Lowe 2008, and https://headlandarchaeology.com/hostage-stone-to-star-in-new-viking-exhibition/.

[60] Personal communication from Dr. Sven Kalmring, Zentrum für Baltische und Skandinavische Archäologie, Stiftung Schleswig-Holsteinische Landesmuseen, Schloss Gottorf, Schleswig, Germany, see also Westphalen 2002, pp. 185–187, Schietzel 2014 pp. 550–551, and Raffield 2019 pp. 7–8, 15.

[61] Westphalen 2002 pp. 185–187, esp. p. 186 with further references.

[62] Kalmring 2010 p. 406: "Fesseln werden mit Kriegsgefangenen und/oder Sklaven in Verbindung gebracht, die zumeist in den islamischen Raum verhandelt wurden. Den Fesselfunden nach zu urteilen scheint der Sklavenhandel offenbar über den Hafen abgewickelt worden zu sein und für Haithabu eine richtige Rolle gespielt haben" (The fetters are associated with prisoners of war and/or slaves, most of whom were traded in the Islamic region. Judging from the shackles, the slave trade appears to have been carried out via the port and played an important role for Haithabu).

[63] Nørlund 1948 Pl. XXXII:1, cf. Raffield 2019 p. 7. See also the Excursus on Trelleborg.

[64] Nørlund 1948 p. 134. Nørlund writes: "To the riding gear must also be counted the XXXII, 1 reproduced cylinder-shaped clasp, which certainly is a lock/fetter for a horse, whereby one of the forelegs of the horse is linked to, for example, the rein, so that it was not able to run away. The shackle of the cylinder lock is with a chain linked to a big, bent shackle, which in each of its eyes has a three-sided ring" (*Til ridetøjet maa endelig ogsaa henregnes den XXXII, 1 gengivne cylinderlaas og lænke, som vist er en hestelaas, hvormed hestens ene forben lænkedes til f.eks. tømmen, saa den ikke var i stand til at løbe bort. Cylinderlaasens bøjle er ved en lænke forbundet med en stor krum bøjle, som i hvert af sine øjer har en tresidet ring.*)

(a)

(b)

Fig. 14.12a and b Iron shackles and fetters from Haithabu/Hedeby, Germany, which have been interpreted to have been used for war captives or slaves. (Museum für Archäologie Schloss Gottorf, Landesmuseen Schleswig-Holstein; thanks to Dr. Volker Hilberg.)

Fig. 14.13 Iron shackle from Trelleborg, Sjælland, Denmark. (The National Museum of Denmark.)

grube), and Nørlund dates the fetter to "probably" the early Middle Ages (hence c. 1100–1300).

In the light of the previously cited passage from the Gulathing Law, about the farmer's best thralls being two females (*ambátt* and *seta*) and two males (*þjónn* and *bryti*), and the passage from the Frostathing Law about there being three thralls (or servants) at an ordinary farm in Trøndelag, it seems we can assume that singular thralls existed also on the farms of well-off farmers and perhaps also of ordinary farmers. In other words, we can set up an alternative model of explanation, which *may* find support in new excavations made in Iceland. The archaeologist Orri Vésteinsson has excavated in, among other places, Sveigakot, where he has dug out small pit-houses with fireplaces. He interprets these as houses that may have been inhabited by thralls or perhaps workers. Similar pit-houses seem to have been common at Icelandic farms. Orri reckons that many slaves were captured in Ireland and were taken to Iceland during the settlement period in order to help colonize the country, slaves whom he reckons to have been freed virtually immediately so that they became tenants.[65] I see two problems in this model: partly, we do not know whether those who inhabited these pit-houses were free or unfree (they could presumably be inhabited by both); partly, Iceland may not be the best example with which to compare eastern Scandinavia during the same period. The conditions of the settlement period in particular must have been fundamentally different from those governing eastern Scandinavia in the Viking Age. However, I find Orri's interpretation interesting and worthy of consideration.

[65] Personal communication from Dr Orri Vésteinsson, Háskóli Íslands.

A similar interpretation has recently been put forward by the archaeologist Martin Hansson, who is analyzing three large farms, actually estate-like farms, in southern and central Sweden.[66] One of them, Lockarp in Skåne, is an estate-like farm from the Vendel Period and the Viking Age, where the archaeologists have found (some of) the aforementioned Baltic ceramics, and it is on this basis that Mats Roslund has identified a pottery production by female slaves of Slavic origins.

However, the most exciting case, in this connection, is a very large estate-like farm, Sanda in Uppland, Sweden (Fig. 14.14). During the Viking Age the estate consisted of five or six long-houses, and several pit-houses. During the second half of the tenth century until the middle of the twelfth century the situation changed, in that especially a lot of smaller houses were erected, as many as thirty smaller houses existing at the same time. We are undoubtedly dealing with a Viking Age and twelfth-century estate, a very large farm, which was abandoned around 1150–1200. Torun Zachrisson interprets the smaller houses as slave dwellings,[67] and Martin Hansson seems to agree.

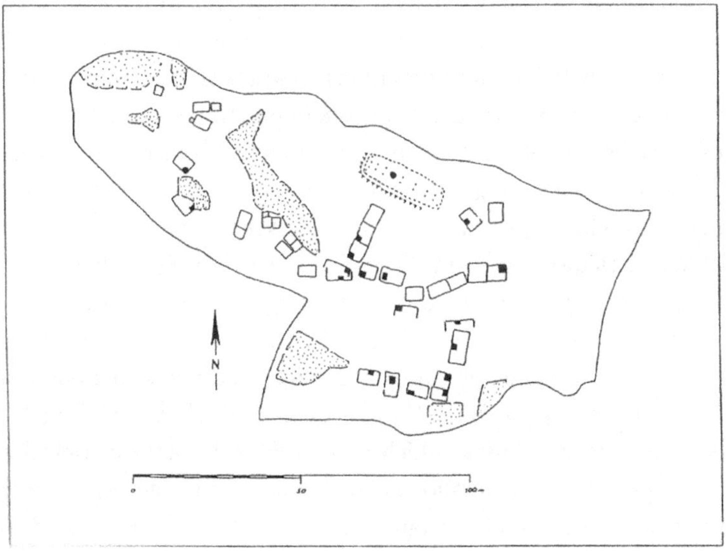

Fig. 14.14 A plan of the excavated Viking Age Sanda estate in Uppland, central Sweden, with the long-house and several small pit-houses, with a hearth (small black squares), which have been interpreted as dwellings for slaves. (After Åqvist 1992 p. 321 ill. 7.)

[66] Hansson 2014.
[67] Zachrisson 2003 pp. 98–99.

I think especially the Sanda case is illuminating. We cannot, of course, be sure that the people living in these thirty small houses were of an unfree status, hence slaves, and not a judicially free workforce on the estate, but I am prepared to follow Zachrisson and Hansson in their interpretation. It also fits the model or theory I am pursuing in this book, namely that slaves predominantly were to be found on estate-like large farms of the Sanda kind in the Viking Age and the twelfth and thirteenth centuries.

As was pointed out in the introduction to this chapter, it is extremely difficult to obtain knowledge about slaves and slavery from archaeological material. That someone who was decapitated and buried should by way of definition be a slave cannot at all be assumed. Instead, many of the decapitated individuals seem to be criminals who had committed serious offenses. The few indications that we do have are, rather, the double burials where it has been possible to establish that one individual was decapitated or otherwise mutilated, which has led the excavators to believe that such persons were thralls. Now and then it has been stated that especially pit-houses may have served as houses for thralls,[68] or that the smaller houses found at excavations of entire Danish villages, for example Sødding near Esbjerg in Jutland, which appear to be adjoined to the long-houses, may have housed servants or thralls.[69] Both interpretations seem plausible, and both, indeed, are supported by the Sanda case. However, in practical terms it is impossible to prove whether or not we are dealing with judicially unfree individuals.

A particularly interesting possibility for discovering slaves in archaeological material has been presented by Frands Herschend, following excavations of the Eketorp ringfort in Öland, Sweden.[70] Some of the byres that were excavated within the fortification contained a single fireplace in one corner as well as finds that point toward habitation (Fig. 14.15). The reasonable interpretation is that servants, presumably thralls, lived here. This observation can then be linked to one of the thrall's names of *Rígsþula*, *Fjósnir* 'one who lives/spends time in the byre', which may support this archaeological interpretation. A similar interpretation is presented by Svante Norr in his attempt to identify an extra room in certain long-houses from the period of AD the second to the sixth century as rooms that may have housed thralls.[71]

[68] See for example Roesdahl 1980 p. 28.
[69] Roesdahl 1980 p. 65.
[70] Personal communication from Frands Herschend, cf. Nordström and Herschend 2003 pp. 85 ff.
[71] Norr 1996.

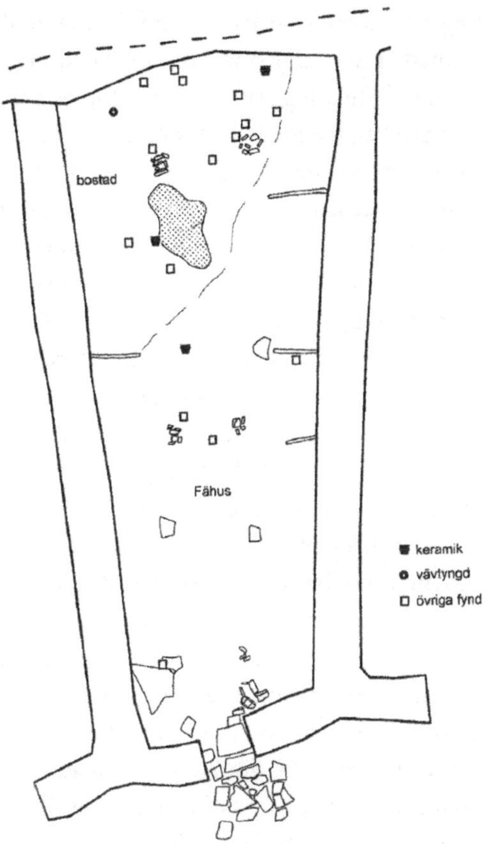

Fig. 14.15 A plan of a byre, excavated in the Eketorp ring-fortress on Öland, Sweden, with a hearth in one corner, which excavators have interpreted as a dwelling place for slaves. (From Herschend and Nordström 2003 p. 63.) Legend: the "pot" Pottery; "ring" Loom weight; "square" Other objects.

If this interpretation of the inhabited section of certain byre houses in Eketorp as the living quarters of thralls is correct, then one may wonder how people managed to make the slaves stay put and not run away. Perhaps they were chained by their necks or feet during the night, which could then be linked to the word *fräls*, that is to say "free neck," so that what characterized a freed slave was that he or she was not chained by the neck anymore. Another alternative, mentioned previously, was that they were marked with mutilated ears, noses, tongues, or other visible body parts, which meant that the social control within society prevented their escape.

At the interesting settlement near Paviken on the island of Gotland in the Baltic, which contained finds of craftsmanship and boatbuilding, excavations revealed a strange grave.[72] In a shallow pit, a skeleton was crammed. On top of it there seem to have been some boards or a heavy layer of soil. The deceased was apparently shoved into the pit and landed on the stomach with the back much bent. The skeleton was dated to the tenth century (AD 940 ± 95). Considering the simple grave and the anything but pious positioning of the deceased one would think that this was someone of low social standing or an outsider, perhaps a thrall.[73]

In the next chapter I discuss Dagfinn Skre's theory regarding prehistoric society in Norway wherein certain (peripheral) farms in areas controlled by a prehistoric aristocracy were run by slaves. It is one of the more elaborate theories involving a slave population. As I will expand on, I can see alternative possibilities and slightly modify the theory into a model, which in the main follows Skre's in terms of presenting a hierarchical society, with main farms and smaller dependent farms, but which I would consider more likely to have been run by farmers (akin to "tenants") rather than by slaves.

In other words, it seems especially difficult to establish the existence of slaves within archaeological materials, in particular the existence of slaves within a Scandinavian socio-agrarian system of prehistoric times. Actually, in my opinion, only the double graves and the probable existence of thralls living in byres, as has been supposed from excavations of Eketorp in Öland, and potentially the female "pottery slaves" and the many small houses at the estate-like farms, such as Sanda and Sødding, have any reasonable proof value, or rather valid indications. Hopefully the use of stable isotopes and ancient DNA will, as in the case of Flakstad, help us to identify individuals who display a different (nutritionally inferior) diet pattern than the rest of the buried population in double graves, and potentially give hints as to ethnic differences and individuals coming from distant parts of the world.

If we then assume that the decapitated and bound individuals who were placed inside of someone else's grave, in double burials, should be regarded as slaves, which appears likely and is moreover supported by contemporary eyewitness accounts in the shape of Ibn Fadlan's description as well as those

[72] Lundström 1981 p. 120.

[73] This grave links up with the aforementioned prone burials as Kopparsvik, Gotland, analyzed by Toplak (2018).

found in literary Norse sources,[74] certain important deductions can be made on the basis of this. For example, it gives us insights into the eschatology of pre-Christian religion.

A contextually interesting episode occurs in the passage from *Landnámabók* (64) cited previously, which treats the burial at *Ásmundarleiði* where Ásmundr expresses his wish to be rid of his slave inside the grave since, as he emphasizes, it is better to be alone than to live (in the next world, that is!) with such bad company.[75] Apparently, people reckoned with a chthonic realm that one must travel to after death and where one needed personal possessions, food, domestic animals, horse, and wife, concubine, or slave. But above all, these graves appear to prove the existence of thralls within Scandinavian society, unfree people of no legal standing whose social position nonetheless remains obscure to us. In the same way as there were horses, dogs, falcons, and other living beings, there existed thralls who were the property of someone and who could be put to death and placed inside such people's graves.

The Old Norse sources can be compared, for example, to what Caesar writes in *De Bello Gallico* (6:19) about how a deceased Gallic chieftain is provided in his grave with slaves and subordinates whom he was fond of as well as domestic animals and possessions. Leif Nordenstorm has, furthermore, pointed out how the Lithuanian grand duke Germont in 1271 had his father, Swintorog, cremated according to old heathen customs and deposited into his grave swords, bow and arrows, falcons, dogs, and horses as well as his father's beloved slaves.[76] This custom, of putting to death the slaves of a deceased to let them follow their master into the grave, recurs already among the Egyptians[77] and seems to be quite common in some cultures that believe in the existence of a chthonic realm and regard death as a journey to another place.[78]

[74] See Nordenstorm 1994.

[75] *Landnámabók* (*Hauksbók*) ch. 60; cf. Nordenstorm 1994 p. 268.

[76] Nordenstorm 1994 p. 269. The existence of slaves (*þeowan*) in the neighboring country of Estonia is evidenced already in Wulfstan's travel description in King Alfred's translation of Orosius from about the 890s (*Ottar och Wulfstan* p. 25)

[77] Spencer 1982.

[78] The custom of killing slaves to accompany their master to "the spiritual world," is hence not uncommon. It has inter alia been described among Indian tribes on the Pacific Coast of North America. W. C. MacLeod (1929 p. 107) notes "Ordinarily slaves were killed merely that the deceased might have slave labor to wait on him in the other world. The richer the deceased had been, the more slaves were sent to accompany him. Favorite slaves of the master were those usually selected." The methods

Strontium isotope analyses of teeth, such as the one conducted on the buried persons at Flakstad (see earlier), and which can reveal from where the deceased might come, have also been done at a gravefield outside of the ring-fortress Trelleborg, in Sjælland, Denmark. The grave field contains more than 150 graves, where three were mass graves (one with eleven individuals, two with five in each).[79] The majority of the buried people were males in their 20s–40s. The analyses of Douglas Price and his team show that the population at the Trelleborg fortress, as represented by the burials, was an army consisting of young adult males, who were accompanied by some women and children.[80] Samples from teeth were taken from forty-eight individuals, who were identified as coming from northern Scandinavia and from south of the Baltics.[81]

This corresponds with analyses from Trelleborg of pottery and ceramics, as well as other objects such as combs and spindle whorls, which seem to have an origin in Slavic areas on the south coast of the Baltic Sea.[82] In the same way, but at the ring-fortress at Fyrkat on Jutland, many finds have parallels in eastern Europe.[83] To this picture we have to add that finds of Slavic, Baltic, and eastern provenance are seldom in the material from Aggersborg,[84] which

used when killing slaves at these occasion show how "dehumanized" they were in these cultures (MacLeod 1929 p. 108):

> In the Puget Sound area and below on the Columbia river slaves were sometimes starved to death; sometimes tied to the corpse and left thus to starve—in which case if the slave was not dead within three days he was ordered strangled to death by another slave. On the Columbia also a slave's arms might be tied behind him and another slave ordered to stab the victim. Sometimes slave mortuary victims were merely thrown into the river and drowned. Among the Chinook and the Makah the slain slave was sometimes interred. Among the Shuswap and the Thompsons of the plateau it seems that slaves were usually buried alive under the corpse. With the northern Tlingit a slave might be cremated along with the corpse of his master.
>
> We have one vivid description of an actual Chinook funeral with mortuary immolations. A chief's twenty-year-old daughter had died. The corpse was wrapped in a mat and placed in a canoe-coffin. The father of the dead girl ordered a slave bound hand and foot and tied to the corpse; then both bodies, living and dead, were enfolded in a second mat, the slave's head being allowed to protrude in order that he might be able to breathe. It was then ordered that if within three days the slave was still alive in the coffin that another slave should strangle him, using a cord for the strangling.

[79] Nørlund 1948, Price et al. 2011 p. 478–479.

[80] Price et al. 2011 p. 482.

[81] Price et al. 2011 pp. 483–487; cf. Gardeła (2019 pp. 248–249), who has also highlighted the find of a T-shaped axe ("beard axe") found in one of the burials here at Trelleborg, which has direct parallels in northeasten Germany and Poland.

[82] Hermann (ed.) 1974, Brather 2001 pp. 188–201, Dobat 2010.

[83] Roesdahl 1975, 1977 p. 150.

[84] Madsen and Sindbæk 2014 pp. 228–232, this is also reemphasized in Anne Pedersen's summary of the finds from Aggersborg, the paucity of finds from the Baltic and Eastern (Slavic) area, and instead the close contact with southern Norway and northwest Europe (Pedersen 2014 pp. 362–363).

hence is a memento. What the analyses from the Danish ring-fortress reveal is that this was a population that can be described as an army, consisting of people from not only Denmark, but also northern Scandinavia and Slavic areas south of the Baltics. However, whether they were slaves or whether slaves were to be found in this material, is inconclusive, as discussed in the Excursus.

One new and spectacular phenomenon, which recently has seen a lot of attention in archaeological research as well as in public, are the around one hundred buried individuals from the Viking Age who have had their teeth modified, where the front teeth have been filed in one or several horizontal lines (Fig. 14.16a and b).[85] One such individual was found at Trelleborg,[86] other individuals, seen in a "slave" context and found in burials discussed earlier, include the potential "slave" in the grave with the "Elk-man" in Birka and in the grave at Bollstanäs. This could be taken as an indication that this custom of filed teeth was a way of branding a slave, and this has been mentioned in research,[87] however, individuals with this kind of modified teeth have also been found in burials at central-places and even within the Birka garrison. Hence, it is probably not possible to see this custom as a way of branding a slave, it probably had some other function in viking society: a way of communicating some group affiliation to a retinue or a trade guild, viking "fashion," rite of passage to prove one's manhood, or what have you.[88]

Finally, a new source that will be important in future discussion of Scandinavian slavery and the ethnic background of potential slaves is—building on the groundbreaking research by Professor Kári Stefánsson, Reykjavík (ex. Harvard) on the human genome and genetic drift—ancient DNA analyses of buried individuals, especially found in double graves. This research has been conducted by Professor Agnar Helgason, Reykjavík, and his colleagues, and they have presented us with some new evidence of ethnic background for Viking Age settlers in the North Atlantic region.

When analyzing Y-chromosome variation, according to three haplogroups (1, 2, and 3) among 181 Icelanders, 233 Scandinavians, and 283 Gaels from Ireland and Scotland—where Icelandic haplogroup-1 chromosomes are assumed to have a Gaelic origin, and most Icelandic haplogroup-2 and -3

[85] Bennike and Alexandersson 2003, Arcini 2005, Kjellström 2014, Toplak 2015, Radon 2019a, 2019b.

[86] Arcini et al. 1991, Radon 2019b p. 34.

[87] Kjellström 2014 pp. 54–55.

[88] For a discussion of this research regarding modified teeth, see Randon 2019a and 2019b with references.

(a)

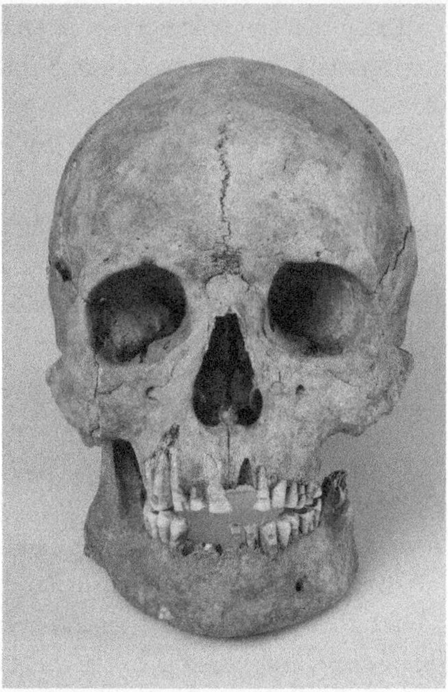

Fig. 14.16a An example of modified, filed teeth, in this case from burial 25 in a cemetery at Torget, Slite, Othem, Gotland. (Photo: Gabriel Hildebrand, Historical Museum/SHM [CC BY].)

(b)

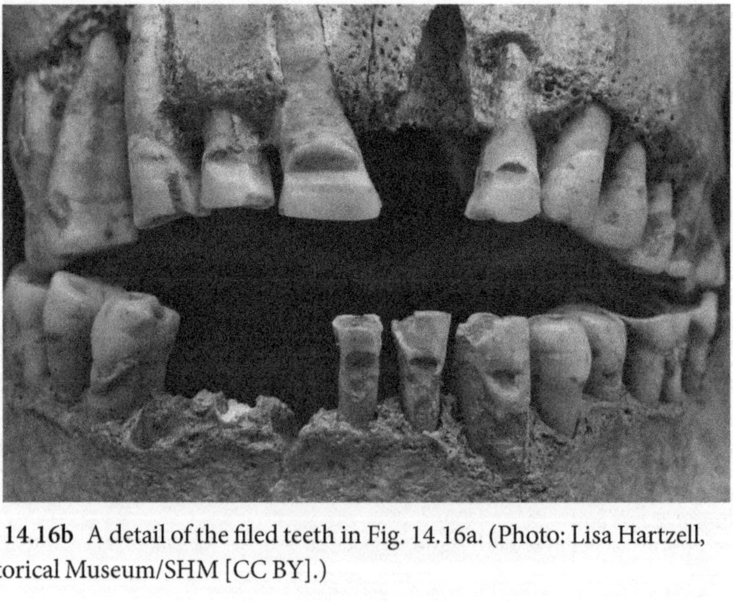

Fig. 14.16b A detail of the filed teeth in Fig. 14.16a. (Photo: Lisa Hartzell, Historical Museum/SHM [CC BY].)

chromosomes indicate a Scandinavian origin—the data suggest that 20–25 percent of Icelandic founding males had Gaelic ancestry, with the remainder having Norse ancestry.[89]

This is to be compared to another analysis—of ancient mitochondrial DNA (mtDNA variation)—regarding the background of female first settlers in Iceland, where mtDNA for 401 Icelandic individual females were compared with more than 12,500 other Europeans, and which suggest that the majority of Icelandic founding females may have originated from the British Isles,[90] in a later article specified at 62 percent from Scotland and Ireland.[91] From these two studies, on the basis of the evidence from the two uniparental markers (Y-chromosome and mtDNA), it is therefore possible to propose that the Icelandic founding population comprised a majority of males carrying Scandinavian Y-chromosomes and females carrying Gaelic mtDNA lineages. The researchers furthermore propose that: "In addition to purely Scandinavian males and Gaelic females, many of these Icelandic founders are likely to have been the offspring of admixed family groups formed by Scandinavian males and Gaelic females in the British Isles prior to the settlement of Iceland."[92]

This result is recently reconfirmed in two studies, one in which mtDNA sequences were taken from sixty-eight early medieval Icelandic skeletal remains,[93] and a second in which genome sequence data from twenty-seven ancient Icelanders were analyzed. Both studies demonstrated a combination of Norse, Gaelic, and admixed individuals who, interestingly, are much more similar to the source population in Scandinavia and the British Isle than to contemporary Icelanders—obviously a result of a millennium of extensive genetic drift.[94] These newer results showing evidence for a shift toward more Norse ancestry over time in Iceland could potentially be explained by a reproductive disadvantage for Gaelic slaves during the first generations of settlement.[95]

In another paper from 2005 Agnar Helagson and his team of researchers have analyzed Y-chromosomal and mtDNA variation in the North Atlantic region with regard to the genetic background of the Orkney and Shetland

[89] Agnar Helgason et al. 2000b.
[90] Agnar Helgason et al. 2000a.
[91] Sunna Ebenesersdóttir et al. 2018 p. 1028.
[92] Agnar Helgason et al. 2000b p. 715.
[93] Agnar Helgason et al. 2009.
[94] Sunna Ebenesersdóttir et al. 2018.
[95] Personal communication from Professor Agnar Helgason, Reykjavík.

population.[96] Their findings indicate an overall Scandinavian ancestry of approximately 44 percent for Shetland and approximately 30 percent for Orkney, which contrasts with the situation for the Western Isles, where the overall Scandinavian ancestry is less (approximately 15 percent) and where there is a disproportionately high contribution from Scandinavian males. As the previous results have shown, Iceland exhibits both the greatest overall amount of Scandinavian ancestry (55 percent) and the greatest discrepancy between Scandinavian male and female components. While Orkney and Shetland may have been settled primarily by Scandinavian family groups, due to the closeness to mainland Scandinavia, lone Scandinavian males, who later established families with female subjects from the British Isles, may have been prominent in areas more distant from their homeland such as the Hebrides and Isle of Man.

These DNA results indicate that we must reckon with a large proportion of females coming to Iceland during the Viking Age. However, we cannot know whether these women were brought there as slaves or (judicially free) wives.[97] Some were more or less certainly taken as slaves in the Gaelic speaking region, which would chime with what the Icelandic sagas so often describe, but some probably voluntarily followed their Scandinavian husbands as wives. This latter, I imagine, must have been the predominant situation in Orkney and Shetland—an intermarrying between Scandinavian males and Orcadian women.

Hence, although DNA analysis has opened up a new and important avenue for research in the Viking world, it is still very difficult to get clear-cut evidence for the existence of slaves in the material. The main contribution, which has revolutionized Viking studies, is the—what seems to be robust—evidence of a large proportion of female with a background in Celtic areas as being among the first settlers on Iceland.

[96] Goodacre et al. 2005, cf. Agnar Helgason et al. 2001.
[97] See also Raffield et al. 2017a and 2017b.

15

The Rise and Fall of Scandinavian Thraldom

When Did Slavery Appear in Scandinavia?

It is to be observed that slavery takes place
in all societies at their beginning,
and proceeds from that tyrannic disposition
which may almost be said to be natural to mankind.
Whatever form of government was established,
it was a part of its constitution that slavery should be continued.

—Adam Smith, *Lectures on Justice, Police, Revenue and Arms . . . 1763*, —Oxford 1896, p. 96

The disappearance of European slavery constitutes one of the questions regarding which there is as yet no consensus.[1] Marxist historians claim that slavery vanished with the fall of Rome, that is in the fifth century, and the emergence of feudal Europe. The influential French historian Georges Duby, who in his analysis places himself close to his predecessor Marc Bloch, holds the opinion that slavery ceased in the eleventh century. Others place themselves somewhere between those two dates in their respective analyses.

In Scandinavia, thraldom is generally regarded as coming to an end first in Iceland during the twelfth century, then in Norway during the latter part of the same century, or at least sometime before 1270,[2] followed by Denmark, which is assumed to have had slavery still in the thirteenth century.[3]

[1] Cf. Goetz 1993 and Rio 2017.
[2] Iversen 1997 p. 277.
[3] Karras 1993 p. 599.

Thraldom. Stefan Brink, Oxford University Press. © Oxford University Press 2021.
DOI: 10.1093/oso/9780197532355.003.0015

With regard to Sweden, it is a little simpler. By all appearances, slavery, or thraldom, decreased in importance during early medieval times, presumably because of changes in agricultural land use.[4] With the issuing of the Skara Charter in 1335 we have most likely a date for the abolition of slavery within this country.[5] Following this royal decree, people were no longer allowed to keep thralls. In other words, slavery gradually lost its importance during the twelfth and thirteenth centuries and ceased to exist in the early fourteenth century.[6]

While the end of thraldom is thus a known historical phenomenon, its origins in Scandinavia are entirely unknown. In order to say anything about this opaque problem, we have to settle for some assumptions and specific analogies.

Relatively few people have dared speculate about when and how slavery arose, alternatively arrived, in Scandinavia. The archaeological evidence is, as has been made clear, scant and problematic. The written accounts leave us high and dry; they are far too late. Nor can anything be detected from the treatment of Scandinavia by classical authors. Slavery or allusions to slavery practically go unmentioned.

From a general perspective, if we are to follow the influential eighteenth-century Scottish Enlightenment philosopher and economist, often called "the father of Liberalism," Adam Smith, slavery is found "in all societies at their beginning" (see epigraph), and it has been suggested by Smith and many others that slavery can arise when certain conditions apply. Henry Marsh proposed that at least three such conditions should exist within society: (1) personal, that is to say individual, ownership; (2) experience of domesticating animals in order to use them for work purposes; and (3) the occurrence of war, which has always constituted the most significant method of acquiring new slaves.[7] These conditions, however, present a very uneven chronology; war and conflicts have probably always existed between different peoples, the domestication of animals began in the Stone Age, while individual ownership in Scandinavia may not appear until the Iron Age, perhaps even the Late Iron Age,[8] which is why the premise of such a proposal

[4] On this, see especially Lindkvist 1979 and Lindkvist and Myrdal (eds.) 2003.

[5] Hasselberg 1944.

[6] It is notable that slavery continued in the neighboring Baltic states until the end of the Middle Ages, see Selart 2013.

[7] Marsh 1974 p. 13.

[8] The Historian Bjørn Poulsen (2012 p. 455) is even more cautious: "We cannot be certain that private land ownership in our sense existed before the eleventh century." The question of when we can

remains unconvincing in terms of explaining the appearance of slavery in Scandinavia. Most early scholars discussing the genesis of slavery perceived a connection between slavery and some level of economy, with the assumption that in a hunting–gathering society slaves were not necessary or useful both because it was difficult to control them and because slavery was unprofitable, instead slavery was introduced with agriculture.[9] Anthropological research, especially, claims this cannot be correct,[10] but I tend to agree with Detlef Gronenborn and Michael Zeuske that the emergence of slavery is in some way linked to the Neolithization, settledness, and the emergence of a sedentary culture.[11] However, the genesis of dependencies and slavery is much more complex and blurred.

For Europe, for a somewhat later period, we have ancient Greek slavery, which perhaps could be characterized as a "personal servitude," although inferior to the free—*instrumentum vocale* "things that can speak" as they were—they were tied to a certain master, family, and house, working the fields and gardens or in the households. In a way they were "a sort of extension of the master's person, an instrument."[12] This kind of slavery continued in early Rome, but something seems to happen around the fourth and third centuries BC, with a new "kind" of slavery. During these centuries a new agrarian economic system emerged in Rome, with large-scale employment of servile laborers working fields. Hence, a new kind of slave developed, who did not have a "personal" affiliation to a master or his *familia*.[13] And this new slavery became the kind of forced labor seen in the following millennium in Europe.

As was common in earlier times, scholars were happy to construct—in our eyes—very bold hypotheses, as did Emil Sommarin (1917) in a neat little study of the institution of thraldom in Scandinavia. He stresses that the precondition for the keeping of thralls to emerge is the existence of war and that people thus captured come to be exploited as thralls. In the case of Sweden this supposedly happened in such a way that the kingdom arose through the

assume private ownership of land is a decisive problem for anyone trying to understand premedieval Scandinavian society, but a notoriously difficult question, see also, e.g., Widgren 1995.

[9] See the discussion by Kopytoff 1982 p. 209, cf. Zeuske 2019:1 pp. 269–272.

[10] See, e.g., MacLeod 1928, 1929, Siegel 1945, Leach 1967.

[11] Gronenborn 2001, Zeuske 2018 p. 42.

[12] Cuffel 1966 p. 332.

[13] These aspects were discussed by Professor Pierangelo Buongiorno, Lecce/Münster, in a lecture at the Bonn Center for Dependency and Slavery Studies, Bonn University, January 27, 2020.

joining together of separate provinces, which in turn constituted joined-together districts and other smaller regions, and these smallest units were supposedly based on tribes who were nomadic. With this we must assume that Sommarin is placing the actions in the Stone Age. As part of the fighting that must have taken place in connection with the economic exploitation of the landscape, prisoners may have been taken who were mercilessly put to death. "A great step forward in civilization," says Sommarin, "was made when people hit on the idea of sparing the lives of war captives and using the prisoners to carry out work in the service of the victors."[14] Since the author bases his study on *Rígsþula*, he is able to establish that "the swarthy thrall child did not have the same pure Nordic blood in its veins as did the ruddy farm boy with the gleaming eyes."[15] In other words, the precondition for a class separation within society was basically a "separation of race," which in turn builds on the notion that thralls were originally suppressed people of a different race.

Even earlier, I. S. Landtmanson had come to the same conclusion, namely that the most important means "by which thraldom could arise must, at least in olden times, have been by way of taking war prisoners."[16] In this respect, Landtmanson differs from another authority whom he relies on in his study, namely Matth. Calonius, whose early work on thralls from 1780 emphasizes that thraldom initially emerged by way of free people voluntarily entering slavery.[17]

In the 1930s and 1940s, the archaeologist Sune Lindqvist had the courage to express himself on this topic in some synthesizing works. In the publication *Svenskarna i heden tid* (1935) ("Sweden in Pagan Times") he holds the opinion that since slavery existed as an important element in classical—Greek and Roman—societies, which influenced Scandinavia, there was reason to suppose "that already the first agricultural people of our country used thralls."[18] In other words, he reckoned that slavery existed already in Neolithic agricultural societies in Scandinavia, and to him it was logical to imagine that "the construction of the huge megalithic graves, the great mounds

[14] Sommarin 1917 p. 9: *Ett stort framsteg i civilisationen var det man gjorde, då man fann på att skona krigsfångars liv för att använda de fångna till utförande av arbete i segrarens tjänst.*
[15] *svartmuskiga trälbarnet hade ej samma rent nordiska blod i ådrorna som den rödlätte bondpojken med de tindrande ögonen, loc. cit.*
[16] Landtmanson 1897 p. 5: *på hvilka träldom kunde uppkomma, torde väl hafva, åtminstone i äldre tider, varit fångenskap i krig.*
[17] Calonius 1780 p. 142.
[18] Lindqvist 1935 p. 178: *att redan de första jordbrukarna i vårt land nyttjade trälar.*

and monuments of the Bronze Age [were] thrall-made just like the pyramids of Egypt."[19] In his publication *Svenskt forntidsliv* (1944) ("Prehistoric Life in Sweden") Lindqvist, almost a decade on, throws himself into even grander pronouncements, yet again using *Rígsþula* as his starting point, apparently considering this poem an allegory wherein the three social orders appear as metaphors for the following three time periods in Scandinavia:

thralls = "the swine-herding makers of pitted-ware ceramics from the Late Stone Age"
"*the confident farmers*" = "the boat-axe period or Bronze Age environment"
noblemen and chieftains = "the large farmers and emerging kingships during the Migration and Vendel Periods"[20]

Thus, he finds that thraldom was part of Stone Age society. But he goes even further. "These similarities become much more than mere coincidence if we consider that the majority of slaves that existed in Scandinavia by the close of the heathen period presumably descended from earlier populations who were suppressed by the Battle Axe people (or at least that the thrall institution as such went back to the yoke, which was laid upon the former)."[21] On the other hand, free men and the families of their kings and chieftains supposedly descended from the victorious Battle Axe culture. Sune Lindqvist's hypotheses are probably representative of a fairly general scholarly trend belonging to the 1930s and 1940s in Sweden wherein concepts such as *ancestral homeland* (*Urheimat*), *race*, *folk element*, and so on made up self-evident aspects of the scientific terminology,[22] and in which it was reckoned that the Battle Axe culture of the Stone Age was a people coming in from the outside (of a different "race" from the indigenous population) who defeated the native peoples, of the Pitted Ware culture, and conquered their land.

[19] *uppförandet av de stora megalitgravarna, av bronsålderns mäktiga högar och kummel [var] trälgöra precis som byggandet av Egyptens pyramider, loc. cit.*

[20] Lindqvist 1944 p. 283: *trälarna = "yngre stenålderns svinskötande gropkeramiker"; "det trygga bondefolket" = "båtyxetidens eller bronsålderns miljö"; stormän och hövdingar = "folkvandrings- och Vendeltidens uppsvenska storbönder och kungar."*

[21] *Dessa likheter bli mer än en tillfällighet, om vi besinna, att huvudmassan av de slavar, som funnos i Norden vid hednatidens slut, förmodligen härstammade från de äldre folkelement, som kuvades av stridsyxfolken (eller åtminstone att trälinstitutet som sådant gick tillbaka på det ok, som lades på de förra), loc. cit.*

[22] For more details on this, see Alkarp (2009 pp. 345–354), which is a brilliantly executed "honor rescue" of Sune Lindqvist, who is regarded by some scholars and scientific journalists as a Nazi or at least—to use a favorite rhetorical expression of politicians wanting to discredit someone without having substantial proof—as someone who was "fishing in murky waters."

In other words, Sommarin and Lindqvist had very similar opinions when it comes to explaining the causes of thraldom and the origins of thralls: thralls are obtained through war and conquest and it is a characteristic trait of theirs that they belong to another ethnic group ("race"), [23] which differs markedly in terms of appearance from the remaining, free population. These authors saw slavery as very ancient, a system that seemed to have existed in society ever since the Stone Age.

Against such a point of view it is possible to argue, as E. A. Thompson has done, that it must have been rather hard to keep pure work slaves in northern Europe in olden times, say during pre-Roman Iron Age and earlier. The culture, for sure, was to a large extent sedentary, that is to say a settled farming culture, but there was a high degree of lability and mobility in society. It must have been difficult to exercise control over slaves. Furthermore, the agricultural methods were not particularly suited for the use of slaves. No large farms, such as the slave-run *latifundia* that existed in the Roman Empire, appear to have existed in Scandinavia during the Early Iron Age, although this hypothesis might be contradicted in the future.

In his book *Passages from Antiquity to Feudalism*, which was used particularly in the 1970s as an academic textbook for history, the Marxist historian Perry Anderson presents an elaborate theory of what slavery looked like in Scandinavia, a theory that acquired great impact during the contemporary, radical and conformist period of the seventies. Anderson holds that the key to early Scandinavian society lies in the viking raids, which he regards as plunder expeditions in search of slaves. He believes, paradoxically, that these viking raids and the capture of slaves contributed to maintaining the "primitive" societal structure of Scandinavia; Scandinavia, he says, was the last societal formation in Europe in which slaves were a common and vital part of society. Slavery was the very foundation of societal structure and the pillar of viking life. He develops this by claiming that it was exactly this common and widespread slavery that made possible the emergence of an aristocracy that was able to obtain a foothold alongside the large class of free farmers. It was the agricultural productivity of slaves and their "surplus labor" that laid the

[23] Readers might find it curious that I always have quotation marks around the word "race," a word unproblematic to use in the Anglo-Saxon speaking world, but which has been a taboo word, an n-word, in especially Sweden since the Second World War, never used in decent language, neither as an analytical term in *academia*. This has changed in recent years, still not among the general public, but among socio-cultural opinion producers and in certain academic disciplines, such as Critical Theory, Post-Colonial Studies, "Whitness studies," etc., a rhetorical drift under the influence of especially American academic discourse.

foundation for this landowning upper class, which therefore did not need to "exploit" the free farmers and make serfs of them. The continued import of slaves via the viking raids was the reason why Scandinavia never developed into feudal states with serfdom.

When we today in postconformist times dare to throw off the ideological glasses of the seventies, we find many flaws in this theoretical construction. First, we have no source material to support all aspects of the theory; it is simply a hypothetical construct, an attempt at a synthesis. For example, we have no obvious evidence that large estates based on slave work existed during the Viking Age.[24] Nor do we know whether the vikings who participated in an extensive slave trade actually brought these slaves back home to Scandinavia. A more reasonable hypothesis is that they, as soon as the possibility arose, traded these captives for money and silver, by demanding ransom for hostages or by selling them at slave markets. Such a hypothesis could find support in the large amounts of silver from the Viking Age that have been excavated as buried treasure in Scandinavia—especially in Gotland.

The hypothesis is also backed up by some Arabic writers, such as Ibn al-Athīr (*Izz ad-Dīn Ibn al-Athīr*), and his work *al-Kāmil fī 't-Ta'rīkh*. Ibn al-Athīr was an Iraqi scholar who, circa 1231, collected and reworked earlier annalistic scholarship from the ninth and tenth centuries, among other things dealing with customs and economic activities of the Rūs in the ninth and tenth centuries. He is—as noted by William E. Watson[25]—not so interested in the trading, but instead in the warlike Rūs and their raiding in the Caspian region. In one of the accounts discussed (and translated by Watson) the Rūs are involved in a battle at Barda'a up the Kura River in 943. They besieged the town for a while, but then left Barda'a with some of the booty. They had left many dead warriors after the battle and they had been buried with their weapons, they had also buried wives and slaves after the dead warriors, Ibn al-Athīr tells us. But regarding ransom he has the following interesting to say:

> They gathered those who remained in the Friday Mosque, and they said to the remaining townsmen: "You can either ransom yourselves or we will kill you." A Christian came forth and settled on twenty dirhams for each man.

[24] An attempt to identify such large slave-run estates in southern Småland is carried out by Clas Tollin (1999 p. 19 and *passim*).
[25] See Watson 2001.

> But the Rūs did not keep to their bargain, except for the sensible ones, after they realized that they would not receive anything for some townsmen. They massacred all of those [for whom they could receive no ransom], and only a few fled from the massacre. The Rūs then took the valuables of the people and enslaved the remaining prisoners, and took the women and enjoyed them.[26]

Again, one gets the impression that the goal of the Rūs was not to take slaves per se, but to take hostages and steal their valuables, if they had any, and then demand ransom for the hostages (if no ransom was paid, they killed them, as in this case, or took them to slave markets and sold them off, as in other cases), except for the women whom they kept as concubines ("and enjoyed them"). In other words, their aim was to obtain silver and women (concubines).

Recently Mary A. Valante (2013) discussed slave trading in Early Viking Age northwest Europe and presented a number of remarkably unsubstantiated statements, such as: "some [captive men] of course were sold to Scandinavia and Iceland where they worked fields, tended animals, and otherwise helped farmwork."[27] One wonders what sources or evidence—apart from perhaps the problematic poem *Rígsþula*—Valante builds this argument on? To my knowledge this can at best be an assumption, a hypothesis, but not a "fact," as presented here. The same goes for the statement: "Vikings also targeted them [monasteries] to capture literate young males who could be turned into eunuchs and sold off to the east."[28] This may be a probable assumption, but do we have any evidence of this in the written sources? And to state that Ruth Mazo Karras' (1998) work on medieval slavery in Scandinavia "is the most important work analyzing the uses and origins of slaves in Scandinavian lands during the Viking Age," is a kind nod to a good book on the topic, but one that was, in terms of complexity, depth and breadth, challenged by Tore Iversen's *Trelldommen* (1997). And referring to Mazo Karras that "very rarely, women might be concubines" is remarkable, in the light of the aforementioned Arabic sources and also several Icelandic sagas where Icelanders, *rūs* and *varangians* are said to have taken women as concubines. However, Valante's concluding hypothesis,[29] that the vikings'

[26] Watson 2001.
[27] Valante 2013 p. 175.
[28] Valante 2013 p. 175.
[29] Valante 2013 p. 187.

many raids of and deliberate focus on monasteries and ecclesiastical centers should probably be seen in relation to the huge demand for eunuchs in the Byzantine and especially Arab world from the ninth century and onward is probably well-founded. I think this is another piece in the puzzle, which helps to explain the vikings' engagement in large-scale slave trade, probably already as early as the end of the eighth century.

The Norwegian professor of archaeology Dagfinn Skre has put forward a theory about an early "(kind of) slave society" in Scandinavia, more specifically in Romerike, Norway.[30] He proposes a model for a settlement situation based on the establishment of a few large farms on the best soil at the beginning of the first millennium. Around the middle of the first millennium the settlement expanded by establishing a number of smaller farms in more peripheral areas, farms that Skre assumes were dependent on the large farms. He imagines the smaller farms to have been run by slaves to an extent (large?), a conclusion he bases on continental Frankish analogies from the same time period as well as place-name evidence analyzed by Tore Iversen, who says that certain place-names apparently indicate that "thralls" can be dated as early as the Roman Iron Age and even earlier.

However, doubts may be raised as to whether continental and especially Frankish analogies, which must then be taken from the later centuries (AD 600–900), are suitable in this context. They represent a new, emerging feudal societal system with a new type of social as well as agrarian structure that was then introduced into Scandinavia toward the end of the Viking Age and above all during the following centuries. Nor does Iversen's toponymical analysis stand up as an argument. It is not possible to show that place-names indicative of "thralls" can be traced to the Early Iron Age. Furthermore, these potential names are, indeed, so rare that they can hardly be used as an argument in a discussion such as this, and the few names that do exist seem rather to be dated to the thirteenth and fourteenth centuries, in some cases perhaps the Viking Age.

Skre's archaeological argumentation is more solid. He is able to demonstrate that there are grave mounds near the large farms while such do not exist in the vicinity of smaller farms. His interpretation is that the few graves that are found by the large farms represent the deceased owners who were then in possession of the farm and its land. This means that not everyone on a farm who died was buried in a mound. Visible mounds are often lacking

30 Skre 2002; cf. Skre 1998 *passim* for in-depth analyses.

from the smaller farms in Romerike. Skre's interpretation is that these were run by slaves who received no burial at all and consequently no mounds. This interpretation *might* be right. But in my belief, the theory can hardly be applied to Scandinavia generally, perhaps only to settlements in agriculturally affluent areas in Norway. In, for example, the Mälar Valley in central Sweden practically all villages and farms of prehistoric origins have their own grave fields, not just individual mounds, and this also goes for small hamlets and peripheral individual farms. Furthermore, John Ljungkvist, who has studied estate-like large farms in central Sweden in the same period, concludes, after thorough analyses, that it is most doubtful whether such estates where driven by slaves during the second half of the first millennium.[31]

If this model with smaller farms in Romerike run by slaves is valid, then we probably are presented with the problem raised by Thompson (mentioned earlier) and his claim that it must have been hard to get slaves to stay put on a peripherally situated farm and to run it. They could not be chained in any way, and the risk of such slaves running away must have been high.[32] Already Plato realized this and in his *Republic* (9:578d–578e) he employs a rich man with many slaves as a metaphor for a city (= state) with its leaders and inhabitants, and asks the question: How come the rich man does not feel threatened by and afraid of his slaves; well, because the rich man can count on the support of his peers in the city if anything like a slave revolt were to take place. But let us imagine, continues Plato, the removal of a rich man with, say, fifty slaves or more away from the city to a remote place where there are no other free men to help this rich man. Can you imagine, asks Plato, the terror that rich man would experience in such a situation? He would immediately start praising his slaves, keep on the right side of them, give them all sorts of promises and grant them their freedom. There is no other alternative, concludes Plato. I think that Plato here touches on a vital aspect of slaveholding, namely that a sole farmer could only with great difficulty suppress other human beings, as some sort of human cattle, without them reacting violently. This problem with runaway slaves is also known from Anglo-Saxon England. Regarding this matter, Dorothy Whitelock has laconically stated: "Slaves often ran away," and "It proved particularly difficult to prevent slaves from running away to join the Danish forces during the periods of Viking ravages."[33] In an attempt to stop this the Anglo-Saxon laws, such as

[31] Ljungkvist 2006 pp. 104–105.
[32] Cf. Iversen 1997 p. 232–233.
[33] Whitelock 1952 p. 110.

Æthelstan's (924–939), enforced harsh penalties, for example that the runaway slave should be stoned to death.

Another parallel, however, which does support Skre's theory is presented by recent research from northern Europe,[34] which shows that also unfree people could occupy "tenant farms," that is small farming units dependent on some main farm, something Tacitus had already described (*Germania* ch. 25), hence the Continental *servi casati*, the *liti*, the *aldii*, etc., or "housed slaves." And furthermore, many slaves in Anglo-Saxon England must be understood to have lived in separate houses, farms, probably on peripheral, marginal land, such as the *cotsetla*, and the Kentish *laet*. The slave had certain rights by custom, and could earn his own money during his free time. Even a swineherd should annually have a little pig, a bondwoman eight pounds of corn, a sheep or threepence, and so on, and a Christmas and an Easter food-allowance, which means they could build up a little fortune to be able to buy their freedom.[35] So the conclusion is pending; there are arguments that speak in favor of Skre's model, but also some doubts that must be kept in mind.

There is yet another question that in my opinion needs to be discussed in connection with Skre's analysis. He believes that slaves were never given any "official" burial and that there were therefore never any mounds raised over them, which seems to be a sound and probable stance. However, I can easily imagine that such "thralls" as Tolir from Hovgården in Adelsö, the king's *bryti*, that is (presumably) estate manager, who had a rune stone raised after his king, as well as Tófi, also a *bryti*, in Randbøl in Denmark, who had a rune stone raised after his wife, could very well be honored with their own grave mounds, although they were obviously "slaves." It is therefore likely that Skre has in mind pure work slaves, chattel slaves. However, the important point made by, among others, Tore Iversen in his analysis, is exactly the variable status of "slaves" in ancient times, something the present work also emphatically expresses.

Attempting thus to modify Skre's interesting theory—by removing the toponymic aspect and questioning the problematic Frankish analogues—the archaeological part of the argument remains. I think a slightly different model to the hypothesis of "slaves" running peripheral farms (that lack graves) could be proposed. Perhaps we are dealing instead with a particular burial custom whereby, as Skre assumes, only the owners of the "main farm"

[34] See, e.g., Hammer 2002.
[35] Whitelock 1952 p. 109.

were given burial mounds, while a farmer on a smaller farm dependent on the nobleman's farm, or why not a free farmer on a small farm, was not given a grave.[36] Such a model could be applicable to parts of Norway and northern Sweden, where fairly uniform burial customs are found,[37] but hardly to eastern central Sweden, which shows a different burial custom during the Late Iron Age (c. 600–1050). We thus end up with a rather traditional model of colonization, which Norwegian scholars like Magnus Olsen and Andreas Holmsen previously considered, wherein secondary farms were in a relationship of dependency to a "mother farm" from which they successively sprung.[38] We would then have no need of slaves for such a model, but instead farmers (akin to the situation of the historical tenant farms), of whom some may have been unfree, who ran farms owned by other people.

During the Stone Age and Bronze Age the need for slaves was in all likelihood even smaller in Scandinavia. One wonders how slaveholding would have operated within a mobile society of hunter-gatherers or in a mobile society based on slash-and-burn agriculture with elements of domesticated animals.[39] These societies on the contrary had, as is often stressed, a high degree of equality and egalitarianism, which also contradicts any slavery.

I therefore believe that there are grounds for supposing that slavery—or perhaps a new type of slavery, if we dare reckon with a previous type of slavery—was introduced in Scandinavia subsequent to the Scandinavians' intimate contacts with the Roman Empire, during the first centuries AD. It is, after all, known that Scandinavia was at this time more or less flooded by new tools, jewelry, ideas, concepts, and words, all of which emanated from the Roman Empire on the continent.[40] Here was a slavery in operation, which the Scandinavians must have encountered, and here were above all slaves, a trading item that merchant Scandinavians by no means precluded the chance to both buy and sell. There is, in other words, reason to believe that foreign slaves came into Scandinavia due to the lively contacts that existed between Rome and Scandinavia during the Roman Iron Age, perhaps not as

[36] A generally accepted view within archaeology today is that, of course, not all people within prehistoric society were given burials or, even better, a marked grave such as a visible mound or similar. The understanding—and quantifying—of this great and complex problem has been thoroughly analyzed by Frands Herschend 2009 pp. 33–136.

[37] Cf. the burial practice for northern Sweden, e.g., Liedgren 1992 *passim*.

[38] On this theory, see, e.g., Pilø 2005.

[39] For a discussion on potential slavery in hunter-gatherer cultures, see also Zeuske 2019 pp. 193–282, esp. 269–272.

[40] See, e.g., Brink 2002b, 2002c, 2002d, Hedeager and Tvarnø 1991; Andersson and Herschend 1997, with references.

regular farming slaves, but more as exclusive and exotic elements within the households of the ruling classes at the time.

However, there is in my opinion also another factor, which is significant to the understanding of the emergence and contents of thraldom in Scandinavia during prehistoric times, namely, the participation through agreement and contract by Germanic peoples and therefore also Scandinavians—perhaps involving oath-taking—as soldiers in the Roman army. It must have been strange news to these people to experience how, at the transition into a Roman legionary or some sort of auxiliary unit, a person was ascribed certain privileges, but above all many restrictions that regulated his social and legal status within a hierarchical society.[41] I think that this circumstance came to greatly influence the social and legal practices of Scandinavia over the subsequent centuries, until the Christian societal structure and canon law begin to permeate Scandinavia, presumably from about AD 1000 and onward. In this societal order, then, a person could voluntarily enter a position of service wherein his social status was perhaps higher than that of a free man, but certainly much more legally binding and repressive than for a free man, wherein the autonomy of the individual was limited and the possibility of making decisions the way a free man did was transferred to a superior, wherein the ultimate idea was to enter into a contract whereby one's life was by definition left in the hands of a superior.

It is perhaps a precondition for slaveholding partly that there be aggressions within society, or rather between societies, which lead to the taking of captives (who could be enslaved), and partly that society was sedentary, that is to say it was a stationary farming society, with cultivation and with a low degree of nomadic behavior.[42] Moses I. Finley, who studied Roman slavery in great detail, reckons that slavery can arise when private ownership of land exists, the workforce needed exceeds what one family can provide, a relatively extensive and developed production exists, and there is a market for, and a lack of, manpower for hire within society.[43]

Based on archaeology there is no way of claiming with any degree of certainty that slaves existed in the Stone Age, but what about the Bronze Age? This has been discussed by the archaeologist and Bronze Age expert Professor

[41] On the intensive contacts between Rome and Scandinavia, see, e.g., Hedeager 1978, 1987, Lund Hansen 1987, Hedeager and Tværnø 1991, and Andersson and Herschend 1997.

[42] On this, see Nieboer 1910; cf. Phillips 1985 p. 9. For a well-founded general critique of Nieboer, see MacLeod 1929 (with further refs. on p. 91 n. 2), Patterson 1977 p. 33, and Goody 1980 pp. 22 ff. See also the discussion in Olsson 1999 pp. 9–10.

[43] Finley 1980 p. 86.

Kristian Kristiansen.[44] From the knowledge we have about Neolithic culture and Bronze Age society, a change within society—the establishment of greater hierarchy—took place during these periods. The Bronze Age witnesses the emergence of an obvious ruling class, which manifests itself in the form of large three-aisled long-houses, luxury goods and wealthy grave goods, often in the shape of neat and elaborate bronze weapons, and with monumental grave mounds. At archaeological excavations of settlements carried out especially in Denmark, exactly such longhouses surrounded by smaller houses and farms have been found. This is interpreted as a kind of "large household system" wherein a chieftain controls and possibly "owns" the farms surrounding the longhouse. The model is based on the idea that farmers occupy the smaller farms and give part of their surplus production to the chieftain who can then use this to acquire items of prestige and weapons. The societal model is in many ways, then, similar to the model generally descriptive of the Iron Age. Kristiansen says that those who occupied the smaller farms and worked the land were "slaves," but stresses that we naturally cannot know whether they were "free" or "unfree." A similar conclusion is reached by Mats Olsson based on a model of how a society develops.[45] This is, probably, correct.

The problem is, as Kristiansen clearly points out, we do not know what the situation was like for those who lived at the bottom of the societal pyramid during the Bronze Age. The analytical tools we have at our disposal are terms and concepts belonging to historical times. We do not know whether these analytical tools are adequate for describing Bronze Age society. We do not know what the circumstances of dependency were like between the chieftain and his subjects, nor what were the circumstances of landownership for the cultivated land. We do not know whether it is appropriate for us to use the legal description "unfree." However, it seems reasonable to imagine that there was an economic exploitation of those at the bottom of the social hierarchy. How repressive this dominance was we can only speculate about, such as the extent to which this was a kind of "patron–client" relationship or pure slavery. If we can reckon with some sort of "slavery" during the Bronze Age then it is not impossible that this had very different qualities and operational methods than what we later encounter in the Iron Age.

[44] See, e.g., Kristiansen 2006, 2007, 2009.
[45] Olsson 1999 p. 18.

It is, furthermore, difficult to imagine slavery within a nomadic hunter-gatherer culture. In other words, one possibility could be that a Scandinavian slavery may have arisen during pre-Roman times, in the so-called Celtic Iron Age, or perhaps in the Early Roman Iron Age. One chronological anchor in this is the Roman historian Tacitus, who in his book on the Germanic tribes (AD 98) tells of how these people had slaves, whether or not his use of the term *servus* referred specifically to unfree slaves. It is, however, well known that Tacitus' text on the Germanic tribes must be approached cautiously. He had an agenda when he wrote it, which was to show how decadent the Romans had become, while the Germanic tribes represented vitality and a natural state, which the Romans had lost completely.[46] Tacitus' *Germania* is therefore in many ways a Roman morality play wherein Roman society and culture are "showcased" against a Germanic background. Tacitus' statements about Germanic slavery must therefore be critically assessed. They may be a transposition that Tacitus makes, with no actual bearings. On the other hand, exchanges between the Roman Empire and the Germanic tribes are so extensive, in various ways, that the format of a Roman household with slaves may very well have been taken up by Germanic societies, even if such a system had not existed there previously.

A hypothesis that I find reasonable is that a slavery—or perhaps a *new type* of slavery—may very well have been introduced into northern European societies from the more developed and socially complex Rome. This would then have happened during the centuries surrounding the birth of Christ, maybe most likely in the first centuries AD (known in Scandinavia as the Roman Iron Age). This hypothesis finds support in the research by the Italian legal historian and classicist Pierangelo Buongiorno (discussed earlier) of a "new kind of slavery" around the third century BC, based on the introduction of a new large-scale agriculture, and the idea presented by the Dutch legal historian Herman van den Brink that Roman slavery is actually a rather late phenomenon, which only appears as a general social phenomenon when we can reckon with an urbanization of society, which takes place during Etruscan times on the Italian peninsula. He believes, then, that the Romans took over slavery as well as the term *servus* from the Etruscans.[47]

If we can reckon with some kind of existing slavery in Scandinavia in the first millennium, I am today inclined to see a (totally?) new surge of slavery

[46] See, e.g., Lund 1991, 2007 and Damtoft Poulsen 2018 pp. 24–29 with further refs.
[47] van den Brink 1974 p. 45.

and slave trading by Scandinavians during the Early Viking Age (starting probably during the early ninth century or even the eighth century). The reason for this is the following:

One of the more intensely discussed problems during the centuries after the Fall of Rome is the "Pirenne thesis." The Belgian historian Henri Pirenne famously came up with the idea that the rising power of Islam and the Arabs blocked Europe in the Mediterranean from trading in the East; the old trading system broke down. Economically speaking, the Mediterranean became a "dead sea" in the eighth and ninth centuries regarding trade, at least for Europe. According to Pirenne, Europe therefore turned its back on the Mediterranean, the old *Mare Nostrum*, and the old trading routes with the East were cut off. Instead Europe started to focus on agriculture and small-scale trading in the Atlantic. The Early Middle Ages were therefore looked on as a time of commercial stagnation and cultural isolation.[48]

In his book *Origins of the European Economy: Communications and Commerce, A.D. 300–900* (2001), Michael McCormick challenges Pirenne's theory, especially regarding an eastern Mediterranean trade. The written sources, which Pirenne built his theory on, are more or less silent regarding trade between AD 700 and 900; merchants and ships seem to simply have disappeared.[49] However, as McCormick demonstrates, those who wrote these kinds of sources, monks and clergy, had no particular interest in such secular, ephemeral, and earthly matters, therefore, these sources provide no information on trading. Instead McCormick turns to other sources such as archaeological evidence, for example coins and precious jewelry, relics of saints and holy places, and luxury items such as spices, silk, and drugs, which he finds are abundant during this period in western Europe. Of course, the Europeans had to pay for these items, but with what? To this question he poses the intriguing fact that we have, in this period, an ever-growing influx of silver into western Europe; the Carolingian economy became more and more monetized. He boils all of this down—geographically speaking—to one important place in Europe at the time, namely Venice.[50] Here we find traded goods of silk, spices, drugs, Arab gold, and silver, which seems to hint at Europe running a positive trade balance. Hence, what was Europe producing in abundance circa 800, McCormick asks, that was so important

[48] See Pirenne 1936 and 1939, in a way continued by Duby 1968; *pace* especially Hodges and Whitehouse 1983, and Hodges 1982 and 2012.

[49] McCormick 2002a p. 28.

[50] McCormick 2002a p. 40.

to the Arab economy that the Europeans gained a surplus from trade, and the answer he gives is *slaves*. It is well known, as was discussed in a previous chapter, that slavery was crucial to the Muslim economy; some in production, but even more important was domestic and military slavery. Plenty of slaves were captured during the Muslim conquest of new territories,[51] but at the end of the victorious Umayyad dynasty (AD 661–750) the supply of slaves started to dry up and the following Abbasids had to turn to large-scale purchasing of slaves. Hence, as McCormick demonstrates, there was money to be made in exporting slaves to the Arab world, and perhaps *the* most important point in Europe for this trade in the ninth century was Venice.

However, there was a crux with this slave trade. There was a sentiment in the Western Church at this time against slave trade, and treaties were being written by the Church and Frankish rulers forbidding buying, selling, and transport of Christians into foreign enslavement. These treaties and this involvement by the Church and secular rulers obviously did not stop the Venice slave trade, but this kind of sentiment in the upper echelons in society and these attempts to prevent Christians being sold off as slaves must have been an obstacle for Christian slave traders in the eighth and ninth centuries.

Exactly at this point in history, Scandinavians begin to make their presence felt all around Europe, trading and raiding. Since slavery was endemic to and widespread within European society, the idea was not unknown to emergent vikings, who thus began to take part in this lucrative business. While the resistance put up by the Church and the Frankish rulers against capturing and selling off Christians as slaves, which must have been a nuisance to at least the slave traders in Europe, this did not concern the pagan Scandinavian vikings. Here, they must have felt, was an economic *niche* for them to capitalize on. In all likelihood, they quickly became a major player in this business, ruthlessly raiding, taking hostages, and demanding ransoms; and if no ransom was paid, they took the poor people to slave markets in Europe and in the East and sold them off for silver. We know that the Muslim slave armies consisted mostly of whites—Turks, Caucasians from the East, Slavs and Europeans from the West—and we find them in the East and in al-Andalus; for example, as the palace guards by the Umayyad Caliph al-Hakim in Córdoba and the Abbasid Caliph al-Mu'tasim in Iraq.[52]

[51] See also Lewis 1990 p. 62

[52] Lewis 1990 pp. 63 and 65.

This became a most lucrative industry, and I am of the opinion that taking part in this slave-trading economy was the main driving force for the viking expansion in the eighth and ninth centuries. I would not be surprised if proof were to emerge that the Scandinavian vikings rapidly became the dominant players in this inhuman business. But, as I have stressed several times in this book, I do not think they took part in this slave trade in order to send slaves back home to Scandinavia; instead, they sold them off as quickly as possible—for silver.

16

The Status of Slaves in Prehistoric Scandinavian Society

An Attempt at a Summary

Experience has proved it: of all forms of breeding,
that of human cattle is one of the hardest.

—Marc Bloch, in *The Cambridge Economic History of Europe*, 1940, p. 221

I have here striven to expose the problems inherent in attempts at defining and properly describing slavery and unfree status in Scandinavia. Researchers must constantly move within an evaluative scale of gray in which one must take into account aspects relating to the right to one's own life, to move freely, to decide about one's own choice of partner, to make decisions about one's own body, to decide what one produces, to live in a context of kinships, and so on. Various forms of lack of freedom have existed over time and continue to exist today. The right to decide on one's own partner for life can by no means be taken for granted even today, an abomination that was reintroduced also into Scandinavia in recent decades. Most Scandinavians would, moreover, have felt themselves tied to their farms and lands over the centuries; for these people, industrialization and urbanization became the road to freedom, a freedom from being fettered to the parish, the village, the farm, and the land. [1] What characterizes slavery and thraldom, however, is

[1] There is a notion today—even among many academic scholars—that people in earlier Scandinavian society were allowed to travel freely, and were constantly moving around, so that it was a fluid and an "open" society. This is an unfortunate way of transferring a politically treasured idea of today, where we want to be an open, welcoming, borderless, globalized, and generous society, to earlier societies, so that we can use these allegedly "open" societies as a model for how our society should be: "We have always been . . ." Unfortunately, this was not the case. At least from the sixteenth century

Thraldom. Stefan Brink, Oxford University Press. © Oxford University Press 2021.
DOI: 10.1093/oso/9780197532355.003.0016

that a human being is deprived of *all* aspects of freedom, to the extent that the slave/thrall is no longer considered human, but instead an "object," a socially dead implement.

As I emphasized early in this book, it is a mistake to study the forms of slavery and lack of freedom belonging to ancient times alongside modern slavery, especially American slavery. One result of the discussion presented thus far is precisely the establishment of the existence in ancient times of sliding transitions between degrees of freedom and lack of freedom as well as of dependent and independent states of service. Scandinavia is probably no different in this respect from ancient Greece and Rome. As Keith Hopkins pointed out: "there was in the ancient world no clear cut-off point between dependent and independent or between free and slave. There was instead a continuum of status and duties."[2] And in the same way Chris Wickham argues:

> The slave mode of production of course needs slaves, as defined in legal terms, for such a totalizing economic control presupposes a denial of rights to the workers involved; but *servi*, *ancillae*, *mancipia* do not have to be organized according to the slave mode. Plenty of tenants throughout the ancient and medieval periods were referred to in these words (and their analogues in other languages), and were unfree in legal terms, but their *economic* relationship to their lords was effectively identical to that of their free tenant neighbours. I would argue that the de facto economic autonomy that such tenants had as peasants was more important than their legal unfreedom, and that slaves in the slave mode were on the other side of a divide from them. For this reason, I shall avoid calling unfree tenants "slaves," restricting this terminology to the slave mode.[3]

In other words, it becomes clear that, in order to comprehend the social hierarchies of different societies, it is necessary to study the social totality; but the

(perhaps even earlier) until 1860 you had to have a passport, a "parish passport," to travel to a neighboring county, even sometimes another parish in Sweden. Such passports could be commissioned by the local fiscal (*landsfiskal*), bailiff (*kronofogde*), or even the parish priest, and you had to report your arrival to the bailiff in the capital in that county you passed through or came to, and so on (see Lövgren 2018). Even in the middle of the ninteenth century 90 percent of the Swedish population, as mentioned earlier, were living on farms in the countryside (see SCB HSS p. 45), this was indeed a very "closed" and static society.

[2] Hopkins 1967 p. 167; the same argument is made by Moses I. Finley (1964 pp. 233–249).
[3] Wickham 2005 pp. 261–262.

scope of this book does not allow the space for that. One such social aspect that has been emphasized in recent times within gender-research is the similarities between women and slaves in terms of their social and legal status in, for example, classical antiquity.[4] Similarly, research into the classical cultures has noted the likeness between slaves and minors (cf. Latin *puer* 'boy, son', but also 'slave'), especially those who were orphaned and therefore lacked any kin-group.

It is probably impossible to overstate the impact, strength, and pervasiveness of the legacy of classical antiquity and Roman law and its use of definitions of a person as a commodity. It is in this respect notable that both of the monotheistic cultures that grew out of Late Antiquity, i.e., the Christian and the Islamic worlds, largely adopted Roman legal concepts of property and ownership. However, as has been intimated earlier, we are essentially blind as to whether other, polytheistic, premodern cultures shared the same, or at least similar, concepts of law, property, and ownership. How did interpersonal dependencies function in the Neolithic and the Bronze Age, for example? What seem to be the only shared factor in all societies are strong asymmetrical dependencies in which humans exploited their fellow humans by means of physical violence. In most cases, we must assume, people were being forced to perform labor. This can be labeled as "strong asymmetrical dependency" to avoid the black-and-white dichotomy of slavery and freedom.[5] By using such an approach, we are able to explore what lies between these two binaries: convicts, servants, prisoners of war, serfs, and coerced labor as well as people held in all other kinds of bondage, from socially high-ranking slaves to chattel slaves at the bottom of society.

An excellent example of this problem has been described by Edmund Leach.[6] In Old Indian society (as still today) the different groups, castes,

[4] On these aspects, see, e.g., Joshel and Murnaghan (eds.) 1998.

[5] This very useful concept of *asymmetrical dependency* has been introduced by the research group, the Bonn Cluster of Excellence "Beyond Slavery and Freedom." Their working definition is:

> Dependencies between actors are based on the ability of one actor to control the actions and the access to resources of another. This type of control over actions and access to resources is often reciprocal, and in this case, it is compatible with the autonomy of both actors. So the existence of strong asymmetries between actors is decisive for the loss of autonomy of one of them. In addition, this asymmetrical dependency between actors has to be supported by an institutional background that ensures that the dependent actor normally cannot change their situation by either going away ("exit") or by articulating protest ("voice").

(www.dependency.uni-bonn.de/en/our-research/research-objective, accessed November 27, 2019).

[6] Leach 1967 p. 12.

in society were defined in terms of social life. The lowest castes showed great likeness to slaves known from Europe, with a practically lifelong lack of freedom or at least a vital dependency on a master; they were socially despised and were given the heaviest and most degrading work-tasks. But they nonetheless had rights. They could, first and foremost, expect the help of their lords during bad times.

At the beginning of the nineteenth century, India was ruled by British colonial administrators. During this period, especially in the 1820s, eager supporters of freedom and opponents of slavery led a successful campaign against slavery and in favor of personal freedom back in England. The British administrators in India were gradually influenced by the vigorous discussions in their homeland and had the ambition to change India, too. These lowest castes came to be identified with a system of slavery and therefore new laws were introduced which prohibited the "feudal" lords from exercising legal power over their subjects; this was a truly philanthropic, conscientious and liberal western European move to improve for others on what we have seen far too many times, even today.[7] But what happened in India was that the situation *worsened* for the lowest castes following the intervention of the British administrators into a socially complex system, which they had not properly understood. Previously, the "feudal" lords had been bound by a social "contract" to provide for their subjects, to offer economic protection to even those of the lowest social standing, and to feed them during times of crisis. The British attempt to increase "freedom" in India, a social improvement, caused a financial and legal deterioration for the socially lowest people.

A kind of "original state" or a very archaic society with slavery can be discerned through etymological analyses of words for "slave," as the French etymologist Emile Benveniste has done.[8] Following an in-depth analysis of words for "slave," he found that a fundamental semantic aspect must have been 'foreigner', someone coming from the outside, an unknown person. One category of meaning that emerges consists of words indicating how someone is "taken," supposedly above all during warfare, such as Latin *captus*, *captivus*,[9] Goth. *frahunþans*, ON *haptr*, and, as mentioned previously, among indigenous Indian tribes a generic term for a slave was *Pawnee*, although the slave could have belonged to some other tribe. Another consists

[7] A recent example is Carsten Jensen's analysis of the situation in and of Western efforts in Afghanistan (*Dagens Nyheter* January 12, 17, and 19, 2011; Jensen and Hammer 2014).
[8] Benveniste 1973 pp. 289 ff.
[9] Cf. Bobrycki 2015 p. 60.

of words for neighboring peoples, OE *wealh*, OSw *est*, or words borrowed from neighbouring peoples, such as Latin *servus*, Greek *doûlos*, or words for simply 'foreigner', 'enemy', meanings which are, of course, very close to 'guest'. This can be illustrated through the fact that Latin *hostis* 'enemy' (cf. English *hostility*) can be placed alongside the etymologically related Latin *hospes* 'guest' (cf. *hospital* and English *hospitality*), where the latter word has a direct counterpart in Goth. *gasts* as in English *guest*.

What we encounter here is an "introverted" heliocentric society that focuses on its own group, while outsiders are potential enemies. One's own group was essential; it defined one's social belonging. And the basic social group seems at the earliest stages to have been the family.[10] Not belonging to any social group or a family was the equivalent of being socially dead, as Orlando Patterson has put it. The original significance of the family is made clear by words such as Latin *familia*, which is acknowledged to refer to a kin-based group of close relatives; in modern Scandinavia, mother, father, and child, but in our old farming society an extended family inclusive of grandparents, unmarried aunts, and more. From the beginning, we can see that kinship within a *familia* was hardly defining. The latter word derives from *famulus*, which was a word for a 'slave' or a 'servant' (within a family, a household), constructed on a collective suffix so that a *familia* seems originally to have referred to those who served within the one family, a *familia* that included *famuli* (pl. of *famulus*) consisted not only of slaves but also of wife, children, and other, more or less loosely connected people who were all obliged to obey the head of the family, *paterfamilias*,[11] who had the ultimate autocratic, legal power over his subjects, the *patria potestas*. According to Richard Saller, the everyday use of *familia* referred initially only to 'slaves'.[12] In other words, in such an archaic society there may not have been any great difference between a slave within the *familia* and, for example, a son (Latin *puer* 'son', but also 'slave'). Other words belonging to the same semantic sphere include *lord* (< *hlāfweard* 'bread-keeper'), *lady* (< *hlæfdige*, the mistress of a household, lit. 'bread-baker') and the Scandinavian *bryti* (< [*hlaf-*] *brutjan* 'bread-breaker'), alluding to the symbolic function of bread within the family's or the group's food-collective.[13]

[10] See Brink 2008; cf. Henrion 1941–1942, Herlihy 1991, Saller 1996, Moggi and Cordiano (eds.) 1997.

[11] See, e.g., Much 1937 pp. 167–168, Buongiorno 2017, Zeuske 2019 pp. 298–299, 643.

[12] Saller 1996 p. 115.

[13] On this, see Brink 2008; cf. Kauffmann 1910 pp. 20 ff.

Slavery later changed due to the expansion of the Roman polity. Following all wars in newly conquered areas there was a steady stream of captive slaves. These might become work slaves, in mines and at large estates (*latifundia*), but also better-off household slaves and even administrators (*ministeriales*) high up in the Roman management (*servi principis* who were part of *familia Caesaris*).[14] Slavery changes its nature; it becomes differentiated and more complex. This complicated mosaic of different kinds of slaves, with different work-tasks and different social standing, can, I believe, be traced also in Scandinavia during the Iron Age, a period in many respects inspired by the Roman empire during the first half of the first millennium. One socio-agrarian difference was that Scandinavians during this period presumably had no parallels to the Roman system of *latifundia* and slave-based large farms, and if such did exist they were in all likelihood very few, which may be the reason why pure work slaves (cf. Eng. *chattel slavery*, *chain-gangs*) seem not to have played any significant role in Scandinavia, if they ever existed here.[15] Instead, I promote the hypothesis that slaves were generally quite rare in prehistoric Scandinavian society—not at all to be compared with for example the slave societies in ancient Greece and the Roman Empire, nor with the south American chattel slavery—in which they perhaps primarily constituted a sort of prestigious item and a work force at estates, and therefore existed *mainly* among the upper classes of society. I hold this hypothesis to be supported by the archaeological source-material and by the linguistic analysis of terms for 'slave' carried out here. On the other hand, there must have been slaves on farms, in the household and as farmhands working in the fields, and at certain places, such as early *emporia* and trading places, such as Birka, it is not improbable that there were proportionally large quantities of slaves, as bonded craftsmen or kept assembled to be sold off.

In concluding my reflections on Scandinavian thraldom, I must say a few words on source-criticism and evaluate the possibilities for historical reconstruction. To begin with, it must be asked whether it is fair to make use of the meanings of terms during historical time as well as their etymological meanings, that is their original meanings. Since language is in a constant state of flux—languages never cease to develop—it may seem daring to base anything on the current and original meanings of words when attempting to reconstruct, as is the case here, a societal condition during a given period,

[14] Weaver 1972, Schumacher 2001a.

[15] Future archaeological research might prove this assumption wrong.

in our case the Viking Age (AD 800–1100), or (more generously) the period from the (Scandinavian) Late Iron Age into the High Middle Ages (c. 600–1300). That terms could undergo drastic changes even during such a short time-span is evident from many of the terms analyzed previously—*bryti*, *deja*, *ambótt*, and so forth. The important aspect of this linguistic analysis is that it is generally possible to trace the semantic development of a word, from an original meaning established by or presumed from etymological analysis to the meaning we find in literate times—and in Scandinavia that means the (Scandinavian) Middle Ages (thus c. 1100–1500). It is, then, not a development that is easy to trace in prehistory, but, surprisingly often, a logical semantic chain of development can be constructed for a word. In other words, the linguistic analysis should highlight source-critical problems and problems of reconstruction that seem possible to overcome. For obvious reasons, there will always be a chronological uncertainty in relation to a linguistic analysis of preliterary times, but on the other hand we do not need to beware of distorted interpretations and pure falsifications with which we may be confronted when it comes to grappling with written sources.

During the nineteenth century, it was possible (fairly unashamedly) to bring together information from thirteenth-century Icelandic sagas and legal material from Scandinavian provincial laws from the twelfth, thirteenth, and fourteenth centuries and thereby obtain a rather sizable corpus of information on which to build reconstructions. In our times, the available source-material has, as is well known, shrunk severely for the serious scholar. A source-critical historian such as Niels Skyum-Nielsen has disqualified the Icelandic saga-literature as worthless when it comes to obtaining historical information about thraldom.[16] According to Skyum-Nielsen, the sagas relate only the saga-writer's views on slavery, which belong to the time when the saga was written, the thirteenth century and thereabouts. Of course, this is a relevant point, even if it is clear that some information about thralls can, in fact, be obtained from this category of sources; the problem is how to evaluate what goes back to earlier times and what is the interpretation of posterity.[17] Instead, Skyum-Nielsen has ascribed tremendous significance

[16] Skyum-Nielsen 1979 p. 129: "On the whole it must be said that these sources were written so late that they rarely provide reliable information. They can, on the other hand, be used as 'monuments.' They tell us something of the attitude the authors, the originators, had towards slavery."

[17] This is an important and current research problem with which many philologists and literary historians struggle. A stimulating and programmatic article analyzing this problem was written by Preben Meulengracht Sørensen (1991).

to our earliest laws: "The laws are and must remain the main source."[18] As I pointed out before, the laws are nonetheless problematic; the example of *bryti* illustrates this in a striking way. In some laws and legal clauses, the *bryti* appears unfree, in others he is a free tenant, at times an esteemed royal administrator. The current interpretation is that those examples in which the *bryti* appears with the status of a thrall constitute older elements within the laws. The scant runic evidence seems to contradict this or at least force us to revise our views on the social standing of slaves in Scandinavian prehistoric times (i.e., the Viking Age and earlier). What can be learned from this clarification is that not even the laws are reliable sources for reconstruction-work. The legal clauses mentioning thralls must be evaluated and carefully discussed. It is apparent that there are old elements in our provincial laws,[19] but this does not mean that one can take for granted that legal clauses mentioning, for instance, *brytar* in the context of thraldom are necessarily legal relicts. I think it is to be mistaken—not to say impossible—to focus, the way Skyum-Nielsen and others do, exclusively on the legal sources when the issue is a historical reconstruction of thraldom.[20] That is to let oneself and others be lulled by false certainty. This implies that a modern study such as that by Ruth Mazo Karras (1988) also becomes somewhat problematic in the light of this particular scholarly attitude, since she mainly relies on Icelandic saga-material and early laws. The only way forward is, in my opinion, to involve all available potential source-material: runic inscriptions, medieval records, Old Scandinavian literary texts, archaeology, provincial laws, contemporary terminology alongside etymological considerations, and, not least, historical and anthropological comparisons.[21]

In this context, it is interesting to dig out observations made by the Lund philologist Ivar Lindquist about half a century ago. While commenting on Tacitus's *Germania* (ch. 44), he treated also the famous passage on the thrall, the weapon-guardian, among the *Suionum* (the "Swedes"). "Regarding

[18] Skyum-Nielsen moderated this later in his work, when he problematized the source-value of the laws (Skyum-Nielsen 1979 p. 145).

[19] See, e.g., Foote 1987, cf. Brink 2013b, 2014d.

[20] It goes without saying that our laws lend themselves readily to the study of the abolition of slavery, giving rules for how one was to be freed. In this case, the laws are contemporary with the historical event. It is therefore natural that so much of the historical scholarship on Scandinavian slavery has focused on exactly its final stages: the granting of freedom (see Nevéus 1974 and Iversen 1997).

[21] I.e., approaching the issue from the diametrically opposite point, attempting to reach a reasonable synthesis in which the studied elements and snippets of sources are taken into account so as not to try to pick out "obvious" sources and base arguments on the far too few fragments of knowledge they contain. For this theoretical approach, see, e.g., Meulengracht Sørensen 1991 and Brink 1992–1993, 1996a pp. 49–50.

this thrall," Lindquist began,[22] "it should perhaps be mentioned, although it is of minor importance, that it seems to be not entirely impossible for a Germanic scholar to trace the ultimate reason for this bizarre story. We do have several pieces of evidence to show how the primitive Germanic language constructed terms for the concept of 'civil servant'. This has in remarkably many cases happened through the adjustment of words that originally had a contemptible meaning."[23] Lindquist then brought up the example of *bryti*, which may refer to a thrall or a foreman as well as a royal-farm manager. Moreover, Lindquist pointed out the word *marskalk* (English *marshall*), which literally means 'horse-thrall' and also the word Swedish *ämbete* 'office' is brought to the fore, a term and an "office" that "undoubtedly entailed 'thraldom' from the very beginning."

Ivar Lindqust was very often inventive in his writings. In this case, I think he showed great foresight and put his finger on a very central aspect, namely the origins of the institution of thraldom. In my opinion, it is no coincidence that it is precisely from the philological perspective that observations of this kind can be made, since the written material is too late and too flimsy, and the archaeological material is practically silent. The etymological conclusions the philologist is able to draw are what throw a clarifying light onto prehistoric Scandinavian slavery.

One final question—which is unfortunately practically impossible to answer—concerns the numbers of thralls in Scandinavian society during the Viking Age. We have seen that, in the Scandinavian Middle Ages (beginning c. 1100), the lives of thralls were regulated in our oldest provincial laws. We can establish that thralls presumably existed as unfree workers on farms. However, it is not clear how common this was, whether each farmer had one or more thralls, or whether thralls existed mainly among the more affluent layers of society. From thirteenth-century Icelandic sagas, on the other hand, we get the clear impression that thralls, predominantly foreign captives or bought slaves, were owned by noblemen and the social upper classes. By the same sagas we are told of Scandinavians who carried out rather extensive

[22] Lindquist 1944 p. 225. His argument was pointed out to me by Professor Gösta Holm, Lund, partly in print (Holm 1985 pp. 151 ff.), partly in conversation, for which I here express my gratitude.

[23] Lindquist 1944 p. 225. *På tal om denne träl må det kanske nämnas, fastän det är av underordnad vikt, att det inte lär vara alldeles omöjligt för en germanist att utpeka den yttersta anledningen till denna bisarra historia. Vi har dock flera bevis på hur primitiva germanska språk vet att skapa sig termer för idéen 'ämbetsman'. Det har i påfallande många fall skett genom att för det lämpa ord i språket, som från början har en låg klang.*

See also regarding this slave, who was given the task of guarding the weapons, Henrik Schück (1905 pp. 116–117) and Elias Wessén (1969 pp. 29–30).

trading in slaves. Captives were taken in Britain and Ireland, and the great contemporary slave markets were sought out in order to convert the stolen people into gold and silver. Against this can be placed the information in the Frostathing Law about how an "ordinary" farm in Trøndelag consisted of twelve cows, two horses, and three thralls (or perhaps servants), which, if this legal clause can be considered normative rather than conditional, would indicate that almost all farmers had thralls, which is probably unlikely to have been the case. Moreover, it may not be certain that the word "man's man," that is to say a man (who works for another) man, which is the term used in the relevant passage of the Frostathing Law, necessarily is equivalent to 'thrall'; perhaps 'servant' or 'farmhand' are equally possible translations here.[24] Jørn Sandnes has, nonetheless, used this information in the Frostathing Law to calculate how many thralls existed in Norway during the Central Middle Ages and he has calculated an approximate figure of 50,000–75,000 thralls, which according to Claus Krag is way too high.[25]

Another aspect is that, if there were many slaves in Viking Age Scandinavia, then at the abolition of the institution of thraldom a huge group of migrant people should have appeared. Not everyone would have been incorporated into the family or as tenants on newly established farms in the outfield, although this probably happened to a variety of extents, but there would in such circumstances have been great numbers of people with no attachments to land or family. It can probably be assumed that a slave who had been badly treated by his owner was unlikely to have remained on the farm after obtaining his freedom. If we can reckon with such a development, it would be strange if this had not been noticed during the period after the abolition. But, as far as is known, there is no evidence at all of such vagabond hordes of freed slaves.[26]

In light of the preceding analysis, I hypothesize that thralls were actually rather uncommon in the Scandinavian farming society of the Viking Age.[27] This hypothesis rests mainly on indications from proper Scandinavia. Iceland differs perhaps—or even certainly—from eastern Scandinavia in

[24] See Krag 1982 p. 210; for alternative views, see Sandnes 1983 p. 81.

[25] Krag 1982 p. 210.

[26] Cf. Anners 1957 p. 9, with references.

[27] Similar views have been presented already by Edv. Bull (1931:2 pp. 15–16), Andreas Holmsen (1961 pp. 70–71, 184), Claus Krag (1982, 1983), Birgit and Peter Sawyer (1993 p. 132), and recently also Thomas Lindkvist: "If a slave society once existed . . . the significance of slavery lay not in its quantity" (Lindkvist 2003 p. 19), while researchers such as Jørn Sandnes (1979, 1983), Kåre Lunden (1976 pp. 268 ff.) on Norway, and Vilhelm Moberg (1970 p. 38) on Sweden, reckon with a sizable slave-population and a great economic importance of slavery in Scandinavia.

many respects. The saga evidence and the DNA analyses mirrors perhaps a larger number of slaves in Viking-Age Iceland than in eastern Scandinavia. From these sources we may estimate that Iceland saw a large influx of Celtic people, as wives, farmhands and slaves. Future DNA analyses in eastern Scandinavia may in the same way indicate that we had a similar large influx of people from abroad, perhaps mainly from the east. But at the moment we have very little evidence that can substantiate this.

That a single common farmer should own one or more work thralls must have been quite unusual, although it certainly must have occurred. Instead, I take the view that thralls in many ways constituted a kind of "prestigious property," or rather that slaves were both "economic capital" and "social capital,"[28] so that large farmers, noblemen, and chieftains were able to keep partly work thralls and household-thralls on their great farms, partly servants of various standing in their entourage.[29] This could be compared to the slave system in the Middle East (discussed previously), and also renaissance and early modern Europe, where "slaves were a luxury item."[30] The great numbers of slaves that the Scandinavians handled were probably sold as quickly as possible at slave-markets and converted into more easily handled goods such as jewelry and (above all) precious metals, gold and especially silver.[31]

The "slave" was in my opinion for the vikings—and their "economy"—more of a *commodity* than an *instrument for production*. They were used for trading transactions in Europe and the East and not primarily for agrarian production in Scandinavia.

This hypothesis finds support in the particularly sparse archaeological material. From the Stengade excavations, which have been interpreted as the cemetery of an ordinary Danish village in the Viking Age, one grave stands out from the rest. This is a large chamber-grave containing a tall, weapon-equipped youngster. In his grave there also lay a man who had been decapitated and whose hands and feet were tied together, arguably his slave. Nowhere else in this cemetery is anything similar found; no indications of

[28] Cf. Kopytoff 1982 p. 218, with refs.

[29] A similar viewpoint has been expressed in general terms with regard to slaveholding by William D. Phillips Jr. (1985 p. 8): "As servants, guards, and sexual partners, their [the slaves'] primary function in many cases was to demonstrate the wealth and luxury enjoyed by their owners."

[30] Kopytoff 1982 p. 223.

[31] Similar conclusions have also been drawn by Claus Krag (1982 p. 214), who even held that he had sufficient evidence for saying: *formålet kan ha vært å kreve løsepenger mer enn å ta treller. . . . Om løsepenger ikke ble betalt, slo vikingene ofte fangene ihjel* ("the purpose may have been to demand ransom more than to capture slaves. . . . If the ransoms were not paid, the vikings often killed their prisoners").

the burial of slaves are found in the more ordinary graves. I think that this can be taken as an indication that slaves occurred predominantly among the upper social classes, that they were considered "prestigious property." Scandinavian society during the Viking Age hardly merits, in my opinion, the label of a "slave society."[32] Instead, slaves were presumably mostly for the affluent people, and furthermore to be found on farms (and estates, if we can count on estate-like agrarian production units in prehistoric Scandinavia) as some kind of farmhands and maidens.

This is supported by the fact that the sister of King Canute the Great (1016–1035) was considered an infamous slavemonger in England. She seems to have supplied slaves for several aristocratic households in Denmark and, as William of Malmesbury wrote in his *De gestis regum Anglorum*, not least among them beautiful concubines.[33]

Such a hypothesis would also, I think, find support in anthropological analogies. From the analyses carried out on various kinds of slave societies, it is very clear that extensive slaveholding requires a certain level of "complexity" within society, an agrarian-economic system that necessitates a large slave population.[34] The Roman empire and the eighteenth-century American plantation-economy can be mentioned as examples. In the former there existed a very large number of slaves as work slaves at *latifundia*, in mines, and as household-workers in people's homes. In the latter, the need for manual labor in cotton-plantations was very great. Here, slaves had a significant economic function within society.

In societies of lesser economic "complexity," as among the Maori of New Zealand, North American Indians, and so on, slaves had a different socioeconomic function; they constituted a sort of "prestigious property" and were found predominantly among the leading groups of society. William Christi MacLeod cites an observation from 1815 regarding the North American Clayoquot Nootka tribe:[35]

> Only the king and chiefs have slaves, the common people being prevented from holding them either from their inability to purchase them, or, as I am

[32] For a definition of a "slave society," see especially Moses I. Finley's many contributions and also the earlier discussion; also Lenski and Cameron (eds.) 2018.

[33] *quod dicebatur agmina mancipiorum, in Anglia coempta, Danemarchiam solere mittere, puellas præsertim quas decus et ætas pretiosiores facerent*, William of Malmesbury, *De gestis regum Anglorum*, vol. 2, ed. W. Stubbs (London 1887) p. 200; Gjessing 1862 p. 123, Holm 1986 p. 343.

[34] See Gronenborn 2001 p. 21.

[35] MacLeod 1928 p. 638.

> rather inclined to think, from its being considered as the privilege alone of the former to have them, especially as all those made prisoners in war belong either to the king or to the chiefs who have captured them, each one holding such as have been *taken by himself and his slaves.*

One can say that in the former examples, slavery was financially conditioned, in the latter socially conditioned.

To continue on this theme, slaves were not for everyone—not even in a proper "slave society," such as the one in classical Rome. It has recently been calculated that the top 1.5 percent of the population, hence the "super rich," in the Roman Empire owned about half of all slaves during the late Empire.[36]

My opinion is that the agrarian-economic system of Viking Age Scandinavia did not require a high degree of slaveholding, for the reasons already stated.[37] When the Scandinavian society became gradually "feudalized," on the other hand, which took place primarily in the (Scandinavian) High Middle Ages, there was potentially an economic need for slaves within the emergent estate-system, with work thralls on main farms and possibly "tenants" of some sort on dependent farms. This development seems to be discernible during the twelfth and thirteenth centuries also in Sweden, but relatively quickly this system changed, apparently for economic reasons, so that slaveholding was abolished and replaced with the more lucrative and easily maintained tenant system, with rent-paying "semifree" farmers on tenant farms. The preconditions for extensive slaveholding in the form of great numbers of work slaves is (on this reading of the evidence) unlikely ever to have existed in medieval Scandinavia.

What we think can be defined as slave shackles or fetters have, to my knowledge, never been found in Iron Age "farming communities," during excavations of settlements and burials in relation to farms or hamlets, instead the very few we know of come from proto-towns and slave markets, such as Birka, Haithabu/Hedeby, Dublin, and a Danish fortress, Trelleborg. This could be taken as an indication that the existence of chattel slavery, and the need to keep someone fettered at a farm, may have been uncommon or looked upon as unnecessary.

On the other hand, the slave—the thrall—was important in Scandinavian society during—especially, I think—the Viking Age, but for a different, social

[36] Harper 2011 p. 59; cf. Rio 2017 p. 5.
[37] See similar conclusion in Gustafsson 2013 p. 74.

reason. A thrall constituted the social and moral contrast to a free man.[38] A thrall had no possibility of obtaining honor or worth, had no family or kin—crucial concepts within Viking Age society. This polarity was important in order to validate the social order, not just in viking society, but as a general observation.[39] I agree here with Alice Rio, who, on this theme, has written: "Unfree status was capable of fulfilling many functions, in areas as diverse as labour, honour and display, or sexual gratification. Like any other generic characterization of a human relationship, it operated at many different levels."[40] Rio continues by making a valid comparison between unfreedom and other social bonds, such as kinship (in a way an antithesis to slavery), a form of social institution that varies considerably between cultures and also over time. Like slavery it is a kind of power relationship where the primary function is to make a distinction between "us and them," hence insiders and outsiders.[41] If you were "inside" of the family or kin, you had a certain protection and inclusion in that society, if you were "outside" you were, in the kind of societies we are dealing with here, in a very exposed position, in the extreme case, you were considered to be "socially dead," to cite Orlando Patterson again.

All in all, it seems time has come to present a new model (or different options) for what society looked like in terms of its social, economic, and legal aspects, with regard not just to Scandinavia but also to Europe at large for the period in question, the second half of the first millennium. Recently, the Dutch archaeologist Frands Theuws has conducted an important discussion focusing on this, and his opinions concur with mine.[42] He has argued that the elite-controlled model of society, with which historians have worked ever since Marc Bloch and which has been developed in a recent publication by Chris Wickham,[43] is perhaps not so well suited to what the archaeologists unearth. The old maxim that the farmers of Europe were predominantly semifree tenants or unfree slaves in a repressive "lord–subject" relationship can and should, according to Theuws, be modified. Instead, he has proposed to put forward the farmer as a relatively free agent, akin to the role and status that farmers had in northern Spain and southern France, as Pierre Bonnassie

[38] See also Meulengracht Sørensen 1993 p. 161 and Karras 1988 pp. 159–160, 165 ff.

[39] See Patterson 1982 p. 47 and Wyatt 2000 p. 341.

[40] Rio 2017 p. 11.

[41] Rio 2017 pp. 11–12; for Scandinavia see, e.g., Wennerström 1933, Munktell 1943, Fenger 1971, Jacoby 1974, Byock 1993, Breisch 1994, Hansen 2000, Riisøy 2014.

[42] Theuws ms.

[43] Bloch 1921, 1933, 1947, 1961, 1967, 1975, Wickham 2005.

has argued.[44] I take the view that Theuws here touches on a new and productive way of thinking that will force us to consider the period in a radically new light.

In this new "model" it is my opinion that the role of the "free" farmer, the farmer who was taxed by the crown, and who was not a semifree, serf-like tenant, must be highlighted much more. Researchers—especially in the 1950s and 1960s—necessarily criticized the romantic idea of an early medieval (here in the European sense) society made up by equal free farmers,[45] and correctly noted that also the early society was hierarchical to different degrees, but during this clean-up operation, in their eagerness they also threw out the baby with the bathwater. It has been more or less impossible—with the risk of losing your academic credibility—to emphasize the role of also the "free farmer" during the last couple of decades, but I am not the only one to take this stance. Today there are several historians and archaeologists who have argued in the same way.[46]

In an attempt to find a new state-of-the-art regarding the settlement structure and social dependencies in the period circa 800–1200, several scholars have discussed whether there is a continuation between the Viking Age and the Early Middle Ages in Scandinavia, whether there were estates and manors already in the Viking Age, or if these emerged later. [47] Many tend to elaborate on Viking Age large magnates or demesne farms that were slave-driven, and I think this is a valid possibility. I tend to agree with Bjørn Poulsen, who suggests:

> The size of the group of slaves, *trælle*, which existed well into the thirteenth century, is not easy to measure but it is very likely that they constituted a vital workforce on the larger farms. This strongly suggests that in the old

[44] See Bonnassie 1989 and 1991. A view similar to Theuws' is expressed by another archaeologist, Joachim Henning (2003); building on the important work by Michael McCormick (2001), he proposes a break up of the prevailing model where the Roman *villae* continued after the collapse of the Roman Empire with permanent labor forces (slaves): "The key factors for the new system were a technological base which in part reached a nearly nineteenth-century level of quality (not of quantity), and the increasing number of relatively autonomous and self-managing peasants organized mainly in villages, a growing interest of these food producers in their own daily work, and finally, a high degree of freedom in the rural world" (p. 274).

[45] See, e.g., Reuter 1978 p. 11 with refs.

[46] For Sweden: esp. Rahmqvist 1986, 1996, 2002, 2007, Brink 1994, 2014a; for Denmark: Bøgh 2007, Hybel and Poulsen 2008; and the important discussion by P. Sawyer 2002 pp. 173, 185, 189, Gelting 2005, Poulsen and Sindbæk 2011, and Poulsen 2012 on the distinction in esp. Denmark of *bønder*, legally free farmers, legally free tenants, etc.

[47] See the discussion by Poulsen and Sindbæk 2011, and the following articles in that volume.

agrarian system before the eleventh century, there were only free farmers, *bønder*, and their unfree bailiffs [*brytar*] assisted by slaves.[48]

I am more hesitant in seeing an extensive occurrence of slaves on "tenant" farms, for the simple reason that it is impossible to prove whether these were free or unfree farmers.[49]

As has been stressed several times in this volume, it is possible to see in the concept of the *thrall* a more nuanced semantic content than "unfree slave." It may have referred to some sort of dependent relationship between a superior person and his servants, subjects, as in a "patron–client" relationship. The servants or clients may, whether by force or voluntarily, have ended up in a constant or coincidental position of dependency or service. This could have the form of taking on the task (more or less serf-like) of running a farm as a tenant; to assist in trading journeys; to be "employed" as a craftsman, perhaps a blacksmith, by some superior person; to serve as a warrior for some nobleman or king, for which role an oath of allegiance was presumably sworn and possibly even entering some kind of legal position as an individual. Some unique legal clauses from the Guta Law (the law for the inhabitants of the island of Gotland in the Baltic) (§ 2, 6, and 16) are of great interest in this context, since they state that thraldom could be limited to a specified period of time:[50]

Þa en ambatnu manns werþr slikt mal kennt, þa leggir engin henni maira fe framm, þan siex oyra penninga. Þa en han werþr full, þa byti drotin firi hana siex oyra penninga ok legg a bak henni siex wintr sen mali ier inntr.

If such a case is brought against someone's female slave, no one is to lay any higher fine against her than six öre in coin. If she is found guilty, then her master is fined six öre in coin on her behalf, and six years are added after her time of slavery is complete.

Weþr þrel eþa ambatn manns um helgan dag a werki takin, þa bytir drotin firi þaun þria oyra, en þaun yrkin þria wintr sen mali ir inntr.

[48] Poulsen 2012, p. 456.
[49] This was also the conclusion by Peter Sawyer 2002, pp. 173, 185, 189.
[50] Old Gotlandic text from Säve 1859; English translation by Christine Peel (2015, pp. 37, 40, and 48).

If a male or female slave is caught working on a holy day, their master is fined three öre on their behalf, and they are to have their time of slavery extended by three years.

Wn þrel þann, sum ort hafr mala, þa taki frelsi firi kirkiu-durum miþ soknamanna witnum, ok siþan warþer þrel sir sielfr, hwat sum hann gierir.

But a slave who has worked through his time of slavery is to embrace his freedom at the church door with the witness of the parishioners and then the slave is himself responsible for his actions.

It is clear from the Guta Law that a thrall could, naturally, not compensate and regulate an offense himself; it was his owner who must do so. Instead, the thrall's time in thraldom was extended, which must be taken to mean that this period of time had been specified prior to that person entering thraldom.[51]

A person could bind himself and accept wages as a "soldier" in the service of some nobleman or king, and (in so doing) he was probably required to swear an oath of loyalty and thereby enter a new legal status as an individual. Such persons are probably identifiable with the assumed words for "warriors"—found in a number of place names—who must have existed in prehistoric Scandinavian society and who can be traced as *karlar*, *rekkar/*rinkar*, *sveinar/svennar*, and *þegnar/tegnar* in place names. Older attested meanings, and Old English and Old Frankish parallels, show that these warriors and soldiers were in the service of a king, bishop, or nobleman. Here, therefore, we are dealing with a "patron" and several kinds of "clients." A *sven* (ON *sveinn*) could be a young warrior or a young man (corresponding to Latin *puer*), for in, for example, Old High German the word referred to a "young (swine)herd," and in Old Scandinavian it could also refer to a "thrall." A *karl* had a certain legal status in society, while a **rinkr* had an even more elevated position, if one judges by, among other things, the excavated grave of a warrior from the Vendel Period (AD 600–800) in the village of Rickeby in Vallentuna parish, in the province of Uppland, Sweden.[52] A *thegn*, finally, can be assumed to have belonged to the nobility within society. All categories nonetheless found themselves in a dependent relationship, in a position of service. One of the great merits of Tore Iversen's dissertation on Norwegian thraldom[53] is that

[51] *Guta Lag*, ed. C. Peel (2016); cf. Hasselberg 1944 p. 56 and Skyum-Nielsen 1979 p. 133.
[52] See Sjösvärd 1989.
[53] Iversen 1997.

he highlighted the shifting social positions of the Scandinavian thrall within the societal hierarchy. Not all unfree people can have lived at the bottom of society. Iversen has here pointed to the Old Norwegian *ármaðr*, the legally unfree royal steward during the Middle Ages, who had economic, legal, and military functions within the local administration.[54]

This chimes entirely with the situation known from the European continent where unfree people or slaves could be made to fulfill a service for someone. It is well known that, for the many privately owned churches that existed in northern Europe during the second half of the first millennium, the church owner, *patronus*, could choose to place an unfree man, hence a slave—alternatively a son—as the priest in his church. The reason was, of course, that the church owner then had complete control of his property; he owned both the church and the priest. But this simultaneously tells us something about the social position of unfree people of the Early Middle Ages in northern Europe. We are presumably so blinded by (above all) the American slavery of the eighteenth and nineteenth centuries, as well as the well-known classical Roman slavery, that it becomes unbelievably hard to perceive the system of degrees of what is here called *asymmetrical dependency*, which existed in the second half of the first millennium in northern Europe and in Scandinavia.

It is likewise praiseworthy that Iversen has emphasized the mobility that existed within society. People obviously moved upward and downward within the societal pyramid. A free man can for various reasons have accepted subjecting himself to another man, that is to say, entered into a more or less unfree position, as a thrall or a servant. The reason may have been economic or legal in nature. Through an oath of loyalty or a legally binding contract, an individual could place himself in an unfree situation or a particular, inferior position of service, as a *þræll*, *ambátt*, *ármaðr*, *bryti* or *karl*, **rinkr* or *þegn*, or as someone unable to work perhaps due to old age.

In other words, it appears reasonable to assume that a young man was able to more or less voluntarily choose to be taken on as a warrior or a guard for a nobleman or king, to become part of such a man's retinue. From what we can discern regarding such warrior groups during the Early Middle Ages in northern Europe, a person entered into a sort of "contract" with his patron, an oath was sworn, presumably containing the message of doing one's best at all times, of defending the king or nobleman's life at all cost, of obeying his commands and subjecting oneself to his private jurisdiction, to the extent of practically putting one's own life into the hands of the king or nobleman.[55]

[54] Iversen 1997 p. 167–180, Poulsen and Orning 2019 p. 217.

[55] On the formerly so attentively discussed, but controversial (due to many especially German researcher's ideological background), institution of *hird*, *Männerbund*, *Comitatus*, etc., see the

The king or nobleman accepted the young man into his entourage whereby the latter came to enjoy the rights offered in the form of plunder during campaigns, a place in the chieftain's hall during feasting and presumably not least access to unfree women for sexual purposes.[56] Exactly his ability to buy and keep women for sexual purposes and at the disposal of these crowds of young men further strengthened the position of the king or nobleman in the male hierarchy.[57]

The word *varangian*, ON *væringi*, Swedish *väring*, Russian *varjagu/varjazi*, Greek *varangoi*, and Arabic *warank*, should probably be explained against this background. The word was the designation for a Scandinavian who had gone on viking expeditions in the east, particularly one who had entered the royal guard of the Byzantine emperor in Constantinople.[58] The word appears to derive from a Proto-Nordic **wāragangja-*, containing the word ON *vár* 'oath, agreement, loyalty' and the verb ON *ganga* (< **gangjan*) 'to go', thus 'someone entering an agreement, taking an oath'.[59] We have here an obvious example of how a young Scandinavian man was able by oath to become accepted as a warrior into an entourage, someone's guard, and thereby subject himself to someone else's private jurisdiction.

In so doing, this young man changed his legal and social position. In a social sense, this must, of course, have been a rapid journey up the ladder of class hierarchy; he found himself in the hall belonging to and in the constant presence of the nobleman or king. In legal terms, he renounced certain rights, for example the free man's freedom and right to decide over his own life. A poor freeholder might be living socially as a thrall, but legally he had a free man's rights. A young warrior in a guard, ON *karl*, *drengr*, or *rekkr* (OSw *rinker*), certainly had a socially elevated position (physical nearness to the king or nobleman and the right to exercise repression and physical power), but he was limited in terms of his legal rights, which he had put into the hands of a king or nobleman who exercised his own jurisdiction over his

important analysis by Joseph Harris (1993), especially of Otto Höfler's *Kultische Geheimbünde der Germanen* (1934), and with numerous references.

[56] Cf. Schlesinger 1953 pp. 70, 231, 235 ff., Karras 1994 p. 21, and especially Wyatt 2009 pp. 61 ff.

[57] Wyatt 2009 p. 131 and *passim*, see also the review by Brink 2011.

[58] See, e.g., Sigfús Blöndal 1978 and the overview articles in *Varangians* and *Varangian guard* in Wikipedia.

[59] Stender-Petersen 1953 pp. 89 ff., de Vries 1962 pp. 671–672, Lägreid 1984 pp. 101–102, and Andersson 2006; cf. Parducci 2007 for a potential Langobardic link.

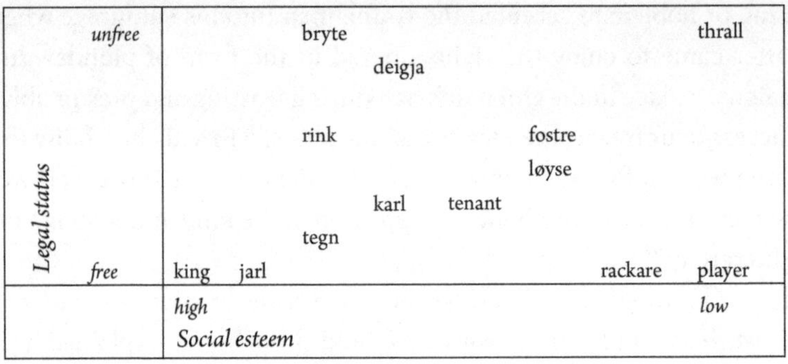

Fig. 16.1 An attempt to describe the social web in Viking Age Scandinavia, indicating placement in the web depending on legal freedom contra unfreedom, and high and low social esteem.

guard. Moreover, in the Gothic *Passio St. Saba* (Passion of St. Sabas the Goth) the guard of a king or chieftain is referred to as his "slaves."[60]

This circumstance provides a good illustration of the previously mentioned travel account by Ibn Fadlan regarding his encounter with the Rūs, that is to say (probably) Swedish viking traders, on the banks of the Volga in the early tenth century. When Ibn Fadlan describes what he knows of the king of the Rūs, he says that the king in his "castle" (which must be understood as his royal hall) "keeps company with four hundred of his bravest and most trusted companions," which in all likelihood is best interpreted as a large group of warriors, a retinue or a royal guard, constantly in the presence of the king and living with him. And then follows the important piece of information: "they die when he dies and they offer their lives to protect him."[61] They have, in other words, dedicated their lives to the king and probably sworn by oath to fight for their king even unto death. They are, in a word, "varjags," who have pledged themselves to and voluntarily accepted the private jurisdiction of their lord.

Another issue to consider in this connection is that people who occupied different levels of the societal pyramid had different legal statuses (Fig. 16.1). A free, but outlawed person lacked all legal (and social) rights, since he had been excommunicated, placed outside the society and the

[60] See Enright 1996 p. 203 n. 31. For a Swedish translation of the Greek text of Saint Saba's martyrdom, see Flemberg 1992. I think there is reason to once again pay attention to the well-known Viking Age fortresses of Trelleborg, Nonnebakken, Fyrkat, etc., the ring fortresses that are referred to as *trelleborgar*, in the light of the arguments I present here (hence, see *Excursus Trelleborg*, in what follows).

[61] Montgomery 2000 p. 21.

protection of the law. Legally speaking, then, an outlaw was worse off than a thrall, who was in every way part of a social community and had a certain amount of protection through his master. A bit further up the social scale were migrants, vagabonds, wandering men (OSw *løskamaþer* sg.) and women, and performers or players, that is, wandering "artists." These people were, for sure, under the protection of the criminal law, but they had such a low social standing that their legal status was practically nonexistent, since they did not possess the fundamental characteristics of honor, reputation, and home, that is, they were not attached to a farm, household, or settled family. These people could be treated as forcefully and degradingly as anything, which is made clear for instance by the famous "Player's Right" of the Older Västgöta Law:

> *Þattæ ær lecara rætar.*
> *Uarþær lekæri barþær þæt skal e vgilt uaræ. Varþær lekari sargarþær þen sum mæþ gighu gangar allær mæþ fiþlu far allær bambu. þa skal kuighu taka otamæ ok flytiæ up a bæsing. þa skal alt har af roppo rakæ. ok siþæn smyriæ. þa skal hanum fa sko nysmurþæ. þa skal lekærin takæ quighuna vm roppo. maþær skal til huggæ mæþ huassi gesl. Gitær han haldit. þa skal han hauæ þæn goþa grip. ok niutæ sum hundær græss. Gitær han eigh haldit. havi ok þole þæt sum han fek skama ok skaþæ biði alþrigh halldær ræt æn huskonæ hudstrukin.*[62]

> This is the Player's Right
> If a player is beaten, that shall always be unpunished. If a player, someone who walks around with a Jew's harp or travels around with a fiddle or a drum, is wounded, then one shall take an untamed heifer and bring it up on the *bäsing.* [63] Then one shall shave off all the hair from the tail and then lubricate it. Then one shall give him [the player] newly lubricated shoes. Then the player shall grab the tail of the heifer, and a man shall flog [the heifer] with a sharp whip. If he can hold her, then he shall have the good animal and enjoy it, as a dog enjoys grass. If he cannot hold her, he shall have and endure what he got, shame and harm. He can never ask for greater rights than a flogged slave-woman.[64]

[62] VgL, Collin and Schlyter (eds.) 1827 p. 67.
[63] The word *bäsing* here refers apparently to a 'hill, mound', cf. Olson 1916 p. 260.
[64] My translation.

In this way, it was possible even by law to harass and expose a player to public scorn, which shows that a migrant and a player were practically without any legal rights—he had no more rights "than a flogged slave-woman"! Only a free man, a freeholder, had full legal protection.[65]

With these examples, we seem able to turn the spotlight to the fluidity of the social and legal situation during the Viking Age and the succeeding centuries in Scandinavia, such as I have argued in the present book. After the introduction of the new Christian religion in Scandinavia and the establishment of the Church (roughly the eleventh to the fourteenth centuries), the roles became more cemented and the anchoring within various social strata became more static, while the situation was more fluid in the Vendel Period and the Viking Age (c. 600–1100). This latter period, then, presented the opportunity for remarkable leaps up the social ladder as well as the possibility of placing oneself in—or forcefully ending up in—a state of lacking freedom (or a state of asymmetrical dependency). With the arrival of the Church onto the stage alongside the "feudalization" of society, the societal climate changed radically and became more static. If you wanted to climb the social ladder in this new society your greatest chance of success was to educate yourself as a priest.

Pax vobiscum.

[65] Cf. Anners 1957. This legal clause about players in medieval Sweden has recently been given a new and interesting interpretation, by Dr Lisa Collinson, Aberdeen, that not only widens the perspective considerable but also puts the citation in a new and more convincing context.

17
Excursus *Trelleborg*

Thus far I have deliberately avoided discussing the Danish ring-fortresses called *Trelleborg* or *Trælleborg*. The ring-fortresses are some of the most enigmatic features of the Viking Age; all seem to have been built between circa 970 and circa 980, and were in use for an astonishingly short period of time, only ten to fifteen years.[1] It seems obvious that these names and fortresses should have a central position in any discussion of slaves in Scandinavia, since we must assume that the first element of the name is Da. *træl*, ON *þræll*. The reason for avoiding the topic thus far is that the fortresses and the name are actually difficult to analyze and understand.

To start with the name, *Trælleborg*,[2] we find—apart from the name of the ring-fortress on Sjælland and the name of a town in Skåne—at least thirty such names in Denmark and Skåne, Sweden. Furthermore, according to *Hákonar saga herðibreiðs*,[3] in Snorri Sturluson's *Heimskringla*, there was also a *Þrælaborg* just south of Oslo in Norway.[4] There is another one, interestingly enough, in the vicinity of Novgorod in Russia, mentioned in the so-called Privileges at Novgorod from 1228–1229 written in Low German as *Dhrelleborch*,[5] and according to Alexander Bugge mentioned in 1268 as a place in southern Russia between Ladoga and Novgorod, on the right bank of the river Volchov.[6] The most mysterious example is to be found in south-western France, some forty kilometers from Rochefort and the Atlantic, north of Bordeaux (Fig. 17.1). Today the name is *Taillebourg*, but in 1007 it was written *Traillebrucense* and in 1074 *Tralliburgo*.[7] This name has been dismissed as having nothing to do with the *Trælleborg* group,[8] but I think that

[1] Nørlund 1948, Roesdahl and Sindbæk 2014a p. 208. For an overview of different theories of how these ring-fortresses have been interpreted and been given an historical explanation, see Roesdahl and Sindbæk 2014b.
[2] The most in-depth analysis of the name *Trelleborg*/*Trælleborg* is Knudsen 1948.
[3] See https://skaldic.abdn.ac.uk/db.php?id=131&if=default&table=text.
[4] Snorri Sturluson, *Heimskringla*, vol. 3, pp. 367–368, cf. Ståhl 1957 col. 163.
[5] Sartorius 1830:2, p. 29.
[6] A. Bugge 1918 p. 91.
[7] Knudsen 1948 pp. 196–197, Mariotti et al. 2005 p. 326.
[8] Jørgensen 1995 p. 7, *pace* Brøndum-Nielsen 1974 p. 9.

DOI: 10.1093/oso/9780197532355.003.0017

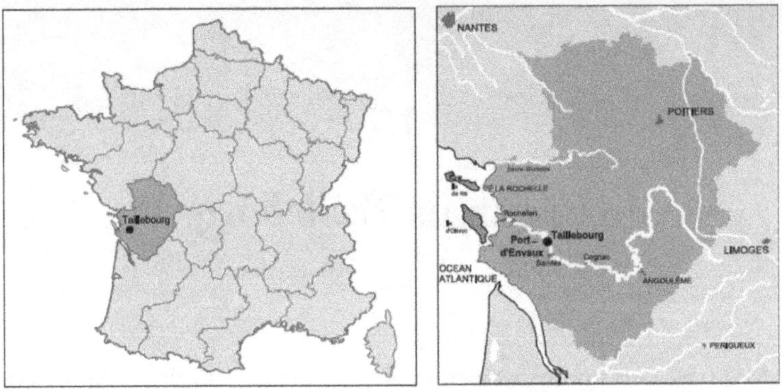

Fig. 17.1 The situation of the potential Trelleborg in southern France, Taillebourg at Port d'Envaux. (After Mariotti et al. 2005 p. 300.)

is a rushed conclusion. The reason for this is some very interesting archaeological excavations at this site by the river Charente.[9] At Taillebourg and Port d'Envaux archaeologists have found Viking Age finds and weapons, definitely of Scandinavian origin. We know, of course, that viking Scandinavians frequently were there, and had winter camps in the region. It is therefore not possible, as I see it, to dismiss this *Taillebourg* as a potential *Trælleborg* in a Gallicized (and slightly corrupt) form.

What we are dealing with are late tenth-century—and regarding their construction—unique ring-fortresses, which are found in southern Scandinavia. The most famous ones are Trelleborg (Fig. 17.2) and the newly discovered Borgring on Sjælland; Nonnebakken (beneath! the city of Odense) on Fyn; Fyrkat and Aggersborg in Jutland; Trelleborg (today a town) and Borgby in Skåne, southern Sweden; and possibly another one in Helsingborg, Skåne. Together with these seven (potentially eight) known *trelleborgar*, there are as many as forty names in southern Scandinavia: *Trelleborg*, *Trælleborg*, *Trælborg*, etc., twenty-eight of them in present-day Denmark, which potentially could denote a fortification.[10]

First we ask, is the name *Trælleborg* young or late? Can it have been given in the Viking Age? To discuss this we have to conduct an onomastic analysis of the names.

The most famous *Trælleborg* in Hejninge sn, Slagelse hd, western Sjælland, has no medieval name forms apart from a transcription from 1607 of a letter

[9] Mariotti et al. 2005.
[10] Knudsen 1948, DS 24 p. 68 and Jørgensen 1995 pp. 10–11.

Fig. 17.2 The Viking Age fortress Trelleborg, Sjælland, Denmark. (Photo: Niels Elswing, National Museum, Copenhagen, CC-BY-SA.)

from 1487, when it is written *Trelborg* (which mirrors a language form more from c. 1600, than from the late Middle Ages).

The Swedish city of *Trelleborg* has many medieval forms: *in Treleburg* 1257 trans., *Threlæburgh*, *Threlleburgh* 1291 or., *Thrælæyeburgh*, *threlleburgensi*, *Threlleburg* 1291 or., *in Træleborgh* 1299 trans. 1494, *Thrælæborgensis* 1320 or., *Thrælæburgh* 1335 or., *Thræleb[u]rg* 1334–1366 or., *Thrælæborgh* 1344 or., in *thræleburgh* 1358 or., etc.[11] This name is an indication that we are dealing with an old, probably Viking Age name.

[11] For sources for the medieval name forms for the Swedish *Trelleborg*, see the Swedish digital place-name register at the *Institute for Language and Folklore*, Uppsala: http://www.isof.se/sprak/namn/ortnamn/ortnamnsregistret/sok-i-registret.html.

Other Danish place-names, *Træleborg* etc., are: *Trælborg*, Brede sn, Tønder, Højer & Lø hd, Jutland (*Trelburg* c. 1412 or., *Trelborg* 1479 or.); *Trælborg*, Lødderup sn, Morsø Sønder hd, Jutland (*Trelldige* 1528 trans. 1591, *Trelborrig* 1664); *Trælleborg* Enge (a nature name), Åstrup sn, Falster Sønder hd, Falster (*Trelleborg* 1509, *Treelburg Eng* 1532), etc.[12] For many of these twenty-eight Danish names there are at these locations legends, records, or reminiscences of a fortress or some rampart,[13] hence there are reasons to believe that there have been more than the seven (potentially eight) known *trælleborgar*. Finally, we have the name *Þrælaborg* (c. 1160) in Oslo mentioned in *Heimskringla*, the Russian *Dhrelleborch* (< OSw *Þrælaborg*) and the potential French *Taillebourg*, written *Traillebrucense* in 1007.

This analysis intimates that a place name *Trælleborg* probably has an origin in the Viking Age.

Since we know (and have discussed previously) that there are very few Scandinavian place names beginning with *Træl-*, the second question is: Does the name *Trælleborg* indicate the existence of an appellative *trælleborg*, or have the many names *Trælleborg* been given from one famous, eponymous *Trælleborg*? In the first case we have to reckon with an existing appellative, in the latter case a name transfer.[14] Since we are not aware of the existence of an appellative **trælleborg*, the most plausible assumption is that one of the major *trælleborgar* is the "progenitor," the *eponym*, and what first springs to mind as a realistic supposition would be to identify this with *Trælleborg* on Sjælland, from which the rest of the place-names of this kind have taken its name. However, the Danish onomastician, Bent Jørgensen, has, in his discussion of the name *Trælleborg*, instead highlighted the (today) Swedish town of *Trelleborg* as the "progenitor," with some rather ingenious arguments. First, it has a geographically central position, connecting trade routes to the Baltic and the East, to Germany and Haithabu in the south, and to Norway, the North Sea, and the West in the north and west. Second, it would make the occurrence of a *Trælleborg* (*Dhrelleborch*) near Novgorod in Russia and in the Oslo fjord seem logical. And third, it could also explain why the three other ring-fortresses in the west (on Fyn and Jutland) don't have the name

[12] For the sources for the Danish names and their early name forms, see Knudsen 1948 pp. 189–195, DS, and Jørgensen 1995 pp. 10–11.

[13] Se Knudsen 1948 pp. 189–195, Andersen 1992 pp. 23–28, Madsen and Jeppesen 1993, and Jørgensen 1995 p. 10.

[14] Cf. the discussion on name transfer, etc., in Brink 2016.

**Trælleborg*. So, what do I think? Well, Jørgensen has some valid points for his hypothesis, but I rest my case; I don't know.

The third question is: Why *þræll*? How can we semantically understand the first element in these names? What immediately springs to mind is, of course, the word *þræll* meaning 'slave', but there are actually also other possibilities. Several of these have been discussed for the name *Trælleborg* in research especially by archaeologists but also by some linguists. An interpretation of the first element in the name is intimately tied to how we historically understand these ring-fortresses, about which there is still no consensus.[15] There seems, however, to be a consensus today that it must have been the king, obviously king Harald Bluetooth, who was behind the construction of these ring-fortresses, and also some other fortified constructions during the same period, i.e., c. 970s–980s.

The interpretations so far have been based on four main questions:

1. whether the fortresses had a defensive or an offensive function;
2. whether they were built against foreign enemies or for control of the indigenous population;
3. whether they were built in answer to a particular military crisis or in relation to a long-term strategy of control of the kingdom;
4. whether they had a strictly military function or also fulfilled civil functions.[16]

Out from this, let's enumerate some possibilities that have been discussed in research:

i. *Trælle*—refers to 'thralls, slaves'.[17] If we are dealing with captured slaves, used as chattel slaves, they might either have been detained within these fortresses, as a kind of gathering enclosure of captives, or have been used for building the fortresses as forced labor. The former hypothesis seems rather far-fetched (but *has* been aired in previous research), however, it seems unfathomable that someone would build such huge and complex constructions just to fence-in captive slaves. What could speak in favor of the latter hypothesis is the fact that the construction seems to

15 See Roesdahl and Sindbæk 2014b.
16 Here I am citing Roesdahl and Sindbæk 2014b p. 383–384.
17 Knudsen 1948 p. 211, 213; cf. Ståhl 1957 col. 163.

have taken place during a relatively short period of time, which would demand a very large workforce. Such demand of large-scale manpower could have been provided by slaves. A caveat might be that we don't know what the slave trade looked like around the 970s, was it as intensive and extensive as (we think it was) in the ninth and tenth centuries?

ii. *Trælle*—refers to 'dependent warriors in a retinue'. This is a somewhat far-fetched idea, where the word *þræll* could have referred to a royal public servant (of which we, admittedly, have no evidence);[18] it was intimated earlier as regarding warriors in a retinue who lose their personal judicial capacity as a "free man," because they are under a king's or a chieftain's jurisdiction. And especially, as discussed earlier, if the retinue at these ring-fortresses were made up of, not local men, but men coming from many places, in Scandinavia, the Baltic, and from Slavic areas, that could have resulted in them being called—perhaps pejoratively—*þrælar* among the local population.

iii. *Trælle*—could refer to a 'beam, pole, or buttress'. This idea was proposed by Johs. Brøndum-Nielsen (1974). His interpretation is focusing not on the actual fortress and its ramparts, but the special kind of long-houses found at these fortresses, which we call "long-house of the Trelleborg type," (Fig. 17.3) and which have the characteristics that they have bended or arched sides of the house with a long row of outer transversed buttresses. Brøndum-Nielsen is of the opinion that this unique construction detail, the buttress, has been called a *thræll.* The word is not known in older Scandinavian languages, but he is highlighting a compound ODa *bævertræl* 'beaver-thrall', a (as I understand it) unique and very dubious word,[19] and also he is pointing to a construction detail in the Viking Age long-houses, called *dvergr* for a joist,[20] as some kind of parallel. Bent Jørgensen dismisses this interpretation straight off, and I am inclined to follow him on this. There is, as far as I am aware, no known word **þræll* in the Old Scandinavian languages for some construction detail in a house or a fortress.

[18] Cf. Knudsen 1948 p. 212.
[19] Cf. Jørgensen 1995 p. 6.
[20] See Terry Gunnell's discussion of *dvergr* in a hall building (Gunnell 2001 pp. 20-22).

Fig. 17.3 The reconstructed long-house at Trelleborg, Slagelse, Sjælland, Denmark, with its outer row of buttresses. (CC BY-SA 3.0.)

iv. *Trælle*—could have been used as an ethnic term for a 'Slav', or a translation by Scandinavians of the ethnic term *Slav* with *þræll*. This idea has been discussed by Gunnar Knudsen.[21] The problem with this hypothesis is that we have no evidence whatsoever that a free Slavic person might have been called *þræll*, or that *Slav* could have been translated as *þræll*. This hypothesis seems very far-fetched.

v. *Trelle*—refers to 'thralls, slaves', but the name was, although old, not contemporary with the fortresses, but rather given some generations later, when some legend or idea had become so popular that slaves had been used to build the fortresses or had been kept there. This idea is impossible to either prove or dismiss.

Alexander Bugge is the one who has come up with the most elaborate explanation to the name(s). In his opinion, the Russian *Dhrelleborch* is the original one! His arguments are: There are many fortresses in the Slavic region on the Baltic coast in the Viking Age. The word for a "Slav" was in Old Slavic *slověninъ*; inhabitants in Novgorod were thus known in the old Novgorodian Law ("Russkaja Pravda"). The Lat. *schlavus* 'slave' comes from Gr. *σκλάβος* 'Slav', but could also in Byzantinic times denote 'slave, prisoner of war'. In Byzantium the Scandinavian *væringar* (Scandinavian palace

[21] Knudsen 1948 pp. 198–200.

guard) picked up the Gr. *σκλάβος* 'slave, prisoner of war' and brought it to Kiev and Novgorod. When they came to the Volchov river they found a small Slavic fortified settlement, which they therefore called "The fortress of the Slavs." But from Byzantium the Swedes knew that *slověninъ* also meant 'slave', whereby they called the Slavic fortified settlement OSw *þrælaborg*. Then, when the Scandinavians had left the Volchov area, the Russians translated and Russified the name to *cholopij gorodokъ* 'the settlement of the slaves'. During the time when the famous Norwegian *Haraldr Harðráði* spent time in Novgorod and the Volchov area, he had learned about the fortified settlement of *þrælaborg* and when he came home to Norway and founded Oslo he had just outside of the town, a fortress built, similar to the one he had seen in Russia, and called it *þrælaborg*. Then from Oslo and Norway this name "migrated" to Denmark and gave name to all the "trælleborgar" there. Hence, according to Bugge's ingenious idea, the name *Trælleborg* is from the beginning a folk etymological reinterpretation of "the fortress of the Slavs," and the origin is to be found in "Scandinavianized" Russia (in the Volchov region) and the "progenitor" Dhrelleborch, and the word then was taken to Norway and then to Denmark.[22] I have seen no one in later research who has picked up Bugge's idea,[23] which indeed seems far-fetched.

So, what do I think? I tend to agree with, for example, Bent Jørgensen that the most plausible interpretation of the first element in the name *Trælleborg* is *þræll* 'slave'. Hence, the word-semantical analysis seems fairly robust. I also think that it is a valid hypothesis to assume one of the *Trælleborg*s is the eponym, the "progenitor," for the other names, whether *Trelleborg* in Skåne or *Trælleborg* on Sjælland (or even *Dhrelleborch* in Russia!). The problem comes when attempting a name-semantical analysis; *þræll*s in *Þrælaborg*, doing what? Perhaps the least controversial hypothesis would be: used as forced labor of building the fortresses. But I have to admit I wouldn't bet too many cents or pennies on this. The name *Trælleborg*, found in southern Scandinavia, in Russia and potentially in southern France, as well as these ring-fortresses, are truly enigmatic.[24]

[22] A. Bugge 1918 pp. 93–95, cf. Ståhl 1957 col. 163.

[23] The only one I have found, who has referenced Bugge's hypothesis as a possibility to explain the names, is Elof Hellquist (1948 p. 1234).

[24] I hence agree with the conclusion of Gunnar Knudsen (1948 p. 214) in his analysis of the name *Trelleborg* when he says: "But although we with fairly high security may be able to conclude the meaning of the two elements [in the compound, i.e., *træl* 'slave' and *borg* 'fortress'], which the name consists of, there are several other puzzles, which we hardly ever will find the solution for" (*Men selv om vi med ret stor sikkerhed kan fastslaa betydningen af de to led, som navnet bestaar af, rummer det flere andre gaader, som vi vel næppe nogensinde finder løsningen paa*).

APPENDIX 1

Historical and Archaeological Periods in Europe

In Scandinavia they use a different periodization than in the rest of Europe. In this book the Scandinavian periodization is used, hence Prehistory ends with the end of the Viking Age (1050–1100), and the Middle Ages is consequently between circa 1100 and 1500. See the simplified Table of Historical (and Archaeological) periods that follow.

Table A.1 Table of Historical (and Archaeological) Periods

	Stone Age	*Bronze Age*	*Iron Age (IA)*		*Roman Period*	*Middle Ages*			
Central Europe	> 1800 BC	1800–700 BC	700–15 BC Hallstadt 700–450 BC	La Tène 450–15 BC	100 BC–AD 400	Early Middle Ages 400–1000 Migration Period 400–600	High Middle Ages 1000–1300	Late Middle Ages 1300–1500	
Britain	> 2100 BC	2100–700 BC	800–15 BC		50 BC–AD 400	Anglo-Saxon Period 400–1066	Norman Period > Middle Ages 1066– > 1500		
Scandinavia	> 1500 BC	1700–500 BC	500 BC–AD 400 Pre-Roman IA 500–100 BC		Roman IA 100 BC–AD 400	Migration Period 400–600	Vendel Period (Sw) Germanic IA (Da) Merovingian IA (No/Fi) 600–800	Viking Age 800–1050/1100	Middle Ages 1100–1500

APPENDIX 2

Development of Indo-European Languages

To be able to follow especially the discussion of languages, language history, and etymology, a reader might need a "crash course" in language history. Language historians still use a nineteenth-century theoretical tool we call the "language family tree." Although often criticized as too simplistic, it still fulfills its function.

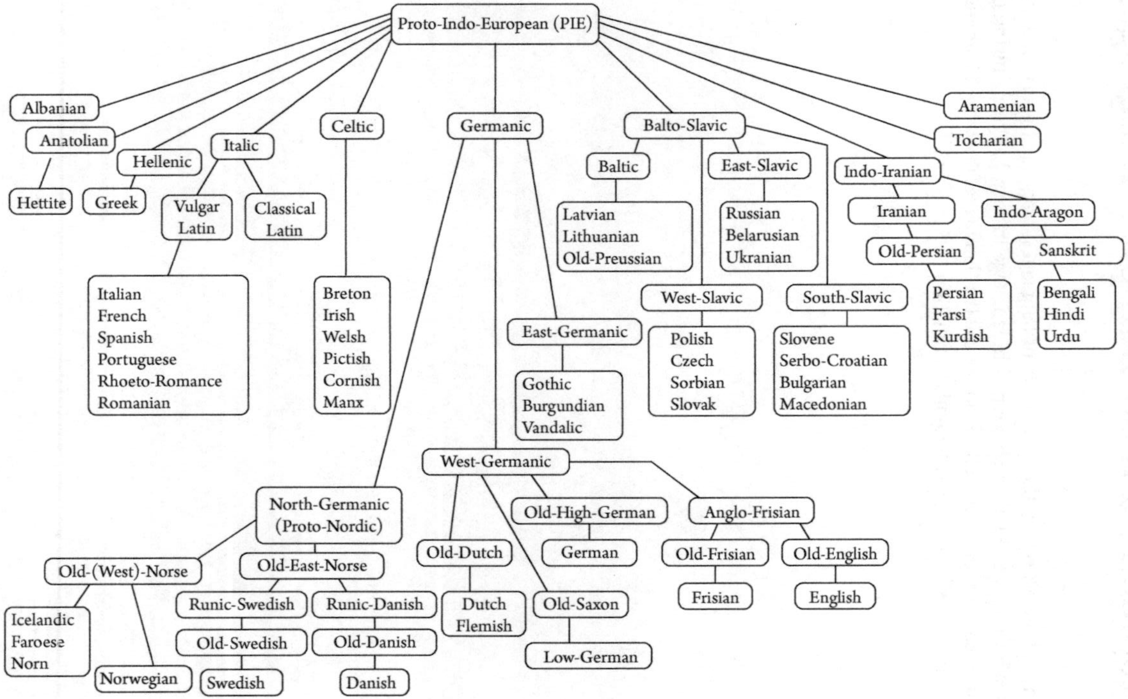

Simplified Language Tree for the Indo-European languages.

We start with the ancient common ancestor, *Proto-Indo-European* (PIE), which is a reconstructed language that has been possible to deduce from languages on the Euro-Asian continent. The genesis of this ancestral language-group is heavily debated, one old idea is that it comes from the area around the Indus river, a recent one (the Kurgan hypothesis) from the steppe north of the Black Sea. This PIE language spread westward and then split up into *Anatolian*, *Albanian*, *Hellenic* (i.e., Proto-Greek), *Indo-Iranian* (resulting in Iranian, Sanskrit, etc.), *Italic* (which split up into Classical Latin and Vulgar Latin, which is the mother of Romanian, French, and other Romance dialects), *Celtic* (with the dialects Irish, Pictish, Breton, Welsh, etc.), *Balto-Slavic*, *Tocharian*, *Armenian*, and *Germanic*. These early split-ups of the PIE language took place over two thousand years ago.

The *Proto-Germanic* (PGmc), which we are able to reconstruct thanks to early runic inscription and also words found in classical authors' works, emerges circa 500 BC–AD 200 or earlier. In the first half of the first millennium PGmc splits up into three dialects, *East Germanic* (i.e., *Gothic* [Goth.], *Burgundian*, *Vandalic*), which ceases to exist c. AD 400, *West Germanic* (which splits up into *Old-High-German* (OHG), the mother of modern *German*; *Old-Saxon* (OSax) or *Old-Low-German* (OLG), the mother of dialects spoken in northern Germany; *Anglo-Frisian*, the mother of *Old-Frisian* (OFr) and *Old-English* (OE); and *Old-Dutch* (ODu), evolving into modern *Dutch* and *Flemish*. *North Germanic*, which we also call *Proto-Nordic*, emerges as a language in the first half and the middle of the first millennium, and is possible to reconstruct mainly via the runic inscriptions made with the Early Germanic or Proto-Nordic runes (the 24-type Futhark).

This Proto-Nordic language starts to split up around AD 800 into two dialects, one in the west *Old* (*West*) *Norse* (ON or OWN), and one in the east *Old-East-Norse* (OEN), or *Old-East-Scandinavian*. We can follow this split-up of Proto-Nordic in runic inscriptions from circa 800—as on the famous Rök runestone—and onward. Old Norse is the language in which the famous Icelandic sagas and Old Norse poetry are written, but we also find it in early documents and literature in Norway. Old Norse has become "The Latin of the North" for students interested in the Old Norse literature, and is taught at many universities around the world. The Old-East-Norse is what we find on Swedish and Danish viking runestones (with the 16-type Futhark), but in the twelfth century the Danish language starts to divide, resulting in *Old Danish* (ODa), which diverges from the somewhat more "archaic" *Old Swedish* (OSw), with an older predecessor (during the Viking Age) in *Runic Swedish*. What then happens especially with Old Danish and Old Swedish is that these languages from circa thirteenth century are heavily influenced by *Low-German* (during the Hanseatic Period), and then in the fifteenth century (in Danish earlier than in Swedish) they undergo a simplification of the grammatical system (esp. case) and a reduction of word length, which eventually results in modern *Danish* (Da) and *Swedish* (Sw).

List of Abbreviations

acc.	accusative
Da.	Danish
dat.	dative
dial.	dialect
Eng.	English
f.	feminine
Gall.	Gallic
gen.	genitive
Germ.	German
Goth.	Gothic
hd.	herred/härad ("hundred")
Ir.	Irish
Icel.	Icelandic
KB	Royal Library
Latv.	Latvian
Lith.	Lithuanian
m.	masculine
mbyn.	man's byname
ME	Middle English
MLG	Middle Low German
mn.	man's name
MNo.	Middle Norwegian
MSlov.	Modern Slovenian
MSw.	Middle Swedish
n.	neuter
No.	Norwegian
nom.	nominative
OCelt	Old Celtic
ODa	Old Danish
OE	Old English
OHG	Old High German
OIcel	Old Icelandic
OInd	Old Indic
OIr	Old Irish
or.	original
OSax	Old Saxon

OSlav	Old Slavic
OSw	Old Swedish
PIE	Proto-Indo-European
pl.	plural
PGmc	Proto-Germanic
Raä	Swedish National Heritage Board, Stockholm (*Riksantikvarieämbetet*)
sg.	singular
Slav.	Slavic
sn.	sogn/socken ("parish")
Sw.	Swedish
voc.	vocative
WGerm.	West Germanic

Bibliography

Primary Sources and Collections

Very useful online tools for early Scandinavian primary sources are *Early North Data Service* (https://skaldic.abdn.ac.uk//m.php) and *The Scaldic Project* (https://skaldic.abdn.ac.uk//m.php?p=skaldic), both created and maintained by Dr. Tarrin Wills, The Arnamagnaean Commission, University of Copenhagen.

Adam of Bremen = Adam of Bremen, *Gesta Hammaburgensis ecclesiæ pontificum*, ed. by Bernhard Schmeidler (Monumenta Germaniae Historica: Scriptores rerum Germanicarum, 2), 3rd ed., Hannover: Hahn, 1917; repr. 1977. [IN TRANS.: *History of the Archbishops of Hamburg–Bremen: Adam of Bremen*, trans. by Fr. J. Tchan, New York: Columbia University Press, 2002.]

Ágrip = *Ágrip af Nóregskonungasǫgum—A Twelfth-Century Synoptic History of the Kings of Norway*, ed. and trans. with an introduction by M. J. Driscoll, 2nd ed., London: Viking Society for Northern Research, 2008.

AM = The Arnamagnæan Collection, Department of Scandinavian Research, University of Copenhagen, Denmark, and Stofnun Árna Magnússonar í íslenskum fræðum/The Árni Magnússon Institute for Icelandic Studies, Reykjavík, Iceland.

The Annals of St-Bertin = *Ninth-Century Histories*, vol. 1: *The Annals of St-Bertin*, trans. and com. by Janet L. Nelson, Manchester & New York: Manchester University Press, 1991.

Aristotle, *Politics*, trans. by H. Rackham, new ed. (Loeb Classical Library, 264), Cambridge, MA: Harvard University Press, 1944 (http://www.perseus.tufts.edu).

Bede's Ecclesiastical History of England, a revised trans., with intro, life, and notes by A. M. Sellar, London: George Bell and Sons, 1907.

Beowulf = *Beowulf and The Fight at Finnsburg*, ed. by Fr. Klaeber (https://sourcebooks.fordham.edu/basis/beowulf-oe.asp), accessed Nov. 30, 2017. [IN TRANS.: Seamus Heaney, *Beowulf: A New Verse Translation*, New York & London: W. W. Norton & Comp., 2000.]

Caesar, *De bello Gallico* = *C. Iuli Caesaris De bello Gallico*, ed. by T. Rice Holmes, New York: Arno Press, 1979.

Code of Hammurabi (Code of Hammurabi online: http://www.wsu.edu/~dee/MESO/CODE.HTM).

The Complete Sagas of the Icelanders, 5 vols, gen. ed. Viðar Hreinsson, Reykjavík: Leifur Eiríksson Publishing, 1997.

DD = *Diplomatarium Danicum*, 1–, publ. by Det danske sprog- og litteraturselskab, København: Reitzel, 1938 ff.

DGLL = *Danmarks gamle landskabslove med kirkelovene*, 10 vols, publ. by Det danske sprog- og litteraturselskab under ledelse af Johs. Brøndum-Nielsen, København: Gyldendal, 1933–1961.

DGL = *Danmarks gamle love paa nutidsdansk*, 3 vols, by Erik Kroman and Stig Iuul, København: Gad, 1945–1948.

Die Gesetze der Angelsachsen, ed. by F. Liebermann, Halle: Savigny-Stiftung, 1903–1916.

DR = *Danmarks runeindskrifter*, ed. by Lis Jacobsen and Erik Moltke, København: E. Munksgaard, 1942.

DS = *Diplomatarium Suecana: Svenskt diplomatarium*, 1–, Stockholm: Kungl. Vitterhets, Historie och Antikvitetsakademien/Riksarkivet, 1829 ff.

Edda = *Edda. Die Lieder des Codex Regius nebst Vervandten Denkmälern*, ed. by Gustav Neckel, 3rd ed. (Germanische Bibliothek, 2:9), Heidelberg: Carl Winter, 1936. [IN TRANS.: *The Poetic Edda*, 3 vols, ed. with trans, intro., and com. by Ursula Dronke, Oxford: Clarendon, 1969–2011; *The Poetic Edda*, trans. with an intro. and notes by Carolyne Larrington, Oxford: Oxford University Press, 1999.]

Egil's saga = *Egils saga Skallagrímssonar*, tilligemed Egils större kvad, publ. by Finnur Jónsson (Samfund til udgivelse af gammel nordisk literatur, 17), København: Samfund til udgivelse af gammel nordisk literatur, 1886–88. [IN TRANS.: *Egil's saga*, trans. with an intro. by Hermann Pálsson and Paul Edwards (Penguin Classics), Harmondsworth: Penguin, 1976, and "Egil's Saga," ed. and trans. by Bernhard Scudder, in *The Complete Sagas of the Icelanders*, vol. 1, gen. ed. Viðar Hreinsson, Reykjavík: Leifur Eriksson Publishing, 1997, pp. 33–177.]

Eyrbyggja saga = "The Saga of the People of Eyri," ed. and trans. by Judy Quinn, in *The Complete Sagas of Icelanders*, vol. 5, gen. ed. Viðar Hreinsson, Reykjavík: Leifur Eriksson Publishing, 1997, pp. 131–218.

FrL = *Frostatingslagen*. [OLD NORWEGIAN TEXT: "Den ældre Frostathings-Lov," *Norges Gamle Love indtil 1387*, vol. 1, ed. by R. Keyser and P. A. Munch, Christiania: Norsk historisk kjeldeskrift-institutt, 1846; IN TRANSLATION: *The Earliest Norwegian Laws: Being the Gulathing Law and the Frostathing Law*, trans. by Lawrence M. Larson (Records of civilization, 20), New York: Morningside Heights, 1935.]

Gísla saga Súrssonar, ed. by Agnete Loth (Nordisk filologi, A: 11) København: Munksgaard, 1956.

GL = *Guta Lag and Guta Saga: The Law and History of the Gotlanders*, ed. by Ch. Peel, (Routledge Medieval Translations; Nordic Medieval Laws), Abingdon & New York: Routledge, 2015, see also Peel 1999 and 2009.

Grágás = *Grágás. Islændernes Lovbog i Fristatens Tid udg. efter det konglige Bibliotheks Haandskrift . . . af Vilhjálmur Finsen for det nordiske Literatur-Samfund*, 2 vols, Kjøbenhavn: Det Nordiske Literatur-Samfund, 1852; *Grágás efter det Arnnmagnæanske Haandskrift Nr. 334 fol. . . .* ed. by Vilhjálmur Finsen, Kjøbenhavn, 1879; *Grágás. Stykker, som findes i det Arnamagnæanske Haanskrift Nr. 351 fol. . . . og en Række andre Haandskrifter . . .* ed. by Vilhjálmur Finsen, Kjøbenhavn: Komissionen for det Arnamagnæanske Legat, 1883; *The Codex Regius of Grágás. . .*, ed. by Páll Eggert Ólason (Corpus coducum Islandicoru medii aevi, 3), Reykjavík, 1932. [IN TRANS.: *Laws of Early Iceland: Grágás; The Codex Regius of Grágás with Material from Other Manuscripts*, 2 vols, trans. by A. Dennis, P. Foote, and R. Perkins (University of Manitoba Icelandic studies), Winnipeg: University of Manitoba Press, 1980, 2000.]

GuL = *Gulatingslagen*. [OLD NORWEGIAN TEXT: "Den ældre Gulathings-Lov," *Norges Gamle Love indtil 1387*, vol. 1, ed. by R. Keyser and P. A. Munch, Christiania: Norsk historisk kjeldeskrift-institutt, 1846; *Den eldre Gulatingslova*, ed. by B. Eithun, M. Rindal and T. Ulset (Norrøne tekster, 6), Oslo: Riksarkivet, 1994; IN TRANSLATION: *The Earliest Norwegian Laws: Being the Gulathing Law and the Frostathing Law*, trans. by Lawrence M. Larson (Records of Civilization, 20), New York: Morningside Heights, 1935; *The Older Gulathing Law*, ed. and trans. by Erik Simensen (Medieval Nordic Laws), Abingdon & New York: Routledge 2021.]

Guta Lag and *Guta Saga*, see *GL* and Peel 1999 and 2009.
Hálfs saga ok Hálfsrekka, ed. by Hubert Seelow (Stofnun Árna Magnússonar á Íslandi, 20), Reykjavík: Stofnun Árna Magnússonar á Íslandi, 1981.
Hrólfs saga kraka ok kappa hans, in *Fornaldarsögur Norðurlanda*, ed. by Guðni Jónsson and Bjarni Vilhjálmarsson (online at: http://heimskringla.no/wiki/Hrólfs_saga_kraka_ok_kappa_hans). [IN TRANS: *The Saga of King Rolf Kraki*, trans. with an intro. by Jesse Byock, London, Penguin, 1998.]
King Æthelberht's Law, see *Die Gesetze der Angelsachsen*, ed. Liebermann, or *The Laws of the Earliest English Kings*, ed. Attenborough.
The Laws of the Earliest English Kings, trans. and ed. by F. L. Attenborough, Cambridge: Cambridge University Press, 1922.
Ldn = *Landnámabók Íslands*, udg. efter de gamle håndskrifter af det Nordiske Oldskriftselskab [by] Finnur Jónsson, København: Det Konglige Nordiske Oldskriftselskab, 1925.
Lex Baiuwariorum (Monumenta Germaniae Historica. Legvm Sectio, 1: Leges Nationvm Germanicarum, 5:2), Hannoverae, 1926 (https://www.dmgh.de/mgh_ll_nat_germ_5_2/index.htm#page/(III)/mode/1up).
Lex Frisionum, ed. (and trans. to German) by K. A. Eckhardt and A. Eckhardt (Monumenta Germaniae Historica. Fontes Iuris Germanici Antiqui . . ., 12), Hannover: Hahn, 1982. [LATIN TEXT AND ENGLISH TRANSLATION: http://www.keesn.nl/lex/.]
Lex Salica, ed. by K. A. Eckhardt (Monumenta Germaniae Historica. Legvm Sectio, 1: Leges Nationvm Germanicarum, 4:2), Hannoverae, 1969 [http://www.dmgh.de/].
Liebermann, see *Die Gesetze der Angelsachsen*.
Liutprandi Antapodosis (Monumenta Germaniae Historica, 5: Scriptorum tomus, 111), Hannover, 1839.
NGL = *Norges gamle Love indtil 1387*, 1–, Christiania: Norsk historisk kjeldeskrift-institutt, 1846 ff.
Njáls saga (or *Brennu-Njáls saga*) = "Njals Saga," ed. and trans. by Robert Cook, in *The Complete Sagas of Icelanders*, vol. 3, gen. ed. Viðar Hreinsson, Reykjavík: Leifur Eriksson Publishing, 1997, pp. 1–220.
OAUs = Dialect collections in former Ortnamnsarkivet in Uppsala, now SOFI, Uppsala, Sweden.
Ög = *Östergötlands runinskrifter* (Sveriges runinskrifter, 2), Stockholm: Kungl. Vitterhets, Historie och Antikvitetsakademien, 1911–1918.
ÖgL = *Östgötalagen*: *Codex iuris Ostrogotici* = *Östgöta-lagen*, ed. by H. S. Collin and C. J. Schlyter (SGL, 2), Stockholm: P. A. Norstedt & Söner, 1830.
Óláfs saga Tryggvasonar = *Snorri Sturluson*, *Heimskringla*, vol. 1: *The Beginnings to Óláfr Tryggvasonar*, ed. and trans. by Alison Finlay and Anthony Faulkes, 2nd ed., London: Viking Society for Northern Research, 2016.
The Older Västgöta Law = Corpus iuris sueo-gotorum antiqui. Samling af Sweriges gamla lagar, vol. 1: *Westgötalagen. Codex iuris vestrogotici, cum notis criticis, variis lectionibus, glossariis locupletissimis ac indicibus nominum propriorum/ Westgöta-lagen*, ed. by. H. S. Collin and C. J. Schlyter, Stockholm: Z. Haeggström, 1827.
OSD = *Ordbok över Sveriges dialekter*, 1–, Uppsala: Ordbok över Sveriges dialekter, 1991 ff.
OSDs = Collections to Ordbok över Sveriges dialekter, SOFI, Uppsala: SOFI.
Ottar og Wulfstan. To rejsebeskrivelser fra vikingetiden, trans. and com. by Niels Lund, Roskilde: Vikingeskibshallen, 1983.
Pactus = *Pactus Legis Salicae*, ed. by K. A. Eckhardt (Monumenta Germaniae Historica. Leges, 4:1), Hannover, 1962 [http://www.dmgh.de/].

Plato, *Laws*, I–VI, trans. by R. G. Bury (Loeb Classical Library, 187), Cambridge, MA: Harvard University Press, 1926 [http://www.perseus.tufts.edu].

Plato, *The Republic*, I–V, trans. by P. Shorey (Loeb Classical Library, 237), Cambridge, MA: Harvard University Press, 1937 [http://www.perseus.tufts.edu].

Prokopios, *The Wars of Justinian*, trans. by H. B. Dewing, rev. with an intro. and notes by A. Kaldellis, Indianapolis/Cambridge: Hackett Publ. Co., 2015.

Rives, J. B., 1999. *Tacitus Germania*, trans. with Introduction and Commentary, Oxford: Clarendon Press.

The Saga of King Rolf Kraki, see *Hrólf Kraki*.

Saxo Grammaticus = *Saxo Grammatics. The History of the Danes*, 2 vols, trans. by Peter Fisher, ed. by Hilda Ellis Davidson, Cambridge: D. S. Brewer, 1979–1980.

SDHK = *Svenskt Diplomatariums huvudkartotek* (Swedish Diplomatarium's Main Index) (online at: http://sok.riksarkivet.se/sdhk).

SGL = *Sweriges gamla lagar: Corpus iuris sueo-gotorum antiqui. Samling af Sweriges gamla lagar*, 1–13, ed. by H. S. Collin and C. J. Schlyter, Stockholm: Haeggström, 1827–1877.

SHM Coll. = http://mis.historiska.se/mis/sok/sok.asp? (Searchable database of the Collection of archaeological objects, etc., at the Historical Museum, Stockholm.)

Skj = *Den norsk-islandske skjaldedigtning*, A: *Tekst efter håndskrifterne* I–II; B: *Rettet tekst med tolkning*, I–II, ed. by Finnur Jónsson, København: Nordisk forlag, 1912–1915.

Snorra Edda = *Snorri Sturluson, Edda: Prologue and Gylfaginning*, ed. by Anthony Faulkes, London: Viking Society for Northern Research, 1988; *Snorri Sturluson, Edda: Skáldskaparmál*, 2 vols, ed. by Anthony Faulkes, London: Viking Society for Northern Research, 1998; *Snorri Sturluson, Edda: Hattatal*, 2nd ed., ed. by Anthony Faulkes, London: Viking Society for Northern Research, 2007. [IN TRANS.: *Edda, Snorri Sturluson*, trans. and ed. by Anthony Faulkes, London: Dent, 1987.]

Snorri Sturluson, *Heimskringla*, 3 vols (Íslenzk Fornrit, 26–28), 3rd ed., Reykjavík: Hið Íslenzka Fornritafélag, 2002.

SOFI = Institutet för språk och folkminnen (The Institute of Languages and Folk Memories), Uppsala, Sweden.

Sö = *Södermanlands runinskrifter* (Sveriges runinskrifter, 3), Stockholm: Almqvist & Wiksell international, 1924–1936.

Tacitus *Germania* = *Tacitus*: *Agricola and Germany*, trans. with intro. and notes by Anthony R. Birley (Oxford World's Classics), Oxford: Oxford University Press, 1999; see also Rives 1999. [SWEDISH TRANS.: *Germania, Cornelius Tacitus*, ed. by Alf Önnerfors, 3rd ed. Stockholm: Natur & kultur, 1969.]

Tamm, Ditlev, and Helle Vogt (eds.), 2016. *The Danish Medieval Laws: The Laws of Scania, Zealand and Jutland* (Routledge Medieval Translations; Nordic Medieval Laws), Abingdon & New York: Routledge.

The Travels of Reverend Ólafur Egilsson. The Story of the Barbary Corsair Raid on Iceland in 1627, trans. from the original Icelandic text and ed. by Karl Smári Hreinsson and Adam Nichols, Washington, DC: The Catholic University of America Press, 2016.

U = *Upplands runinskrifter* 1–4 (Sveriges runinskrifter, 6–9), Stockholm: Almqvist & Wiksell International, 1940–1958.

Ulpian *Digest* = *Iustiniani Digesta*, Recognovit Theodorus Mommsen/Retractavit Paulus Krueger (Corpus Iuris Civilis, 1), Berlin, 1954 [http://web.upmf-grenoble.fr/Haiti/Cours/Ak/].

VA = LATIN: *Vita Ansgarii: Accedit vita Rimberti, auctore Rimberto*, ed. by G. Waitz (Monumenta Germaniae historica. Scriptores rerum Germanicarum), Hannover:

Hahn, 1988 (1884); [IN TRANS.: *Rimbert: Life of Anskar, the Apostle of the North, 801–865*, ed. by Charles H. Robinson; http://www.fordham.edu/halsall/basis/anskar.asp#seriesint].

Varro, *La Lingua Latina* = Varro, *On the Latin Language*, 2 vols, trans. by R. G. Kent (Loeb Classical Library, 333–334), Cambridge, MA: Harvard University Press, 1938.

Vg = *Västergötlands runinskrifter*, 1–5 (Sveriges runinskrifter, 5), Stockholm: Almqvist & Wiksell international, 1940–1970.

VgL = *Västgötalagen*: *Westgötalagen. Codex iuris vestrogotici, cum notis criticis, variis lectionibus, glossariis locupletissimis ac indicibus nominum propriorum. Westgöta-lagen*, ed. by H. S. Collin and C. J. Schlyter (SGL, 1), Stockholm, 1827. [IN SWEDISH TRANS.: Holmbäck, Åke och Wessén, Elias, *Svenska landskapslagar*, 5: *Äldre Västgötalagen, Yngre Västgötalagen . . .*, Stockholm: Geber, 1946; IN ENGLISH TRANS.: *The Västgöta Laws*, ed. by Thomas Lindkvist (Medieval Nordic Laws), Abingdon & New York: Routledge, 2021.]

Secondary Sources and Studies

Abels, Richard, 1988. *Lordship and Military Obligation in Anglo-Saxon England*, London: British Museum Publications.

Aebisher, Paul, 1936. "Les premiers pas du mot *sclavus* = esclave," *Archivum Romanicum* 20: 484–490.

Agnar Helgason, Eileen Hickey, Sara Goodacre, Vidar Bosnes, Kári Stefánsson, Ryk Ward, and Bryan Sykes, 2001. "mtDNA and the Islands of the North Atlantic: Estimating the Proportions of Norse and Gaelic Ancestry," *American Journal of Human Genetics* 68: 723–737.

Agnar Helgason, Charles Lalueza-Fox, Shyamali Ghosh, Sigrún Sigurðardóttir, Maria Lourdes Sampietro, Elena Gigli, Adam Baker, Jaume Bertranpetit, Lilja Árnadóttir, Unnur Þorsteinsdóttir, Kári Stefánsson, 2009. "Sequences from first settlers reveal rapid evolution in Icelandic mtDNA pool," *PLoS Genetics* 5(1): e1000343–e1000343.

Agnar Helgason, Sigrún Sigurðardóttir, Jeffrey R. Gulcher, Ryk Ward, and Kári Stefánsson, 2000a. "mtDNA and the Origin of the Icelanders: Deciphering Signals of Recent Population History," *American Journal of Human Genetics* 66: 999–1016.

Agnar Helgason, Sigrún Sigurðardóttir, Jayne Nicholson, Bryan Sykes, Emmeline W. Hill, Daniel G. Bradley, Vidar Bosnes, Jeffery R. Gulcher, Ryk Ward, and Kári Stefánsson, 2000b. "Estimating Scandinavian and Gaelic Ancestry in the Male Settlers of Iceland," *American Journal of Human Genetics* 67: 697–717.

Ahnlund, Nils, 1935. "Träldomens dödsår i Sverige," *Svenska Dagbladet* 25.6.1935. [Reprinted in: *Svenskt och nordiskt från skilda tider*, Stockholm: Norstedt, 1943.]

Alkarp, Magnus, 2009. *Det Gamla Uppsala. Berättelser och metamorfoser kring en alldeles särskild plats* (Opia, 49), Uppsala: Institutionen för arkeologi och antik historia, Uppsala universitet.

Almqvist, Bo, 1965–1974. *Norrön niddiktning. Traditionshistoriska studier i versmagi*, 2 vols (Nordiska texter och undersökningar, 21, 23), Stockholm: Almqvist & Wiksell.

Althoff, Gerd, 1984. *Adels- und Königsfamilien im Spiegel Ihrer Memorialüberlieferung. Studium zum Totengedenken der Billunger und Ottonen* (Münstersche Mittelalter-Schriften, 47), München: Wilhelm Fink Verlag.

Amitai, Reuven, 2006. "Slavery, Military," in *Medieval Islamic Civilization. An Encyclopedia*, vol. 2, ed. by Josef W. Meri, pp. 755–757, New York & London: Routledge.

Amitai, Reuven, and Christoph Cluse, 2017. *Slavery and the Slave Trade in the Eastern Mediterranean (c. 1000–1500 CE)* (Mediterranean Nexus 1100–1700. Conflict, Influence and Inspiration in the Mediterranean Area, 5), Turnhout: Brepols.

Amory, Frederic, 2001. "The Historical Worth of Rígsþula," *Alvíssmál* 10:3–20.

Andersen, Harald, 1960. "Hovedstaden i riget," *Nationalmuseets arbejdsmark* (Copenhagen): 13–35.

Andersen, Harald, 1992. "De glemte borge", *Skalk* 1992(1): 19–30.

Andersen, Per, 2014. "'The Truth Must Always Be Stronger'. The Introduction and Development of *Næfnd* in the Danish Provincial Laws," in *New Approaches to Early Law in Scandinavia*, ed. by S. Brink and L. Collinson (Acta Scandinavica, 3), pp. 7–36, Turnhout: Brepols.

Andersen, S. W., 1995. "Lejre – skibssætninger, vikingegrave og Grydehøj," *Aarbøger for nordisk Oldkyndighed og Historie* (1993): 7–137.

Anderson, Perry, 1996. *Passages from Antiquity to Feudalism*, new ed., London: Verso.

Andersson, Kent, and Frands Herschend, 1997. *Germanerna och Rom* (Opia, 13), Uppsala: Institutionen för arkeologi och antik historia, Uppsala universitet.

Andersson, Theodore M., 1964. *The Problem of Icelandic Saga Origins. A Historical Survey* (Yale Germanic Studies, 1), New Haven: Yale University Press.

Andersson, Theodore M., 1967. *The Icelandic Family Saga. An Analytic Reading* (Harvard Studies in Comparative Literature, 28), Cambridge, MA: Harvard University Press.

Andersson, Theodore M., 2003. *The Growth of the Medieval Icelandic Sagas, 1180–1280*, Ithaca, NY: Cornell University Press.

Andersson, Theodore M., and William Ian Miller, 1989. *Law and Literature in Medieval Iceland. Ljósvetninga Saga and Valla-Ljóts Saga*, Stanford: Stanford University Press.

Andersson, Thorsten, 1993. "Sakrala personnamn – eller profana? Klassifikations- och gränsdragningsproblem i det gamla nordiska personnamnsförrådet," in *Personnamn i nordiska och andra germanska fornspråk*, ed. by L. Peterson (NORNA-rapporter, 51), pp. 39–60, Uppsala: Norna.

Andersson, Thorsten, 2006. "Waräger. Sprachlich," *RGA* 33: 252–256.

Andreau, Jean, and Raymond Descat, 2006. *Esclave en Grèce et à Rome*, Paris: Hachette.

Androshchuk, Fedir, 2005. "En man i Osebergsgraven?," *Fornvännen* 100: 115–128.

Androshchuk, Fedir, and Vladimir Zotsenko, 2012. *Скандиавские древносми Южной Руси* [Scandinavian Antiquities of Southern Rus'], Paris: Ukrainian Committee for Byzantine Studies.

ANF = *Arkiv för nordisk filologi*, 1–, Lund: Gleerup, 1888 ff.

Angermann, Norbert, 1997. "Wergeld," *Lexikon des Mittelalters* 8: 2203–2204.

Anners, Erik, 1957. "Götalagarnas Lekarerätt – en keltisk influens?," *Rättshistoriska studier* 2, pp. 8–25, Stockholm: Nerenius & Santérus.

Anthony, Sean W., 2012. *The Caliph and the Heretic. Ibn Saba' and the Origins of Shi'ism* (Islamic History and Civilization, 91), Leiden & Boston: Brill.

Antonsen, Elmer H., 1975. *A Concise Grammar of the Older Runic Inscriptions* (Sprachstrukturen. Reihe A: Historische Sprachstrukturen, 3), Tübingen: Niemeyer.

Antonsen, Elmer H., 1987. "The Oldest Runic Inscriptions in the Light of New Finds and Interpretations," in *Runor och runinskrifter* (Kungl. Vitterhets Historie och Antikvitets Akademien. Konferenser, 15), pp. 17–28, Stockholm: Almqvist & Wiksell International.

Antonsen, Elmer H., 2002. *Runes and Germanic Linguistics* (Trends in Linguistics. Studies and Monographs, 140), Berlin & New York: Mouton de Gruyter.

Arcini, Caroline, 2005. "The Vikings Bare Their Filed teeth," *American Journal of Physical Anthropology* 128: 727–733.

Arcini, Caroline, et al., 1991. "Vikingatida hantverkare med slipspår på tänderna," *Populär arkeologi* 9: 19–21.

Arnoux, Mathieu, 2014. "Effacement ou abolition? Réflexion sur la disparition de l'esclavage dans l'Europe non méditerranéenne (XIe–XIVe siècles)", in *Mediterranean Slavery Revisited (500–1800)/Neue Perspectiven auf mediterrane Sklaverei (500–1800)*, ed. by Stefan Hanss and Juliane Schiel, pp. 49–74, Zürich: Chronos Verlag.

Åqvist, Cecilia, 1992. "Pollista and Sanda. Two Thousand-Year-Old Settlements in the Mälaren Region," with a contribution by Lena Flodin, in *Rescue and Research. Reflections of Society in Sweden 700–1700 A.D.*, ed. by L. Ersgård, M. Holmström, and K. Lamm, pp. 310–333, Stockholm: Riksantikvarieämbetet.

Authén-Blom, Grete, 1981. "Bryte," *RGA* 4: 27.

Auður Magnúsdóttir, 2001. *Frillor och fruar. Politik och samlevnad på Island 1120–1400* (Avhandlingar från Historiska institutionen i Göteborg, 29), Göteborg: Historiska institutionen, Universitetet i Göteborg.

Auður Magnúsdóttir, 2008. "Women and Sexual Politics," in *The Viking World*, ed. by Stefan Brink in coll. with Neil Price, pp. 40–48, London: Routledge.

Backhaus, Wilhelm, 1974. *Marx, Engels und die Sklaverei. Zur ökonomischen Problematik der Unfreiheit* (Geschichte und Gesellschaft. Bochumer Historische Studien), Düsseldorf: Pädagogischer Verlag Schwann.

Bagge, Sverre, 1987. *Political Thought of the King's Mirror* (Mediaeval Scandinavia. Supplements, 3), Odense: Odense University Press.

Bagge, Sverre, Michael H. Gelting, and Thomas Lindkvist (eds.), 2011. *Feudalism. New Landscapes of Debate* (The Medieval Countryside, 5), Turnhout: Brepols Publishers.

Bailey, A. M., and F. R. Llobera, 1981. *The Asiatic Mode of Production*, London: Routledge & Kegan Paul.

Bales, Kevin, 1999. *Disposable People. New Slavery in the Global Economy*, Berkeley, Los Angeles, & London: University of California Press.

Bammesberger, Alfred, 2002. "On the Prehistory of Old English *hlæfdige*," *Language Sciences* 24: 213–219.

Barker, Hannah, 2016. "Purchasing a Slave in Fourteenth-Century Cairo. Ibn Afkānī's *Book of Observation and Inspection in the Examination of Slaves*," *Mamluk Studies Review* 19: 1–23 [online: http://mamluk.uchicago.edu/MSR_XIX_2016_Barker.pdf].

Barnes, Michael, 1984. "The New Runic Finds from Illerup and the Question of the Twenty-Second Rune," *Saga och Sed*: 59–76.

Barry, Kathleen, 1984. *Female Sexual Slavery*, New York & London: New York University Press.

Bartlett, Robert, 1986. *Trial by Fire and Water. The Medieval Judicial Ordeal*, Oxford: Clarendon Press.

BB = [*Bezzenbergers*] *Beiträge zur Kunde der indogermanischen Sprachen*, Göttingen, 1877–1906.

Beck, Heinrich, 1999. "Hagestoltz," *RGA* 13: 352–354.

Beck, Jan-Wilhelm, 1998. *"Germania" – "Agricola." Zwei Kapitel zu Tacitus' zwei kleinen Schriften. Untersuchungen zu ihrer Intention und Datierung sowie zur Entwicklung ihres Verfassers* (Spudasmata, 68), Hildesheim: Olms.

Becker, Jeffery A., and Nicola Terrenato (eds.), 2011. *Roman Republican Villas. Architecture, Context and Ideology*, Ann Arbor: University of Michigan Press.

Benedictow, Ole Jørgen, 1996. "The Demography of the Viking Age and the High Middle Ages in the Nordic Countries," *Scandinavian Journal of History* 21: 151–182.

Bennike, Pia, 1985. *Palaeopathology of Danish Skeletons. A Comparative Study of Demography, Disease and Injury*, Copenhagen: Akademisk Forlag.

Bennike, Pia, and Jørgen Christoffersen, 1981. "Et hoved kortere," *Skalk* 1981(3): 10–13.

Bennike, Pia, and Verner Alexandersen, 2003. "Dental Modification in the Past," in *A Tooth for a Tooth. Seminar for Odontologists, Osteologist and Archaeologists, May 28th 1998*, ed. by E. Iregren and L. Larsson, pp. 85–100, Lund: Department of Archaeology and Ancient History, University of Lund.

Benveniste, Emile, 1973. *Indo-European Language and Society* (Studies in General Linguistics), London: Faber & Faber.

Beringer, Walter, 1961. "Zu den Begriffen für 'Sklaven' und 'Unfreie' bei Homer," *Historia* 10(3): 259–291.

Beringer, Walter, 1982. "'Servile Status' in the Sources for Early Greek History," *Historia* 31(1): 13–32.

Berg, Johan, 2003. *Gods och landskap. Jordägande, bebyggelse och samhälle i Östergötland 1000–1562* (Meddelanden från Kulturgeografiska institutionen, Stockholms universitet, 120), Stockholm: Kulturgeografiska institutionen, Stockholms universitet.

Bergen, C. (ed.), 2005. *The Mysterious Bog People*, 2nd ed., Zwolle: Waanders.

Birkebaek, Frank, 1982–1983. *Danmarkshistorien. Vikingetiden*, 2 vols., København: Sesam.

Biuw, Anita, 1992. *Norra Spånga. Bebyggelse och samhälle under järnåldern* (Monografier utgivna av Stockholms stad, 76), Stockholm: Kommittén för Stockholmsforskning.

Björkman, Erik, 1900. *Scandinavian Loan-Words in Middle English* (Studien zur Englischen Philologie, 7), Halle: Niemeyer.

Björkman, Erik, 1910. *Nordische Personennamen in England in Alt- und Frühmittel-Englischer Zeit. Ein Beitrag zur Englischen Namenkunde* (Studien zur Englischen Philologie, 37). Halle a. S.: Verlag von Max Niemeyer.

Björkman, Erik, 1919. "Zu einigen Namen im *Beowulf*: *Breca, Brondingas, Wealhtheo(w)*," *Anglia. Beiblatt* 30: 170–180.

Björn Þorsteinsson, 1966. *Ný Íslandssaga*, Reykjavík: Heimskringla.

Bjorvand, Harald, and Frederik Otto Lindeman, 2007. *Våre arveord. Etymologisk ordbok*, rev. ed. (Inst. for sammenlignende kulturforskning. Serie B: Skrifter, 105), Oslo: Novus.

Blackburn, Robin, 1988. *The Overthrow of Colonial Slavery 1776–1848*, London: Verso.

Blackburn, Robin, 1996. "Slave Exploitation and the Elementary Structures of Enslavement," in *Serfdom & Slavery. Studies in Legal Bondage*, ed. by M. L. Bush, pp. 158–180, London: Longman.

Blair, John, 1991. *Early Medieval Surrey. Landholding, Church and Settlement before 1300*, Gloucester: Sutton.

Blindheim, Charlotte, and Birgit Heyerdahl-Larsen, 1995. *Kaupang-funnene*, vol. 2: *Gravplassene i Bikjholbergene/Lamøya. Undersøgelsene 1950–57. Del A. Gravskikk* (Norske Oldfunn, 16), Oslo: Universitetets Oldsaksamling.

Bloch, Marc, 1921. "Serf de la glèbe," *Revue Historique* 136: 220–242.

Bloch, Marc, 1933. "Liberté et servitude personelles au moyen âge, particulièrement en France contribution à une étude des classes," *Annuario de Historia del Derechio Espanol* 10: 19–115. [IN TRANS.: Bloch 1975, pp. 33–92.]

Bloch, Marc, 1947. "Comment et pourquoi finit l'esclavage antique," *Annales d'Histoire Economique et Sociale* 2(1): 30–44, 2(2): 161–170.

Bloch, Marc, 1961. *Feudal Society*, 2 vols, trans. by L. A. Manyon, London: Routledge & K. Paul.

Bloch, Marc, 1967. *Land and Work in Mediaeval Europe. Selected Papers*, trans. by J. E. Anderson, London: Routledge & K. Paul.

Bloch, Marc, 1975. *Slavery and Serfdom in the Middle Ages. Selected Essays by Marc Bloch*, trans. by W. R. Beer (Publications of the Center for Medieval and Renaissance Studies, UCLA, 8), Berkeley, Los Angeles, & London: University of California Press.

Bloom, Jonathan, and Sheila Blair, 2002. *Islam. A Thousand Years of Faith and Power*, New Haven: Yale University Press.

Bobrycki, Shane, 2015. "A Hypotethical Slave in Constantinople. Amalarius's Liber Officialis and the Mediterranean Slave Trade," *Haskins Society Journal* 26 (2014): 47–67.

Bodel, John, 2011. "Slave Labour and Roman Society," in *The Cambridge World History of Slavery*, vol. 1: *The Ancient Mediterranean World*, ed. by Keith Bradley and Paul Cartledge, pp. 311–336, Cambridge: Cambridge University Press.

Boehler, Maria, 1930. *Die altenglischen Frauennamen* (Germanische Studien, 98), Berlin: Verlag Dr. Emil Ebering.

Bøgh, Anders, 2007. "Bundones regis. Selvejerbøndernes antal og funktioner, især i senmiddelalderen," in *Konge, kirke og samfund. De to øvrighedsmagter i dansk senmiddelalder*, ed. by Agnes Arnórsdóttir, Per Ingesman, and Bjørn Poulsen, pp. 117–150, Århus: Aarhus Universitetsforlag.

Bonnassie, Pierre, 1989. "Consommation d'aliments immondes et cannibalisme de survie dans l'Occident du Haut Moyen Age," *Annales* 44(5): 1035–1056.

Bonnassie, Pierre, 1991. *From Slavery to Feudalism in South-Western Europe*, trans. by J. Birrell, Cambridge: Cambridge University Press.

Bosl, Karl, 1978. "'Noble Unfreedom'. The Rise of the *ministeriales* in Germany," in *The Medieval Nobility. Studies in the Ruling Classes of France and Germany from the Sixth to the Twelfth Century*, ed. by Timothy Reuter (Europe in the Middle Ages. Selected Studies, 14), pp. 291–311, Amsterdam, New York, & Oxford: North Holland Publ. Co. [trans. from Karl Bosl, *Die Grundlagen der modernen Gesellschft im Mittelalter*, vol. 1, chap. 5, part 3 (Monographien zur Geschichte des Mittelalters, 4:1), pp. 190–211, Stuttgart: Anton Hiersemann Verlag, 1972.]

Bosworth, Joseph, and T. N. Toller, *ASD. An Anglo-Saxon dictionary . . .*, Oxford: Clarendon, 1882–1898.

Bosworth, Joseph, and T. N. Toller, *ASD* Suppl. *An Anglo-Saxon dictionary . . . Supplement*, Oxford: Clarendon, 1921.

Bovill, E. W. 1968. *The Golden Trade of the Moors*, 2nd ed., London & Oxford: Oxford University Press.

Bradley, Keith R., 1989. *Slavery and Rebellion in the Roman World, 140 B.C.–70 B.C.*, Bloomington, Indianapolis, & London: Indiana University Press.

Bradley, Keith R., 1994. *Slavery and Society at Rome*, Cambridge: Cambridge University Press.

Bradley, Keith R., 2000. "Animalizing the Slave: The Truth of Fiction," *Journal of Roman Studies* 90: 110–125.

Bradley, Keith R., and Paul Cartledge (eds.), 2011. *The Cambridge World History of Slavery*, vol. 1: *The Ancient Mediterranean World*, Cambridge: Cambridge University Press.

Brady, Niall, 1994. "Labor and Agriculture in Early Medieval Ireland: Evidence from the Sources," in *The Work of Work. Servitude, Slavery, and Labor in Medieval England*, ed. by A. J. Frantzen and D. Moffat, pp. 128–149, Glasgow: Cruithne Press.

Brate, Erik, 1884. *Nordische lehnwörter im Orrmulum*, Halle. [Also in: *PBB* 10.]

Brate, Erik, 1887. *Äldre Vestmannalagens ljudlära* (Upsala Universitets Årsskrift 1887. Filosofi, Språkvetenskap och Historiska vetenskaper, 3), Uppsala: Akademiska bokhandeln.

Brather, S., 2001. *Archäologie der westlichen Slawen. Siedlung, Wirtschaft und Gesellschaft im früh- und hochmittelalterlichen Ostmitteleuropa* (Ergänzungsbände zum Reallexikon der germanischen Altertumskunde, 30), Berlin: de Gruyter.

Braune, Wilhelm, 1973. *Gotische grammatik*, 18th ed., ed. by Ernst A. Ebbinghaus (Sammlung kurzer grammatiken germanischer dialekte, A:1), Tübingen: Niemeyer.

Breen, Gerard, 1999. "'The Wolf Is at the Door'. Outlaws, Assassins, and Avengers Who Cry 'Wolf!'," *Arkiv för nordisk filologi* 114: 31–43.

Breisch [Ney], Agneta, 1994. *Frid och fredlöshet. Sociala band och utanförskap på Island under äldre medeltid* (Studia historica Upsaliensia, 174), Uppsala: Historiska institutionen, Uppsala universitet.

Bresson, Alain, 1997. "Remarques préliminaires sur l'onomastique des esclaves dans la Rhodes antique," in *Schiavi e dipendenti nell'ambito dell'oikos e della familia: atti del 22. Colloquio Girea. Pontignano (Siena), 19–20 novembre 1995*, ed. by M. Moggi and G. Cordiano (Studi e testi di stori antica, 8), pp. 117–126, Pisa: ETS.

Brett, Stephen F., 1994. *Slavery and the Catholic Tradition. Rights in the Balance* (American University Studies, Ser. 5. Philosophy, 157), New York: P. Lang.

van den Brink, Herman, 1974. *The Charm of Legal History* (Studia Amstelodamensia ad epigraphicam, ius antiquum et papyrologicam pertinentia, 3), Amsterdam: Hakkert.

Brink, Stefan, 1991. "Sockenbildningen i Sverige," in *Kyrka och socken i medeltidens Sverige*, ed. by O. Ferm (Studier till Det medeltida Sverige, 5), pp. 113–142, Stockholm: Riksantikvarieämbetet.

Brink, Stefan, 1992–1993. "Var står onomastiken idag? En epistemologisk betraktelse," *Namn og nemne* 9/10: 7–30.

Brink, Stefan, 1994. *Hälsinglands äldsta skattelängd. Hjälpskattelängden "Gärder och hjälper" från år 1535* (Skrifter utgivna genom Ortnamnsarkivet i Uppsala. Ser. C. Källskrifter, 2), Uppsala: Ortnamnsarkivet.

Brink, Stefan, 1996a. "Forsaringen – Nordens äldsta lagbud," in *Beretning fra femtende tværfaglige vikingesymposium* (Det tværfaglige vikingesymposium, 15), ed. by E. Roesdahl and P. Meulengracht Sørensen, pp. 27–55, Højbjerg: Hikuin.

Brink, Stefan, 1996b. "Political and Social Structures in Early Scandinavia. A Settlement-Historical Pre-Study of the Central Place," *Tor. Journal of Archaeology* 28: 235–281.

Brink, Stefan, 1997a. "Names and Naming of Slaves," in *The Historical Encyclopedia of World Slavery*, vol. 2., ed. by J. P. Rodriguez, pp. 454–456, Santa Barbara, CA: ABC-Clio.

Brink, Stefan, 1997b. "Västsvenska namnmiljöanalyser," in *Ortnamn i språk och samhälle*, ed. by S. Strandberg (Nomina Germanica, 22), pp. 61–84, Uppsala: Uppsala universitet.

Brink, Stefan, 2002a. "Slavery in Scandinavia, as Reflected in Names, Runes and Sagas," in *Slavery across Time and Space. Studies in Slavery in Medieval Europe and Africa*, ed. by P. Hernæs and T. Iversen (Trondheim Studies in History, 38), pp. 107–128, Trondheim: Dept. of History, NTNU.

Brink, Stefan, 2002b. "Nordic Language History and Archaeology," in *The Nordic Languages*, vol. 1, ed. by O. Bandle (HSK – Handbücher zur Sprach- und Kommunikationswissenschaft), pp. 317–324, Berlin & New York: de Gruyter.

Brink, Stefan, 2002c. "Sociolinguistic Perspectives and Language Contacts in Proto-Nordic," in *The Nordic Languages*, vol. 1, ed. by O. Bandle (HSK – Handbücher zur Sprach- und Kommunikationswissenschaft), pp. 685–690, Berlin & New York: de Gruyter.

Brink, Stefan, 2002d. "Sociolinguistic Perspectives in the Transitional Period between Proto-Nordic and Old Nordic," in *The Nordic Languages*, vol. 1, ed. by O. Bandle (HSK – Handbücher zur Sprach- und Kommunikationswissenschaft), pp. 761–768, Berlin & New York: de Gruyter.

Brink, Stefan, 2005. "Verba Volant, Scripta Manent? Aspects of the Oral Society in Scandinavia," in *Literacy in Medieval and Early Modern Scandinavian Culture*, ed. by P. Hermann (Viking Collection, 16), pp. 59–117, Odense: Odense University Press.

Brink, Stefan, 2008. *Lord and Lady – Bryti and Deigja. Some Historical and Etymological Aspects of Family, Patronage and Slavery in Early Scandinavia and Anglo-Saxon England* (The Dorothea Coke Memorial Lecture in Northern Studies 2005), London: Viking Society for Northern Studies.

Brink, Stefan, 2011. "[Review of:] David Wyatt, *Slaves and Warriors in Medieval Britain and Ireland, 800–1200* (Leiden & Boston: Brill, 2009)," *Early Medieval Europe* 19(3): 373–375.

Brink, Stefan, 2013a. "[Review of:] Olof Holm, *Självägarområdenas egenart* (Stockholm, 2012)," *Bebyggelsehistorisk tidskrift* 66: 94–98.

Brink, Stefan, 2013b. "The Creation of a Scandinavian Provincial Law. How was it done?," *Historical Research* 86(233): 432–442.

Brink, Stefan, 2014a. "Skatteböndernas roll under medeltiden," [*Swedish*] *Historisk tidskrift* 2014: 71–78.

Brink, Stefan, 2014b. "Bryten," in *Medeltida storgårdar*, ed. by O. Karsvall and K. Jupiter (Acta Academiae Regiae Gustav Adolphi, 131), pp. 59–82, Uppsala: Kungl. Gustav Adolfs akademi.

Brink, Stefan, 2014c. "The Hälsinge Law between South and West, King and Church, and Local Customs," in *New Approaches to Early Law in Scandinavia*, ed. by Stefan Brink and Lisa Collinson (Acta Scandinavia, 3), pp. 37–56, Turnhout: Brepols.

Brink, Stefan, 2014d. "The Origins of the Swedish Medieval Laws. A State of the Art, from My Perspective," in *How Nordic Are the Nordic Medieval Laws? Ten Years After*, ed. by P. Andersen et al., pp. 129–144, Copenhagen: Djøf Publ.

Brink, Stefan, 2016. "Transferred Names and Analogy in Name-Formation," in *The Oxford Handbook of Names and Naming*, ed. by C. Hough, pp. 158–166, Oxford: Oxford University Press.

Brink, Stefan, 2019a. "*K(i)æfsir* in the Old Västgöta and Östgöta Laws," in *Tidens landskap. En vänbok till Anders Andrén*, ed. by C. Ljung et al., pp. 137–138, Lund: Nordic Academic Press.

Brink, Stefan, 2019b. "Gekauft, geraubt, verdingt. Spurensuche zum Sklaventum," in *Die Wikinger. Entdecker und Eroberer*, ed. by Jörn Staecker and Matthias Toplak, pp. 161–172, Berlin: Ullstein.

Brink, Stefan, 2021, "Slavery in Medieval Scandinavia. Some Points of Departure," in *Viking Age Trade. Silver, Slaves and Gotland*, ed. by Jacek Gruszczyński, Marek Jankowiak, and Jonathan Shepard, pp. 40–56, Abingdon: Routledge.

Brink, Stefan, ms. *Äldre administrativ och territoriell indelning i Hälsingland* [unpublished manuscript].

Brockmeyer, Norbert, 1979. *Antike Sklaverei* (Erträge der Forschung, 116), Darmstadt: Wissenschaftliche Buchgesellschaft.

Bromberg, Erik I., 1942. "Wales and the Medieval Slave Trade," *Speculum* 17: 263–269.

Brøndum-Nielsen, Johs., 1950. *Gammeldansk grammatik*, 1: *Vokalisme*, 2nd ed., København: Schultz.

Brøndum-Nielsen, Johs., 1952, "Bidrag til Dansk Sproghistorie," *Acta Philologica Scandinavica* 21: 35–53.

Brøndum-Nielsen, Johs., 1974. "Navnet Trælleborg," in *Festskrift til Kristian Hald* (Navnestudier udg. af Institut for Navneforskning, 13), pp. 9–12, København: Akademisk Forlag.

Brunt, P. A. 1971. *Italian Manpower 225 BC–AD 14*, Oxford: Clarendon Press.

Buchwitz, Wolfram, 2012. *Servus alienus heres: Die Erbeinsetzung fremder Sklaven im klassischen römischen Recht* (Forschungen zum römischen Recht, 56), Köln: Böhlau.

Buck, C. D., 1949. *A Dictionary of Selected Synonyms in the Principal Indo-European Languages*, Chicago: University of Chicago Press.

Bugge, Alexander, 1905. *Vesterlandenes indflydelse paa nordboernes og særlig nordmændenes ydre kultur, levesæt og samfundsforhold . . .* (Videnskabsselskapet i Kristiania. II, Historisk-filosofisk Klasse. Skrifter 1904:1), Christiania: Videnskabsselskapet i Kristiania.

Bugge, Alexander, 1918. "En Björkö i Sydrusland," *Namn och bygd* 6: 77–103.

Bugge, Sophus, 1873. "To nyfundne norske Rune-Indskrifter fra den ældre Jærnalder," *Kristiania Videnskabs Selskabs Forhandlinger* (1872): 310–332.

Bugge, Sophus, 1896. "Oldnorske sammensætninger paa *nautr*," in *Sproglig-historiske studier tilegnede professor C. R. Unger*, pp. 12–29, Kristiania: Aschehoug.

Bugge, Sophus, 1905. "Oldnorske sammensætninger paa *-nautr*. Nye bemærkninger," *ANF* 21(NF 17): 261-273.

Bull, Edv., 1931. *Det norske folks liv og historie*, 2: *Fra omkring 1000 til 1280*, Oslo: Aschehoug.

Bullough, A. A., 1991. *Friends, Neighbours and Fellow-drinkers. Aspects of Community and Conflict in the Early Medieval West* (H. M. Chadwick Memorial Lectures, 1), Cambridge: Dept. of Anglo-Saxon, Norse and Celtic, University of Cambridge.

Buongiorno, Pierangelo, 2017. "Famulus," in *Handwörterbuch der Antiken Sklaverei (HAS)*, vol. 1, ed. by J. Deissler et al. (Forschungen zur Antiken Sklaverei begr. von Joseph Vogt . . . Beiheft, 5), col. 923, Stuttgart: Franz Steiner Verlag.

Bush, Michael L., 1996. "Serfdom in medieval and modern Europe: a comparison," in *Serfdom & Slavery. Studies in Legal Bondage*, ed. by M. L. Bush, pp. 199–224, London & New York: Longman.

Byock, Jesse, 1993. "Outlawry (in Free State Iceland)," in *Medieval Scandinavia. An Encyclopedia*, ed. by Ph. Pulsiano, pp. 460–461, New York: Garland.

Cacho, Lydia, 2012. *Slavery Inc. The Untold Story of International Sex Trafficking*, with a foreword by Roberto Saviano, London: Portobello.

Calissendorff, Karin, 1982–1983. "Ortnamn i uppländsk bruksbygd," *Upsala Nya Tidning* 30.8.1983 [here cited from: *Ortnamnssällskapets i Uppsala Namnspalten i UNT* (1), Uppsala: Ortnamnssällskapet i Uppsala].

Calonius, Matth., 1780. *De prisco in patria servorum jure*, Åbo. [LATER TRANS. TO SWEDISH: *Om de forne Trälarnes Rätt i Swerige*, Jönköping, 1836.]

The Cambridge World History of Slavery, vol. 1–, gen. eds. K. Bradley et al., Cambridge: Cambridge University Press, 2011 ff.

Cameron, Kenneth Neill, 1973. *Humanity and Society. A World History*, Bloomington: Indiana University Press.

Cameron, Kenneth, 1980. "The Meaning and Significance of Old English *walh* in English Place-Names" (with two appendices by M. Todd and J. Insley), *Journal of English Place-Name Society* 12 (1979–1980): 1–53.

Carlsson, Lizzie, 1942. "Nyckeln som rättslig symbol," *Rig* 25: 80–99.

Carlton, David A., 2019. *Semantic Shift in Old English and Old Saxon Identity Terms* (Western University. Electronic Thesis and Dissertation Repository. 6183. https://ir.lib.uwo.ca/etd/6183.)

Casares, Aurelia Martín, 2014. "Maghrebian Slaves in Spain. Human Trafficing and Insecurity in the Early Modern Western Mediterranean," in *Mediterranean Slavery Revisited (500–1800)/Neue Perspectiven auf mediterrane Sklaverei (500–1800)*, ed. by Stefan Hanss and Juliane Schiel, pp. 97–117, Zürich: Chronos Verlag.

Cavaciocchi, Simonetta (ed.), 2013. *Schiavitù e servaggio nell'economia europea. Secc. X–XVIII / Serfdom and Slavery in the European Economy 11th–18th Centuries* (Fondazione Instituto Internazionale di Storia Economica "F. Datini" Prato. Serie II: Atti delle "Settimane di Studi" e altri Convegni, 45), Firenze: Firenze University Press.

CDOEE = *Concise Dictionary of English Etymology*, ed. T. F. Hoad, Oxford: Oxford University Press, 1996.

Chagnon, Napoleon A., 2013. *The Yanomamö*, 6th ed.: The Legacy Edition, Belmont, CA: Wadsworth.

Charpentier, A., 1896. *Om sytning*, Helsingfors: Helsingfors universitet.

Charles-Edwards, Thomas M., 1972. "Kinship, Status and the Origins of the Hide," *Past and Present* 56(1): 3–33.

Charles-Edwards, Thomas M., 2000. "*The Continuation of Bede*, s.a. 750. High-Kings, Kings of Tara and *Bretwaldas*," in *Seanchas. Studies in Early and Medieval Irish Archaeology, History and Literature in Honour of Francis J. Byrne*, ed. by Alfred P. Smyth, pp. 137–145, Dublin: Four Courts.

Cheyette, F. L., 2002. "George Duby's *Mâconnais* after fifty Years. Reading It Then and Now," *Journal of Medieval History* 28: 291–317.

Christensen, Tom, 1981. "Gerdrup-Graven," *Romu*, 2. *Årsskrift fra Roskilde Museum*: 19–28.

Christensen, Tom, and Pia Bennike, 1983. "Kvinder for fred?," *Skalk* 1983(3): 9–11.

Claesby–Vigfússon = *An Icelandic-English Dictionary*, initiated by Richard Cleasby, subsequently revised, enlarged, and completed by Gudbrand Vigfusson, 2nd ed. with a supplement by Sir William A. Cragie containing many additional words and references, Oxford: Clarendon, 1957.

Clarence-Smith, William G., 2014. "Slavery in Early Modern Russia," in *Mediterranean Slavery Revisited (500–1800)/Neue Perspectiven auf mediterrane Sklaverei (500–1800)*, ed. by Stefan Hanss and Juliane Schiel, pp. 119–142, Zürich: Chronos Verlag.

Clarke, Duncan, 1999, *Slaves & Slavery*, London: Grange.

Clunies Ross, Margaret, 2006. "Poet into Myth: Starkaðr and Bragi," *Viking and Medieval Scandinavia* 2: 31–43.

COD = *The Concise Oxford Dictionary of Current English Adapted by H. W. Fowler and F. G. Fowler from the Oxford Dictionary*, new rev. ed. publ. by H. W. Fowler, Oxford: Oxford University Press, 1931.

Collinson, Lisa, 2017. "Welsh Law in Thirteenth-Century Sweden: Women, Beasts, and Players," *Speculum* 92(3): 755–786.

Conermann, Stephan, forthcoming. "Slavery in the Mamluk Empire," in *The Cambridge World History of Slavery*, vol. 2: *500–1420*, ed. by David Richardson, Stanley Engerman, David Eltis, and Craig Perry, Cambridge: Cambridge Univeristy Press.

Constable, Olivia Remie, 1996. *Trade and Traders in Muslim Spain. The Commercial Realignement of the Iberian Penninsula, 900–1500*, Cambridge: Cambridge University Press.

Cosack, Erhard, and Peter Kehne, 1999. "Ein Archäologisches zeugnis zum germanisch-römischen Sklavenhandel?," *Archäologisches Korrespondenzblatt* 29(1): 97–109.

Cuffel, Victoria, 1966. "The Classical Greek Concept of Slavery," *Journal of the History of Ideas* 27(3): 323–342.

Curschmann, F., 1900. *Hungersnöte im Mittelalter. Ein Beitrag zur deutschen Wirtschaftgeschichte des 8. bis 13. Jahrhunderts* (Leipziger, aus dem Gebiet der Geschichte. Studien, 6:1), Leipzig: B. G. Teubner.

Damico, Helen, 1984. *Beowulf's Wealhtheow and the Valkyrie Tradition*, Madison: University of Wisconsin Press.

Damtoft Poulsen, Aske, 2018. *Accounts of Northern Barbarians in Tacitus' Annales. A Contextual Analysis* (Studia Graeca et Latina Lundensia, 24), Lund: Faculty of Humanities and Theology, Centre for Languages and Literature, Lund University.

Davidson, Julia O'Connell, 2013. "Troubling Freedom: Migration, Debt, and Modern Slavery," *Migration Studies*: 1–20.

Davies, Wendy, 1996. "On Servile Status in the Early Middle Ages," in *Serfdom & Slavery. Studies in Legal Bondage*, ed. by M. L. Bush, pp. 225–246, London: Longman.

Davis, David Brion, 1966. *The Problem of Slavery in Western Culture*, Ithaca, NY, & London: Cornell University Press.

Davis, David Brion, 1984. *Slavery and Human Progress*, New York & Oxford: Oxford University Press.

Davis, David Brion, 2001. "Slavery: White, Black, Muslim Christian," *New York Review of Books*, July 5, 2001.

Davis, David Brion, 2014. *The Problem of Slavery in the Age of Emancipation*, New York: Alfred A. Knopf.

Derrick, Jonathan, 1975. *Africa's Slaves Today*, London: Allen and Unwin.

Devroey, Jean-Pierre, 2006. *Puissants et misérables. Système social et monde paysan dans l'Europe des Francs (VIe–IXe siècles)* (Mémoires de la Classe des lettres. Académie royale de Belgique. Collection in 8° Sér. 3, 40), Bruxelles: Academie Royale de Belgique.

Diebold, A. Richard, 1987. "Linguistic Ways to Prehistory," in *Proto-Indo-European: The Archaeology of a Linguistic Problem. Studies in Honor of Marija Gimbutas*, ed. by S. Nacev Skomal and E. C. Polomé, pp. 19–71, Washington, DC: Institute for the Study of Man.

Dillmann, François Xavier, 2003. "Rígsþula," *RGA* 24: 619–28.

DMA = *Dictionary of the Middle Ages*, 12 vols, New York: Scribner, 1982–1989.

Dobat, Andres Siegfried, 2010. "The State and the Stranger. The role of External Forces in a Process of State Formation in Viking Age South Scandinavia (*ca.* 900–1000)," *Viking and Medieval Scandinavia* 5: 65–104.

Dockès, Pierre, 1982. *Medieval Slavery and Liberation*, trans. by. A. Goldhammer, London: Methuen.

Dørum, Knut, 1999. "Leilendingsforhold, føydalisme og statsutvikling," *Heimen* 1999(1): 45–60.

Douget, Jean-Paul, 2016. *Les philosophes et l'esclavage*, Paris: Éditions Kimé.

Dovring, Folke, 1951. *De stående skatterna på jord 1400–1600* (Acta Regiae Societatis humaniorum litterarum Lundensis, 49), Lund: Gleerup.

Dronke, Ursula, 1992. "Eddic Poetry as a Source for the History of Germanic Religion," in *Germanische Religionsgeschichte. Quellen und Quellenprobleme* (Ergänzungsbände zum RGA, 5), ed. by H. Beck, D. Ellmers, and K. Schier, pp. 656–684, Berlin & New York: de Gruyter.

Dronke, Ursula, 1997. *The Poetic Edda*, 2: *Mythological Poems*, Oxford: Clarendon Press.

DS = *Danmarks Stednavne* 1–, København: Københavns Universitet. Institut for Navneforskning 1922 ff.

Duby, Georges, 1953. *La société aux XIe et XIIe siècles dans la région mâconnaise* (Bibliothèque générale de l'Ecole pratique des hautes études, 6e section), Paris: Armand Colin.

Duby, Georges, 1968. *Rural Economy and Country Life in the Medieval West*, trans. by. C. Postan, London: Edward Arnold.

Duby, Georges, 1973. *Guerriers et paysans VII–XIIe siècle. Premier essor de l'économie européenne*, Paris: Gallimard.

Duby, Georges, 1980. *The Three Orders. Feudal Society Imagined*, trans. by A. Goldhammer, Chicago: University of Chicago Press.

Duggan, Anne J., 2003. "Servus servorum Dei," in *Adrian IV The English Pope (1154–1159)*, ed. by B. Bolton and A. J. Duggan, pp. 181–213, Aldershot: Ashgate.

Dumont, Christian, 1987. *Servus, Rome et l'esclavage sous la république* (Collection de l'École française de Rome, 103), Rome: École française de Rome.

Dumville, David, 1997. "The Terminology of Overkingship in Early Anglo-Saxon England," in *The Anglo-Saxons from the Migration Period to the Eighth Century. An Ethnographic Perspective*, ed. J. Hines, pp. 345–365, Woodbridge, Suffolk, UK: Boydell Press/San Marino, R.S.M.: Center for Interdisciplinary Research on Social Stress.

Dunn, Stephen P., 1982. *The Fall and Rise of the Asiatic Mode of Production*, London: Routledge.

Düwel, Klaus, 2006. "Tjurkö. § 3 Runologisch," *RGA* 31: 14–16.

Eckhardt, Karl August, 1927. *Die Lex Baiuvariorum. Eine textkritische Studie* (Untersuchungen zur Deutschen Staats- und Rechtsgeschchte, 138), Breslau: Marcus.

Einar Ól. Sveinsson, 1962. *Íslenzkar bókmenntir í fornöld*, vol. 1, Reykjavík: Almenna Bókafélagið.

Eisenberg, Daniel, 2003. "Slavery," in *Medieval Iberia. An Encyclopedia*, ed. by E. M. Gerli, pp. 758–759, New York & London: Routledge.

Ekbo, Sven, 1947. "Nordiska personbinamn under vikinga- och medeltid," in *Personnamn*, ed. by A. Janzén (Nordisk kultur, 7), pp. 269–284, Stockholm: Bonnier.

Ekwall, Eilert, 1953. "Tribal Names in English Place-Names," *Namn och bygd* 41: 129–177.

Elgqvist, Eric, 1963. "Något om måla-bebyggelsen i Älmeboda och ett fåtal andra socknar på blekingegränsen," *Älmebodaboken*: 17–34.

Eltis, David, and Stanley L. Engerman (eds.), 2011. *The Cambridge World History of Slavery*, vol. 3: *AD 1420–AD 1804*, Cambridge: Cambridge University Press.

Engdahl, Kerstin, 1990. *Människooffer i gravar i Skandinavien under yngre järnålder*, Stockholm. ["C-uppsats" in archaeology at University of Stockholm.]

Enright, Michael J., 1996. *Lady with a Mead Cup. Ritual, Prophecy, and Lordship in the European Warband from La Tène to the Viking Age*, Dublin: Four Courts Press.

EOI = *The Encyclopaedia of Islam*, 12 vols, new ed., Leiden: Brill, 1960–2004.

EOI Gloss. & Index = *The Encyclopaedia of Islam*, new ed. *Glossary and Index of Technical Terms to Volumes I–VIII*, compiled by J. van Lent, ed. by P. J. Bearman, Leiden: Brill, 1997.

Epstein, Steven A., 2001. *Speaking of Slavery. Color, Ethnicity, and Human Bondage in Italy*, Ithaca & London: Cornell University Press.

Erdem, Y. Hakan, 1996. *Slavery in the Ottoman Empire and Its Demise, 1800–1909*, London & New York: St. Martin's Press.

Erhardt, H., 1997. "Wergeld," *Lexikon des Mittelalters* 8: 2202–2203.

Ericsson, Alf, 2012. *Terra mediaevalis. Jordvärderingssystem i medeltidens Sverige* (Acta Universitatis agriculturae Sueciae, 2012: 81), Uppsala: Swedish University of Agricultural Sciences.

Eriksson, Benny, 2017. "Ny arkeologisk teknik avslöjar ett ogästvänligt Birka," *SVT Nyheter/Vetenskap* (publ. October 7, 2017): https://www.svt.se/nyheter/vetenskap/ett-arbetslager-befolkat-av-slavar.

Erslev, Kristian, 1898. *Valdemarernes Storhedstid*, København: Jacob Erslevs Forlag.

Esders, Stefan, 2011. "'Eliten' und 'Strafrecht' im frühen Mittelalter. Überlegungen zu den Bußen- und Wergeldkatalogen der *Leges barbarorum*," in *Théories et pratiques des élites au haut Moyen Âge*, ed. by François Bougard, Hans-Werner Goetz, and Régine Le Jan (Collection Haut Moyen Âge, 13), pp. 261–282, Turnhout: Brepols.

Esders, Stefan, 2015. "*Wergild* and Social Practice in the Early Middle Ages. A 9th-Century Reichenau Fragment and Its Context," in *Entre texte et histoire. Études d'histoire médiévale offertes au professeur Shoichi Sato*, ed. by Osamu Kano and Jean-Loup Lemaitre, pp. 117–127, Paris: Éditions de Boccard.

Esposito, John L. (ed.), 1999. *The Oxford History of Islam*, New York: Oxford University Press.

Evans, Susan T., 2008. *Ancient Mexico and Central America. Archaeology and Culture History*, 2nd ed., New York: Thames & Hudson.

Falk, Hjalmar, 1886. "Oldnorske etymologier," *ANF* 3: 339–344.

Falk, Hjalmar, and Alf Torp, 1903–1906. *Etymologisk Ordbog over det Norske og det Danske Sprog*, Kristiania: Aschehoug.

Fanning, Steven, 1991. "Bede, Imperium, and the Bretwaldas," *Speculum* 66: 1–26.

Faroqhi, Suraija, 2017. *Slavery in the Ottoman World: A Literature Survey*, Berlin: EB Verlag.

Faull, Margaret Lindsey, 1975. "The Semantic Development of Old English *wealh*," *Leeds Studies in English* 8: 20–44.

Feist, Sigmund, 1939. *Vergleichendes Wörterbuch der Gotischen sprache . . .*, 3rd ed., Leiden: Brill.

Fenger, Ole, 1971. *Fejde og mandebod. Studier over slægtsansvaret i germansk og gammeldansk* ret, Copenhagen: Juristforbundet.

Fick, August, Hjalmar Falk, and Alf Torp, 1909. *Vergleichendes Wörterbuch der indogermanischen Sprachen*, vol. 3: *Wortschatz der germanischen Spracheinheit*, unter Mitwirkung von Hjalmar Falk gänzlich umgearb. von Alf Torp, Göttingen: Vandenhoeck & Ruprecht.

Fidjestøl, Bjarne, 1999. *The Dating of Eddic Poetry. A Historical Survey and Methodological Investigation*, ed. by Odd Einar Haugen (Bibliotheca Arnamagnaeana, 41), København: Reitzel.

Finberg, H[erbert], P. R., 1964. *Lucerna. Studies in Some Problems in the Early History of England*, London & New York: Macmillan.

Finberg, H[erbert], P. R., 1976. *The Formation of England 550–1042*, London: Hart-Davies.

Finkelman, Paul, and Joseph C. Miller (eds.), 1998. *Macmillan Encyclopedia of World Slavery*, 2 vols, New York: Macmillan.

Finley, Moses I. (ed.). 1960. *Slavery in Classical Antiquity. Views and Controversies*, Cambridge: Heffer.

Finley, Moses I., 1964. "Between Slavery and Freedom," *Comparative Studies in Society and History* 6: 233–249.

Finley, Moses I., 1972. "The Extent of Slavery," in *Slavery. A Comparative Perspective; Readings on Slavery from Ancient Times to the Present*, ed. by R. W. Winks, pp. 3–15, New York: New York University Press.

Finley, Moses I., 1978. *The World of Odysseus*, new ed., New York: Viking.

Finley, Moses I., 1980. *Ancient Slavery and Modern Ideology*, London & New York: Chatto & Windus.

Finley, Moses I., 1981. *Economy and Society in Ancient Greece*, ed. by B. D. Shaw and R. Saller, London: Chatto & Windus.

Finnur Jónsson, 1920. *Den oldnorske og oldislandske litteraturs historie*, vol. 1, 2nd ed., København: Gad.

Fischer, Chr., 1979. "Moseligene fra Bjældskovdal," *Kuml*: 7–44.

Fischer Drew, Katherine, 1956. "Notes on Lombard Institutions," *Rice Institute Pamphlet* 43(2): 3–100.

Fischer Drew, Katherine, 1988. *Law and Society in Early Medieval Europe*, 6: *The Family in Frankish Law*, London: Variorum.

Fischer Drew, Katherine, 1991. *The Laws of the Salian Franks*, Philadelphia: University of Pennsylvania Press.

Fisher, Alan, 1980. "Chattel Slavery in the Ottoman Empire," *Slavery & Abolition* 1(1): 25–41.

Fisher, Humphrey J., 2001. *Slavery in the History of Muslim Black Africa*, New York: New York University Press.

Fitzgerald, William, 2000. *Slavery and the Roman Literary Imagination*, Cambridge: Cambridge University Press.

Flemberg, Johan, 1992. "The Martyrdom of Saint Sabas the Goth, translated into Swedish and English," *Tor* 24: 165–175.

Fontaine, Janel Marie, 2017. *Slave Trading in the British Isles and the Czech Lands, 7th–11th Centuries* (Unpubl. PhD-dissertation, King's College, London. Online at: https://kclpure.kcl.ac.uk/portal/).

Foote, Peter, 1975. "Træl," *KL* 19: 13–19.

Foote, Peter, 1977. "Þrælahald á Íslandi. Heimildakönnun og athugasemdir," *Saga. Tímarit Sögufélags* 15: 41–74.

Foote, Peter, 1987. "Reflections on *Landabrigðisþáttr* and *Rekaþáttr* in *Grágás*," in *Tradition og historieskrivning. Kilderne til Nordens ældste historie*, ed. by K. Hastrup and P. Meulengracht Sørensen (Acta Jutlandica, 63:2), pp. 53–64, Aarhus: Aarhus universitetsforlag.

Foote, Peter, and David Wilson, 1970. *The Viking Achievement*, London: Sidgwick & Jackson.

Förstemann, Ernst, 1900. *Altdeutsches Namenbuch*, 1: *Personnamen*, 2nd ed., Bonn: P. Hanstein.

Fourquin, Guy, 1988. "Serfs and Serfdom. Western European," *DMA* 11: 199–208.

Frantzen, Allen J., 1994. "The Work of Work. Servitude, Slavery, and Labor in Medieval England," in *The Work of Work. Servitude, Slavery, and Labor in Medieval England*, ed. by Allen J. Frantzen and Douglas Moffat, pp. 1–15, Glasgow: Cruithne Press.

Frazer, Alfred (ed.), 1998. *The Roman Villa. Villa Urbana* (University Museum Monographs, 101), Philadelphia: University Museum, University of Pennsylvania.

Freudenthal, Axel Olof, 1895. *Östgötalagen. Med förklaringar* (Skrifter utgivna av Svenska litteratursällskapet i Finland, 29), Helsingfors: Svenska litteratursällskapet i Finland.

Fridell, Staffan, 1992. *Ortnamn på -ryd i Småland* (Acta Academiae Regiae Gustavi Adolphi, 60), Uppsala: Kungl. Gustav Adolfs akademi.

Fridell, Staffan, 1996. "Ortnamn och bebyggelsehistoria på Bolmsö," *Ortnamnssällskapets i Uppsala årsskrift*: 5–29.

Fridell, Staffan, 2013, see Larsson and Fridell 2013.

von Friesen, Otto, 1913. *Upplands runstenar. En allmänfattlig öfversikt*, Uppsala: Akademiska bokhandeln.

Frings, Theodor, 1942. "sl und scl," *PBB* 66: 227–231.

Fritzner = Fritzner, Johan, 1972–1973. *Ordbog over det gamle norske sprog*, 4 vols, 4th ed., Oslo,

Fry, Donald K., 1977. "Polyphemus in Iceland," in *The Fourteenth Century*, ed. by Paul E. Szarmach and Bernard S. Levy (Acta, 4), pp. 65–86, Binghamton: Center for Medieval and Early Renaissance Studies, State University of New York at Binghamton.

Fuglestad, Finn, 1979. "Earth-Priests, 'Priest-Chiefs' and Sacred Kings in Ancient Norway, Iceland and West Africa. A Comparative Essay," *Scandinavian Journal of History* 1979(4): 47–74.

Fulk, R. D., 1988. "Unferth and His Name," *Modern Philology* 85 (1987–1988): 113–127.

Gansum, Terje, 2002. "Fra jord til handling," *Plats och praxis. Studier av nordisk förkristen ritual*, ed. by K. Jennbert, A. Andrén, and C. Raudvere, pp. 249–286, Lund: Nordic Academic Press.

García Losquiño, Irene, 2015. *The Early Runic Inscriptions. Their Western Features* (Berkeley Insights in Linguistics and Semiotics, 92), New York et al.: Peter Lang.

Gardeła, Leszek, 2011. "Buried with Honour and Stoned to Death? The Ambivalence of Viking Age Magic in the Light of Archaeology," *Analecta Archaeologica Ressoviensia* 2009(4): 339–375.

Gardeła, Leszek, 2013. "The Headless Norsemen. Decapitation in Viking Age Scandinavia," in *Motyw głowy w dawnych kulturach w perspektywie porównawczej/The Head Motif in Past Societies in a Comparative Perspective*, vol. 1 (Międzynarodowe Spotkania Interdyscyplinarne "Motywy Przez Wieki"/International Interdisciplinary Meetings "Motifs through the Ages," 1), ed. by Leszek Gardeła and Kamil Kajkowski, pp. 88–155, Bytów: Muzeum Zachodniokaszubskie w Bytowie.

Gardeła, Leszek, 2017. *Bad Death in the Early Middle Ages. Atypical Burials from Poland in a Comparative Perspective* (Collectio Archaeologica Ressoviensis, Tom. 36), Rzeszów: Wydawca.

Gardeła, Leszek, 2019. "Gegenseitige Einflüsse. Skandinavier und Westslawen," in *Die Wikinger. Entdecker und Eroberer*, ed. by Jörn Staecker and Matthias Toplak, pp. 238–251, Berlin: Ullstein.

Gardner, Jane F., 2011. "Slavery and Roman Law," in *The Cambridge World History of Slavery*, vol. 1: *The Ancient Mediterranean World*, ed. by Keith Bradley and Paul Cartledge, pp. 414–437, Cambridge: Cambridge University Press.

Garlan, Yvon, 1988. *Slavery in Ancient Greece*, trans. by J. Lloyd, Ithaca, NY, & London: Cornell University Press.

Garnsey, Peter, 1996. *Ideas of Slavery from Aristotle to Augustine*, Cambridge: Cambridge University Press.

Gelting, Michael H., 1988. "Europæisk feudalisme og dansk 1100–1200-tal," in *Kongemagt og samfund i middelalderen. Festskrift til Erik Ulsig på 60-årsdagen 13. februar 1988*, ed. by Poul Enemark, Per Ingesman, and Jens Villiam Jensen (Arusia-historiske skrifter, 6), pp. 3–17, Århus: Arusia – Historiske Skrifter.

Gelting, Michael H., 2002. "Féodalisation sans féodalité dans le Danemark médiéval: Une question mal posée?," in *Die Gegenwart des Feudalismus/Présence du féodalisme et présent de la féodalité/The Presence of Feudalism*, ed. by Natalie Fryde, Pierre Monnet, and Otto Gerhard Oexle, pp. 137–151, Göttingen: Vandenhoeck & Ruprecht.

Gelting, Michael H., 2005. "Legal Reform and the Development of Peasant Dependence in Thirteenth Century Denmark," in *Forms of Servitude in Northern and Central Europe. Decline, Resistance, and Expansion*, ed. by Paul Freedman and Monique Bourin, pp. 343–367, Turnhout: Brepols.

Girsch, Elizabeth Stevens, 1994. "Metaphorical Usage, Sexual Exploitation, and Divergence in the Old English Terminology for Male and Female Slaves," in *The Work of Work. Servitude, Slavery, and Labor in Medieval England*, ed. by Allen J. Frantzen and Douglas Moffat, pp. 30–54, Glasgow: Cruithne Press.

Gísli Sigurðsson, 1988. *Gaelic Influence in Iceland. Historical and Literary Contacts. A Survey of Research* (Studia Islandica, 46), Reykjavík: Bókaútgáfa Menningarsjóðs.

Gissel, Svend, 1981. "Bryte," *RGA* 4: 26–27.

Gjessing, A. [Gustav Antionio], 1862. "Trældom i Norge," *Aarbøger for nordisk Oldkyndighed og Historie*: 28–322.

Glob, P. V., 1965. *Mosefolket. Jernalderens mennesker bevaret i 2000 år*, København: Gyldendal. [Trans. by Rupert Bruce-Mitford, *The Bog People*, London: Faber and Faber, 1998.]

Goetz, Hans-Werner, 1993. "Serfdom and the Beginnings of a 'Seigneurial System' in the Carolingian Period. A Survey of the Evidence," *Early Medieval Europe* 2: 29–51.

Goetz, Hans-Werner, 2003. "[Review of] C. I. Hammer, *A Large-Scale Slave Society of the Early Middle Ages. Slaves and Their Families in Early Medieval Bavaria* (2002)," *American Historical Review* 108(3): 893–894.

Gonzales, Antinio, 1997. "Esclaves, affranchis et 'familia' dans la 'correspondance' de Pline le jeune. Hiérarchies internes et promotions liées aux services," in *Schiavi e dipendenti nell'ambito dell'oikos e della familia : Atti del 22. Colloquio Girea: Pontignano (Siena), 19–20 novembre 1995*, ed. by M. Moggi and G. Cordiano (Studi e testi di stori antica, 8), pp. 329–376, Pisa: ETS.

Goodacre, S., Agnar Helgason, J. Nicholson, L. Southam, L. Ferguson, E. Hickey, E. Vega, K. Stefánsson, R. Ward, B. Sykes, 2005. "Genetic Evidence for a Family-Based Scandinavian Settlement of Shetland and Orkney during the Viking Periods," *Heredity* 95(2): 129–135.

Goody, Jack, 1976. *Production and Reproduction. A Comparative Study of the Domestic Domain* (Cambridge Studies in Social Anthropology, 17), Cambridge: Cambridge University Press.

Goody, Jack, 1980. "Slavery in Time and Space," in *Asian and African Systems of Slavery*, ed. by J. L. Watson, pp. 16–42, Oxford: Blackwell.

Göransson, Sölve, 1961. "Om planmässighet i Hälsinglands kulturlandskap jämte en kommentar om geometriska kartskalor," *Ymer* 1960(4): 277–285.

Gordon, E. V., 1935. "*Wealhþeow* and Related Names," *Medium Ævum* 4: 169–175.

Gordon, Matthew S., and Kathryn A. Hain, 2017. *Concubines and Courtesans. Women and Slavery in Islamic History*, New York: Oxford Univeristy Press.

Gordon, Murray, 1987. *Slavery in the Arab World*, New York: New Amsterdam.

Grace, John, 1975. *Domestic Slavery in Western Africa*, London & New York: Barnes and Noble.

Gräslund, Anne-Sofie, 1991–1992. "Runstenar – om ornamentik och datering [1]–2," *Tor* 22/23: 113–140 and 177–201.

Gräslund, Anne-Sofie, 1998. "Ornamentiken som dateringsgrund för Upplands runstenar," in *Innskrifter og datering* (Senter for middelalderstudier. Skrifter, 8), pp. 73–91, Trondheim: Tapir.

Gräslund, Anne-Sofie, 2006. "Dating the Swedish Viking-Age Runes Stones On Stylistic Grounds," in *Runes and Their Secrets. Studies in Runology*, ed. by M. Stoklund et al., pp. 117–139, Copenhagen: Museum Tusculanum Press, University of Copenhagen.

Gräslund, Bo, 2018. *Beowulfkvädet. Den nordiska bakgrunden* (Acta Academiae Regiae Gustavi Adolphi, 149/ Opia, 64), Uppsala: Institutionen för arkeologi och antik historia.

Green, D. H., 1965. *The Carolingian Lord. Semantic Studies on Four Old High German Words: Balder, Frô, Truthin, Hêrro*, Cambridge: Cambridge University Press.

Green, D. H., 1998. *Language and History in the Early Germanic World*, Cambridge: Cambridge University Press.

Greenidge, C. W. W., 1958. *Slavery*, London: Allen and Unwin.

Grimm, Jacob, and Wilhelm Grimm, *Deutsches Wörterbuch*, 33 vols, 2nd ed. München: Deutscher Taschenbuch Verlag.

Gronenborn, Detlef, 2001. "Zum (möglichen) Nachweis von Sklaven/Unfreien in prähistorischen Gesellschaften Mitteleuropas," *Ethnographisch-Archäologische Zeitschrift* 42: 1–42.

Grünert, H., 1969. "Zu den Anfängen und zur Rolle der Sklaverei und des Sklavenhandels im ur- und frühgeschichtlichen Europa, speziell bei den germanischen Stämmen," *Ethnographisch-archäologische Zeitschrift* 10: 501–515.

Gschnitzer, Fritz, 1964. *Studien zur griechischen Terminologie der Sklaverei*, vol. 1: *Grundzüge des vorhellenistischen Sprachgebrauchs* (Akademie der Wissenschaften und der Literatur. Abhandlungen der Geistes- und sozialwissenschaftlichen Klasse, 13), Weisbaden: Steiner.

Gschnitzer, Fritz, 1976. *Studien zur griechischen Terminologie der Sklaverei*, vol. 2: *Untersuchungen zur Älteren, inbesondere homerischen sklaventerminologie* (Forschungen zur antiken Sklaverei, 7), Weisbaden: Steiner.

Guenther, Rigobert, 1960. "Etr. *serve* – lat. *servus*. Ein Deutungsversuch," *Acta Antiqua Academiae Scientiarum Hungaricae* 8: 45–50.

Gunnell, Terry, 2001. "*Hof*, Halls, *Goðar* and Dwarves: An Examination of the Ritual Space in the Pagan Icelandic Hall", *Cosmos. The Journal of the Traditional Cosmology Society* 17(1): 3–36.

Gurevich, Aaron (Ya.), 1992. *Historical Anthropology of the Middle Ages*, Cambridge: Polity Press.
Gustafsson, Bo, 1986. *Det antika slaveriets nedgång* (Uppsala Papers in Economic History, 10), Uppsala: Dept. of Economic History, Uppsala University.
Gustafsson, Ny Björn, 2009. "För folk och fä. Om vikingatida fjättrar och deras användning," *Fornvännen* 104(2): 89–96.
Gustafsson, Ny Björn, 2013. *Casting Identities in Central Seclusion Aspects of non-ferrous metalworking and society on Gotland in the Early Medieval Period* (Theses and Papers in Scientific Archaeology, 15), Stockholm: Archaeological Research Laboratory, Stockholm University.
Hadjinicolaou-Marava, Anne, 1950. *Rescherches sur la vie des esclaves dans le Monde Byzantine* (Collection de l'institut Francais d'Athène, 45). Athène: L'Institut Francais d'Athène.
Hagland, Jan-Ragnar, and Jørn Sandnes, 1994. "Om lova og lagdømmet," in *Frostatingslova*, ed. and trans. by J. R. Hagland and J. Sandnes, pp. ix–li, Oslo: Det norske samlaget.
Hald, Kristian, 1957. "Bryde som personnavn og i stednavne," *KL* 2: 273–274.
Hallakarva, Gunnora, ms. *The Vikings and Homosexuality* (http://www.fordham.edu/halsall/pwh/gayvik.html).
Hämeen-Anttila, Jaakko, 2914. "The Umayyad State - an Empire?," in *Imperium und Reiche in der Weltgeschichte. Epochenübergreifende und globalhistorische Vergleiche*, vol. 1: *Imperien des Altertums, Mittelalterliche und frühneuzeitliche Imperien*, ed. by M. Gehler and S. Pittl, pp. 538–557, Weisbanen: Harrassowitz Verlag.
Hammer, Carl I., 2002. *A Large-Scale Slave Society of the Early Middle Ages. Slaves and Their Families in Early Medieval Bavaria*, Aldershot: Ashgate.
Hansen, Lars Ivar, 2000. "Slektskap som innfallsvinkel til førmoderne samfunn," in *Holmgang. Om førmoderne samfunn. Festskrift til Kåre Lunden*, ed. by A. Eidsfeldt et al. (Tid og tanke, 4), pp. 103–32, Oslo: Historisk institutt, Universitetet i Oslo.
Hansson, Martin, 2014. "Att hysa folk på gården. Ett försök till byggnadsarkeologi," in *Medeltida storgårdar*, ed. O. Karsvall and K. Jupiter (Acta Academiae Regiae Gustav Adolphi, 131), pp. 165–187, Uppsala: Kungl. Gustav Adolfs akademi.
Harper, Kyle, 2011. *Slavery in the Late Roman World, AD 275–425*, Cambridge: Cambridge University Press.
Harris, Joseph, 1986. "Review of Damico 1984," *Speculum* 61: 400–403.
Harris, Joseph,1993. "Love and Death in the *Männerbund*. An Essay with Special Reference to the *Bjarkamál* and *The Battle of Maldon*," in *Heroic Poetry in the Anglo-Saxon Period. Studies in Honour of Jess B. Bessinger Jr.*, ed. by H. Damico and J. Leyerle, pp. 77–114, Kalamazoo: Medieval Institute Publications. [Reprinted in: *"Speak Useful Words or Say Nothing". Old Norse Studies by Joseph Harris*, ed. by Susan E. Deskis and Thomas D. Hill (Islandica, 53), Ithaca, NY: Cornell University Library, 2008.]
Harrison, Dick, 2006. *Slaveri. En världshistoria om ofrihet. Forntiden till renässansen*, Lund: Historiska media.
Harvey, F. D., 1988. "Herodotus and the Man-Footed Creature," in *Slavery and Other Forms of Unfree Labour*, ed. by L. Archer, pp. 42–52, London: Routledge.
Hasselberg, Gösta, 1944. "Den s.k. Skarastadgan och träldomens upphörande i Sverige," *Västergötlands fornminnesförenings tidskrift* 5(3): 51–90.
Hasselberg, Gösta, Stig Iuul, and Kauko Pirinen, 1959. "Flatföring," *KL* 4: 414–417.
Haubrichs, Wolfgang, 2004. "Eine neue Wormser Inschrift aus der Zeit um 500 und die frühen Personennamen auf germ **þewaz* 'Diener,'" in *Entstehung des Deutschen.*

Festschrift für Heinrich Tiefenbach, ed. by A. Greule, E. Meineke, and C. Thim-Mabrey, pp. 153–172, Heidelberg: Winter.

Hauck, Karl, 1950. "Rituelle Speisegemeinschaft im 10. und 11. Jahrhundert," *Studium Generale* 3(11): 611–621.

Hawting, G[erald] R., 2000. *The First Dynasty of Islam. The Umayyad Caliphate AD 661–750*, 2nd ed., London: Routledge.

Hedeager, Lotte, 1978. "A Quantitative Analysis of Roman Imports in Europe North of Limes and the Question of Roman-Germanic Exchange," in *New Directions in Scandinavian Archaeology*, ed. by K. Kristiansen and C. Paludan-Müller, pp. 191–216, Copenhagen: National Museum of Denmark.

Hedeager, Lotte, 1987. "Empire, Frontier and the Barbarian Hinterland. Rome and Northern Europe from AD 1–400," in *Centre and Periphery in the Ancient World*, ed. by M. Rowlands, M. T. Larsen, and K. Kristiansen, pp. 125–140, Cambridge: Cambridge University Press.

Hedeager, Lotte, and Henrik Tvarnø, 1991. *Det Europæiske Hus*, vol. 2: *Romerne og Germanerne*, København: Gyldendal.

Hellberg, Lars, 1975. "Ortnamnen och den forntida sveastaten," in *Inledningar till NORNAs fjärde symposium Ortnamn och samhälle på Hanaholmen den 25.–27.4.1975* [dupl.].

Hellberg, Lars, 1979. "Forn-Kalmar. Ortnamnen och stadens förhistoria," in *Kalmar stads historia*, vol. 1: *Kalmarområdets forntid och stadens äldsta utveckling. Tiden intill 1300-talets mitt*, ed. by I. Hammarström, pp. 119–166, Kalmar: Kulturnämnden i Kalmar.

Hellberg, Lars, 1984–1985. "Aktuell forskning om tuna-namnen 1–5," *Upsala Nya Tidning* (6.11.1984; 20.11.1984; 4.12.1984; 26.2.1985; 12.3.1985) [here cited from: *Ortnamnssällskapets i Uppsala Namnspalten i UNT*, 3, Uppsala: Ortnamnssällskapet i Uppsala, 1985].

Heller, Rolf, 1988. "Bemerkungen zu den 'irischen' Namen in der Laxdölasaga," *ANF* 103: 142–149.

Hellie, Richard, 1982. *Slavery in Russia 1450–1725*, Chicago & London: University of Chicago Press.

Hellquist, Elof, 1922. *Svensk ordbildningslära från historisk synpunkt*, Lund: Gleerup.

Hellquist, Elof, 1948. *Svensk etymologisk ordbok*, 3rd ed., Lund: Gleerup.

Hemmendorff, Ove, 1984. "Människooffer. Ett inslag i järnålderns gravritualer, belyst av ett fynd i Bollstanäs, Uppland," *Fornvännen* 79: 4–12.

Hemmer, Ragnar, 1932. "Vad förstår Östgötalagen med en gävträl?," *Tidskrift utg. av Juridiska föreningen i Finland* 68: 229–237.

Hempl, George, 1901. "Etymologies," *American Journal of Philology* 22(4): 426–428.

Henning, Joachim, 1992. "Gefangenenfesseln im slawischen Siedlungsraum und der europäischen Sklavenhandel im 6. Bis 12. Jahrhundert. Archaäologisches zum Bedeutungswandel von 'sklabos-sakaliba-slavus,'" *Germania* 70: 403–426.

Henning, Joachim, 2003. "Slavery or Freedom? The Cause of Early Medieval Europe's Economic Advancement," *Early Medieval Europe* 12: 269–277.

Henning, Samuel, 1930. "Träldomens försvinnande och de svenska landskapslagarna," [Swedish] *Historisk tidskrift* 50: 86–95.

Henninger, J., 1987. "Sacrifice," in *The Encyclopedia of Religion*, vol. 12, pp. 544–557, New York: Macmillan.

Henrion, R., 1941–42. "Des origines du mot Familia," *L'antiquité classique* 10 (1941): 37–69; 11 (1942): 253–290.

Herlihy, David, 1985. *Medieval Household*, Cambridge, MA: Harvard University Press.

Herlihy, David, 1991. "Family," *American Historical Review* 96(1): 1–15.

Hermann, Joachim (ed.), 1974. *Die Slawen in Deutschland. Geschichte und Kultur der slawischen Stämmer westlich von der Oder und Neisse vom 6. bis 12. Jahrhundert.* Ein Handbuch, 3rd ed., bearb. in einem Autorenkollektiv von Hans Holm Bielfeldt, Berlin: Akademie.

Herschend, Frands, 2000. "Ship Grave Hall Passage. The Oseberg Monument as Compound Meaning," in *Old Norse Myths, Literature and Society. The Proceedings of the 11th International Saga Conference 2–7 July 2000, University of Sydney*, ed. by G. Barnes and M. Clunies Ross, pp. 142–151, Sydney: Centre for Medieval Studies, University of Sydney.

Herschend, Frands, 2009. *The Early Iron Age in South Scandinavia. Social Order in Settlement and Landscape* (Opia, 46), Uppsala: Dept. of Archaeology and Ancient History, Uppsala University.

Hesselman, Bengt, 1913. *Västnordiska studier*, 2: *En nordisk och västgermansk slutljudsregel* (Skrifter utgivna av Kungl. Humanistiska vetenskapssamfundet i Uppsala, 15:2), Uppsala.

Heusler, Andreas, [1906] 1969. "Heimat und Alter der eddischen Gedichte," in Andreas Heusler, *Kleine Schriften*, vol. 2, pp. 165–194, Berlin: de Gruyter [also in: *Archiv für das Studium d. neueren Sprachen und Litteraturen* 116 (1906): 249–281].

A Historical Guide to World Slavery, ed. by S. Drescher and S. L. Engerman, New York & Oxford: Oxford University Press, 1998.

Hildebrand, Hans, S. M. *Sveriges medeltid. Kulturhistorisk skildring*, 2 vols, Stockholm, 1879–1898.

Hill, Thomas D., 1986. "Rígsþula: Some Medieval Christian Analogues," *Speculum* 61(1): 79–89.

Hill, Thomas D., 1990. "'Wealhtheow' as a Foreign Slave: Some Continental Analogues," *Philological Quarterly* 69: 106–112.

Hjärne, Erland, 1947. "Roden. Upphovet och namnet. Området och jarlen," *Namn och bygd* 35: 1–96.

Hodges, Richard, 1982. *Dark age economics. The origins of towns and trade A.D. 600-1000*, London: Duckworth.

Hodges, Richard, 1989. "Archaeology and the Class Struggle in the First Millennium A.D.," in *The Birth of Europe. Archaeology and Social Development in the First Millennium A.D.*, ed. by K. Randsborg (Analecta Romana Instituti Danici. Supplementum, 16), pp. 178–187, Rome: L'Erma di Bretschneider.

Hodges, Richard, 2012. *Dark age economics. A new audit*, London: Bloomsbury Academic.

Hodges, Richard and David Whitehouse, 1983. *Mohammed, Charlemagne and the origins of Europe*, London: Duckworth.

Hodkinson, Stephen, 1997. "Servile and Free Dependants of the Classical Spartan 'Oikos'," *Schiavi e dipendenti nell'ambito dell'oikos e della familia: Atti del 22. Colloquio Girea: Pontignano (Siena), 19-20 novembre 1995*, ed. by M. Moggi and G. Cordiano (Studi e testi di stori antica, 8), pp. 45–71, Pisa: ETS.

Höfler, Otto, 1934. *Kultische Geheimbünde der Germanen*, Frankfurt am Main: M. Diesterweg.

Hofmann, Dietrich, 1955. *Nordisch-englische Lehnbezeihungen der Wikingerzeit* (Bibliotheca Arnamagnæana, 14), København: Munksgaard.

Holck, Per, 2006. "The Oseberg Ship Burial, Norway: New Thoughts on the Skeletons from the Grave Mound," *European Journal of Archaeology* 9: 185–210.

Holm, Gösta, 1985. "Ivar Lindquist," *Årsbok för Vetenskaps-Societeten i Lund*: 151–161.

Holm, Poul, 1986. "The Slave Trade of Dublin, Ninth to Twelfth Centuries," *Peritia: Journal of the Medieval Academy of Ireland* 5: 317–345.

Holmbäck, Åke, and Elias Wessén, 1933. *Östgötalagen och Upplandslagen* (Svenska landskapslagar, 1), Stockholm: Geber.

Holmbäck, Åke, and Elias Wessén, 1943. *Skånelagen och Gutalagen* (Svenska landskapslagar, 4), Stockholm: Geber.

Holmbäck, Åke, and Elias Wessén, 1946. *Äldre Västgötalagen, Yngre Västgötalagen, Smålandslagens kyrkobalk samt Bjärköarätten* (Svenska landskapslagar, 5), Stockholm: Geber.

Holm-Olsen, Ludvig, 1974. *Norges litteraturhistorie*, vol. 1, Oslo: Cappelen.

Holm-Olsen, Ludvig (ed.), 1983. *Konungs Skuggsjá*, 2nd ed. Oslo: Norsk Historisk Kjeldeskrift-institutt.

Holm-Olsen, Ludvig (ed.), 1987. *The King's Mirror: AM 243 a fol.* (Early Icelandic Manuscripts in Facsimile, 17), Copenhagen: Rosenkilde and Bagger.

Holmquist Olausson, Lena, 1990. "'Älgmannen' från Birka. Presentation av en nyligen undersökt krigargrav med människooffer," *Fornvännen* 85: 175–182.

Holmsen, Andreas, 1961. *Norges historie. Fra de eldste tider til eneveldets innførelse i 1660*, Oslo, Bergen & Tromsø: Universitetsforlaget.

Holthausen, F., 1934. *Altenglisches etymologisches wörterbuch* (Germanische bibliothek, 4:7), Heidelberg: Carl Winter.

Hoops, Johannes, 1908. "Zur Etymologie von ne. LADY," *Englische Studien* 39: 467.

Hopkins, Keith, 1967, "Slavery in Classical Antiquity," in *Caste and Race. Comparative Approaches*, ed. by A. de Reuck and J. Knight, pp. 166–177, London: Wiley.

Hopkins, Keith, 1978, *Conquerors and Slaves* (Sociological Studies in Roman History, 1), Cambridge: Cambridge University Press.

Hough, Carole, 1999. "Wergild," in *The Blackwell Encyclopedia of Anglo-Saxon England*, ed. by M. Lapidge et al., pp. 469–470, Oxford: Blackwell.

van Houts, Elisabeth, 2004. "The Vocabulary of Exile and Outlawry in the North Sea Area around the First Millennium," in *Exile in the Middle Ages. Selected Proceedings from the International Medieval Congress*, ed. by L. Napran and E. van Houts (International Medieval Research, 13), pp. 13–28, Turnhout: Brepols.

Høverstad, Th., 1909. "Trællenavnet Hjalli", *Maal og Minne*: 101–102.

Hubbard, R. Glenn, and Tim Kane, 2013. *Balance: The Economics of Great Powers from Ancient Rome to Modern America*, New York: Simon & Schuster.

Hyams, Paul R., 1980. *Kings, Lords and Peasants in Medieval England. The Common Law of Villeinage in the Twelfth and Thirteenth Centuries* (Oxford Historical Monographs), Oxford: Clarendon Press.

Hybel, Nils, and Bjørn Poulsen, 2008. *The Danish Resources c. 1000–1550. Growth and Recession*, Leiden & Boston: Brill.

İnalcık, Halil, 1979. "Servile Labor in the Ottoman Empire," in *The Mutual Effects of the Islamic and Judeo-Christian Worlds. The East European Pattern*, ed. by A. Ascher, B. K. Kiraly, and T. Halasi-Kun (Studies on Society in Change, 3), pp. 25–43, Brooklyn, NY: Brooklyn College Press.

ÍO = *Íslenzk orðabók*, ed. by Árni Böðvarsson, Reykjavík: Menningarsjóðs, 1963.

Iversen, Frode, 1999. *Var middelalderens lendmannsgårder kjerner i eldre godssamlinger? En analyse av romlig organisering av graver og eiendomsstruktur i Hordaland og Sogn og Fjordane* (Arkeologiske avhandlinger og rapporter fra Universitetet i Bergen, 4), Bergen: Akeologisk institutt, Universitetet i Bergen.

Iversen, Ragnvald, 1973. *Norrøn grammatik*, 7th ed., rev. by E. Fjeld Halvorsen, Oslo: Tano.

Iversen, Tore, 1995. "Fremveksten av det norske leilendingvesenet - en forklaringsskisse," *Heimen* 1995(3): 169–180.

Iversen, Tore, 1997. *Trelldommen. Norsk slaveri i middelalderen* (Historisk institutt. Universitetet i Bergen. Skrifter, 1), Bergen: Historisk institutt. Universitetet i Bergen.

Iversen, Tore, 2003. "Fra trell til leilending - frigivning, bosetning og herredømme i Norge, Norden og Vest-Europa i tidlig middelalder," in *Trälar. Ofria i agrarsamhället från vikingatid till medeltid*, ed. by Th. Lindkvist and J. Myrdal, pp. 22–49, Stockholm: Nordiska museet.

Jacoby, Karl, 1994. "Slaves by Nature? Domestic Animals and Human Slaves," *Slavery & Abolition* 15: 89–97.

Jacoby, Michael, 1974. *Wargus, vargr "Verbrecher" "Wolf" eine sprach- und rechtsgeschichtliche Untersuchung* (Studia Germanistica Upsaliensia, 12), Uppsala: Almqvist Wiksell.

Jankowiak, Marek, 2013. "Two Systems of Trade in the Western Slavic Lands in the 10th Century," in *Economies, Monetisation and Society in the West Slavic Lands 800–1200 AD*, ed. by M. Bogucki and M. Rebkowski (Wolinskie Spotkania Mediewistyczne, 2), pp. 137–148, Szczecin: Szczecin University.

Jansson, Tore, 2013. *Germanerna: Myten, historien, språken*, Stockholm: Norstedts.

Jensen, Carsten, and Anders Sømme Hammer, 2014. *"Alt dette kunne vært unngått". En reise gjennom det nye Afghanistan*, Oslo: Press.

Jesch, Judith, 2005. "Memorials in Speech and Writing," *Hikuin* 32: 95–104.

Jessen, Mads Dengsø, and Jesper Olsen, forthcoming. "Regulated Deviancy: Ritual Executions at Viking Age Tissø as Indications of a Complex Judicial Culture."

Jew, Daniel, Robin Osborne, and Michael Scott (eds.), 2016. *M. I. Finley. An Ancient Historian and His Impact* (Cambridge Classical Studies), Cambridge: Cambridge University Press.

Jochens, Jenny, 1991. "The Illicit Love Visit: An Archaeology of Old Norse Sexuality," *Journal of the History of Sexuality* 1: 357–392.

Jochens, Jenny, 1999. "Race and ethnicity in the Old Norse world," *Viator. Medieval and Renaissance Studies* 30: 79–103.

John, Eric, 1966. *Orbis Britanniae, and other studies* (Studies in early English history, 4), Leicester: Leicester University Press.

Jolliffe, J. E. A., 1937. *The Constitutional History of Medieval England, from the English settlement to 1485*, London [4th ed., London: Black, 1961].

Johannesson, Kurt, 1978. *Saxo Grammaticus. Komposition och världsbild i Gesta Danorum* (Lychnos-Bibliotek. Studier och källskrifter utgivna av Lärdomshistoriska Samfundet, 31), Stockholm: Almqvist & Wiksell International.

Jón Hnefill Aðalsteinsson, 1984. "Önnungar," *Úr Sögu. Tímariti Sögufélags* 22: 31–40.

Jón Hnefill Aðalsteinsson, 1986. "The Position of Freed Slaves in Medieval Iceland," *Saga-Book* 22: 33–49.

Jón Jóhannesson, 1969. *Islands historie i mellomalderen. Fristatstida*, trans. by Hallvard Magerøy, Oslo, Bergen, & Tromsø: Universistetsforlaget.

Jonsson, Ingvar, 1971. *Jordskatt och kameral organisation i Norrland under äldre tid* (Kungl. Skytteanska samfundets handlingar, 9), Umeå: Umeå universitet.

Jonsson Haurdal, Thorir, 2013. "Integration and Disintegration: The 'Norse' in Descriptions of the Early Rus," in *Norman Tradition and Transcultural Heritage. Exchange of Cultures in the "Norman" Peripheries of Medieval Europe*, ed. by Stefan Burkhardt and Thomas Foerster, pp. 279–294, Farnham: Ashgate.

Jørgensen, Bent, 1994. *Stednavneordbog*, 2nd ed., Copenhagen. Gyldendal.

Jørgensen, Bent, 1995. "Et gensyn med navnet Trælleborg," in *Fjortende tværfaglige Vikingsymposium. Københavns Universitet*, ed. by G. Fellows-Jensen and N. Lund, pp. 5–11, Aarhus: Hikuin and Afdeling for Middelalder-arkæologi.

Jørgensen, Lars, and Lisbeth Pedersen, 1996. "Vikinger ved Tissø. Gamle og nye fund fra et handels- og håndverkscenter," *Nationalmuseets arbejdsmark* (Copenhagen): 22–36.

Jørgensen, Poul Johannes, 1974. *Dansk Retshistorie*, 6th ed., Copenhagen: Gad.

Joshel, Sandra R., 2010, *Slavery in the Roman World*, Cambridge: Cambridge University Press.

Joshel, Sandra R., and Sheila Murnaghan (eds.), 1998. *Women and Slaves in Greco-Roman Culture. Differential Equations*, London & New York: Routledge.

Jurasinski, Stefan, 2007. "The Feminine Name *Wealhtheow* and the Problem of Beowulfian Anthroponymy", *Neophilologus*, 91: 701–705.

Jürgs, Michael, 2014. *Sklavenmarkt Europa. Das Milliardengeschäft mit der Ware Mench*, München: C. Bertelsmann.

Kahane, Henry, and Renée Kahane, 1962. "Notes on the Linguistic History of *Sclavus*," in *Studi in onore di Ettore Lo Gatto e Giovanni Maver* (Collana di Ricerche slavistiche, 1), pp. 345–360, Firenze: Sansone.

Källström, Magnus, 2015. "Kungen, bryten och märket. Till tolkningen av runblocket U 11 vid Hovgården på Adelsö och något om runstenarnas placering," *Saga och sed*: 67–86.

Kalmring, Sven, 2010. *Der Hafen von Haithabu* (Die Ausgrabungen in Haithabu, 14), Neumünster: Wachholtz Verlag.

Karg-Gasterstädt, Elisabeth, 1942. "Ahd. thiu und thiorna," *PBB* 66: 291–326.

Karras, Ruth Mazo, 1988. *Slavery and Society in Medieval Scandinavia*, New Haven: Yale University Press.

Karras, Ruth Mazo, 1990. "Concubinage and Slavery in the Viking Age," *Scandinavian Studies* 62: 141–162.

Karras, Ruth Mazo, 1992. "Servitude and Sexuality," in *From Sagas to Society. Comparative Approaches to Early Iceland*, ed. by Gisli Pálsson, pp. 289–304, Enfield: Hisarlik.

Karras, Ruth Mazo, 1993. "Slavery," in *Medieval Scandinavia. An Encyclopedia*, ed. by Ph. Pulsiano et al. (Garland Reference Library of the Humanities, 934/ Garland Encyclopedias of the Middle Ages, 1), pp. 266–268, New York & London: Garland.

Karras, Ruth Mazo, 1994. "Desire, Descendants, and Dominance: Slavery, the Exchange of Women, and Masculine Power," in *The Work of Work. Servitude, Slavery, and Labor in Medieval England*, ed. by A. J. Frantzen and D. Moffat, pp. 16–29, Glasgow: Cruithne Press.

Kaser, Max, 1971. *Das römische Privatrecht*, vol. 1: *Das altrömische, das vorklassische und klassische Recht* (Rechtsgeschichte des Altertums, im Rahmen des Handbuchs der Altertumswissenschaft, 3:3), 2nd ed., München: Beck.

Kauffmann, Friedrich, 1910. "Altdeutsche Genossenschaften," *Wörter und Sachen* 2: 9–42.

Kelly, Fergus, 1988. *A Guide to Early Irish Law* (Early Irish Law Series, 3), Dublin: Dublin Institute for Advanced Studies.

Keynes, Simon, 1992. "Rædwald the Bretwalda," in *Voyages to the Other World. The Legacy of Sutton Hoo*, ed. by Calvin B. Kendall and P. S. Wells, pp. 103–123, Minneapolis: University of Minnesota Press.

Keynes, Simon, 1999. "Bretwalda," in *The Blackwell Encyclopaedia of Anglo-Saxon England*, ed. by Michael Lapidge et al., p. 74, Oxford: Blackwell.

Kirby, D. P., 1967. *The Making of Early England*, London: Batsford.

Kjellström, Anna, 2014. "Spatial and Temporal Trends in New Cases of Men with Modified Teeth from Sweden (AD 750–1100)", *European Journal of Archaeology* 17(1): 45–59.

KL = *Kulturhistoriskt lexikon för nordisk medeltid från vikingatid till reformationstid*, 22 vols, Malmö, København & Oslo: Roskilde & Bagger, 1956–1978.

Kluge, Friedrich, 1899. *Nominale Stammbildungslehre der altgermanischen Dialekte*, 2nd ed. (Sammlung Kurzer Grammatiken Germanischer Dialekte. Ergänzungsreihe, 1), Halle: Max Niemeyer.

Kluge *EW* = Friedrich Kluge, *Etymologisches Wörterbuch der deutschen Sprache*, bearb. von Elmar Seebold, 23rd ed., Berlin & New York: de Gruyter, 1995; 24th ed., Berlin & New York: de Gruyter 2002.

Kluge, F., and F. Lutz, 1898. *English Etymology. A Select Glossary Serving and an Introduction to the History of the English Language*, Strassburg: Trübner.

Knirk, E. James, 2011. "Hogganvik-Innskriften. En hard runologisk nøtt," *Viking* 74: 25–39.

Knudsen, Gunnar, 1948. "Navnet Trælleborg," in Poul Nørlund, *Trelleborg* (Nordiske Fortidsminder, 4:1), pp. 189–214, København: Det Kongl. Nordiske Oldskriftselkab.

Koch, Axel, 1898. "Studier i de nordiska språkens historia," *ANF* 14: 213–270.

Koch, Axel, 1905. "Ett par ordbildningsspörsmål i fornnordiska språk, 2: Fornnordiska komposita på *-nautr*, *-nøter*," *ANF* 21(NF 17): 112–124.

Kolendo, J., 1981. "L'esclavage et la vie sexuelle des hommes libres à Rome," *Index* 10: 288–297.

Konstan, David, 1975. "Marxism and Roman Slavery," *Arethusa* 8(1): 145–169.

Kopytoff, Igor, 1982. "Slavery," *American Review of Anthropology* 11: 207–230.

Kopytoff, Igor, and Suzanne Miers, 1977. "African 'Slavery' as an Institution of Marginality," in *Slavery in Africa. Historical and Anthropological Perspectives*, ed. by S. Miers and I. Kopytoff, pp. 3–84, Madison: University of Wisconsin Press.

Korth, Georg, 1970. "Zur Etymologie des Wortes 'Slavus' (Sklave)," *Glotta* 48(1/2): 145–153.

Kousgård Sørensen, John, 1984. *Patronymer i Danmark*, vol. 1: *Runetid og Middelalder* (Navnestudier udg. af Institut for Navneforskning, 23), København: Akademisk forlag.

Kousgård Sørensen, John, 1989. "Om personnavne på -vi/-væ og den førkristne præstestand. Med nogle overvejelser over en omstridt passage i Glavendrup-stenens indskrift," *Danske studier*: 5–33.

Krag, Claus, 1982. "Treller og trellehold," [*Norsk*] *Historisk tidsskrift* (Oslo) 61: 209–227.

Krag, Claus, 1983. "Trelleholdet. Et svar til Sandnes, Iversen og Lunden," [*Norsk*] *Historisk tidsskrift* (Oslo) 61: 362–368.

Krause, Wolfgang, 1966. *Die Runeninschriften im älteren Futhark*, 1: *Text*, with the participation of Herbert Jankuhn (Abhandlungen der Akademie der Wissenschaften in Göttingen. Philologisch-historische Klasse 3. Folge, 65:1), Göttingen: Vandenhoeck & Ruprecht.

Krebs, Christopher B., 2011. *A Most Dangerous Book. Tacitus's* Germania *from the Roman Empire to the Third Reich*, New York: Norton.

Kristiansen, Kristian, 2006. "Cosmology, Economy and Long-Term Change in the Bronze Age of Northern Europe," in *Ecology and Economy in Stone Age and Bronze Age Scania*, ed. by Karl-Göran Sjögren, pp. 149–171, Lund: Raä.

Kristiansen, Kristian, 2007. "The Rules of the Game. Decentralised Complexity and Power Structures," in *Socialising Complexity: Approaches to Power and Interaction in the Archaeological Record*, ed. by S. Kohring and S. Wynne-Jones, pp. 60–75, Oxford: Oxbow.

Kristiansen, Kristian, 2009. "Premieres Aristocraties. Pouvoir et metal a l'age du Bronze," in *L'Europe. Un continent redécouvert par l'archéologie*, ed. by Jean-Paul Demoule, pp. 73–83, Paris: Gallimard.

Kristensen, Inge Kjær, and Pia Bennike, 2001. "Kumle Høje," *Skalk* 2001(3): 12–15.

Krogmann, Willy, 1938. "Adel und Udel," *Zeitschrift für deutsche Philologie* 63: 189–191.

Krömmelbein, Thomas, 1994. "Die Spitzenstellung des Geirmundar þáttr heljarskinns innerhalb der Kompilation Sturlunga Saga," *Alvíssmál* 4: 33–50.

Kroonen, Guus, 2013. *Etymological Dictionary of Proto-Germanic* (Leiden Indo-European Etymological Dictionary Series, 11), Leiden: Brill.

Kuhn, Hans, 1973. "Amt. 1. Sprachliches," *RGA* 1: 258.

Kunt, I. Metin, 2014. "Ottoman White Eunuchs as Palace Officials and Statemen (1450–1600)," in *Mediterranean Slavery Revisited (500–1800)/Neue Perspectiven auf mediterrane Sklaverei (500–1800)*, ed. by Stefan Hanss and Juliane Schiel, pp. 325–336, Zürich: Chronos Verlag.

Lägreid, Annalies, 1984. "The Scandinavians in Russia. On the extra-linguistic factors in the language contact between North Germanic and East Slavic peoples in the early middle ages," in *Scandinavian Language Contacts*, ed. by P. Sture Ureland and Iain Clarkson, pp. 97–110, Cambridge: Cambridge University Press.

Lambertini, Renzo, 1984. "L'etymologia di *servus* secondo i giuristi latini," in *Sodalitas. Scritti in onore di Antonio Guarino*, vol. 5, Napoli: Jovene.

Landtmanson, Isak Sven, 1897. *Träldomens sista skede i Sverige* (Skrifter utgivna av K. Humanistiska vetenskapssamfundet i Uppsala, 5:6), Uppsala.

Larsson, Lars-Olof, 1980. *Småländsk bebyggelsehistoria*, I:1:3: *Konga härad* (Acta Wexionensia. Serie 1. History & Geography, 1:3), Växjö: Högskolan i Växjö.

Larsson, Mats G., and Staffan Fridell, 2013. "Runristningen på Hovgårdsstenen," *Saga och sed*: 95–109.

Lauffer, Siegfried, 1956–1957. *Die Bergwerkssklaven von Laureion*, 2 vols. (Akademie der Wissenschaften und der Literatur. Abhandlungen der Geistes- und sozialwissenschaftlichen Klasse 1955:12, 1956:11), Mainz & Wiesbaden.

Launaro, Alessandro, 2011. *Peasants and Slaves. The Rural Population of Roman Italy (200 BC to AD 100)*, Cambridge: Cambridge University Press.

Lazzaro, Lucino, 1993. *Esclaves et affranchis en Belgique et Germanies Romaines d'après les sources épigraphiques* (Annales Littéraires de l'Université de Besançon, 430), Paris: Belles Lettres.

Leach, Edmund, 1967, "Caste, Class and Slavery: The Taxonomic Problem," in *Caste and Race. Comparative Approaches*, ed. by A. de Reuck and J. Knight, pp. 5–16, London: J. & A. Churchill Ltd.

Lehmann, Winfred P., 1986. *A Gothic Etymological Dictionary*, Leiden: Brill.

Lenski, Noel, and Catherine M. Cameron (eds.), 2018. *What is a Slave Society? The Practice of Slavery in Global Perspective*, Cambridge: Cambridge University Press.

LEW = *Lateinisches etymologische Wörterbuch*, 2 vols, ed. by A. Walde, 3rd rev. ed. by J. B. Hofmann (Indogermanische Bibliothek, 2: Wörterbücher, 1), Heidelberg: Carl Winter, 1938–1956.

Lewis, Bernard, 1990. *Race and Slavery in the Middle East. An Historical Enquiry*, New York and Oxford: Oxford University Press.

Lexikon des Mittelalters, 9 vols, München: Artemis/Lexma, 1980–1998.

Lexicon Poeticum, 2nd ed., by Finnur Jónsson, København: Møller, 1931.

Lichtheim, G., 1963. "Marx and the 'Asiatic Mode of Production'," *St. Anthony's Papers* 14: 86–112.

Lidén, Evald, 1894. *Vermischtes zur Wortkunde und Grammatik* (Språkvetenskapliga sällskapets i Upsala förhandlingar 1891–94, 1:4. Bil. D/Uppsala universitets årsskrift 1894: Filosofi, språkvetenskap och historiska vetenskaper, 2). [Also printed in: *BB* 21: 93–118.]

Liebermann, Felix, [1898]–1916. *Die Gesetze der Angelsachsen*, Halle: Niemeyer.

Liedgren, Lars, 1992. *Hus och gård i Hälsingland. En studie av agrar bebyggelse och bebyggelseutveckling i norra Hälsingland Kr.f.-600 e.Kr.* [*House and Farm in Hälsingland. A Study of Agrarian Settlement and Settlement Development in Northern Hälsingland AD 1-600*] (Studia archaeologica Universitatis Umensis, 2), Umeå: Umeå universitet.

Lind, P. H., 1905–1915. *Norsk-isländska dopnamn ock fingerade namn från medeltiden*, Uppsala & Leipzig: Lundequistska bokhandeln.

Lindkvist, Thomas, 1979. *Landborna i Norden under äldre medeltid* (Studia Historica Upsaliensis, 110), Uppsala: Historiska inst., Uppsala universitet.

Lindkvist, Thomas, 2003, "Från träl till landbo: Uppkomsten av det medeltida godssystemet i Europa och Norden," in *Trälar. Ofria i agrarsamhället från vikingatid till medeltid*, ed. by Th. Lindkvist and J. Myrdal, pp. 9–21, Stockholm: Nordiska museet.

Lindkvist, Thomas, and Janken Myrdal (eds.), 2003. *Trälar. Ofria i agrarsamhället från vikingatid till medeltid* (Skrifter om skogs- och lantbrukshistoria, 17), Stockholm: Nordiska museet.

Lindquist, Ivar, 1940. *Religiösa runinskrifter, 2: Sparlösastenen* (Skrifter utg. av Kungl. Humanistiska Vetenskaps-Samfundet i Lund, 24), Lund.

Lindquist, Ivar, 1944. "Kungadömet i hednatidens Sverige," in *Festskrift till Jöran Sahlgren 8/4 1944*, ed. by K. G. Ljunggren et al., pp. 221–234, Lund. [Also printed in: *ANF* 58: 221–234.]

Lindqvist, Sune, 1935. *Svenskarna i heden tid*, Stockholm: Bonnier.

Lindqvist, Sune, 1944. *Svenskt forntidsliv*, Stockholm: Bonnier.

Lindroth, Hjalmar, 1916. "Estnisk bosättning i Sverige under äldre tider," *Ymer* 36: 194–214.

Liwoch, Radosław, and Michael Müller-Wille, 2012. "'Druzhina' Graves Dating to the Time around AD 1000," *Archäologisches Korrespondenzblatt* 42: 421–438.

Ljung, Cecilia, ms. "Världsliga och kyrkliga krav. Äktenskap, samlevnad och oäkta barn i Äldre Västgötalagen och Upplandslagen."

Ljunggren, Karl Gustav, 1951. "Fsv. *male*, nysv. *måle*," *ANF* 65 (1950): 178–194.

Ljungkvist, John, 2006. *En hiar atti rikr. Om elit, struktur och ekonomi kring Uppsala och Mälaren under yngre järnålder* (Aun, 34), Uppsala: Institutionen för arkeologi och antik historia, Uppsala universitet.

Locke, John, 1690. *Two Treatises of Government* (*The Second Treatise of Government*), London: Awnsham Churchill. [Also: *Two Treatises of Government by John Locke*; a critical edition with an introduction and apparatus criticus by Peter Laslett, 2nd ed., Cambridge: Cambridge University Press, 1967.]

Löffler, Heinrich, 1995, "Namen von Freien und Unfreien," *Namenforschung. Ein internationales Handbuch zur Onomastik*, ed. by E. Eichler et al., pp. 1296–1300, Berlin & New York: de Gruyter.

Lönnroth, Lars, 2006. *Njals saga* [translated and with an introduction], Stockholm: Atlantis.

Lövgren Anna-Brita, 2018. *Staten och folk på väg. Pass i Sverige från Gustav Vasas tid till 1860*, Lund: Nordic Academic Press.

Lowe, Christopher, 2008. *Inchmarnock. An Early Historic Island Monastery and Its Archaeological Landscape*, Edinburgh: Society of Antiquaries of Scotland.

Löwenborg, Daniel, 2010. *Excavating the Digital Landscape. GIS Analyses of Social Relations in Central Sweden in the 1st Millennium AD* (Aun, 42), Uppsala: Dept. of Archaeology and Ancient History, Uppsala University.

Loyn, H. R., 1955. "Gesiths and Thegns in Anglo-Saxon England from the Seventh to the Tenth Century," *English Historical Review* 70: 529–549.

Loyn, H. R., 1991. *Anglo-Saxon England and the Norman Conquest*, 2nd ed., London & New York: Longman.

Lucas, Henry S., 1930. "The Great European Famine of 1315, 1316, and 1317," *Speculum* 5: 343–377.

Łukaszewicz, Adam, 1998. "De Sclavinis et slavis . . . ," *Dialogues d'histoire ancienne* 24(2): 129–135.

Lund, Allan A., 1991. "Zur Gesamtinterpretation der 'Germania' des Tacitus," in *Aufstieg und Niedergang der römischen Welt. Geschichte und Kultur Roms im Spiegel der neueren Forschung*, vol. 2, 33:3: *Sprache und Literatur*, ed. by Wolfgang Haase, pp. 1857–1988, Berlin: de Gruyter.

Lund, Allan A., 1995. *Germanenideologie im Nationalsozialismus. Zur Rezeption der "Germania" des Tacitus im "Dritten Reich,"* Heidelberg: Winter.

Lund, Allan A., 2007. "Zur interpretatio Romana in der, 'Germania' des Tacitus," *Zeitschrift für Religions- und Geistesgeschichte* 59(4): 289–310.

Lund Hansen, Ulla, 1987. *Römischer Import im Norden. Warenaustausch zwischen dem Römischen Reich und dem freien Germanien während der Kaiserzeit unter besonderer Berücksichtigung Nordeuropas* (Nordiske fortidsminder. Serie B 10), København: Det Kongelig nordiske Oldskriftselskab.

Lunden, Kåre, 1976. *Norge under Sverreætten 1177–1319* (Norges historie, 3), Oslo: Cappelen.

Lundkvist, Artur, 1978. *Slavar för Särkland*, Stockholm: Bonnier.

Lundström, Per, 1981. *De kommo vida. Vikingars hamn vid Paviken på Gotland* (Sjöhistoriska museets rapportserie, [15]), Stockholm: Statens sjöhistoriska museum.

MacLeod, William Christie, 1928. "Economic Aspects of Indigenous American Slavery," *American Anthropologist* 30: 632–650.

MacLeod, William Christie, 1929. "The Origin of Servile Labor Groups," *American Anthtropologist* 31: 89–113.

Macmillan Encyclopedia of World Slavery, ed. by P. Finkelman and J. C. Miller, New York: Macmillan, 1998.

Madsen, Hans Jørgen and Jens Jeppesen, "Et slot ved navn Trælborg," *Skalk* 1993(1): 9–12.

Madsen, Hans Jørgen, and Søren M. Sindbæk, 2014. "The Finds: Pottery," in *Aggersborg. The Viking-Age Settlement and Fortress*, ed. by E. Roesdahl, S. M. Sindbæk, A. Pedersen, and D. Wilson (Jutland Archaeological Society. Publications, 82), pp. 214–234, Århus: Aarhus University Press.

Maitland, Frederic William, 1897. *Domesday Book and Beyond. Three Essays in the Early History of England*, Cambridge: Cambridge University Press.

Mallory, J. P., and D. Q. Adams, 1997. *Encyclopedia of Indo-European Culture*, London: Fitzroy Dearborn.

Manco, Albert, 2008. "On the Toponym *Schiava* 'Slave'," *Indogermanische Forschungen* 113: 271–283.

Manning, Patrick, 1990. *Slavery and African Life. Occidental, Oriental, and African Slave Trades* (African Studies Series, 67), Cambridge: Cambridge University Press.

Mariotti, Jean-François, Annie Dumont, Vivien Mathé, Adrien Camus, François Lévêque, Anne Nissen Jaubert, Olivia Hulot, Sandra Greck, and Béatrice Szepertyski, 2005. "Prospection du lit mineur et des bergessur le site médiéval de Taillebourg – Port-d'Envaux (Charente-Maritime). Un secteur d'activité lié à la Charente," *Aquitania* 21: 299–336.

Marmon, Shaun E. (ed.), 1999. *Slavery in the Islamic Middle East*, Princeton: Marcus Weiner.

Marsh, Henry, 1974. *Slavery and Race. A Story of Slavery and Its Legacy for Today*, Newton Abbot: David and Charles.

Marstrander, Carl J. S., 1925. "Træll," in *Heidersskrift til Marius Hægstad fraa vene og læresveinar 15de Juli 1925*, pp. 173–176, Oslo: Norli.

Masson, Olivier, 1972. "Les noms de esclaves dans la Grece Antique," in *Actes du Colloque 1971 sur l'Esclavage* (Centre de Researches d'Histoire Ancienne, 6), pp. 9–23, Paris.

Mazor, Amir, 2015. *The Rise and Fall of a Muslim Regiment. The Mansuriyya in the First Mamluk Sultanate, 678/1279–741/1341* (Mamluk Studies, 10), Göttingen: V&R Unipress/Bonn University Press.

McCormick, Michael, 2001. *Origins of the European Economy. Communcations and Commerce, A.D. 300–900*, Cambridge: Cambridge University Press.

McCormick, Michael, 2002a. "New Light on the 'Dark Ages': How the Slave Trade Fuelled the Carolingian Economy," *Past and Present* 177: 17–54.

McCormick, Michael, 2002b. "Verkehrswege, Handel und Sklaven zwischen Europa und dem nahen Osten um 900: Von der Geschichtsschreibung zur Archäologi?," *Europa im 10. Jahrhundert. Archäologie einer Aufbruchszeit*, ed. by J. Henning, pp. 171–180, Mainz am Rhein: von Zabern.

McFarlane, Bruce, Steve Cooper, and Miomir Jaksic, 2005. "The Asiatic Mode of Production – A New Phoenix (Part 2)," *Journal of Contemporary Asia*, 35(4): 499–536.

McKee, Sally, 2014. "The Familiarity of Slaves in Medieval and Early Modern Households," in *Mediterranean Slavery Revisited (500–1800)/Neue Perspectiven auf mediterrane Sklaverei (500–1800)*, ed. by Stefan Hanss and Juliane Schiel, pp. 501–514, Zürich: Chronos Verlag.

McKinnell, John, 2001. "[Review of] Ursula Dronke (ed. and trans.), *The Poetic Edda*, 2: *Mythological Poems* (Oxford 1997)," *Alvíssmál* 10: 116–128.

McTurk, Rory, 1997. "Marie de France, Geirmundar þáttr Heljarskinns, and Reader-Respons Criticism," in *Hugur. Mélanges d'histoire, de littérature et de mythologie offerts à Regis Boyer pour son 65e anniversaire*, ed. by C. Lecouteux and O. Gouchet, pp. 193–209, Paris: Presses de l'Université de Paris-Sorbonne.

Mees, Bernhard, 1998. "Celtic Influence in the Vocabulary of Hierarchy during the Common Germanic Period," *Zeitschrift der Savigny-Stiftung für Rechtsgeschichte. Germanistische Abteilung* 115: 361–388.

Meißner, Rudolf, 1933. "Rígr," *Beiträge zur Geschichte der deutschen Sprache und Literatur* 57: 109–130.

Ménage, Victor L., 1991. "*Devşirme*," in *Encyclopaedia of Islam*, vol. 1, pp. 210–213, Leiden: Brill.

Menges, Karl H., 1983. "Wieder einmal zu poln. 'kobieta', weibliche Person; Frau," *Zeitschrift für Slavische Philologie* 43(2): 400–406.

Meulengracht Sørensen, Preben, 1980. *Norrønt nid. Forestillingen om den umandige mand i de islandske sagaer*, Odense: Odense universitetsforlag.

Meulengracht Sørensen, Preben, 1991. "Håkon den gode og guderne. Nogle bemærkninger om religion og centralmagt i det tiene århundrede- og om religionshistorie og kildekritik," in *Høvdingesamfund og Kongemagt*, ed. by P. Mortensen and B. M. Rasmussen (Fra Stamme til Stat, 2), pp. 235–244, Århus: Jysk Arkæologisk Selskab.

Meulengracht Sørensen, Preben, 1993. *Fortælling og ære. Studier i islændigesagaerne*, Århus: Århus universitetsforlag.

Michalsen, T., and Sv. Stech Jr., 1963. "Det slaviske ordet 'otrok' og dets germanske ekvivalenter," *ANF* 78: 232–240.

Miller, Edward, and John Hatcher, 1978. *Medieval England. Rural Society and Economic Change 1086–1348*, London & New York: Routledge.

Miller, Joseph C., 2002. "The Historical Contexts of Slavery in Europe," in *Slavery across Time and Space. Studies in Slavery in Medieval Eurpe and Africa*, ed. by P. Hernæs and T. Iversen (Trondheim Studies in History, 38), pp. 1–57, Trondheim: Dept. of History, NTNU.

Miller, Joseph C., 2012. *The Problem of Slavery as History. A Global Approach*, New Haven: Yale University Press.

Miller, William Ian, 1988. "Ordeal in Iceland," *Scandinavian Studies* 60: 189–218.

Miller, William Ian, 1990. *Bloodtaking and Peacemaking. Feud, Law and Society in Saga Iceland*, Chicago & London: Longman.

Mire, Lawrence, 1985. "Al-Zubayr Pasha and the Zariba Based Slave Trade in the Bahr al-Ghazal 1855–1879," in *Slaves and Slavery in Muslim Africa*, 2nd ed., ed. by J. R. Willis, pp. 101–122, London: Frank Cass.

Mishin, Dmitrij, 1998. "The Saqaliba Slaves in the Aghlabid State," *Annual Journal of Medieval Studies at CEU*, ed. by M. Sebök (Department of Medieval Studies, 1996–1997), pp. 236–244, Budapest: Central European University.

Moberg, Lennart, 1984. *Konungastyrelsen. En filologisk undersökning* (Samlingar utgivna av Svenska fornskriftssällskapet. Serie 1: Svenska skrifter, 255 = 69:2), Uppsala: Svenska fornskriftssällskapet.

Moberg, Vilhelm, 1970. *Min svenska historia berättad för folket. Från Oden till Engelbrekt*, Stockholm: Norstedt.

Moggi, Mauro, and Giuseppe Cordiano (eds.), 1997. *Schiavi e dipendenti nell'ambito dell'oikos e della familia: Atti del 22. Colloquio Girea: Pontignano (Siena), 19–20 novembre 1995* (Studi e testi di storia antica, 8), Pisa: ETS.

Moltke, Erik, 1981. *Runes and Their Origin. Denmark and Elsewhere*, trans. by Peter Foote, Copenhagen: Nationalmuseets forlag.

Montgomery, James E., 2000. "Ibn Faḍlān and the Rūsiyyah," *Journal of Arabic and Islamic Studies* 3: 1–25.

Montgomery, J[ames] E., 2008. "Arabic Sources on the Vikings," in *The Viking World*, ed. by Stefan Brink in coll. with Neil Price, pp. 550–561, London: Routledge.

Moriarty, Michael, 2011. *Disguised Vices. Theories of Virtue in Early Modern French Thought*, Oxford: Oxford University Press.

Morris, Ian, 1998. "Remaining Invisible. The Archaeology of the Excluded in Classical Athens," in *Women and Slaves in Greco-Roman Culture. Differential Equations*, ed. by S. R. Joshel and S. Murnaghan, pp. 198–220, London & New York: Routledge.

Mowafi, Reda, 1981. *Slavery, Slave Trade and Abolition Attempts in Egypt and the Sudan 1820–1882* (Lund Studies in International History, 14), Lund: Esselte studium.

Much, Rudolf, 1937. *Die Germania des Tacitus* (Germanische Bibliothek, 1:5:3), Heidelberg: Carl Winter.

Munkhammar, Lars, 2003. "'Turkrånet' var Heimaeys stora olycka," *Svenska Dagbladet* (Under strecket) 13.11.2003.

Munktell, H., 1943. "Till frågan om fredlöshetens utveckling," *Uppsala Universitets Årsskrift* 1943(3): 143–165.

Murphey, Rhoads, 1999. *Ottoman Warfare, 1500–1700*, London: UCL Press.

Müllenhoff, Karl, 1870–1908. *Deutsche Altertumskunde*, 5 vols, Berlin: Weidmannsche Buchhandlung.

Myrdal, Janken, 1999. *Det svenska jordbrukets historia*, vol. 2: *Jordbruket under feodalismen 1000–1700*, Stockholm: Natur och kultur/LT.

Myrdal, Janken, 2011. "Milking and Grinding, Digging and Herding. Slaves and Farmwork 1000–1300," in *Settlement and Lordship in Viking and Early Medieval Scandinavia*, ed. by Bjørn Poulsen and Søren Michael Sindbæk (The Medieval Countryside, 9), pp. 293–307, Turnhout: Brepols.

Myrdal, Janken, and Clas Tollin, 2003. "Brytar och tidigmedeltida huvudgårdar," in *Trälar. Ofria i agrarsamhället från vikingatid till medeltid*, ed. by Th. Lindkvist and J. Myrdal, pp. 133–168, Stockholm: Nordiska museet.

Naumann, Elise, Maja Krzewińska, Anders Götherström, and Gunilla Eriksson, 2013. "Slaves as Burial Gifts in Viking Age Norway? Evidence from Stable Isotope and Ancient DNA Analyses," *Journal of Archaeological Science* 41: 533–540.

Nazmi, Ahmad, 1998. *Commercial Relations between Arabs and Slavs (9th–11th Centuries)*, Warszawa: Wydawnictwo Akademickie.

Nehlsen, Hermann, 1984. "Mancipia," in *Handwörterbuch der deutschen Rechtsgeschichte*, vol. 3, ed. by A. Erler and E. Kaufmann, pp. 219–230, Berlin: Erich Schmidt Verlag.

Nehlsen, Hermann, 2001. "Die *servi*, *ancillae* und *mancipia* der Lex Baiuvariorum. Ein Beiträge zur Geschichte der Sklaverei in Bayern," in *Fünzig Jahre Forschungen zur Antiken Sklaverei an der Mainzer Akademie 1950–2000*, ed. by Heinz Bellen und Heinz Heinen (Forschungen zur Antiken Sklaverei, 35), pp. 505–521, Stuttgart: Franz Steiner Verlag.

Neidorf, Leonard, 2018. "Wealhtheow and Her Name: Etymology, Characterization, and Textual Criticism," *Neophilologus* 102: 75–89.

Nelson, Janet L., 1986. *Politics and Ritual in Early Medieval Europe* (Hambledon History Series, 42), London: Hambledon. [First chapter (pp. 1–48) also printed as: "Queens as Jezebels: Brunhild and Balthild in Merovingian History," in *Medieval Women. Dedicated and Presented to Rosalind M. T. Hill on the Occasion of her Seventieth Birthday*, ed. by D. Baker (Studies in Church History. Subsidia, 1), pp. 31–77, Oxford: Blackwell, 1978.]

Nelson, Janet L., 1997. "The Frankish Empire," in *The Oxford Illustrated History of the Vikings*, ed. by P. Sawyer, pp. 19–47, Oxford & New York: Oxford University Press.

Nerman, Birger, 1969. "Rígsþulas ålder," *ANF* 84: 15–18.

Neumann, Günter, and Henning Seemann (eds.), 1992. *Beiträge zum Verständnis der Germania des Tacitus* (Bericht über die Kolloquien der Kommission für die

Altertumskunde Nord- und Mitteleuropas im Jahr 1986, 2; Abhandlungen der Akademie der Wissenschaften in Göttingen. Philologisch-historische Klasse, F:3, 195), Göttingen: Vandenhoeck & Ruprecht.

Nevéus, Clara, 1974. *Trälarna i landskapslagarnas samhälle. Danmark och Sverige* (Studia Historica Upsaliensia, 58), Uppsala: Uppsala universitet.

Nieboer, Herman J., 1910. *Slavery as an Industrial System. Ethnological Researches*, 2nd ed., Haag.

Nielsen, Hans Frede, 1993. "On Case-Form Endings in the Earliest Runic Personal Names," in *Personnamn i nordiska och andra germanska fornspråk*, ed. by L. Peterson (NORNA-rapporter, 51), pp. 85–93, Uppsala: Norna.

Nielsen, Hans Frede, 2000. *The Early Runic Language of Scandinavia. Studies in Germanic Dialect Geography* (Indogermanische Bibliothek, 1), Heidelberg: Carl Winter.

Nielsen, Hans Frede, 2004. "Om Danmarks tidligste sproghistorie – i tværvidenskabelig belysning," in *Namenwelten. Orts- und Personennamen in historischer Sicht*, ed. by S. Brink, L. Elmevik, and A. van Nahl (Ergänzungsband der RGA, 44), pp. 638–651, Berlin & New York: de Gruyter.

Nielsen, Niels Åge, 1976. *Dansk etymologisk ordbog*, 3rd ed., København: Gyldendal.

Nilsson, Bertil, 2001. "Gudsdomar i Skandinavien under vikingatid och medeltid," in *Kontinuitäten und Brüche in der Religionsgeschichte*, ed. by M. Stausberg (Ergänzungsband der RGA, 31), pp. 503–535, Berlin & New York: de Gruyter.

NO = *Norrøn Ordbok*, 4th ed. Oslo: Det norske samlaget, 1990.

NoB = *Namn och bygd. Tidskrift för nordisk ortnamnsforskning*, 1–, Uppsala: Kungl. Gustav Adolfs Akademi, 1913 ff.

Nordberg, Andreas, 2002. "Vertikalt placerade vapen i vikingatida gravar," *Fornvännen* 97: 15–24.

Nordberg, Michael, 1988. *Profetens folk. Stat, samhälle och kultur i Islam under tusen år*, Stockholm: Tiden.

Norden, Eduard, 1923. *Die germanische Urgeschichte in Tacitus Germania*, 3rd ed., Leipzig: Teubner.

Nordenstorm, Leif, 1994. "Dödande vid begravningar. Ett inslag i järnålderns gravritualer i komparativ religionshistorisk belysning," *Fornvännen* 89: 265–278.

Nordström, Karin, and Frands Herschend, 2003. "Det ideologiska inslaget i väven," in *Trälar. Ofria i agrarsamhället från vikingatid till medeltid*, ed. by Th. Lindkvist and J. Myrdal, pp. 50–76, Stockholm: Nordiska museet.

Noreen, Adolf, 1892. "Mytiska beståndsdelar i Ynglingatal," in *Uppsalastudier tillegnade Sophus Bugge på hans 60-åra födelsedag den 5 januari 1893*, pp. 194–225, Uppsala: Almqvist & Wiksell.

Noreen, Adolf, 1923. *Altisländische und Altnorwegische Grammatik*..., (Samlung kurzer Grammatiken germanischer Dialekte 4: Altnordische Grammatik, 1), 4th ed., Halle: Niemeyer.

Noreen, Erik, 1926. *Den norsk-isländska poesin*, Stockholm: P. A. Norstedt.

Nørlund, Poul, 1948. *Trelleborg* (Nordiske fortidsminder, 4:1), København: Nordisk forlag.

Norr, Svante, 1996. "A Place for Proletarians? A Contextual Hypothesis on Social Space in Roman and Migration Period Long-Houses," *Current Swedish Archaeology* 4: 157–164.

Norrby, Robert, 1905. *Ydre härads gårdnamn*, Stockholm: P. A. Norstedt.

Ó Corráin, Donnchadh, 1997. "Ireland, Wales, Man, and the Hebrides," in *The Oxford Illustrated History of the Vikings*, ed. by P. Sawyer, pp. 83–109, Oxford: Oxford University Press.

Ödeen, Nils, 1927. *Studier i Smålands bebyggelsehistoria. Ett bidrag till svensk ortnamnsforskning*, Lund.

Odenstedt, Bengt, 1990. *On the Origin and Early History of the Runic Script. Typology and Graphic Variation in the Older Futhark* (Acta Academiae regiae Gustavi Adolphi, 59), Uppsala: Kungl. Gustav Adolfs akademi.

Odenstedt, Bengt, 1995. "Nuns and Midwives, Slaves and Adulteresses: Old English Terms Denoting Women," in *New Trends in Semantics and Lexicography*, ed. by H. Kardela and G. Persson (Umeå Studies in the Humanities, 127), pp. 131–143, Umeå: Umeå universitet.

O'Donoghue, Heather, 1997. "Viking Raiders and Irish Slaves: The Outsider in Native Traditions," in *Amico Amici. Gad Rausing den 19 maj 1997*, ed. by J. Ellerström, pp. 97–109, Lund: Signum.

Øeby Nielsen, Gunhild, 2004. *Magt og mentalitet, kontinuitet og brud i tiden for religions- og kulturskiftet ca. 950-1200 belyst ud fra runesten og deres fundforhold*. [Dupl. PhD diss. in Medieval Archaeology at the University of Aarhus.]

Øeby Nielsen, Gunhild, 2005. "De danske runestens oprindelige plads," *Kuml*: 121–144.

OED[2] = *The Oxford English Dictionary*, 20 vols, ed. by J. A. Simpson and E. S. Weiner, 2nd ed., Oxford: Oxford University Press, 2005.

Ohlmarks, Åke, 1983. *Fornnordiskt lexikon*, 2nd ed., Stockholm: Tiden.

von Olberg, Gabriele, 1983. *Freie, Nachbarn und Gefolgsleute. Volkssprachliche Bezeichnungen aus dem sozialen Bereich in den frühmittelalterlichen Leges* (Europäische Hochschulschriften, 1. Deutsche Sprache und Literatur, 627), Frankfurt am Main: Peter Lang.

von Olberg, Gabriele, 1987. "Zum Freiheitsbegriff im Spiegel volkssprachliger Bezeichnungen in den frühmittelalterlichen Leges," in *Akten des 26. Deutschen Rechtshistorikertages*, ed. by D. Simon (Ius Commune. Sonderhefte: Studien zur Europäischen Rechtsgeschichte, 30), pp. 411–425, Frankfurt am Main: Vitorio Klostermann.

von Olberg, Gabriele, 1991. *Die volkssprachigen Wörter der Leges barbarorum, 2: Die Bezeichnungen für soziale Stände, Schichten und Gruppen in den Leges barbarorum* (Arbeiten zur Frühmittelalterforschung, 11), Berlin & New York: de Gruyter.

von Olberg, Gabriele, 2000. "Kebse," *RGA* 16: 347–352.

Olsen, Magnus, 1926. *Ættegård og helligdom. Norske stedsnavn socialt og religionshistorisk belyst* (Instituttet for sammenlignende kulturforskning. Serie A. Forelesninger, 9a), Oslo: H. Aschehoug & Co.

Olson, Emil, 1916. *De appellativa substantivens bildning i fornsvenskan. Bidrag till den fornsvenska ordbildningsläran*, Lund: Gleerup.

Olsson, Ingemar, 1976. *Gotlands Stavgardar – en ortnamnsstudie* (Gotlandica, 10), Visby: Press.

Olsson, Mats, 1999. *Vikingatida träldom. Om slaveriets plats i Skandinaviens ekonomiska historia* (Lund Papers in Economic History, 67), Lund: Department of Economic History, Lund University.

Orel, Vladimir, 2003. *A Handbook of Germanic Etymology*, Leiden & Boston: Brill.

Otterbjörk, Roland, 1965. "Det äldsta originalbrevet på svenska," *Namn och bygd* 53: 122–133.

Ould Ciré, Mohamed Yahya, 2014. *La Mauritanie. Entre l'esclavage et le racisme* (Quête du sens), Paris: L'Harmattan.

Parducci, Domenico, 2007. "Gli stranieri nell'alto medioevo. Appunti sul cap. 367 dell'Edictum Rothari," *Mirator* 1: 1–10.

Pârvulescu, Adrian, 2010. "Lat. *servus*," *Indogermanische Forschungen* 115: 190–197.

Patterson, Orlando, 1977. "The Structural Origins of Slavery. A Critique of the Nieboer–Domar Hypothesis from a Comparative Perspective," in *Comparative Perspectives on Slavery in New World Plantation Societies*, ed. by V. D. Rubin and A. Tuden (Annals of the New York Academy of Sciences, 292), pp. 12–34, New York: New York Academy of Sciences.

Patterson, Orlando, 1982, *Slavery and Social Death. A Comparative Study*, Cambridge, MA: Harvard University Press.

Patterson, Orlando, 1991. *Freedom*, vol. 1: *Freedom in the Making of Western Culture*, London: Tauris.

PBB = (H. Paul and W. Braune's) *Beiträge zur Geschichte der deutschen Sprache und Literatur*, Halle (Saale), 1874–1979.

Pearson, Cathy, 2005. "[Review of] C. I. Hammer, *A Large-Scale Slave Society of the Early Middle Ages: Slaves and Their Families in Early Medieval Bavaria* (2002)," *Speculum* 80(2): 582–584.

Pedersen, Anne, 2014. "The Finds: Summary," in *Aggersborg. The Viking-Age Settlement and Fortress*, ed. by E. Roesdahl, S. M. Sindbæk, A. Pedersen, and D. Wilson (Jutland Archaeological Society. Publications, 82), pp. 361–364, Århus: Aarhus University Press.

Pedersen, Ellen Anne, and Mats Widgren, 1998. *Det svenska jordbrukets historia*, vol. 1: *Jordbrukets första femtusen år*, Stockholm: Natur och kultur/LT.

Peel, Christine, 1999. *Guta Saga. The History of the Gotlanders* (Viking Society for Northern Research. Text Series, 12), London: Viking Society for Northern Research, University College London.

Peel, Christine, 2009. *Guta Lag. The Law of the Gotlanders* (Viking Society for Northern Research. Text Series, 18), London: Viking Society for Northern Studies, University College London.

Peel, Christine, 2015. *Guta Lag and Guta Saga. The Law and History of the Gotlanders* (Nordic Medieval Laws), London: Routledge.

Pelteret, David A. E., 1981. "Slave Raiding and Slave Trading in Early England," *Anglo-Saxon England* 9: 99–114.

Pelteret, David A. E., 1985. "Slavery in Anglo-Saxon England," in *The Anglo-Saxons. Synthesis and Achievement*, ed. by J. D. Woods and D. A. E. Pelteret, pp. 116–133, Waterloo, On.: Wilfrid Laurier University Press.

Pelteret, David A. E., 1995. *Slavery in Early Mediaeval England. From the Reign of Alfred until the Twelfth Century* (Studies in Anglo-Saxon History, 8), Woodbridge: Boydell.

Pelteret, David A. E., 2002. "A Missing Half-Millennium. The Beginning and End of Slavery in Early Medieval England," in *Slavery across Time and Space: Studies in Slavery in Medieval Europe and Africa*, ed. by P. Hernæs and T. Iversen (Trondheim Studies in History, 38), pp. 69–95, Trondheim: Dept. of History, NTNU.

Pelteret, David A. E., 2014. "Slavery," in *The Wiley Blackwell Encyclopedia of Anglo-Saxon England*, 2nd ed., ed. by M. Lapidge et al., pp. 436–437, Oxford: Wiley Blackwell.

Perdue, Theda, 1979. *Slavery and the Evolution of Cherokee Society, 1540–1866*, Knoxville, Tenn.: University of Tennessee Press.

Perrin, C. E., 1955. "Le Servage en France et en Allemagne," in *Relazioni del X Congresso international di scienze storichi*, vol. 3: *Storia del medioevo*, pp. 213–245, Firenze: G. C. Sansoni.

Persson, Per, 1912. *Beiträge zur indogermanischen Wortforschung* (Skrifter utgivna av Kungl. Humanistiska vetenskapssamfundet i Uppsala, 10:[1]–2), Uppsala: Akademiska bokhandeln.

Peterson, Lena, 2004. "Reflections on the Inscription **laguþewa** on Shield-Handle Mount 3 from Illerup," in *Namenwelten. Orts- und Personennamen in historischer Sicht*, ed. by S. Brink, L. Elmevik, and A. van Nahl (Ergänzungsbände zum RGA, 44), pp. 659–677, Berlin & New York: de Gruyter.

Peterson, Lena, 2007. *Nordiskt runnamnslexikon*, 5th ed., Uppsala: Institutet för språk och folkminnen.

Peterson, Lena, *LUP. Lexikon över urnordiska personnamn* [http://www.sofi.se/images/NA/urnord.pdf].

Pettersson, Björn, 1959. *Stilstudier i de svenska landskapslagarna* (Studier i nordisk filologi, 49), Helsingfors: Svenska litteratursällskapet i Finland.

Phillips, William D., 1985. *Slavery from Roman Times to the Early Transatlantic Trade*, Manchester: Manchester University Press.

Phillips, William D., 1996. "Continuity and Change in Western Slavery. Ancient to Modern Times," in *Serfdom & Slavery. Studies in Legal Bondage*, ed. by M. L. Bush, pp. 71–88, London: Longman.

Pilarczyk, Ian C., 1996. "Between a Rock and a Hot Place. Issues of Subjectivity and Rationality in the Medieval Ordeal by Hot Iron," *Anglo-American Law Review* 25: 87–112.

Pilø, Lars, 2005. *Bosted, urgård, enkeltgård. En analyse av premissene i den norske bosetningshistoriske forskningstradisjon på bakgrunn av bebyggelsearkeologisk feltarbeid på Hedemarken* (Oslo Archaeological Series, 3), Oslo: Institutt for arkeologi, kunsthistorie og konservering, Universitetet i Oslo.

Pirenne, Henri, 1936. *Economic and social history of medieval Europe*, trans. by Ivy E. Clegg, London: K. Paul, Trench, Trubner & co.

Pirenne, Henri, 1939. *Mohammed and Charlemagne*, trans. by Bernard Miall, London: George Allan & Unwin

PLRE = *Prosopography of the Later Roman Empire*, 3 vols (in 4), by A. H. M. Jones, J. R. Martindale, and J. Morris, Cambridge: Cambridge University Press, 1971–1992.

Pohl, Heinz-Dieter, 2013. "Slawen/Slowenen/Windische und Deutsche/Nemci," *Kultur Land Menschen – Die Kärntner Landsmannschaft* 2013(9/10): 6–11 (online: http://members.chello.at/heinz.pohl/Slawenname.htm).

Pokorny, Julius, 1959. *Indogermanisches etymologisches Wörterbuch*, Bern & München: Francke.

Poly, J.-P., and E. Bournazel, 1980. *La mutation féodale* (Nouvelle Clio, 16), Paris: PUF.

Pomeroy, Sarah B., 1975. *Goddesses, Whores, Wives and Slaves. Women in Classical Antiquity*, New York: Dorset Press.

Pons-Sanz, Sara M., 2007. "A Reconsideration of Wulfstan's Use of Norse-Derived Terms: The Case of Þræl," *English Studies* 88: 1–21.

Pons-Sanz, Sara M., 2013. *The Lexical Effects of Anglo-Scandinavian Linguistic Contact on Old English* (Studies in Early Middle Ages, 1), Turnhout: Brepols.

Postan, Michael M., 1954. *The Famulus. The Estate Labourer in the XIIth and XIIIth Centuries* (Economic History Review. Supplements), Cambridge: Cambridge University Press.

Poulsen, Bjørn, 2012. "A Classical Manor in Viking Age and Early Medieval Denmark?," *Revue belge de philologie et d'histoire* 90(2): 451–465.

Poulsen, Bjørn, ms. "The Free *bønder* of Scandinavia – Who Were They?"

Poulsen, Bjørn, and Hans Jacop Orning, 2019. "Holding Royal Office and the Creation and Consolidation of the Elites in Scandinavia c. 1050–1250," in *Nordic Elites in Transformation, c. 1050–1250*, vol. 1: *Material Resources*, ed. by Bjørn Poulsen, Helle Vogt, and Jón Viðar Sigurðsson, pp. 212–247, Abingdon & New York: Routledge.

Poulsen, Bjørn, and Søren Michael Sindbæk, 2011. "Settlement and Lordship in Viking and Early Medieval Scandinavia," in *Settlement and Lordship in Viking and Early Medieval Scandinavia*, ed. by Bjørn Poulsen and Søren Michael Sindbæk (The Medieval Countryside, 99), pp. 1–28, Turnhout: Brepols.

Price, Douglas T., Karin Margarita Frei, Andres Siegfried Dobat, Niels Lynnerup, and Pia Bennike, 2011. "Who Was in Harold Bluetooth's Army? Strontium Isotope Investigation of the Cemetery at the Viking Age Fortress at Trelleborg, Denmark," *Antiquity* 85: 476–489.

Price, Neil, 2005. "Sexualität," *RGA* 28: 244–257.

Price, Neil, 2010. "Passing into Poetry. Viking-Age Mortuary Drama and the Origins of Norse Mythology," *Medieval Archaeology* 54: 123–156.

Price, Neil, 2014. "Nine Paces from Hel. Time and Motion in Old Norse Ritual Performance," *World Archaeology* 46(2): 178–191.

de la Puente, Cristina, 2006. "Slaves and Slave Trade, Western Islamic World," in *Medieval Islamic Civilization. An Encyclopedia*, vol. 2, ed. by Josef W. Meri, pp. 758–762, New York & London: Routledge.

Radon, Jenny, 2019a. *Filade tänder. I ljuset av sina sammanhang. En studie av individer med modifierade tänder i Skandinavien under yngre järnålder* ([Master-dissertation, Dept. of Archaeology and Ancient History, Uppsala University, VT 2019).

Radon, Jenny, 2019b. "Skandinaviska tandmodifieringar i nytt ljus," *Situne Dei. Årsskrift för Sigtunaforskning och historisk arkeologi*: 34–51.

Raffield, Ben, 2019. "The Slave Markets of the Viking World. Comparative Perspectives on an 'Invisible Archaeology,'" *Slavery & Abolition* (online: https://doi.org/10.1080/0144039X.2019.1592976).

Raffield, Ben, Neil Price, and Mark Collard, 2017a. "Male-Biased Operational Sex Ratio and the Viking Phenomenon. An Evolutionary Anthropological Perspective on Late Iron Age Scandinavian Raiding," *Evolution and Human Behaviour* 38: 315–324.

Raffield, Ben, Neil Price, and Mark Collard, 2017b. "Polygyny, Concubinage, and the Social Lives of Women in Viking-Age Scandinavia," *Viking and Medieval Scandinavia* 13: 165–209.

Rahmqvist, Sigurd, 1986. "Gamla Uppsala by – Upplands största," in *Uppsala stads historia*, vol. 7, ed. by Herbert Lundh, pp. 254–271, Uppsala: Uppsala kommun.

Rahmqvist, Sigurd, 1996. *Sätesgård och gods. De medeltida frälsegodsens framväxt mot bakgrund av Upplands bebyggelsehistoria* (Upplands fornminnesförenings tidskrift, 53), Uppsala: Upplands fornminnesförening.

Rahmqvist, Sigurd, 2002. "Medeltida bondebygd i Rytterne," *Västmanlands fornminnesförening och Västmanlands läns museum. Årsskrift* 78: 113–124 [= *Nya anteckningar om Rytterns socken: Medeltidsstudier tillägnade Göran Dahlbäck*].

Rahmqvist, Sigurd, 2007. "Medeltid i Tierp," in *Land och samhälle i förändring: uppländska bygder i ett långtidsperspektiv* (Riksantikvarieämbetet. UV GAL/Societas archaeologica Upsaliensis), pp. 715–720, Uppsala: Upplandsmuseet.

Randsborg, Klavs, 1980. *The Viking Age in Denmark. The Formation of a State*, London: Duckworth.

Randsborg, Klavs, 1986. "The Study of Slavery in Northern Europe. An Archaeological Approach," *Acta Archaeologica* 55 (1984): 155–160.

Reichert, Hermann, 1987. *Lexikon der altgermanischen Namen*, 1: *Text* (Österreichische Akademie der Wissenschaften. Schriftenreihe der Kommission für Altgermanistik. Thesaurus Palaeogermanicus, 1:1), Wien: Verlag der Österreichischen Akademie der Wissenschaften.

Reinach, Julien, 1960. *Ébauches d'une mancipation* (Collection d'études anciennes), Paris.

Reuter, Timothy, 1978. "Introduction," in *The Medieval Nobility. Studies in the Ruling Classes of France and Germany from the Sixth to the Twelfth Century*, ed. by Timothy Reuter (Europe in the Middle Ages. Selected Studies, 14), pp. 1–16, Amsterdam, New York & Oxford: North Holland Publ. Co.

Reynolds, Andrew, 2009. *Anglo-Saxon Deviant Burial Customs*, Oxford: Oxford University Press.

Reynolds, Susan, 1994. *Fiefs and Vassals. The Medieval Evidence Reinterpreted*, Oxford & New York: Oxford University Press.

RGA = *Reallexikon der germanischen Altertumskunde, begr. von Johannes Hoops*, ed. by H. Bech et al., 37 vols, 2nd ed. Berlin: de Gruyter, 1972–2008.

Rietz = Rietz, Johan Ernst, 1867. *Svenskt dialektlexikon. Ordbok öfver svenska allmogespråket*, Lund.

Rihll, Tracy, 1996. "The Origin and Establishment of Ancient Greek Slavery," in *Serfdom & Slavery. Studies in Legal Bondage*, ed. by M. L. Bush, pp. 89–111, London: Longman.

Riis, Thomas, 1970. "Villici og coloni indtil 1340. Et forsøg på en begrebsanalyse," in *Landbohistoriske studier tilegnede Fridlev Skrubbeltrang* (Landbohistoriske skrifter, 4), pp. 1–20, København: Landbohistorisk Selskab.

Riise Kristensen, Jens, 2003. *Barbariet tur retur*, København: Ørby.

Riisøy, Anne Irene, 2014. "Outlawry. From Western Norway to England," in *New Approaches to Early Law in Scandinavia*, ed. by S. Brink and L. Collinson (Acta Scandinavica, 3), pp. 101–129, Turnhout: Brepols.

Rio, Alice, 2017. *Slavery after Rome, 500–1100*, Oxford: Oxford University Press.

Rivers, Theodore John, 1986. *Laws of the Salian and Ripuarian Franks* (AMS Studies in the Middle Ages, 8), New York: AMS Press.

Rix, Helmut, 1994. *Die Termini der Unfreiheit in den Sprachen Alt-Italiens* (Forschungen zur antiken Sklaverei, 25), Stuttgart: Franz Steiner Verlag.

Robinson, F. C., 1964. "Is Wealhtheow a Prince's Daughter?," *English Studies* 45: 36–39.

Rodriguez, Junius P. (ed.), 1997. *The Historical Encyclopedia of World Slavery*, 2 vols., Santa Barbara, CA: ABC-Clio.

Roesdahl, Else, 1975. "Eastern Imports at the Viking Fortress of Fyrkat, Denmark," in *Rapports du IIIe congrès international d'archéologie slave*, ed. by B. Chropovsky, pp. 665–669, Bratislava: Veda.

Roesdahl, Else, 1977. *Fyrkat. En jysk vikingeborg*, vol. 2: *Oldsagerne og gravpladsen*, København: Det Kongl. Nordiske Oldskriftselskab.

Roesdahl, Else, 1980. *Danmarks vikingetid*, København: Gyldendal.

Roesdahl, Else, and Søren M. Sindbæk, 2014a. "The Dating of Aggersborg," in *Aggersborg. The Viking-Age Settlement and Fortress*, ed. by E. Roesdahl, S. M. Sindbæk, A. Pedersen, and D. Wilson (Jutland Archaeological Society. Publications, 82), pp. 203–208, Århus: Aarhus University Press.

Roesdahl, Else, and Søren M. Sindbæk, 2014b. "The Purpose of the Fortress," in *Aggersborg. The Viking-Age Settlement and Fortress*, ed. by E. Roesdahl, S. M. Sindbæk,

A. Pedersen, and D. Wilson (Jutland Archaeological Society. Publications, 82), pp. 383–386, Århus: Aarhus University Press.

Rooth, Erik, 1963. "Käfig und Kebse. Ein etymologischer Versuch," in *Festgabe für Ulrich Pretzel zum 65. Geburtstag dargebracht von Freunden und Schülern*, pp. 301–307, Berlin.

Roslund, Mats, 2005. "Transcending Borders. Social Identity in the Middle Ages and in Medieval Archaeology," *ARHEO. Glasilo arheološkega društva Slovenije* 23 (Ljubljana: Slovensko arheolosko drustvo): 63–78.

Roslund, Mats, 2007. *Guests in the House. Cultural Transmission between Slavs and Scandinavians 900 to 1300*, Leiden: Brill.

Roslund, Mats, 2021. "A Geography of Slavery. Ceramic networks and communities in the Lake Mälaren valley, Sweden AD c. 950 to 1150," in *Vikings Across Boundaries*, vol. 2: *Viking-Age Transformations*, ed. by Hanne Lovise Aanestad et al., pp. 259–284, London & New York: Routledge.

Roslund, Mats, in press. "Tacit Knowing of Thralls – Style Negotiation among the Unfree in 11th and 12th C. Sweden," in *Archaeology, Syncretism, Creolisation*, ed. by T. Clack, Oxford: Oxford University Press.

Roslund, Mats, ms. "Legacy of the Disowned. Finding *ambátts* in High Medieval Scania and Östergötland through Ceramic Production."

Roth, A., 1997. "Wergeld," *Lexikon des Mittelalters* 8: 2199–2201.

Rothenhöfer, Dieter, 1967. *Untersuchungen zur Sklaverei in den ostgermanischen Nachfolgestaaten des Römischen Reiches*, Tübingen [diss.].

Roux, Paul, 1910. *La question agraire en Italie. Le latifundium romain*, Paris: Félix Alcan.

Russo, John Paul, 1999. "The Sicilian Latifundia," *Italian Americana*, 17(1): 40–57.

Saller, Richard, 1996. "The Hierarchical Household in Roman Society. A Study of Domestic Slavery," in *Serfdom & Slavery. Studies in Legal Bondage*, ed. by M. L. Bush, pp. 112–129, London: Longman.

Samson, Ross, 1994. "The End of Early Medieval Slavery," in *The Work of Work. Servitude, Slavery, and Labor in Medieval England*, ed. by A. J. Frantzen and D. Moffat, pp. 95–119, Glasgow: Cruithne Press.

Sandnes, Jørn, 1979. "Bondesamfunnet," in *Vår fjerne fortid. Norges kulturhistorie*, vol. 1, ed. by Ingrid Semmingsen et al., pp. 33–68, Oslo: Aschehoug.

Sandnes, Jørn, 1983. "'Tolv kyr, to hester og tre træler'. Litt om omfanget av træleholdet i Norge i vikingetid og tidlig kristen tid," [*Norsk*] *Historisk Tidsskrift* (Oslo) 1983(1): 79–82.

Sandnes, Jørn, 2000. "Bønder, herrer og treller. Hvordan var egentlig det gammelnorske samfunnet?," *Heimen* 2000(3): 195–210.

SAOB = *Svenska akademiens ordbok*, 1–, Lund: Gleerup, 1898 ff.

Sartorius, G. F., 1830. *Urkundliche Geschichte des Ursprunges der Deutschen Hanse*, 2 vols., ed. by J. M. Lappenberg, Hamburg: F. Perthes.

Säve, Carl, 1859. *Gutniska Urkunder. Guta Lag, Guta Saga och Gotlands Runinskrifter språkligt behandlade*, Stockholm: Norstedt.

Sawyer, Birgit, and Peter Sawyer, 1993. *Medieval Scandinavia. From Conversion to Reformation circa 800–1500*, Minneapolis: University of Minnesota Press.

Sawyer, Peter, 1997a. "The Age of the Vikings and Before," in *The Oxford Illustrated History of the Vikings*, ed. by P. Sawyer, pp. 1–18, Oxford & New York: Oxford University Press.

Sawyer, Peter, 1997b. "The Viking Legacy," in *The Oxford Illustrated History of the Vikings*, ed. by P. Sawyer, pp. 250–261, Oxford & New York: Oxford University Press.

Sawyer, Peter, 2002. *Da Danmark blev Danmark. Fra ca. år 700 til ca. 1050*, 2nd ed. (Gyldendal og Politikens Danmarkshistorie, 3), Copenhagen: Gyldendal.

Sawyer, Roger, 1986. *Slavery in the Twentieth Century*, London & New York: Routledge & Kegan Paul.

Sayers, William, 1996. "Vifill - Captive Gael, Freeman Settler, Icelandic Forbear," *Ainm* 6 (1994–1995): 46–55.

Scardigli, Piergiuseppe, 2002. "Contact with Non-Germanic Languages, 1: Relations to the West," in *The Nordic Languages. An International Handbook of the History of the North Germanic Languages*, vol. 1, ed. by O. Bandle et al. (Handbücher zur Sprach- und Kommunikationswissenschaft, 22:1), pp. 572–582, Berlin & New York: de Gruyter.

SCB HSS = *Historisk Statistik för Sverige/ Historical Statistics of Sweden*, vol. 1: *Befolkningen/Population*, 2nd ed. (SCB Statistiska Centralbyrån/National Central Bureau of Statistics), Stockholm: AB Allmänna Förlaget, 1969.

Scheidel, W. 1997. "Quantifying the Sources of Slaves in the Early Roman Empire," *Journal of Roman Studies* 87: 156–169.

Scher, Steven P., 1963. "Rígsþula as Poetry," *Modern Language Notes* 78(4): 397–407.

Schiavone, Aldo, 2013. *Spartacus*, trans. by Jeremy Carden, Cambridge, MA: Harvard University Press.

Schiel, Juliane, and Stefan Hanss, 2014. "Semantics, Practices and Transcultural Perspectives on Mediterranean Slavery," in *Mediterranean Slavery Revisited (500–1800)/Neue Perspectiven auf mediterrane Sklaverei (500–1800)*, ed. by Stefan Hanss and Juliane Schiel, pp. 11–23, Zürich: Chronos Verlag.

Schietzel, Kurt, 2014. *Spurensuche Haithabu. Archäologische Spurensuche in der frühmittelalterlichen Ansiedlung Haithabu: Dokumentation und Chronik 1963–2013*, Neumünster: Wachholtz Verlag.

Schjødt, Jens Peter, 2010. "Ibn Fadhlan's Account of a Rus Funeral. To What Degree Does It Reflect Nordic Myths?," in *Reflections on Old Norse Myths*, ed. by P. Hermann, J. P. Schjødt, and R. Tranum Kristensen (Studies in Viking and Medieval Scandinavia, 1), pp. 133–148, Turnhout: Brepols.

Schlaifer, Robert, 1936. "Greek Theories of Slavery from Homer to Aristotle," *Harvard Studies in Classical Philology* 47: 165–204

Schlaug, Wilhelm, 1962. *Die altsächsischen Personnamen von dem Jahre 1000* (Lunder germanische Forschungen, 34), Lund: Gleerup & Munksgaard.

Schlesinger, Walter, 1953. "Herrschaft und Gefolgschaft in der germanisch-deutschen Verfassungsgeschichte," *Historische Zeitschrift* 176: 225–275.

Schlyter *Gloss.* = Schlyter, C. J., *Glossarium ad Corpus iuris Sueo-Gotorum antiqui = Ordbok till Samlingen af Sweriges gamla lagar* (Corpus iuris sueo-gotorum antiqui. Samling af Sweriges gamla lagar, 13), Lund, 1877.

Schnall, Jens Eike, and Rudolf Simek (eds.), 2000. *Speculum regale. Der altnorwegische Königsspiegel (Konungs skuggsjá) in der europäischen Tradition* (Studia Medievalia Septentrionalia, 5), Vienna: Fassbinder.

Schönfeld, M. 1965. *Wörterbuch der altgermanischen Personen- und Völkernamen, nach der Überlieferung des klassischen Altertums*, 2nd ed. (Germanische Bibliothek. 3 Reihe: Wörterbücher), Heidelberg: Winter.

Schrader, O., 1896. "Etymologisch-Kulturhistorisches," in *Philologische Studien. Festgabe für Eduard Sievers*, pp. 1–11, Halle: Niemeyer.

Schramm, Gottfried, 1957. *Namenschatz und Dichtersprache. Studien zu den zweigliedrigen Personennamen der Germanen* (Ergänzungshefte zur Zeitschrift für vergleichende Sprachforschung, 15), Göttingen: Vandenhoeck & Ruprecht.

Schröder, Heinrich, 1906. "Beiträge zur deutschen wortforschung II," *Zeitschrift für deutsche Philologie* 38: 518–528.

von Schroeder, Leopold, 1893. "Indogermanisches Wergeld," in *Festgruss an Rudolf von Roth* . . . , ed. by E. Kuhn, pp. 49–52, Stuttgart: W. Kohlhammer.

Schtaerman [Štaerman/ Штаерман], Elena Michajlovna, 1969. *Die Blütezeit der Sklavenwirtschaft in der römischen Republik*, trans. by Maria Bräuer-Pospelova (Übersetzungen ausländischer Arbeiten zur antiken Sklaverei, 2), Wiesbaden.

Schumacher, Leonhard, 2001a. *Sklaverei in der Antike. Alltag und Schicksal der Unfreien*, München: Beck.

Schumacher, Leonhard, 2001b. "Hausgesinde – Hofgesinde. Terminologische Überlegungen zur Funktion der *familia Caesaris* im 1. Jh. n. Chr.," in *Fünzig Jahre Forschungen zur Antiken Sklaverei an der Mainzer Akademie 1950–2000*, ed. by Heinz Bellen und Heinz Heinen (Forschungen zur Antiken Sklaverei, 35), pp. 331–352, Stuttgart: Franz Steiner Verlag.

Schulte, Michael, 2011. "Die sprachliche Deutung der Hogganvik-Inschrift. Ergänzungen zum vorläufigen Bericht," *Amsterdamer Beiträge zur älteren Germanistik* 67: 57–68 [= *Festschrift für Arend Quack zum 65. Geburtstag*].

Schulte, Michael, 2013. "The Norwegian Hogganvik Stone as an Emblem of Social Status and Identity," *JONA: Journal of the North-Atlantic*, Special vol. 4: 120–128.

Schultz, Warren C., 2006. "Mamluks," in *Medieval Islamic Civilization. An Encyclopedia*, vol. 2, ed. by Josef W. Meri, pp. 470–472, New York & London: Routledge.

Schweinfurth, George, 1874. *The Heart of Africa. Three Years of Travels and Adventures in the Unexplored Regions of Central Africa*, vol. 1, trans. by E. E. Frewer, London: Sampson Low.

Schück, Henrik, 1905. *Studier i Ynglingatal*, Uppsala: Almqvist & Wiksell.

Scott, B. G., 1978. "Iron 'Slave-Collars' from Lagore Crannog, Co. Meath," *Proceedings of the Royal Irish Academy: Archaeology, Culture, History, Literature* 78: 213–230.

von See, Klaus, 1961. "Das alter der Rígsþula," *Acta Philologica Scandinavica* 24 (1957–1961): 1–12.

von See, Klaus, 1964. *Altnordische Rechtswörter. Philologische Studien zur Rechtsauffassung und Rechtsgesinnung der Germanen* (Hermaea. Germanische Forschungen. N.F., 16), Tübingen: Max Niemeyer Verlag.

von See, Klaus, 1981. *Edda, Saga, Skaldendichtung. Aufsätze zur skandinavischen Literatur des Mittelalters* (Skandinavistische Arbeiten, 6), Heidelberg: Carl Winter.

Seebohm, Frederic, 1890. *The English Village Community Examined in Its Relations to the Manorial and Tribal Systems and to the Common or Open Field System of Husbandry. An Essay in Economic History*, 4th ed. London.

Seebohm, Frederic, 1911. *Tribal Custom in Anglo-Saxon Law*, London: Longmans, Greens, and Co.

Seelow, Hubert, 1994. "Der Geirmundar þáttr Heljarskinns in der Sturlunga saga," in *Samtíðarsögur/The Contemporary Sagas. Preprint of Papers for the Ninth International Saga Conference*, vol. 2, ed. by Sverrir Tómasson et al., pp. 698–711, Akureyri.

Segal, Ronald, 2003. *Islam's Black Slaves. A History of Africa's Other Black Diaspora*, London: Atlantic.

Seiler, Anton, 2001. *I skuggan av båtgravarna. Landskap och samhälle i Vendels socken under yngre järnålder*, 2 vols (Theses and Papers in Archaeology, B:7–8), Stockholm: Arkeologiska forskningslaboratoriet, Stockholms universitet.
Seiler, Anton, 2003. "I guldsmedens tjänst. Spår av träldomen i gravmaterialet från östra Mellansverige under yngre järnålder," in *Trälar. Ofria i agrarsamhället från vikingatid till medeltid*, ed. by Th. Lindkvist and J. Myrdal (Skrifter om skogs- och lantbrukshistoria, 17), pp. 77–87, Stockholm: Nordiska museet.
Seip, Didrik Arup, 1929. "Valþiófr og Valþiúfr," *ANF* 44: 159–163 [= *Studier tillägnade Axel Koch*, Lund: Gleerup, 1929].
Seip, Didrik Arup, 1957. "Böter," *KL* 2: 533–537.
Selart, Anti, 2013. "Slavery in the Eastern Baltic in the 12th–15th Centuries," in *Schiavitù e servaggio nell'economia europea. Secc. XI–XVIII / Serfdom and Slavery in the European Economy 11th–18th Centuries*, ed. by Simonetta Cavaciocchi (Fondazione Instituto Internazionale di Storia Economica "F. Datini" Prato. Serie II: Atti delle "Settimane di Studi" e altri Convegni 45), pp. 352–364, Firenze: Firenze University Press.
Sen, Subhadra Kumar, 2004. "On *þius," *General Linguistics* 41(1): 265.
Sha'bān, Muḥammad 'Abd al-Ḥayy Muḥammad, 1970. *The 'Abbāsid Revolution*, Cambridge: Cambridge University Press.
Shaw, Brent D., 2001. *Spartacus and the Slave Wars. A Brief History with Documents*, trans., ed. and with an introduction, Boston, MA: Bedford.
Shields, Kenneth Jr., 2006. "Gothic *þius* - Once Again," *Indogermanische Forschungen* 111: 285–291.
Shippey, Tom, 2010. "Hrólfs saga kraka and the Legend of Lejre," in *Making History. Essays on the Fornaldarsögur*, ed. by Martin Arnold and Alison Finley, pp. 17–32, London: Viking Society for Northern Research.
Sides, Braden, 2017. "A Life's Worth: Reexamining Wergild in the Anglo-Saxon Royal Law Codes (c. 600–1035)," *The Expositor: A Journal of Undergraduate Research in the Humanities* 15 (online: http://digitalcommons.trinity.edu/eng_expositor/15).
Siegel, Bernard J., 1945. "Some Methodological Considerations for a Comparative Study of Slavery," *American Anthropologist* 47: 357–392.
Sievers, Edvard, 1909. "Ags. *hlæfdige*," *PBB* 34: 576–579.
Sievers, Edvard, 1927. "Ags. *hlæfdige*," *PBB* 50: 16–17.
Sigfús Blöndal, 1978. *The Varangians of Byzantium. An Aspect of Byzantine Military History*, trans., rev., and rewritten by Benedikt S. Benedikz, Cambridge: Cambridge University Press.
Simek, Rudolf, 1993. *Dictionary of Northern Mythology*, trans. by Angela Hall, Woodbridge: Brewer.
Sindbæk, Søren M., and Bjørn Poulsen (eds.), 2011. *Settlement and Lordship in Viking and Early Medieval Scandinavia* (The Medieval Countryside, 9), Turnhout: Brepols.
Sjösvärd, Lars, 1989. *HaukR – en rinker från Vallentuna. Arkeologisk undersökning av fornlämning 27, Rickeby, Vallentuna sn, Uppland* (Raä. UV Rapport 1989:2), Stockholm: Riksantikvarieämbetet.
Skaarup, Jørgen, 1972. "Rejsekammeraten," *Skalk* 1972(1): 4–9.
Skaarup, Jørgen, 1976. *Stengade II. En langelandsk gravplads med grave fra romersk jernalder og vikingetid* (Meddelelser fra Langelands museum), Rudkøbing: Langelands museum.

Skautrup, P., 1934. "Fylling på sandemænd," in *Studier tilegnede Verner Dahlerup paa Femoghalvfjerdsaarsdagen*, ed. by P. Andersen, A. Hansen, and P. Skautrup, pp. 231–243, Aarhus: Universitetsforlaget.

Skeat, W. W., 1882. *A Concise Etymological Dictionary of the English Language*, Oxford: Clarendon.

Skovgaard-Petersen, Inge, 1994. "Samfundsudviklingen i perioden 800–1200," in *Norden og Europa i vikingetid og tidlig middelalder*, ed. by N. Lund, pp. 27–43, København: Museum Tusculanum.

Skre, Dagfinn, 1998. *Herredømmet. Bosetning og besittelse på Romerike 200–1350 e. Kr.* (Acta humaniora, 32), Oslo: Scandinavian University Press.

Skre, Dagfinn, 2002. "The Role of Slavery in Agrarian Production in Norway, 200–1100 AD," in *Slavery across Time and Space. Studies in Slavery in Medieval Europe and Africa*, ed. by P. Hernæs and T. Iversen (Trondheim Studies in History, 38), pp. 147–158, Trondheim: Dept. of History, NTNU.

Skre, Dagfinn, 2014. "Fri er den 'som fri kommer til verden'. Om friheten i vikingetiden," in *Ja, vi elsker frihet. En antologi*, ed. by Svein H. Gullbekk, pp. 172–179, Oslo: Dreyer.

Skre, Dagfinn, 2017. "Monetary Practices in Early Medieval Western Scandinavia (5th–10th Centuries AD)," *Medieval Archaeology* 61(2): 277–299.

Skrubbeltrang, Fridlev, 1957. "Bryde," *KL* 2: 269–272.

Skyum-Nielsen, Niels, 1979. "Nordic Slavery in an International Setting," *Mediaeval Scandinavia* 11 (1978–1979): 126–148.

Smith, A. H., 1956. *English Place-Name Elements*, 2 vols, Cambridge: Cambridge University Press.

Smith, J. T., 1997. *Roman Villas. A Study in Social Structure*, London: Routledge.

Söderwall = Söderwall, K. F., *Ordbok öfver svenska medeltids-språket*, Lund, 1884–1918.

Solin, Heikki, 1971. *Beiträge zur Kenntnis der griechischen Personennamen in Rom*, vol. 1 (Commentationes Humanarum Litterarum, 48), Helsinki: Societas Scientiarum Fennica.

Solin, Heikki, 1990. *Namenpaare. Eine Studie zur römischen Namengebung* (Commentationes Humanarum Litterarum, 90), Helsinki: Societas Scientarum Fennica.

Solin, Heikki, 2001. "Griechische und romische Sklavennamen. Eine vergleichende Untersuchung," in *Fünzig Jahre Forschungen zur Antiken Sklaverei an der Mainzer Akademie 1950–2000*, ed. by Heinz Bellen und Heinz Heinen (Forschungen zur Antiken Sklaverei, 35), pp. 307–330, Stuttgart: Franz Steiner Verlag.

Sommarin, Emil, 1917. *Träldomen i Norden. Ett blad ur den svenska arbetarklassens äldsta historia*, 2nd ed. (Verdandis småskrifter, 104), Stockholm: Verdandi.

SOSk = *Ortnamnen i Skaraborgs län*, 18 vols., by I. Lundahl (Sveriges ortnamn, 6), Uppsala: Lundequistska bokhandeln, 1950–1981.

Spencer, A. J. 1982. *Death in Ancient Egypt*, Harmondsworth: Penguin.

Spurkland, Terje, 2005. *Norwegian Runes and Runic Inscriptions*, trans. by B. van der Hoek, Woodbridge: Boydell Press.

Stafford, Pauline, 1983. *Queens, Concubines and Dowagers. The King's Wife in the Early Middle Ages*, London: Batsford Academic and Educational.

Ståhl, Harry, 1948. *Ortnamnen i Hallands län*, vol. 1: *Bebyggelsenamnen i södra Halland* (Sveriges ortnamn), Uppsala: Ortnamnsarkivet i Uppsala.

Ståhl, Harry, 1957. "Borgnamn," *KL* 2: 163–165.

Ståhle, Carl Ivar, 1946, *Studier över de svenska ortnamnen på -inge* (Skrifter utg. av Kungl. Gustav Adolfs Akademi, 16), Uppsala: Lundequistska bokhandeln.

Ståhle, Carl Ivar, 1965. "Lagspråk," *KL* 10: 167–177.

Stein, Dorothy K., 1978. "Women to Burn: Suttee as a Normative Institution," *Sign* 4: 253–268.

Steinsland, Gro. 1991. *Det hellige bryllup og norrøn kongeideologi. En analyse av hierogami-myten i Skírnismál, Yngligatal, Háleygjatal og Hyndluljóð*, Oslo: Solum.

Steinsland, Gro. 2004. "Myten om kongen i historien om religionsskiftet i Norge," in *Religionsskiftet i Norden*, ed. by Jón Viðar Sigurðsson, Marit Myking, and Magnus Rindal (Occasional Papers. Skriftserie 6/2004), pp. 63–101, Oslo, Akademika.

Stender-Petersen, Adolf, 1953. *Varangica*, Aarhus: Lunos.

Stenton, F. M., 1971. *Anglo-Saxon England*, 3rd ed., Oxford: Oxford University Press.

Stiles, Paula R., 2006. "Slaves and Slave Trade, Eastern Islamic World," in *Medieval Islamic Civilization. An Encyclopedia*, vol. 2, ed. by Josef W. Meri, pp. 757–758, New York & London: Routledge.

Stoklund, Marie, 1985. "De nye runefund fra Illerup ådal og en nyfundet runeindskrift fra Vimose," *Danske studier*: 5–24.

Stoklund, Marie, 1987. "New Inscriptions from Illerup and Vimose," in *Runor och runinskrifter* (Kungl. Vitterhets Historie och Antikvitets Akademien. Konferenser, 15), pp. 280–300, Stockholm: Almqvist & Wiksell International.

Stoklund, Marie, 1995. "Die Runen der römischen Kaiserzeit," in Ulla Lund Hansen, *Himlingøje—Seeland—Europa. Ein Gräberfeld der jüngeren römischen Kaiserzeit auf Seeland, seine Bedeutung und internationalen Beziehungen* (Nordiske Fortidsminder, B:13), pp. 317–341, København: Det Kongelige Nordiske Oldskriftselskab.

Strickland, Matthew, 1992. "Slaughter, Slavery and Ransom: The Impact of the Conquest on Conduct in Warfare," in *England in the Eleventh Century. Proceedings of the 1990 Harlaxton Symposium*, ed. by C. Hicks (Paul Watkins Medieval Studies, 12/Harlaxton Medieval Studies, 2), pp. 41–60, Stamford: Paul Watkins.

Strid, Jan Paul, 2006. *Från Mumsmålen till Duvemåla. Den svenska måla-kolonisationen under medeltiden. En topolingvistisk studie* (Runica et mediævalia. Opuscula, 10), Stockholm: Sällskapet Runica et mediævalia.

Ström, Folke, 1973. *Nið, ergi and Old Norse moral attitudes* (The Dorothea Coke Memorial Lecture in Northern Studies 1973), London: Viking Society for Northern Studies.

Strömbäck, Dag, 1935a. *Sejd. Textstudier i nordisk religionshistoria* (Nordiska texter och undersökningar, 5), Stockholm: Geber.

Strömbäck, Dag, 1935b. "Till Codex Wormianus av Snorre-Eddan. Textkritiska och lexikaliska bidrag till dess Wb-redaktion," *ANF* 51: 90–120.

Stylegar, Frans-Arne, 2007. "The Kaupang Cemeteries Revisited," in *Kaupang in Skiringssal*, ed. by Dagfinn Skre (Norske Oldfunn, 22), pp. 86–126, Århus: Aarhus University Press.

Sundqvist, Olof, 2002. *Freyr's Offspring. Rulers and Religion in Ancient Svea Society* (Historia religionum, 21), Uppsala: Acta Universitatis Upsaliensis.

Sunna Ebenesersdóttir, Marcela Sandoval-Velasco, Ellen D. Gunnarsdóttir, Anuradha Jagadeesan, Valdís B. Guðmundsdóttir, Elísabet L. Thordardóttir, Margrét S. Einarsdóttir, Kristjan H. S. Moore, Ásgeir Sigurðsson, Droplaug N. Magnúsdóttir, Hákon Jónsson, Steinunn Snorradóttir, Eivind Hovig, Pål Møller, Ingrid Kockum, Tomas Olsson, Lars Alfredsson, Thomas F. Hansen, Thomas Werge, Gianpiero L. Cavalleri, Edmund Gilbert, Carles Lalueza-Fox, Joe W. Walser III, Steinunn

Kristjánsdóttir, Shyam Gopalakrishnan, Lilja Árnadóttir, Ólafur Þ. Magnússon, M. Thomas P. Gilbert, Kári Stefánsson and Agnar Helgason, 2018. "Ancient Genomes from Iceland Reveal the Making of a Human Population," *Science* 360 (6392): 1028–1032.

Svennung, J[osef], 1962. "Svearnas ö och Sithonerna hos Tacitus," *Fornvännen* 57: 193–211.

Sweet, Henry, 1880. "Disguised Compounds in Old English," *Anglia* 3: 151–154. [Also printed in: *Collected Papers of Henry Sweet*, ed. by H. C. Wyld, pp. 220–223, Oxford: Clarendon, 1913.]

Tamm, Ditlev, and Helle Vogt (eds.), 2016. *The Danish Medieval Laws. The Laws of Scania, Zealand and Jutland* (Routledge Medieval Translations), Abingdon & New York: Routledge.

Tamm, Fredrik, 1890–1905. *Etymologisk svensk ordbok*, Upsala: Edv. Berling.

Tengvik, Gösta, 1938. *Old English Bynames* (Nomina Germanica, 4), Uppsala: Almqvist & Wiksell.

Thalmann, Wilhelm G., 1998. *The Swineherd and the Bow. Representations of Class in the Odyssey*, Ithaca, N.Y.: Cornell University Press.

Thalmann William G., 2001. "Female Slaves in the *Odyssey*," in *Women and Slaves in Greco-Roman Culture, Differential Equations*, ed. by S. R. Joshel and Sh. Murnaghan, pp. 22–34, London & New York: Routledge.

Theuws, Frands, ms. *The Free and Unfree of the Historians and the Rural Population of the Archaeologists*. [Unpublished paper at the conference *Law and Archaeology*, Carlsbergsakademien, Copenhagen, Dec. 7–8, 2010.]

Thompson, E. A., 1957. "Slavery in Early Germany," *Hermathena* 89: 17–29.

Thompson, Hugh, 1993. "Iron Age and Roman Slave-Shackles," *Archaeological Journal* 150: 57–168.

Tibiletti, Gianfranco, 1955. "Lo sviluppo del latifondo in Italia dall'epoca Gracca al principio del' impero," in *Storia dell'antichità. Relazioni del X Congresso Internationale di Scienze Storiche*, vol. 2, pp. 235–292, Firenze: G. C. Sansoni.

Toch, Michael, 2014. "Was There a Jewish Slave Trade (or Commercial Monopoly) in the Early Middle Ages," in *Mediterranean Slavery Revisited (500–1800)/Neue Perspectiven auf mediterrane Sklaverei (500–1800)*, ed. by Stefan Hanss and Juliane Schiel, pp. 421–444, Zürich: Chronos Verlag.

Toledano, Ehud R., 1982. *The Ottoman Slave Trade and Its Suppression: 1840–1890*, Princeton: Princeton University Press.

Toledano, Ehud R., 1998. *Slavery and Abolition in the Ottoman Middle East*, Washington, DC: University of Washingtion Press.

Tollin, Clas, 1999. *Rågångar, gränshallar och ägoområden. Rekonstruktion av fastighetsstruktur och bebyggelseutveckling i mellersta Småland under äldre medeltid* (Meddelanden från Kulturgeografiska institutionen vid Stockholms universitet, 101), Stockholm: Stockholms universitet.

Tomich, Dale W., 2004. *Through the Prism of Slavery. Labor Capital, and World Economy*, Lanham, MD: Rowman & Littlefield.

Toplak, Matthias, 2015. "Prone Burials and Modified Teeth at the Viking Age Cemetary of Kopparsvik. The Changing of Social Identities at the Treshold of the Christian Middle Ages," *Analecta Archaeologica Ressoviensia* 10: 77–97.

Toplak, Matthias, 2018. "Deconstructing the Deviant Burials – Kopparsvik and the Rite of Prone Burials in Viking Age Scandinavia," *META: Medeltidsarkeologisk tidskrift*: 79–141.

Torp *NEO* = Alf Torp, *Nynorsk etymologisk ordbok*, Kristiania: Aschehoug, 1919.
Tovar, Antinio, 1971. "Lat. *seruus*, ein Indogermanisches Wort," in *Sprache und Geschichte. Festschrift für Harri Meier zum 65. Geburtstag*, ed. by E. Coseriu and W.-D. Stempl, pp. 557–562, München: Fink.
Trakulhun, Sven, 2014. "Formen institutionalisierter Unfreiheit in Siam. Historische Semantik und gesellschaftliche Praxis (16.–19. Jahrhundert)," in *Mediterranean Slavery Revisited (500–1800)/Neue Perspectiven auf mediterrane Sklaverei (500–1800)*, ed. by Stefan Hanss and Juliane Schiel, pp. 163–183, Zürich: Chronos Verlag.
Třeštík, D., 2001. "'Eine große Stadt der Slawen namens Prag': Staaten und Sklaven in Mitteleuropa im 10. Jahrhudert," in *Boleslaw II: Der tschechische Staat um das Jahr 1000*, ed. by Petr Sommer (Colloquia mediaevalia Pragensia, 2), pp. 93–138, Prague: Filosofia.
Tsigaridas Glørstad, Zanette, Jakob Johansson, and Frans-Arne Stylegar, 2011. "Minnelund og monument. Runestein på Hogganvik, Mandal, Vets-Agder," *Viking* 74: 9–24.
Turley, David, 2000. *Slavery*, Oxford: Blackwell.
Þorsteinn Helgason, 1997. "Historical Narrative as Collective Therapy: The Case of the Turkish Raid in Iceland," *Scandinavian Journal of History* 22: 275–289.
Urbainczyk, Theresa, 2008. *Slave Revolts in Antiquity*, Stockfield: Acumen.
Valante, Mary A., 2013. "Castrating Monks: Vikings, the Slave Trade, and the Value of Eunuchs," in *Castration and Culture in the Middle Ages*, ed. by Larissa Tracy, pp. 174–187, Cambridge: Boydell & Brewer.
Varga, Eugen, 1967. "Über die asiatische Produktionsweise," *Jahrbuch für Wirtschaftsgeschichte* 1967(4): 181–204.
Velschow, H. M., 1840. "Om Bryderne," [*Dansk*] *Historisk Tidsskrift* (Copenhagen) 1(1): 112–147.
Vendell, Herman, 1894. *Terminologin i Äldre Västgöta- ock Östgöta-lagarne. Sammanställd*, Helsingfors.
Vendryes, Joseph, 1935. "À propos de lat. servus," *Bulletin de la Société de Linguistique de Paris* 36: 124–130.
Verlinden, Charles, 1943. "L'origine de *Sclavus* = Esclave," *Bulletin du Cagne: Archivum Latinitatis Medii Aevi* 17 (1942): 97–128.
Verlinden, Charles, 1955–1977. *L'esclavage dans l'Europe médiévale*, 2 vols. (Werken uitgegeven door de Faculteit van de Letteren en Wijsbegegeerte, Rijksuniversiteit te Gent, 119, 162), Gent: Rijksuniversiteit te Gent.
Verlinden, Charles, 1979. "Ist mittelalterliche Sklaverei ein bedeutsamer demographischer Faktor gewesen?," *Vierteljahrschrift für Sozial- und Wirtschaftsgeschichte* 66(2): 154–164.
Verlinden, Charles, 1988. "Slavery, Slave Trade," *DMA* 11: 334–340.
Vikstrand, Per, 2001. *Gudarnas platser. Förkristna sakrala ortnamn i Mälarlandskapen* (Acta Academiae Regiae Gustavi Adolphi, 77), Uppsala: Kungl. Gustav Adolfs akademi.
Vikstrand, Per, 2009. "Förkristna sakrala personnamn i Skandinavien," *Studia anthroponymica Scandinavica* 27: 5–31.
Vinogradoff, Paul, 1911. *The Growth of the Manor*, London: George Allan.
Vittinghoff, F., 1960. "Die Theorie des historischen Materialismus über den 'antiken Sklavenhalterstaat'. Probleme der Alten Geschichte bei den 'Klassikern' des Marxismus und in der modernen sowjetischen Forschung," *Saeculum* 11: 89–131.

Vlassopoulos, Kostas, 2009. "Slavery, Freedom and Citizenship in Classical Athens: Beyond a Legalistic Approach," *European Review of History-Revue européenne d'histoire* 16(3): 347–363.

Vlassopoulos, Kostas, "Finlay's Slavery," in *M. I. Finley. An Ancient Historian and His Impact*, ed. by D. Jew et al., pp. 76–99, Cambridge: Cambridge University Press.

Vlastos, Gregory, 1941. "Slavery in Plato's *Republic*," *Philosophical Review* 50(3): 289–304.

Vogt, Joseph, 1957. *Struktur der antiken Sklavenkriege* (Akademie der Wissenschaften und der Literatur. Abhandlungen der Geistes- und Sozialwissenschaftlichen Klasse, 1957:1), Mainz & Wiesbaden: Steiner.

Vogt, Joseph, 1965. *Sklaverei und Humanität. Studien zur Antiken Sklaverei und ihrer Erforschung* (Historia. Zeitschrift für alte Geschichte. Einzelschriften, 8), Wiesbaden: Steiner.

Vogt, Joseph, 1975. *Ancient Slavery and the Ideal of Man*, trans. by Th. Wiedemann, Cambridge, MA: Harvard University Press

Vogt, Joseph, 1983. *Sklaveri und Humanität. Studien zur Antiken Sklaverei und ihrer Erforschung*, Ergänzungzheft zur 2. erweiterten Aufl. (Historia. Zeitschrift für alte Geschichte. Einzelschriften, 44), Wiesbaden: Steiner.

Volkmann, Hans, 1961. *Die Massenversklavungen der Einwohner eroberter Städte in der hellenistisch-römischen Zeit* (Akademie der Wissenschaften und der Literatur. Abhandlungen der Geistes- und sozialwissenschaftlichen Klasse, 1961:3), Mainz & Wiesbaden: Akademie der Wissenschaften und der Literatur.

de Vries, Jan, 1962. *Altnordisches etymologisches Wörterbuch*, 2nd ed., Leiden: Brill.

de Vries, Jan, 1967. *Altnordische Literaturgeschichte*, vol. 2: *Die Literatur von etwa 1150 bis 1300, die Spätzeit nach 1300* (Grundriß der germanischen Philologie, 16), 2nd ed., Berlin: Walter de Gruyter.

Wagner, Veruschka, 2017. "şirmerd, Mosiye und Payidār - Sklaven im frühmodernen Istanbul, dokumentiert in den lokalen Gerichtsregistern," in *Sklaveri in der Vormoderne. Beispiele aus aussereuropäischen Gesellschaften*, ed. by Stephan Conermann (Dhau. Jahrbuch für aussereuropäische Geschichte, 2), pp. 83–97, St. Ingbert: Röhrig Universitätsverlag.

Wakeford, J., 1984. "Two *walh* Names in the Fields of Kingston," *Surrey Archaeological Collections* 75: 251–256.

Walde-Pokorny = Walde, Alois, 1927–1932. *Vergleichendes Wörterbuch der indogermanischen Sprachen*, publ. and ed. by Julius Pokorny, Berlin: Gruyter.

Warmind, Morten L., 1995. "Ibn Fadlan in the Context of His Age," in *The Ship as Symbol in Prehistoric and Medieval Scandinavia*, vol. 1, ed. by O. Crumlin-Pedersen and B. Munch Thye, pp. 131–138, Copenhagen: National Museum.

Watson, Alan, 1987. *Roman Slave Law*, Baltimore & London: Johns Hopkins University Press.

Watson, James L. (ed.), 1980. *Asian and African Systems of Slavery*, Oxford: Blackwell.

Watson, William E., 2001. "Ibn al-Athīr's Accounts of the Rūs: A Commentary and Translation," *Canadian-American Slavic Studies* 35: 423–438. [Online: https://deremilitari.org/2014/08/ibn-al-athirs-accounts-of-the-rus-a-commentary-and-translation/.]

Watts, V. E., and E. F. M. Prince, 1982. "OE *walh* in English Place-Names, an Addendum," *Journal of the English Place-Name Society* 14 (1981–1982): 32–36.

Weaver, P. R. C., 1972. *Familia Caesaris*, Cambridge: Cambridge University Press.

Weber, Max, 1924. *Gesammelte Aufsätze zur Sozial- und Wirtschaftgeschichte*, Tübingen: Mohr.

Weigand, Friedrich Ludwig Karl, 1909. *Deutsches Wörterbuch*, 5th ed., Giessen: Töpelmann.

Wennerström, Torsten, 1933. "Fredlösheten. Några rättshistoriska och filologiska synpunkter," *Vetenskapssocietetens i Lund årsbok*: 53–85.

Wergeland, Agnes M., 1900–1902. "Slavery in Germanic Society during the Middle Ages," *Journal of Political Economy* 9(1) (1900): 98–120; 9(3) (1901): 398–422; 10(2) (1902): 230–254.

Wessén, Elias, 1922. *Svensk ordbildningslära från historisk synpunkt*, Lund: C.W.K. Gleerups förlag.

Wessén, Elias, 1927. *Nordiska namnstudier* (Uppsala universitets årsskrift 1927. Filosofi, språkvetenskap och historiska vetenskaper, 3), Uppsala: Lundequistska bokhandeln.

Wessén, Elias, 1945. "Gutalagen," in *Boken om Gotland. Minnesskrift med anledning av Gotlands återförening med Sverige genom freden i Brömsebro den 13 augusti 1645*, vol. 1: *Gotlands historia fram till år 1645*, ed. by. M. Stenberger, pp. 165–177, Visby: AB Sylve Norrbys Bokhandel.

Wessén, Elias, 1979. *De nordiska språken*, 11th ed., Stockholm: AWE Geber.

Wessén, Elias, 1966. *Isländsk grammatik*, 2nd ed., Stockholm: Svenska bokförlaget.

Wessén, Elias, 1969. "Nordiska folkstammar och folknamn. En översikt," *Fornvännen* 64: 14–36.

Westermann, William Linn, 1942. "Industrial Slavery in Roman Italy," *Journal of Economic History* 2: 149–163.

Westermann, William Linn, 1943. "Slavery and the Elements of Freedom in Ancient Greece," *Bulletin of the Polish Institute of Arts and Sciences in America* 1943:1(2): 332–347.

Westermann, William Linn, 1955. *The Slave Systems of Greek and Roman Antiquity* (Memoirs of the American Philosophical Society, 40), Philadelphia: The American Philosophical Society.

Westermann, William Linn, 1968, "Slavery and the Elements of Freedom in Ancient Greece," in *Slavery in Classical Antiquity. Views and Controversies*, ed. by Moses I. Finley, pp. 17–32, New York. [First published in: *Quarterly Bulletin of The Polish Institute of Arts and Sciences in America* 1943:1(2): 1–16.]

Westphalen, Petra, 2002. *Die Eisenfunde von Haithabu* (Die Ausgrabungen in Haithabu, 10), Neumünster: Wachholtz Verlag.

Whitelock, Dorothy (ed. and trans.), 1930. *Anglo-Saxon Wills*, Cambridge: Cambridge University Press.

Whitelock, Dorothy, 1952. *The Beginnings of English Society*, Harmondsworth: Penguin.

Whitelock, Dorothy, 1979. "General Introduction," in *English Historical Documents* vol. 1: *c. 500–1042*, 2nd ed., ed. by D. Whitelock, pp. 1–105, London and New York: Routledge.

Wickham, Chris, 2005. *Framing the Early Middle Ages. Europe and the Mediterranean 400–800*, Oxford: Oxford University Press.

Wickert-Micknat, Gisela, 1983. *Unfreiheit im Zeitalter der homerischen Epen* (Forschungen zur antiken Sklaverei, 16), Wiesbaden: Steiner.

Widengren, Geo, 1971. *Religionernas värld*, Stockholm: Almqvist & Wiksell.

Widgren, Mats, 1995. "Individuellt eller kollektivt ägande i bondesamhällen?," in *Äganderätten i lantbrukets historia*, ed. by Mats Widgren (Skrifter om skogs- och lantbrukshistoria, 8), pp. 5–16, Stockholm: Nordiska museet.

Widgren, Mats, 1998. "Kulturgeografernas bönder och arkeologernas guld - finns det någon väg till en syntes?," in *Centrala platser, centrala frågor*, ed. by B. Hårdh and L. Larsson (Uppåkrastudier, 1), pp. 281–296, Stockholm: Almqvist & Wiksell International.

Widgren, Mats, 2003. "Trälar, landbor och hövdingar under järnåldern - vad säger fältmaterialet?," in *Trälar. Ofria i agrarsamhället från vikingatid till medeltid*, ed. by Th. Lindkvist and J. Myrdal, pp. 118–124, Stockholm: Nordiska museet.

Wiedemann, Thomas E. J., 1981. *Greek and Roman Slavery*, London: Croom Helm.

Wiedemann, Thomas E. J., 1987. *Slavery* (Greece & Rome. New surveys in the Classics, 19), Oxford: Clarendon.

Wikander, Stig, 1978. *Araber, vikingar, väringar* (Svenska humanistiska förbundet, 90), Lund: Svenska humanistiska förbundet.

Wikström af Edholm, Klas, 2020. *Människooffer i myt och minne. En studie av offerpraktiker i fornnordisk religion utifrån källtexter och arkeologiskt material*, Åbo: Åbo Akademis förlag.

Wilde-Stockmeyer, Marlis, 1978. *Sklaverei auf Island. Untersuchungen zur rechtlich-sozialen Situation und literarischen Darstellung der Sklaven im skandinavischen Mittelalter* (Skandinavistische arbeiten, 5), Heidelberg: Carl Winter.

Williams, Carl O., 1937. *Thraldom in Ancient Iceland*, Chicago: University of Chicago Press.

Williams, Henrik, 2001. "From Meldorf to Haitabu: Some Early Personal Names from Schleswig-Holstein", in *Von Thorsberg nach Schleswig*, ed. by Klaus Düwel, Edith Marold, and Christiane Zimmermann, pp. 149–166, Berlin: de Gruyter.

Williams, Phil (ed.), 1999. *Illegal Immigration and Commercial Sex. The New Slave Trade*, London & Portland, OR: Frank Cass.

Willis, John Ralph (ed.), 1985. *Slaves and Slavery in Muslim Africa*, 2 vols., London: Frank Cass.

Witzenrath, Christoph, 2016. "Slavery in Medieval and Early Modern Eurasia: An Overview of the Russian and Ottoman Empires and Central Asia," in *Eurasian Slavery, Ransom and Abolition in World History, 1200–1860*, ed. by Ch. Witzenrath, pp. 1–77, London & New York: Routledge.

Wood, Ian N., 1983. *The Merovingian North Sea* (Occasional Papers on Medieval Topics, 1), Alingsås: Viktoria.

Woolf, Henry Bosley, 1939. *The Old Germanic Principles of Name-Giving*, Baltimore: Johns Hopkins Press.

Wormald, Patrick, 1983. "Bede, the *Bretwaldas* and the origins of the *Gens Anglorum*," in *Ideal and Reality in Frankish and Anglo-Saxon Society*, ed. by P. Wormald, pp. 99–129, Oxford: Blackwell.

Wormald, Patrick, 1997. "Wergild," *Lexikon des Mittelalters* 8: 2201–2202.

Wormald, Patrick, 1998. "Feuds and Wergild," in *Medieval England: An Encyclopedia*, ed. by Paul Szarmach et al., pp. 297–298, New York: Garland.

Wrede, Ferdinand, 1886. *Über die Sprache der Wandalen. Ein Beitrag zur germanischen Namen- und Dialektforschung* (Quellen und Forschungen zur Sprach- und Kulturgeschichte der germanischen Völker, 59), Berlin.

Wright, Joseph, 1910. *Grammar of the Gothic Language*, Oxford: Clarendon.

Wulf, Fred, 1994. "Runenmeisternamen," *Proceedings of the Third International Symposium on Runes and Runic Inscriptions*, ed. by J. Knirk (Runrön, 9), pp. 31–42, Uppsala: Institutionen för nordiska språk, Uppsala universitet.

Wührer, K., 1981. "Bryte," *RGA* 4: 25–26.

Wyatt, David, 2000. "The Significance of Slavery: Alternative Approaches to Anglo-Saxon Slavery," *Anglo-Norman Studies* 23: 328–347.

Wyatt, David, 2009. *Slaves and Warriors in Medieval Britain and Ireland, 800–1200* (The Northern World, 45), Leiden & Boston: Brill.

Yavetz, Zvi, 1988. *Slaves and Slavery in Ancient Rome*, New Brunswick & Oxford: Transaction Books.

Yilmaz, Gulay, 2009. "Becoming a Devshirme: The Training of Conscripted Children in the Ottoman Empire," in *Children in Slavery through the Ages*, ed. by Gwyn Campbell, Suzanne Miers, and Joseph C. Miller, pp. 119–134, Ohio: Ohio University Press.

Yorke, Barbara, 1981. "The Vocabulary of Anglo-Saxon Overlordship," *Anglo-Saxon Studies in Archaeology and History* 2: 171–200.

Young, Jean I., 1933. "Does Rígsþula Betray Irish Influence?," *ANF* 49: 97–107.

Zachrisson, R[obert], E., 1927. *Romans, Kelts and Saxons in Ancient Britain. An Investigation into the Two Dark Centuries, 400–600, of English History* (Skrifter utgivna av K. Humanistiska vetenskapssamfundet i Uppsala, 24:12), Uppsala.

Zachrisson, Torun, 2003. "De osynliggjorda. Om trälar i arkeologisk forskning," in *Trälar. Ofria i agrarsamhället från vikingatid till medeltid*, ed. by Th. Lindkvist and J. Myrdal, pp. 88–102, Stockholm: Nordiska museet.

Zeuske, Michael, 2018. *Sklaverei. Eine Menschheitsgeschichte von der Steinzeit bis heute*, Ditzingen: Reclam.

Zeuske, Michael, 2019. *Handbuch Geschichte der Sklaverei. Eine Globalgeschichte von den Anfängen bis zur Gegenwart*, 2 vols, 2nd ed., Berlin: de Gruyter.

Zilfi, Madeline C., 2010. *Women and Slavery in the Late Ottoman Empire. The Design of Difference*, Cambridge: Cambridge University Press.

Index of Persons

Index

Old-norse letters: Þ, þ is a voiceless *th*, pronounced as in *thing*. Ð, ð is a voiced *dh*, pronounced as in *these*. Ǫ, ǫ is a vowel derived from *u*-mutation (*u-Umlaut*; vowel fronting) of an *a* (e.g. *vǫr* f. < *waru-*), probably pronounced as /ø/ in Old Icelandic (in modern Icelandic developed to /œ/, spelt *ö*).

Alphabet: The index is alphabetised accordingly: a/å/ä/æ/á, b, c, d (ð=dh), e/é, f, g, h, i/í, j, k, l, m, n, o/ö/ø/ó, p, q, r, s, t (þ=th), u/ú, v, w, x, y/ý, z, ǫ/ǭ [to the typesetter: this ǭ should be an ǫ with an acute accent, ǫ + ´]

Note: Some very often-occurring words are not in the Index, such as slave, slavery, slaving, thrall/ þræll, thraldom, free, freedom, unfree.